ASSYRIOLOGICAL STUDIES • *No. 25*

THE ORIENTAL INSTITUTE OF THE UNIVERSITY OF CHICAGO

Thomas A. Holland • *Editor*

with the assistance of Thomas G. Urban

THE HITTITE STATE CULT OF THE TUTELARY DEITIES

GREGORY McMAHON

THE ORIENTAL INSTITUTE OF THE UNIVERSITY OF CHICAGO

ASSYRIOLOGICAL STUDIES • No. 25

CHICAGO • ILLINOIS

Library of Congress Catalog Card Number: 91–60344

ISBN: 0–918986–69–9
ISSN: 0066–9903

The Oriental Institute, Chicago

Published 1991. Printed in the United States of America.

To my wife Melinda

TABLE OF CONTENTS

PREFACE

This volume represents a thorough revision of my doctoral dissertation completed at the Oriental Institute of the University of Chicago in May of 1988. It therefore necessarily reflects an immense amount of encouragement, correction, and guidance from my dissertation committee of Professors Harry A. Hoffner, Jr., Hans G. Güterbock, Ahmet Ünal, and Thomas McClellan, at that time all on the faculty or staff of the Oriental Institute. I have retained some of the personal element inherent in a closely supervised dissertation by referring to personal communications throughout the monograph. It would be impossible to credit my committee with every correction and idea which they shared; I have tried to do so for certain important concepts.

This work represents an attempt to study all the religious textual material available on the Hittite tutelary deities and to analyze the role they played in the official state cult as celebrated in the capital and at provincial cult centers. I have not attempted to evaluate the many tutelary deities in all of their occurrences in every genre of Hittite text beyond the survey presented in *Chapter 1*. The use of titles and names of tutelary deities in personal names is beyond the scope of this work. The basis of the work is extensive philological research in the cuneiform archives left by the Hittites over 3,000 years ago. The work on texts which are completely edited in the chapters devoted to different festivals is based on a year of research in the Hittite tablet archives in the museums of Istanbul, Ankara, and Berlin. That work with the tablets was supplemented with research in the lexical files of the *Chicago Hittite Dictionary*, which provided convenient access to the entire published corpus of Hittite tablets for research on individual deities or Hittite words that required in-depth analysis.

A word of caution is in order concerning the conclusions reached in this volume. The nature of the Hittite archives is such that the amount and type of textual material which is available to us is dependent on accidents of preservation and discovery. Unlike historical archives of more recent cultures that have been continuously maintained up to the present day, the Hittite tablet archives were buried underground for more than three millennia. The Hittite capital, Ḫattuša, has not been completely excavated, and we simply cannot know what portion of the preserved corpus of Hittite material has been discovered. Shelf lists from the archives list many festivals and rituals the actual texts of which have not yet been discovered or identified. Of what has been discovered a portion has yet to be published. Therefore a work such as this, which relies to some extent on the frequency of occurrences of particular deities in the texts and assumes that we have representative samples of at least most of the major Hittite cultic texts, must carry with it the caveat that new discoveries of tablets or temples or cult objects may alter our reconstruction. Part of the attraction of Hittitology as a discipline is the intellectual flexibility which it requires, the certain knowledge that only a portion of the evidence is available, that more is constantly being discovered, and that theories will have to be revised. Our understanding of cultic activity at the local level especially may change as additional sites outside the capital continue to be investigated.

The work has two main focuses. The first is a broad review of the evidence for the role of all tutelary deities in the cult. The discussion draws on evidence from the corpus of festivals, rituals, prayers, cult inventories, and mythology, as well as various genres of "secular" texts. I have created a provisional outline of the types of tutelary deities, the kinds of cultic activities performed for them, and their position vis-à-vis the other gods in the Hittite pantheon.

The second focus of this monograph is a contribution to the continuing process of establishing our sources for the study of Hittite religion by editing a number of the festival texts. A study of the cults for tutelary deities must utilize as sources all types of religious texts, but the texts in which the Hittites described specific cult ceremonies will be our most important source. The festivals which I have chosen for extensive work are ones which were or at least may have been celebrated primarily for one or more tutelary deities. A number of fragmentary cult texts having to do with tutelary deities which cannot be fitted into the scheme of one of the larger festivals are included in *Appendix A*. The editing of texts from any ancient Near Eastern culture requires intensive philological investigation into certain words or phrases central to the meaning or difficult of translation. Selected words which required special attention are treated individually in *Appendix B*.

Because part of this work involves making English translations of Hittite religious texts available to the non-Hittitologist interested in ancient Near Eastern religious, social, or intellectual history, I have tried to be sensitive to the varied audience to which this monograph will appeal. Much of the work must remain fairly technical and address itself to other Hittite scholars. I hope, however, that the discussions in *Chapter 1* and the English translations of *Chapters 2–5* will be of use to non-Hittitologists. Citations of reference works abound, and a word is in order concerning these. Laroche's *Catalogue des Textes Hittites* is a systematic cataloguing of all published Hittite tablets, in which texts are assigned a modern title and a number. This standardizes the names by which we identify festivals, rituals, treaties, etc. Laroche's work in identifying festival texts for tutelary deities was the starting point for my research. In the *Introduction* I provide a revised schema of the texts for *CTH* 681–685, Laroche's "Cultes de ^{d}KAL." Hittite lexicography is still in a rather fluid state as attested by the three major dictionary projects[1] being carried on simultaneously to supplement the admirable *Hethitisches Wörterbuch* of Friedrich published in 1952. The newer dictionaries benefit greatly from the hundreds of tablets published since Friedrich's work, but for many words Friedrich remains the only dictionary available.

Any exercise in scholarship is a cooperative effort that benefits from a multiplicity of perspectives, and it is with gratitude that I acknowledge those who helped guide this work. I offer here my sincerest thanks to my advisor Professor Harry Hoffner, who not only taught me Hittite and supervised my dissertation but also graciously extended to me the use of the lexical files of the *Chicago Hittite Dictionary* for my research. Professors Hoffner and Güterbock also allowed me to utilize early drafts of individual *CHD* articles. The dictionary project has been funded by the National Endowment for the Humanities. I wish to express my deep appreciation also to Professor Hans G. Güterbock, who gave generously of his time and unparalleled experience in guiding and correcting my work and also provided me with examples from his field transliterations of unpublished material. I also extend my thanks to the other members of my committee, Professors Ahmet Ünal and Thomas McClellan, each of whom carefully helped guide me through the various stages of preparing this work. Dr. Richard Beal read the entire manuscript more than once and checked all my references. I thank him for his meticulous care and the excellent ideas he offered along the way. Any errors which remain in the work are naturally my sole responsibility. I am grateful also to Professor Robert Dankoff, who introduced me to the joys of Turkish and thus facilitated my research in Turkey. I would in addition like to thank the other members of the faculty and my classmates at the Oriental Institute, who shared with me the wonder and fascination of the ancient Near East. I acknowledge a special debt of

1. In Chicago the *Hittite Dictionary of the Oriental Institute of the University of Chicago* (*CHD*), in Munich the second edition of the *Hethitisches Wörterbuch* (*HW*^{2}), and in Los Angeles (UCLA) the *Hittite Etymological Dictionary* (*HED*).

gratitude to Ron Gorny, who accompanied me in explorations of the Hittite homeland, provided much-needed guidance in the archaeology of ancient Anatolia, and shared my passionate enthusiasm for things Hittite.

My work here and abroad has been aided by numerous fellowships. I wish to thank the American and Turkish Fulbright Commissions and the American Research Institute in Turkey, all of whom helped make possible my research in Turkey. The Mrs. Giles Whiting Foundation provided generous support of my research and study in the crucial last year of my doctoral program. I am grateful also to the Turkish Department of Antiquities for allowing me to work in their museums, and I extend my appreciation to the staffs of the İstanbul Arkeoloji Müzeleri and the Anadolu Medeniyetleri Müzesi in Ankara for their kindness and help in my work in Turkey. I particularly would like to thank Veysel Donbaz and Fatma Yıldız of the Istanbul museum tablet archives, who extended their friendship as well as professional assistance throughout my year in Turkey.

I also wish to acknowledge my gratitude to Professor Heinrich Otten, who gave me access to important unpublished sources. While I worked at the Vorderasiatisches Museum in Berlin I was aided by the director, Professor Liane Jakob-Rost, and Dr. Evelyn Klengel, both of whom very willingly facilitated my work with the tablets there. Professor Horst Klengel of what was then the Akademie der Wissenschaften der DDR has very kindly allowed me to utilize an unpublished tablet fragment which has greatly aided my understanding of the relevant text.

The revision of the dissertation has been generously funded by my present academic home, the University of New Hampshire. The UNH Center for Humanities provided a summer grant which gave me the necessary time to revise the manuscript. The Central University Research Fund awarded me a travel grant to return to Chicago to confer during the revising process with Professors Hoffner and Güterbock and with the editors of the Oriental Institute Press. I would also like to thank Tom Holland and Tom Urban of the Oriental Institute for their diligence and expertise in the preparation of the manuscript.

Finally I would like to thank my parents for their unceasing encouragement and support of every kind over years of bringing this project to fruition and to express my deep appreciation to my wife Melinda, without whose constant support, encouragement, and sacrifice this work would never have been possible.

LIST OF BIBLIOGRAPHIC ABBREVIATIONS*

AANL	*Atti della Accademia Nazionale dei Lincei Rendiconti della Classe di Scienze morali, storiche e filologiche, Serie 8*
ABoT	*Ankara Arkeoloji Müzesinde bulunan Boğazköy Tabletleri.* Istanbul 1948
AfO	*Archiv für Orientforschung*
AHw	W. von Soden, *Akkadisches Handwörterbuch*
AION	*Annali dell'Istituto Universitario Orientale di Napoli*
AIΩN	*Annali del Seminario di Studi del Mondo Classico Sezione Linguistica.* (Istituto Universitario Orientale di Napoli)
AJA	*American Journal of Archaeology*
Alakš.	Treaty of Muwatalli with Alakšandu, edited in *SV* 2: 42–102
AlHeth	H. A. Hoffner, Jr., *Alimenta Hethaeorum.* (*AOS* 55) New Haven 1974
Alp, *Beamt.*	S. Alp, *Untersuchungen zu den Beamtennamen im hethitischen Festzeremoniell.* Leipzig 1940
Alp, *Tempel*	S. Alp, *Beiträge zur Erforschung des hethitischen Tempels. Kultanlagen im Lichte der Keilschrifttexte.* Ankara 1983
AM	A. Götze, *Die Annalen des Muršiliš.* (*MVAeG* 38) Leipzig 1933
ANET	J. B. Pritchard, ed., *Ancient Near Eastern Texts Relating to the Old Testament.* 3rd ed., with suppl. Princeton 1969
AnOr	*Analecta Orientalia*
AnSt	*Anatolian Studies* (Journal of the British Institute of Archaeology at Ankara)
AnYayın	*Ankara Üniversitesi Dil ve Tarih-Çoğrafya Fakültesi Yayınları*
AO	*Der Alte Orient*
AOAT	*Alter Orient und Altes Testament*
AOATS	*AOAT, Sonderreihe*
AOF	*Altorientalische Forschungen*
AOS	*American Oriental Series*
ArOr	*Archiv Orientální*
AS	*Assyriological Studies*
AU	F. Sommer, *Die Ahhiyavā-Urkunden.* Munich 1932

*The abbreviations used are in general those of the *Chicago Hittite Dictionary.* I also have striven for consistency by following *Chicago Hittite Dictionary* style in my citations of primary sources and secondary works.

BagM	*Baghdader Mitteilungen*
Balkan, *İnandık*	K. Balkan, *İnandık'ta 1966 yılında bulunan eski Hitit çağına ait bir bağış belgesi.* Ankara 1973
Beal, Diss.	R. Beal, *The Organization of the Hittite Military* (Ph.D. diss., University of Chicago). Chicago 1986
Bel Madg.	*BĒL MADGALTI* instr., ed. *Dienstanw.*
Belleten	*Türk Tarih Kurumu Belleten*
Bildbeschr.	C.-G. von Brandenstein, *Hethitische Götter nach Bildbeschreibungen in Keilschrifttexten.* (*MVAeG* 46.2) Leipzig 1943
BiOr	*Bibliotheca Orientalis*
Bittel, *Hethiter*	K. Bittel, *Die Hethiter.* Munich 1976
Bo	Inventory numbers of Boğazköy tablets excavated 1906–12
Bo year/ ...	Inventory numbers of Boğazköy tablets excavated 1968–
BoHa	*Boğazköy-Ḫattuša, Ergebnisse der Ausgrabungen*
Borger, *AOAT* 33	R. Borger, *Assyrisch-babylonische Zeichenliste.* (*AOAT* 33) Neukirchen-Vluyn 1978
Bossert, *Heth.Kön.*	H. T. Bossert, *Ein hethitisches Königssiegel.* Berlin 1944
BoSt	*Boghazköi-Studien*
BoTU	E. Forrer, *Die Boghazköi-Texte in Umschrift.* (*WVDOG* 41/42) Leipzig 1922, 1926
CAD	*The Assyrian Dictionary of the Oriental Institute of the University of Chicago.* Chicago 1956–
Carter, Diss.	C. Carter, *Hittite Cult Inventories* (Ph.D. diss., University of Chicago). Chicago 1962
CHD	*The Hittite Dictionary of the Oriental Institute of the University of Chicago.* Chicago 1980–
Chrest.	E. H. Sturtevant and G. Bechtel, *A Hittite Chrestomathy.* Philadelphia 1935
Coşkun, *Kap isimleri*	Y. Coşkun, *Boğazköy metinlerinde geçen bazı seçme kap isimleri.* (*AnYayın* 285) Ankara 1979
CRRAI	*Compte rendu de la ... Rencontre Assyriologique Internationale* (cited by date of congress, not date of publication)
CTH	E. Laroche, *Catalogue des textes hittites*, 2nd ed. Paris 1971
Dienstanw.	E. von Schuler, *Hethitische Dienstanweisungen für höhere Hof- und Staatsbeamte.* (*AfO* Beiheft 10) Graz 1971
DLL	E. Laroche, *Dictionnaire de la langue louvite.* Paris 1959
DMOA	*Documenta et Monumenta Orientis Antiqui*
Dressler, *Plur.*	W. Dressler, *Studien zur verbalen Pluralität.* Vienna 1968
Dupp.	Treaty of Muršili II and Duppi-Tešub, edited in *SV* 1:1–48
EHGl	H. A. Hoffner, Jr., *An English-Hittite Glossary* (*RHA* XXV/60). Paris 1967
Engelhard, Diss.	D. Engelhard, *Hittite Magical Practices: An Analysis* (Ph.D. diss., Brandeis University). Waltham 1970
Erimḫuš	Lexical series erimḫuš = *anantu*
Erimḫuš Bogh.	Boğazköy version of Erimḫuš
Ertem, *Fauna*	H. Ertem, *Boğazköy metinlerine göre Hititler devri Anadolu'sunun Faunası.* Ankara 1965
Ertem, *Flora*	H. Ertem, *Boğazköy metinlerine göre Hititler devri Anadolu'sunun Florası.* Ankara 1974

FHG	*Fragments hittites de Genève* (*RA* 45:131–38, 184–94; *RA* 46:42–50, 214). Paris 1951–52
FHL	*Fragments hittites du Louvre*, in *Mém. Atatürk* (1982) 73–107
Forsch.	E. Forrer, *Forschungen*. Berlin 1926–29
FsAkurgal	*Akurgal'a Armağan (Festschrift Akurgal)*. Ankara 1987–89
FsBittel	*Beiträge zur Altertumskunde Kleinasiens. Festschrift für Kurt Bittel.* Mainz 1983
FsFriedrich	*Festschrift J. Friedrich zum 65. Geburtstag gewidmet.* Heidelberg 1959
FsGüterbock	*Anatolian Studies Presented to Hans Gustav Güterbock on the Occasion of his 65th Birthday.* Istanbul 1973
FsGüterbock^2	*Kaniššuwar: A Tribute to Hans G. Güterbock on His Seventy-fifth Birthday May 27, 1983.* Chicago 1986
FsKantor	*Essays in Ancient Civilization Presented to Helene J. Kantor.* Chicago 1989
FsLacheman	*Studies on the Civilization and Culture of Nuzi and the Hurrians in Honor of Ernest R. Lacheman.* Winona Lake, Indiana 1981
FsLaroche	*Florilegium Anatolicum: Mélanges offerts à Emmanuel Laroche.* Paris 1979
FsNeumann	*Serta Indogermanica: Festschrift für Günter Neumann zum 60. Geburtstag.* (*IBS* 40) Innsbruck 1982
FsOtten	*Festschrift Heinrich Otten.* Wiesbaden 1973
FsOtten^2	*Documentum Asiae Minoris Antiquae. Festschrift für Heinrich Otten zum 75. Geburtstag.* Wiesbaden 1988
FsReiner	*Language, Literature and History: Philological and Historical Studies Presented to Erica Reiner.* (*AOS* 67) New Haven 1987
Gilg.	Gilgameš epic
GLH	E. Laroche, *Glossaire de la langue hourrite* (*RHA* 34–35). Paris 1976–77
Goetze, *Kl*	A. Goetze, *Kleinasien*, 2nd ed. Munich 1957
GsKronasser	*Investigationes philologicae et comparitativae. Gedenkschrift für Heinz Kronasser.* Wiesbaden 1982
Gurney, Schweich	O. R. Gurney, *Some Aspects of Hittite Religion.* (The Schweich Lectures 1976) Oxford 1977
Haas, *KN*	V. Haas, *Der Kult von Nerik.* Rome 1970
Haas-Thiel, *AOAT* 31	V. Haas and H. Thiel, *Die Beschwörungsrituale der Allaituraḫ(ḫ)i und verwandte Texte.* Neukirchen-Vluyn 1978
HAB	F. Sommer und A. Falkenstein, *Die Hethitisch-akkadische Bilingue des Ḫattušili I.* Munich 1938
Ḫatt.	Apology of Ḫattušili III, cited by column and line in A. Götze, *Hattušiliš. Der Bericht über seine Thronbesteigung nebst den Paralleltexten.* (*MVAG* 29.3) Leipzig 1925
HbOr	*Handbuch der Orientalistik*
HE	J. Friedrich, *Hethitisches Elementarbuch.* Heidelberg: Part 1 1960, 2nd. ed. 1974; Part 2 1967
HED	J. Puhvel, *Hittite Etymological Dictionary.* Berlin 1984–
Heth.u.Idg.	E. Neu and W. Meid, eds., *Hethitisch und Indogermanisch: Vergleichende Studien zur historischen Grammatik und zur dialektgeographischen Stellung der indogermanischen Sprachgruppe Altkleinasiens.* Innsbruck 1979
HFAC	G. Beckman and H. A. Hoffner, *Hittite Fragments in American Collections* (*JCS* 37 [1985] 1–60)
HG	J. Friedrich, *Die hethitischen Gesetze.* Leiden 1959, 2nd ed. 1971

HHB	H.-S. Schuster, *Die hattisch-hethitischen Bilinguen I/1.* (*DMOA* 17) Leiden 1974
Hipp.heth.	A. Kammenhuber, *Hippologia hethitica.* Wiesbaden 1961
HT	*Hittite Texts in the Cuneiform Character in the British Museum.* London 1920
HTR	H. Otten, *Hethitische Totenrituale.* Berlin 1958
Ḫuqq.	The Treaty of Šuppiluliuma with Ḫuqqana, edited in *SV* 2:103–63
HW	J. Friedrich, *Hethitisches Wörterbuch.* Heidelberg 1952(–54)
HW 1., 2., 3. Erg.	J. Friedrich, *Hethitisches Wörterbuch 1.–3. Ergänzungsheft.* Heidelberg 1957, 1961, 1966
HW²	J. Friedrich and A. Kammenhuber, *Hethitisches Wörterbuch,* 2nd ed. Heidelberg 1975–
IBoT	*İstanbul Arkeoloji Müzelerinde Bulunan Boğazköy Tabletleri(nden Seçme Metinler)* 1–4. Istanbul 1944, 1947, 1954, 1988
IBS	*Innsbrucker Beiträge zur Sprachwissenschaft*
IF	*Indogermanische Forschungen*
Illu.	Illuyanka Myth
IM	*Istanbuler Mitteilungen*
Izi	Lexical series izi = *išātu* (*MSL* 13:154–226)
Izi Bogh.	Boğazköy version of Izi (*MSL* 13:132–47)
JANES	*Journal of the Ancient Near Eastern Society*
JAOS	*Journal of the American Oriental Society*
JBL	*Journal of Biblical Literature*
JCS	*Journal of Cuneiform Studies*
JESHO	*Journal of the Economic and Social History of the Orient*
JIES	*Journal of Indo-European Studies*
JKF	*Jahrbuch für kleinasiatische Forschungen* (= *Anadolu Araştırmaları*)
Josephson, *Par.*	F. Josephson, *The Function of Sentence Particles in Old and Middle Hittite.* Uppsala 1972
JNES	*Journal of Near Eastern Studies*
Kammenhuber, *Materialien*	A. Kammenhuber, *Materialien zu einem hethitischen Thesaurus.* Heidelberg 1973–
Kaškäer	E. von Schuler, *Die Kaškäer.* Berlin 1965
KBo	*Keilschrifttexte aus Boghazköi*
KlF	*Kleinasiatische Forschungen,* ed. F. Sommer and H. Ehelolf
KUB	*Keilschrifturkunden aus Boghazköi*
Kum.	H. G. Güterbock, *Kumarbi. Mythen vom churritischen Kronos.* Zürich-New York 1946
Kup.	Treaty of Muršili II with Kupanta-ᴰKAL, edited in *SV* 1:95–181
KZ	*Zeitschrift für Vergleichende Sprachforschung* ("*Kuhns Zeitschrift*")
Laroche, *HH*	E. Laroche, *Les hiéroglyphes hittites I.* (Unmarked number following "*HH*" refers to a sign number) Paris 1960
Laroche, *Myth.*	E. Laroche, *Textes mythologiques hittites en transcription* (*RHA* XXIII/77, XXVI/82). Paris 1965, 1968
Laroche, *Onom.*	E. Laroche, *Recueil d'Onomastique Hittite.* Paris 1951
Laroche, *Rech.*	E. Laroche, *Recherches sur les noms des dieux hittites* (*RHA* VII/46). Paris 1947

Lebrun, *Hymnes*	R. Lebrun, *Hymnes et prières hittites.* Louvain-la-neuve 1980
Lebrun, *Samuha*	R. Lebrun, *Samuha, foyer religieux de l'empire hittite.* Louvain-la-neuve 1976
LS	K. Riemschneider, *Die hethitischen Landschenkungsurkunden* (*MIO* 6: 321–81). Berlin 1958
Madd.	A. Götze, *Madduwattaš.* (*MVAeG* 32.1) Leipzig 1928
Man.	Treaty of Muršili II with Manapa-ᴰU, edited in *SV* 2:1–41
MAOG	*Mitteilungen der Altorientalischen Gesellschaft*
Mašt.	Ritual of Maštigga against family quarrels (CTH 404); 2Mašt. cited according to the edition of L. Rost, *MIO* 1 (1953) 348–67
MAW	S. N. Kramer, ed., *Mythologies of the Ancient World.* Garden City, New York 1961
MDOG	*Mitteilungen der deutschen Orient-Gesellschaft zu Berlin*
Melchert, Diss.	H. C. Melchert, *Ablative and Instrumental in Hittite* (Ph.D. diss., Harvard University). Cambridge, Massachusetts 1977
Mém.Atatürk	*Mémorial Atatürk: Études d'archéologie et de philologie anatoliennes.* Paris 1982
Meriggi, *HhGl*	P. Meriggi, *Hieroglyphisch-hethitisches Glossar,* 2nd. ed. Wiesbaden 1962
Mestieri	F. Pecchioli Daddi, *Mestieri, professioni e dignità nell'Anatolia ittita.* Rome 1982
MIO	*Mitteilungen des Instituts für Orientforschung*
MRS	*Mission de Ras Shamra*
MSL	B. Landsberger et al., *Materialien zum sumerischen Lexikon.* Rome
MSS	*Münchener Studien zur Sprachwissenschaft*
MVAeG	*Mitteilungen der Vorderasiatisch-ägyptischen Gesellschaft*
MVAG	*Mitteilungen der vorderasiatischen Gesellschaft*
NF	Neue Folge
NH	E. Laroche, *Les Noms des Hittites.* Paris 1966
NH Suppl.	E. Laroche, "Les noms des Hittites: supplément" (*Hethitica* 4 [1981] 3–58)
NHF	*Neuere Hethiterforschung,* ed. G. Walser. Wiesbaden 1964
OA	*Oriens Antiquus*
Oettinger, *Stammbildung*	Norbert Oettinger, *Die Stammbildung des hethitischen Verbums.* Nürnberg 1979
OIP	*Oriental Institute Publications*
OLP	*Orientalia Lovaniensia Periodica*
OLZ	*Orientalistische Literaturzeitung*
Or	*Orientalia, New Series*
Otten, *Puduḫepa*	H. Otten, *Puduḫepa: Eine hethitische Königin in ihren Textzeugnissen.* Mainz 1975
Otten, *Tel.*	H. Otten, *Die Überlieferungen des Telipinu-Mythus.* (*MVAeG* 46.1) Leipzig 1942
Pap.	F. Sommer and H. Ehelolf, *Das hethitische Ritual des Pāpanikri von Komana.* (*BoSt* 10) Leipzig 1924
Popko, *Kultobjekte*	M. Popko, *Kultobjekte in der hethitischen Religion (nach keilschriftlichen Quellen).* Warsaw 1978
PRU	*Le palais royal d'Ugarit* (subseries of *MRS*). Paris 1955–
RA	*Revue d'Assyriologie et d'Archéologie orientale*
Records	P. H. J. Houwink ten Cate, *The Records of the Early Hittite Empire (c. 1450–1380 B.C.).* Leiden 1970

RGTC 6	G. F. del Monte and J. Tischler, *Répertoire géographique des Textes Cunéiformes*, vol. 6. Wiesbaden 1978
RHA	*Revue hittite et asianique*
RLA	*Reallexikon der Assyriologie und Vorderasiatischen Archäologie*. Berlin 1928–
RS	Ras Shamra Text, inventory number
RSO	*Rivista degli Studi Orientali*
SAOC	*Studies in Ancient Oriental Civilization*
SBo	H. G. Güterbock, *Siegel aus Boğazköy* I, II. (*AfO* Beiheft 5, 7) Berlin 1940, 1942 (reprint 1967)
SCO	*Studi Classici e Orientali*
SHAW	*Sitzungsberichte der Heidelberger Akademie der Wissenschaften*
SMEA	*Studi micenei ed egeo-anatolici*
StBoT	*Studien zu den Boğazköy-Texten*
StMed	*Studia Mediterranea*
Süel, *Direktif Metni*	A. Süel, *Hitit kaynaklarında tapınak görevlileri ile ilgili bir direktif metni*. Ankara 1985
Sürenhagen, *Staatsv.*	D. Sürenhagen, *Paritätische Staatsverträge aus hethitischer sicht*. (*StMed* 5) Pavia 1985
SV	J. Friedrich, *Staatsverträge des Hatti-Reiches in hethitischer Sprache* 1, 2. (*MVAeG* 31.1, 34.1) Leipzig 1926, 1930
Targ.	Treaty of Muršili II with Targašnalli, edited in *SV* 1:51–94
Taw.	Tawagalawa letter, edited in *AU*
Tel.pr.	Telipinu proclamation
Tel.myth	Telipinu myth
THeth	*Texte der Hethiter*
Tischler, *HEG*	J. Tischler, *Hethitisches etymologisches Glossar*. (*IBS* 20) Innsbruck 1977–
Tunn.	A. Goetze, *The Hittite Ritual of Tunnawi*. New Haven 1938
Untersuchungen	W. Orthmann, *Untersuchungen zur Späthethitische Kunst*. Bonn 1971
UF	*Ugarit-Forschungen*
Ugar.	*Ugaritica*
Ullik.	H. G. Güterbock, "The Song of Ullikummi, Revised Text of the Hittite Version of a Hurrian Myth" (*JCS* 5:135–61; 6:8–42). New Haven 1961–62
VAT	Inventory numbers of tablets in the Staatliche Museen in Berlin
VBoT	*Verstreute Boghazköi-Texte*, ed. A. Götze. Marburg 1930
VIO	*Veröffentlichungen des Instituts für Orientforschung der Deutsche Akademie der Wissenschaften*
WO	*Die Welt des Orient*
WVDOG	*Wissenschaftliche Veröffentlichungen der deutschen Orient-Gesellschaft*
WZKM	*Wiener Zeitschrift für die Kunde des Morgenlandes*
Yaz^2	*Das hethitische Felsheiligtum Yazılıkaya*. (*BoHa* 9) Berlin 1975
ZA	*Zeitschrift für Assyriologie und vorderasiatische Archäologie*

LIST OF GENERAL ABBREVIATIONS

abl.	ablative
acc.	accusative
col.	column
dat.	dative
diss.	dissertation
d.-l.	dative-locative
DN	divine name
dupl(s).	duplicate(s)
e.	edge
ed.	edition, edited by
eras.	erasure
Erg.	Ergänzungsheft
f(f).	following
fasc.	fascicle
fest.	festival
frag.	fragment
GN	geographical name
instr.	instruction(s)
l.e.	left edge
Lief.	Lieferung
MH	Middle Hittite
MS	Middle Hittite Script
NH	New Hittite
NS	New Hittite Script
OH	Old Hittite
OS	Old Hittite Script
par.	parallel
pl.	plate(s)
PN	personal name
TOS	Typical Old Script
tr.	translation, translated (by)
translit.	transliteration, transliterated (by)
×	indicates an inscribed sign
o	space within a lacuna for a sign
x	illegible sign
=	equivalences in duplicates, lexical texts and bilinguals
§	paragraph in cuneiform text
*	denotes an unattested form
[ ]	encloses material lost in a break in the tablet
[( )]	encloses material restored from a duplicate text
⌈ ⌉	partly broken
< >	omitted by scribal error
<( )>	omitted by scribal error and restored from a duplicate
« »	to be omitted
/	end of line in cuneiform text
//	marks morpheme boundaries
:	single- or double-wedge marker (Glossenkeil). Used to indicate foreign words in a Hittite text.
x+1	indicates that the first line of a transliteration is not the original first line because the top of the tablet is broken away
′	after a line number indicates that the line numbering reflects only the preserved lines of a broken tablet

INTRODUCTION

General

Much of Hittite official life revolved around the cult, the system of state-sponsored festivals designed to ensure regular and appropriate offerings to the gods.[1] Festivals in this sense are cult ceremonies often lasting several days, which are the primary shared religious expression of the Hittites.[2] Although the state had a well developed system of priests and other functionaries, the king and queen played the most prominent role in most festivals. The festival descriptions as they have come down to us written in cuneiform on clay tablets specify in great detail the materials and mode of offerings, the kinds of cult liturgy to be performed, and the places of celebration. Investigation into the nature of the Hittite state reveals that among a Hittite monarch's responsibilities the one that was perhaps most essential was that of maintaining the state's relationship with its deities by providing for and performing the requisite cult ceremonies. A rather full religious calendar prescribed a yearly cycle of these festivals. Further evidence bearing on the centrality of the cult comes from the oracle texts in the state archives, in which very often the Hittites question a god as to whether his anger stems from the forgetting of cult offerings.

The activities of the cult took place at a variety of sacred loci. The Hittite capital, Ḫattuša, is a city of temples large and small, with attached storerooms and tablet archives. Within the temple cella was a series of "holy places" that received libations and offerings. Many major festivals involved cult journeys or processions of king and queen, priests, and gods within the capital or to sacred spots outside the city. Sacred groves or springs might be the locus of a deity. Many deities had a cult stela (*ḫuwaši*) out in the countryside at which offerings would be made. Those offerings might be beer or wine or other unidentified beverages, meat, bread, or cheese. The great variety of offering breads alone testifies to the diversity within the cult.

1. For general remarks on Hittite religion see Gurney, *Some Aspects of Hittite Religion* (Oxford, 1977) and Güterbock, "Hittite Religion," pp. 81–109 in Vergilius Ferm, ed., *Forgotten Religions* (New York, n.d.).
2. Hittitologists follow the Hittites themselves in distinguishing between festivals (EZEN), group religious ceremonies designed to worship and provide offerings to the gods, and rituals (SISKUR), magical procedures often performed by and for individuals to address specific maladies.

Tablets of festival descriptions make up a large portion of the extant Hittite corpus. The nature of a cultic description is such that these tablets can be difficult to place chronologically within the four centuries of the Hittite kingdom. Unlike historical texts, which often can be dated by events or allusions to known individuals, the festivals usually exist in many copies written over a period of centuries, changing little if at all during that time. The primary means for establishing the date of a festival tablet are the types of gods mentioned, the characteristics of the language, and the paleography of the script. None of the festivals edited in this volume is on the grand scale of a festival like the thirty-eight days of the Festival of the AN.TAḪ.ŠUM plant, but they are in most cases state festivals celebrated by the kingdom's religious institution. Some Hittite festivals are intended to be universal, dedicated to the entire pantheon; others are performed for a particular deity. The cult descriptions edited herein contain festivals of both types. The texts describing the cult, while often repetitious in their descriptions of offerings, provide a penetrating insight into the Hittite perception of the world, a world ruled by gods who must be fed and propitiated, who must at any cost be provided with their ordained offerings and ceremony.

TUTELARY DEITIES

Among the gods of the Hittite pantheon were a number of deities who were thought of as "tutelary" or "protective" deities. This is not a uniquely Hittite concept, as many cultures revere and attempt to propitiate gods who are supposed to be guardian spirits over personal well-being, nature, the home, a sacred locus, a particular activity, etc.[3] The Mesopotamians revered protective spirits who watched over one's person and served as patron deities.[4] Two of the Sumerian words for these deities were LAMMA and ALAD, whose Akkadian equivalents were *lamassu* and *šēdu*.[5] It is in fact the Sumerian logogram LAMMA[6] which the Hittites used in writing the titles of many of their protective deities. They used this logogram not as a name but as a title, "the Tutelary Deity," or to represent an Anatolian name such as Inara, whose name is sometimes written with this sign, usually with a phonetic complement, for example ^{D}LAMMA-*aš* or ^{D}LAMMA-*ri*.[7]

The notion of protective deities is of great antiquity in Anatolia. Kutlu Emre identifies the lead statuettes found in houses from the Old Assyrian colony period as protective

3. See for example descriptions of such gods among the Romans in Hammond and Scullard, eds., *The Oxford Classical Dictionary* (Oxford, 1970), on Genius, p. 461; Juno, pp. 568–69; Lares, pp. 578–79; and Penates, pp. 797–98.
4. For a summary of the Mesopotamian tutelary deities see von Soden, *BagM* 3 (1964) 148–56 and Foxvog, Heimpel, and Kilmer, *RLA* 6 (1980–83) 447–53. Foxvog et al, p. 448, comment on the ubiquitous presence of protective deities in Mesopotamian religion: "Any person, god, place or even object could have a LAMMA."
5. See the Erimḫuš vocabulary *KBo* 26.25(+)*KBo* 1.35 iii 3′–4′, discussed in *Chapter 1*.
6. The KAL sign, Borger, *AOAT* 33A #322. The reading LAMMA is derived from lexical texts such as the one cited above.
7. Steiner, *RLA* 3 (1957–71) 548, and Laroche, *RLA* 6 (1980–83) 456, note the complexity of the Hittite use of ^{D}LAMMA, which denotes not one specific god but a type of god.

deities for the houses, probably the "your god, our god" referred to in the documents.[8] The evidence of seals from the pre-Hittite period also indicates the antiquity of the association of certain gods with the stag, the sacred animal of the tutelary deity in the Hittite period.[9] There are seals from the Old Assyrian period which show a deity on a stag, armed with weapons, with a hare and/or bird in its hand.[10] This is the same iconography attested for certain Hittite tutelary deities (see below) and demonstrates the continuity of cult representation from the *kārum* period into the Hittite kingdom, a continuity based on the Hittites' extensive borrowing of gods, cults, and iconography from the Hattians, their Anatolian predecessors.

The appropriate English translation for the title ᴰLAMMA has proved somewhat elusive. In German ᴰLAMMA is usually translated "Schutzgott," which is convenient and conveys the meaning as well as any other translation. There is, however, no one-word English equivalent for "Schutzgott"; I have chosen in general to utilize the term "tutelary deity."[11] The translation intentionally conveys the rather general connotations of the Hittite term.

The iconography of tutelary deities is fairly well known, thanks to the well-attested use of a *kurša-* (hunting bag) as a cult image[12] and several descriptions of images from cult inventories.[13] The description of ᴰLAMMA LÍL matches so well with a number of extant representations that we can identify a number of images of tutelary deities in the preserved art of the Hittites,[14] for example the Yeniköy relief,[15] Karasu,[16] the Hacı Bebekli relief,[17] and a relief from Arslantepe.[18] Güterbock notes that the god on the stag and the

8. *Anatolian Lead Figurines and Their Stone Moulds* (Ankara 1971) 154.
9. Old Assyrian seals noted by Güterbock, *Belleten* VII/1 (1943) 316.
10. N. Özgüç, *The Anatolian Group of Cylinder Seal Impressions from Kültepe* (Ankara 1965) 66–67, Orthmann, *Untersuchungen* 262. The relevant seals are reviewed and discussed by Crepon, *Hethitica* 4 (1981) 131–37.
11. ᴰLAMMA is also sometimes translated "patron deity" in English, "dieu protecteur" in French, "divinità tutelare" in Italian, and "koruyucu tanrı" in Turkish. Laroche, *RLA* 6 (1980–83) 455, points out that even "Schutzgott" is a makeshift term which does not completely describe the nature of these deities.
12. See *Chapter 4* and *Appendix B* sub *kurša-*.
13. Discussed under ᴰLAMMA, ᴰLAMMA ᵁᴿᵁḪatenzuwa, ᴰLAMMA ᴳᴵŠŠUKUR, and ᴰLAMMA LÍL in *Chapter 1.*
14. See the discussion in *Bildbeschr.* 78–82 and the list of late Hittite material in Orthmann, *Untersuchungen* 258–63, with accompanying plates. Orthmann provides a recent overview of the iconography in the late period, with examples, and discusses the problems of identifying all the pertinent reliefs as tutelary deities. In addition to Orthmann's list Yazılıkaya #32, Karasu, the Schimmel rhyton, and seal #386 in von der Osten, *Ancient Oriental Seals in the Collection of Mr. Edward T. Newell* (p. 58, pl. XXVI), represent tutelary deities. The identification of these images as tutelary deities is discussed by Przeworski, *Syria* 21 (1940) 69–71, and Güterbock, *SBo* II (1947) 15–17, *Belleten* VII/1 (1943) 313–16, *Or* 15 (1946) 494–95, and *FsBittel* 207–08.
15. Bittel, *Hethiter* pl. 247.
16. Hellenkemper and Wagner, *AnSt* 27 (1977) 167–73.
17. Orthmann, *Untersuchungen* 258, Hellenkemper and Wagner, *AnSt* 27 (1977) 170, pl. XXXIIb.
18. *Bildbeschr.* pl. III figure 10.

hieroglyphic stag-god must be the cuneiform ᴰLAMMA.[19] The iconography may include the god represented (1) standing on its sacred animal the stag, (2) armed with bow and sword, (3) holding a bird, often an eagle, on his outstretched hand,[20] and (4) holding an animal, often a hare, upside down.

The iconography is not consistent and shows many variations in the representations within a fairly clear group of similar images. Orthmann[21] provides a table of the variations and similarities of this group. Headgear is not always the expected high horned helmet of divinity. The bow may be replaced by a spear or axe or staff. Güterbock[22] indicates from the evidence of gods such as the moon god that at Yazılıkaya the sacred animal may be omitted, as is the case with the Tutelary Deity (#32) in that sanctuary's divine procession. The significance of the animal held upside down by the god is open to some question. In Orthmann's table these animals are referred to as "Beutetier," the results of the hunt. This contributes to our association of the tutelary deities with the hunt. Güterbock[23] notes that the hare and the eagle could either be the fruit of the hunt or a representation of the beasts of the field as an indication of what the Tutelary Deity of the Countryside protects. As there are some reliefs in which a god holds a hare or other animal upside down while raising a weapon to strike it, I would interpret the animal suspended from the Tutelary Deity's hand as the prey, Orthmann's "Beutetier."

The variations in iconography suggest that in the images we have to do with a variety of deities of the same general type, which fits well with the textual evidence of many different manifestations under the general rubric of tutelary deity. Przeworski[24] infers from these differing representations a group of related gods reflecting local manifestations. Güterbock[25] also derives from the lack of uniformity the idea that different gods are represented in this group.

Although there are a great variety of tutelary deities in the Hittite pantheon, they may be reduced to the following types:

I. Deities whose actual name is written out in the text.
II. A deity whose title is written simply ᴰLAMMA without any further specification. This is the most problematic to the modern scholar because the Hittites did not use this title to denote the same deity throughout the history of its usage. It is sometimes

19. *SBo* II 16, where Güterbock points out that like many hieroglyphs, this sign evolved, and may take the form of the whole stag, the head, or the antler. In *Belleten* VII/1 (1943) 213–14, he adduces other evidence such as the unpublished tablet 544/f for the connection of the stag with the tutelary deity. In *FsBittel* 207 he reiterates the use of the antler as a name-hieroglyph for the Tutelary Deity. This sign is used for human and divine names on seals and monuments. See also Laroche, *HH* 102.

20. Güterbock, *Belleten* VII/1: 315, cites two seals which show a seated deity with a bird on its hand and the antler, the hieroglyphic sign for tutelary deity, as inscription.

21. *Untersuchungen* 260.

22. *Belleten* VII/1: 298.

23. *Belleten* VII/1: 313.

24. *Syria* 21 (1940) 70–71.

25. *Belleten* VII/1: 316.

used for Inar(a), an originally Hattic goddess, and at other times for a god who is clearly male. I have translated this unspecified title ᴰLAMMA as "the Tutelary Deity."

III. Deities who are identified by title in the form ᴰLAMMA plus (geographical name), for example ᴰLAMMA ᵁᴿᵁKaraḫna.

IV. Deities whose title is of the form ᴰLAMMA plus (non-GN) epithet. The epithet is usually formed with a genitive construction and may therefore precede the ᴰLAMMA element (normal Hittite syntax) or follow it (Sumerian or Akkadian syntax), for example ᴰLAMMA.LÍL = ᴰLAMMA *ṢĒRI* = *gimraš* ᴰLAMMA, "the Tutelary Deity of the Countryside."

The Hittites' own awareness of the unusual nature of this large group of gods who had the same title and were distinguished only by individual epithets is most clearly seen in the Festival for All the Tutelary Deities,[26] whose ostensible purpose was to name and provide offerings for all of the tutelary deities.

Probably all of the tutelary deities whose names we know are Hattic in origin. That tutelary deities were important in the religion of the pre-Hittite Anatolian peoples may be inferred from the evidence cited above and the survival of these Hattic gods in Hittite rituals, festivals, and prayers. In many ceremonies they continue to enjoy their offerings to the accompaniment of singing in the pre-Hittite Hattic language. The origins of the deities who are known to us in the texts only by title cannot so easily be discerned. Given the eclectic nature of the Hittite religious mind, it is likely that this plethora of tutelary deities exists precisely because the Hittites borrowed such gods (along with other deities) from many of the peoples with whom they came in contact.

The tutelary deities are normally grouped together when they occur in lists, especially in the lists of oath-deities in the treaties. Some of them indeed are minor deities who are only rarely if ever attested by themselves, occurring almost invariably in a group with other tutelary gods. Some of the offering or oath deity lists are of course more complete than others and include a larger range of the tutelary deities. Partly because Hittite uses a common gender for both masculine and feminine it is often impossible to determine the sex of a particular tutelary deity.[27] A deity such as Inara, whose name is often written with the LAMMA sign, is female,[28] but there are other tutelary deities represented by the same logogram who are male.[29] The question of the gender of various gods is taken up in *Chapter 1* in the discussions of individual tutelary deities. I have purely as a convention generally used the pronoun "he" and the noun "god" to denote a tutelary deity without necessarily implying anything about the gender of the divinity. Where the gender is known it is indicated.

26. *CTH* 682; see *Chapter 3*.
27. As Laroche, *JCS* 1 (1947) 196, notes the pre-Hittite Hattians also did not indicate the sex of their deities.
28. Laroche, *Rech.* 82, *Onom.* 79.
29. Laroche, *Onom.* 81.

The tutelary deities occur in all types of cultic texts as well as texts of other genres. In the present work I have edited or discussed texts which I consider the most important sources for our understanding of this group of deities. *Chapters 2-5* treat the major festivals dedicated primarily to tutelary deities. In *Appendix A* fragments of festival texts having to do with tutelary deities are discussed. Evidence for the cult of the tutelary deities from other texts is assembled in *Chapter 1*, and some conclusions are offered in *Chapter 6*.

TEXT SCHEME OF THE FESTIVALS FOR THE TUTELARY DEITIES

The following text scheme represents a revision of Laroche's initial work of identifying and cataloguing all of the Hittite tablets (*CTH* 681–685) that contain festivals for tutelary deities, a collection of tablets that Laroche titles "Cultes de dKAL." The revisions and additions to Laroche's text scheme are the result of the publication of many new tablets since *Catalogue des Textes Hittites* appeared, and of my identifying some of his fragments (*CTH* 685) with known festivals.

CTH 681. Festivals of Karaḫna (*Chapter 2*)

1. Bo 3298+*KUB* 25.32+*KUB* 27.70+1628/u
2. *IBoT* 1.5

CTH 682. The Festivals for All the Tutelary Deities (*Chapter 3*)

The Festival of Group Offerings

1. A. *KUB* 2.1.
   B. *KBo* 2.38. Column ii? duplicates 1.A (*KUB* 2.1) ii 35–50.
   C. *KUB* 44.16+*IBoT* 3.69. Columns i–iii describe offerings, column v duplicates 1.A (*KUB* 2.1) ii 22–41, vi duplicates 1.A (*KUB* 2.1) iii 46–iv 23.
   D. Bo 6113. Duplicates 1.A (*KUB* 2.1) iv 22–v 8.
   E. *KBo* 22.189. Column i lost, column ii duplicates 1.C (*KUB* 44.16+*IBoT* 3.69) ii 8′–25′, but the reverse does not duplicate the main text *KUB* 2.1.
   F. *KUB* 11.21. Obverse ii and iii too broken to place, reverse v 15′–25′ duplicates 1.E (*KBo* 22.189) iii 3–13.[30]
   G. *IBoT* 4.73. Duplicates 1.E (*KBo* 22.189) v 6′–11′.
   H. 754/t. Duplicates 1.C (*KUB* 44.16+*IBoT* 3.69) ii 7′–14′=1.E (*KBo* 22.189) ii 1–7.

The Festival of Individual Offerings

2. A. *KBo* 11.40. Column i is parallel to 1.A (*KUB* 2.1) i 47–51.
   Column ii is parallel to 1.A (*KUB* 2.1) ii 15–24.
   Column v probably parallels lost portions of 1.A (*KUB* 2.1) v.
   Column vi 1–8 are parallel to 1.A (*KUB* 2.1) vi.

30. Identified by George Moore, *JAOS* 102 (1982) 180.

B. *KUB* 40.108. Column ii duplicates 2.A (*KBo* 11.40) i 18′–26′; column v is parallel to 1.A (*KUB* 2.1) iv 7–10 and fills in some of the missing portions of 2.A(*KBo* 11.40).
C. *KUB* 40.101. Duplicates 2.A (*KBo* 11.40) v 1′–23′.
D. *KUB* 40.107+*IBoT* 2.18. Column i may be from the early part of the festival. Reverse iv 17′–30′ duplicate 2.A (*KBo* 11.40) vi 2′–18′.
E. *KBo* 12.60. Parallel to 1.A (*KUB* 2.1) iii 8–15, probably duplicate to missing portions of 2.A (*KBo* 11.40) obverse iii. It is not an indirect join to *KBo* 11.40.
F. *KUB* 55.25. Parallel to 1.A (*KUB* 2.1) iii 29–35 and probably duplicates some of the missing 2.A (*KBo* 11.40) obverse iii.

Texts of Uncertain Attribution

3. *KBo* 12.59. Similar to 1 (Festival of Group Offerings) and 2 (Festival of Individual Offerings).
4. *KUB* 51.36.
5. *KUB* 52.100.

CTH 683. The Festivals for Renewing the ^{KUŠ}*kurša*-s (*Chapter 4*)

1. *KUB* 55.43.
2. A. *KBo* 13.179.
   B. *KBo* 22.168. Duplicates 2.A (*KBo* 13.179) ii 2′–13′.
3. *KUB* 7.36.[31]
4. *KUB* 20.13.[31]
5. A. *KBo* 21.89+*KBo* 8.97.[31]
   B. *IBoT* 2.69.[31] Obverse i duplicates 5.A (*KBo* 21.89+*KBo* 8.97) i 10′–18′. Reverse too small to interpret.

CTH 684. The Festivals for the Tutelary Deities of the River (*Chapter 5*)

1. A. *KUB* 9.21.
   B. *ABoT* 3. Duplicates 1.A (*KUB* 9.21) 8′–10′ and adds two lines after 1.A (= *KUB* 9.21) breaks off.
2. *IBoT* 1.2
3. A. *KUB* 51.79.
   B. *IBoT* 2.19. Duplicates 3.A (*KUB* 51.79) rev! 10′–15′.
   C. 412/s(+?)457/s. Obverse duplicates 3.A (*KUB* 51.79) obv! 4′–15′. Reverse 1′–7′ duplicate 3.A (*KUB* 51.79) rev! 14′–18′.
4. A. *KUB* 44.2. Parallel to 3.A (*KUB* 51.79) rev! 7′–13′.
   B. *KUB* 44.3. Adds one line to the beginning of 4.A (*KUB* 44.2) and duplicates 1′–7′ of that tablet.

31. Catalogued by Laroche as *CTH* 685, "Fragments de fêtes pour les dieux KAL."

CTH 685. Fragments of Festivals for Tutelary Deities (*Appendix A*)

KUB 7.40
KUB 9.17
KUB 10.29
KUB 10.93
KUB 12.52
IBoT 2.22
IBoT 3.18
KBo 8.59
KUB 44.24
KUB 51.40
KUB 53.11

CHAPTER 1

TUTELARY DEITIES AND THEIR CULTS

General Comments

As mentioned in the *Introduction*, tutelary deities may be referred to either by name, such as Zitḫariya, or by the title LAMMA, with or without an epithet. We have the evidence of lexical texts such as the Erimḫuš text A. *KBo* 26.25(+)*KBo* 1.35 iii 3′–4′ with the duplicate B. *KBo* 13.1+*KBo* 1.44 iv 35–36[1] for the reading of the KAL sign: Sumerian [^{D}LAMM(A)] = Syllabic *la-am-ma* = Akkadian *LA-MA-SÚ* = Hittite ^{D}LAMMA-*aš*[2] / [^{D}ÁLA(D)][3] = *a-la* = *ŠE-E-DU*[4] = *tar-pí-iš*. Both LAMMA and ÁLAD (ALA in this text) are readings of the same sign (KAL), indicated by the syllabic column in text A. For further comment on ^{D}ALA(D) see sub Ala on page 11.

The Hittite column of B reads *a-an-na-ri-iš* instead of ^{D}LAMMA-*aš*. The word *annari-* is not completely understood. Otten, *MDOG* 94 (1963) 19, suggests as a meaning "männliche Potenz." Puhvel, *HED* 1–2: 62, translates it "strength, force, vigor." Kammenhuber, *HW*^{2} 79, does not give a translation. In the Festival for All the Tutelary Deities[5] *annari-* and *tarpi-* are associated together, both in rare or unique *a*-stem forms. They occur in a genitival relationship with ^{D}LAMMA that is not consistent with text B's

1. Edition *MSL* 17 (1985) 115, in which *KBo* 13.1+*KBo* 1.44 is the main text. *KBo* 26.25(+)*KBo* 1.35 is text A$_5$ in *MSL* 17. *KBo* 13.1+ lacks the column of syllabic Sumerian. *KBo* 13.1+*KBo* 1.44 is also edited by Otten and von Soden, *StBoT* 7.
2. *MSL* 17: 115 n. 36 (3) gives the equation ^{D}KAL-*aš* = ^{D}*Inaraš* for the Hittite column of A. I read ^{D}LAMMA-*aš* based on the syllabic Sumerian column. The correct Hittite reading may very well be ^{D}*Inaraš*, but Inara is not always the Hittite deity behind the logogram LAMMA. On ^{D}LAMMA-*aš* = ^{D}*Inaraš* see pp. 24–27 below.
3. Borger, *AOAT* 33A p. 226, gives a value ÁLAD for the KAL sign. In Mesopotamia the KAL×BAD sign, ALAD in Borger *AOAT* 33A #323, is the regular Sumerogram for Akkadian *šēdu*. Deimel, *Pantheon Babylonicum* (Rome, 1914) 154, had at an early date recognized a reading *A-la-ad* = *še-e-du* for the KAL sign. In this Boğazköy lexical text the syllabic Sumerian column gives the Hittite pronunciation ALA.
4. Text B iv 35: *ŠE-DU*.
5. *KUB* 2.1 obv. iii 1–2 (*Chapter 3*).

equation of ^{D}LAMMA with *annariš*. Von Soden[6] notes that in Mesopotamia the paired tutelary deities *LAMASSU* and *ŠĒDU* together were benevolent but *ŠĒDU* by itself usually evil.[7] Hoffner[8] suggests a similar pattern for *annari-* and *tarpi-*, noting especially that the two together form one protective spirit. Hittite *tarpi-* by itself seems to be evil. Otten and von Soden[9] adduce additional evidence, partly from unpublished sources, to demonstrate that *annari-*[10] and *tarpi-* often occur together and that *tarpi-* alone is evil. Despite the evidence of copy B of the lexical text, we cannot assume that *annari-* is the Hittite or Luwian word invariably underlying ^{D}LAMMA. The evidence of the *a*-stem complementation for many ^{D}LAMMA occurrences (including text A of the vocabulary) argues against it. The parallelism of *LAMASSU* and *ŠĒDU* = *annariš* and *tarpiš* conditioned the pairing of the latter in text B, but if the equivalence ^{D}LAMMA = *LAMASSU* = *annariš* were universal we would expect ^{D}LAMMA to occur regularly with ^{D}ÁLAD or *tarpiš*, which it does not. Perhaps the *annariš* comes simply from confusion with ^{D}*Inaraš* (^{D}LAMMA-*aš*) of text A. Such a confusion of the two is attested by the ^{D}*In-na-ri* for expected *annari* in the unpublished tablet 453/d.

Most tutelary deities are associated with a location or a particular object or being. Some of them show close connections with the hunting bag (*kurša-*) and the dog-men, who are hunters or dog-handlers, and are to be associated with the hunt. Güterbock[11] interprets the EZEN *ḫurnayayaššar* attested in the cult inventory for ^{D}LAMMA of Karaḫna[12] as possibly meaning "Festival of the Hunt." One of the most obvious characteristics of the tutelary deities is the great diversity of their manifestations. The nature of a tutelary deity easily lends itself to the diversification of this god type as new deities, in the form ^{D}LAMMA plus epithet, are created. This tendency to expand the number of tutelary deities is most obvious in the Festival for All the Tutelary Deities, treated in *Chapter 3*. This text is apparently an attempt by the Hittites to codify in written form their concept of the tutelary deity in the late period.[13]

6. *BagM* 3 (1972) 149–50.
7. In Mesopotamia ^{D}LAMMA = *LAMASSU* is female and ^{D}ALAD = *ŠĒDU* is male. Exceptions to this are noted by Foxvog, Heimpel, and Kilmer, *RLA* 6 (1980–83) 447, who cite Assyrian evidence to indicate that LAMMA may sometimes be male.
8. *JNES* 27 (1968) 64–66.
9. *StBoT* 7 (1968) 29–31.
10. In 453/d obv. 4 (*StBoT* 7: 29) replaced by ^{D}*In-na-ri*.
11. *FsKantor* 118.
12. *KUB* 31.35 i 21.
13. The unique or rare titles of tutelary deities in this festival are not treated individually in this chapter; their discussion is reserved for the treatment of the text itself in *Chapter 3*.

TUTELARY DEITIES WITH KNOWN NAMES

^{D}Ala[14]

There is a Mesopotamian deity ^{D}ALAD whose name is written with the ÁLAD (KAL) sign or with the ALAD (KAL×BAD) sign. In the Boğazköy lexical text cited at the beginning of this chapter the syllabic column for ÁLAD gives the pronunciation *a-la*. This raises the question as to whether the deity whose name is usually written ^{D}*A-a-la-*[15] in the Hittite texts is to be identified with ^{D}ÁLAD of the lexical text. Laroche[16] implies his understanding of ^{D}Ala as separate from the ^{D}ÁLAD of the lexical text by placing Ala (as Aala) under his very general rubric "Divinités Asianiques" instead of under "Idéogrammes." This also indicates his caution in not identifying Ala as either a Hattic or Hittite deity. Kammenhuber[17] does not consider the possibility that Ala is the Mesopotamian deity ^{D}ALAD and suggests that Ala is a newly created consort for the male tutelary deity ^{D}LAMMA in the late period. The writing of doubled *a* at the beginning of the name would be unnecessary in representing a Sumerian divine name, and we would expect the Hittites to use the logogram anyway if they were referring to the Mesopotamian deity. The *a*-stem complementation for this name is not consistent with the Hittite reading *tarpiš* given in the lexical text above as the equivalent for ^{D}ÁLAD. In Anatolia ^{D}Ala is female, while the Mesopotamian ^{D}ALAD = *ŠĒDU* is male. As noted above, *tarpi-* by itself, without *annari-*, is an evil, not a protective demon. This is good evidence for understanding ^{D}ALAD as distinct from Ala, as Ala never has a malevolent persona. The Anatolian deity ^{D}Ala must have been confused with the Sumerian ^{D}ALAD in the lexical text, conditioning the syllabic Sumerian spelling *a-la* without final *d* for the KAL sign in that vocabulary. Evidence for the antiquity of Ala in the cult in Anatolia may be seen in her inclusion in a ritual featuring Hattic cult singing[18] and in an Old Script cult text.[19] As detailed below, ^{D}Ala in her few attestations in the Hittite corpus occurs both with and without ^{D}LAMMA.

Ala was not one of the "standard" group of tutelary deities listed among the oath-deities in the treaties.[20] She does however occur once in a late treaty (Tudḫ. IV), in the middle of the standard group of tutelary deities, between ^{D}LAMMA ^{URU}*ḪATTI* and ^{D}Karzi.[21] There is one example of a masculine personal name ^{m}*A-a-la-a*, whose daughter occurs in

14. This deity receives a short treatment in Laroche, *Rech.* 78. There is no "Ala" article in *RLA* because the first volume antedated the discovery of ^{D}Ala in Hittite texts.
15. Case endings ^{D}*A-a-la-aš* and ^{D}*A-a-la-an* are attested.
16. *Rech.* 78.
17. *ZA* 66 (1976) 85.
18. *KBo* 29.211 i 7′–12′, discussed below.
19. *KUB* 43.23 rev. 38–42, discussed below.
20. For example *KBo* 5.3+*KBo* 19.43++ i 48–49 (Ḫuqq.), *KUB* 19.49+*KUB* 26.36+ iv 2–4 (Man.), and *KUB* 21.1+*KBo* 19.73a++ iv 10–11 (Alakš.).
21. *KBo* 4.10 obv. 54 (Ulmi-Tešub treaty).

broken context in a list of women,[22] but as Laroche indicates[23] this is not an argument that Ala is masculine, as other names such as ^{m}Inara indicate that a man might have a name which was identical with a feminine divine name.

Besides these two examples in non-cultic type texts, Ala occurs exclusively in texts of primarily religious nature. Ala is paired with ^{D}LAMMA in *KUB* 43.23, a text which Laroche catalogues in his supplement to *CTH* under number 820, "Bénédictions pour le labarna-roi." Reverse 38–42 reads: 2 NINDA.KUR$_4$.RA GÍD.DA 1 NINDA.KUR$_4$.RA LIBIR 1 GAL GEŠTIN 1 MÁŠ.GAL *ANA* LÚ.MEŠ *ŠA* ^{D}LAMMA ^{D}LAMMA ^{D}*A-a-la* "Two 'long' thick breads, one 'old' thick bread, one cup of wine, (and) one billy-goat to the men of the Tutelary Deity, the Tutelary Deity, (and) Ala." The tablet *KUB* 43.23 is written in Old Script and is thus firm evidence for the antiquity of Ala in the Hittite pantheon and the antiquity of the pairing of the Tutelary Deity and Ala. The "men of the Tutelary Deity" are not otherwise attested but are presumably cult personnel of this deity, although it is unusual for personnel to be receiving offerings.

In Muwatalli's prayer to the Stormgod *piḫaššašši*,[24] this goddess occurs as ^{Df}Alaš[25] in a paragraph naming the gods of Karaḫna, including the Tutelary Deity of Karaḫna. This text is instructive, because the unusual writing of her name with both DINGIR and feminine determinatives confirms that Ala is indeed a goddess, while causing us to wonder why it was felt necessary to specify that she was female. Was there some confusion among the Hittites, or perhaps rather some variation from place to place, as to the nature or gender of this deity? We also observe in this text a paired LAMMA tutelary deity and Ala tutelary deity at the same town, and we learn that Ala was important enough at Karaḫna to be mentioned individually and not simply grouped together with the main body of male and female gods of Karaḫna.

In addition to this list of deities in a prayer, Ala occurs several other times in texts which are primarily lists, such as cult inventories. The cult inventory text *KUB* 38.1[26] describes cult items belonging to Ala. In l.e. 1–2 we read: x ^{URU}*Wiyanauwanta ANA* ^{D}LAMMA EZ[EN o o *AN*]*A* ^{D}*A-la* EZEN *TEŠ*[*I*?[27] o o o o D]Ù-*at* DINGIR-*LIM-tar″ma na*[*wi*? "At(?) Wiyanauwanta a fest[ival of x] for the Tutelary Deity, a spr[ing] festival for Ala [...i]s done. The divine images, however, not y[et..."[28] Again we see a LAMMA tutelary deity and an Ala tutelary deity together in a provincial city. The parallel prescription of a festival for each god testifies to the prominence of Ala in the local cult. A

22. *KBo* 10.10 obv. iv 29.

23. *Rech.* 82–83.

24. *KUB* 6.45+*KUB* 30.14 ii 5–6 with duplicate *KUB* 6.46 ii 48.

25. The writing ^{Df}*A-la-a-aš* is unusual and is sufficiently faint on the tablet that the copyist suggested it may have been meant to be erased. The duplicate has ^{Df}*A-la-aš* and is also partially erased.

26. Line ii 25′–26′: ^{D}*A-la*, edited by von Brandenstein, *Bildbeschr.* as text 2, trans. by Rost, *MIO* 8 (1963) 180.

27. Implied by Rost in her translation and based on her collation.

28. Güterbock, *FsBittel* 208, interprets this section as a statement that although Ala had a festival at Wiyanawanta, she still had no cult image there.

cult image (DINGIR-*LIM-tar*) was not, apparently, part of the equipment when the inventory was taken. This same pair is attested as the gods for the city Kalašmitta in a text detailing royal gifts.[29] In this text the king establishes temples and deportees to be dedicated to the service of these gods in this provincial city. Ala is paired with a different tutelary deity in a ritual fragment:[30] ⌜^{D}⌝LAMMA [*Ṣ*]*ERI* GUB-*aš* ^{D}*A-la-an-na* G[UB?-*aš ekuzi nu*? ^{L}]$^{Ú.MEŠ}$[NA]R ^{URU}*Kaniš* SÌR-*RU* "[He drinks] the Tutelary Deity of the [co]untryside and Ala, standing. The sin[ge]rs of Kaneš sing." Ala occurs once in a list of Hurrian gods, as [^{D}]*A-a-la-aš* in broken context in *KBo* 14.141 ii 2′.

In actual festival texts Ala is quite rare. The festival fragment *KUB* 55.12 ii? 13′–14′ [ ] *ANA* ^{D}LAMMA x[...] [ ] ^{D}*A-a-la-ya* [...] provides little information beyond a further example of the pair ^{D}LAMMA ^{D}Ala. Another example of this pairing, again emphasized by the conjunction *-ya* "and," occurs in the following passage: ^{LÚ}MUḪALDIM *tuḫḫuišnit* ^{NA_4}*ḫuwašiya* EGIR-*pa šuppiaḫḫi* LUGAL-*uš* 1 NINDA.KUR$_4$.RA SA$_5$ *ANA* ^{D}LAMMA ^{D}*A-a-la-ya paršiya nu* ZAG-*az kuit* $\frac{1}{2}$-*AM ḫarzi n″at* ZAG-*aš″pat ḫarzi na″at* ZAG-*az″pat dai* GÙB-*laz″ma kuit* $\frac{1}{2}$-*AM ḫarzi n″at* GÙB-*laz″pat katta dai* "The cook re-purifies(?) the stela with *tuḫḫueššar*.[31] The king breaks one red thick bread to the Tutelary Deity and Ala. The half which he holds on the right, he holds on that same right. He places it on that same right side. The half which he holds on the left, however, he puts down on that same left side" *KUB* 20.99 ii 6–10 (Festival at Šareššа). The divine pair ^{D}LAMMA and Ala received offerings at Šareššа as well, and we learn from this text that this pair probably did not have a temple at this cult center, but only a stela.

The text in which Ala plays a major role is the Festival for All the Tutelary Deities, *CTH* 682, for which see *Chapter 3*. This text uses Ala as a generic title instead of a name and claims to provide offerings for all the "Ala deities." Most copies of the text are late, and it may be a late composition, done under Tudḫaliya IV. It seems to be an attempt to extend to their logical limits all the functions and attributes of both the LAMMA tutelary deity and of Ala. I have understood this festival as a unique experiment in theology and not necessarily a reflection of the general Hittite conception of Ala in earlier periods. The many copies datable to the reign of Tudḫaliya IV attest to that king's great interest in religion and the importance of the state cult.

The attestations of Ala are few in number and indicate the small role which she played in the Hittite cult. The premise that the Anatolian Ala is female is based on one occurrence of her name as ^{Df}Alaš and on the pairing with ^{D}LAMMA, who in Anatolia is often male. Her appearance only once in an oath-deity list points up her absence from the "standardized" pantheon. In many of her occurrences she is paired with the Tutelary Deity, both in the state cult and at provincial cult centers. The occurrence of this pair in the Old

29. *KUB* 48.105 rev. 14–15, ed. Archi and Klengel, *AOF* 7 (1980) 145 and 149.

30. *KBo* 29.211 i? 7′–8′. The same pair receives offerings later in the same ritual, column iv? 6′–10′.

31. The *-ya* on *ḫuwašiya* is difficult to interpret. Güterbock suggests to me that EGIR-*pa* = *appa* could conceivably stand for *appan* here and mean "behind," if *ḫuwašiya* is to be taken as a d.-l. form. The *-ya* could also be a conjunction, "the stela also," after the king used the *tuḫḫueššar* in ii 3, in which case *appa* should probably be understood as "again."

Script text *KUB* 43.23 rev. 38–42 indicates the early date from which the Hittites put them together. Because Ala is female and the Tutelary Deity seems to be male,[32] it is clear from these occurrences that these two were often viewed as a divine couple.[33]

Ḫapantali(ya)

An important tutelary deity of Hattic origin is Ḫapantali(ya). As Laroche and Otten[34] point out, this god appears primarily in lists of oath deities, in myths and in festivals. In the treaties he occurs in a group of tutelary deities which is fairly standardized, for example: ᴰLAMMA ᴰLAMMA ᵁᴿᵁ*ḪATTI* ᴰ*Zitḫariya[š]* ᴰ*Karziš* ᴰ*Ḫapandaliyaš* ᴰLAMMA ᵁᴿᵁ*Garaḫnan* ᴰLAMM[A.LÍ]L ᴰLAMMA ᴷᵁŠ*kuršaš*.[35] He is attested from the earliest period; there is at least one Old Assyrian text in which a personal name *Ḫa-ba-ta-li* occurs.[36]

In the mythology, Ḫapantali(ya) occurs in the myth of the Moon That Fell From Heaven,[37] next to the Tutelary Deity as one of the assembly of gods in the Telipinu myth,[38] and in the myth of the Missing Stormgod.[39] The god is an active participant in the disappearing deity myth preserved on the Maşat tablet edited by Güterbock[40] and is part of an unidentified mythological fragment.[41] As befits Ḫapantali(ya)'s Hattic origins, he occurs only in the older Anatolian myths and not in the later Hurrian myths.

Ḫapantali(ya) occurs once in a prayer—in a list of gods, next to Karzi[42]—but not in a context that provides any information about his nature. He also occurs one time in a dream of Puduḫepa, again next to Karzi in a list of gods.[43] The context is broken and again provides no information about Ḫapantali(ya)'s nature. However, Ḫapantali(ya)'s occurrence in these later texts does demonstrate that he remained a part of the pantheon into the Empire period.

By far the majority of references to Ḫapantali(ya) are in the cultic texts. He occurs in a variety of festival texts, usually as one of a group of gods receiving offerings, a group that

32. See discussion of unspecified ᴰLAMMA below.
33. This was pointed out by Laroche, *Rech.* 78, but without comments as to the earliest appearance of this couple.
34. Laroche, *Rech.* 22–23, and Otten, *RLA* 4: 111. As Otten notes, we do not have enough evidence to determine the sex of this deity.
35. *KBo* 5.3+*KBo* 19.43++ i 48–49 (Ḫuqq.). The Egyptian language version of the Ḫattušili III-Ramesses II treaty has this group minus ᴰLAMMA; see *ANET* 201 with n. 16 and 17.
36. Cited in Stephens, *Personal Names from Cuneiform Inscriptions of Cappadocia* (New Haven, 1928) 39, and Laroche, *NH* #282.
37. *KUB* 28.5 obv. 15b, translit. Laroche, *Myth.* 1: 75.
38. *KUB* 17.10 ii 32, translit. Laroche, *Myth.* 1: 35–36.
39. 277/w 6′, restored based on the parallel passage in the Telipinu myth.
40. *JKF* 10 (1986) 205–14.
41. *KUB* 57.105 iii 3.
42. *KUB* 6.45 i 55–56 with duplicate *KUB* 6.46 ii 21 (Prayer of Muwatalli to the Stormgod *piḫaššašši*).
43. *KUB* 31.77 iii 3′.

normally includes the familiar companions ᴰLAMMA and Karzi. As might be expected, he is included among the gods who receive offerings in the Hattic-based Festivals of Teteš̮ḫabi.[44] In each case where the text is preserved, Ḫapantali(ya) is paired with ᴰLAMMA, and this pair receives its own drink offerings and bread offerings. This pairing of the Tutelary Deity and Ḫapantaliya in the offerings ceremonies is a theme in other festivals, for example the KI.LAM Festival.[45] The same pair is also attested in the Festival celebrated by a DUMU-*aš*.[46] The pair receives drink offerings in an unassigned festival fragment in a ceremony in which the "singer of Ḫatti" sings.[47]

Similar to this pairing of Ḫapantali(ya) with ᴰLAMMA in the festivals is the pairing of Inar with Ḫapantali(ya). A parallel situation in which these two alone receive offerings can be seen in the KI.LAM Festival[48] and in an unidentified festival fragment.[49] In the KI.LAM Festival Ḫapantali(ya) can be paired either with Inar or ᴰLAMMA and always occurs with one or the other of these two deities.[50] ᴰLAMMA and Inar do not both occur in any text of the KI.LAM; the texts with Ḫapantali(ya) and ᴰLAMMA are OH/NS, while those with Ḫapantali(ya) and Inar are OH/MS or OS. Apparently in the later copies of this festival the scribes have replaced Inar with ᴰLAMMA; Ḫapantali(ya) is consistently paired with this tutelary deity. This substitution is implied in Singer's remark that Ḫapantali(ya) always occurs with "ᴰInar/KAL."[51]

One of the reasons why we cannot make a good case for a divine couple Inar and Ḫapantali(ya) is that the latter god in other texts is frequently paired with Karzi[52] and the Tutelary Deity of Ḫatti.[53] Of course such "pairings" may be nothing more than a group of two, just as other deities can occur in groups of two without necessarily being a couple. Ḫapantali(ya) also receives offerings once in conjunction with the name of the king.[54] He is listed in groups of three or more in a number of festival texts, including again *KBo* 4.13, the AN.TAḪ.ŠUM Festival fragment in which he occurs in a number of different arrangements of deities. These gods are usually the gods with whom he is listed in the

44. *KBo* 19.161 i 6′, ii 1′, *KBo* 19.163 iii 14 (OH/NS), and *KBo* 20.46 iv 3′ (OS?).
45. *KBo* 10.26 i 6–7 (OH/NS), translit. Singer, *StBoT* 28 (1984) 42; *KBo* 25.176 obv. 18 (OH/NS), translit. Singer *StBot* 28: 93.
46. *KBo* 25.43 rev. 4′ and *KUB* 53.26 ii? 7′.
47. *KUB* 20.100 obv. iii? 5–7.
48. *KBo* 20.33+ obv. 13–14 (OH/MS), translit. Singer, *StBoT* 28 (1984) 89; *KBo* 22.195 ii! 10′ (OH/MS) with duplicate *KBo* 20.5+ ii 13′ (OS), translit. Singer, *StBoT* 28: 34.
49. *KBo* 30.32 obv. 3.
50. Noted by Singer, *StBoT* 28: 235.
51. *StBoT* 28: 235.
52. For example, *KBo* 4.13 ii 12′ (AN.TAḪ.ŠUM Festival?).
53. *KBo* 4.13 iv 40. The pairing of Ḫapantali(ya) with two different deities in the same festival suggests that he was not strongly associated with any one god.
54. *KUB* 55.18 ii 13′–16′ (festival fragment): EGIR-*anda-ma* ᴰ*Ḫapantaliyan ŠA* LUGAL-*ya ŠUM-an IŠTU* GAL.GIR$_4$ *ekuzi* GIŠ ᴰINANNA.GAL SÌR-*RU* "Then he drinks Ḫapantaliya and the name of the king with a bitumen cup. (They play) the large Inanna instrument and sing."

oath-deity lists: the Tutelary Deity, the Tutelary Deity of Ḫatti, Karzi, and Zitḫariya. In the festival fragment *KUB* 55.12 iii? 3–7 he is associated (in broken context) with the Tutelary Deity of Karaḫna. It is in fact the normal pattern for Ḫapantali(ya) to receive offerings in a festival only as part of a group of gods, and that group is almost always composed of other tutelary deities.[55] One of the few examples in which he occurs among a group of deities which are of a diverse nature is *IBoT* 1.29 obv. 63–67 (EZEN *ḫaššumaš*), in which he occurs with a group of Hattic deities.

It is clear from his presence in the oath-deity lists from the Empire period that Ḫapantali(ya) continued to be a part of the pantheon to the end of the Hittite Empire. This supposition is strengthened by his presence in various newer festival texts cited above as well as in the New Hittite text *KUB* 27.1, the Festival for Ištar of Šamuḫa. In lines i 64–67 Ḫapantaliya[56] occurs in a group of ten different tutelary deities, once again following Karzi in the list. Another instructive text for the place of Ḫapantali(ya) in the later Hittite pantheon is *KUB* 2.1 i 42–44, the Festival for All the Tutelary Deities. In these lines near the end of the first column, Ḫapantaliya and Karzi (as Karši) are listed (along with a great many tutelary deities identified by various epithets) among all the names of the tutelary deities.

Ḫašgala[57]

This god appears to be a Hattic deity; Otten so identifies him, and Laroche puts him in his "Proto-Hittite" classification. Neither cites any evidence, but we may point out the *KUB* 28.103 vi 4′ occurrence, which is in a fragment of festival containing Hattic, and *KUB* 53.3 i 13′–15′, in which offerings to Ḫašgala are accompanied by the Hattic exclamation "*aḫa*" and by breaking *takarmu-* bread, which Hoffner suggests is probably Hattic.[58] None of this evidence conclusively proves that Ḫašgala is a deity of the pre-Indo-European Hattian population, but there is nothing to suggest otherwise. He occurs exclusively receiving offerings in festivals. He occurs both by himself[59] and with other gods not known to be tutelary deities.[60] In the *KUB* 28.103 passage the next paragraph has to do with the priest of the Tutelary Deity of the Hunting Bag, so here Ḫašgala is in close proximity to another Tutelary Deity, although not apparently in a list of tutelary deities as in the *kurša-* Festival texts discussed below.

55. For example *KUB* 2.13 v 4–9 (OH?/NS), Festival of the Month.
56. Spelled ᴰ*Ḫa-pa-la-li-ya* in the main text, ᴰ*Ḫ*[*a*]*-ba-an-ta-li-ya* in the duplicate *KUB* 27.64 ii 37 (NH).
57. See Laroche, *Rech.* 24, and Otten, *RLA* 4 (1972–75) 134. Laroche cites only the passage *KUB* 28.103 vi 4′ (festival fragment containing Hattic, *CTH* 744), ᴰ*Ḫa-aš-qa-*[, as all of the other occurrences of this god occur in texts published after *Rech.* was completed. Now that we know of a god by this name, however, we may understand this passage as another occurrence of his name.
58. *AlHeth* 185.
59. *KUB* 53.3 i 13′ (Festival for Telipinu) and possibly *HFAC* 60:3′ (fest. frag.).
60. *KUB* 53.14 ii 2 (Festival for Telipinu); *KUB* 55.18 ii 7′ (fest. frag.); and *KBo* 20.101:9′ (fest. frag.).

Ḫašgala is included here because he receives offerings in two different texts of the *kurša*- Festival[61] among a number of tutelary deities. In *KBo* 21.89+*KBo* 8.97 i 18′, in the form ^{D}*Ḫa-aš-ga-la-a-i*, he occurs in a list of gods receiving offerings, between the Tutelary Deity of Ḫatenzuwa[62] and the Tutelary Deity of Zapatiškuwa. He occurs as ^{D}*Ḫa-aš-ga-la-a-an* in *KUB* 55.43 iv 23′, between the same two gods in a similar list. I also restore his name in *KUB* 55.43 ii 24, in the analogous slot in the offerings list of that column. One other probable occurrence is *KUB* 55.43 ii 31, where the broken beginning of the line is almost certainly to be read [^{D}*Ḫa-aš-g*]*a-la-a-an*, which in turn suggests restoring his name in the analogous place in the column iv-left edge list, which I do in the broken away portion at the beginning of l.e. 1. From these several occurrences of Ḫašgala in lists of tutelary deities, we may infer that he as well is a tutelary deity, but the paucity and nature of attestations do not allow us to define his nature further.

Inara

See the discussion of ^{D}LAMMA without epithet below.

Kantipuitti

This god is attested only a few times, several of which are in texts presently unpublished.[63] Two festivals in which he appears represented by a *kurša*- indicate that he is a tutelary deity: NIN.DINGIR*⸗ma šarā INA* É ^{KUŠ}*kuršaš paizzi piran* ^{D}*Kantipuittiyaš* ^{KUŠ}*kuršaš iyatta* $^{\text{LÚ.MEŠ}}$*ḫapeš ú-nu-wa*!?*-an-t*[*e-eš*?] *iyanta* LÚ.MEŠ ^{URU}*Anunuw*[*a* SÌR]-⌈*RU*⌉ $^{\text{SAL.MEŠ}}$*zintuḫiyaš* EGIR-*a*[*n* SÌR]-⌈*RU*⌉ $^{\text{SAL.MEŠ}}$*arkammiyaleš* ^{GIŠ}*arkammi galgalturi* GUL-*aḫḫannieškanzi* "The NIN.DINGIR goes up to the house of the hunting bags. The hunting bag of Kantipuitti goes before. The *ḫapiya*- functionaries, adorned(?), proceed. The men of Anunuw[a si]ng. The female singers [si]ng afterwa[rds]. The female *arkammi*- players play the *arkammi*- and *galgalturi*- instruments" *KBo* 10.27 iii 10′–17′ (Festival naming the NIN.DINGIR); LÚ.MEŠ ^{É}*ḫešta* ^{KUŠ}*kuršan kuiš karpan ḫarzi nu⸗šši* 1 ^{TÚG}BÁR *pianzi* § *ŠA* ^{D}*Kantipuitti*[64] ^{KUŠ}*kuršan kuiš karpan* (eras.) *ḫarzi nu⸗šši* 2 ^{TÚG}BÁR *pianzi* "They give one 'rough garment'[65] to the men of the *ḫešta*- building who[66] have carried the hunting bag. § They give two 'rough garments' to the one who has carried the *kurša*- of Kantipuitti" *KUB* 10.13 iii 16′–21′ (KI.LAM outline tablet).[67] In each case the *kurša*- of Kantipuitti must be the cult image of the god in the form of a hunting bag. Since the hunting bag is an

61. See *Chapter 4*.
62. See note to the transliteration of *KBo* 21.89+*KBo* 8.97 i 18′ in *Chapter 4* on this restoration.
63. See the comprehensive article by Otten, *RLA* 5 (1976–80) 390, for the unpublished material. Bo 2622 is now *KUB* 56.51. Laroche, *Rech.* 83, comments on Kantipuitti briefly.
64. The duplicate *KBo* 25.176 rev. 16′ has ^{LÚ}*kán-te-pu-it-ti*.
65. See Singer, *StBoT* 27 (1983) 91.
66. The duplicate *KBo* 25.176 rev. 14′ has singular LÚ ^{É}*ḫešta*, which agrees with the singular relative pronoun *kuiš*, and the *-ši* of *nu⸗šši*.
67. Duplicate to *KBo* 25.176, translit. by Singer, *StBoT* 28 (1984) 94.

image normally used for tutelary deities, we may posit that Kantipuitti is a tutelary deity. *KUB* 56.51 i 7–14 describe ceremonies for Kantipuitti in association with the temple of the Tutelary Deity.

Kappariyamu

This deity is only attested in a few examples, all of them in festivals.[68] Laroche's proposed identification of this deity with Ḫatepinu is the only evidence we have that she is female, but we may accept that as a working hypothesis. Her very scant attestation would be understandable if she did indeed also go by the name Ḫatepinu as Laroche suggests. In a fragment of a festival for tutelary deities she is associated with the *kurša*- symbol.[69] She appears also in a festival fragment[70] in a context which provides little to supplement our knowledge about her. She occurs after Inar[71] and Ḫapantaliya, both tutelary deities. She is followed, however, by Telipinu, which is one of the reasons why Laroche, *Rech.* 27, tentatively identifies her with Ḫaṯepinu, Telipinu's consort. She is attested in the KI.LAM Festival in broken context together with ᴰTaḫantiu.[72] Her appearances in the *kurša*-Festival[73] indicate that she is a minor tutelary deity who occurs in a triad with the Tutelary Deity of Tatašuna and the Tutelary Deity of Tašḫapuna.[74]

Karzi[75]

Karzi precedes Ḫapantali(ya) in lists of tutelary deities, occurring with that god in all of his attestations where the text is preserved. The converse, however, is not true; Ḫapantali(ya) sometimes occurs without Karzi. Karzi is included in the oath-deity lists of a number of Empire period treaties,[76] in the prayer of Muwatalli to the Stormgod *piḫaššašši*,[77] and in queen Puduḫepa's dream.[78]

68. See Laroche, *Rech.* 27, on the morphology of the name, her origins in the town Kappa/eri, and her probable identification with Ḫatepinu. See also Frantz-Szabó, *RLA* 5 (1976–80) 400.
69. *KUB* 53.11 ii 9′, 18′, 25′, and 31′. See discussion of this sub *KUB* 53.11 in *Appendix A.*
70. A = *KUB* 20.39 v? 14′, B = *KBo* 11.35 rev. 3.
71. ᴰLAMMA in text B.
72. Lost in A = *KUB* 2.3 iv 12′, supplied by E = Bo 2505 iv 4–5, translit. Singer, *StBoT* 28 (1984) 68.
73. *KUB* 55.43 ii 17 and iv 16′; *KUB* 7.36 rev. rt. 4′ and 16′; and *KBo* 21.89+*KBo* 8.97 iv 17′. See *Chapter 4.*
74. See the further discussion of Kappariyamu and this triad in *Appendix B* sub *kipikkišdu.*
75. See Laroche, *Rech.* 84, and Otten, *RLA* 5 (1976–80) 459. Laroche does not categorize him as Hattic, but rather as "Asianique" (i.e., of uncertain origin). Bossert, *Heth.Kon.* 52–53, and Güterbock "Hittite Religion" in Ferm, ed. *Forgotten Religions* (New York, n.d.) 92, note his Hattic origin. *KUB* 2.13 v 5–9, in which his drink offering is accompanied by cult singing in Hattic, is good evidence for this.
76. Including the Egyptian language version of the Ḫattušili III-Ramesses II treaty, translated by Wilson, *ANET* 201, as "the god of *Karzis.*"
77. *KUB* 6.45 i 55.
78. *KUB* 31.77 iii 3′.

Of the festivals in which he occurs, several are significant for our understanding of this god. His presence in the AN.TAḪ.ŠUM fragment *KBo* 4.13 ii 12′, if I am correct in dating it as Old Hittite,[79] would indicate his role in the state cult from an early period. His presence in the New Hittite Festival of Ištar of Šamuḫa[80] is good evidence that he continued to receive offerings in the cult down into the Empire period and that he, along with other tutelary deities, was included in the Hurrian-influenced cult at Šamuḫa. Another significant passage for Karzi is *KUB* 40.107+ i 26′–28′, one of the texts of the Festival for All the Tutelary Deities. Here he and Ḫapantali(ya) each receive a billy-goat as an offering. In the very late text *KUB* 2.1 i 44 (Tudḫaliya IV) Karzi (as Karši) is cited as one of the names of the tutelary deities. A suggestion of Franz Steinherr's to Güterbock (cited in *Yaz*² 175) involves reading the hieroglyphic name of Yazılıkaya god #32 as ᴰ*Kar-ti* for Karzi. While this is not impossible, Güterbock notes the difficulty of such a reading and interpretation.

Zitḫariya

This is the best attested of the tutelary deities whose names are known. Laroche[81] points out his place in the oath-deity lists with the other tutelary gods, after Karzi and Ḫapantali(ya).[82] He notes the existence of a city Zitḫara, from which this god took his name, and the theophoric mountain names ḪUR.SAGZittaḫariya and ḪUR.SAGZitḫarunuwa. He cites a Hattic word *zitḫar* which reinforces the idea that this is an originally Hattic deity. Otten[83] concurs that Zitḫariya is Hattic.

There is some confusion about Zitḫariya's home city. In the Detailed Annals of Muršili II[84] the king describes Ḫatenzuwa as Zitḫariya's city. The *kurša*- Festival text[85] makes it clear that Zitḫariya and the Tutelary Deity of Ḫatenzuwa are distinct deities, so Zitḫariya, if he originates in Ḫatenzuwa, is not the only tutelary deity of the city. Two text fragments mention Zitḫariya and the city Ḫalenzuwa (a common variant of Ḫatenzuwa) together, but both of them are very broken and do not allow us to determine what they originally said about the relationship between the two. In a cult inventory text[86] Tudḫaliya IV describes how Ḫalenzuwa had deteriorated, and how he rebuilt the city. This included making a new cult image, an image of Zitḫariya as a hunting bag (*kurša*-), with a sundisk of gold on it.[87]

79. The sentence particle *ta*, although not used exclusively, occurs throughout the text. The text also consistently uses *natta* instead of *ŪL*.
80. *KUB* 27.1 i 65, ed. Lebrun, *Samuha* 77 and 88.
81. *Rech.* 40.
82. He also appears before these gods, as in *KUB* 19.50++ iv 7–8 (Man.), *KBo* 22.34 iii 18′–19′ (Dupp.), and *KBo* 5.3+KBo 14.43++ i 48–49 (Ḫuqq.).
83. *FsFriedrich* 355, 357.
84. *KUB* 19.39 ii 7–8, ed. *AM* 167–64.
85. *KUB* 55.43 i 1–27, see *Chapter 4*.
86. *KUB* 38.35 i 1–5, ed. Jakob-Rost, *MIO* 9 (1963) 195–96.
87. This sounds a bit like the renaming of the *kurša*-s in the festival treated in *Chapter 4*, with the difference that the *kurša*- Festival was a regularly instituted procedure while Tudḫaliya's

The king also had a temple built. In the third paragraph, i 9–10, a statue of gold or silver (the text breaks after KÙ) of the Tutelary Deity of Ḫalenzuwa is described. Thus down to the very late period of the Hittite Empire Zitḫariya and the Tutelary Deity of Ḫatenzuwa remained distinct, but each had a cult at that city. Muwatalli's prayer to the Stormgod *piḫaššašši*,[88] however, confuses the issue slightly. Among the deities who are addressed are: [(D)Z]*itḫariyaš* DU KARAŠ DUMU DU DLAMMA KUŠ*kuršaš* (eras.) [ ]x ḪUR.SAG.MEŠ ÍD.MEŠ *ŠA* URU*Zitḫara* "[Z]itḫariya, the Stormgod of the Army the son of the Stormgod, the Tutelary Deity of the Hunting Bag, [ ]x, (and) the mountains (and) rivers of the city Zitḫara." Here in a post-Muršili text Zitḫariya is associated with the town Zitḫara and addressed as one of its gods. Zitḫara very well may be the original home of Zitḫariya, but at some point he added a cult center at Ḫatenzuwa in addition to the one at Zitḫara.

Popko[89] takes a different view, citing the prominence of Zitḫariya in the Ritual at an Enemy Border, discussed below, as evidence that he received a special reverence in the north. As he locates Zitḫara in the far south, in Kizzuwatna, Popko suggests that only later, when Zitḫariya's homeland had been lost to the Kaškeans, did the Hittites suggest (in Muwatalli's prayer) that Zitḫariya came from Zitḫara. This does not fit with del Monte's assertion[90] with good evidence that Zitḫara is to be located in the Halys basin not far from Ḫattuša. Nor does Popko's assertion that Zitḫariya is not attested in the Old Hittite corpus take into account the possible OH?/NS dating for *KUB* 2.13, a tablet of the Festival of the Month, in which Zitḫariya receives offerings to the accompaniment of chanting in Hattic.[91]

This god shows an extremely close connection with the *kurša*-.[92] In the *kurša*- Festival and the cult inventory mentioned above, Zitḫariya's cult image is the hunting bag (*kurša*-). In a ceremony of the AN.TAḪ.ŠUM Festival,[93] Zitḫariya's offering is placed on the hunting bag. The cult inventory *KUB* 38.35 i 1–5 cited above makes it clear that when Tudḫaliya IV made a new cult image for this god it took the form of a *kurša*-. This association conditions an unusual use of his name; among the holy places that receive libations in many Hittite festivals the *kurša*- is often included. There are occasions, however, when in this standard list the name Zitḫariya occurs in place of the *kurša*-. This occurs mostly in the

reconditioning of the cultic equipment at Ḫatenzuwa was prompted by the state of disrepair into which it had fallen.

88. *KUB* 6.45 i 59–60.

89. *Kultobjekte* 111–12.

90. *RGTC* 6: 513–14.

91. *KUB* 2.13 v 4–9.

92. Güterbock, *NHF* 67–68, notes this close association, especially the fact that the offering materials for Zitḫariya were normally provided by the Temple of the *kurša*-s. Popko, *Kultobjekte* 111, also discusses this and suggests that the only cult image Zitḫariya ever had was a *kurša*-. Houwink ten Cate, *FsOtten*² 190, notes that the *nuntarriyašḫaš* Festival for Zitḫariya takes place in the Temple of the *kurša*-s. See Güterbock, *FsKantor* 113–19, for the *kurša*- as hunting bag and *Appendix B* for discussion of this cult item.

93. *KBo* 19.128 ii 35–37, ed. Otten, *StBoT* 13 (1971) 6–7.

AN.TAḪ.ŠUM Festival.[94] The *kurša-* as the cult image of Zitḫariya represented that god, and the god could therefore be referred to simply as the *kurša-*. Here the name Zitḫariya is used in place of *kurša-* because of this close association of the two. In the only other example of a specific *kurša-* cult image being used this way the Hittites used the *kurša-* of Kappariyamu as one of the holy places in a series of offerings.[95]

Zitḫariya occurs somewhat rarely in rituals but is involved in at least two. In the Great Substitution Ritual[96] he occurs immediately after the Tutelary Deity of the Hunting Bag (ᴰLAMMA ᴷᵁŠ*kuršaš*). This is interesting because in the renaming ceremony of the *kurša-* Festival[97] the old hunting bag of Zitḫariya is given the new name of "the Tutelary Deity of the Hunting Bag" and sent off to a provincial cult center. One might therefore have thought that these two deities would not occur together, but the renamed Zitḫariya symbol was sent to Tuḫuppiya, and there is no reason to think that there would not be another Tutelary Deity of the Hunting Bag located in the capital.

The other ritual in which Zitḫariya plays a role is the Ritual at an Enemy Border.[98] In this text Zitḫariya is perceived as the god most offended by the Kaškean incursions, presumably because the lost territory is his homeland,[99] and he is therefore singled out for the chief role in the early portion of the ritual. While one sheep is sacrificed to all the gods, a second sheep is sacrificed for Zitḫariya alone.[100] When the practitioner prepares to address the gods, he bows to "Zitḫariya (and) all the gods."[101] That Zitḫariya was considered the primary god threatened by the Kaškeans is indicated by the fact that the practitioner feels compelled to remind the other deities that it was not Zitḫariya alone from whom the lands were taken, but all the gods.[102]

Zitḫariya is well attested in the Hittite cult, receiving offerings in many different festivals both in the capital and in the countryside. He is associated in one festival with cult functionaries who bark,[103] reminiscent of the barking dog-men who play such an important role in the *kurša-* Festival devoted partially to him. Unlike tutelary deities like Ḫapantali(ya) and Karzi, he was considered important enough to receive offerings on an individual basis.[104] When he does appear as part of a group of deities in the cult, it is

94. *KBo* 4.13+ iii 21′, *KUB* 11.22 obv. iii 3′+81/t obv. iii 17′, and *KUB* 20.42 ii 9. An additional example, *KUB* 51.75:4′, is a fragment of a festival and could belong to the AN.TAḪ.ŠUM.

95. See the discussion of the evidence for this in *Appendix A* sub *KUB* 53.11, §§9′–12′.

96. *KUB* 17.14 obv. 13′, ed. Kümmel, *StBoT* 3 (1967) 58–60.

97. *KUB* 55.43 i 20–27; see *Chapter 4*.

98. *CTH* 422: A = *KUB* 4.1, B = *KUB* 31.146. Von Schuler, *Kaškäer* 168, calls this text "Ritual vor Beginn eines Feldzuges gegen die Kaškäer."

99. Noted by Popko, *Kultobjekte* 111.

100. *KUB* 4.1 i 8–9.

101. *KUB* 4.1 i 19–20.

102. *KUB* 4.1 i 24–29. In i 24 Zitḫariya's name is spelled ᴰ[*Z*]*i-ip-ḫa-ri-ya*, possibly just a scribal slip, but explained by Laroche, *Rech.* 40, as a means of avoiding the *-tḫ-* combination foreign to Hittite.

103. *KUB* 20.90 iv 2–5 (festival fragment naming the NIN.DINGIR).

104. See for example *KBo* 4.13+ iv 19 and vi 5; and *KBo* 19.128 ii 11, ed. Otten, *StBoT* 13 (1971) 4–5.

usually with other tutelary deities, although he does also occur with the Stormgod[105] and in groups of diverse deities.[106]

Hittite deities often moved around the various cult sites as part of certain ceremonies, and for Zitḫariya we have several good references to his movements among the sacred loci. In the Festival of Haste he was [taken(?)] into the house of the hunting bags.[107] This is not unexpected, since the *kurša-* Festival tells us that this was his official locus. It is noteworthy rather in that it implies that he had been moved from the house of the hunting bags to some other cultic place for a ceremony, possibly the temple of Ziparwa. He also goes into the É *ḫ*[*uḫḫaš*] in the Festival of Haste.[108] In a fragment of festival celebrated by the queen[109] the (*kurša-* of) Zitḫariya is hung up in the *ḫalentu-* building. As is discussed in *Appendix B* sub *kurša-* the hunting bag as a cult image moved among temples and cult centers as a regular part of the KI.LAM, AN.TAḪ.ŠUM, and *nuntarriyašḫaš* festivals.[110]

The god is associated with cultic singing in Hattic[111] and has a "great festival" performed just for him in his temple.[112] This text in which a "great festival" for Zitḫariya is prescribed demonstrates another point of contrast between Zitḫariya and some of the more minor Hattic tutelary deities, namely that he has a temple. The Festival of Haste provides additional evidence for this, as the king goes into the temple of Zitḫariya.[113] In the text describing the Spring Festival at Tippuwa Zitḫariya goes into his temple for the AN.TAḪ.ŠUM Festival.[114] Zitḫariya was an important deity in the AN.TAḪ.ŠUM Festival, as evidenced by the passage at the end of that festival's outline tablet, which refers to "the AN.TAḪ.ŠUM Festival of Zitḫariya." The text also mentions a temple of Zitḫariya and a *karimmi-* building for him.[115] An oracle about festivals[116] mentions a festival specifically for Zitḫariya after the king returns from campaign and returns Zitḫariya to his temple. In this case offering materials are to be supplied from the palace. Thus Zitḫariya has his own temple, a festival, and is sufficiently important to the king's safety that he is taken on campaign.[117]

105. *KBo* 13.135:13′ (Thunder Festival?).
106. *KBo* 12.135 vii 1′–17′ (divine list fragment).
107. *KBo* 14.76 i 13′.
108. *IBoT* 4.81(+)34/t+*KBo* 3.25 i 4–5, with duplicate *KUB* 9.16 i 4–5. 34/t is from *ZA* 64 (1975) 246.
109. 315/t i 12′–14′, ed. Alp, *Tempel* 228–31, and discussed in *Appendix B* sub *kurša-*.
110. Noted by Güterbock, *NHF* 68.
111. *KUB* 44.12 v 4′–5′ (Festival of the Month?).
112. *KUB* 25.27 ii 18–70 (*CTH* 629, "Regular Festival").
113. *KBo* 22.228:13′–14′, ed. Alp, *Tempel* 180–81.
114. *KUB* 10.18 ii 10–13 with duplicate *KUB* 10.17 ii 5–8.
115. *KBo* 10.20 iv 24–27, ed. Güterbock, *JNES* 19 (1960) 84–87. Lines 25–26: [(*I*)]*NA* É-*ŠU apēl* ^{É}*karimmi paišk*[(*aita*)]. Güterbock translates "'one goes to his temple, (that is) to his own temple (in Hattusa).'"
116. *ABoT* 14 v 11′–20′.
117. Zitḫariya's importance in accompanying the king on campaign is pointed out by Popko, *Kultobjekte* 112, and Houwink ten Cate, *FsOtten*² 180.

Zitḫariya's tutelary, or protective, nature is also manifest from references to a Zitḫariya of a person.[118] A Zitḫariya of the king receives offerings once in the Spring Festival at Mt. Tapala.[119] The Zitḫariya of the king also occurs in a list of deities in a fragment of a treaty or protocol[120] and receives offerings during the AN.TAḪ.ŠUM Festival.[121] Most interesting of the few examples of such a deity is the occurrence of both a Zitḫariya of the king and a Zitḫariya of the queen in the festival of Ištar of Šamuḫa: 1 NINDA.SIG LUGAL ᴰ*Zittaḫariyaš* KI.MIN (i.e., *paršiya*) 1 NINDA.SIG *ŠA* SAL.LUGAL ᴰ*Zitḫariyaš* KI.MIN.[122] The ending *-aš* on this name is odd, as one would expect a dative-locative case here. This is probably another example of the scribe forgetting what he was writing and not consistently putting the elements of the list in the proper case. It is somewhat problematic that there is no indication that LUGAL is to be taken as genitive, but the parallel example with SAL.LUGAL is good evidence that LUGAL was intended to be genitive as well. Laroche takes the deities in line 64 not as tutelary deities of the king and queen but as a god and goddess of (the town) Zitḫara.[123] Other examples of tutelary deities of the king and the queen suggest to me, however, that these also are intended to be personal tutelary deities. Line 66 of this text refers to a ᴰLAMMA LUGAL, so the king has both a personal Zitḫariya and a personal LAMMA tutelary deity. See below for discussion of ᴰLAMMA LUGAL. There is at least one other occurrence of a Zitḫariya of the queen, in the Festival celebrated by the queen mentioned above.[124] It is not only royalty who have a Zitḫariya; as part of the AN.TAḪ.ŠUM Festival a Zitḫariya of the NIN.DINGIR priestess receives an offering loaf.[125]

TUTELARY DEITIES WITH THE TITLE ᴰLAMMA

Many tutelary deities are known to us not by name but by the designation ᴰLAMMA. The following discussion of these deities is organized according to the three basic types noted in the *Introduction*: simple ᴰLAMMA, ᴰLAMMA GN, and ᴰLAMMA plus non-GN epithet.

ᴰLAMMA WITHOUT EPITHET

I translate this title as "the Tutelary Deity." A possible reading Kurunta is proposed by Houwink ten Cate[126] on the basis of texts in which the name ᴰLAMMA-*a*- seems to refer to

118. This is not unique; there are a few examples of other deities not specifically tutelary being associated with a person. There is attested, for example, a "Stormgod of Ašmunikal."

119. 755/t ii 17′–21′.

120. *KBo* 12.69:9′.

121. *KUB* 41.55 obv. 8′–9′.

122. *KUB* 27.1 i 64 (NH), ed. Lebrun, *Samuha* 77 and 88.

123. *Rech.* 40.

124. 315/t i 7′–14′, ed. Alp, *Tempel* 228–30, and discussed in *Appendix B* sub *kurša-*.

125. *KBo* 19.128 ii 11, ed. Otten, *StBoT* 13 (1971) 4–5.

126. *The Population Groups of Lycia and Cilicia Aspera during the Hellenistic Period* (Leiden, 1961) 128–30, especially 130 n. 3.

Kurunta, king of Tarḫuntašša. This is certainly a possible Luwian reading, but it would not fit the complementation ᴰLAMMA-*ri* that is attested throughout the Festival for All the Tutelary Deities and in other texts such as *KUB* 44.2:6′. This complementation as evidence for a confusion of the Tutelary Deity with Inara is discussed below. This suggested equivalence of ᴰLAMMA with Kurunta was not picked up or commented on by Otten in his *RLA* article on Kurunta.[127] Laroche accepts Kurunta as a possible late form in his *RLA* article on LAMMA.[128]

One cult inventory describing an anthropomorphic cult image of this god is extant: ᴰLAMMA ALAM LÚ GUB-*an* IGI-*ŠU* KÙ.GI GAR.RA ZAG-*za* ŠU-*za marin* KÙ.BABBAR *ḫarzi* GÙB-*za* ŠU-*za ARITUM ḫarzi* "The Tutelary Deity, a man, standing, his eyes inlaid with gold, in (his) right hand he holds a silver *mari*- spear, in (his) left hand he holds a shield."[129] It is probably unspecified ᴰLAMMA who is the god represented in the great outdoor sanctuary at Yazılıkaya.[130] The accompanying hieroglyphic name cannot yet be read but the antler sign indicates that this is a tutelary deity.

ᴰLAMMA occurs in basically the same types of texts as the other tutelary deities. We should note, however, that it is not certain that all the occurrences of "AN KAL" are to be read ᴰLAMMA. The most obvious possible exception is in the myth of the "Kingship of KAL" (*CTH* 343). In this myth, which belongs to the Kumarbi cycle, the title or name of the god who seizes control of heaven is written ᴰKAL. He is a Hurrian god not necessarily related to the earlier Hittite pantheon. For this reason and because he does not seem to behave like a tutelary or protective deity in the myth, scholars hesitate to equate him with the Tutelary Deity and render his name ᴰKAL.[131] However, Hoffner points out to me that the fact of the gods themselves being offended by his behavior after his accession to kingship may indicate that they had expected something different from him, something more in keeping with the character of a patron deity. We therefore cannot say definitely that this is not also the Tutelary Deity.

There has been some confusion as to the name(s) underlying the logogram ᴰLAMMA. The reading Inara[132] for this logogram was proposed as early as 1926 by Forrer.[133] Otten notes the alternation of ᴰLAMMA and Inara in duplicates of the Illuyanka myth.[134] This alternation can be seen in that myth for example in *KUB* 17.6 i 14 (OH/NS) ᴰ*I-na-ra-aš* ≐

127. *RLA* 6 (1980–83) 372.

128. *RLA* 6 (1980–83) 458–59.

129. *KUB* 38.2 ii 24′–26′, ed. von Brandenstein, *Bildsbeschr.* 8–9, Rost, *MIO* 8 (1963) 176.

130. God #32; see Bittel, *Yaz²* 137–38, pl. 21.2, 57, Güterbock, *Yaz²* 174–75. This could also be the Tutelary Deity of Ḫatti.

131. See Güterbock, *MAW* 161–64, and Kammenhuber, *ZA* 66 (1976) 81–82.

132. On this deity see Laroche, *Rech.* 82–83, 100; von Schuler in H. W. Haussig, ed. *Wörterbuch der Mythologie* (Stuttgart, 1965) 178–79; Kammenhuber, *ZA* 66 (1976) 68–88, and idem, *RLA* 5 (1976–80) 89–90.

133. *Forsch.* 1: 10 n. 2.

134. *AfO* 17 (1954/1956) 369.

KBo 12.84 i 1 (OH/NS) ^{D}LAMMA-*aš*,[135] as well as the myth of Inara, *KUB* 33.63 rev. 5 (OH/NS) ^{D}*I-n*]*a-ra-aš* = *KUB* 36.51 rev. 7′ (OH/NS) ^{D}LAMMA.[136] In these texts Inara is the original god, and it is ^{D}LAMMA who has been inserted in her place in some late copies. It therefore has been thought that Inara was the Tutelary Deity in the Old Hittite period. This would mean that the oldest form of the Tutelary Deity among the Hittites was female, which is interesting in light of the fact, mentioned in this chapter's introduction, that in Mesopotamia ^{D}LAMMA = Akkadian *LAMASSU* is female. The later Hittite concept of ^{D}LAMMA as male would then be due to a development within Hittite cultural history rather than a fundamental difference between Anatolian and Mesopotamian perceptions. Kammenhuber[137] rejects this identification of ^{D}LAMMA and Inara in the early period, pointing out that this would require some "altheth. 'Originale'" (that is Old Script) evidence to verify the existence of ^{D}LAMMA in the Old Hittite period, evidence which she does not find.

KUB 43.23[138] is an Old Script text which provides evidence for an Old Hittite ^{D}LAMMA. Reverse 38–42 reads: 2 NINDA.KUR$_4$.RA GÍD.DA 1 NINDA.KUR$_4$.RA LIBIR 1 GAL GEŠTIN 1 MÁŠ.GAL *ANA* LÚ.MEŠ *ŠA* ^{D}LAMMA ^{D}LAMMA ^{D}*A-a-la* "Two 'long' thick breads, one 'old' thick bread, one cup of wine, (and) one billy-goat to the men of the Tutelary Deity, the Tutelary Deity, (and) Ala." Instead of strengthening the equation Inara = Old Hittite ^{D}LAMMA, however, this passage indicates an Old Hittite pairing of ^{D}LAMMA and ^{D}Ala. In the Empire period ^{D}LAMMA and ^{D}Ala are attested as a divine couple, ^{D}LAMMA as the male and ^{D}Ala as the female deity.[139] The *KUB* 43.23 passage indicates that this divine pair goes back to the Old Hittite period and therefore implies that the ^{D}LAMMA was male already in this period. Although there is no question that ^{D}LAMMA is often used, at least in New Script tablets, for ^{D}Inara, more than one "Hittite" name could underlie this logogram, and we must accept the evidence for an Old Hittite male tutelary deity written ^{D}LAMMA. The very existence of the female ^{D}Ala as an Old Hittite tutelary deity suggests that tutelary deities in the early period could be female, and Inara may therefore also have been a tutelary deity. Hoffner points out to me that in the Old Hittite Illuyanka myth Inar(a)'s activities in providing abundance at a feast and in making (hunting?) trips to the steppe (*gimraš*) would be consistent with what we know of the activities of a tutelary deity. If she were a tutelary deity the confusion in the New Hittite period between her and ^{D}LAMMA would be understandable.

135. Ed. Beckman, *JANES* 14 (1982) 14 and 18. See p. 20 on his dating of the various copies of the myth to the Empire period.

136. Translit. Laroche, *Myth.* 1: 155.

137. *ZA* 66 (1976) 71.

138. *CTH* 820: "Bénédictions pour le labarna-roi," cited also in the discussion on Ala.

139. See comments on this above sub ^{D}Ala and in Güterbock, *FsBittel* 208, and Kammenhuber, *ZA* 66 (1976) 72f. The Festival for All the Tutelary Deities, edited in *Chapter 3*, is good evidence for this pairing. Güterbock earlier in Ferm, ed. *Forgotten Religions* (New York, n.d. [ca. 1950]) 92 had suggested without specifying time period that the tutelary deities written with the LAMMA ideogram were male gods.

In the late period ^{D}LAMMA is definitely masculine, as is most obvious in the cult inventory entry describing his cult image as that of a man.[140] Other evidence includes the occurrence of the divine pair ^{D}LAMMA and Ala in a cult inventory for Wiyanawanta[141] and more extensively in the Festival for All the Tutelary Deities. Kammenhuber[142] comments on the male tutelary deity portrayed in this festival. In addition the Tutelary Deity at Yazılıkaya and elsewhere in the extant cult images is clearly male.

The evidence that ^{D}LAMMA is male must be reconciled with the fact that this logogram in the New Hittite period is often complemented for a reading *Inara-*.[143] One possible pre-New Hittite example is *KUB* 41.10, the reverse of which contains a list of gods in the Ritual for the Stormgod of Kuliwišna. All of the LAMMA tutelary deities are complemented ^{D}LAMMA-*ri*. If I am correct in dating this tablet Middle Script, this would be an early example of ^{D}LAMMA as Inara. Alternation between ^{D}LAMMA and Inara occurs in New Script copies of older texts as well as New Hittite texts. ^{D}LAMMA-*ri* for example occurs throughout *KUB* 2.1, a Tudḫaliya IV text. *KUB* 51.79 rev! 12′ (OH/NS?) has ÍD-*aš* ^{D}*Inaran* where the parallel *KUB* 44.2:5′–6′ (?/NS) has ÍD-*aš-š*[*a*] ^{D}LAMMA-*ri*.[144] *KUB* 44.3, the Middle Script? duplicate to *KUB* 44.2, has uncomplemented [^{D}LAM]MA ÍD. It therefore is possible that here the tutelary deity of the river was originally written ^{D}LAMMA, which later copyists interpreted as Inara in the New Script copies *KUB* 44.2 and *KUB* 51.79. *KUB* 44.16 ii 16′, *I*[*NA* É ^{D}LAMM]A shows the variant ^{D}*Inaraš parna* in *KBo* 22.189 ii 8.[145] The substitution of ^{D}LAMMA for Inar(a) in the later copies of the KI.LAM Festival is noted above under Ḫapantali(ya). The same alternation can be seen in two unidentified festival fragments which duplicate each other: *KBo* 11.35 rev. 2–3: ^{D}LAMMA ^{D}*Ḫa-pa-an-t*[*a-li-ya*] ^{D}*Kap-pa-ri-ya-mu*; *KUB* 20.39 v? 13′–14′: ^{D}*I-na-ar* ^{D}*Ḫ*[(*a-pa-an-t*)*a-li-ya*] ^{D}*Kap-pa-ri-ya-m*[*u*]. Laroche, *RLA* 6 (1980–83) 455, points out that the logogram KAL (LAMMA) has the meaning "strong" and explains the confusion of ^{D}LAMMA and Inara as a folk etymology connecting Inara with *innarawanza* "strong." Kammenhuber[146] explains the use of Inara as the reading for ^{D}LAMMA in the late period as a product of the confusion between ^{D}LAMMA and Inara that occurred in the Empire period, the same confusion which led to writing ^{D}LAMMA for Inara in New Script copies of Illuyanka. She notes without comment that ^{D}LAMMA = Inara occurs in the Festival for All the Tutelary Deities as a male tutelary deity. This is true if we read ^{D}*Inari* for the many occurrences of ^{D}LAMMA-*ri* in that festival. It is at least possible that some other name

140. *KUB* 38.2 ii 24′–26′, ed. von Brandenstein, *Bildbeschr.* 8–9, Rost, *MIO* 8 (1963) 176.

141. *KUB* 38.1 l.e. 1–2, ed. von Brandenstein, *Bildbeschr.* text 2, trans. Rost, *MIO* 8 (1963) 182.

142. *ZA* 66 (1976) 85.

143. Laroche, *Onom.* 79–81, sums up the situation by noting that although Inara definitely is one possible reading for ^{D}LAMMA, this logogram also stands for male gods and obviously covers a diverse group of gods. He quite rightly cautions against mechanically reading Inara for all occurrences of ^{D}LAMMA.

144. See *Chapter 5* for these festival texts.

145. Both Festival for All the Tutelary Deities, edited in *Chapter 3* with commentary on the possibly early date of their composition.

146. *ZA* 66 (1976) 72–77.

ending in *-r* + stem vowel underlies this writing. The use of ^{D}LAMMA to denote a tutelary deity goes back to the Old Hittite period as seen in the Old Script Benediction for Labarna *KUB* 43.23. Inar(a) is a pre-Hittite Hattic goddess who plays a prominent role in the Hattian-based mythology of the Old Hittite period. In the Empire period the Hittites confused these two, putting ^{D}LAMMA in Inara's place in mythological texts, and perhaps switching each for the other in the festival offering prescriptions.

One explanation for ^{D}LAMMA as Inara in the late period and for expressions such as the "Inara of the River" in the *KUB* 51.79 passage is that Inara by the Empire period was a common noun. Perhaps Inara was always a noun with a semantic range of "protection, guarding," used as a name, or it may have been an originally Hattic divine name borrowed by the Hittites which in later usage became a common noun. This development is already discernible in an OH/OS or MS lot oracle[147] in which one of the "lots" is ^{URU}*Ḫattušaš* ^{D}*Inareš*, "the *inara* s of Ḫattuša," where plural "*inara* s" is not a proper name but rather a noun.

The LAMMA logogram was also used as a common noun designating a type of deity, as in the Festival for All the Tutelary Deities, *KUB* 2.1 i 42, *ANA ŠUM*$^{\text{ḪI.A}}$ ^{D}LAMMA *ḫumandaš* "to the names of all the tutelary deities." Such a usage is also seen in an oracle on the king's campaigns,[148] in which one of the lots is ^{D}LAMMA.ḪI.A "the tutelary deities." In the prayer of Muršili II to all the gods,[149] among similar expressions like ^{D}IM.ḪI.A *ḫumanteš* "all the Stormgods" (line 6′) is the phrase ^{D}LAMMA.MEŠ *ḫumanteš*, "all the tutelary deities." ^{D}LAMMA's protective nature can be seen in an OH/MS text of uncertain category: *uk*-*war*-*an*-*ši* ^{D}LAMMA *maniyaḫḫun* "'I assigned him to him (as) a protective deity.'"[150] Here ^{D}LAMMA is not a title, but a common noun denoting the generic concept "protective deity."

^{D}LAMMA as a common noun occurs with possessive suffixes. This occurs for example in the Festival for the Underworld Deities,[151] in which in consecutive paragraphs, each describing short ceremonies, the palace attendant (DUMU.É.GAL) calls out the title "the Stormgod" and then ^{D}LAMMA-*aš*-*miš* "my tutelary deity." In an Old Hittite historical fragment[152] in broken context ^{D}LAMMA-*KUNU* "your (pl.) tutelary deity" is preserved. The tutelary deity as a kind of guardian angel occurs twice in similar formulas in the Instructions for Temple Personnel:[153] *takku parkuešteni šumel* ^{D}LAMMA-*KUNU takku paprišteni*-*ma nu*-*šmaš*-*at* SAG.DU-*aš waštul* "If you (pl.) are innocent, (it is) your (pl.) protective deity, but if you are guilty, it (is) a capital sin for you" (iv 32, cf. also line 54).

147. *KBo* 18.151 obv? 11–13, ed. Ünal and Kammenhuber, *KZ* 88 (1974) 164–65.
148. *CTH* 561: *KUB* 5.1 ii 94–95.
149. *CTH* 379: *KUB* 31.121 i! 11′.
150. *KBo* 9.114:10′ OH/MS?, ed. *CHD* sub *maniyaḫḫ-* 3b3′.
151. *CTH* 645: *KUB* 20.24 iv 8′–11′.
152. *KBo* 3.23 rev. 3′.
153. *CTH* 264: *KUB* 13.4 iv 32, 54, ed. Sturtevant, *Chrest.* 164–65, and Süel, *Direktif Metni* 80–85.

Although the LAMMA logogram can be a common noun, in the great majority of cases the use of ^{D}LAMMA without any accompanying epithet or modifier is a title used to refer to one particular deity, whom I call "the Tutelary Deity."[154] He occurs primarily in lists of deities, usually other tutelary deities, both among the oath deities in treaties and among groups of gods who receive offerings in the festivals. He is included in the major state cults, but his role is restricted to witnessing the oaths of treaties and receiving offerings. He is attested from the earliest period, as evidenced by his appearance in the Old Script text *KUB* 43.23 rev. 41 (Benediction for the Labarna).

Like many of the other tutelary deities, ^{D}LAMMA is one of the standard oath deities in the treaties, occurring in the New Hittite treaties as the first of the group of tutelary deities, but in two Middle Hittite treaties with the Kaškeans he occurs without the other tutelary deities. In *KUB* 23.77a+*KUB* 13.27+ obv. 3 he occurs as the third of the "gods of Ḫatti" after the Sungod and Stormgod. The only other tutelary deity witness in this treaty is the Tutelary Deity of Karaḫna (line 4). In *KUB* 40.36+*KUB* 23.78+ ii 5′ he occurs fourth in the list, after the Sungod, the Stormgod, and ZA.BA$_4$.BA$_4$. In the Middle Hittite period, when the list of oath-deities was not fully developed or nearly as extensive as it was in the Empire period, ^{D}LAMMA was one of the primary gods of Ḫatti, along with the Sungod and Stormgod. By the Empire period he merely has first place among the tutelary deities in the lists.

In the prayers as in the treaties we see ^{D}LAMMA not only in the texts in which many tutelary deities occur but also in texts where he or he and the Tutelary Deity of Ḫatti are the only tutelary deities mentioned. Again this preference can be seen in the Middle Hittite period, as the Tutelary Deity occurs in the prayer of Kantuzili[155] and the prayer of Arnuwanda and Ašmunikal.[156] In the latter ^{D}LAMMA again occurs third in the list after the Sungod and Stormgod. ^{D}LAMMA is also prayed to individually in Muršili II's prayer to all the gods,[157] in which all the tutelary deities, except for the Tutelary Deity and the Tutelary Deity of Ḫatti, are covered with the phrase ^{D}LAMMA.MEŠ *ḫumanteš* "all the tutelary deities."

The Tutelary Deity frequently played a role in Hittite magic, occurring in many different rituals. He was included in rituals for other gods; for example, the Ritual for the Stormgod of Kuliwišna,[158] in which the gods are regularly grouped under the rubric DINGIR.MEŠ *ḫumandaš*, except for the Stormgod of Kuliwišna (the main god of the ritual), Ištar, and the Tutelary Deity. He occurs in major state rituals such as the

154. This is done with the understanding that some of these occurrences may refer to Inara. Those that can be shown to be Inara are not considered here.

155. *CTH* 373: *KUB* 30.10 obv. 4, rev. 20.

156. *CTH* 375: *FHL* 3+*KUB* 31.123 obv. 9.

157. *CTH* 379: *KUB* 31.121+*KUB* 48.111 i 11′.

158. *KBo* 15.35+*KBo* 15.33 i 5′; *KBo* 15.36+*KBo* 21.61 ii 15.

"Totenrituale,"[159] the Ritual at an Enemy Border,[160] and the Old Hittite Ritual Against Curse.[161] ^{D}LAMMA's range of influence can be inferred not only from his inclusion in rituals for provincial gods such as the Stormgod of Kuliwišna but also from the occurrences of his name in "foreign" rituals, magic performed by practitioners not native to Ḫatti and containing conjurations in foreign languages.[162] There is also a tablet catalogue[163] which lists a ritual perhaps dedicated to the Tutelary Deity: 1 *ṬUP*[(*PU* INIM ^{f}*Anna*)]*nna* ^{SAL}ŠU.GI ^{URU}*Zigazḫura* [(*mān* ^{D}LAMMA-*an*) *mug*]*anzi* "One tablet, the words of Annanna, the old woman of Zigazḫura, 'when they invoke the Tutelary Deity.'" This could also be interpreted as a generic use of the title ^{D}LAMMA: "... when they invoke a tutelary deity."

The evidence of the festival texts demonstrates that the Tutelary Deity was a major god of the pantheon involved throughout the entire range of the Hittite state cult, receiving offerings in all the major festivals such as the KI.LAM, AN.TAḪ.ŠUM, *nuntarriyašḫaš*, etc. His fairly prominent position in the procession of state gods at the cult center of Yazılıkaya also attests to his importance in the pantheon. The use of his spear as a cult symbol in the KI.LAM Festival is commented on below in the discussion of the Tutelary Deity of the Spear. ^{D}LAMMA like Zitḫariya was at times taken out during cultic ceremonies and transported to cult loci outside his temple. An example of an unusual cult ceremony involving such a journey occurs in a large unidentified cult fragment: [LUGAL-*uš*″*ka*]*n*? *katta* KÁ.GAL *ašušaš paizzi* [*nu*?″*k*]*an maḫḫan ANA* ÍD ^{D}LAMMA *šer* [*par*]*a arnuwanzi n*″*an*″*kan* ^{GIŠ}GIGIR-*az* [*katt*]a *uwatanzi nu*″*kan IŠTU* GAL KÙ.BABBAR [*kue*]*z*[164] *akkuškit šaštann*″*a* [*nu*″*uš*″*š*]*i*? *para pianzi maḫḫan*″*ma*″*aš*″*kan* [*ANA*? Í]D *kattanta ari* (bottom of column) "[The kin]g(?) goes down to(?) the *ašuša*- gate. When they bring the Tutelary Deity forth to the river on top,[165] they carry him down on a chariot. The silver cup from [whic]h he used to drink, and the bed, they give [them] forth [to hi]m(?).[166] When, however, he arrives down at the river[167]....[168] Another example of this is *KUB* 9.17 (edited in *Appendix A*), depending on the interpretation of the text. One interpretation is that a god travels by chariot to Taurіša, Ḫaḫiša, and other local cult centers, a god that context indicates was the Tutelary Deity. See the comments to *KUB* 9.17 in *Appendix A*.

159. *CTH* 450, e.g., *KUB* 30.25+*KUB* 34.68+*KUB* 39.4 obv. 34, ed. Otten, *HTR* 26–27; *KUB* 39.33 ii 7, ed. Otten, *HTR* 114–15.
160. *CTH* 422: *KUB* 4.1 i 3.
161. *KBo* 10.37 ii 7′, 13′, 18′, iii 39, 41, 42.
162. For example *KUB* 7.1+*KBo* 3.8 iii 13 (Ritual of Wattiti), translit. Laroche, *Myth.* 1: 169; and *KUB* 17.15 ii 19′ (Conjuration containing Luwisms).
163. *KUB* 5.1+*KUB* 31.45+ i 22–23, with duplicate *KUB* 30.58 obv! 7′–8′(+)*KBo* 14.68 i 21′, ed. Laroche, *CTH* pp. 158–59.
164. This restoration as well as the ideas on *šer* and *kattanta* with ÍD expressed in the translation were suggested by Güterbock.
165. That is, perhaps at the top of a high riverbank?
166. That is, the god?
167. Perhaps at the water's edge as opposed to up on top of the riverbank as in the second sentence.
168. *KUB* 20.2 iv 24′–30′.

Although the Tutelary Deity is ubiquitous in the state cult, there are very few references to his cultic equipment or personnel. The cult inventory discussed above describes an anthropomorphic cult image of this god. A fragment of cult inventory[169] mentions an É ^{D}LAMMA, "Temple of the Tutelary Deity" several times in descriptions of festivals. However it is not discernible from this broken fragment where this temple is located, whether in the capital or in a provincial city. A temple of the Tutelary Deity, probably in the capital, is clearly attested in *KUB* 9.17:5′; see *Appendix A*. An É $^{\text{NA}_4}$*ḫekur* ^{D}LAMMA at the capital is attested in Muršili's Prayer about the Tawannana.[170]

A throne or chair of the Tutelary Deity is mentioned in the Ritual of Wattiti. It is first described as being bound: *ŠA* ^{D}LAMMA ^{GIŠ}ŠÚ.A *ḫamikta* "He (the Great River) bound the Tutelary Deity's throne/chair,"[171] and then it is released: *ŠA* ^{D}LAMMA ^{GIŠ}ŠÚ.A *lattat*.[172] The Tutelary Deity had a spear associated with him that was used in some of the festivals, discussed below in the section on ^{D}LAMMA ^{GIŠ}ŠUKUR.[173]

We do not have a great deal of evidence for cult personnel for this god. A "singer of the Tutelary Deity" is attested once in the Old Hittite KI.LAM Festival.[174] This singer plays the wooden INANNA instrument in a ceremony that involves beaded hunting bags,[175] a procession of images of wild animals coming in, and the dog-men. In this ceremony, in which things relating to the hunt predominate, the singer of the Tutelary Deity makes his only appearance attested so far in the texts. The other functionary attested for ^{D}LAMMA is a priest (^{LÚ}SANGA) who occurs in a variety of festivals.[176]

We have a certain amount of ambiguous evidence for the cult of ^{D}LAMMA in the provinces. This title occurs in various local festivals in all periods. The problem is whether to understand the title ^{D}LAMMA in a text describing a provincial cult as "the Tutelary Deity" or to understand it as the tutelary deity of that particular cult center. It is likely that in a festival text intended to be celebrated at the local level there would be no need to modify the ^{D}LAMMA title, as it would be understood as the tutelary deity of that particular area. However, the occurrence of both ^{D}LAMMA GN and ^{D}LAMMA in local cult texts, for

169. *KBo* 26.223:5′, 7′, 9′.

170. *CTH* 70: *KUB* 14.4 ii 5′, ed. Güterbock apud Laroche, *Ugar.* 3 (1956) 102–03. Güterbock suggested that the É $^{\text{NA}_4}$*ḫekur* ^{D}LAMMA might be something similar to an ^{É}NA$_4$ DINGIR-*LIM*, "mausoleum," pointing out that the context in Muršili's prayer made the general sense "graveyard" clear. He has since indicated to me in a personal communication that he is no longer sure of this, as ^{D}LAMMA presumably did not have a mausoleum. We should perhaps simply translate this term literally as "the stone house of the Tutelary Deity."

171. *KBo* 3.8+*KUB* 7.1 iii 13.

172. *KBo* 3.8+*KUB* 7.1 iii 31. See *CHD* sub *la-* 6c on this text, translating "the throne of ^{d}LAMMA."

173. See the description of the ^{D}LAMMA's image which mentions the *mari-* spear in his right hand, *KUB* 38.2 ii 24′–26′, discussed above.

174. *KBo* 10.25 vi 12′, translit. Singer, *StBoT* 28 (1984) 53.

175. $^{\text{NA}_4}$*kunnanaš* ^{KUŠ}*kuršeš* as a beaded hunting bag is suggested by Güterbock, *FsKantor* 116 with n. 23.

176. For example, *KBo* 30.87 obv. 12′ (Festival Celebrated by the Prince); *KBo* 10.23 v 9 (KI.LAM Festival); *KBo* 4.9 ii 13, 14, 20, 27, 28 (AN.TAḪ.ŠUM Festival for ZA.BA$_4$.BA$_4$); *KUB* 53.16 i 7′ (fest. frag.). See Pecchioli Daddi, *Mestieri* 360, for the priest of the Tutelary Deity.

example ^{D}LAMMA ^{URU}Karaḫna and ^{D}LAMMA in the cult inventory for Karaḫna,[177] indicates that at least sometimes ^{D}LAMMA in provincial cult practice denotes "the Tutelary Deity."

^{D}LAMMA is featured especially in the Festival at Šareššа.[178] The occurrence of this title in various other local festivals indicates that he was worshipped in Tuḫumiyara,[179] Arinna,[180] Zippalanda,[181] and Šamuḫa.[182] The Festival of Tuḫumiyara is an Old Hittite text containing sections in Hattic that show the antiquity of the worship of a local tutelary deity or the Tutelary Deity in provincial towns. Another Hattic-based festival in which ^{D}LAMMA plays a part is that of Tetešḫabi.[183] ^{D}LAMMA was also worshipped in later local festivals and in festivals that show Hurrian influence. He occurs for example in a Festival of Tešub of Aleppo, a New Hittite festival.[184]

We also have evidence of cultic paraphernalia for ^{D}LAMMA from the provinces. An É ^{NA_4}*ḫekur* ^{D}LAMMA is mentioned several times in an oracle concerning the cult of the god of Arušna.[185] There was also one of these buildings at Zippalanda, as seen in the Festival celebrated there.[186] A temple of the Tutelary Deity of Karaḫna is discussed below in the comments on that god. Not only did the local tutelary deity have a temple at Karaḫna, but a cult inventory for that city includes ^{D}LAMMA as one of the gods for whom there was also a temple, as opposed to the gods whose cult locus was simply a *ḫuwaši-* stela.[187]

Although ^{D}LAMMA had a temple at Karaḫna, there were a number of cult sites where he had only a stela. In the Festival at Šareššа part of the cult ceremony is performed at the stela of the Tutelary Deity.[188] A stela of this god with the prescribed offerings to be provided during the Spring Festival is listed in a cult inventory cataloguing the stelae of various gods.[189] In another cult inventory text[190] ^{D}LAMMA is listed among the gods who have stelae in the towns of Iššanašši (i 33′) and Mallitta (iv 15′–17′). Thus the Tutelary Deity is a sufficiently important member of the pantheon to be worshipped throughout the provinces as well as in the capital, either at a temple or, more frequently, at a cult stela.

177. *KUB* 38.12 ii 5, iii 13′–16′.
178. *CTH* 636: *KUB* 20.99 ii 18, 19, 25.
179. Festival of Tuḫumiyara: *CTH* 739, *KUB* 12.8 ii 6′.
180. The Great Festival of Arinna: *CTH* 634, *KUB* 25.9 ii 8′, iv 22.
181. *CTH* 635: fest. frag., *KBo* 22.209 rev. 7′.
182. Autumn Festival for Ištar of Šamuḫa: *CTH* 711, *KBo* 11.28 obv. iii 34′.
183. *CTH* 738: *KBo* 19.161 i 6′.
184. *KBo* 14.142 i 9.
185. *CTH* 566: *KUB* 22.70 obv. 13, 20, 73.
186. *CTH* 635: *KBo* 22.209 rev. 7′.
187. *KUB* 38.12 iii 13′–16′.
188. *CTH* 636: *KUB* 20.99 ii 18, 19, 25.
189. *KUB* 12.2 iii 5–6, ed. Carter, Diss. 77, 84.
190. *KUB* 38.6 i 33′, iv 15′–17′, restored from the duplicate *KUB* 38.10, ed. Rost, *MIO* 8 (1963) 187–88, 196.

We note above that when the Tutelary Deity appears in oath-deity lists in treaties, he is almost always in the group of tutelary deities. In the festivals and rituals he often receives offerings by himself, as well as appearing in groups that can include a great variety of other gods. There is however a certain tendency in many cult texts to associate the Tutelary Deity with the Sungod(dess) and Stormgod as a special group of three, either as the first three in a longer list of deities or as a discrete group. This may be seen in the occurrence of this triad in Old Hittite texts such as the Festival of Tuḫumiyara[191] and the Ritual Against Curse.[192] In the latter text these three are specifically named together, with the remainder of the pantheon disposed of under a phrase like "the thousand gods" or "all the gods." Because these texts are Old Hittite we may posit a relative antiquity to this grouping and to the prominent place of the Tutelary Deity. That they are written in New Script allows the possibility that this triad is a late modification, but the evidence of the treaties discussed above indicates that ᴰLAMMA tends to be *less* prominent in the Empire period. This may be due to an increased proportion of Hurrian over Hattic cultural influence on the Hittite cult in the Empire. The older treaties such as the Middle Hittite Treaty with the Kaškeans[193] place the Tutelary Deity in a triad with the Sungod and Stormgod as the first three of the gods of Ḫatti. In the Festival of the Month this same group plus Mezzulla occurs at the beginning of a list of offerings of NINDA.KUR$_4$.RA.

Not only in the festivals but also in ritual texts is this same triad discernible. In "private" rituals such as that of Pupuwanni this group occurs as the first three of the gods of whom clay figures are made.[194] In state rituals such as the Totenrituale, they appear together (with the Sungoddess of the Earth making a fourth) receiving drink offerings.[195] In the Ritual by the Enemy Border these three are specifically mentioned before the phrase DINGIR.MEŠ-*naš ḫuman*[*d*]*aš* "all the gods."[196] In this text the Sun deity is specified as the Sungoddess of Arinna; in most other examples it is ᴰUTU-*un* (Ištanun) or simply ᴰUTU.

This divine group may also be seen at least once in the prayers, in the Prayer of Arnuwanda and Ašmunikal.[197] It also occurs in the local cults, as evidenced particularly in the cult inventories. The list of the gods of the city Ḫapatḫa, for example, begins with these three, followed by ZA.BA$_4$.BA$_4$ and a local deity.[198] In a cult inventory for Wiyanawanta and other towns this group appears immediately before or immediately after the local deity (divine mountain) whose cult is being described.[199] In *KBo* 2.13 rev. 2′ the sun deity of the group is again identified as the Sungoddess of Arinna. In rev. 5′ of that text, there are four

191. *CTH* 739: *KUB* 12.8 ii 6′ (OH/NS).
192. *CTH* 429: *KBo* 10.37 ii 7′, 13′, 18′, iii 39 (OH/NS).
193. *CTH* 139: *KUB* 23.77a+*KUB* 13.27+ obv. 3 (MH/MS).
194. *CTH* 408: *KUB* 41.3 obv. 20′–22′.
195. *KUB* 39.33 iii 7–9, ed. Otten, *HTR* 115.
196. *CTH* 422: *KUB* 4.1 i 3 (MH/NS).
197. *CTH* 375: *FHL* 3+*KUB* 31.123 obv. 9.
198. 15/r v 15′–17′ (cult inventory fragment).
199. *CTH* 505: *KBo* 2.7 obv. 12′, ed. Carter, Diss. 91, 97; *KBo* 2.13 rev. 2′, 5′, ed. Carter, Diss. 108, 113.

gods instead of three, as both the Sungoddess of Arinna and the Sungod of the Heavens are included in the group.

The great number of references to ^{D}LAMMA indicate his important role in both cultic and non-cultic contexts. A good example for this is his occurrence in the Prayer of Muršili to all the gods, in which the one or two most important deities of a particular title are mentioned specifically and the rest covered with an all-inclusive term: [^{D}]LAMMA ^{D}L[AMMA ^{URU}*ḪAT*]*TI* ^{D}LAMMA.MEŠ *ḫumanteš* ^{D}*IŠTAR* ^{D}[*IŠTAR*...]^{D}UTU-*ŠI* ^{D}*IŠTAR* ^{URU}*Šamuḫa* ^{D}*IŠTAR*$^{ḪI.A}$ *ḫu*[*manteš*] ^{D}*Telipinuš* ^{D}*Telipi*!$^{ḪI.A}$ *ḫ*[*uma*]*nteš* ^{D}ZA.BA$_4$.BA$_4$ ^{D}ZA.BA$_4$.BA$_4$ *ḫumanteš*.[200] In Muršili's day ^{D}LAMMA and ^{D}LAMMA ^{URU}*ḪATTI* were the two tutelary deities most prominent in the texts, and the occurrence of ^{D}LAMMA in many texts as part of a threesome of which the other two were the most important gods in the pantheon indicates not only the Tutelary Deity's first rank among all the tutelary deities but his very high position in the Hittite pantheon as well.

^{D}LAMMA Plus Geographical Name

Some of the tutelary deities specified by locality played a major role in the Hittite state cult, while many others are very poorly attested in the festival texts discovered at the capital. Much of this is due to the nature of these gods; presumably all of them had a cult center and a festival dedicated to them at their home city, but since our textual evidence comes from the capital they do not play such a major role in the extant festivals. Those attested in the texts from Ḫattuša appear either as lesser deities in state festivals or in copies of festivals to be performed at their respective local cult centers.

^{D}LAMMA ^{URU}Ḫatenzuwa[201] and ^{D}LAMMA ^{URU}Zapatiškuwa

These gods play a central role in the *kurša-* Festival treated in *Chapter 4*, which describes the replacing of the old *kurša-* (cult symbol) of ^{D}LAMMA ^{URU}Ḫatenzuwa and its subsequent renaming as ^{D}LAMMA ^{URU}Zapatiškuwa. The Tutelary Deity of Ḫatenzuwa, obviously not originating in Ḫattuša, by some point in the Middle Hittite era (the text is MH) had become sufficiently important at the capital that the cult symbol was permanently housed there and a festival established for the regular replacing of that symbol. We would thus expect this god to occur in other texts on the basis of his stature in the capital, while we would expect to hear less of the Tutelary Deity of Zapatiškuwa, who is sent to the provinces. This turns out to be the case on the basis of our present evidence. The Tutelary Deity of Zapatiškuwa occurs only in these passages in the main text of the *kurša-* Festival. The Tutelary Deity of Ḫatenzuwa, by contrast, occurs in other fragments of festivals for tutelary deities.[202] He also occurs in at least one other festival, where the god received

200. *CTH* 379: *KUB* 31.121+Bo 5728 i! 11′–15′.

201. This city name is written both Ḫatenzuwa and Ḫalenzuwa; see del Monte, *RGTC* 6: 102–03, for attested orthographies.

202. *KUB* 20.13 iv 10′, edited in *Appendix A*; *KBo* 21.89:10′, 15′ with duplicate *IBoT* 2.69:9′, edited in *Chapter 4*. The name ^{D}*Ḫatenzawu* is attested clearly only in *KUB* 10.29:7′ (^{D}*Ḫa-ti-en-za-wu*$_{ú}$*-ú*), with a

drink and bread offerings from a prince in the course of the festival.[203] He is also among the gods listed in a prayer of Muwatalli,[204] showing that his position was sufficiently important to be included in a royal prayer, although this list is quite long and includes many other gods as well. This god also occurs in a cult inventory text of Tudḫaliya IV[205] in which a statue of gold or silver is being described. This is an interesting development in light of this god's close connection with the *kurša-* and the elaborate ceremony detailed in the main text of the *kurša-* Festival for ritually renewing the *kurša-* as his cult symbol. Apparently by this late period (Tudḫaliya IV) the *kurša-* had been replaced as a cult symbol by a statue of precious metal. We may perhaps view Tudḫaliya's religious reforms partially as an attempt to standardize cult representations by replacing the unusual hunting bag with the more common anthropomorphic statue.[206]

^{D}LAMMA ^{URU}*ḪATTI*

The Tutelary Deity of Ḫatti[207] is the best attested tutelary deity of this type. He occurs in lists of deities in a great number of Empire period historical texts. He is regularly one of the oath gods for treaties, including apparently the Egyptian language version of the international treaty between Ḫattušili III and Ramesses II.[208] In oracle texts he also occurs more than any other tutelary deity except simple ^{D}LAMMA. In the oracles he is addressed only as one of a group of gods with the Stormgod of Ḫatti and others who are being questioned as to why they are angry with the Hittites.[209]

---

possible second occurrence in *KUB* 58.13 obv. 6′, ^{D}*Ḫa*]-*ti-en-za*-⌈*wu*$_{ú}$⌉-[*u*]*n*, noted by Popko, *KUB* 58 Inhaltsübersicht and index. This name probably represents a god to be equated with ^{D}LAMMA ^{URU}Ḫatenzuwa. See Laroche, *Rech.* 24, for commentary and *Appendix A* for *KUB* 10.29.

203. The Festival Celebrated by a Prince, *CTH* 647: 316/t rev. 1.

204. *KUB* 6.46 ii 36.

205. *KUB* 38.35 i 9, see Jakob-Rost, *MIO* 9 (1963) 196.

206. Van Loon, *Anatolia in the Second Millennium B.C.* (Leiden, 1985) 29 notes that after Tudḫaliya's reforms most deities had anthropomorphic images. The exception which he does not note is Zitḫariya, who at the same city of Ḫatenzuwa had a new hunting bag image rather than an anthropomorphic one.

207. Written ^{D}LAMMA ^{URU}*ḪA-AT-TI*, e.g., *KUB* 2.13 v 5 (Festival of the Month, OH?/NS), *KUB* 14.16 i 28 (Detailed Annals of Muršili, NH); ^{D}LAMMA ^{URU}*ḪAT-TI*, e.g., *KBo* 26.166 ii 15′ (cult inventory fragment), *KUB* 18.25 i 12 (lot oracle); and ^{D}LAMMA ^{URU}KÙ.BABBAR-*TI*, e.g., *KUB* 6.45 i 51 (Prayer of Muwatalli to the Stormgod *piḫaššašši*). I translate ^{D}LAMMA ^{URU}*ḪATTI* as "the Tutelary Deity of Ḫatti" on analogy with gods such as ^{D}U ^{URU}*ḪATTI* "the Stormgod of Ḫatti." However, because ^{URU}*ḪATTI* is the Akkadogram for the city Ḫattuša, and since with all the other tutelary gods of the type ^{D}LAMMA GN the GN is a city name, this should perhaps be translated "the Tutelary Deity of Ḫattuša." The form ^{URU}*Ḫa-at-tu-ša-aš* ^{D}*I-na-re-eš*, "the tutelary deities of Ḫattuša," in *KBo* 18.151 obv? 11 (lot oracle, OH/OS or MS) is an early example of Inara used as a common noun to denote "tutelary deity," and is also the only example to date of a tutelary deity of syllabically written Ḫattuša. Although properly the land of Ḫatti is written KUR ^{URU}*ḪATTI*, the capital Ḫattuša is often to be identified with the land of Ḫatti, so ^{D}LAMMA ^{URU}*ḪATTI* should be understood as the tutelary deity of the capital, and, by extension, of the land of Ḫatti.

208. See Wilson's comments on Goetze's interpretation of this in *ANET* 201 with n. 16.

209. *KUB* 16.34 i 1–3, *KUB* 16.82+ i 1–5, *KUB* 18.25 i 12–15.

The Tutelary Deity of Ḫatti also occurs twice in cult inventory texts, in broken contexts which tell us that offerings to his image were listed as part of the inventory.[210] In one text this is in Ḫattuša, in the other the context is a paragraph about the deities of Kizzimara. Although he is tutelary deity of the capital, he also has cult images and is worshipped in the provinces. In the prayer of Muršili to all the gods he is listed among the gods.[211] He occurs immediately after "the Tutelary Deity" (simple ⁽ᴰ⁾LAMMA) and is the only other tutelary deity singled out for individual mention. His occurrence in this text alongside ᴰLAMMA shows that ᴰLAMMA ᵁᴿᵁ*ḪATTI* and ᴰLAMMA are two distinct deities, a fact which is borne out by numerous other examples of these two divine names occurring together. The Hattic tutelary deities such as Ḫapantali(ya) and Zitḫariya, to whom Muwatalli prays in his prayer to the Stormgod *piḫaššašši*, as well as all the other tutelary deities, are not mentioned separately in Muršili's prayer but are subsumed under the rubric ᴰLAMMA.MEŠ *ḫumanteš* "all the tutelary deities."

We have mentioned that in Muwatalli's prayer most of the tutelary deities are not mentioned separately by name. The exception to this is the Tutelary Deity of Ḫatti, who is placed rather with the major deities such as the Stormgod of Ḫatti and the Sungod of Ḫatti.[212] Once again this god has preeminence over the other tutelary deities, showing his high position in the state pantheon during the late Hittite period. His importance in the late period is underscored by his inclusion in the lists of gods to receive offerings in the Festival of Ištar of Šamuḫa.[213] This text is not further evidence of his being singled out from among the other tutelary deities, however, because he is simply one in a list of these deities, which includes some of the early Hattic tutelary deities. His inclusion in a list of Hurrian gods[214] is, however, an example of his special status among the tutelary gods in this late period, as he was taken over as a Hurrian god as well. Another example of his inclusion in a Hurrian cultic text is the Festival of Tešub of Aleppo,[215] in which ᴰLAMMA and ᴰLAMMA ᵁᴿᵁ*ḪATTI* are the only two tutelary deities included in the great list of gods to receive offerings, a list which includes Hittite, Hurrian, and Mesopotamian deities.

There is little evidence for his role in the cult in the early period; he seems to have become prominent only in the Empire period. The antiquity of his position in the pantheon is however suggested by a ceremony in the Festival of the Month[216] in which he and some Hattic tutelary deities receive offerings while the singer chants in Hattic. Although his prominence among the tutelary deities in the later period is clear, his position relative to the entire state pantheon is not so prominent. He does not play as active a role in the cult as one might expect based on the evidence from other text genres. He receives offerings in

210. *KBo* 12.140 obv. 2, *KBo* 26.166 ii 15.
211. *KUB* 31.121+*KUB* 48.111 i! 11′.
212. *KUB* 6.45 i 50–53 with duplicate *KUB* 6.46 ii 14–18.
213. *KUB* 27.1 i 64–67, ed. Lebrun, *Samuha* 77 and 88.
214. *KUB* 34.102+ ii 11–15′, iii 32′–35′.
215. *KBo* 14.142 i 9.
216. *KUB* 2.13 v 4–9 (OH?/NS).

several different festivals, almost invariably as one of a group. That group is always other tutelary deities, not the major state gods in whose company he occurs in the Muwatalli prayer mentioned above. The only occasions in which he receives individual offerings are in two festival fragments. In a fragment of the AN.TAḪ.ŠUM Festival[217] he occurs in broken context between the Sungod, Mezulla, and the Stormgod of Zippalanda before him and Ḫapantali(ya) after him. In an unidentified festival fragment[218] he receives individual offerings on the same scale as the Stormgod of Ḫatti and the Sungoddess of Arinna and third in line after them.

There are few references to cultic equipment and personnel for this deity. A priest of the Tutelary Deity of Ḫatti is attested several times, all in one fragment of a festival dedicated to tutelary deities.[219] It is uncertain whether this text reflects the situation at a local cult center or at the capital. A temple of the Tutelary Deity of Ḫatti is mentioned just once.[220] The context is broken, but it is clear that the king enters this temple to make offerings.

^{D}LAMMA ^{URU}Karaḫna

One of the most important of these provincial tutelary deities was the Tutelary Deity of Karaḫna. I understand this particular local tutelary deity as a goddess on the evidence of the Egyptian language version of the Ḫattušili III-Ramesses II treaty, in which "the goddess of the town of Karahna"[221] witnesses the treaty oaths. Goetze[222] identifies this goddess as the Tutelary Deity of Karaḫna; the Egyptian scribe may have been mistaken in recording this unfamiliar deity in the feminine in the Egyptian text,[223] but in the absence of evidence to the contrary it is likely that ^{D}LAMMA ^{URU}Karaḫna is a goddess. She is known to us better than most because of the existence of a text for a festival performed at Karaḫna and of a cult inventory text for this goddess. Her origins in the Hattic milieu are suggested by Beckman[224] on the basis of the Birth Ritual *KUB* 30.29 obv. 9–15, in which ^{D}LAMMA-<*az*> ^{URU}Karaḫna occurs as one of the gods in a mythological conjuration. She is the only tutelary deity of a locality besides ^{D}LAMMA ^{URU}*ḪATTI* to appear regularly in the lists of oath-deities in the New Hittite treaties.[225] She was an important oath deity down to the very end of the Hittite state, as evidenced by her occurrence in a protocol of

217. *IBoT* 2.61 v 3–6.
218. *KUB* 20.2 obv. iii 1–9.
219. *KUB* 53.11 i 6′, ii 7′, iii 24, ed. *Appendix A*.
220. *KUB* 51.26 rt. col. 15′ (cult inventory).
221. Translation Wilson, *ANET* 201 with n. 17.
222. Apud Wilson, *ANET* 201 n. 17.
223. Kammenhuber, *ZA* 66 (1976) 84–85, notes this evidence on the sex of ^{D}LAMMA in the treaty and the possibility of error.
224. *StBoT* 29 (1983) 29 with n. 38.
225. For example, A = *KUB* 19.49+*KUB* 26.36+ iv 3, B = *KUB* 19.50 iv 8 (Man.); *KBo* 5.3+*KBo* 19.43++ i 49 (Ḫuqq.).

Šuppiluliuma II.[226] She occurs in Muwatalli's Prayer to the Stormgod *piḫaššašši* between the Stormgod of Karaḫna, with whom she is associated by cult center, and Ala, with whom she shares the characteristic of being a tutelary deity. The importance of the city Karaḫna is evidenced by its inclusion as one of the cities whose gods are specifically addressed in this prayer.[227] Also in the Empire period she appears in the Festival of Ištar of Šamuḫa[228] among an extended list of tutelary deities, showing that she also was active in the late period and held a sufficiently important position in the pantheon to be in a Hurrian festival.

Two texts which establish this deity's importance in the Hittite cult are the cult inventory of the Tutelary Deity of Karaḫna[229] and the Festivals of Karaḫna.[230] The cult inventory details equipment and personnel for other deities in addition to ^{D}LAMMA ^{URU}Karaḫna, but the beginning of the text indicates that the inventory was done at Karaḫna and for its chief deity, probably its tutelary deity. From the text we learn that at least twenty-six people served this one goddess[231] in addition to one priest (^{LÚ}SANGA) assigned to her.[232] In terms of cult buildings the text refers to temples of the Tutelary Deity and the Stormgod of the city: 2 É.DINGIR-*LIM* ^{D}LAMMA ^{URU}*Karaḫna* ^{D}U ^{URU}*Karahn*[*a*] "Two temples, of the Tutelary Deity of Karaḫna (and) the Stormgod of Karaḫn[a]."[233]

For the text describing the Festivals of Karaḫna see the discussion in *Chapter 2* below. The text itself describes offerings to many gods, with the Tutelary Deity of Karaḫna just one among them, but the colophon indicates the location for the festival as Karaḫna.

This particular tutelary deity seems quite important because of the festivals for her cult center and because she had her own cult inventory. The existence of a copy of her festival in the capital may indicate that it held a particularly important place in the cult calendar and was noted at the capital. Any deity who was the principal god of a local cult center normally had a festival dedicated to him or her. The cult inventory text is also something we would expect for most provincial cult centers. However, ^{D}LAMMA ^{URU}Karaḫna is the only localized tutelary deity besides ^{D}LAMMA ^{URU}*ḪATTI* who regularly appears in the oath-deity lists. This may be the best evidence of all for the special status of this particular tutelary deity in the state pantheon.

226. *ABoT* 56 ii 11.

227. *KUB* 6.45+*KUB* 30.14+1111/z ii 5–6, Otten and Rüster, *ZA* 64 (1975) 242–43.

228. *KUB* 27.1 i 67, ed. Lebrun, *Samuha* 77 and 88.

229. *CTH* 517: *KUB* 38.12 with duplicate *KUB* 38.15, partially ed. Darga, *RHA* XXVII/84–85 (1969) 5–20 (*Belleten* XXXIII/132 [1969] 493–504) and Rost, *MIO* 8 (1963) 200–01.

230. *CTH* 681: Bo 3298+*KUB* 25.32+*KUB* 27.70+1628/u; see Dinçol and Darga, *Anatolica* 3 (1969–70) 99–118 and *Chapter 2* below.

231. *KUB* 38.12 i 11: ŠU.NIGIN 26 $^{LÚ.MEŠ}$*ḫilammateš*.

232. *KUB* 38.12 ii 1.

233. *KUB* 38.12 ii 5. Rost, *MIO* 8 (1963) 201, interpreted this as a double temple, for which there is the precedent of Temple 1 at Boğazköy, but 2 É DINGIR-*LIM* should mean "two temples."

^{D}LAMMA ^{URU}Tauriša[234]

This is one of the best known of the local tutelary deities because the thirty-second day of the AN.TAḪ.ŠUM Festival involves a journey to the grove of Tauriša and a festival for this god.[235] The description of cultic activities for this day of the festival not only features the Tutelary Deity of Tauriša but includes offerings for other gods as well. From his inclusion in the AN.TAḪ.ŠUM cult journey in the environs of Ḫattuša Popko makes the likely suggestion that this god may have come from the Hattic tradition.

This inclusion of the local festival for the Tutelary Deity of Tauriša in a major state festival is clear evidence of the great importance ascribed to this god and his cult by the official state religion. However, we do not find many other references to this god in texts other than this one festival. He does occur in a few festival fragments, mostly in broken context.[236] He occurs once among a number of other gods in a liver oracle.[237] Again the context tells us little about this deity, except that in this particular case he was included in a text that is late and includes other better known local gods such as the Stormgod of Aleppo. The god also occurs in a fragment of a Kizzuwatnean ritual[238] in a list of mostly Hurrian deities and in the Hittite version of a Luwian mythological text.[239] There are possible examples of a priest of this deity in *KUB* 12.52 i 3 and 4, and ii 2. See that text in *Appendix A* for comments. The attestations of the Tutelary Deity of Tauriša indicate that he was part of the earliest Hittite cultic tradition with a local cult considered sufficiently important to be included in the AN.TAḪ.ŠUM Festival, and that he was active in the late period as seen in his inclusion in texts of the Hurrian and Luwian traditions.

Summary: Tutelary Deities of the Type ^{D}LAMMA plus Geographical Name

There are other tutelary deities of cities, none of which are well attested in the sources. The Tutelary Deities of Tatašuna and Tašḫapuna are among the gods who receive offerings in the *kurša*- Festival and are discussed under *kipikkišdu* in *Appendix B*. In the portion of the Festival Celebrated by a Prince[240] which takes place in the city of Kaštama, the priest of the Tutelary Deity lifts the *kurša*- of the tutelary deity of that city. Tutelary deities of Ankuwa, Ḫurma, Kalašmitta, Maḫḫut[...], Pitamma, Wašḫa[ni(?)], and Wiyanawanta[241] are attested, but the evidence is insufficient for us to say much about them.

234. See Popko, *AOF* 8 (1981) 329–31.

235. *CTH* 617: see especially the colophon *KUB* 2.8 vi 4–6, *mān⸗za* LUGAL-*uš INA* ^{GIŠ}TIR ^{URU}*Tauriša ANA* ^{D}LAMMA ^{URU}*Tauriša* [EZE]N AN.TAḪ.ŠUM^{SAR} *iyazi* "When the king performs the AN.TAḪ.ŠUM festival in the grove of Tauriša for the Tutelary Deity of Tauriša."

236. *KUB* 9.17 obv. 13′; *KUB* 12.52 i 3′, 4′, both ed. *Appendix A*; *IBoT* 2.67:6′.

237. *KUB* 5.6+*KUB* 18.54 iv 12–15 (NH).

238. *KBo* 8.97 obv. 17.

239. *KBo* 9.127+*KUB* 36.41 i 13, translit. Laroche, *Myth.* 1: 172–73, ed. Popko, *AOF* 8: 329–30.

240. *CTH* 647, *KUB* 20.80 iii 14–15, noted by Popko, *Kultobjekte* 112 with no. 74.

241. The cult inventory *KUB* 38.1 ii 1–9 describes for Wiyanawanta one or two ^{D}LAMMA LÍL, "Tutelary Deity of the Countryside" images, and in l.e. 1–2 inventories a festival for unspecified ^{D}LAMMA. Del Monte, *RGTC* 6: 483, notes the existence of a Tutelary Deity of Wiyanawanta.

There are some tutelary deities of this type in the Festival for All the Tutelary Deities who are unique to that text.[242] A subset of this type of tutelary deity is attested in the one occurrence of ᴰLAMMA URU-*LIM-ya* "and the Tutelary Deity of the City."[243] This may refer to the Tutelary Deity of Ḫatti, although it may also have meant the tutelary deity of some particular city mentioned earlier in the text.

This type of god, the tutelary deity of a specific place, presents certain problems in our understanding of them. They are recognizable in the texts by title, but they probably also had names. We may know the names of some of them without realizing that they are to be correlated with those LAMMA titles. In the Hittite pantheon there is a plethora of localized deities like this, with the "Stormgod of GN" for example attested for many cities. Some cities had a well-known principal deity, for instance the Sungoddess of Arinna or Ištar of Šamuḫa. Given the nature of a tutelary deity, one may wonder if "LAMMA" was ever used to indicate the primary deity of a particular place. For instance could ᴰLAMMA ᵁᴿᵁKaraḫna simply be interpreted as the principal deity of Karaḫna, whoever that might have been, who would naturally take a protective attitude towards her city and could therefore perhaps be considered a tutelary deity of that city, or is she a specific goddess with protective functions?

In my opinion the evidence indicates that we should consider ᴰLAMMA GN a title denoting a specific god, "the Tutelary Deity of GN" and not "a tutelary deity of GN = principal deity of GN." Evidence for this includes for example the possible double temple for the Stormgod and the Tutelary Deity of Karaḫna cited above. The Stormgod of Karaḫna may well have been that city's chief deity, and he is kept separate from the Tutelary Deity of the city. The cult inventories also refer specifically to images of or festivals for the tutelary deity of a particular place in addition to other important local deities.

ᴰLAMMA PLUS EPITHET

Tutelary Deities of Objects

ᴰLAMMA ᴷᵁŠ*kuršaš*

"The Tutelary Deity of the Hunting Bag"[244] is perhaps the most important of the tutelary deities with non-GN epithet. The *kurša-* Festival shows how closely related the hunting bag was to some tutelary deities, as four different tutelary deities each had a *kurša-* as their cult symbol. One of these four is the "Tutelary Deity of the Hunting Bag."

242. See Archi, *SMEA* 16 (1975) 103–05, and *Chapter 3* below.

243. *IBoT* 3.18:4′ (fragment of a festival for the tutelary deities), edited in *Appendix A*.

244. See Popko, *AOF* 2 (1975) 67–68 with n. 17, and idem, *Kultobjekte* 112–13. The title is written once ᴷᵁŠ*kuršaš* ᴰLAMMA-*an* in *KUB* 30.54 i 8′ (X *ṬUP-PU* catalogue, translit. Laroche, *CTH* p. 178) and once ᴷᵁŠ*kuršaš* ᴰLAMMA-*ri*, in *KUB* 41.40 rev. 15′ (Ritual for the Stormgod of Kuliwišna). See Güterbock, *FsKantor* 113–19, and *Appendix B* sub *kurša-* for the translation "hunting bag."

This deity occurs many times in a variety of text genres. Like many of the other tutelary deities, he occurs as an oath deity in several treaties.[245] In the prayer of Muwatalli to the Stormgod *piḫaššašši* he is addressed not with the main group of tutelary deities but with Zitḫariya and the sacred mountains and rivers of Zitḫara.[246] This close connection between Zitḫariya and the Tutelary Deity of the Hunting Bag is apparent also in the *kurša*- Festival, in which Zitḫariya's old *kurša*- becomes the ᴰLAMMA ᴷᵁŠ*kuršaš*.[247]

The Tutelary Deity of the Hunting Bag was involved in the state cult, although not in the large number of different festivals in which more major deities are seen. He receives drink offerings in at least two fragments of the AN.TAḪ.ŠUM Festival[248] and receives a male goat, a major item, as a sacrifice in another fragment of the same festival.[249] In this example his title is written *ANA* ᴰLAMMA ᴷᵁŠ*kuršaš* EN-*i* "to the Tutelary Deity, the lord of the hunting bag," or "to the Tutelary Deity of the Hunting Bag, the lord." He also appears in the *kurša*- Festival as the new name for the former *kurša*- of Zitḫariya, but he is not mentioned explicitly in the preserved portions of the text which describe the cultic offerings of the festival. He receives bread offerings in *KBo* 25.88:10′ (Festival of Moon and Thunder): *nu* ᴸᵁ́AZU 1 NINDA.SIG *kuršaš* ᴰLAMMA-*ri parš*[*iya*] "The seer bre[aks] one thin bread for the Tutelary Deity of the Hunting Bag." He is included in the very broken list of tutelary and other deities receiving offerings in *KUB* 52.100 (line 6′) that may be a fragment of the Festival for All the Tutelary Deities.[250] That this god was worshipped throughout the entire Hittite historical period may be inferred from his occurrence in both a festival fragment containing extensive sections in Hattic[251] and in the Festival for Ištar of Šamuḫa, a late text for a Hurrian-based cult.[252] In the former example the ᴸᵁ́SANGA ᴰLAMMA ᴷᵁŠ*gurš*[*aš*] is mentioned, the only attestation of a priest for this god.

In addition to these attestations in festival texts, this deity appears in several tablet catalogues that refer to as yet undiscovered/unidentified festival or ritual texts in which he played a prominent role. In *KUB* 30.60+*KBo* 14.70 i 21′–22′[253] we read: DUB 2 KAM *QATI ŠA* ᴰLAMMA ᴷᵁŠ*kuršaš MAḪRU ṬUPPU* NU[.GÁL] [*m*]*ān*″*za* LUGAL-*uš* ᴰLAMMA ᴷᵁŠ*kuršan apašila* DÙ-*zi* "Second tablet, finished, of the Tutelary Deity of the Hunting Bag. The first tablet [is] not [there]. (Titled:) 'When the king himself worships the Tutelary Deity, the Hunting Bag.'" This festival, performed by the king for this deity, is otherwise

245. For example *KUB* 19.49+*KUB* 26.36+ iv 4 (Man.); *KBo* 5.3+*KBo* 19.43++ i 49 (Ḫuqq.).

246. *KUB* 6.45 i 59–60.

247. *CTH* 683.1, *KUB* 55.43 §5, edited in *Chapter 4*.

248. *KBo* 19.128 v 50′, ed. Otten, *StBoT* 13 (1971) 14–15; *KUB* 54.78 rev. 4′–5′.

249. *KBo* 4.13+ i 11′.

250. See *Chapter 3* for this text.

251. *KUB* 28.103 vi 6′.

252. *KUB* 27.1 i 66, ed. Lebrun, *Samuha* 77 and 88.

253. DUB X KAM catalogue, translit. Laroche, *CTH* p. 154.

unknown to us. In *KUB* 30.54 i 6′–14′[254] three consecutive paragraphs describe festivals for this god, the last of which involves carrying *kurša*-s up to some place which is broken away in the tablet. In *KUB* 30.65+34/i++ ii 7–8[255] we have a description of a ritual of invocation for the Tutelary Deity of the Hunting Bag.

Besides this catalogue entry describing a ritual for this deity, we have ritual texts in which he occurs. Although he occurs in other rituals,[256] the importance of this deity is most clearly evidenced by the Ritual of Anniwiyani[257] and the Ritual for the Tutelary Deity of the Hunting Bag,[258] in each of which he is featured as one of the primary gods addressed in the ritual procedure.

ᴰLAMMA KARAŠ

The Tutelary Deity of the Army plays a much smaller role in the festivals and in Hittite culture in general than one might expect. The ᴰLAMMA KARAŠ or *tuziyaš* ᴰLAMMA-*ri* occurs once in a fragment of an offerings list,[259] once in the fourth plague prayer of Muršili II,[260] and once in the Festival for All the Tutelary Deities.[261] In each of those cases he occurs only in a long list of gods and is not singled out for special treatment. There are no indications of special prayers or offerings for him at all. This is probably because among the Hittites the idea that the gods in general ran before them in battle was an integral part of their theology,[262] and they therefore did not develop very fully the concept of a specific tutelary deity for the army.

ᴰLAMMA MÁ.URU.URU$_6$

All three pieces of hunting equipment in the cult scene on the Schimmel rhyton,[263] the hunting bag, the quiver, and the spear, have tutelary deities attested in the textual material. Of these the Tutelary Deity of the Quiver is the most scantily attested, occurring in only three festival texts.[264] From these we may determine that this deity at times received offerings, for example a male goat in the Karaḫna Festival, but did not play a role in the

254. Catalogue: X *ṬUP-PU*, translit. Laroche, *CTH* p. 178.
255. Catalogue: X *ṬUP-PU*, ed. Laroche, *CTH* pp. 169–70.
256. For example, the Royal Substitution Ritual, *KUB* 17.14 obv. 15′, ed. Kummel, *StBoT* 3 (1967) 58–60, and the Ritual for the Stormgod of Kuliwišna, *KUB* 41.40 rev. 15′.
257. *CTH* 393, ed. Sturtevant, *Chrest.* 112–17.
258. *CTH* 433, part of which is edited by Rosenkranz, *Or* 33 (1964) 238–56.
259. *KBo* 17.82 obv? 14.
260. *KUB* 14.13+ i 11.
261. *CTH* 682, see *Chapter 3*. The *tuziyaš* ᴰLAMMA-*ri* occurs in *KUB* 2.1 ii 73 and its duplicates.
262. See especially the annals of Muršili passim.
263. Discussed in *Appendix B* sub *kurša*-.
264. Bo 3298+*KUB* 25.32+ i 29 (Festivals of Karaḫna, see *Chapter 2*); *KUB* 34.93 obv? 12′ (fragment naming the SAL.MEŠ *zintuḫeš*), written ᴰLAMMA ᴷᵁŠÉ.MÁ.URU$_6$; and 320/t:2′ (fest. frag.). Although the Festival for All the Tutelary Deities as preserved does not include a ᴰLAMMA of the quiver, it does specify an Ala of the quiver in *KUB* 2.1 iv 4 with duplicate *KUB* 44.16 vi 7′.

major state festivals. The Tutelary Deity of the Quiver did not become important in the cult, while the hunting bag and the spear both functioned as cult symbols in the festivals, and therefore the tutelary deities of these objects had a significantly greater role in the cult.

DLAMMA GIŠŠUKUR

This god appears in a well-preserved cult inventory text in which his image is described as being a wooden figurine of a seated man, with a height of one hand, three fingers, and a fingernail.[265] The text specifies that there is no daily offering bread or monthly festival for this deity but does list the required materials for his offerings at the fall and spring festivals, to be provided by the "men of the spear." He also occurs in a cult inventory of idols in the towns[266] in a long list of gods for a particular town, whose name is broken away. Another example of his presence in local festivals is his occurrence immediately after the Tutelary Deity of Karaḫna in the list of deities receiving animal sacrifices in the Festivals of Karaḫna.[267] This god also receives offerings in a few other festivals[268] but does not occur regularly in the state cult. He does however show up in festivals for tutelary deities. He is included as one of the gods in the Festival for All the Tutelary Deities.[269] He also receives offerings along with a number of other tutelary deities in the *kurša-* Festival.[270] In *KUB* 40.110 rev. 2′ his offerings are accompanied by the barking of the "dog-men."

There is some possible confusion between this deity's name, written DLAMMA GIŠŠUKUR, and the phrase GIŠŠUKUR DLAMMA which occurs in certain major state festivals.[271] In each case bread offerings are given to the GIŠŠUKUR DLAMMA, always by a palace attendant (DUMU É.GAL or GAL DUMU.MEŠ É.GAL), and always for this object alone. Is this to be understood as "the spear of the Tutelary Deity," or is it to be understood as Hittite syntax and translated "the Tutelary Deity of the Spear?" Singer[272] comments on the importance of spears as cult symbols in the procession involved in the KI.LAM Festival, and it seems to me that this phrase must be understood as the description of a cult object of the Tutelary Deity that receives its own offerings in certain festivals. I would distinguish the (cultic) spear of the Tutelary Deity (GIŠŠUKUR DLAMMA) from the Tutelary Deity of the Spear (DLAMMA GIŠŠUKUR) obviously associated with the hunt. The spear is one of the three pieces of hunting paraphernalia from the Schimmel rhyton cult scene, all of which have tutelary deities attested in the texts.

265. *KUB* 38.19+*IBoT* 2.102 obv. 9′–14′, ed. Rost, *MIO* 8 (1963) 203–04.
266. *KUB* 38.10 iv 16, translit. Rost, *MIO* 8 (1963) 196.
267. *KUB* 25.32+ i 28; see *Chapter 3.*
268. *KUB* 40.110 rev. 2′ with duplicate 158/o (fest. frag.), ed. Otten and Rüster, *ZA* 68 (1978) 277; 743/t rev. 5′, *KUB* 10.21 ii 5 (fest. frag.).
269. *KUB* 2.1 ii 14. See *Chapter 3.*
270. *KUB* 55.43 ii 31, [l.e. 1]; *KBo* 21.89+*KBo* 8.97 iv 20. See *Chapter 4.*
271. *KBo* 27.42 ii 21–25 (KI.LAM Festival), translit. Singer, *StBoT* 28 (1984) 57; *KBo* 4.9 v 11–14, *KUB* 25.1 i 7–10 (AN.TAḪ.ŠUM Festival, 16th day).
272. *StBoT* 27 (1983) 89–91.

Miscellaneous Tutelary Deities of Objects

A number of tutelary deities are attested in only one or two examples each. There is a Tutelary Deity of the Pot Stand (*zeriyalli-*) attested once in a cult inventory text,[273] in which the offerings for him and the Stormgod of Zipalanda for the Autumn Festival are specified. There is also one example of a ^{D}LAMMA *INBU*, "Tutelary Deity of Fruit," who occurs in a duplicate of a text of the Nerik cult, alternating with ^{D}LAMMA[274] and receiving drink and bread offerings.

There are some less well understood tutelary deities of the type LAMMA plus noun. There is one example of a ^{D}LAMMA ^{GIŠ}NÍG.KA$_9$.[275] The word NÍG.KA$_9$ with a GIŠ determinative is otherwise unknown at Boğazköy or anywhere else. The Akkadian for NÍG.KA$_9$ is *nikkassu*, translated in the *CAD*[276] "account, accounting," or "property, assets, wealth." As inventories and accounts were kept on wooden tablets at Ḫattuša, perhaps ^{GIŠ}NÍG.KA$_9$ refers to such an inventory, and ^{D}LAMMA ^{GIŠ}NÍG.KA$_9$ should be translated "the Tutelary Deity of the Inventory."[277]

A ^{D}LAMMA *aniyattaš* is also attested, but only in the Ašḫella ritual.[278] This deity appears in only one section of the ritual, in which two male goats are sacrificed to him and he receives three drink offerings. This is the only tutelary deity sacrificed to in this ritual. The title of the god is perhaps best translated "the Tutelary Deity of the Ritual Equipment," which is approximately the same as Dinçol's "Kurban Malzemesinin Koruyucu Tanrısı."[279]

Tutelary Deities of Locations

^{D}LAMMA É.ŠÀ

The "Tutelary Deity of the Inner Chamber" occurs in the Luwian-based tablet of Lallupiya.[280] He occurs between *ŠA* É[...DN] and *ḫilamnaš* ^{D}[...], two other architectural terms. The deity is otherwise unattested, but compare É.ŠÀ-*aš* ^{D}x[...].[281]

273. *KUB* 42.87 v 16′.

274. *IBoT* 3.127:4′, main text *KUB* 58.11 rev. 4′, ed. (as Bo 2710) Haas, *KN* 216–17.

275. *KBo* 30.125 iii 9, festival fragment with Luwian and Hurrian divine names. This name is not read by Otten and Rüster in the *KBo* 30 indices to divine names. The final sign is the SANGA sign, read KA$_9$ in Borger, *AOAT* 33A #597.

276. N vol. 2: 223.

277. Hoffner, personal communication.

278. See Dinçol, *Belleten* XLIX/193 (1985) 1–40, for an edition of this text.

279. *Belleten* XLIX/193: 25.

280. *CTH* 771: *KUB* 25.37+*KUB* 51.9 iv 9′.

281. *KUB* 12.42 i 4.

^{D}LAMMA ḪUR.SAG.MEŠ

These deities, attested in a Middle Hittite Kizzuwatnean evocatio,[282] are somewhat analogous to the Tutelary Deity of the River. Mountains, like rivers are often divine; in *KUB* 15.34 iii 48–55, all the mountains, the Tutelary Deities of the Mountains, and the male gods of the mountains are invited to eat and drink of the offerings. The Tutelary Deity or Deities of the Mountains are distinct from the mountains themselves in the Hittite mind. In the Spring Festival at Mt. Tapala[283] both Mt. Tapala and the Tutelary Deity of Mt. Tapala receive offerings. The tutelary deity of a divine being may be worshipped alongside the divine being itself.

^{D}LAMMA ÍD

The Tutelary Deity of the River[284] occurs once in a cult inventory description of a festival,[285] with a sheep specified as the sacrifice for him. Beyond that, he occurs in the thirty-second day of the AN.TAḪ.ŠUM Festival (for the Tutelary Deity of Tauriša) and in texts which have been classified as festivals for the Tutelary Deity of the River.[286] We should point out a difference here between tutelary deities of places like the inner chamber and a Tutelary Deity of the River. Rivers are often mentioned in cultic texts as divinities; a specific river such as the Maraššanta was treated as a god, or rivers in general could be invoked as divine. Thus with the Tutelary Deity of the River we may have the concept of the tutelary deity of another deity, discussed in more detail below.

^{D}LAMMA LÍL

The Tutelary Deity of the Countryside is related to the hunt and derives much of his importance from his association with it. His name is written ^{D}LAMMA.LÍL, ^{D}LAMMA *ṢĒRI*, and *gimraš* ^{D}LAMMA. This god is especially important in establishing the link between the text attestations and extant cult representations. In *KUB* 38.1 ii 1′–6′[287] his cult image is described as that of a male deity standing on a stag, with a bow in his right hand, an eagle and hare in his left, and a sword. This fits so closely with several extant relief

282. *CTH* 330: *KUB* 15.34 iii 50′–51′, ed. Haas and Wilhelm, *AOATS* 3 (1974) 200–01, English translation *ANET* 351–53.
283. *CTH* 593: 755/t ii 4′–6′.
284. Written ^{D}LAMMA ÍD, e.g., *KUB* 2.8 ii 8 (AN.TAḪ.ŠUM Festival, 32nd day) and ÍD-*aš* ^{D}LAMMA, e.g., *KUB* 9.21:3′ (Festival for Tutelary Deities of the River). Laroche, *Rech.* 101, gives a spelling ^{D}LAMMA ÍD-*aš* with six references. None of his cited references, however, have such a spelling. *KUB* 20.2 iv 25, which reads...*ANA* ÍD ^{D}LAMMA..., is to be understood as "...the Tutelary Deity to the river...." *KUB* 2.8 v 28 does not have the Tutelary Deity of the River at all, and the other four examples read ^{D}LAMMA ÍD.
285. *KBo* 26.193 iv 7′–9′.
286. See *Chapter 5* for discussion of these festivals and this deity.
287. A cult inventory, ed. in *Bildbeschr.* 14–15, translated by Rost, *MIO* 8 (1963) 179–80.

images of the "god on the stag"[288] that they have been identified as the Tutelary Deity of the Countryside. Nimet Özgüç connects the "Hunting God" of the Kültepe seals with ᴰLAMMA LÍL, described by her as "the god who protects hunters in the fields."[289] The god on the stag on the Schimmel rhyton could be this god.[290] The problematic broken entry in the inventory (*KUB* 38.1 ii 7′–9′), which lacks the name of the god whose image is described, opens the possibility that the Tutelary Deity of the Countryside could take more than one form. Güterbock in a review of von Brandenstein's *Bilbeschr.*[291] in 1946 stated definitely that this entry described another ᴰLAMMA LÍL, the second of whom stood on an *awiti-* (a winged lion-sphinx?). Almost forty years later[292] he noted the difficulties of the passage, indicating that it could be a second representation of ᴰLAMMA LÍL or another god worshipped together with ᴰLAMMA LÍL.

The great variety of local festivals in which he receives offerings demonstrate how widespread was this god's cult. In the Spring Festival at Mt. Tapala he receives drink offerings from the king and queen, whose presence signifies the importance of this ceremony on the level of the state cult.[293] He receives both drink and bread offerings in the Ritual for the Stormgod of Kuliwišna.[294] In this ritual he receives offerings together with Ištar of the countryside, and the offerings are accompanied by chanting in Hurrian. As befits a god of the open countryside he seems to have been worshipped primarily out in the provinces and not much in the capital. He occurs as one of a group of gods listed as having cult stelae (*ḫuwaši-*) in the provinces.[295] His significance in the later period is indicated by his inclusion in the late Festival of Ištar of Šamuḫa. His importance in a Hurrian-influenced cult such as this is evidenced also by the Hurrian chanting with his offerings mentioned above.

That this god played a role in the "Hittite" cult as well as that of the Hurrian milieu may be seen from the ceremonies in which his offerings were accompanied by the chanting of the singers of Kaneš. This is evident in the description of offerings for this god at Mt. Tapala[296] and in a ceremony of the AN.TAḪ.ŠUM Festival which takes place in the capital.[297] In a fragment of ritual[298] the Tutelary Deity of the Countryside is paired with Ala, the goddess discussed above, who is normally (at least in the later period) seen with the

288. For example Yeniköy, Hacı Bebekli, Karasu; see *Introduction.*

289. *The Anatolian Group of Cylinder Seal Impressions From Kültepe* (Ankara, 1965) 67.

290. Güterbock, *FsBittel* (1983) 207, expressed reservations about this identification, but in *FsKantor* (1989) 114 he states that this must be the "tutelary deity of the open country." The god is labeled in hieroglyphs with the antler logogram and an unidentified sign.

291. *Or* 15 (1946) 494.

292. *FsBittel* (1983) 207.

293. *KUB* 20.48 vi 7–9.

294. *KBo* 15.36+ iii 7′–8′, *KUB* 41.0 rev. 8′–9′.

295. *KUB* 38.10 iv 3, translit. Rost, *MIO* 8 (1963) 196.

296. *KUB* 20.48+ vi 7–9.

297. *KBo* 19.128 v 16′–20′, ed. Otten, *StBoT* 13 (1971) 14–15.

298. *KBo* 29.211 i? 7′, vi? 7′.

Tutelary Deity. Unique among the tutelary deities is ^{D}LAMMA LÍL's role in communicating directly with the king by appearing to him in a dream requesting offerings.[299]

^{D}LAMMA ^{GIŠ}TIR

"The Tutelary Deity of the Grove" occurs in the list of gods detailed in the festival fragment *KUB* 52.100:2′.[300] Sacred groves were often a focus of activity in local cults and might therefore like rivers and mountains be expected to have tutelary deities. A priest of the Tutelary Deity of the Grove (^{LÚ}SANGA ^{D}LAMMA ^{GIŠ}TIR) is in fact attested for a particular local cult, that of Karaḫna, in the cult inventory of the Tutelary Deity of Karaḫna.[301] There could be a local Stormgod of the Grove as well, as in the thirty-second day of the AN.TAḪ.ŠUM Festival.[302] There the ^{D}U ^{GIŠ}TIR is one of the deities who receives drink and bread offerings. That ^{D}LAMMA ^{GIŠ}TIR is the title of a specific deity may be seen in the list of cultic personnel in the above-mentioned cult inventory text, where a priest (^{LÚ}SANGA) of the Tutelary Deity of the Grove occurs. In this local cult the sacred grove was an important locus for cultic ceremonies, important enough to have a priest dedicated to its tutelary deity.

Miscellaneous Tutelary Deities of Locations

There are a few other tutelary deities of locations. However, judging by the very few attestations of each, most of these are probably not specific deities like the Tutelary Deity of the Countryside but are examples of ^{D}LAMMA used as a common noun to denote the protectors of individual places. They occur almost exclusively in cultic texts. Unexpectedly, there are no tutelary deities of this type in the Festival for All the Tutelary Deities except for *KUB* 52.100, which names a number of tutelary deities, including some of the type ^{D}LAMMA of a location. In line 5′ we have the title ^{D}LAMMA *AŠRI*, "Tutelary Deity of the Place." In the same list (line 4′) is the title ^{D}LAMMA É.DINGIR-*LIM*, "the Tutelary Deity of the Temple." Again this god is otherwise unattested. In *KUB* 2.1 iii 20 and *KUB* 56.51 i 1–6 the otherwise unknown Tutelary Deity of the *ḫuwapra*- building receives a ceremony of offerings.[303]

299. *KUB* 48.122+*KUB* 15.5 iv 7–8.

300. *Chapter 3*, text 5.

301. *CTH* 517: *KUB* 38.12 ii 2.

302. *KUB* 2.8 v 22.

303. See the footnote to the translation of *KUB* 2.1 iii 20 in *Chapter 3*.

Tutelary Deities of Beings

ᴰLAMMA LUGAL

The king and queen are, with one exception,[304] the only people who have specific personal tutelary deities in the textual evidence as preserved. A Zitḫariya of the king and of the queen is discussed above. ᴰLAMMA LUGAL, the Tutelary Deity of the King, occurs several times in the cult inventories; his occurrence in a description of cult images[305] is the only evidence (in broken context) we have for a cult representation of this god. He occurs once in a list of gods in a prayer[306] and once in a ritual.[307]

It is in the cult that this god appears most, taking an active role in at least two major state festivals. He is included in a list of tutelary deities in one festival fragment.[308] He is seen most often in the AN.TAḪ.ŠUM Festival, although so far only in fragments that have not been fitted into the festival calendar.[309] He receives drink and/or bread offerings also in the Festival of Procreation,[310] in the Nerik cult,[311] and in the Festival for Ištar of Šamuḫa.[312] Although the Hittites were careful to supply him with offerings in certain festivals and thereby ensure his good will, he was not one of the major tutelary gods. Rather he was simply one of the rank and file of the Hittite pantheon, while individual Hittite kings sometimes took as their "patron deity" some particular deity, such as Muršili and the Sungoddess of Arinna, or Ḫattušili III and Ištar of Šamuḫa.

Tudḫaliya IV provides a unique exploration of possible variations on the theme of a tutelary deity of the king in the Festival for All the Tutelary Deities.[313] Here not only is there a tutelary deity of the king, but offerings are provided for the tutelary deity of the king's shoulder, body, weapon, heroism, etc., with a number of analogous Ala deities as well. This text represents the logical conclusion of the idea that the king's well-being is synonymous with that of the state and therefore should be protected as thoroughly as possible.

ᴰLAMMA UR.MAḪ

The Tutelary Deity of the Lion is the only tutelary deity of an animal attested in the pantheon. He occurs twice in the corpus. In a description of a festival in an oracle about

304. See discussion of personal Zitḫariya above.
305. *KUB* 38.19+*IBoT* 2.102 obv. 1.
306. *KUB* 6.45 ii 56 (Prayer of Muwatalli to the Stormgod *piḫaššašši*).
307. *KUB* 41.10 rev. 17′–18′ (Ritual for the Stormgod of Kuliwišna).
308. *KUB* 52.100, edited as *CTH* 682.5 in *Chapter 3*.
309. That is, among the texts which Laroche catalogues as *CTH* 625, specifically *KBo* 4.13+ ii 14′, iii 32, iv 18 and 42; *KBo* 19.128 ii 3 and 31, ed. Otten, *StBoT* 13 (1971) 4–7.
310. *CTH* 633: EZEN *ḫaššumaš*, *IBoT* 1.29 obv. 16 and 27.
311. *CTH* 678: *KUB* 59.32 rev? iii 3, ed. (as Bo 3112) Haas, *KN* 313 and Otten, *StBoT* 13 (1971) 31.
312. *CTH* 712: *KUB* 27.1 i 66, ed. Lebrun, *Samuha* 77 and 88.
313. Main text *KUB* 2.1, edited in *Chapter 3*.

festivals[314] the context is broken but indicates the performing of a festival in the É UR.MAḪ, an otherwise unattested cult building. This follows two paragraphs of description of a Festival at Mt. Piškurunuwa, so this ceremony with the Tutelary Deity of the Lion may also have been a very localized ceremony performed only there. The only other example of this deity occurs in an unassigned festival fragment[315] in broken context. One cannot determine whether this is a fragment of a state or local cult, but two references to the rarely attested Stormgod of Ḫulašša probably indicate a local festival for this god, again suggesting that the Tutelary Deity of the Lion is a local manifestation only.

Tutelary Deities of Divine Beings

The few examples of tutelary deities of the type ᴰLAMMA of (divine name) indicate that a god or goddess could itself have a tutelary deity. The earliest example of this type of deity occurs in the Old Hittite Prayer to the Sungoddess of the Earth,[316] in the title *taknaš* ᴰUTU-*aš* ᴰLAMMA-*ŠU* "the Tutelary Deity of the Sungoddess of the Earth." The Stormgod of Zipalanda may have had a tutelary deity: *mān* ⌈ŠE$_{12}$⌉-*anti* ITU 12 KAM ᴰ.ᴷᵁŠ*kurša*[*š*] *ŠA* ᴰU ᵁᴿᵁ*Zipalanda ANA* KASKAL.IM.GÀL.LU *paizzi* "If in the [wi]nter, in the twelfth month, the hunting bag of the Stormgod of Zipalanda goes on the south road" *KUB* 10.75+*KUB* 20.25:2–5 (Journey of the *kurša*- in Winter), ed. Güterbock, *JNES* 20 (1961) 92. As Güterbock points out, another interpretation is possible; this could also mean "... the hunting bag goes on the south road of the Stormgod of Zipalanda." A Tutelary Deity of Ištar of Šamuḫa appears in a New Hittite Autumn Festival[317] in which the tutelary deity receives drink and bread offerings to the accompaniment of singing in Hurrian. This deity plays no role in other festivals and is obviously a development of this local cult which emphasizes the hometown Ištar.

ŠA ᴰ7.7.BI ᴰLAMMA

There is apparently a Tutelary Deity of the Pleiades (ᴰ7.7.BI). In the Spring Festival at Mt. Tapala[318] there is a paragraph in which ᴰ7.7.BI, [M]aliya(?), and the Tutelary Deity of ᴰ7.7.BI ([*Š*]*A* ᴰ7.7.BI ᴰLAMMA) receive some unspecified offering three times. The paragraph is parallel to the one preceding it (discussed above sub ᴰLAMMA ḪUR.SAG.MEŠ) in which Mt. Tapala and the Tutelary Deity of Mt. Tapala receive offerings together. To be distinguished from the Tutelary Deity of ᴰ7.7.BI are the examples of a "heptad of the Tutelary Deity," for example *KBo* 4.13+ i 14′ (AN.TAḪ.ŠUM frag.): ᴰLAMMA-*aš* ᴰ7.7.BI. Such a construction is not unusual, as heptads of other deities are known, for example ᴰUTU-*aš* ᴰ7.7.BI;[319] *ŠA* ᴰU ᴰ7.7.BI;[320] and ᴰ7.7.BI *ŠA* ᴰ*IŠTAR*.[321]

314. *CTH* 568: *KUB* 22.27 iv 37, duplicates *KBo* 24.118+ vi 27′, 706/t:9′.
315. *KBo* 25.191 rev? 10′.
316. *CTH* 371: *KBo* 7.28 i 17.
317. *CTH* 711: *KBo* 11.28 v 11′–13′. Written ᴰ[LA]MMA *ŠA* ᴰ*IŠTAR*.
318. *CTH* 593: 755/t ii 7′–11′.
319. *KBo* 4.13+ i 13′ (AN.TAḪ.ŠUM frag.).
320. *KUB* 28.4 iii 17 (Moon That Fell From Heaven).
321. 103/r:3′, 10′ (Ištar cultic text), ed. Lebrun, *Samuha* 189–90.

^{D}LAMMA ^{D}GAZ.BA.A

A tutelary deity of Ḫuwaššana occurs in the Great Substitution Ritual,[322] in a long list of deities: [^{D}]É.A ^{D}DAM.KI.NA ^{D}LAMMA ^{D}*IŠTAR* ^{D}GAZ.BA.A ^{D}LAMMA ^{D}GAZ.BA.A ^{D}LAMMA ^{KUŠ}*kuršaš* ^{D}*Zitḫariy*[*aš*]. The duplicate, *IBoT* 3.36:1′, has, instead of ^{D}LAMMA ^{D}GAZ.BA.A, the syllabic writing [^{D}LAMMA ^{D}*Ḫuwašša*]*naš*. The Tutelary Deity of Ḫuwaššana also occurs in the cult of the goddess Ḫuwaššana. The important role of ^{D}LAMMA *šarlaimmi-* in Ḫuwaššana's cult is discussed below; the only other tutelary deity among the gods worshipped at her city Ḫupišna is this Tutelary Deity of Ḫuwaššana. The two best examples of this are two passages from fragments of the *witaššiyaš* Festival.[323] This title may be restored elsewhere in these festival texts. As in the case of the Autumn Festival for Ištar of Šamuḫa we observe that at the level of a local cult, the primary god or goddess of that cult could have a tutelary deity who also received offerings.

Tutelary Deities with Adjectival Epithet

^{D}LAMMA *innarawanza*

This deity is contrasted with ^{D}LAMMA *lulim*(*m*)*i-* in the Anniwiyani Ritual. Sturtevant translates ^{D}LAMMA *innarawanza* as "manly(?)" in opposition to his proposed "effeminate(?)" for ^{D}LAMMA *lulim*(*m*)*i-*.[324] Puhvel translates *in*(*n*)*arawant-* "strong, forceful, rigorous" and translates this title as "potent L(AMMA)."[325] This deity, so important in the Anniwiyani Ritual as a symbol for masculinity, occurs only in this ritual and plays no role in the state cult.

^{D}LAMMA *lulim*(*m*)*i-*

This title, like that discussed above, is apparently a local one used only in one or two texts. The epithet cannot yet be definitively translated.[326] This god's occurrences are restricted almost exclusively to the Anniwiyani Ritual. Sturtevant translates "^{D}KAL, the effeminate(?)" on the basis of context.[327] This god does occur in some tablet catalogues,[328] including entries for the Anniwiyani Ritual, and for the Ritual of Ḫuwarlu. *KUB* 30.65++ ii 4 reads [1 *ṬUPPU man*″*za* ^{D}LAMM]A *lulimmin* DÙ-*anzi* "One tablet, when they worship the *lulimmi-* Tutelary Deity," indicating that there was a festival or perhaps a ritual of the same

322. *CTH* 421: *KUB* 17.14 obv. 12′–13′, ed. Kummel, *StBoT* 3 (1967) 60–61. Cf. also ^{D}GAZ.BA.A.A ^{D}LAMMA ^{D}GAZ.BA.[A.A...], *KBo* 29.194:4′ (rit. frag.).

323. *CTH* 692: *KBo* 29.82(+)*KBo* 14.95 iv 9′ and *KBo* 29.99 i 13′.

324. *Chrest.* 109, 111.

325. *HED* 1–2: 368 sub *in*(*n*)*arawant-*.

326. *CHD lulim*(*m*)*i-*, with previous literature.

327. *Chrest.* 107–17.

328. *KUB* 30.65+34/i++ ii 4, 11, ed. Laroche, *CTH* pp. 169–70, and possibly *KUB* 30.50++ v 19, ed. Laroche, *CTH* p. 167 (both X *ṬUP-PU* catalogues.)

type as that of Anniwiyani for this god, the text of which has not yet been discovered or identified.

DLAMMA *šarlaimi-*

"The Exalted Tutelary Deity" is a god confined exclusively to the cult of Ḫuwaššana in the city Ḫupišna.[329] He occurs in the *witaššiyaš* Festival, the *šaḫḫan* Festival, and many fragments of festivals for Ḫuwaššana. He receives offerings as part of a group of gods,[330] paired with ZA.BA_4.BA_4,[331] and he also was sufficiently important in the cult to have a cult ceremony performed for him alone.[332]

The importance of this deity in the Ḫuwaššana cult at Ḫupišna can be seen not only in the fact that he sometimes received individual offerings but also in that he had a temple and cult personnel. É DLAMMA *šarlaimi-* is attested several times in texts describing this cult.[333] In each case this temple occurs as part of the phrase LÚ.MEŠ É DLAMMA *šarlaimiyaš* "the personnel of the Exalted Tutelary Deity's Temple." In the *witaššiyaš* fragment (*KUB* 27.49 iii 10–12) these personnel occur in a group with other cult functionaries such as the male Ḫuwaššana priests (LÚ.MEŠ*ḫuwaššanalaš*) and the singers who are to perform a drink offering. In the *šaḫḫan* Festival (*KBo* 14.89+*KBo* 20.112 i 2′) they are part of a different group of cult personnel who are called the "lords of the gods" and are all called into an unspecified house/temple. In a fragment of the Ḫuwaššana cult (*KBo* 29.65 iv 13′–19′) they are one part of a large group of personnel for whom offering tables are set up. It is interesting to note that except for a mention of the LÚ.MEŠ É DINGIR-*LIM* in *KUB* 27.49 iii 11, all the other cult personnel described in this text have specific titles such as SAL*ḫuwaššannalli*; it is only the functionaries attached to the temple of the Exalted Tutelary Deity who have no native title, but are called "the men of the Exalted Tutelary Deity's temple." This might indicate that this deity was a later or outside addition, whose functionaries did not fit into the available local categories of cultic personnel and so have only a descriptive title and not a native term. This god is a good example of a tutelary deity who plays no role in the state cult but is one of the central deities of a provincial cult.

wašḫazza DLAMMA

This epithet may be a Luwian dative plural and is discussed in the note to the translation of Bo 3298+*KUB* 25.32+*KUB* 27.70+ i 27 in *Chapter 2*.

329. On *šarlaimi-* see Laroche, *DLL* 86. The DLAMMA D*šarlaim*[*i-*] in *KBo* 16.100:13′ (fragment of Ḫuwaššana cult) is presumably a scribal error.

330. For example *KBo* 29.99 i 12′ and *KBo* 29.82(+)*KBo* 14.95 iv 8′ (fragments of *witaššiyaš* Festival).

331. *KUB* 77.66 ii 22, with duplicate *KBo* 29.69:22′ (*witaššiyaš* fragments).

332. *KBo* 29.82 iii 8′–12′ (*witaššiyaš* fragment); *KBo* 29.89+ *KBo* 20.68 iv 31′–33′ (*šaḫḫan* Festival).

333. *KUB* 27.49 iii 11 (*witaššiyaš* fragment); *KBo* 14.89+*KBo* 20.112 i 2 (*šaḫḫan* Festival); *KBo* 29.65 iv 19′; and *KBo* 24.27:9′ (Ḫuwaššana cult fragments).

ᴰLAMMA GAL

"The Great Tutelary Deity" occurs twice in the Ištanuwian thunder chant,[334] receiving offerings in one passage and occurring in a Luwian passage whose meaning is obscure. His only other occurrence is in a cult inventory of Stormgods,[335] in which he is simply one of many deities whose regular offerings are listed.

OTHER TUTELARY DEITIES

There are also a number of tutelary deities detailed only in the Festival for All the Tutelary Deities, discussed in *Chapter 3*. These deities govern activities, attributes, belongings, and body parts of the king, as well as mountains and rivers of the Hittite kingdom. Most are attested only in this festival and indicate an attempt by the Hittites to extend the concept of the tutelary deity into new areas. See Archi's[336] categorization of these deities and the discussion in *Chapter 3*.

DISCUSSION

The manifestations of the tutelary deity among the Hittites are many and diverse. Some, such as the Tutelary Deity of the Hunting Bag and Tutelary Deity of the Countryside, are associated with the hunt. Several cities of the Empire are attested with their own tutelary deity; many more probably had one which does not appear in the state archives. In addition to the tutelary gods inherited from the Hattian pantheon known to us by name the Hittites recognized many protective deities represented by the title ᴰLAMMA. Laroche[337] points out how varied is the Hittite use of this logogram, and Güterbock[338] in 1943 recognized that several deities underlie the hieroglyphic and cuneiform word signs. In the early period the Tutelary Deity (ᴰLAMMA) occupied a fairly prominent place in the pantheon as seen in his occasional inclusion in a triad with the Stormgod and Sun deity in older treaties. By the Empire period he was not so prominent among the oath deities who guaranteed the treaties, and his location in the procession of gods at the sanctuary of Yazılıkaya built at the end of the kingdom represents a kind of middle position within the pantheon.

The tutelary deities may be personal, but they also protect various aspects of nature or specific locations ranging from a single room or building to the entire state. Despite the potential of the tutelary deities for personal protective qualities, none of the kings who enjoys the special patronage or protection of one deity receives it from a tutelary deity.[339] Muršili II was guided by the Sungoddess of Arinna, Muwatalli by the Stormgod, and

334. *KBo* 4.11:6, 56, transliterated in *DLL* 164.
335. *KBo* 2.16 obv. 4, 9.
336. *SMEA* 16 (1975) 89–117, especially 95–105.
337. *Syria* 31 (1954) 113.
338. *Belleten* VII/1: 316.
339. The "Spezialgötter" of several kings are noted by Kammenhuber, *ZA* 66 (1976) 85.

Ḫattušili III by Ištar of Šamuḫa. Even Tudḫaliya IV, who perhaps sponsored the extensive Festival for All the Tutelary Deities treated in *Chapter 3*, chose Šarruma as his protector on the permanent monument which he erected at Yazılıkaya.[340] As the many figurines and references to "our god" from the Old Assyrian period demonstrate, the tradition of a personal or household tutelary god is an ancient Anatolian response to the vagaries of human existence. However, for the Hittite king at the center of a powerful Empire, his personal deity was invariably a state god of a stature appropriate to his august majesty.

340. On a seal noted by van Loon, *Anatolia in the Second Millennium B.C.* (Leiden, 1985) 47 pl. XLVa Tudḫaliya is encircled by the protective arm of the Stormgod.

CHAPTER 2

THE FESTIVALS OF KARAḪNA

THE TEXTS

CTH 681.1: Bo 3298+*KUB* 25.32+*KUB* 27.70+1628/u

Bo 3298+*KUB* 25.32+*KUB* 27.70+1628/u is a large four column tablet in a good state of preservation. The two large pieces, *KUB* 25.32 and *KUB* 27.70, are both in Istanbul and are physically joined together. The fragment 1628/u, containing the left edge of lines 47′–51′ of column iii, is in Ankara and has therefore not been glued into its place in the tablet. Bo 3298, containing column i 1–20, is also in Ankara. The surface of the tablet is in general well preserved.

There is a seal impression in the middle of the reverse, on which Dinçol and Darga comment briefly in their edition (p. 118). The seal is also published in copy in Bittel and Güterbock, *Boğazköy* 1 (1935) pl. 29.10, and as *SBo* II 92. In the literature on this seal it is usually cited as *SBo* II 92. The "hare" sign on the seal is discussed by Bittel and Güterbock in *Boğazköy* 1: 45 and by Güterbock in *SBo* II: 18. The seal itself has been discussed and interpreted by several different scholars. Laroche in 1956[1] compared it to the seal on RS 17.231 and to Boğazköy socle 2, reading the name on the *KUB* 25.32 seal as HARE+spur-*mi* = Tabrami. He connected this name with the Tabrammi of RS 17.337, who was a contemporary of Tudḫaliya IV, and thus dated *KUB* 25.32 to that king's reign. At that time he read only the name on the seal, not commenting on the other signs. Four years later,[2] while not giving a transliteration of the whole seal, Laroche read the name on the RS 17.231 seal as "LIÈVRE+*ra-mi* = cun. ^{m}*Tap-ra-am-mi*; même personnage à Boğazköy, *SBo* II 92 (= KUB XXV.32) ..." This reinforces his suggestion about the identification of the Ras Shamra Tabrammi with that of the *KUB* 25.32 seal.

1. *Ugar.* 3 (1956) 151–52.
2. *HH* 115 2a.

Meriggi, *HhGl* (1962) 201 no. 121, transliterates all the signs on the seal. He reads "(G 176)[3]–121-*r-mi-ku-wi*?." G 176 = *HH* 441 is the sign at the top of the seal and 121 is the HARE sign in Meriggi's list. He apparently confuses the PALACE signs on either side of HARE (*HH* 254) with *ku* (*HH* 423). He also reads SCRIBE (*HH* 326) as *wi*?. Although Meriggi does not interpret this transliteration any further here, his understanding of the name as Taprammi is made clear in *HhGl* 213 no. 220b. He did not recognize the logograms PALACE and SCRIBE on the seal. Güterbock[4] goes beyond the reading of the name to an interpretation of the logograms written to the left and right (PALACE) and under (SCRIBE) the name, which he understands as a compound, "Palast-Schreiber." More recently[5] Güterbock utilizes the evidence of the sign *HH* 254 ("PALACE") on the RS 17.231 seal to suggest that the logogram may stand for the title *ša rēši*, a palace official, and to read on the *KUB* 25.32 seal two titles for Tap(a)rami, *ša rēši* and scribe.

Based on this previous work on the seal, we may now read it in its entirety as "G 176 = *HH* 441 (an ornamentation?) / HARE+spur-*mi* = Tap(a)rami / *ša rēši* / scribe." Laroche's identification of this man Tap(a)rami with that of the RS 17.231 seal, although quite likely, is not certain. The seal on *KUB* 25.32 is different from and much simpler than that of RS 17.231. They may of course have belonged to the same person, who would have commissioned different seals as his title changed. This would explain the difference between his title(s), which in the *KUB* 25.32 seal include "scribe" and in RS 17.231 do not.

The script of this tablet is quite distinctive and facilitated the identifying of the three joins made so far for this text. The signs are small and somewhat sloppy. The scribe was not at all proficient; the tablet is full of erasures and extra wedges where he apparently wrote over mistakes without completely erasing them. There is very little consistency to the sign shapes, and the spacing of the signs is extremely uneven, with frequent large spaces between signs that all belong to the same word.

The tablet shows consistent late NS forms for the signs. The *ik*, *da*, and URU signs show their latest forms. The absence of any examples of older *li* or *ḫa* (i.e., with two winkelhakens) is another indication of late NS. Corroborating evidence for a late NS dating includes the use of AŠ for *INA* (many examples), the use of UGU for *šarā* (ii 50, iii 13′, 29′ (twice), iv 14), and *liš* as li_x (ii 20). See table 1 in *Appendix C* for specific sign shapes. The late script is further evidence that the seal on the tablet belonged to a contemporary of Tudḫaliya IV.

The text Bo 3298+*KUB* 25.32+*KUB* 27.70+1628/u, according to its colophon, records the festivals of Karaḫna. Laroche[6] labels this text simply "Fêtes de Karahna" but puts it under the more general rubric "Cultes de ᵈKAL." The text is in fact not a festival exclusively dedicated to the Tutelary Deity of Karaḫna, but she is the only deity mentioned in the text who is specifically associated with Karaḫna. The Tutelary Deity of Karaḫna is a

3. That is, sign number 176 in Güterbock's sign list in *SBo* II.
4. *IM* 17 (1967) 67.
5. *AnSt* 33 (1983) 30 with nn. 13–14.
6. *CTH* 681.

prominent goddess among the tutelary deities of cities and is discussed in *Chapter 1.* This text provides a good example of what a provincial festival was like, a festival not part of the cult celebrated at the capital but important for the maintenance of piety among the Hittites throughout their empire and not just at its political and religious center. The festival provides offerings to the entire pantheon of this particular town, with a few gods of surrounding cult centers singled out for more particular attention. It thus is meant to ensure harmonious relations with all the gods of the region, only one of which is the tutelary deity of this particular town.

The text has been edited by Dinçol and Darga, *Anatolica* 3 (1969–70) 99–118.[7] Page numbers cited for Dinçol and Darga refer to this edition. The unpublished join piece 1628/u was utilized by Dinçol and Darga in their work on this text. I would like to thank Professor Heinrich Otten for graciously sending me a prepublication version of his hand copy of this fragment, so that I was able to check this piece for myself in preparing a new transliteration and translation. The fragment furnishes the beginnings of lines iii 47–52.

Since Dinçol and Darga's edition appeared, Hoffner has discovered another join to this tablet and has generously allowed me to use his discovery in my work on this text. The new fragment, Bo 3298, fits into the top of column i; its last three lines join the first three lines of *KUB* 25.32 i. The addition of this join adds twenty lines to the first column. Dr. Evelyn Klengel very kindly allowed me to look at this unpublished piece during my work in Berlin, and Professor Horst Klengel also provided a photograph of the text. This tablet fragment is now in Ankara. On the basis of this major new join and the results of my collations of the tablets in Istanbul and Berlin I have prepared a new transliteration of the tablet and an English translation. Although the new join piece does not actually preserve the top edge, comparison with column ii, whose top edge is preserved in *KUB* 27.70 ii, indicates that there is only room for about twenty lines above the 1′ of *KUB* 25.32 i. The colophon indicates that this is the first and only tablet of festival description, and yet the first paragraph as preserved does not look like an introductory paragraph. It is thus conceivable that there was a very short paragraph before this one or at least another line or two introducing the text. There is however very little room for what are only conjectural additional lines, so I have taken the first line of Bo 3298 as line 1 of the tablet.

7. Other scholars cite passages from this text in various other publications. *KUB* 25.32 i 10′–14′ is transliterated by Bossert, *Heth.Kön.* 55. *KUB* 25.32 iv 8–11 is transliterated and translated by Alp, *Anadolu* 2 (1957) 18, where he also transliterates *KUB* 27.70 iii 3′–4′, now iii 37′–38′ in the joined text. Dressler, *Plur.* 181–82, transliterates and translates *KUB* 25.32 iv 8–9. *KUB* 25.32 i 4′–19′ is transliterated by Danmanville, *RHA* XX/70 (1962) 55. *KUB* 27.70 ii 19–21 is transliterated and translated by Coşkun, *Kap İsimleri* 14. Dinçol and Darga note places where Bossert's and Danmanville's transliteration differs from their own, but they do not comment on the passages worked on by Alp or Dressler.

Bo 3298+*KUB* 25.32+*KUB* 27.70+1628/u

Transliteration[8]

Obverse i

§1 [o o o o o] É? x[
[o o pár-š]i-ya na-an-kán [*A*]-*N*[*A*
[o o o o]x [

---

§2 [o o o]x BAL-ti na-an-kán *A-NA* DUGḫ[ar-ši-ya-al?[9] ME-i KAŠ GEŠTIN BAL-ti]
[na-an *IŠ-TU* ?] DUGḫar-ši-ya-al[10] *ŠA* ZÍZ da-a-an-zi n[a-at-kán?]
[o o o o]x [o] GIŠ!?gur-ta-li iš-ḫu-wa-an-zi ma-⌈x-x⌉[o o]
[GIŠgur-ta-li *IŠ-TU* GAD] ⌈ka⌉-ri-ya-an-zi GIŠgur-ta-li-za IGI-zi [pal-ši?]
[o o o o o-] ⌈zi⌉ EGIR-*ŠU* DUMU.É.GAL kar-pa-an-zi [Ø]
[na-at AŠ É LÚ[11] NA4]ARÀ pé-e-da-a-i LÚ.MEŠNAR pí-an ḫ[u-ya-an-zi]
[nu *A-NA* DUGḫar-ši]-ya-al UZUNÍG.GIG ti-an-zi 3 NINDAta-wa-ra[-al]
[pár-ši-ya nu-ká]n!? me-ma-al še-er iš-ḫu-wa-a-an-zi [Ø]
[na-at-kán? *A-NA*] DUGḫar-ši-ya-al EGIR-pa ti-ya-an-zi [Ø]
[ta wa-ga-a-t]a[12] ḫal-zi-ya 3-*ŠU* a-ku-wa-an-zi [Ø]
[o o o o o] ⌈pár-ši⌉-ya na-at-kán *A-NA* DUGḫar-ši-ya-al ZÍZ EGIR-pa [ti-ya-a]n?-zi[13]
[UD 1 KAM?[14] o o-]at

---

§3 [ma-a-an lu-kat-]ta GIŠ⌈IG⌉ ḫé-e-ša-an-zi KUŠNÍG.BÀR ME-an-zi [Ø]
[LUGAL-uš AŠ É].ŠÀ DINGIR-*LIM* pa-iz-zi 1 GUD ŠE 2 UDU [Ø]
[tar-ša-a]n-zi-pa an-da É.ŠÀ DINGIR-*LIM* ḫu-u-kán-zi [Ø]
[o o o o]da-a!-an-zi 3 NINDAta-wa-ra-al NINDA.Ì.E.DÉ.A me-ma-a[l]
[o o o AŠ] ⌈É⌉.ŠÀ DINGIR-*LIM* EGIR-pa da-a-i [Ø]

---

8. The join piece Bo 3298 adds twenty to the Dinçol and Darga column i line numbers.
9. Or DUG*ḫ*[*ar-ši-ya-li*$_x$.
10. The form *ḫar-ši-ya-al* is not cited by Friedrich in *HW*, although he cites the occurrence of DUG*ḫar-ši-ya-li*$_x$ (as DUG*ḫarsiyališ*) in this text, line ii 20. Without the examples from the join piece Bo 3298, there was almost no evidence for a form *ḫaršiyal* except for line ii 22 of *KUB* 27.70. The join piece now adds three more examples of *ḫar-ši-ya-al*, in lines i 5, 10, and 14. We may therefore posit an *l*-stem form *ḫaršiyal* for this word in addition to Friedrich's *ḫaršiyalli-*. On DUG*ḫaršiyalli-* see most recently Coşkun, *Kap İsimleri* 9–16.
11. Or SAL.
12. The trace fits *-t*]*a* quite well; the passage is restored from i 45 and ii 35.
13. From intercolumnium of *KUB* 27.70, labeled obverse i 1′.
14. The indication of the end of the first day of the festival is not preserved. In §§10 and 11, the last two paragraphs of column i, the tablet is broken in such a way that there could have been a short line denoting the end of day one in either of these paragraphs. There is a similar space here in i 15, and the following paragraph, if correctly restored, indicates the beginning of a new day in the ceremony.

Bo 3298+*KUB* 25.32+*KUB* 27.70+1628/u

Translation

Obverse i

§1 The few preserved words indicate that the text begins in its first paragraph with offerings and their preparation.

§2 He sacrifices. [...] x. [He places(?)]it in the s[torage] vessel. [He libates beer and wine(?).] They take [it from] the wheat storage vessel. They pour [...] into the *kurtali-* vessel. x[...] They cover [the *kurtali-* vessel with a cloth]. The *kurtali-* vessel the first [time] he/they [...]. Afterwards the palace attendant lifts (it).[15] He carries [it into the house of the mil]ler.[16] The singers r[un] in front. They place liver(s) [in the stor]age vessel. [He breaks] three *tawara[l]* breads and pours meal over (them). They place [them] back[17] in the storage vessel. [A "tidbi]t" is called out. They drink three times. He breaks [(a bread type)]. They [place] it back in the wheat storage vessel. [They ...] it.

§3 [When it daw]ns, they open the door. They remove[18] the curtain. [The king] goes [into the inner] chamber of the god. At the [*tarša*]*nzipa* of the inner chamber of the god they slaughter one fattened ox (and) two sheep. They take [...]. He takes three *tawaral* breads, sweet oil cake, meal [(and) ...] back [into] the inner chamber of the god.

15. The Hittite has a singular noun and a plural verb. The singular verb in the following sentence, in which the subject is probably still the palace attendant, indicates that the verb here should be singular.

16. This may be male or female; see the note to the transliteration of i 9.

17. See *Commentary* below for a description of the problems in translating the phrase *ANA* ^{DUG}*ḫaršiyal* EGIR-*pa tianzi* and similar phrases that occur throughout the festival description.

18. Literally "take."

Bo 3298+*KUB* 25.32+*KUB* 27.70+1628/u

Obverse i (*transliteration cont.*)

§4 21 LUGAL-uš-kán *I*[*Š-TU*] É.ŠÀ pa-ra-a ú-iz-zi na-aš[19] pí-an ḫ[u-e-ek]-zi[20]
22 UGULA $^{LÚ.MEŠ}$MUḪALDIM š[a-o o] šu-up-pí-aḫ-ḫi UGULA $^{LÚ.MEŠ}$MUḪALDIM LUGAL-i túḫ-ḫ[u-i-šar]
23 pa-ra-a e!-e[p-z]i ták-kán túḫ-ša[-i?]

§5 24 1 GUD ŠE (eras.) 7 UDU 2 ⌈SILA$_4$ *A*-⌉[*NA* (DN)]
25 1 UDU *A-NA* ^{D}UTU ^{URU}TÚL-n[a 1] UDU [*A-NA* (DN) 1 UDU *A-NA* ^{D}*IŠTAR* ^{URU}Ša-mu]-ḫa[21]
26 1 UDU *A-NA* ^{D}Hé-pát mu-šu-ni 1 U[DU *A-NA* (DN) 1 UDU *A-NA* (DN)]
27 1 UDU *A-NA* ^{D}LAMMA wa-aš-ḫa-az-za 1 [UDU *A-NA* (DN) 1 UDU *A-NA* ^{D}LAMMA?](-)x-ma-ti[22]
28 1 MÁŠ.GAL *A-NA* ^{D}LAMMA ^{URU}Ka-ra-aḫ[-na 1 MÁŠ.GAL *A-NA* ^{D}LAMMA ^{GIŠ}]ŠUKUR
29 1 MÁŠ.GAL *A-NA* ^{D}LAMMA MÁ.URU.URU$_6$ 1 MÁŠ.[GAL *A-NA* (DN)]
30 1 UDU *A-NA* ^{D}U.KARAŠ 1 UDU *A-NA* ^{D}U.⌈GUR[23] 1 UDU⌉[*A-NA* ^{D}Z]A.BA$_4$.BA$_4$
31 1 MÁŠ.GAL *A-NA* ^{D}Pi-ir-wa 1 UDU[24] ^{D}Aš-ka-ši-pa 1 UDU ^{D}[SAL.LUGAL]
32 1 UDU *A-NA* DINGIR.MEŠ É.DINGIR-*LIM* 1 UDU *A-NA* ^{D}Ḫal-ki 1 UDU ⌈^{D}⌉[Te-l]i-pí-nu
33 1 UDU *A-NA* ^{D}30 1 UDU *A-NA* ^{D}An-ta-li-ya 1 UDU [^{D}Im]-mar-ni-za
34 1 SILA$_4$ ^{D}MAḪ-ni 1 UDU ^{D}Gul-ša-aš 1 UDU ^{D}Ḫa-[ša-mi]-li
35 1 UDU *A-NA* DINGIR.MEŠ ^{URU}Ḫa-ši-iq-qa-ša-na-u-wa-an-d[a]

19. The tablet clearly has *na-aš*. We might expect the verb *ḫuwāi-* in the break, which would require emending the text to *na-at pí-an ḫ*[*u-u-ya-an*]*-zi* "They run before." If the pronoun is correct, we should not restore *ḫuwai-* in the break, as the king is never attested with *piran ḫuwai-*. I therefore restore *ḫuek-* "slaughter." This fits with the remainder of the paragraph.

20. From intercolumnium of *KUB* 27.70, there labeled obverse i 3′.

21. Dinçol and Darga restore ^{D}UTU ^{URU}*Ša-mu*]*-ḫa* at the end of this line, but as they point out (p. 100 n. 6) a sun deity of Šamuḫa is not otherwise attested. They infer his/her existence from the fact that lines ii 19–54 describe a ceremony for ^{D}UTU which takes place in Šamuḫa (written Šapuḫa). Worship of the Sungod in Šamuḫa need not, however, imply the existence of a Sungod of Šamuḫa. I therefore restore Ištar of Šamuḫa. There is too much space in this line for only one deity in the break.

22. Dinçol and Darga, in their commentary on this line (p. 112), suggest the possibility of reading the end of the line as [… ^{D}LAMMA] ^{GIŠ}DAG-*ti*. The sign which they read DAG quite definitely does not have a broken vertical. In addition, the first sign preserved after the break is not consistent with a reading GIŠ. Perhaps a place name is to be read here: "[the Tutelary Deity of]x-*mati*."

23. Dinçol and Darga read this name as ^{D}U.GUR; Danmanville, *RHA* XX/70 (1962) 55, reads ^{D}LIŠ. The traces would allow ^{D}LIŠ ⌈x⌉, i.e., Ištar with an epithet. ^{D}*IŠTAR* LÍL would be unlikely, as this goddess is probably to be restored at the end of line 36. ^{D}U.⌈GUR⌉ is certainly a possible reading if we take note that the U sign is written over an incomplete erasure. I read ^{D}U.⌈GUR⌉ here because of the rarity of the use of ^{D}LIŠ for Ištar, especially in a text that also uses the *IŠTAR* sign, and because I cannot postulate a likely epithet for Ištar which fits the traces.

24. Danmanville, *RHA* XX/70 (1962) 55, transliterated *A-NA* here, as well as twice in line 34, where the tablet does not have it.

Bo 3298+*KUB* 25.32+*KUB* 27.70+1628/u

Obverse i (*translation cont.*)

§4 The king comes o[ut] of the inner chamber and he [sacrific]es(?) in front. The overseer of the cooks purifies [...]. The overseer of the cooks hol[ds] forth *tuḫḫ[ueššar]* to the king. He separa[tes(?)] (it).

§5 One fattened ox, seven sheep, two lam[bs] t[o DN ...], one sheep to the Sungoddess of Arinn[a, one] sheep [to DN, one sheep to Ištar of Šamu]ḫa, one sheep to Ḫepat the True,[25] one sh[eep to DN, one sheep to DN], one sheep to the *wašḫazza* Tutelary Deity,[26] one [sheep to DN, one sheep to the Tutelary Deity of ...]x-*mati*,[27] one billy goat to the Tutelary Deity of Karaḫ[na, one billy goat to the Tutelary Deity of the] Spear, one billy goat to the Tutelary Deity of the Quiver, one [billy] goat [to DN], one sheep to the Stormgod of the Army, one sheep to Nergal, one sheep [to Z]A.BA_4.BA_4, one billy goat to Pirwa, one sheep (to) Aškašipa, one sheep (to) [Kattaḫḫa], one sheep to the gods of the temple, one sheep to the Grain Deity, one sheep (to) [Tel]ipinu, one sheep to the Moongod, one sheep to Antaliya, one sheep (to) [the Im]marni deities,[28] one lamb to the Mother Goddess, one sheep to the fate deities, one sheep to Ḫa[šami]li, one sheep to the gods of Hašiqqašanauwand[a],[29]

25. See *CHD* sub $^{(d)}$*muš(u)ni*.

26. See the Dinçol and Darga comment on this title (p. 112 of their edition). To the occurrences which they cite add *KBo* 21.54+*KBo* 30.174 (fragment naming ^{D}Zenkuruwa) 9′: *ŠA* ^{D}LAMMA *wa-aš-ḫ[a-*; 10′: *ANA* ^{D}LAMMA *wa-aš-ḫa-za*; and 21′:]x *wa-aš-ḫa-za* ^{D}LAMMA-*ya*. The word *wašḫaz(z)a* in all its attestations occurs with ^{D}LAMMA and is obviously an epithet for a tutelary deity or deities. The contexts in which it occurs are too few and indistinct to allow us to say what this epithet might mean. Laroche, *DLL* 109, cites this word under *wašḫa-* "maitre?" but in *DLL* 160 translates it in *KUB* 35.107 iii 10 as "dame(?)." In *NH* 327 he analyzes it as a derivative *wašḫa(n)t-* from *wašḫa/i-* and notes that his translation "dame(?)" is only a conjecture. He also suggests that the word is an epithet "de la déesse ^{d}KAL." His evidence in *NH* 326 that *wašḫa/i-* is an element only in feminine names is an indication that this particular tutelary deity is feminine. The case ending appears to be a Luwian dative plural ending *-nza* that has assimilated to *-zza*.

27. Or perhaps "[the Tutelary Deity] of the Throne." See Dinçol and Darga's commentary (p. 112) and my comments on line i 27.

28. Laroche, *DLL* 51, cites this as a plural acc./dat.(?) of "divinités de la campagne," but there is really too little evidence to enable us to identify these deities specifically.

29. The gods of this city are attested only here and in the AN.TAḪ.ŠUM Festival, *KBo* 4.13 i 37. See *RGTC* 6: 94.

Bo 3298+*KUB* 25.32+*KUB* 27.70+1628/u

Obverse i (*transliteration cont.*)

§5 36 1 UDU *A-NA* ^{fD}Ḫa-a-ša-la 1 UDU *A-NA* ^{D}*IŠTAR*[LÍL]
(*cont.*) 37 1 UDU *A-NA* ^{D}*IŠTAR* ^{URU}Ta-pí-ni-qa 1 UDU ad-da-aš [DINGIR.MEŠ-a]š!?[30]
38 1 UDU *A-NA* ^{D}A-pa-a-ra 1 UDU *A-NA* $^{ḪUR.SAG}$Za-a-a
39 1 MÁŠ.GAL *A-NA* ḪUR.SAG GAL 1 MÁŠ.GAL *A-NA* $^{ḪUR.SAG}$Ta-pa-a-la
Z[A]G.GAR.RA ḫu-u-kán-zi

---

§6 40 2 ⌈SILA$_4$⌉ ^{D}U ^{URU}Zi-pa-la-an-da *IŠ-TU* É.ŠÀ pa-ra-⌈a⌉ [ú-d]a-an-zi
41 [nu-ká]n *A-NA* ZAG.GAR.RA EGIR-pa ti-ya-an-zi [*A-NA* ^{D}]U? KÁ.GAL
42 [BAL]-an-zi nu-kán NINDA.Ì.E.DÉ.A me-ma-al še-er [iš-ḫ]u-wa-an-zi
43 [nam-m]a-aš 1 NINDA.KU$_7$ 40 NINDA ta-wa-ra-al *A-NA* ZAG.GAR.RA-n[i] ti-an-zi
44 [nu B]AL-an-zi *IŠ-TU* KAŠ GEŠTIN ta-wa-al [wa-a]l-ḫi[31]

---

§7 45 [na-at *A-NA*] ^{GIŠ}ZAG.GAR.RA ti-an-zi wa-ga-a-ta [ḫ]al-zi-ya
46 [3?-*ŠU* a-ku-w]a-an-zi[32] 3 NINDA.KUR$_4$.RA pár-ši-ya na-aš-kán $^{[GI]Š}$ZAG.GAR.RA
ti-an-zi

---

§8 47 [nu an]-dur-za x[o o] AŠ[33] É ^{LÚ}NINDA.DÙ.DÙ pé-[da]-i (eras.)
48 [*Ú-UL*]-pát-at-kán[34] [ka-r]i-ya-an-zi $^{LÚ.MEŠ}$⌈NAR⌉ [pí]-an ḫu-u-i-ya-an-zi
(Uninscribed space for 4 lines.)

---

30. Although Dinçol and Darga read the end of this line [DINGIR.MEŠ], there is a trace visible on the right side of this break at the end of the line, and that trace is not good for a reading ME]Š. It looks more like the end of an *i* or *az*. The phrase, *addaš* [DINGIR]-*i* "to the god of the ancestors," would fit spacing and trace well. The expected plural d.-l. *addaš* [DINGIR.MEŠ-*a*]*š* makes sense but does not fit the trace well and may be too long for the available space in the break.

31. Dinçol and Darga restore [KAŠ GEŠTIN] at the beginning of this line, which is too long for the break and necessitates emending the line considerably, as they have done: "[KAŠ GEŠTIN] BAL-*an-zi* <*BI-IB-RI* $^{ḪI.A}$-*kán*> *IŠ-TU* KAŠ GEŠTIN *ta-wa-al wa-al-ḫi* <*šu-un-na-an-zi*> '[Beer (and) wine] they libate. <They fill the rhyta> with beer, wine, *tawal*, (and) *walḫi*.'" No emendation is required with the transliteration suggested above, which could be translated, "They [li]bate, with beer, wine, *tawal* (and) *walḫi*."

32. Restored on the basis of Dinçol and Darga and the similar passage ii 35–36. The space in the break is tight for this restoration. Collation indicates a definite horizontal trace before *an*, which fits -*w*]*a*- and eliminates the possible restoration [BA]L-*an-zi* suggested by the similar spacing in i 44.

33. The Sumerogram AŠ for the Akkadian *INA* is used frequently throughout this text.

34. Dinçol and Darga read *na-at-kán* as the beginning of the line, but the left edge of the tablet is broken away here and there is space for one or two signs to the left of the preserved edge. They restored two signs in the same space in the line above. In line 48 the first preserved sign does not look like *na*, but more like *nu* or *pát*. I posit a restoration that fits the space and signs and makes sense. It is also possible that a noun (probably a logogram) began the clause. [^{UZU}NÍ]G.GIG!-*kán* would only barely fit the signs but would make sense; see ii 9.

Bo 3298+*KUB* 25.32+*KUB* 27.70+1628/u

Obverse i (*translation cont.*)

§5 (*cont.*) one sheep to the Ḫašala River, one sheep to Ištar of the [Countryside], one sheep to Ištar of Tapiniga, one sheep to the Ancestral [God]s(?), one sheep to Apāra, one sheep to Mt. Zā, one billy goat to the great mountain, (and) one billy goat to Mt. Tapala, (at/on) the altar they sacrifice.

---

§6 They [br]ing forth two lambs of the Stormgod of Zipalanda out of the inner chamber and place (them) back on the altar. They [sacrifice] (them) [to] the Stormgod of the Gate. They [sca]tter sweet oil cake (and) meal over them. [The]n they place them, (and) one sweet bread (and) forty *tawaral* loaves, on the altar. They libate, with beer, wine, *tawal,* (and) [*wa*]*lḫi,*

---

§7 and place [them] (on) the altar. A "tidbit" is called out.[35] They [drink 3(?) times]. He breaks three thick breads and they place them (on) the altar.

---

§8 [In]side(?) he c[ar]ries x[...] into the house of the baker. They [do not(?) co]ver that same one.[36] The singers run [in f]ront.

---

35. This is the only text where *wagata-* occurs without a NINDA determinative. See Hoffner, *AlHeth* 188, for examples of ^{NINDA}*wagata-* and the likelihood that this word is from the verb *wak-* "to bite." Neu, *StBoT* 26 (1983) 208, proposes "Brotbissen(?)." Dinçol and Darga translate "Der Imbiss!" It is possible, in light of the lack of any other occurrences of *wagata-* without NINDA determinative, that this text's scribe, who made mistakes throughout the tablet, for some reason neglected to write the determinative but intended ^{NINDA}*wagata-* in i 25 and ii 35. However, in view of the recurrence of the phrase *waganna ḫalziya*, it also seems possible that the scribe may have somehow understood *wagata* without determinative as approximately equal to *waganna*. The phrase with *ḫalziya* would then be "a 'tidbit' is called out" instead of "a 'biting' is called out."

36. Or perhaps "They cover the [li]ver(s)"? See commentary on i 48 (n. 34 above) for possible readings of the Hittite.

Bo 3298+*KUB* 25.32+*KUB* 27.70+1628/u

Obverse i (*transliteration cont.*)

§9 49 [o o o o o o o pár-š]i-ya ^{Ú}ip-pi-ya-an
50 [$^{\text{TU}_7}$mar-ḫa-an ti-an-zi nu-kán[37]] 4 NINDA.UTÚL ku-it pár-ši-ya-an-na-a-i
51 [nu-kán 4 a-na-ḫi da-a-a]n-zi ta-at ^{GIŠ}ZAG.GAR.RA-ni ME-⸢i⸣[Ø][38]
52 [o o o o o *IŠ-TU B*]*I-IB-RI* GUB-aš <3-*ŠU* a-ku-wan-an-zi> 3 NINDA.KUR$_4$.RA
53 [pár-ši-ya na-aš-kán ^{GIŠ}ZAG.GAR.RA t]i-an-zi

---

§10 54 [KAŠ GEŠTIN ta-wa-al wa-al-ḫi 4?-*ŠU*] ši-pa-an-da-an-zi
55 [nu-kán EGIR-pa DINGIR.MEŠ ḫu-u-m]a-an-te-eš ir-ḫa-a-an-zi

---

§11 56 [o o o o o o o o o o ša]r?-ra-an-zi
57 [o o o o o o o o o o] da-an-zi
58 [o o o o o o o o o o o] pé-e-da-an-z[i]

(bottom of tablet)

Obverse ii (*transliteration*)

§12 1 [o o o o o o o]-uš e-ez-za-i UZU-kán
2 [o o o o o o ḫ]a-an-da-an-zi ta (eras.)[39] ^{D}7.7.BI [BAL-an]-zi
3 [o o o o o o] x[40] ^{DUG}*KU-KU-UB* ta-wa-la-kán ar-ḫa
4 [o o o o o o] ḫa-aš-ta-i-ma ar-ḫa BIL-an-zi[41]
5 [o o o o o ḫ]a-aš-ši an-da ši-pa-an-da-an-zi
6 [ta 1 NINDA *LA-A*]*B-KU* pár-ši-ya-an-zi na-an-kán GUNNI ti-an-zi
7 [na-an-kán za-nu-w]a-an-zi 3 NINDA.KUR$_4$.RA pár-ši-ya (eras.)
8 [nu-kán? x[42] ^{NINDA}]ḫa-a-li i-ya-an-zi

---

§13 9 ⸢^{UZU}⸣NÍG.GIG.ḪI.A-kán ka-ri-ya-an-zi na-at UGU ME-an-zi
10 na-at AŠ É ^{LÚ}MUḪALDIM[43] pé-e-da-an-zi (eras.) UD 2 KAM

---

37. Dinçol and Darga suggest the restoration [*mar-ḫa-an ti-an-zi*] at the beginning of this line. This is almost certainly correct, as $^{(\text{TU}_7)}$*marḫa-* frequently occurs with the *ippiya-* plant. However, there is more space than this at the beginning of the line.
38. There is not enough space at the end of this line for Dinçol and Darga's reading *d*[*a-a-i*]. Collation of the tablet shows a vertical wedge exactly in the crease of the left line of the intercolumnium, after which comes the horizontal, which in the copy is drawn as a continuation of the preceding *ni* sign.
39. The signs *na-at* are erased.
40. Probably meant to be erased.
41. Dinçol and Darga read *ne-an-zi*. I read instead BIL-*an-zi* because burning up the bones is attested fairly frequently in rituals and festivals and thus makes good sense here.
42. A number.
43. The *mu* sign of ^{LÚ}MUḪALDIM looks as if the scribe started to write ^{LÚ}NINDA.DÙ.DÙ and then changed it to ^{LÚ}MUḪALDIM.

Bo 3298+*KUB* 25.32+*KUB* 27.70+1628/u

Obverse i (*translation cont.*)

§9 [...] he [br]eaks. [They set out] *ippiya*- plant (and) [*marḫa*-stew]. Th[ey take four samples[44]] of the four stew-breads which one regularly breaks, and he places them on the altar. <They drink> [DN] <3 times> [from a rh]yton, standing. [He breaks] three thick breads. They place [them (on) the altar].

§10 They libate [beer, wine, *tawal*, (and) *walḫi* 4(?) times]. [Then] they treat al[l the gods] with offerings in sequence.

§11 [...] they [dist]ribute. [...] they take. [...] they carry.

(bottom of tablet)

Obverse ii (*translation*)

§12 He eats the [...]s. The flesh [...] they prepare. They [sacrifice] (it) (to) the Pleiades. [...] And a jar of *tawal* away [...] The bones, however, they burn up. [...] they libate into the [h]earth. They break [one moi]st [bread] and place it (on) the hearth. They [coo]k [it(?)]. He breaks three thick breads. They make [x]*ḫali* [breads].

§13 They cover the livers and take them up. They carry them to the house of the cook. Second day.

44. Puhvel, *HED* 1–2 (1984) 57–58, suggests that the word *anaḫi*- could be either Hurrian or Luwian, although in his review of *HW*^{2}, Lief. 1, in *JAOS* 97 (1977) 597, he refers to *anaḫi*- as "Hurrian-based." Laroche, *GLH* (1976) 48–49, cites *anaḫi*- as a Hurrian word but suggests that it is a borrowing from Luwian. Already in *RHA* XXVIII (1970) 70 Laroche had suggested that this word was originally Luwian and not Hurrian. The word is rather common in festivals and rituals. Hoffner, *AlHeth* (1974) 151, commenting on the problem of choosing between the readings ^{NINDA}*anaḫi* or 4 *anaḫi*, suggests that the examples in *KUB* 25.32+ were probably not ^{NINDA}*anaḫi*. Kammenhuber, *HW*^{2} Lief. 1 (1975) 73b, suggests that the examples in this text are to be read neither ^{NINDA}*anaḫi* nor 4 *anaḫi*, but NINDA *anaḫi* "des Brotes Kostprobe." Hoffner notes, *AlHeth* 151 n. 6, that in some texts NINDA is distinguished from 4 by an indentation of the middle vertical, but this tablet contains definite examples of NINDA with and without an indented middle vertical, so this criterion cannot be used to decide the question of whether to read NINDA or 4 before *anaḫi* in this text. Either is possible, but since in each case the samples are specified as being warmed bread and stew-bread the reading NINDA *anaḫi* as a further specification of the type of sample offering seems less likely than a reading 4 *anaḫi*.

Bo 3298+*KUB* 25.32+*KUB* 27.70+1628/u

Obverse ii (*transliteration cont.*)

§14 11 *I-NA* UD 3 KAM ma-a-an lu-kat-ta ^{GIŠ}IG ḫé-e-ša-an-zi
12 ^{KUŠ}NÍG.BÀR da-an-zi ta *I-NA* UDUN ḫal-zi-ya ^{NINDA}a-a-a-n NINDA.UTÚL
13 ku-e pár-ši-ya-an-na-i nu-kán 4 a-na-ḫi da-aš-kán-zi na-at-kán ^{GIŠ}ZAG.GAR.RA
14 EGIR-pa zi-ik-ki-iz-zi *IŠ-TU BI-IB-RI* 3-*ŠU* a-ku-wa-an-zi
15 3 NINDA.KUR$_4$.RA pár-ši-ya na-aš-kán ^{GIŠ}ZAG.GAR.RA-ni EGIR-pa ti-an-zi
16 DINGIR.MEŠ ir-ḫa-a-at-ti a-ku-wa-an-zi

---

§15 17 ŠU.NIGIN 1 GUD.ÁB ŠE![45] 1 GUD.⸢AMAR 30⸣ UDU.NITÁ 2 SILA$_4$ 8 MÁŠ.GAL
18 ŠU.NIGIN.GAL 40 UDU.ḪI.A UD 3 KAM tuḫ-ḫu-uš-ta

---

§16 19 ma-a-an lu-uk-kat-ta LUGAL-uš AŠ É.ŠÀ DINGIR-*LIM* pa-iz-zi
20 (eras.) 1 NINDA.KUR$_4$.RA *LA-AB-KU* pár-ši-ya na-an-kán *A-NA* ^{DUG}ḫar-ši-ya-li$_x$ ZÍZ ME-i
21 ⸢KAŠ⸣ GEŠTIN BAL-ti (eras.)

---

§17 22 [nu *IŠ-TU* ^{DUG}]ḫar-ši-ya-al ZÍZ da-a-an-zi na-at-kán ^{GIŠ}gur-ta-li
23 iš-ḫ[u-wa-an]-zi ^{GIŠ}gur-ta-li-kán *IŠ-TU* GAD ka-ri-ya-an-zi
24 na-at AŠ ⸢É⸣ [LÚ[46] $^{\text{NA}_4}$]ARÀ pé-e-da-an-zi $^{\text{LÚ.MEŠ}}$NAR pí-an DÙ-ta-ri[47]

---

45. This sign looks more like 50 than ŠE. However, 51 calves have not been sacrificed, nor would reading 50 agree with the grand total of 40 "sheep" (small livestock).

46. Or SAL; a female miller is also attested in the Hittite corpus. In the similar passage in i 9 the critical sign is also lost, so we cannot use it to restore this passage.

47. This DÙ-*ta-ri* must from context represent *iyantari* "they go." Kümmel, *StBoT* 3 (1967) 106–07, explains the possible confusion of DÙ = *iya-* "to make" with DU = *iya-* "to go" in his commentary on *KBo* 15.9 iv 28, where one encounters DÙ-*at-ta-ri*. He cites the passage here from the Karaḫna festivals as another example of this "Ideogrammübertragung."

Bo 3298+*KUB* 25.32+*KUB* 27.70+1628/u

Obverse ii (*translation cont.*)

§14 On the third day, when it dawns, they open the door. They remove[48] the curtain. "In the oven" is called out.[49] They take four samples of the warmed bread (and) the stew-bread which one regularly breaks, and he puts them back (on) the altar. They drink from a rhyton three times. He breaks three thick breads. They place them back on the altar. They drink the gods in order.[50]

§15 A total of one fattened cow, one calf, thirty rams, two lambs, (and) eight billy goats. A grand total of forty small livestock.[51] The third day is ended.

§16 When it dawns the king goes into the inner chamber of the god. He breaks one moist thick bread. He places it in the wheat storage vessel. He libates beer and wine.

§17 [From] the storage vessel they take wheat(?).[52] They p[ou]r it into the *kurtali*-vessel. They cover the *kurtali*-[53] vessel with a linen cloth and carry it to the house of the [mi]ller. The singers go before it.

48. Literally "take."

49. This expression, which occurs once in each of the various festival proceedings described in this text (except in the third one, where it is probably in the broken section at the end of column ii), is somewhat unusual. It always occurs immediately before the taking of sample-offerings of the ceremonial breads. Since these sample-offerings always include "warmed bread," it seems likely that the point of calling out "In the oven" is to let the celebrants know that the offering bread is in the oven being warmed and therefore the ceremony is almost ready to begin.

50. Friedrich, *HW* (1952) 83, cites *irḫatti* as a Luwian form of *irḫa-* and translates "in der Reihe, rings herum." Laroche, *DLL* (1959) 52, cites a Luwian word *irḫatt-* "série, cercle," and gives the examples from this text as dative. He gives only two other possible attestations of this Luwian word. Its meaning seems clear from the context in this text and its relation with the verb *irḫai-* in the meaning "provide with offerings in sequence." Laroche, *RHA* IX/49 (1948–49) 22, translates *irḫatti* in *KUB* 25.32+ as "à la ronde."

51. Literally "sheep," but this is to include the other small animals in the grand total.

52. The point of this paragraph seems to be that wheat is taken from a *ḫaršiyal*, into which thick bread broken as an offering has previously been placed, and taken to the miller in a ceremonial procession with singers. This wheat is presumably ground into meal, although the text does not specify what is done with it. Meal (*memal*) is utilized in the offerings to the Sungod described in the next paragraph, so perhaps we should understand §16 as an explanation of the preparation of such meal. I thus translate ZÍZ here not as part of a genitive construct with *ḫaršiyal*, but rather as the object of *da-*.

53. This word occurs in ii 22 and 23 as ^{GIŠ}*gur-ta-li*. Friedrich, *HW 3. Erg.* 21, under his lemma *kurtal*, cites both these occurrences as singular dative-locative. In ii 22 it is dative-locative, but this second occurrence, in ii 23, is singular nominative-accusative. Friedrich lists *kurtali* as a possible form for the singular nominative-accusative of this word and in fact has more examples of *kurtali* than of *kurtal* as the nom.-acc. form.

Bo 3298+*KUB* 25.32+*KUB* 27.70+1628/u Obverse ii (*transliteration cont.*)

§18 25 ^{D}UTU-un-kán kat-[ta-an ^{G}]^{IŠ}⌈TIR⌉-ni pé-e-da-an-zi
26 na-an *A-NA* ^{NA_4}ZI.K[IN EGIR-pa t]i-ya-an-zi
27 1 GUD ŠE 7 UDU 1 SILA$_4$ ši-pa-[an-da-an-zi]
28 ta ^{NA_4}ZI.KIN-ši ḫu-u-kán-zi [^{UZU}šu-up-pa t]i-an-zi
29 2? ^{NINDA}dan-na-aš pár-ši-ya-an-zi ^{UZU}NÍG.⌈GIG⌉ [ka-ri-ya-a]n-zi
30 1 NINDA.KU$_7$ (eras.) 12 ^{NINDA}ta-wa-ra-al NINDA.Ì.E.DÉ.A me-ma-al 1 NINDA.KUR$_4$.RA KU$_7$
31 na-at-kán *A-NA* ^{NA_4}ZI.KIN ^{D}UTU EGIR-pa ti-an-zi
32 KAŠ! GEŠTIN wa-al-ḫi mar-nu-wa-an 4-*ŠU* BAL-⌈an-zi⌉
33 *BI-IB-RI*$^{ḪI.A}$-kán *IŠ-TU* GEŠTIN šu-un-na-an-⌈zi⌉
34 na-aš-kán *A-NA* ^{NA_4}ZI.KIN ^{D}UTU EGIR-pa ti-an-zi
35 1 DUG KA.DÙ ti-an-zi ta wa-ga-ta ḫal-zi-ya
36 3-*ŠU* a-ku-wa-an-zi 3 NINDA.KUR$_4$.RA pár-ši-ya-an-zi na-aš-kán EGIR-pa *A-NA* ^{NA_4}ZI.KIN
37 ti-an-zi

---

§19 38 nu *IŠ-TU* É ^{LÚ}NINDA.DÙ.DÙ NINDA.KUR$_4$.RA ú-da-an-zi
39 nu-kán NINDA.KUR$_4$.RA *IŠ-TU* GAD ka-ri-ya-an-za $^{LÚ.MEŠ}$NAR pí-an
40 ḫu-u-ya-an-zi 3 NINDA.KUR$_4$.RA pár-ši-ya ḫu-u-ma-an-⌈da⌉-aš DINGIR.MEŠ-aš
41 NINDA.Ì.E.DÉ.A (eras.) DÙ-an-zi 3 NINDA.KUR$_4$.RA NINDA.Ì.E.D[É.A]-ya ZAG.GAR.RA ti-an-zi
42 nu KAŠ! GEŠTIN wa-al-ḫi 3-*ŠU* BAL-an-z[i]

---

§20 43 nu *I-NA* UDUN ḫal-zi-ya-ta-ri ^{NINDA}a-a-an NINDA.UTÚL.ḪI.A ku-e
44 pár-ši-ya-an-na-an-zi nu-kán 4 a-na-ḫi da-a-an-zi
45 na-at-kán *A-NA* ^{NA_4}ZI.KIN ^{D}UTU EGIR-pa ti-eš-kán-zi
46 NINDA.Ì.E.DÉ.A-ma *A-NA* LUGAL ti-an-zi NINDA.Ì.E.DÉ.A [d]a-pí-i pí-an-zi
47 *IŠ-TU BI-IB-RI* GUB-aš 3-*ŠU* a-ku-wa-an-zi 3 [NINDA.KUR$_4$.RA pá]r-ši-ya
48 na-aš-kán ^{NA_4}ZI.KIN ti-an-zi (eras.) [ ]
49 DINGIR.MEŠ ḫu-ma-an-te-eš ir-ḫa-ti a-ku-wa-an-z[i]

---

§21 50 DINGIR-*LIM* UGU da-a-an-zi na-<an> AŠ[54] É.DINGIR-*LIM* [pé-e-da-an-zi]
51 ^{UZU}NÍG.GIG-kán ka-ri-ya-an-zi $^{LÚ.MEŠ}$N[AR pí-an ḫu-u-ya-an-zi]
52 ^{UZU}NÍG.GIG *ŠA* DINGIR-*LIM* É ^{LÚ}MUḪALDIM p[é-e-da-an-zi]
53 na-at-kán ^{GIŠ}ZAG.GAR.RA-ni ti-an-zi [Ø?]
54 *I-NA* ^{URU}Ša-pu-ḫa UD 1 KAM [Ø]

One erased line.

---

54. Dinçol and Darga read *na-aš* É DINGIR-*LIM* [*pé-e-da-an-zi*]; the spacing between *na* and *aš* is ambiguous. If there are several gods, as indicated by the plural pronoun -*aš*-, we would have expected DINGIR.MEŠ in the first sentence. The ceremony itself only mentions the Sungod. If he is indeed the only deity being worshipped in this ceremony, the singular form DINGIR in the first sentence of this paragraph is correct, and the text should be emended as above.

Bo 3298+*KUB* 25.32+*KUB* 27.70+1628/u Obverse ii (*translation cont.*)

§18 They carry the Sungod do[wn] to the grove. They place him [back] on the ste[la]. [They] consecra[te][55] one fattened ox, seven sheep, (and) one lamb. They slaughter (them) at the stela and [s]et out [the flesh]. They break two(?) *danna*- breads. The[y cover] the liver(s). (There are) one sweet bread, twelve *tawaral* breads, sweet oil cake, meal, (and) one sweet thick bread. They place them back on the stela (for) the Sungod.[56] They libate beer, wine, *walḫi*, (and) *marnuwan* four times. They fill rhyta with wine and place them back on the stela (for) the Sungod. They place one vessel of KA.DÙ beer. A "tidbit" is called out. They drink three times. They break three thick breads and place them back on the stela.

§19 They bring the thick bread from the house of the baker. The thick bread (is) covered with a linen cloth. The singers run in front (of it). He breaks three thick breads. They make sweet oil cake for all the gods.[57] They place the three thick breads (and) sweet oil cake on the altar. They libate beer, wine, and *walḫi* three times.

§20 "In the oven" is called out. They take four samples of the warmed bread (and) stew-bread which they regularly break, and they place[58] them back on the stela (for) the Sungod. Sweet oil cake, however, they set out for the king. The sweet oil cake they give to [a]ll. They drink three times from a rhyton, standing. He [br]eaks three [thick breads], and they place them (on) the stela. They drink all the gods in order.

§21 They take the god up. [They carry] <him> into the temple. They cover the liver(s). The si[ngers run in front. They carr]y the liver(s) (to) the house-of-the-cook of the god. They place them on the altar. […] In Šamuḫa,[59] one day.

One erased line.

55. Note the use of *šipant-* with animals to mean "consecrate, offer." That this verb does not indicate the actual slaughtering here and in §§22, 24′, 27′, 31′, and 34′ is obvious from the use of *ḫuek-* in the sentence immediately following. See Goetze, *JCS* 23 (1970) 85–92, on the distinction between *šipant-* with an animal object and no sentence particle meaning "sacrifice" and the same verb with an animal object and a particle such as *-kan* meaning "to consecrate." In general the use of *šipant-* in this text follows this rule; the two exceptions are here (ii 28) and iii 49′, in each of which the context makes it clear that despite the lack of a sentence particle, *šipant-* is used to mean "consecrate" and does not imply killing the animal.

56. My understanding of the two occurrences in this paragraph of *ANA* $^{\text{NA}_4}$ZI.KIN ^{D}UTU EGIR-*pa* as "back on the stela (for) the Sungod" instead of taking $^{\text{NA}_4}$ZI.KIN ^{D}UTU as a genitive construction is conditioned by the similar phrase in iii 43′ and 45′, *ANA* $^{\text{NA}_4}$ZI.KIN *taknaš* ^{D}UTU-*i* EGIR-*pa*, in which it is clear that the DN is in the locative.

57. Note the unusual word order; the normal word order would be DINGIR.MEŠ-*aš ḫumandaš*.

58. The verb here is a very unusual iterative form *ti-eš-kán-zi*. The more normal third person plural iterative of *dai-* is *zikkanzi*. There is no obvious reason why the action should call for an iterative verb here, but the iterative is used in similar contexts several times in the description of the festival.

59. The form ^{URU}Šapuḫa in this text is clearly an alternate spelling for ^{URU}Šamuḫa. Del Monte, *RGTC* 6: 339 and 350, cites several other examples of this alternate spelling.

Bo 3298+*KUB* 25.32+*KUB* 27.70+1628/u

Obverse ii (*transliteration cont.*)

§22 55 ma-a-an-za LUGAL-uš ^{D}LAMMA ^{URU}Ma-aḫ-ḫu-ut[(-)[60] i-ya-zi]

56 LUGAL-uš ti-ya-zi nu-kán 1 GUD 9 [UDU *A-NA* ^{D}LAMMA ^{URU}Ma-aḫ-ḫu-ut? BAL-ti]

§23 57 [nu ^{NA_4}ZI.KIN] ḫu-u-kán-z[i ^{UZU}šu-up-pa ti-an-zi]

58 [o o o o o] x x [ ]

(approximately six lines missing from the bottom of the tablet)

Reverse iii (*transliteration*)

(approximately seven lines missing from the top of the tablet)

§24′ x+1 ma-a-an-za LUGAL-uš ^{D}ZA.BA$_4$.BA$_4$-an ⸢i⸣-[ya-zi]

2′ LUGAL-uš ti-ya-zi nu-kán 1 GUD 4 U[DU]

3′ *A-NA* ^{D}ZA.BA$_4$.BA$_4$ BAL-ti ^{NA_4}ZI.K[IN-ši ḫu-u-kán-zi]

4′ ^{UZU}šu-up-pa ti-an-zi 1 ^{NINDA}dan-na-aš 1 NINDA K[U$_7$]

5′ 1 NINDA.KUR$_4$.RA KU$_7$ NINDA.Ì.E.DÉ.A me-ma-al *A-NA* $^{GI[Š}$ZAG.GAR.RA]

6′ ti-an-zi *BI-IB-RI*$^{ḪI.A}$-kán *IŠ-TU* GEŠTIN š[u-un-na-an-zi]

7′ na-aš-kán EGIR-pa ti-an-zi KAŠ GEŠTIN wa-al-ḫi [3?-*ŠU* BAL-an-zi]

§25′ 8′ *I-NA* UDUN ḫal-zi-ya-ri ^{NINDA}⸢a⸣-a-an$^{ḪI.A}$ NINDA.UTÚL.ḪI.A ku-e [pár-ši-ya-an-ni-an-zi]

9′ nu-kán 4 a-na-ḫi da-aš-ká[n-z]i na-at *A-NA* ^{GIŠ}ZAG.GAR.RA ⸢EGIR⸣-[pa]

10′ ti-an-zi *IŠ-TU BI-IB-RI* GUB-aš 3-*ŠU* a-ku-wa-an-zi

11′ 3 NINDA.KUR$_4$.RA pár-ši-ya-an-zi na-aš-kán ^{GIŠ}ZI.KIN-ši[61]

12′ EGIR-pa ti-an-zi DINGIR.MEŠ ḫu-ma-an-te-eš ir-ḫa-ti a-ku-wa-an-z[i]

§26′ 13′ DINGIR-*LUM* ^{UZU}šu-up-pa-ya UGU ME-an-zi na-at AŠ É ^{LÚ}MUḪALDIM

14′ pé-e-da-an-zi UD 1 KAM AŠ $^{ḪUR.SAG}$Ḫu-u-ra

§27′ 15′ ma-a-an-za LUGAL-uš ^{D}U.KARAŠ i-ya-zi

16′ LUGAL-uš ti-ya-zi ták-kán 1 GUD.MAḪ ŠE 4 UDU ŠÀ.BA 1 SILA$_4$

17′ 4 MÁŠ.GAL ŠÀ.BA 1 MÁŠ.TUR *A-NA* ^{D}U.KARAŠ ši-pa-an-ti

60. Or ^{URU}*Ma-aḫ-ḫu-w*[*a*(-). The name is otherwise unattested.

61. Dinçol and Darga read the determinative as NA$_4$, which is the expected determinative for ZI.KIN. However, Güterbock notes in *KUB* 25.32 that this word was written over an incomplete erasure; he is even able to decipher the original word: ^{GIŠ}ZAG.GAR.RA-*ni*. The scribe in changing this word did not do his task fully, neglecting to erase the GIŠ determinative and write NA$_4$ in its place.

Bo 3298+*KUB* 25.32+*KUB* 27.70+1628/u

Obverse ii (*translation cont.*)

§22 When the king [worships] the Tutelary Deity of Maḫḫut[(-)], the king steps (forward) and [consecrates] one ox (and) nine [sheep to the Tutelary Deity of Maḫḫut(-)].

---

§23 They slaughter (them) [(at) the stela and set out the flesh.] [...]x x[...]

(approximately six lines missing from the bottom of the tablet)

Reverse iii (*translation*)

(approximately seven lines missing from the top of the tablet)

---

§24′ When the king wo[rships] ZA.BA$_4$.BA$_4$, the king steps (forward) and consecrates one ox (and) four sh[eep] to ZA.BA$_4$.BA$_4$. [They slaughter] (them) (at) the stela and set out the flesh. They place one *danna-* bread, one swe[et] bread, one sweet thick bread, sweet oil cake, (and) meal on the a[ltar. They fil]l rhyta with wine and put them back. [They libate] beer, wine, (and) *walḫi* [three times].

---

§25′ "In the oven" is called out. They take (iterative) four samples of the warmed bread (and) stew-bread which [they regularly break]. They place them bac[k] on the altar. They drink three times from the rhyton, standing. They break three thick breads and place them back (on) the stela. They drink all the gods in order.

---

§26′ They take up the god and the flesh and carry them to the house of the cook. One day, on Mt. Ḫura.

---

§27′ When the king worships the Stormgod of the Army, the king steps (forward) and consecrates one fattened bull, four sheep among which is one lamb, (and) four billy goats among which is one kid, to the Stormgod of the Army.

Bo 3298+*KUB* 25.32+*KUB* 27.70+1628/u

Reverse iii (*transliteration cont.*)

§28′ 18′ ^{NA_4}ḫu-wa-a-ši ḫu-u-kán-zi ^{UZU}šu-up-pa ti-an-zi

19′ 1 ^{NINDA}dan-na-aš 1 NINDA.KU$_7$ 12 ^{NINDA}ta-wa-ra-al 1 NINDA.KUR$_4$.RA KU$_7$ NINDA.Ì.E.DÉ.A me-ma-al

20′ *A-NA* ^{NA_4}ZI.KIN EGIR-pa ti-ya-zi[62] *BI-IB-RI*-kán *IŠ-TU* GEŠTIN

21′ šu-un-na-an-zi na-aš-kán EGIR-pa ti-ya-zi

22′ KAŠ GEŠTIN wa-al-ḫi 4-*ŠU* BAL-zi![63]

---

§29′ 23′ AŠ UDUN ḫal-zi-ya-ri ^{NINDA}a-a-an$^{ḪI.A}$ NINDA.UTÚL.ḪI.A ku-e

24′ pár-ši-ya-an-ni-an-zi nu-kán a-na-ḫi da-aš-kán-zi

25′ na-at-kán EGIR-pa zi-ik-kán-zi

26′ *IŠ-TU BI-IB-RI* GUB-aš 3-*ŠU* a-ku-wa-an-zi 4 NINDA.KUR$_4$.RA pár-ši-ya

27′ na-aš-kán ^{NA_4}ḫu-wa-a-ši EGIR-pa ti-an-zi

28′ LÚ.MEŠ da-pí-an-te-eš wa-ar-šu-li a-ku-wa-an-zi

---

§30′ 29′ DINGIR-*LUM* UGU ME-an-z[i] ^{UZU}šu-<up>-pa-ya UGU ME-an-zi

30′ na-at AŠ É ^{LÚ}MUḪALDIM pé-e-da-an-zi ^{UZU}šu-<up>-pa-kán ^{GIŠ}ZAG.GAR.RA GIN-zi[64]

31′ ^{D}U.KARAŠ AŠ UD! 1 KAM ^{URU}A-ka-li-ya-aš ^{GIŠ}TIR-ni

---

---

§31′ 32′ ma-a-an-za LUGAL-uš ták-na-aš ^{D}UTU-un i-ya-zi

33′ ⸢LUGAL⸣-uš ti-ya-zi ták-kán kiš-an BAL-ti

34′ 1 GUD.ÁB ŠE 2 UDU ták-na-aš ^{D}UTU-i ⸢BAL-an⸣-zi

35′ ^{NA_4}ZI.KIN!-ši ḫu-u-kán-zi GUD UDU ḫu-u?-[m]a-[a]n?-[da-a]n?

36′ *PA-NI* ^{NA_4}ZI.KIN ti-an-zi

---

62. The text should perhaps be emended to *ti-ya-<an>-zi*, although three closely grouped examples (iii 20′, 21′, 38′) of *ti-ya-zi* where *ti-ya-an-zi* is expected make one cautious about emending. Dinçol and Darga, pp. 114–15, suggest the possibility of "Nasalreduktion" of the regular third person plural form to explain the occurrences of *tiyazi*. Such a phenomenon seems infrequent enough to merit our simply understanding these three examples as mistakes made by a scribe who made many other mistakes as well. Their further explanation of the odd use of DU in iii 30′ as an ideogram for expected *dai-* is not impossible, but see my comment on iii 30′.

63. The complement on BAL is written with an odd sign that looks like a combination of *an* plus *zi* and could be read either BAL-*zi*! or BAL-*an*!-*zi*! Either way it must stand for *šipandanzi*.

64. The unusual writing DU-*zi* where *tiyanzi* is expected is an example of a very rare use of Sumerian GIN (DU) for Hittite *dai-*. Hoffner points out to me one other occurrence of this in the Milawata letter, where GIN is used for *dai-* as "to set (boundaries)." This festival text now provides a second example of this rarely attested equation. See *CAD* K 162b sub *kânu* A 3a for the use of GIN (read GUB by *CAD*) in Mesopotamia for the action of setting up cultic equipment such as censers and sacrificial implements.

Bo 3298+*KUB* 25.32+*KUB* 27.70+1628/u

Reverse iii (*translation cont.*)

§28′ They slaughter (them) at the stela and set out the flesh. They place[65] one *danna*-bread, one sweet bread, twelve *tawaral* breads, one sweet thick bread, sweet oil cake, (and) meal back on the stela. They fill rhyta with wine and put them back. They libate beer, wine, (and) *walḫi* four times.

§29′ "In the oven" is called out. They take (iterative) samples of the warmed bread and stew-bread which they regularly break, and they put (iterative) them back. They drink three times from a rhyton, standing. He breaks four thick breads, and they put them back on the stela. All the men drink in the aroma.[66]

§30′ They take up the god and they take up the flesh. They carry them to the house of the cook. They place the flesh (on) the altar. (For) the Stormgod of the Army, in one day, in the grove of the city Akaliya.[67]

§31′ When the king worships the Sungoddess of the Earth, the king steps (forward) and consecrates (animals) as follows: They consecrate (one) fattened cow (and) two sheep to the Sungoddess of the Earth. They slaughter (them) at the stela. They place a[l]l of the cow (and) sheep before the stela.

65. See comment on iii 30′ in transliteration.

66. Friedrich, *HW 3. Erg.* (1966) 36, suggests "Duft" for *waršula*-. Engelhard, Diss. (1970) 65–66 translates "scent." More recently Güterbock, *JKF* 10 (1986) 212, indicates that he also understands *waršula*- this way, translating "smell, aroma," and proposing the above idea for *waršula*- used with drink offerings.

67. Dinçol and Darga, p. 118, indicate that this city name is among the geographical names in this text which are attested nowhere else in the Hittite corpus. However, Laroche, *NH* p. 269, connects the examples of Akaliya in *KUB* 25.32+ (iii 31′ and 46′, iv 16) with two examples of a city Angaliya or Angalā. Del Monte, *RGTC* 6: 17, accepts this identification and cites the examples from *KUB* 25.32+ under Ankaliya.

Bo 3298+*KUB* 25.32+*KUB* 27.70+1628/u

Reverse iii (*transliteration cont.*)

§32′ 37′ 1 ^{NINDA}dan-na-aš 1 NINDA.KU$_7$ 1 NINDA mi-l[i-i]t-ta-aš[68] NINDA.Ì.E.DÉ!A me-ma-al ^{UZU}ku-du-ur

38′ *A-NA* $^{\text{NA}_4}$ZI.KIN EGIR-pa ti-ya-zi KAŠ GEŠTIN li-im-ma-an BAL-zi

39′ *BI-IB-RI*$^{\text{ḪI.A}}$-kán *IŠ-TU* GEŠ[TIN] šu-un-na-an-zi

40′ 1 DUG KA.⌈DÙ⌉ *PA-NI* [$^{\text{NA}_4}$Z]I.KIN ti-an-zi

---

§33′ 41′ ta AŠ UDUN ḫal-zi-ya-ri 1 ^{NINDA}a-a-an$^{\text{ḪI.A}}$ NINDA.UTÚL$^{\text{ḪI.A}}$

42′ ku-e pár-ši-an-ni-an-zi ták-kán 4 a-na-ḫi da-a-aš-kán-zi

43′ na-at-kán *A-NA* $^{\text{NA}_4}$ZI.KIN ták-na-aš ^{D}UTU-i EGIR-pa zi-⌈kán⌉-zi

44′ *IŠ-TU BI-IB-RI* GUB-aš 9-*ŠU* a-ku-wa-an-zi

45′ 11 NINDA.KUR$_4$.RA pár-ši-ya-an-zi na-aš-kán *A-NA* $^{\text{NA}_4}$ZI.KIN ták-na-aš ^{D}UTU-i

46′ EGIR-pa ti-ya-an-zi AŠ UD 1 KAM AŠ ^{GIŠ}TIR ^{URU}A-ga-li-aš

---

68. The reading 1 NINDA.GE$_6$ [*wa-g*]*a-ta-aš* by Dinçol and Darga is impossible because the sign which they read *-g*]*a-* is preserved mostly as a vertical wedge which cannot fit *ga*. In addition, there is a very clear trace after the GE$_6$ sign, despite the fact that Dinçol and Darga indicate that their *wa* sign is completely lost in the break. There is in fact no space at all between *mi* and the trace following it. Dinçol and Darga, in their commentary on this line, themselves point out that the construction *NINDA.GE$_6$ *wagataš* is otherwise unattested. The signs on the tablet do not support such a reading here either. In this position in similar lists of bread offerings in this text we have 12 ^{NINDA}*ta-wa-ra-al* (ii 30), 1 NINDA.KUR$_4$.RA KU$_7$ (iii 4′–5′) or 12 ^{NINDA}*ta-wa-ra-al* 1 NINDA.KUR$_4$.RA KU$_7$ (iii 19′). Neither ^{NINDA}*tawaral* or NINDA.KUR$_4$.RA KU$_7$ fit the traces here, however.

This passage is cited in the *CHD* sub *milit-* in the morphology section, reading *mi-li?-ta-aš*, which fits the traces quite well, except that the break in the middle of the word may be too large for the *li* sign to bridge and still show traces on either side of the break. For this reason I suggest that this word should be read NINDA *mi-l*[*i-i*]*t-ta-aš*, "bread of honey, honey bread," for which there is sufficient room in the break. Either reading would be the only attestation for a syllabically spelled genitive of *milit-*, although the genitive LÀL-*aš* is attested. There are no other occurrences of NINDA *milittaš*, but NINDA.LÀL "honey bread" (*AlHeth.* 123 and 202) is well attested. Hoffner, *AlHeth* 209, commenting on bread names which allude to their ingredients and pointing out possibilities for the Hittite reading of logographically written bread names, cites as a hypothetical example *milittaš zuwaš* as a possible reading for NINDA.LÀL. Thus the reading NINDA *mi-l*[*i-i*]*t-ta-aš* in this line, although providing a previously unattested spelling of a bread name, is certainly a possible reading and may be the first occurrence of a partially Hittite rendering of NINDA.LÀL.

Bo 3298+*KUB* 25.32+*KUB* 27.70+1628/u

Reverse iii (*translation cont.*)

§32′ They set out one *danna*- bread, one sweet bread, one ho[n]ey bread(?), sweet oil cake, meal, (and) the thigh[69] back on the stela. They libate beer, wine (and) *limma*-beverage. They fill rhyta with wi[ne]. They place one vessel of KA.DÙ beer before the [st]ela.

---

§33′ "In the oven" is called out. They take (iterative) four samples of the warmed breads (and) stew-breads which they regularly break and put (iterative) them back on the stela for the Sungoddess of the Earth.[70] They drink nine times from the rhyton, standing. They break eleven thick breads and place them back on the stela for the Sungoddess of the Earth. In one day, in the grove of the city Agaliya.

---

69. Friedrich, *HW 2. Erg.* (1961) 16, primarily on evidence from *KBo* 11.40, rejects the idea of Alp, *Anadolu* 2 (1957) 16–19, that *kudur* was the part of an animal immediately below the neck, and proposes in its place "Oberschenkel." Goetze, *JCS* 17 (1963) 63, is less specific, suggesting the more general semantic range "part of the leg." Poetto, *KZ* 99 (1986) 220–22, reviews the scholarship on *kudur* and suggests that it has an Indo-European etymology. He adduces possible cognates from Scandinavian languages which would support the identification of *kudur* with the calf of the leg or thigh.

70. Hoffner suggests the possible interpretation of *ANA* ^{NA_4}ZI.KIN *taknaš* ^{D}UTU-*i* as apposition: "on the stela, (namely) the Sungoddess of the Earth." This would indicate an underlying conception of the stela not as an altar for the deity but as the deity itself.

Bo 3298+*KUB* 25.32+*KUB* 27.70+1628/u

Reverse iii (*transliteration cont.*)

§34′ 47′ ma-a-an-za LUGAL-uš ^{D}U É DÙ-zi

48′ LUGAL-uš ti-ya-zi ták-kán ši-pa-an-ti

49′ 1 GUD.MAḪ :pár!-za-ḫa!-⌈na-aš-ši⌉-iš[71] 3 UDU 1 SILA$_4$ 2 MÁŠ.GAL 1 MÁŠ.TUR

50′ *A-NA* ^{D}U É BAL-[an]-zi 8? UDU ^{GIŠ}ZAG.GAR.RA ḫu-kán-zi

51′ 1 UDU *A-NA* ^{D}T[e-li-pí-n]u ^{GIŠ}DÌM ḫu-u-kán-zi

§35′ 52′ [o o o o o o o] x ^{UZU}NÍG.GIG ^{GIŠ}ZAG.GAR.RA

53′ [o o o o o o o ^{GIŠ}]DÌM ti-an-zi

(bottom of tablet)

Reverse iv (*transliteration*)

§36′ 1 [^{UZU}šu-up-pa ti-an]-zi[72] 1 ^{NINDA}dan-na-aš 3 NINDA.KU$_7$ *ŠA*

2 [NIND]A? BABBAR 1 NINDA.KU$_7$ 30 ^{NINDA}ta-wa-ra-al

3 [pár-ši-ya-an-zi NIND]A.Ì.E.DÉ.A-kán me-ma-al ^{GIŠ}ZAG.GAR.RA

4 [EGIR-pa ti-an-z]i *BI-IB-RI*$^{ḪI.A}$-kán šu-un-na-an-z[i]

5 [na-aš-kán EGIR-pa ti]-an-zi

6 [KAŠ GEŠTIN 2?-*ŠU*] BAL- zi

§37′ 7 [^{GIŠ}Z]AG.GAR.RA ti-an-zi

71. The word which Dinçol and Darga read as *:pir!-za-ḫa!-na-aš-ši-iš* in the transliteration is discussed by them in their commentary (p. 115). There they mention the fact that Güterbock had communicated to them that he felt the first sign should be read *pa* and not *pir*! This word bridges the join 1628/u+*KUB* 27.70, with the sign in question being on the fragment 1628/u. Collation of a photograph of that fragment has convinced me that this somewhat unclear sign is not *pir* (UD) but is either *pa* or *pár*. Otten's hand copy shows a *pa* sign. Güterbock's understanding of the word with the first sign read as *pa* is detailed in Dinçol and Darga's commentary. He has since indicated to me that he now prefers the reading *pár* because it provides an attested form for the beginning of this word; see the form *pár-za-ḫa-an-na-aš* cited in Friedrich, *HW 2. Erg.* 21. In light of the evidence of the majority of other attestations of this word, which are spelled with an initial *pí*, it is conceivable that we should read this (and Friedrich's other example of *pár-za-ḫa-an-na-aš*) as *pir*$_x$*-za-ḫa-an-na-aš*. See Laroche, *Ugar.* 5 (1968) 782, on the possibility of positing a *pir*$_x$ value for the BAR sign.

72. Based on a similar sequence in iii 18′f.

Bo 3298+*KUB* 25.32+*KUB* 27.70+1628/u

Reverse iii (*translation cont.*)

§34′ When the king worships the Stormgod of the House, the king steps (forward) and consecrates (animals thus): They consecrate one *parzaḫana*-(?)[73] bull, three sheep, one lamb, two billy goats, (and) one kid to the Stormgod of the House. They slaughter eight animals[74] (on) the altar. They slaughter one sheep to T[elipin]u (at) the pillar.[75]

§35′ […] the liver(s) (on) the altar [… on/before(?)] the pillar they place.

(bottom of tablet)

Reverse iv (*translation*)

§36′ They [set out the flesh(?)]. [They break] one *danna*- bread, three sweet breads of [… (a number)] white [brea]ds, one sweet bread, (and) thirty *tawaral* breads. Sweet oil [cak]e, (and) meal the[y place back] (on) the altar. They fill rhyta and put [them back]. They libate [beer (and) wine 2(?) times].

§37′ They place [… on the a]ltar.

73. Or perhaps *pazaḫana*-. See the comments on the transliteration of iii 49′.

74. Literally "sheep" (UDU), but this is obviously meant to denote the eight animals of various kinds listed in the previous sentence. See the note to the same use of UDU in ii 18 (§15).

75. Dinçol and Darga follow Friedrich, *HW 1. Erg.* 25, in translating ^{GIŠ}DÌM as "Brunnen." See Otten, *IM* 19/20 (1969/1970) 85–91, on ^{GIŠ}DÌM possibly standing for both *kurakki*- and *šarḫuli*-, with evidence for understanding it as an architectural element of a house and translating it as "pillar" or "post." *CAD* M vol. 1: 143 cites the Akkadian word *makūtu* for ^{GIŠ}DÌM and suggests the meaning "pillar(?)." Ünal, *JCS* 40 (1988) 102–04, provides a thorough discussion of pillars in Hittite architecture.

Bo 3298+*KUB* 25.32+*KUB* 27.70+1628/u

Reverse iv (*transliteration cont.*)

§38′ 8 [ta AŠ UDUN ḫal-zi-ya-r]i ^{NINDA}a-a-an$^{\text{ḪI.A}}$ NINDA.UTÚL.ḪI.A ku-e pár-ši-ya-an-z[i]
9 [ták-kán 4 a-na-ḫi-t]a[76] ar-ḫa da-aš-kán-zi na-at-kán ^{GIŠ}ZAG.GAR.RA-⸢ni⸣
10 [EGIR-pa ti-an]-zi ^{UZU}ku-du-ra-kán *A-NA* ^{GIŠ}ZAG.GAR.RA
11 [ti-an-zi *IŠ-TU B*]*I-IB-RI* GUB-aš 3-*ŠU* a-ku-wa-a[n-z]i
12 [4? NINDA.KUR$_4$.RA pár-ši-ya-a]n-zi na-aš-kán ^{GIŠ}ZAG.GAR.R[A-ni EG]IR-pa
13 [ti-an-zi LÚ.ME]Š ḫu-u-ma-an-te-eš wa-a[l-ḫi ta-wa-a]l? NAG-zi

---

§39′ 14 [nu DINGIR-*L*]*IM*!? ⸢$^{\text{UZU?}}$⸣[77]š[u-up-pa-ya] UGU ME-an-zi
15 [na]-at AŠ É ^{LÚ}MUḪALDIM [p]é-e-da-an-z[i]
16 UD 1 KAM AŠ <É>[78] *ŠA* ^{D}U É[-*TIM*] ^{URU}A-ka-⸢li⸣-ya-aš

(blank space of about 13 lines)

Colophon (*transliteration*)

DUB 1 KAM *QA-TI*
ŠA EZEN.M[EŠ]
^{URU}Ga-ra-[aḫ-n]a

76. Alp, *Anadolu* 2 (1957) 18, reads the beginning of this line as [… *na-a*]*t*, as does Dressler, *Plur.* 181. Dinçol and Darga suggest reading [… *a-na-ḫi-t*]*a*, which fits the trace on the tablet better and makes very good sense in the sentence.

77. Lines 13–14 are restored based on the similar context of paragraphs 29′–30′. Although Dinçol and Darga's DINGIR-*L*]*IM* is an excellent suggestion, there is too much space at the beginning of line 14 for just that. There is also a problem in having what looks like a word space between ⸢$^{\text{UZU?}}$⸣ and *š* [*u*-.

78. Dinçol and Darga make the excellent suggestion of reading É without noting that the tablet does not actually have it. The divine name in this line looks like ^{D}LIŠ, but the vertical is faint on the tablet, and ^{D}U É is the god being worshipped in this particular ceremony, so I concur with Dinçol and Darga in reading this as ^{D}U É. The *a* in ^{URU}*A-ka-*⸢*li*⸣*-ya-aš* also has an extra wedge which shows no signs of being erased but should not be there.

Bo 3298+*KUB* 25.32+*KUB* 27.70+1628/u

Reverse iv (*translation cont.*)

§38′ ["In the oven" i]s [called out]. They take (iterative) away [four sample]s of the warmed breads and stew-bread which they break, and the[y place] them [back] on the altar. The thigh also [they place] on the altar. They drink three times [from a r]hyton, standing. They [break 4 thick breads and place] them [ba]ck [on] the altar. Every[one] drinks *wa*[*lḫi* (and) *tawa*]*l*.

---

§39′ They take up the [go]d [and] the fl[esh] and carry them into the house of the cooks. One day, in the <temple> of the Stormgod of the House of the city Akaliya.

(blank space of about 13 lines)

Colophon (*translation*)

One tablet, finished, of the festival[s] of Kara[ḫn]a.

CTH 681.2: *IBoT* 1.5

Bo 1513 = *IBoT* 1.5 is a fragment measuring approximately 5 cm wide by 3.8 cm high. Its surface is fairly well preserved. Its script is quite neat and regular, with very clearly distinct wedges. There is not enough preserved text to allow a dating of the script. We can say, however, that the script is sufficiently different from that of *KUB* 25.32+ to preclude the possibility that this is a join to the main text.

Although Laroche, presumably on the basis of the occurrence of ^{D}U.KARAŠ in line 2′, catalogues *IBoT* 1.5 as part of *CTH* 681, festivals of Karaḫna, there is not enough of the fragment preserved to make any kind of positive identification for it. Dinçol and Darga do not include this piece in their edition because its relationship to *KUB* 25.32+ is too uncertain. A transliteration of the fragment is included below, but the information added by this piece, even if it is part of the same festival descriptions, is negligible.

Transliteration

x+1]x *I-NA* x[
2′]x LUGAL-uš *A-NA* ^{D}U.KA[RAŠ
3′]x 1 AMAR 4 UDU-ya ši-p[a-an-ti
4′]x *A-NA* ^{D}IB[
5′]x ^{D}Ḫal-k[i

COMMENTARY

Dinçol and Darga, in their edition of this text (pp. 116–18), make some comments on the festival described therein. They note that the first part of the tablet, ending with §15′ (ii 17–18), describes a three day festival that included offerings to many gods and was probably held at Karaḫna. Following this three day festival are descriptions of six one day festivals, separated from each other by double paragraph lines and celebrated in several different locations. Dinçol and Darga enumerate these six one day festivals and note that all seven festivals are probably independent of one another. The plural form EZEN.MEŠ in the colophon is adduced as further evidence that these festival descriptions are considered as separate units. This interpretation seems the correct one for understanding the somewhat unusual organization of the tablet. There are none of the references to the king or other cultic personnel going from one place to another which might have indicated that this was a description of a cultic journey. Although the festivals take place in different localities and provide offerings for different gods, the formulas for the offerings and cultic procedure remain very similar throughout the text, indicating that the festivals were probably all performed in the same region with the same basic plan. One distinctive feature in the last festival, that for the Stormgod of the House, is the placing of one sheep at the ^{GIŠ}DÌM, the pillar(?), in addition to the eight sheep at the altar. Whatever the exact meaning of ^{GIŠ}DÌM may be, as noted above in the footnote at the end of §35′ in the translation, it is some kind of architectural element such as "pillar." It is therefore interesting to see the prominence given to this "pillar" when a deity specifically related to the house is worshipped. In the foundation ritual *KUB* 55.26+Bo 7740[79] the Hittites provide offerings at or to the pillars of a house under construction.

Throughout the text there are a number of phrases of the pattern *ANA* (noun) EGIR-*pa tianzi*. The noun is most commonly ^{GIŠ}ZAG.GAR.RA "altar" or ^{NA_4}ZI.KIN "stela," although it can also be other cult items such as a *ḫaršiyal* vessel. The pattern varies somewhat; sometimes *ANA* is absent and the noun has a Hittite phonetic complement indicating dative-locative case, sometimes there is no indication of case for the noun, the form of the verb *dai-* may change, or, rarely, there may even be some other verb. This pattern has caused no little problem in translation and in thus trying to understand the ceremonial activities of the festival and their significance. Possible translations of, for example, *n⸗at ANA* ^{GIŠ}ZAG.GAR.RA EGIR-[*pa*] *tianzi* (iii 9′–10′) could be "They put it behind the altar," or "They put it back on the altar." In favor of the first translation is the syntax that places *appa* (EGIR-*pa*) in the place of a postposition following a noun in the dative-locative, where it could mean "behind." In addition, in none of the cases is there a mention of the offerings having previously been on the altar/stela, so it becomes difficult to understand how they can be put "back." In favor of the second translation is our understanding of *appa* in general as an adverb, the normal postposition "behind" being *appan*.[80] The Hittites did not always observe this distinction, however. In certain cases sense dictates the latter interpretation, such as i 19–20 (§3), where it makes more sense that the celebrants would be putting cereal offerings back into the inner chamber of the god than behind the chamber. An analogous situation may be seen all through the *kurša*- Festival,[81] in which the offerings are put back on the *kurša*-. The syntax is different, but the idea of putting offerings back on the cult object is the same.

Perhaps all of the necessary offering materials were set out on the altars or stelae before the ritual of sacrificing began, which would explain how such offerings could then be placed "back" on the altar. This, however, cannot always be the case, as for example in §20, in which the samples were in the oven immediately before being placed "back" on the stela. In §18, if ii 26 is correctly restored, the Sungod is carried out to the grove where his cult-stela is and then is placed "back" on it. Another difficulty is that sometimes offering materials are simply placed (without *appa*) on the altar or stela. Does this imply that not all offerings were set out ahead of time? In iii 30′ and 36′ the flesh (*šuppa*-) or entire animals are placed on the altar or stela without *appa*. This makes sense when we consider how difficult it would be to keep an animal on an altar before it was sacrificed.

It may not make a great deal of difference whether the offerings, or in one case the god himself (ii 26), is placed on or behind an altar. I have chosen to translate this phrase to express the idea of putting materials back on the altar or stela rather than behind them. In

79. Edited by Ünal, *JCS* 40 (1988) 97–106.

80. Friedrich, *HW* 25, suggests that *appa* could function as a postposition "behind" governing the ablative in some of the laws but notes the more regular postposition *appan*. Kammenhuber, *HW*² 1:148–49 sub *appa* (which includes *appan* and *appanda*), lists *appa* as an adverb and *appan* as the regular postposition.

81. *KUB* 55.43 passim; see *Chapter 4*.

my opinion this presents fewer problems in understanding the process of these ceremonies of offerings.

The city Karaḫna was an important cult center and as such has been discussed by several scholars. Jakob-Rost[82] points out that the Tutelary Deity of Karaḫna was one of only a few deities for whom there was a daily regimen of cult offerings in operation and notes that any city whose deity received daily offerings must be an important cult city. Some of the evidence for Karaḫna as a major cult center is the existence of the cult inventory text for the city.[83] In their article on Karaḫna, in the *Reallexikon der Assyriologie*,[84] Otten and Röllig summarize the cultic activity attested for this city and cite occurrences of the Tutelary Deity of Karaḫna in other texts. The prominence given to the cultic tradition of this city provides an excellent example of the characteristic Hittite tendency to ensure the prosperity of local cults at some distance from the capital, the locus of the state cult. The king's participation in all of the individual festivals to local deities indicates his role in preserving the state's attitude of propitiation to the gods and the fact that those gods must be worshipped at their own cult loci. Del Monte, in the entry for Karaḫna in *RGTC* 6 (1978) 177–80, also gives an indication of the importance of the city. More recently Alp[85] writes on the location of Karaḫna, and, citing evidence from Maşat texts, proposes that Karaḫna is north of and close to Maşat Höyük.

This northern localization of Karaḫna is interesting in light of the deities worshipped in this festival, seen especially in the list of deities who receive offerings in §5 of *KUB* 25.32+. Danmanville[86] suggests that this list reveals a Hurro-Hittite syncretism, although she does not give any details of the Hurrian elements in the list. In fact the partially Hurrian nature of the list of deities in *KUB* 25.32+ §5 is seen only in Ištar of Šamuḫa (i 25) and ᴰḪepat *mušuni* (i 26), a Hurrian goddess with a Hurrian epithet. There is also at least one deity with a Luwian epithet, ᴰLAMMA *wašḫazza* in i 27.[87] Beyond these few names, however, the names of the deities in this list seem all to be part of the Hattic or Hittite tradition. There is also the frequent employment of the Hurrian or Luwian word *anaḫi*, sample-offerings, another example of the inclusion in this festival of later elements from outside the older Hattic sphere.

That the worship of the Tutelary Deity of Karaḫna extended beyond this local cult and its northern homeland is clear from her inclusion in many other texts besides this festival. Otten and Röllig[88] point out that the Tutelary Deity of Karaḫna occurs in *KUB* 30.29 obv. 11, a Birth Ritual,[89] among Hattic gods, and in *KUB* 27.1 i 67, the Festival of Ištar of

82. *MIO* 8 (1963) 170.

83. *KUB* 38.12 with duplicate *KUB* 38.15; see Rost, *MIO* 8 (1963) 200–01; Darga, *RHA* XXVII/84–85 (1969) 5–11; and idem, *İstanbul Üniversitesi Edebiyat Fakültesi Yayınları* no. 1825 (1973) 1–45.

84. *RLA* 5 (1976–80) 403.

85. *FsBittel* (1983) 43–46.

86. *RHA* XX/70 (1962) 56–57.

87. See comments on this word in the footnote to the translation.

88. *RLA* 5: 403.

89. Ed. Beckman, *StBoT* 29 (1983) 22–23.

Šamuḫa,[90] among Hurrian gods. The evidence from the birth ritual has led Beckman to suggest that ᴰLAMMA ᵁᴿᵁKaraḫna might be a Hattic deity.[91] The occurrences of her name among Hurrian gods and the late date for the writing down of these festivals is evidence that her cult remained active throughout the Hittite kingdom, and that she was included in newer cults. See *Chapter 1* for further discussion of the Tutelary Deity of Karaḫna.

The language of the text reflects a mixing of old and new elements. The text is unusual in that frequently Sumerograms are written without any Akkadian preposition or Hittite phonetic complement to indicate their case, although syntax often indicates that their case must be dative-locative. It is possible that this is simply due to the lack of proficiency of the scribe, already noted above in the comments on the script. This text is dated OH/NS by the *CHD*; see for instance *CHD* sub (:)*lim*(*m*)*a*-, morphology section. Melchert[92] also gives this text his equivalent of an OH/NS dating. Some elements of the language definitely indicate an Old Hittite date for the original composition. The location of the festivals around the cult city Karaḫna in the original Hittite homeland, if the northern localization is correct, is consistent with an Old Hittite composition. The use of the sentence particle *ta* in i 43, ii 28, ii 35, and elsewhere is very strong evidence for dating the original composition Old Hittite.

Despite the evidence for an Old Hittite archetype, in the recopying of the text in the late Empire some NH elements crept into the text. For example, there are numerous examples of a plural common accusative enclitic pronoun in -*aš*- instead of -*uš*-, i 46, ii 15, etc. In i 55 and iii 12′ we have *ḫumanteš* as a plural common accusative, and no examples of the expected Old Hittite form *ḫumanduš*. In addition to the later forms of Hittite words, we have in *mušuni*, i 16, at least one definite Hurrian word, the Luwian word *wašḫazza* in i 17, the dative-locative *irḫatti* in ii 16 and iii 12′, which is probably Luwian and Hittite,[93] and repeated use of *anaḫi*, which may be Hurrian or Luwian. These newer elements should be understood as additions by the scribe who copied the tablet in the Empire period, even if the archetype was Old Hittite.

Laroche's identification of the Tap(a)rami named on the *KUB* 25.32+ seal with the Tabrammi mentioned in RS 17.231 and RS 17.337 and his consequent dating of the text to Tudḫaliya IV fit well with the evidence of the script. Although the identification of the Ras Shamra Tabrammi and the *KUB* 25.32+ Tap(a)rami is not certain, it is a very good possibility which Danmanville,[94] and Dinçol and Darga (p. 118) accept. Laroche goes on to suggest that the writing of the festivals of Karaḫna during Tudḫaliya's reign accords well with what we know of the religious reorganization efforts of this king. We know that this reorganization included work at Karaḫna because of the cult inventory for that city now published as *KUB* 38.12 with duplicate *KUB* 38.15 (*CTH* 517).

90. Ed. Lebrun, *Samuha* 77 and 88.
91. *StBoT* 29: 29 n. 38.
92. *Diss.* 65.
93. Cf. Laroche, *DLL* 52 sub *irḫatt*-.
94. *RHA* XX/70 (1962) 56.

The evidence of language, script, and contents indicate that this text is an Old Hittite composition that describes festivals dating to the early years of the Hittite state which was recopied and modified in the time of Tudḫaliya IV in the late thirteenth century. As such it demonstrates the conservative nature of the cult in second millennium Anatolia. Offerings ceremonies which go back not just to the beginning of the Hittite cult, but which, from the evidence of the Hattic divine names, are based on the cult antedating the Hittites, continued to be celebrated in the last days of the Empire. The history of this particular festival description thus epitomizes the Hittite monarch's role in preserving ancient religious traditions from all over the empire, his active participation in maintaining those traditions, and his importance in providing for the continued celebration of those ceremonies right down to the last days of the Hittite Empire.

CHAPTER 3

THE FESTIVAL FOR ALL THE TUTELARY DEITIES

INTRODUCTION

Among the myriad festival texts preserved from the Hittite archives is a unique composition, preserved in numerous copies and two versions, which purports to enumerate and provide offerings for all the tutelary deities recognized by the Hittites.[1] This festival provides a fascinating insight into the Hittite religious perspective, as it apparently creates new tutelary deities to protect everything the writer can think of. Much of the festival description is simply a long listing of tutelary deities designed to protect the interests and life of the king, denoted by the royal title Labarna. Most of these deities are unattested elsewhere. The festival is now preserved in two distinct versions, one in which the gods are listed in large blocks under a few offering prescriptions (The Festival of Group Offerings), and another in which for each god the required offerings are prescribed individually (The Festival of Individual Offerings). Most of the copies of the festival are late, and several, including the main text *KUB* 2.1, mention the king Tudḫaliya IV several times. As discussed in the *Commentary* at the end of this chapter, the original composition may have been earlier than Tudḫaliya IV. The Hittite penchant for seeking out and worshipping all possible manifestations of the divine is illustrated beautifully by this experiment in diversification.

THE TWO VERSIONS OF THE FESTIVAL

The Festival of Group Offerings

I have called this version the Festival of Group Offerings because the texts describing this festival in general contain long lists of deities without specifying offerings for them

1. The text is catalogued by Laroche as *CTH* 682. It is discussed at length by Archi, *SMEA* 16 (1975) 89–117, in an article which includes a transliteration of the main festival text with a translation of individual epithets by category. Page numbers cited for Archi refer to this edition. While acknowledging my debt to Archi and his work on this text, I have included a new reconstruction of two different festivals with transliteration and translation. I also include here other tablets published since his article. See pp. 6f. in the *Introduction* for a complete text scheme.

individually. The emphasis seems to be on the diversity of the deities and not on the ceremony or offerings. I distinguish this from the festival treated later in the chapter, in which the same gods receive their offerings individually. The following reconstruction is based on the evidence of the ways the various duplicate texts overlap. The order is not in every case definite, and there are gaps in the text. The main text *KUB* 2.1 is almost exclusively a list of tutelary deities and specifies almost none of the cult offerings to be provided for those deities.

The reverse of *KUB* 44.16+*IBoT* 3.69 duplicates part of the list contained in the main text, but its obverse preserves part of the festival procedure.[2] Because the colophon is missing in the main text, *KUB* 2.1, we do not know how many tablets were utilized to describe this festival or where in that sequence (if there was more than one tablet) *KUB* 2.1 fell. *KUB* 44.16 cannot be a previous tablet of the same series as *KUB* 2.1, because it duplicates some of that text. Because the reverse of *KUB* 44.16 duplicates part of the obverse of *KUB* 2.1, the obverse of *KUB* 44.16 must be an earlier portion of the festival than *KUB* 2.1. If *KUB* 2.1 was in a series of tablets, the text of *KUB* 44.16 obverse must have duplicated the tablet before *KUB* 2.1 in that series. The preserved beginning of *KUB* 44.16 contains what looks like the usual preparations for a cult ceremony and may therefore be the beginning of the festival. The few preserved words of column iii in *IBoT* 3.69 indicate that column iii was not a list of deities such as is found on the reverse, but rather a description of festival procedure like column ii. The reverse of *KUB* 44.16 probably duplicated the first three columns of the main text, and the three columns of the obverse contained a description of the portion of the festival to be performed before the offerings to the long list of gods preserved in *KUB* 2.1. *KUB* 44.16+*IBoT* 3.69 is probably the first of a two-tablet series of which the second tablet duplicated the reverse of *KUB* 2.1.

KUB 2.1 was probably the second in a series, with a first duplicating the obverse of *KUB* 44.16+*IBoT* 3.69. *KBo* 22.189, whose column ii duplicates column ii of *KUB* 44.16, but whose reverse does not duplicate any part of *KUB* 2.1 but rather contains further descriptions of cult ceremony, seems to be a tablet which contained a cult ceremony to be performed before the lists of *KUB* 2.1. Although much of *KBo* 22.189 is broken away, enough of each column is preserved that we can be certain that the entire tablet (with the possible exception of column vi, which cannot be checked) contained descriptions of festival procedures and not the long list of all the LAMMA and Ala deities which the main text, *KUB* 2.1, contains.

Aside from the references to the king going into the temple of the Tutelary Deity (ii 3) and the temple of Inara (ii 8), there is no mention of tutelary deities in *KBo* 22.189. The only link with the list of LAMMA and Ala deities is *KUB* 44.16, which duplicates *KBo* 22.189 on its obverse (festival descriptions) and duplicates *KUB* 2.1 on its reverse (part of the list of all the tutelary deities). As *KBo* 22.189 has festival procedures in all six columns, it is apparently a fuller description of the festival (or a description of a longer

2. Column v duplicates *KUB* 2.1 ii 22–41, column vi duplicates *KUB* 2.1 iii 46–iv 23. Presumably the lost column iv of *KUB* 44.16 duplicated the first column of the main text.

more extensive festival) than that in *KUB* 44.16. It is likely that either *KBo* 22.189 or one of its duplicates, *KUB* 11.21, *IBoT* 4.73, or 754/t, was originally the first tablet in a series of which *KUB* 2.1, containing the actual list of deities to receive offerings, was the second tablet. Whatever its exact relationship to *KUB* 2.1, *KBo* 22.189 is linked to it by the evidence of *KUB* 44.16 and is therefore an essential source for a portion of this festival before the long offerings lists of *KUB* 2.1. Reverse v of *KUB* 11.21 duplicates *KBo* 22.189 iii and its column iv thus perhaps fills in part of the ceremony lost in *KBo* 22.189 ii. The fragmentary state of all the tablets has required the conflation of exemplars from originally different series.

Text Scheme[3]

A. *KUB* 2.1.
B. *KBo* 2.38. Column ii? duplicates A ii 35–50.
C. *KUB* 44.16+*IBoT* 3.69.[4] Columns i–iii describe offerings, column v duplicates A ii 22–41, vi duplicates A iii 46–iv 23.
D. Bo 6113. Duplicates A iv 22–v 8.[5]
E. *KBo* 22.189. Column i lost, column ii duplicates C ii 8′–25′, but the reverse does not duplicate the main text *KUB* 2.1.[6]
F. *KUB* 11.21. Obverse ii and iii too broken to place, reverse v 15′–25′ duplicates E iii 3–13.[7]
G. *IBoT* 4.73. Duplicates E v 6′–11′.
H. 754/t. Duplicates C ii 7′–14′ = E ii 1–7.

3. Based on the work of Laroche, *CTH* 682, Archi, *SMEA* 16 (1975) 105, and new material.
4. Join published after Archi's article by Laroche, *OLZ* 72 (1977) 33. *IBoT* 3.69 ii x+1–11′ joins *KUB* 44.16 ii 6′–16′. *IBoT* 3.69 provides a small portion of a third column on the obverse, so this tablet may now be recognized as a six column tablet, and the two columns preserved on the reverse of *KUB* 44.16 can be identified as v (labeled iii? in the copy) and vi (iv? in the copy). Archi's iv? under *KUB* 44.16 in his text scheme is now v, and his v? is now vi. Archi, p. 111 n. 57, cites *KUB* 44.16 iv? 11 when he means v? (now secured as vi) 11.
5. Archi, p. 105 n. 25, suggests that this fragment might be part of the same tablet as *KBo* 2.38. Although I could not compare the two directly, collation of both indicates that they could possibly be from the same tablet.
6. *KBo* 22.189 is edited by Lebrun, *Hethitica* 2 (1977) 8–13. He suggests that this text is part of the multi-day festival for the AN.TAḪ.ŠUM plant. He gives, however, no convincing evidence for this, nor does he mention that part of *KBo* 22.189 duplicates *KUB* 44.16, which is firmly linked with *KUB* 2.1, the main text of the Festival of Group Offerings.
7. Identified by George Moore, *JAOS* 102 (1982) 180.

Transliteration

C = *KUB* 44.16+*IBoT* 3.69

Obverse i[8]

§1′x+1 [LUGAL-uš-za KIN.ḪI.A-ta] ḪUB.BI$^{\text{ḪI.A}}$ KÙ.BABBAR
2′ [… da-a-i LUGAL-uš-kán *I-NA*?] É.DU$_{10}$.ÚS.SA ú-iz-zi
3′ [ta-aš ^{É}ḫa-le-en-tu-w]a-aš pa-iz-zi
4′ [GAL DUMU É.GAL ^{GIŠ}kal-mu-]uš LUGAL-i pa-a-i

---

§2′ 5′ [na-aš-ta ^{LÚ}SAGI.A pár-aš-n]a?-u-wa-aš ú-iz-zi
6′ [2 DUMU.MEŠ É.GAL LUGAL-]⸢i⸣ pí-ra-an ḫu-u-ya-an-<te>-eš
7′ [L]Ú.MEŠ UR.BAR.RA-ya
8′ [a-r]a-an-da

---

§3′ 9′ [ ]⸢x x⸣-u-ya[-x-z]i
10′ [*UŠ-K*]*E-EN-NU*?

(the column breaks off)

C = *KUB* 44.16+*IBoT* 3.69

Obverse ii[9]

§4′x+1 x[

---

§5′ 2′ DINGIR.ME[Š
3′ UR.M[AḪ

---

§6′ 4′ ^{LÚ}N[AR
5′ LÚ.MEŠ x[

---

§7′ 6′ na-at x[ ]x
H 7′ UGULA LÚ.MEŠ U[R.BAR.RA i-ya-]at-ta-ri
E ii 8′ ta-at ⸢^{É}⸣[(ar-ki-ú-i)] ⸢ti-ya⸣-an-zi[10]

---

§8′ 9′ na-aš-ta LUGAL-uš [(^{É}ka-t)]a!-pu-uz-ni-az[11]
10′ kat-ta ú-iz-z[i][12]

---

8. Restorations are from the similar texts *KUB* 11.35 i 10′–21′ (Winter Festival) and *KUB* 10.21 i 4–13 (fest. fragment).
9. After a gap of an undetermined number of paragraphs.
10. Restored from text E ii 1: *na-at* ^{É}*ar-ki-ú-i ti-en-zi.*
11. Text E ii 2: ^{É}*ka-ta-pu-uz-na-az*, text H 3′ has -*n*]*a-az*. This word is always attested as a pure *a*-stem except for this example in *KUB* 44.16+.
12. There is no paragraph divider following this word in text E.

Translation

C = *KUB* 44.16+*IBoT* 3.69

Obverse i

§1′ [The king takes his festival attire:] the silver earrings [and ... The king] comes [into] the cultic washing house. [...] He goes into the [*ḫalent*]*u*- building. [The chief palace attendant] gives the [litu]us to the king.

§2′ [... The cupbearer of squat]ting comes. [Two palace attendants] (are) running in front of [the kin]g. [...] and the wolf-men. [...] they [st]and.

§3′ (too fragmentary to translate)

(the column breaks off)

C = *KUB* 44.16+*IBoT* 3.69

Obverse ii[13]

§§4′–6′ (Too fragmentary to translate.)

§7′ Then x[...]x. The overseer of the w[olf]-men [go]es [...]. They step into the passageway.[14]

§8′ The king comes down from the balcony(?).[15]

13. After a gap of an undetermined number of paragraphs.
14. Singer, *StBoT* 27 (1983) 106–11, thoroughly discusses the evidence and previous work on the ^{É}*arkiu*-. He concludes that this word denotes the passageway in the gates. Kammenhuber, *HW*^{2} Lief. 4 (1979) 307–09 does not commit herself as to what type of structure this is. Puhvel, *HED* 1–2 (1984) 148, translates "anteroom, foyer, vestibule," apparently without having Singer's *StBoT* 27 discussion available to him.
15. See Singer, *StBoT* 27 (1983) 116, on the *kattapuzna*- as a porch or balcony near the main exit of the palace. Alp, *Tempel* (1983) 196–97 n. 192, also localizes the *kattapuzna*- near a door by suggesting that it is near the "Vorhalle" and is the place where the king ascends the chariot during the celebration of the festival in *KBo* 10.24 (KI.LAM). Lebrun, *Hethitica* 2 (1977) 14, had earlier suggested that it was a building of the sanctuary but did not adduce any evidence for such a suggestion.

C = *KUB* 44.16+*IBoT* 3.69

Obverse ii (*transliteration cont.*)

§9′ 11′ LUGAL-uš *I-NA*[16] É ^{D}LA[(MMA)] pa-iz-zi 2 DUMU.MEŠ É.GAL
12′ 1 LÚ *ME-ŠE-DI*[17] ^{GIŠ}ŠUKUR A[N].BAR-aš[18] ḫar-zi 1 DUMU É.GAL
13′ AN.BAR-aš ma-a-ri-in[19] ḫ[(ar)]-zi [20]LUGAL-i pí-ra-an
H 14′ ḫu-u-i-ya-an- zi[21]

---

§10′ 15′ LUGAL-uš AN.BAR-aš ma-a-r[(i-i)]n[22] ḫar-zi[23]
16′ [nu? (L)]UGAL-uš *I*-[*NA* É ^{D}LAMM]A pa-iz-zi[24]

- - - - -

§11′ 17′ [(ḫa-an-te-ez-zi KASKAL-*NI* NIN.DINGI)]R-aš
18′ [(UGULA $^{LÚ.MEŠ}$ḫa-pí-ya-aš DUMU É.G)]AL ^{É}ḫi-lam-ni
19′ [(a-ra-an-da)[25]]

- - - - - - - - -

§12′ 20′ [(NIN.DINGIR LUGAL-i ḫi-ik-zi) n]am-ma-aš ^{É}ḫi-i-li-ya-aš
21′ [o o o o o o o] ti-ya-zi[26]

- - - - - - - - - - - -

§13′ 22′ [(DUMU É.GAL *ME-E QA-TI* pé-e-)]da-i
23′ [(LUGAL-uš *QA-TI-ŠU* a-ar-ri GA)]L DUMU.MEŠ É.GAL[27] GAD-an
24′ [(pa-a-i LUGAL-uš *QA-TE*^{MEŠ}-*ŠU* a-an-š)]i[28]

- -

E **§14′** 25′ [(NI)N.DINGI(R ^{É}ḫ)i-(i-l)i ti-ya?-z]i
26′ [o o o o o o -z]i

- -

16. Text E ii 3 omits *INA*.
17. Text E ii 4 has LÚ *ME-ŠE-«ME-ŠE-»DI.*
18. Text E ii 4: AN.BAR ^{GIŠ}ŠUKUR.
19. Text E ii 5: ^{GIŠ}*ma-a-ri-in.*
20. Text E ii 6 before LUGAL-*i* has 1 LÚ *ME-ŠE-DI.*
21. Text E ii 7 has *ḫu-ya-an-te-eš* and no paragraph divider.
22. Text E ii 7: ^{GIŠ}*ma-ri-in.*
23. See Košak, *FsGüterbock*² 126–27 on lines ii 12′–15′.
24. Text E ii 8: LUGAL-*uš* ^{D}*I-na-ra-aš pár-na pa-iz-zi.*
25. From text E ii 11, which has no paragraph divider.
26. Text E ii 12 has, after *ḫikzi*, LUGAL-*uš* ^{É}*ḫi-i-li ti-i-e-zi.* It would be strange here in *KUB* 44.16 to express LUGAL-*uš* when the sentence already contains the enclitic -*aš*- as a subject. LUGAL-*uš* has therefore not been restored in the break in 21′. The form ^{É}*ḫiliyaš* is unique, although its identification as an otherwise unattested *i*-stem form of ^{É}*ḫila-* is indicated by ^{É}*ḫīli* in the duplicate. It is most likely to be a genitive, as dative-locative plural would not make good sense in this sentence. This suggests that whatever was in the break in line 21′ was something denoting a location within the courtyard in a genitive construction with ^{É}*ḫiliyaš.* Both a "gate" (KÁ) and a "door" (IG) of the *ḫila-* are attested, so perhaps "[T]hen he proceeds to the [gate/door] of the courtyard."
27. Text E ii 14: GAL DUMU É.GAL.
28. From text E ii 15, where again there is no paragraph divider.

C = *KUB* 44.16+*IBoT* 3.69

Obverse ii (*translation cont.*)

§9′ The king goes into the temple of the Tutelary Deity. (There are) two palace attendants. One royal bodyguard holds a ŠUKUR-spear of iron; one palace attendant holds a *māri*-spear of iron. They run in front of the king.

§10′ The king holds the *māri*-spear of iron. The king goes in[to the temple of the tutela]ry deity.[29]

§11′ On the first occasion the NIN.DINGIR priestess, the overseer of the *ḫapiya*- men, (and) the palace attendant stand in the gate house.

§12′ The NIN.DINGIR priestess bows to the king. Then he proceeds to the [gate/door] of the courtyard(?).[30]

§13′ The palace attendant carries (in) the hand-water. The king washes his hands. The chief of the palace attendants gives (him) a linen cloth. The king wipes his hands.

§14′ The NI[N.DING]IR priestess [step]s(?) into the courtyard and [...]'s.

29. Text E "temple of Inara."

30. See the footnote to the transliteration of *KUB* 44.16 ii 21′.

C = *KUB* 44.16+*IBoT* 3.69

Obverse ii (*transliteration cont.*)

§15′ 27′ [GAL *MEŠEDI*-ma[31] ^{LÚ}SAGI ^{TÚG}še-e]k-nu-un e-ep-zi
28′ [na-an LUGAL-i pa-ra-a pé-e-ḫu-te-ez-zi ... še-er d]a?-a-i
29′ [o o o o o o o o o o]
30′ [LUGAL-uš pár-ši-ya ta-an *A-NA* ^{LÚ}SAGI E]GIR-pa pa-a-i
31′ [o o o o o o o o o o o o] ⌈x x x⌉

(the column breaks off)

F = *KUB* 11.21

Reverse iv[32] (*transliteration*)

§16′ x+1 UGULA $^{\text{L[Ú.MEŠ}}$MUḪALDIM ^{NINDA}ḫar-za-zu-un]
2′ LUGAL-i? [pa-a-i]
3′ LUGAL-u[š pár-ši-ya]
4′ UGULA $^{\text{LÚ.M[EŠ}}$MUḪALDIM ^{NINDA}ḫar-za-zu-un]
5′ ^{GIŠ}ZAG.GAR.RA[-ni da-a-i]
6′ 1 ^{NINDA}ḫar-za-zu-u[n ḫa-aš-ši-i]
7′ 1 ^{NINDA}ḫar-za-zu-un [^{GIŠ}DAG-ti]
8′ 1 ^{NINDA}ḫar-za-zu-un [^{GIŠ}AB-ya]
9′ 1 ^{NINDA}ḫar-za-zu-un ^{GIŠ}ḫ[a-at-tal-wa-aš]
10′ GIŠ-i 1 ^{NINDA}ḫar-za-zu-un nam-ma [ḫa-aš-ši-i]
11′ ta-pu-uš-za da-a-i

---

§17′ 12′ UGULA $^{\text{LÚ.MEŠ}}$MUḪALDIM me-ma-al LUGAL[-i]
13′ pa-ra-a e-ep-zi
14′ LUGAL-uš me-ma-al ^{GIŠ}ZAG[.GAR.RA-ni]
15′ 6-*ŠU* iš-ḫu-u-wa-a-i

---

§18′ 16′ UGULA $^{\text{LÚ.MEŠ}}$MUḪALDIM me-ma-li-it *AŠ-RI*$^{\text{Ḫ[I.A]}}$
17′ ir-ḫa-iz-zi ḫa-aš-ši-i 1-*ŠU*
18′ ^{GIŠ}DAG-ti 1-*ŠU* ^{GIŠ}AB-ya 1-*ŠU*
19′ ^{GIŠ}ḫa-at-tal-wa-aš GIŠ-i 1-*ŠU*
20′ nam-ma ḫa-aš-ši-i ta-pu-uš-za
21′ 1-*ŠU* iš-ḫu-u-wa-i

---

§19′ 22′ UGULA $^{\text{LÚ.MEŠ}}$MUḪALDIM ta-pí-ša-na-an
23′ ta-wa-la-aš LUGAL-i pa-ra-a e-e[p-zi]
24′ LUGAL-uš-ša-an *QA-TAM* da-a-i
25′ [o o]x iš-ta-na-ni[

(the tablet breaks off)

31. Restorations in §15′ are from the similar texts *KBo* 20.67+ iii 9–10 and *KUB* 20.78 iv 13–14 (both Festival of the Month), and *KBo* 21.85+*KBo* 8.109 i 7–9 (Festival of the Moon and Thunder).
32. After a gap of an undetermined number of paragraphs.

C = *KUB* 44.16+*IBoT* 3.69

Obverse ii (*translation cont.*)

§15′ [The chief royal bodyguard] takes [the cupbearer by (his) clo]ak. [He leads him forth to the king ... on top] he [p]laces. [...] [The king breaks (a bread type).] He gives [it b]ack [to the cupbearer]. [...] ⸢x x x⸣

(the column breaks off)

F = *KUB* 11.21

Reverse iv[33] (*translation*)

§16′ The overseer of the c[ooks gives *ḫarzazu-* bread] to the king. The king [breaks (it)]. The overseer of the c[ooks places *ḫarzazu-* bread on] the altar. One *ḫarzazu-* bread [to the hearth], one *ḫarzazu-* bread [to the throne], one *ḫarzazu-* bread [to the window], one *ḫarzazu-* bread to the wood [of the] do[or bolt], and finally one *ḫarzazu-* bread next [to the hearth], he sets out.

§17′ The overseer of the cooks holds out meal [to] the king. The king scatters the meal six times [on] the alt[ar].

§18′ The overseer of the cooks makes the rounds of the holy places with meal: To the hearth once, to the throne once, to the window once, to the wood of the door bolt once, and finally next to the hearth once he scatters (it).

§19′ The overseer of the cooks hol[ds] out a pitcher of *tawal* to the king. The king takes it in his hand. [...] to the altar [...]

(the tablet breaks off)

33. After a gap of an undetermined number of paragraphs.

F = *KUB* 11.21

Reverse v[34] (*transliteration*)

§20′x+1 [o o o o o]da-a-i

---

§21′ 2′ [UGULA $^{\text{LÚ.MEŠ}}$MUḪALDIM ^{NINDA}ḫar-]za-zu-un L[UGAL-i pa-a-i]

3′ [LUGAL-uš pár-ši-ya] 1 ^{NINDA}[ḫar-]⌈za⌉[-zu-un]

4′ [ḫa-aš-ši-i 1 ^{NINDA}ḫar-z]a[-zu-un ^{GIŠ}DAG-ti]

5′ [1 ^{NINDA}ḫar-za-zu-un ^{GI}]^{Š}AB-ya 1 ^{NINDA}ḫar-za-zu-un

6′ [^{GIŠ}ḫa-at-tal-wa-aš GIŠ-]⌈i⌉ 1 ^{NINDA}ḫar-za-zu-un

7′ [nam-ma ḫa-aš-ši-]⌈i⌉ ta-pu-uš-za da-a-i

---

§22′ 8′ [LUGAL-uš]x-az kat-ta ú-iz-zi

9′ [GAL LÚ.MEŠ GEŠTIN?] 1? ^{DUG}ḫar-ši-ya-al-li

10′ [pa-ra-a e-ep-zi??] pa-iz-zi GAL *ME-ŠE-DI* e-eš-zi

11′ [UGULA $^{\text{LÚ.MEŠ}}$MUḪALDIM?] GAL LÚ.MEŠ GEŠTIN-ya EGIR LUGAL

12′ [i-ya-an-ta-ri]

---

§23′ 13′ [UGULA LÚ.MEŠ ^{GIŠ}BAN]ŠUR 1 NINDA.KUR$_4$.RA LUGAL-i

E iii 14′ [pa-ra-a e-e]p-zi LUGAL-uš *QA-TAM* da-a-i

15′ [UGULA LÚ.MEŠ[35] ^{GIŠ}BAN]ŠUR pár-ši-ya ta-an-kán[36]

16′ [(^{D})^{UG}ḫar-ši-ya-al-l]i da-a-i[37] GAL LÚ.MEŠ GEŠTIN-kán[38]

17′ [(^{D})^{UG}ḫar-ši-ya-a]l-li ki-nu-uz-zi[39]

18′ [GAL LÚ.MEŠ GEŠT]IN!? GAL KÙ.BABBAR LUGAL-i pa-a-i

19′ [LUGAL (GEŠT)]IN ša-ra-a 3-*ŠU* ḫu-it-ti-ya-zi

20′ [(EGIR-*Š*)*U*-ma] 3-*ŠU* la-ḫu-u-wa-i[40]

---

§24′ 21′ [nu (GAL)] DUMU.MEŠ É.GAL GAL KÙ.BABBAR ar-ḫa da-a-i

22′ [na-aš?] GEŠTIN ša-ra-a 3-*ŠU*

23′ [ḫu-it-ti-]ya-zi kat-ta-ya-at

24′ [(3-*ŠU*) l]a!?-ḫu-u-wa-i GAL DUMU.MEŠ É.GAL

E iii 25′ [-t]a ta-pí-ša-ni KÙ.BABBAR

26′ [la-ḫu-u-wa-]⌈i⌉

---

§25′ 27′ [ ]⌈ú-iz⌉-zi

(the tablet breaks off)

34. After a gap of an undetermined number of paragraphs.
35. Text E iii 2: GAL LÚ[.
36. Text E iii 3: *na-an-ša-an.*
37. Paragraph divider in text E.
38. Text E iii 4: GAL.GEŠTIN-*kán.*
39. Text E iii 5: *ki-i-nu-u*[*z-zi*].
40. Text E has no paragraph divider.

F = *KUB* 11.21

Reverse v[41] (*translation*)

§20′ [...] he sets out.

§21′ [The overseer of the cooks gives *ḫar*]*zazu-* [bread to] the k[ing. The king breaks (it).] One [*ḫar*]*za*[*zu-*] bread [to the hearth], one [*ḫarz*]*a*[*zu-*] bread [to the throne, one *ḫarzazu-* bread] to the window, one *ḫarzazu-* bread to [the wood of the door bolt, and finally] one *ḫarzazu-* bread beside [the heart]h.

§22′ [The king] comes down from the x. [The chief of the wine stewards(?) holds out(??)] a storage container. [x] goes. The chief royal bodyguard is (there). [The overseer of the cooks] and the chief of the wine stewards [walk] behind the king.

§23′ [The overseer of the wait]ers [ho]lds [out] one thick bread to the king. The king takes it in his hand. [The overseer of the wait]ers breaks it. He places it in [the storage container]. The chief of the wine stewards breaks [the storage contain]er. [The chief of the wine stew]ards(?) gives a silver cup to the king. [The king] draws up the wine three times. Then he pours it out three times.

§24′ The chief of the palace attendants takes away the silver cup. [He dra]ws the wine up three times, and he pours it down [three times]. The chief of the palace attendants [pour]s [x] into a silver pitcher.

§25′ [...] comes. [...]

(the tablet breaks off)

41. After a gap of an undetermined number of paragraphs.

E = *KBo* 22.189 Reverse iv[42] (*transliteration*)

§26′ x+1 x [LUGAL-i pí-ra-an]
2′ ḫu-u-ya-an-t[e-eš? LUGAL-uš]
3′ a-ra-aḫ-za [ú-iz-zi]

---

§27′ 4′ LUGAL-uš-kán a[n-da]
5′ ^{É}ḫa-le-en-t[u-wa pa-iz-zi]
6′ wa-ga-an-na ḫal-z[i-ya]
7′ LUGAL-uš ^{É}ḫa-le[-en-tu-az kat-ta]
8′ ú-iz-zi 2 DUMU.M[EŠ É.GAL]
9′ 1 ^{LÚ}*ME-ŠE-DI* L[UGAL-i pí-ra-an]
10′ ḫu-i-ya-an-te-e[š a-ša-an-zi]
11′ gal-gal-tu-ri a[r-kam-mi]
12′ LÚ.MEŠ x[SÌR-*RU*]

(bottom of tablet)

E = *KBo* 22.189 Reverse v[43] (*transliteration*)

§28′ x+1 ⸢KAŠ? GEŠTIN? x⸣[
2′ EGIR-pa *PA-NI* tar-ša[-an-zi-pa-aš da-a-i?]
3′ nu ka-a-aš-mi-iš-ša-a ḫal-⸢za-a-i⸣[Ø]

---

§29′ 4′ DUMU.MEŠ É.GAL *ME-E QA-TI* pé-e-da-an-zi
5′ *ŠA* ^{GIŠ}ŠUKUR DUMU É.GAL ḫu-u-up-pa-ra-aš
G 6′ *A-NA* DUMU É.GAL[44] kat-ta-an GÙB-la-az
7′ i-ya-at-ta-ri[45] GAL DUMU.MEŠ É.GAL
8′ GAD-an ḫar-zi GAL *ME-ŠE-DI*-ma[46] ^{GIŠ}ŠUKUR
9′ ḫar-zi na-aš-kán me-na-aḫ-ḫa-an-da
10′ ar-ta-ri (eras.)[47] LUGAL SAL.LUGAL *QA-TE*^{MEŠ}-*ŠU-NU*[48]
G 11′ a-ar-ra-an-zi[49] GAL DUMU.MEŠ É.GAL
12′ GAD-an pa-a-i nu-za ŠU.MEŠ-*ŠU-NU*
13′ a-an-ša-an-zi GAL DUMU.MEŠ É.GAL-kán

(bottom of tablet)

42. After a gap of an undetermined number of paragraphs. Transliterated and translated by Alp, *Tempel*, 236–37.
43. After a gap of an undetermined number of paragraphs.
44. Text G 1′:]⸢1⸣ DUMU[É.GAL] or ⸢*ANA*⸣ DUMU [É.GAL].
45. Text G has a paragraph line here.
46. Text G 4′: GAL *ME-ŠE-DI*.
47. Text G has a paragraph line here.
48. Text G 7′: ŠU.MEŠ-*ŠU*[-*NU*.
49. Text G 8′: ⸢*a*⸣-*ra-an-* [*zi*].

E = *KBo* 22.189

Reverse iv[50] (*translation*)

§26′ x[...] Th[ey] (are) running [in front of the king]. [... The king comes] from outside.

§27′ The king [goes] in[to] the *ḫalentu-* building. Refreshment[51] is cal[led]. The king comes [down out of] the *ḫale*[*ntu-*]. Two [palace] attendants (and) one royal bodyguard [are] running [in front of the kin]g. The *galgalturi-* instrument (and) the *a*[*rkammi-* instrument] (are played). The x[...]-men [sing].

(bottom of tablet)

E = *KBo* 22.189

Reverse v[52] (*translation*)

§28′ Beer, wine, x[and x] back before the *tarš*[*anzipa-* he places]. He ca[lls] "*kašmišša.*"

§29′ The palace attendants carry in hand-water. The palace attendant of the spear walks with the palace attendant of the basin on (his) left. The chief of the palace attendants holds the linen cloth. The chief royal bodyguard, however, holds the spear. He stands in front. The king (and) queen wash their hands. The chief of the palace attendants gives (them) the linen cloth. They wipe their hands. The chief of the palace attendants ... [53]

(bottom of tablet)

50. After a gap of an undetermined number of paragraphs.
51. Literally "for biting."
52. After a gap of an undetermined number of paragraphs.
53. This sentence is continued at the top of reverse vi, now lost.

E = *KBo* 22.189

Reverse vi[54] (*transliteration*)

Colophon

x+1 [ ]-ša-aš?
2′ [*PA*]-*NI* ^{m}A-nu-wa-an-za
3′ [ŠU ^{m}x] *IŠ-ṬUR*

A = *KUB* 2.1

Obverse i (*transliteration*)

(approximately 39 lines missing)[55]

§30′ 40 [o o o o o o o] ^{D}A-la-aš x[
41 [o o o o (-)u]š?-ša-la-am-mi-eš-še gi-im-ra-aš

---

§31′ 42 2 ⸢GUD GAL⸣ *A-NA ŠUM*!$^{ḪI.A}$ ^{D}LAMMA ḫu-u-ma-an-da-aš
43 ne-pí-ša-aš ^{D}LAMMA ^{URU}Ga-ra-ḫa-na-aš-ša
44 ^{D}LAMMA-ri ^{D}Kar-ši ^{D}Ḫa-ba-an-ta-li-ya
45 ^{URU}A-la-tar!-ma-aš[56] ^{D}LAMMA $^{ḪUR.SAG}$Ša-lu-wa-an-da-aš
46 ^{D}LAMMA-ri $^{ḪUR.SAG}$Ša-ar-pa-aš ^{D}LAMMA-ri
47 ^{D}LAMMA ^{URU}Šu-lu-pa-aš-ša ^{URU}Tu-ut-tu-wa-aš
48 ^{D}LAMMA-ri ^{D}LAMMA ^{URU}Ḫa-ra-na
49 ^{D}LAMMA ^{URU}Ša-ri-iš-ša
50 ^{D}LAMMA $^{ḪUR.SAG}$Šu-un-na-ra ^{D}LAMMA ^{ÍD}Ku-um-ma-ra
51 ^{D}LAMMA ^{ÍD}Ši-ḫi-ri-ya ^{D}LAMMA ^{URU}Ḫal-la-at-ta

(bottom of tablet)

54. Only a part of the colophon is preserved from this column. It originally also contained the continuation of reverse v, which ends in mid-sentence.

55. Estimated by Figulla in the copy.

56. Compare iii 36. Both passages are cited by del Monte, *RGTC* 6: 6–7 sub Alatarma. Singer, *ZA* 75 (1985) 110 n. 61, also correctly reads this place name.

E = *KBo* 22.189

Reverse vi[57] (*translation*)

Colophon

[...]x [... b]efore Anuwanza [... the hand of ᵐX] wrote.

A = *KUB* 2.1

Obverse i[58] (*translation*)

(approximately 39 lines missing)

§30′ [ ] Ala x[(-)*u*]*ššalamiešše*(?)[59] of the countryside

---

§31′ Two large oxen to the names of all the tutelary deities: the Tutelary Deity of the Sky and to the Tutelary Deity of Karaḫna, to Karši,[60] to Ḫapantaliya, the Tutelary Deity of Alatarma, to the Tutelary Deity of Mt. Šaluwanda, to the Tutelary Deity of Mt. Šarpa, the Tutelary Deity of Šulupašša, to the Tutelary Deity of Tuttuwa, the Tutelary Deity of Ḫarana, the Tutelary Deity of Šariššа, the Tutelary Deity of Mt. Šunnara, the Tutelary Deity of the River Kummara, the Tutelary Deity of the River Šiḫiriya, (and) the Tutelary Deity of Ḫallatta.

(bottom of tablet)

57. After a gap of an undetermined number of paragraphs.
58. After a gap of an undetermined number of paragraphs.
59. The broken sign in i 41 which Archi reads as *u*]*š*- is uncertain, although his reading does fit the trace. As there is no other example of a word **šallamiešše* or **uššalamiešše*, a reading for the broken sign or for any signs preceding it remains uncertain. It is some attribute of the tutelary deity Ala.
60. Variant for Karzi.

A = *KUB* 2.1

Obverse ii (*transliteration*)

(approximately 8 lines missing)[61]

§32′ 9 [o o o o o o o o o o o o o o -t]a

10 [o o o o o o o o o o o o o]x-ta-aš TÚL-i

11 [o o o o o o o o o o o o *ŠA* La-ba-a]r-na

12 [o o o o o o o o o o o o]x-aš[62]

13 [*ŠA* La-ba-ar-na ^{D}LA]MMA ANŠE.KUR.RA.MEŠ

14 [*ŠA* La-ba-ar-na] ^{D}LAMMA ^{GIŠ}ŠUKUR

15 [*ŠA* La-ba-ar-na $^{Ḫ]UR.SAG}$Iš-ki-ša-aš ^{D}LAMMA-ri

16 [*ŠA* La-ba-ar-na (ḫ)]u-it-na-aš ^{D}LAMMA-aš

17 [*ŠA* La-ba-ar-na (in-n)]a-ra-u-wa-aḫ-ḫu-u-wa-aš ^{D}LAMMA-aš

18 [*ŠA* La-ba-ar-na] ^{UZU}ZAG.UDU-aš ^{D}LAMMA-ri

19 [*ŠA* La-ba-ar-na] :wa-li-pa-at-ta-aš-ši-iš ^{D}LAMMA-aš

20 [*ŠA* La-ba-ar-n]a pa-ra-a ḫa-an-da-an-da-an-na-aš ^{D}LAMMA

21 [*ŠA* La-ba-ar-n]a TI-aš ^{D}LAMMA-ri

C v 22 [*ŠA* La-ba-ar-n]a tar-ḫu-i-la-an-na-aš[63] ^{D}LAMMA-ri

23 [*ŠA* La-ba-ar]-na tu-zi-ya-aš[64] ^{D}LAMMA-ri

24 [*ŠA* La-ba-ar]-na za-aḫ-ḫi-ya-aš ^{D}LAMMA-ri[65]

61. Estimated in the copy. Based on the parallel *KBo* 11.40 i 23′–26′, the lost lines probably continued the names of the provincial tutelary deities, including those of the cities Tidanda and Anza.

62. Read by Archi as ^{D}LAM]A!-*aš*, but collation indicates that the trace is quite different from the other examples of LAMMA, and there is no compelling reason to read it as such.

63. Text C v 1′: UR.SA[G-*na-aš*?

64. Text C v 2′: ^{D}LAMMA KARA[Š.

65. Text C v 3′: ^{D}LAMMA x[. Read by Archi as ^{D}LAMMA-*i*, which is not impossible, but there is a clear space after LAMMA.

A = *KUB* 2.1 Obverse ii (*translation*)

(approximately 8 lines missing)

§32′ 9 [ ] (traces)
10 [ ] to the spring of [ ]x-*taš*
11 [of the Laba]rna?
12 [ ]x-*aš*
13 [the tute]lary deity of horses [of the Labarna],
14 the tutelary deity of the spear [of the Labarna],[66]
15 to the tutelary deity of [M]t. Iškiša [of the Labarna],
16 the tutelary deity[67] of the animals [of the Labarna],
17 the tutelary deity of the strengthening[68] [of the Labarna],
18 to the tutelary deity of the shoulder [of the Labarna],
19 the tutelary deity of the encircling(?)[69] [of the Labarna],
20 the tutelary deity of the divine power[70] [of the Labarn]a,
21 to the tutelary deity of the life [of the Labarn]a,
22 to the tutelary deity of the heroism [of the Labarn]a,
23 to the tutelary deity of the army [of the Labar]na,
24 to the tutelary deity of battle [of the Labar]na,

66. Note the difference in syntax between ii 13 and 14, in which ᴰLAMMA immediately follows *ŠA* Labarna, and most of the rest of the text, in which the regens of *ŠA* Labarna comes immediately after it. The difference probably stems from the fact that in ii 13 and 14 the regens is a Sumerogram without Hittite complement and the phrase was therefore put into a partially Sumerian word order; only partially, because the genitive *ŠA* Labarna still comes first. §31′ shows both kinds of syntax with syllabically written names.

67. There are several occurrences (ii 16, 17, 19, [32], 39) of the form ᴰLAMMA-*aš* in this text. These could conceivably be dative-locative plural "to the tutelary deities," but nominative singular is more likely, as discussed below in the *Commentary*. The same question occurs with the entire list of manifestations of the deity Ala later in the text.

68. See Puhvel, *HED* 1–2: 370, on *innarawaḫḫuwaš* as the genitive of the verbal substantive of a verb *innarawaḫḫ-*. No examples of a finite form of such a verb exist. There is an attested verb *innaraḫ(ḫ)-*, which has a verbal substantive *innaraḫḫuar*, cited by Puhvel, *HED* 1–2: 367 sub *innar-*. The form *innarawaḫḫuwaš* occurs only in this text and its duplicates. There is one example of the nominative form *innarawaḫḫuwar*, in *KBo* 17.60 rev. 10 (Birth Ritual), ed. Beckman, *StBoT* 29 (1983) 60–61, with the translation "fitness."

69. The word *:walipattaššiš*, a Luwian genitival adjective, occurs only here, in iii 45 of this same text, and in parallel text *KBo* 11.40 ii 11′. In the other examples there is no glossenkeil. This lack of other contexts makes it difficult to suggest a meaning. Laroche, *DLL* 105, cites the use of the word as a divine epithet and derives it from the Luwian verb *walip-* "envelopper?" Archi, p. 99, apparently following Laroche, translates "dell'aggiramento(?)."

70. The phrase *parā ḫandandatar* is difficult to translate in a concise English phrase, but it conveys the concept of divine justice or power and the ability to order events. See Hoffner, *Or* 49 (1980) 315–16, on this Hittite phrase. This is a concept normally applied only to the gods; it is unusual or perhaps even unique in this text to speak of the *parā ḫandandatar* of the Labarna. This line could possibly be translated "the Labarna's tutelary deity of divine power." However, as *parā ḫandandatar* is seen as a special protection or power with which the king was endued (see Hoffner in Wiseman, ed., *Peoples of the Old Testament* [Oxford, 1973] 211), it could in some sense be seen as belonging to the king, not as the originator of it but as the receiver.

A = *KUB* 2.1

Obverse ii (*transliteration cont.*)

C v (*cont.*)

25 [*ŠA* La-ba-ar]-na pí-ra-an ḫu-u-i-ya-u-wa-aš[71] ^{D}LAMMA-ri
26 [*ŠA* La-ba-a]r-na ŠU-an ap-pa-an-na-aš ^{D}LAMMA-ri
27 [*ŠA* La-ba]-ar-na ḫal-la-aš-ša-aš ^{D}LAMMA-ri
28 [*ŠA* La-b]a-ar-na ZI-aš ar-nu-um-ma-aš ^{D}LAMMA-ri
29 [*ŠA* La-b]a-ar-na ša-ki-ya-aḫ-ḫu-u-wa-aš ^{D}LAMMA-ri
30 [*ŠA* La]-ba-ar-na aš-ta-aš wa-aš-ta-aš <^{D}LAMMA-ri>[72]
31 [o o]-na-an-ta-aš La-ba-ar-na-aš[73] ^{D}LAMMA-i

71. Text C v 4′: *ḫu-u-ya-u-wa-a[š.*

72. If one tries to take lines 30–31 together, it becomes very difficult to understand the occurrence of two Labarnas in the genitive. The addition of <^{D}LAMMA-ri> solves this problem. The relevant portion of text C v 9′ is broken away, so comparison to the duplicate is not possible.

73. Text C v 10′: *ŠA La-ba-a[r-na.*

A = *KUB* 2.1

Obverse ii (*translation cont.*)

25 to the tutelary deity of running in front[74] [of the Labar]na,
26 to the tutelary deity of holding up the hand [of the Laba]rna,[75]
27 to the tutelary deity of the *ḫallašša*-[76] [of the Lab]arna,
28 to the tutelary deity of the fulfilling of the wish[77] [of the Lab]arna,
29 to the tutelary deity of the omen-giving[78] [of the Lab]arna,
30 <to the tutelary deity> of the *ašta- wašta*-[79] [of the La]barna,
31 to the tutelary deity of the [-]*nanta*- of the Labarna,[80]

74. To provide protection.

75. That is, the deity takes the Labarna by the hand. Compare examples of this in the historical texts, for example Ḫatt. i 21.

76. The only example of a word *ḫal(l)ašša*- outside of this text and its duplicates occurs in *KBo* 8.73 ii 5′ (mythological fragment), where *ḫa-la-aš-ša-an*(-)*ta*[is a body part listed next to the head. Compare also *BĒL ḫa-la-ša*[(-), *KUB* 31.64++ ii 23′ (campaigns of Muršili I). Archi, p. 102, points out that *KBo* 11.40 i 22 has *ḫallaššaš* ^{D}LAMMA-*ri* where *KUB* 2.1 i 51 has ^{D}LAMMA ^{URU}Ḫallatta. Del Monte, *RGTC* 6: 69, cites a city name *Ḫalaš/ta*, with only these two occurrences and the broken word *ḫal-l*[*a* in the duplicate *KUB* 40.108 ii 5′ attested. Given the nature of this list this *ḫallašša*- should not be a GN but would make sense as a body part of the king. The parallel *ḫallaššaš* ^{D}LAMMA-*ri* = ^{D}LAMMA ^{URU}Ḫallatta must have arisen from a similarity between the body part and the city Ḫallatta.

77. Compare Forrer, *KlF* 1 (1930) 275 with n. 2, and Kammenhuber, *HW*^{2} 333a sub *arnu*-, with the translation "dem KAL der Wunscherfüllung des [Herr]schers."

78. The king is never attested as a subject of a finite form of *šakiyaḫḫ*-, and it is unlikely that he would be giving an omen. Therefore this should be understood as "to Labarna's tutelary deity of omen-giving." Goetze, *KlF* 1 (1930) 406–07, understands this as the *šakiyaḫḫuwaš* of Labarna and discusses the difficulties of "Labarna" as a possible subject for the verb *šakiyaḫḫ*-. He translates this verb "einen Erlaß ergehen lassen o(der) ä(hnliches)." Forrer, *KlF* 1 (1930) 275–76, based on his conviction that *šakiyaḫḫuwaš* must depend on Labarna, utilizes this passage to argue a meaning "darken" for *šakiyaḫḫ*-, a translation which has not proved tenable. What is meant is a tutelary deity who oversees the omens and protects the Labarna from evil omens given against him.

79. The phrase *aštaš waštaš* occurs only in this text; here and iii 49, where it stands in a genitive relationship to Ala in the phrase "Ala of *ašta- wašta*-." I can find no other examples of the word *wašta*-. There is a word spelled *a-aš-ta* which Laroche interprets as a Luwian word in his transliteration of *KUB* 35.37++ ii 20′ (Luwian ritual) in *DLL* 172. This may or may not be the same word as the *aštaš* of *KUB* 2.1; even if it is, it is not helpful, as its meaning is not clear in that text either.

80. In this sentence [ ]-*nantaš* could be a participle in the genitive modifying Labarna, with a translation "to the tutelary deity of the [ ]-*nant*- Labarna." The syntax would be unusual, as participles normally follow the words which they modify, but in the very next line this text uses unusual word order with participles.

A = *KUB* 2.1

Obverse ii (*transliteration cont.*)

32 [(^{KUŠ}kur)[81]]-ša-an [š]u?-u-wa-an-za La-ba-ar-na-aš ^{D}L[AMMA-aš]
33 [(an-n)]a-⸢ra⸣-u-[(wa)-aš] La-ba-ar-na-aš ^{D}LAMMA-ri
34 [(*ŠA* ^{L})]^{Ú}⸢*MU-UT-TI* La-ba⸣-ar-na-aš ⸢^{D}LAMMA-⸣[ri]
B 35 [(pa)[82]]-aḫ-ḫu-na-aš ḫa-aš-ša-a[š (LÚ) p]a?-ḫu-ru-la-aš
36 La-ba-ar-na-aš[83] ^{D}LAMMA-i NÍ.TE.ḪI.A-uš[84]
37 uš-ki-ya-u-wa-aš ^{D}LAMMA-i *ŠA* La-ba-ar-na
38 ^{D}LAMMA *ŠA* $^{ḪUR.SAG}$Tu-ut-ḫa-li-ya[85]
39 [(m)]e-ḫu-na-aš[86] ^{D}LAMMA-aš *ŠA* La-ba-ar-na
40 [^{D}LAM]MA te-pa-ú-wa-aš pé-e<-da>-aš la-mar-ḫa-an-da-at-ti-eš
C v 41 *ŠA* La-ba-ar-na la-pa-at-ta-li-ya-aš ^{D}LAMMA-ri[87]
42 *ŠA* [L]a-ba-ar-na a-ra-u-wa-aš ^{D}LAMMA-i[88]
43 *ŠA* [La]-ba-ar-na ú-li-li-ya-aš ^{D}LAMMA-i

81. From text C v 11′.
82. From text C v 14′.
83. Text B ii? 1: ⸢KI⸣.MIN and thereafter a paragraph divider. Text C v 15′: *ŠA La-b*[*a-ar-na*.
84. Text B ii? 2: NÍ.TE-*aš*, text C v 16′: NÍ.TE-*u*[*š*.
85. Text B ii? 3: (collated) $^{ḪUR.SAG}$*Tu-ut-ḫa-li-ya-aš La-b*[*a-ar-na-aš*.
86. Text B ii? 4: *:ku-la-na-aš* KI.MIN ^{D}L[AMMA-*aš*. From *kulani-* HW 115, "auszeichnen?" This occurrence is cited by Laroche, *DLL* 56 sub *kulani-*, as an uncertain form.
87. Text B ii? 5: *La-*[*b*]*a-ar-na-aš* ^{D}LAMMA-*aš* [.
88. Text B ii? 6: *a-ra-*[*u*]*-wa-aš* KI.MIN ^{D}LAMMA-*aš* [.

A = *KUB* 2.1 Obverse ii (*translation cont.*)

32 Labarna's tu[telary] deity who [f]ills the hunting bag,[89]
33 to the tutelary deity of the strong(?)[90] Labarna,
34 [to] the tutel[ary] deity of the Labarna, the warrior,[91]
35–40 to the Labarna's tutelary deity, the fire-tender of the fire (and) hearth,[92] to the tutelary deity of watching over[93] the body of the Labarna, the tutelary deity of Mt. Tudḫaliya, the tutelary deity of time, [the tutel]ary deity of the small place(s) (and) (of[?]) setting a time[94] of the Labarna,
41 to the tutelary deity of the *lapattali*(*ya*)-[95] of the Labarna,
42 to the tutelary deity of getting up of the Labarna,
43 to the tutelary deity of the field(?) of the Labarna,[96]

89. The position of the nominative participle *šuwanza* in the phrase makes it unclear what it is modifying. Archi, p. 109, restores the dative ending ^{D}L[AMMA-*ri*], but Güterbock suggests to me that if the god's title in this particular phrase were nominative, as it is for example in ii 39, the participle could modify the god. If we then take this as a rare example of the participle with an active sense, it could mean "the bag-filling tutelary deity"; see Güterbock, *FsKantor* 117 with n. 34. Because *šuwanza* immediately precedes Labarna, it could also be taken to modify Labarna. The association of tutelary deities with hunting and the chase compels me to understand ^{D}LAMMA-*aš* as the noun being modified; the scribe could not break up the genitive chain *Labarnaš* ^{D}LAMMA-*aš*. Archi, p. 96, translates only the participial phrase out of context and therefore does not discuss the problem of the various cases in the phrase. He also translates the participle as an active form but understands it as the verb *šuwai-*, "to push," translating "che [sp]inge(?) lo scudo" ("who [pu]shes(?) the shield"). If the *kurša-* is a hunting bag, "fill" makes more sense; the *kurša-* is filled in the Telipinu myth/ritual discussed in *Appendix B* sub *kurša-*.

90. On *annarauwaš* see Puhvel, *HED* 1–2: 63, with the translation "forceful." This is the only example of a word *annaru-*; Kammenhuber, *HW*^{2} 79, cites only this occurrence under the lemma **annaru-*, without giving a translation. Archi, p. 97, takes *annarauwaš* as the genitive of a noun **annarauwar.*

91. See *CAD* M, part 2: 313 for this second meaning of *mutu*, which makes more sense than "husband."

92. Archi's [(^{LÚ})*p*]*a*?-*ḫu-ru-la-aš* is restored from text B (*KBo* 2.38) ii? 1. The word *paḫurula-* is attested elsewhere as an implement, usually with a GIŠ determinative. The *-ul* ending is normally for nomina instrumenti, so this may be better interpreted LÚ *paḫurula-*.

93. Archi, p. 97, translates "del vedere le persone." The iterative form should indicate something like "guard" or "watch over." Güterbock, *SBo* II: 9, translates "Dem Schutzgott des Die-Personen-Sehens (Var. des Sehens der Person(en))." Here NÍ.TE.ḪI.A is to be taken as something like "the limbs" = "the body." Text B ii? 2 has a singular form NÍ.TE-*aš*.

94. See *CHD* sub *lamarḫandatt-*, which points out that the formally nominative plural common *lamarḫandatteš* hardly fits the context. If it is a mistake, perhaps a genitive was intended, as the only other example of the word, in iii 46 of this same text, occurs with the Luwian genitival adjective suffix. Archi does not translate this phrase.

95. A hapax legomenon.

96. Although the syntax is identical to other phrases in which the characteristic epithet may be that of Labarna, sense indicates that in this case the epithet applies to ^{D}LAMMA. This phrase is a good example of the problems of interpreting the genitive phrases correctly. On *ulili-* see Hawkins and Morpurgo Davies, *FsGüterbock*^{2} 73–74, who note a close parallelism between *ulili-* and LÍL/*gimra-*, "field." Laroche, *Rech.* 70, equates ^{D}LAMMA *uliliyaš* (sic) in this passage with ^{D}LAMMA *ṢĒRI*, "the Tutelary Deity of the Countryside." Although the evidence does not indicate an exact equivalence, *ulili-* may be in the same semantic range.

A = *KUB* 2.1

Obverse ii (*transliteration cont.*)

44 *ŠA* L[a-b]a-ar-na EGIR-pa a-ša-an-na-<(aš)>[97] ^{D}LAMMA-i
45 *ŠA* L[a-ba-a]r-na ḫa-an-da-⸢at-ta⸣-aš[98] ^{D}LAMMA-i
46 *ŠA* La-b[a-ar]-na i[(š-ḫa)]⸢-šar-wa-an-⸣[(na-a)]š[99] ^{D}LAMMA-i
47 *ŠA* La-ba[-ar]-na ḫa-an-te-ya-aš-ša-aš-ši-iš ^{D}LAMMA-i
48 *ŠA* La-ba-a[r]-na tar-pa-at-ta-aš-ši-iš[100] ^{D}LAMMA-i KI.MIN
49 ša-lu-ba-at-t[a-aš-ši]-iš <^{D}LAMMA-i> KI.MIN nu-un-ta-ra-aš ^{D}LAMMA-i[101]
B 50 *ŠA* La-ba-a[r-n]a ma-ni-in-ku-wa-an ar-nu?-ma-aš[102] ^{D}LAMMA[-i?]
51 *ŠA* La-ba-a[r-n]a iš-ma-aš-šu-wa-la-aš ^{D}LAMMA-i
52 *ŠA* La-ba-a[r-n]a ták-ša-an-na-aš ^{D}LAMMA-i
53 *ŠA* La-ba-ar-na

(bottom of tablet)

97. Text B ii? 7: EGIR-*pa a-ša-an-na-aš* KI.M[IN.
98. Text B ii? 8: *ḫa-an-da-at-ta-aš-ši-i*[*š*.
99. Text B ii? 9: *iš-ḫa-šar-wa-na-aš* KI.M[IN.
100. Text B ii? 10: *:tar-pa-at-ta-aš* KI.M[IN.
101. Text B ii? 11: [*nu-u*]*n-tar-aš* KI.MIN ^{D}LAMMA-*aš*.
102. Text B ii? 12: [*ma-ni-in-*]⸢*ku-wa-an* x⸣[. The last preserved sign does not look like ⸢*ar*⸣ on the copy, but collation indicates it as a good possible reading.

A = *KUB* 2.1

Obverse ii (*translation cont.*)

44 to the tutelary deity of the L[ab]arna's sitting down again(?),[103]
45 to the tutelary deity of the decision of the L[aba]rna,
46 to the tutelary deity of the lordliness[104] of the Lab[ar]na,
47 to the tutelary deity of the *ḫantiyašša*-[105] of the Labarna,
48–49 to the tutelary deity of the *tarpatta*- of the Labarna, <to the tutelary deity> of the *šalubat*[*ta*-][106] of the same (i.e., the Labarna), [to] the tutelary deity of the swiftness[107] of the same,
50 [to] the tutelary deity of the bringing near of the Laba[rn]a,
51 to the tutelary deity of the *išmašuwala*-[108] of the Laba[rn]a,
52 to the tutelary deity of the *takšatar*[109] of the Laba[rn]a,
53 (This line begins a phrase continued in column iii.)

(bottom of tablet)

103. Archi, p. 95, translates EGIR-*pa ašannaš* as "dell'opposizione." Puhvel, *HED* 1–2: 291 and 294, claims *-za appa*(*n*) *eš*- for "resist,"and translates (p. 296) this line "to L(abarna)'s tutelary god of resistance." This is certainly a possible interpretation. However, the evidence which Puhvel presents is not completely convincing, and when we consider this phrase as a contrast to the *arauwaš*, "getting up," of two lines earlier, "sitting down again" makes good sense.

104. The translation "lordliness" was suggested to me by an old file card of Hoffner's in the *CHD* lexical files. More recently Puhvel, *HED* 1–2: 387, conveys the same idea with a translation of this passage. He derives the word from **išḫaššar* "lordship," not from *išḫaššara*- "lady, mistress," as Haas and Thiel, *AOAT* 31 (1978) 121, do. Friedrich, *HW* 85, translates "Freundlichkeit, Höflichkeit," which is followed by Archi in his translation "gentilezza."

105. Archi, p. 96, without giving evidence, translates *ḫantiyaššaššiš* as "del particolare(?)." See the comments on the word *ḫantiyašša*- in *Appendix B*.

106. This word, although partially broken, can be restored with near certainty as Archi has done. It has the Luwian genitival adjective suffix which is so common in this text. There is no other attestation of a word *šalubatta*- or *šalubattašši*- outside this text and the duplicate text B = *KBo* 2.38 ii? 10′. Güterbock, *Or* 25 (1956) 128, reads *šalumatt* [*ašš*] *iš*. The word is not in *HW* or *DLL*.

107. See Friedrich, *ArOr* 6 (1934) 372, "dem Schutzgott der Eile(??)."

108. A hapax legomenon.

109. Archi, p. 98, translates *takšannaš* "della conciliazione" without further comment. Friedrich, *HW* 205, suggests "Vereinigung(?), Gemeinschaft(?)", and in *3. Erg.* 30, "Gleichheit, Ebene." Laroche, *RHA* XXVIII (1970) 26, translates *takšatar* as "plaine," but gives no reasons for his translation. The word occurs in very diverse contexts and is probably not yet sufficiently well understood to translate.

A = *KUB* 2.1

Obverse iii (*transliteration*)

§32′ 1 [o o o o ^{D}L]AMMA-i *ŠA* La[-ba]-ar-na-aš
(*cont.*) 2 [an-na-ra-a]š? tar-pa-aš ^{D}LAMMA[-i]
3 [*ŠA* La-ba-a]r-na KUR-e-aš ḫu-u-[m]a-an-da-aš ^{D}LAMMA-i
4 [*ŠA* L]a-ba-ar-na pé-e-da[-a]š ^{D}LAMMA-i
5 *ŠA* La-ba-ar-na ta-ak-⌈ku⌉-wi$_5$-aš ^{D}⌈LAMMA-i⌉
6 *ŠA* La-ba-ar-na NÍ.TE-aš ^{D}LAMMA-i
7 *ŠA* La-ba-ar-na ZAG-i[š] ^{UZU}ZAG.U[DU-aš ^{D}LAMMA-i]
8 *ŠA* La-ba-ar-na GÙB[-la]-aš ^{UZU}ZAG.UDU[-aš (^{D}LAMMA-i)]
9 *ŠA* La-ba-ar-na $^{ḪU[(R.S)]AG}$Ki-i-ta-u-wa-a[n-ta-aš ^{D}LAMMA-i]
10 *ŠA* La-ba-ar-na [(pí)]-ḫa-la?-ad-da-aš-š[(i-iš)][110]
11 ^{D}LAMMA-i *ŠA* La-⌈ba⌉-ar-na
12 šar-la-⌈at-ta-aš⌉ ^{D}LAMMA-⌈i⌉[
13 *ŠA* L[a-ba-a]r-na ^{GIŠ}TUKUL-aš ^{D}LAMMA-i
14 *ŠA* La-[b]a-a[r]-na mu-wa-ad-da-la-ḫi-da-aš
15 ^{D}LAMMA-i *ŠA* La-ba-ar-na
16 kur-ra-aš(-)tar-ra-aš-ši-iš ^{D}LAMMA-i
17 *ŠA* La-ba-ar-na
18 :pa-ra-aš(-)tar-ra-aš-ši-iš ^{D}LAMMA-i
19 *ŠA* La-ba-ar-na *ŠA* UD.SIG$_5$-ya ^{D}LAMMA-i
20 *ŠA* La-ba-ar-na ^{É}ḫu-u-wa-ap-ra-aš ^{D}LAMMA-i
21 *ŠA* La-ba-ar-na La-ba-ar-na-aš pár-na-aš
22 ^{D}LAMMA-ri *ŠA* La-ba-ar-na
23 ^{D}LAMMA *ŠA* ^{D}UTU-*ŠI* ^{m}Tu-ut-ḫa-li-ya
24 LUGAL.GAL UR.SAG
25 ŠU.NIGIN 1 *ME* 12 *ŠUM*$^{ḪI.A}$ ^{D}LAMMA 1 ^{GIŠ}BANŠUR

---

110. Restorations in iii 8, 9 and 10 from the parallel *KBo* 12.60:1′–4′. Laroche, *DLL* 38, without the duplicate, reads this as *ḫaladaššiš*. Archi, p. 110, reads [(*pí*)]-*ḫa*{-*la/ad*!?}-*ad-da-aš-š*[(*i-iš*)]. Although collation shows that the word's third sign is clearly *la* and is followed by an *ad* sign, Archi suggests reading it with *ad* to be omitted because the parallel *KBo* 12.60:4 has *pí-ḫa-ad-da-aš-ši-iš*. On p. 102 Archi reads the word *piḫaddaššiš*. The word is attested only in these two texts; it seems that one of them has a mistake. Possibly *KUB* 2.1 has added a superfluous *-ad-* sign, as Archi suggests. Perhaps instead *KBo* 12.60 has omitted the *-la-* sign. The word may thus be either *piḫaddaššiš* or *piḫaladdaššiš*.

A = *KUB* 2.1 Obverse iii (*translation*)

§32′ (*cont.*) 1-2 to the [tu]telary deity of the [ ] of the Labarna,[111] [to] the tutelary deity of the *annari-* and *tarpi-* spirit of the Labarna,[112]

3 to the tutelary deity of all the lands of the [Laba]rna,

4 to the tutelary deity of the place [of the L]abarna,

5 to the tutel[ary] deity of the *takkuwi-*[113] of the Labarna,

6 to the tutelary deity of the body of the Labarna,

7 [to the tutelary deity of] the righ[t] should[er] of the Labarna,

8 to the tutelary deity [of] the le[f]t shoulder of the Labarna,

9 [to the tutelary deity of] Mt. Kitawa[nta] of the Labarna,

10–12 to the tutelary deity of the *piḫadda-* of the Labarna, to the tutelary deity of praise of the Labarna,

13 to the tutelary deity of the weapon of the L[aba]rna,

14–16 to the tutelary deity of the awe-inspiring ability(?) of the Labarna, to the tutelary deity of the *kurraštarra-* of the Labarna,[114]

17–18 to the tutelary deity of the *:paraštarra-* of the Labarna,

19 to the tutelary deity of the propitious day of the Labarna,[115]

20 to the tutelary deity of the Labarna's *ḫuwapra-* building,[116]

21–25 to the tutelary deity of the Labarna's "house of Labarna," the Labarna's tutelary deity of His Majesty Tudḫaliya, Great King, hero, a total of 112 names of tutelary deities, one (offering) table.

---

111. "Of the Labarna" is carried over from column ii.

112. Otten, *MDOG* 94 (1963) 19, suggests that *annari-* might signify "männliche Potenz." On *annari-* and *tarpi-* see Hoffner, *JNES* 27 (1968) 61-68, especially 64–66, and Otten and von Soden, *StBoT* 7 (1968) 27–32. Hoffner discusses the other occurrences of these two terms and their significance when paired to denote a single beneficent spirit. Puhvel, *HED* 1–2: 62, and Kammenhuber, HW^2 79, summarize the evidence for *annari-*. Puhvel translates "strength, force, vigor" and Kammenhuber does not give a translation. Neither notes this particular passage, which shows a rare *a*-stem form for both words, although Kammenhuber suggests that the ^{D}*Innari* ^{D}*Tarpi* of the unpublished text 453/d (Otten and von Soden, *StBoT* 7: 29) may be contaminated forms of *a*-stems.

113. Laroche, *DLL* 89, cites a word *dakkui-* "sombre?" but does not include this passage or even this form. He points out that the translation is based only on the similarity to Hittite *dankui-*. Even if *dakkui-* means "dark," line 5 remains difficult to translate; should it be "to the tutel[ary] deity of the Labarna's dark things?" Archi, p. 101, takes *dakkui-* not as an adjective but as an abstract noun, translating "dell'oscurità(?)."

114. Although Archi, p. 110, reads *kur-ra-aš tar-ra-aš-ši-iš* in iii 16, there is not really any word space on the tablet. Laroche, *DLL* 57, reads this as one word, *kur-ra-aš-tar-ra-aš-ši-iš* but does not propose a meaning. Güterbock, *Or* 25 (1956) 128, reads *kurraš* (-) *tarraššiš*. Two lines after this word/phrase, in iii 18, there is a phrase *:paraš tarraššiš*, with a clear word space between *paraš* and *tarraššiš*. The syntax would fit better with one word, so perhaps it is line 18 which is wrong in having a word space.

115. The reason for the *-ya* on UD.SIG$_5$ is unclear.

116. The word ^{É}*ḫuwapraš* occurs only here and in *KUB* 56.51 i 1, 2, and 4. It is not cited in *HW* or *DLL*. It looks like the full grade of a word **hupra-*, from which ^{LÚ}*ḫuprala-* (a potter?) may have been derived. Could the ^{É}*ḫuwapra-* then be a pottery-making shop? There is attested a word *ḫupra-* which seems to be a fabric, cited by Friedrich *HW* 75 and *1. Erg.* 7. It is conceivable that the ^{É}*ḫuwapraš* could also be derived from this.

A = *KUB* 2.1

Obverse iii (*transliteration cont.*)

§33′ 26 1 GUD.ÁB gi-im-ma-ra-aš 3 MÁŠ.GAL
27 ^{D}A-a-la-aš *ŠUM*$^{ḪI.A}$-aš ḫu-u-ma-an-da-aš
28 ^{D}A-a-la-aš ḫu-e-eš-wa-an-na-aš
29 ^{D}A-a-la-aš *ŠA ŠA-ME-E*
30 ^{D}A-a-la-aš *ŠA* MÁŠ.ANŠE
31 ^{D}A-a-la-aš gi-im!-ra-aš
32 ^{D}A-a-la-aš mi-nu-um-ma-aš!
33 ^{D}A-a-la-aš a-aš-šu-la-aš
34 ^{D}A-a-la-aš ^{URU}*ḪA-AT-TI*
35 ^{D}A-a-la-aš KARAŠ
36 ^{D}A-⌈a-la-aš ^{URU}A-la⌉-tar-ma[117]
37 ^{D}A-a[-l]a-aš [*ŠA* $^{ḪU]R.SAG}$Ša-ar-⌈pa⌉
38 ^{D}A-a-la-aš *ŠA* $^{[Ḫ]UR.SAG}$⌈Ša-lu⌉-w[a-an-da]
39 ^{D}A-a-la-aš ^{URU}T[u-u]t-tu
40 ^{D}A-a-la-aš ^{URU}Šu[-l]u-pa-aš-ša
41 ^{D}A-a-la-aš ^{URU}Ḫa-⌈ra⌉-na
42 ^{D}A-a-la-aš gi-im-ma-ra-aš wa-aḫ-nu-w[a-a]n-da-aš
43 ^{D}A-a-la-aš wa-ar-wa-an-ta-li-ya-aš
44 ^{D}⌈A-a⌉-la-aš aš-ša-at-ta-aš-ši-iš
45 ^{D}A-a-la-aš wa-⌈li⌉-pa-at-ta-aš-ši-iš
C vi 46 ^{D}A-a-la-aš la-⌈mar!⌉-ḫa-an-da-at-ta-aš[(-ši-iš)]
47 ^{D}A-a-la[-aš a]n-n[a-r]u-ma-ḫi-ta-aš-ši-i[(š)]
48 ^{D}A-a-la-[aš o o (-)]x-ku-ti-ya«-ya»-at[(-ḫi-ta-aš-ši-iš)]
49 ^{D}A-a-la-aš [aš-t]a-aš wa-aš-ta[(-aš)]

(bottom of tablet)

117. Archi reads this name *A-at-tar-ma*, but it is correctly noted as Alatarma by del Monte, *RGTC* 6: 7, and Singer *ZA* 75 (1985) 110 n. 61.

§33′26–27 one cow (and) three billy goats of the countryside,[118] to all the names of Ala:[119]
28 Ala[120] of life,
29 Ala of the sky,
30 Ala of the animals,
31 Ala of the countryside,
32 Ala of kindliness,
33 Ala of favor,
34 Ala of Ḫatti,
35 Ala of the army,
36 Ala of the city Alatarma,[121]
37 Ala [of] M[t.] Šarpa,
38 Ala of Mt. Šaluw[anda],
39 Ala of T[u]ttu,
40 Ala of Šulupašša,
41 Ala of Ḫarana,
42 Ala of the enclosed(?) countryside,
43 Ala of *warwantali(ya)-*,[122]
44 Ala of the *aššatta-*,[123]
45 Ala of encircling(?),
46 Ala of "setting a time,"[124]
47 Ala of forcefulness/power,[125]
48 Ala of [(-)]x-*kutiyatḫita-*,
49 Ala of *ašta- wašta-*,[126]

(bottom of tablet)

118. This could be either a wild goat or perhaps one pastured on the prairie rather than kept penned near the house.

119. The form ^{D}Alaš here makes sense as a genitive. This first occurrence as ^{D}*A-a-la-aš* in the list may have conditioned the scribe's continued use of this form where we would expect rather a dative-locative form.

120. As discussed below in the *Commentary*, the form of Ala's name throughout this text is written ^{D}*A-a-la-aš*. I understand this as nominative singular as opposed to dative-locative plural.

121. This Ala deity of Alatarma parallels the LAMMA deity of the same city mentioned in *KUB* 2.1 i 45.

122. Archi, p. 97, translates "di colui che genera(?)" ("of him who generates/begets[?]"), connecting *warwantaliyaš* with ^{D}*Warwaliyan*, a name which Laroche, *DLL* 108, cites as a form of *warwala/i-*, translating "semence, progeniture." The word *warwantaliyaš* is sufficiently different in form from *warwala/i-* that it looks to me like a completely different word perhaps best left untranslated.

123. Another hapax legomenon; Laroche, *DLL* 33, cites this passage and compares to Lycian B *esetesi* and A *ehetehi*, "épithètes divines."

124. Archi, p. 96, follows Laroche, *DLL* 40 sub *ḫandai-*, in translating "della decisione immediata." See now *CHD* sub *lamarḫandattašši-* and ii 40 above.

125. Archi, p. 97, translates *annarumaḫitašši-* "della forza virile." Kammenhuber, *HW*^{2} Lief. 1 (1975) 79, cites only this example and translates the line "A(ala) der Hoheitsmacht/Lebenskraft." More recently Puhvel, *HED* 1–2 (1984) 63 sub *annari-*, translates *annarumaḫitaššiš* as "of forcefulness."

126. See the note to *KUB* 2.1 ii 30–31.

A = *KUB* 2.1

Reverse iv (*transliteration*)

---

§33′ 1 ^{D}A-a-la-aš wa-al-li-y[a-a(n-na-aš)]
(*cont.*) 2 ^{D}A-a-la-aš šar-la-at-ta-aš-š[(i-iš)]
3 ^{D}A-a-la-aš *ŠA* ^{GIŠ}BAN ^{D}A-a-l[(a-aš)]
4 *ŠA* ^{KUŠ}MÁ.URU.URU$_6$[127] ^{D}A-a-la-aš x[o o]
5 *ŠA* La-⸢ba-ar-na⸣
6 ^{D}⸢A-a⸣-l[a-aš o]x-da *ŠA* La-ba-ar-na[128]
7 [(^{D}A-a-la-aš pa-r)]a-a ḫa-an-ta-an-ta-an-na-aš
8 [*ŠA* La-ba-ar-na] ^{D}A-a-la-aš
9 [(ša-ra-a ḫal-zi-y)]a-u-wa-aš *ŠA* La-ba-ar-na
10 [^{D}A-a-la-aš o o]x ḫal-zi-ya-u-wa[(-aš)][129]
11 [*ŠA* La-ba-a]r-n[a] ^{D}A-a-la-aš
12 [ŠU-an? ša-r]a-a ap-pa-an-na-aš
13 [o o o La-ba-a]r-na-aš[130]
14 [^{D}A-a-la-aš ḫ]a-an-ta-an-za
15 [^{D}A-a-la-aš]⸢x-nu-u-ga?⸣-na-ši-i[š][131]
16 [^{D}A-a-la-aš] la[-pa-n]a-aš-ši-i[š][132]
17 [o o *ŠA* L]a[-ba-a]r-na
18 [^{D}A-a-la-aš]⸢x-x-x⸣-ra-aš-ši-i[(š)]
19 [*ŠA* La-ba-ar-n]a
20 [^{D}A-a-la-aš (x EGIR-pa DI)]B-an-na[(-aš)][133]
21 [^{D}A-a-la-aš o o o]x-an-na-aš
D 22 [^{D}A-a-la-aš o o o o $^{KU]Š}$kur-š[(a-aš)][134]
C vi 23 [^{D}A-a-la-aš o o o o -w]a?-an[-

127. Text C vi 7′: ^{D}*A*]*-a-la-aš* ^{GIŠ}MÁ.URU.URU$_6$.

128. Text C vi 9′: K]I.MIN.

129. Text C has only one epithet formed with *ḫalzai-*.

130. Text C vi 12′: *a*]*p-pa-an-na-aš* KI.MIN.

131. Text C vi 14′:*-n*]*a-aš.*

132. Text C vi 15′: *-n*]*a-aš-ši-eš.*

133. Archi, p. 112, reads the end of this line [(EGIR-*pa-r*)]*a-an-na*[(*-aš*)], with the restoration from text C, (*KUB* 44.16) vi 17′, and translates (p. 95) this as "dell'avvenire." However, Hoffner, *BiOr* 37 (1980) 201, notes that *KUB* 44.16 vi 17′ (cited by him as iv 17) should be read]x EGIR-*pa* DIB!-*an-na-aš*. *KUB* 2.1 iv 20 can be read DI]B-*an-na*[*-aš.*

134. Restored from text C vi 19′, but only *-š*]*a-aš* is preserved, so the attribution to this particular spot in the main text is not certain. If the *-š*]*a-aš* goes somewhere else, then it is possible that [^{D}*A-a-la-aš šu-wa-an-za* $^{KU]Š}$ *kur-š*[*a-an*] could be restored, which would fit the spacing in text A and would provide a nice parallel to the description of ^{D}LAMMA in ii 32.

A = *KUB* 2.1

Reverse iv (*translation*)

---

§33′ 1 Ala of glory,
(*cont.*) 2 Ala of praise,
3–5 Ala of the bow, Ala of the quiver, Ala of x[…] of the Labarna,
6 Ala of the [ ]x-*da* of the Labarna,
7–9 Ala of the divine power[135] of the Labarna, Ala of the calling up of the Labarna,[136]
10–13 [Ala] of the calling [ ]x [of the Laba]rna, Ala of holding [u]p [the hand(?) …] of the [Laba]rna,
14 [Ala] the just,
15 [Ala of (-)]x-*nugana*-,
16–17 [Ala] of the summer pastures [ ] of the Labarna,
18–19 [Ala] of the x-*ra*- [of the Labarn]a,
20 [Ala] of the refuge,[137]
21 [Ala] of the […]x-*ātar*,
22 [Ala of the …] of the hunting bag,[138]
(lines 23–26 do not preserve enough to identify the particular Ala deities)

135. See note 70 (p. 99 above) on *parā ḫandandatar* and the similar phrase in the list of LAMMA tutelary deities.

136. Archi, p. 95, suggests "del convocare(?)."

137. The translation "of refuge" is Hoffner's, based on the fact that *-za appa epp-* means "to take refuge in."

138. Or perhaps "[Ala who fills] the hunting ba[g]. See note 134 (p. 110 above) to transliteration of iv 22.

A = *KUB* 2.1

Reverse iv (*transliteration cont.*)

D (*cont.*)

24 [^{D}A-a-la-aš o o o o]-an-t[a-
25 [^{D}A-a-la-aš o o o (-)]x-aḫ-ḫu-w[a-[139]
26 [^{D}A-a-la-aš o o o -y]a-aš
27 [(^{D}A-a-la-aš pí-ra-a)]n ḫu-u-i-ya-u-wa-aš
28 [^{D}A-a-la-aš o o]-nu-un ka-ri-ya-u-wa-aš[140]
29 [^{D}A-a-la-aš o o o -]x
30 [^{D}A-a-la]-aš x[- o o -]x[141]
31 [^{D}A-a-l]a-aš ḪUR.SAG.MEŠ-aš ḫu-u-ma-<(an)>-ta-aš[142]
32 [^{D}A-a-l]a-aš ÍD.MEŠ-aš ḫu-u-ma-an-ta-aš[143]
33 [^{D}A-a-l]a-aš du-wa-du-na?<-aš> ḫu-ma-an-ta-aš
34 $^{[D]}$⌈A⌉-a-la-aš šu-up-pí-ya-an-t[a-aš][144]
35 [ḫ]u-u-ma-an-ta-aš ^{D}A-a-la-aš
36 [ ]x-ku-uš-nu-wa-an-ti-iš[145]
37 [^{D}A]-⌈a⌉-la-aš *ŠA* $^{ḪUR.SAG}$Ša-ar-p[a][146]
38 [^{D}A-a-l]a-aš GURUN-aš i-ya-at-na-aš
39 [^{D}A-a-l]a-aš *ŠA* ^{D}UD SIG_5[147]
40 [^{D}A-a-la-aš] ⌈a⌉-[aš-š]a-u-w[a-aš (Z)]I-aš

(bottom of tablet)

139. Text D 4:]x-*iš*.

140. Text D 6: *ka-ri-ya-an-da-aš*.

141. Text D 7 has [ḪUR.SAG.MEŠ-*aš* ^{D}]*A-a-la-aš* ÍD.MEŠ-*aš* ^{D}*A-a-la-aš*, which should correspond with text A iv 29–30. The traces on text A do not, however, fit the text of the duplicate, and text A has the mountains and rivers in fuller form in the following two lines.

142. Text D 8: *ḫu-u-m*]*a-an-da-aš*.

143. Text D 9: *ḫ*[*u-u-m*]*a-an-da-aš*.

144. Text D 11: *šu-up-p*]*é-eš-*⌈*ša*⌉*-an-na-aš ḫu-u-ma-an-da-aš* "of all purity."

145. Text D 12: -]*nu-wa-an-te-eš*.

146. Text D 13: [*ŠA* $^{ḪUR.SA}$]^{G}*Šar-pa a-li-la-an-za i-ya-at-na-za*. Archi reads A.ŠÀ-*la-an-za i-ya-at-na-za* (p. 112 n. 68) and translates "campagna fiorente" (p. 100). The form *alilanza* is not otherwise attested but could be based on *alil* "blossom."

147. Text D 14: UD.KAM-*aš* ^{D}*A-a-la-aš*.

A = *KUB* 2.1

Reverse iv (*translation cont.*)

(lines 23–26 do not preserve enough to identify the particular Ala deities)

27 [Ala] of running [in fr]ont,

28 [Ala] of covering[148] the [ ]-*nu*-,

(lines 29–30 preserve only traces)

31 [Al]a of all the mountains,

32 [Al]a of all the rivers,

33 [Al]a of all the *duwaduna*-,[149]

34–36 Ala of all the springs(?),[150] x-*kušnuwanti*- Ala,

37 Ala of Mt. Šarp[a],

38 [Al]a of abundance of fruit,

39 [Al]a of the propitious day,

40 [Ala of the g]oo[d] [sp]irit,

(bottom of tablet)

148. Archi, p. 96, takes the verbal substantive *kariyauwaš* as being from the verb *kariya*- (Med. 2) "to comply" and translates "dell'accondiscendere(?)."

149. Archi, p. 101, translates "di tutte le doline(?)" on the basis of Gordon's suggestion, *JCS* 21 (1967) 82, that *duwaduna*- is a sink-hole or *düden* (Turkish). Archi, p. 112 n. 65, reads the duplicate Bo 6113:10 (cited by him as 9) as [*du-wa-d*]*u-na*[*-aš*?], which is only just possible. The only other example known to me is the word *du-wa-du-un* in the unpublished tablet 2025/g, cited in Laroche, *DLL* 101, without translation. Gordon points out the significance of these openings to underground watercourses in Anatolian mythology; they may well have had an Ala deity.

150. Archi translates *šuppiyantaš* as "fonti(?)"; see Gordon, *JCS* 21 (1967) 82 with n. 32.

A = *KUB* 2.1

Reverse v (*transliteration*)

---

§33′ 1 ^{D}A-a-la-a[š *ŠA* ^{m}Tu-ut-ḫa-]li-ya[151]
(*cont.*) 2 *ŠA* É L[UGAL? ^{D}A-a-la-aš][152]
3 *ŠA* ^{m}Tu-ut-ḫ[a-li-ya]
4 ŠU.NIGIN *ŠU-ŠI* [*ŠUM*$^{HI.A}$]
5 1 ^{GIŠ}BANŠUR A[D.KID?][153]

---

§34′ 6 1 AMAR GUD.MAḪ [[154]
7 ḫu-u-ma-an[-ta-aš
D 8 x[

(remainder of column broken away)

A = *KUB* 2.1

Reverse vi[155] (*transliteration*)

---

§35′ 1 *ŠA* KUR ^{URU}*ḪAT-TI* ḪUR.SAG.ḪI.A ḫu-u-ma-an-ta-aš
2 KUR-e-aš ḫu-u-ma-an-ta-aš ^{D}UTU-*ŠI*
3 ^{m}Tu-ut-ḫa-li-ya-aš ku-e-eš la-aḫ-ḫi-ya-iš-ki-iz-zi
4 ḪUR.SAG ḫu-u-ma-an-ta-aš *ŠA* KUR ^{URU}*ḪAT-TI*
5 ^{D}UTU-*ŠI* ^{m}Tu-ut-ḫa-li-ya-aš LUGAL GAL
6 ku-e-eš ši-ya-tal-li-iš-ki-iz-zi
7 ḪUR.SAG.ḪI.A ḫu-u-ma-an-te-eš *ŠA* KUR UGU-*TI*
8 ^{D}UTU-*ŠI* ku-e-eš ši-ya-tal-li-iš-ki-iz-zi
9 [^{fD}Ma-a-la[156] ^{f}]^{D}Ma-am-ra-an-ta-aš

(remainder of column broken away)

151. Text D 17:] LUGAL-*aš* (eras.) ^{D}*A-a-la-aš*.
152. Text D 16:]x LUGAL-*wa-aš pár-na-aš* ^{D}*A-a-l*[*a-aš*]. Text D reverses the order of these two deities from that of the main text.
153. What is preserved from text D 18–19 after the last Ala is named is ^{UZU}NÍG.[GIG] / *ti-an-zi*. This text specifies the offerings to be set out for the above-named deities.
154. Text D 20–23 preserves only the middle of the lines and may diverge from the main text at this point. It reads as follows:

20	Ḫ]I.A *ŠA* ḪUR.SAG.ḪI.A[	
21	ši-p]a-an-ti	[
22	^{m}Tu-ut-ḫ]a?-li-ya-aš	[
23	-]aš	[

155. After a gap of an undetermined number of paragraphs.
156. Restored on the basis of the parallel *KBo* 11.40 vi 7′f., which indicates that this last part of the festival was devoted to the deified mountains and rivers of the king's domain. This includes the upper land, the Hurrian lands, Arzawa, Maša, the Luqqa lands, the Kaškean lands, and the land of Ḫatti.

A = *KUB* 2.1

Reverse v (*translation*)

§33′ 1–3 Ala of the palace [of Tudḫa]liya (and) [Ala(?)] of Tudḫ[aliya][157]
(*cont.*) 4–5 Total: sixty [names]; one w[icker(?)] (offering) table.

---

§34′ 6–8 One bull calf [...] [to] all [...] x[...]

(remainder of column broken away)

A = *KUB* 2.1

Reverse vi[158] (*translation*)

---

§35′ 1–3 To all the mountains (and) lands of the land of Ḫatti in which His Majesty Tudḫaliya regularly campaigns/travels,
4–6 to all the mountains of the land of Ḫatti which His Majesty Tudḫaliya, the Great King, hunts,[159]
7–8 to(?)[160] all the mountains of the upper land which His Majesty hunts,
9 [to the Mala river,] the Mamranta river,

(remainder of column broken away)

157. The duplicate text D, Bo 6113:16f., is somewhat broken and therefore difficult to interpret, but enough remains to show a slightly different version of this section: "[...]x to the A[la] deities of the king's house, [...] to the Ala deities of the king, to the Ala deities [...]x, they place liver [on a table(?)]." There follows a paragraph line as in the main text and then references to mountains, libating, and possibly [Tudḫ]aliya. The Bo 6113 version differs from the main text in using Hittite syntax and in most cases the more general word "king" instead of the king's name, Tudḫaliya.

158. After a gap of an undetermined number of paragraphs.

159. See Laroche, *OLZ* 58 (1963) 247, on *šiyatalleški-* as "chase, hunt." Kammenhuber, *ZA* 66 (1976) 73, does not follow this, translating the verb as "to seal." All the occurrences of *šiyatalleški-* are in the various copies of this text, so no other contexts can be brought to bear on this verb. Early drafts of the treatment of this word in the *CHD* separate the verb *šiyatalleški-* from the verb *šiyatalliya-* "to seal," and point out that because all of the occurrences are from these festivals, "hunt" must remain conjectural.

160. The scribe wrote nominative plural *ḫumanteš* instead of dative-locative plural *ḫumantaš* here. This could be because of confusion with the relative pronoun *kuēš*, which, although functioning as an accusative in its clause, is a form which in older Hittite would have been nominative plural.

The Festival of Individual Offerings

The tablets included here describe a festival that rather closely parallels the festival of *KUB* 2.1 and its duplicates. The primary difference is that this festival in general lists offerings for each of the names of ^{D}LAMMA and ^{D}Ala individually, rather than going through a whole list with one group of offerings. The separate treatment of these tablets reflects my understanding of this series of tablets as a different festival or a different version, perhaps earlier, of the ceremony. Although the gods are the same, the specific ceremony described for their worship differs significantly from that of the Festival of Group Offerings described above.

The reconstruction of the numerous tablet pieces for this festival is based on comparison to the parallel passages in *KUB* 2.1, the main text of the Festival of Group Offerings. Most restorations are from *KUB* 2.1. The reconstructed order of the tablets is naturally not certain. Most tentative is the placement of text D, *KUB* 40.107+*IBoT* 2.18 obverse i, at the beginning. This section looks like a description of an early part of a festival, with various ceremonies by cult functionaries described in preparation for the many offerings to be given during in the festival. The slaughtering of animals described in *KUB* 40.107+*IBoT* 2.18 §§2′–4′ and [8′] would make sense as preparations for the diverse flesh offerings described later.

Transliteration

D = *KUB* 40.107+*IBoT* 2.18 Obverse i[161]

§1′ x+1 [ ]x ⸢ḪUR.SAG.ḪI.A⸣
2′ [ḫu-u-ma-an-te-eš ÍD.ḪI.A ḫu-u-ma-an]-t[e-eš *Š*]*A* KUR ^{URU}*ḪA-AT-TI*
3′ [o o o DINGIR.MEŠ ḫu-u-ma-an-]te-eš ⸢*A*⸣[-*N*]*A* 1 ^{GIŠ}BANŠUR

§2′ 4′ [*A-N*]*A ŠUM*$^{ḪI.A}$ ^{D}LAMMA-aš ḫu-u-ma-an-da-aš
5′ [-]⸢e⸣-eš *A-NA Š*[*U*]*M*$^{ḪI.A}$ ^{D}A-a-la-aš ḫu-u-ma-an-da-aš
6′ [ ]x-kán UDU k[u]-i-e-eš
7′ [ḫu-]⸢u⸣-ma-an-da-aš ši-pa-an-da-aš
8′ [na-aš-ta[162] ... pa-ra-a p]é-en-ni-ya-an-zi
9′ [nu pít-tal-wa-an-d]a-an[163] ar-ḫa mar-kán-zi

161. *IBoT* 2.18 joins *KUB* 40.107 on the right side of the obverse at the top and adds part of another column. Because the left edge of *KUB* 40.107 is preserved, the column labeled Vs? in the copy must be column i, so the columns identified as ii and iii in the *IBoT* 2.18 copy should now be i and ii. The space between ii 7′ and 9′ in *IBoT* 2.18 is now shown in the joined text to be another line, line Vs? 7′ of *KUB* 40.107. *IBoT* 2.18 adds one line to the beginning of the text as copied in *KUB* 40.107; line numbers are adjusted accordingly. Some restorations are from similar festival descriptions in *KUB* 32.135+*KBo* 21.85+*KBo* 8.109 iv 14–15 (Festival of the Moon and Thunder) and *KUB* 2.13 ii 55′–56′ and iii 5′–6′ (Festival of the Month). Because too little of obverse ii (preserved on the join piece *IBoT* 2.18) is preserved to allow a coherent transliteration, its description of offerings to the holy places of the temple and to names (of ^{D}LAMMA and Ala?) has not been integrated into the reconstructed festival.

162. Or perhaps [*nu-uš-kán*.

163. Or ... *ḫu-u-ma-an-d*]*a-an*.

Text Scheme[164]

A. *KBo* 11.40. Column i is parallel to *KUB* 2.1 i 47–51.
Column ii is parallel to *KUB* 2.1 ii 15–24.
Column v probably parallels lost portions of *KUB* 2.1 v.
Column vi 1–8 are parallel to *KUB* 2.1 vi.

B. *KUB* 40.108. Column ii duplicates A i 18′–26′; column v is parallel to *KUB* 2.1 iv 7–10 and fills in some of the missing portions of A.

C. *KUB* 40.101. Duplicates A v 1′–23′.

D. *KUB* 40.107+*IBoT* 2.18. Column i may be from the early part of the festival. Reverse iv 17′–30′ duplicate A vi 2′–18′.

E. *KBo* 12.60. Parallel to *KUB* 2.1 iii 8–15, probably duplicate to missing portions of A = *KBo* 11.40 obverse iii. It is not an indirect join to *KBo* 11.40.

F. *KUB* 55.25. Parallel to *KUB* 2.1 iii 29–35 and probably duplicates some of the missing A = *KBo* 11.40 obverse iii.

Translation

D = *KUB* 40.107+*IBoT* 2.18 Obverse i

§1′ [... all] the mountains [al]l [the rivers, al]l t[he ... gods o]f the land of Ḫatti, for one offering table.

---

§2′ [... f]or the names of all the tutelary deities [... -]*eš* for the names of all the Ala tutelary deities [...] who [...] a sheep [...] to [a]ll the [...] he libated. They [d]rive [forth ...] They butcher the [stri]pped (carcass).[165]

---

164. Based on the work of Laroche, *CTH* 682, Archi, *SMEA* 16 (1975) 105, and new material.

165. Or "They butcher the [who]le (carcass)." See note 163 above for possible restorations.

D = *KUB* 40.107+*IBoT* 2.18

Obverse i (*transliteration cont.*)

§3′ 10′ [ta LUGAL-uš e]-ša UGULA $^{\text{LÚ.MEŠ}}$MUḪALDIM $^{\text{LÚ.MEŠ}}$MUḪALDIM[-y]a ḫu-u-ma-an-te-eš

11′ [UDU.ḪI.A o o] ḫu-u-kán-zi $^{\text{LÚ.MEŠ}}$NAR ^{URU}[K]a-ni-iš SÌR-*RU*

§4′ 12′ [1 LÚ *ME*]-*ŠE-DI* pa-iz-zi ta-aš-kán a-ú-li [kat-t]a-an ti-ya-zi

13′ [GIM-a]n? ḫu-u-ke-eš-šar ḫa-an-ti šar-ra-an-zi [1? M]ÁŠ.GAL-kán

14′ [o -z]i [LU]GAL-uš ša-ra-a ti-ya-zi UGULA $^{\text{L[Ú.MEŠ}}$MUḪALDIM]

15′ ta-pí-ša-ni-in KÙ.G[I]x x x x x [na-an]

16′ LUGAL-i pa-ra-a e-ep-zi[Ø?]

§5′ 17′ UGULA $^{\text{LÚ.MEŠ}}$MUḪALDIM iš-ta-na-ni pí-r[a-an ti-ya-zi?]

18′ [UGULA] $^{\text{LÚ.MEŠ}}$MUḪALDIM UGULA LÚ.MEŠ ^{GIŠ}BANŠUR-ya [ ]

19′ ^{LÚ}ALAN.ZU$_9$ me-ma-i ^{LÚ}pal-wa[-tal-la-aš pal-wa-a-iz-zi]

20′ $^{\text{[L]Ú}}$ki-i-ta-aš ḫal-za-a-[i]

§6′ 21′ UGULA $^{\text{LÚ.MEŠ}}$MUḪALDIM ḫa-aš-ši-i 1-*ŠU* ^{GIŠ}DAG-ti [1-*ŠU* ^{GIŠ}lu-ut-ti-ya 1-*ŠU*]

22′ ḫa-tal-wa-aš GIŠ-i 1-*ŠU* nam-ma ḫa-[aš-ši-i ta-pu-uš-za 1-*ŠU* ši-pa-an-ti]

§7′ 23′ [t]a LUGAL-uš e-ša $^{\text{LÚ.MEŠ}}$MUḪALDIM x[

24′ ti-an-zi 3 *ME* MÁŠ.GAL 20 GUD[

25′ *A-NA* GUD-ma pí-ra-an GAL *ME-Š*[*E-DI*

§8′ 26′ ⸢2⸣ MÁŠ.GAL-ma-kán *IŠ-TU* x[

27′ [n]a-aš *A-NA* ^{D}Kar-zi ^{D}Ḫa-pa[-an-ta-li-ya

28′ [p]é-en-ni-ya-an-zi ta-aš-t[a? ḫu-kán-zi]

§9′ 29′ ma-a-an ḫu-ke-eš-šar t[a-ru-up-ta-ri? … na-aš-ta]

30′ [d]a-ga-an-zi-pu-uš [ša-an-ḫa-an-zi

§10′ 31′ [ ]x ta-pí-ša-n[a

32′ [ ]x LUGAL-uš *QA-TAM*[[166]

33′ [ ]x ši-pa-a[n-ti

34′ [ ] x x [

(the tablet breaks off)

166. Or *QA-TAM*[*-MA*.

D = *KUB* 40.107+*IBoT* 2.18

Obverse i (*translation cont.*)

§3′ [The king sits d]own. The overseer of the cooks and all the cooks slaughter [the sheep ...] The singers of Kaneš sing.

§4′ [One royal bo]dyguard goes. He takes his stand [a]t/[ne]ar the sacrificial animal(s)(?).[167] [Whe]n(?) they divide up the slaughtered animals equally, t[hey x one(?) bi]lly goat. The [k]ing steps up. The overseer of the cooks [holds(?)] a pitcher of gold [and ...] He holds [it] forth to the king. [Ø?]

§5′ The overseer of the cooks [steps] bef[ore] the altar. [The overseer] of the cooks and the overseer of the waiters [...] The ALAN.ZU$_9$-man recites. The shou[ter(?)] [shouts(?)]. The *kita*- man calls out.

§6′ The overseer of the cooks [libates] once to the hearth, [once] to the throne, [once to the window,] once to the wood of the door bolt and finally [once next to the h]earth.

§7′ The king sits down. The cooks place x[...] Three hundred billy goats (and) twenty oxen [...] Before the oxen, however, the chief of the royal body[guard ...]

§8′ Two billy goats, however, with x[...] They drive them for Karzi, Ḫapa[ntali,] [DN, and DN. They slaughter (them).]

§9′ When the slaughtering is c[ompleted(?) ... They sweep] the floors.

§10′ [...] a pitcher [...] the king the hand[168][...] he libat[es ...]

(the tablet breaks off)

167. On *auli-* see most recently Kühne, *ZA* 76 (1986) 85–117, who suggests that an original meaning "throat" came to mean "sacrificial animal." He does not discuss this passage, but it does fit well with this idea.

168. Or ... in that w[ay ...

A = *KBo* 11.40

Obverse i[169] (*transliteration*)

§11′ x+1 [ ]x

§12′ 2′ [1 ^{NINDA}tu-u-ḫu-ra-i 1 $^{UZ]U}$BAR.SÌL GUD
3′ [1 ^{DUG}t]a-la-i-mi-iš KAŠ
4′ [^{URU}Šu-l]u-pa-aš-ša-aš ^{D}LAMMA-ri

§13′ 5′ [1 ^{NINDA}t]u-u-ḫu-ra-i 1 ^{UZU}da-a-an-ḫa-aš-ti GUD ZAG[
6′ [1 $^{DU]G}$ta-la-i-mi-iš KAŠ
7′ [^{URU}Tu-u]t-tu-wa-aš ^{D}LAMMA-ri

§14′ 8′ [1 ^{NINDA}t]u-⸢u-ḫu⸣-ra-i 1 ^{UZU}TI GUD
9′ [1 ^{DUG}ta-la-]i-mi KAŠ ^{URU}Ḫa-ra-na-aš ^{D}LAMMA-ri

§15′ 10′ [1 ^{NINDA}tu-u-ḫu-r]a-i ^{UZU}*RA-PA-AL-TUM* GUD-ya
11′ [1 ^{DUG}ta-l]a-i-mi-iš KAŠ
12′ [$^{ḪUR.SAG?}$Š]a-ri-iš-ša-aš[170] ^{D}LAMMA-ri

§16′ 13′ [1 ^{NINDA}tu]-ḫu-ra-i 1 ^{UZU}BAR.DÙ UDU
14′ [1 ^{DUG}ta-l]a-i-mi KAŠ
15′ [$^{ḪUR.SAG}$Šu-u]n-na-ra-aš ^{D}LAMMA-ri

§17′ 16′ [1 ^{NINDA}tu-u-ḫ]u-ra-i ^{UZU}ku-du-úr UDU ZAG-na-an
17′ [1 ^{DUG}]⸢ta-la-i⸣-mi-iš KAŠ
B ii 18′ [^{ÍD}Ku-um-ma-r]a-aš ^{D}LAMMA-i

§18′ 19′ [(1 ^{NINDA}tu-u-)]ḫu-ra-i ^{UZU}da-ḫa-aš-ti UDU ZAG-na-an
20′ [1 ^{DUG}t]a-la-i-mi-iš KAŠ ^{ÍD}Ke-el-la-aš ^{D}LAMMA[171]

§19′ 21′ [(1 ^{NINDA}tu-u-ḫ)]u-ra-i 1 ^{UZU}ku-du-úr UDU IGI-zi
22′ [(1 ^{DUG}t)]a-la-i-mi KAŠ[172] Ḫal-la-aš-ša-aš ^{D}LAMMA-ri

(no paragraph divider in text B)

169. After a gap of an undetermined number of paragraphs.

170. Spacing favors this reading over [^{URU}*Š*]*a-ri-iš-ša-aš*. Del Monte, *RGTC* 6: 357, gives two examples of a $^{ḪUR.SAG}$*Šarišsa*, although he cites this example under the city name, which is expected here with a tutelary deity. One of the two occurrences of Mt. Šarešša is *KUB* 40.101 rev. 2, a duplicate to column v of this tablet. The scribe may have meant the city and written the mountain.

171. Text B ii 3′: ^{D}LAMMA-⸢*i*⸣. The parallel *KUB* 2.1 ii 51 has the river Šiḫiriya instead of Kella.

172. Text B ii 5′: 1 ^{DUG}*ta-la-i-mi-iš* KAŠ.

A = *KBo* 11.40

Obverse i (*translation*)

§11′ Traces only.

§12′ [One *tuḫurai-* bread, one] BAR.SÌL,[173] [one *t*]*alaimi-* jug of beer to the Tutelary Deity of [Šul]upašša,

§13′ [One] *tuḫurai-* [bread], one right "double bone"[174] of an ox, [one] *talaimi-* [ju]g of beer to the Tutelary Deity of [Tu]ttuwa,

§14′ [One] *tuḫurai-* [bread], one ox rib, [one *tala*]*imi-* [jug] of beer to the Tutelary Deity of Ḫarana,

§15′ [One *tuḫur*]*ai-* [bread], one ox haunch, [one *tal*]*aimi-* [jug] of beer to the Tutelary Deity of [Mt(?) Š]arešša,

§16′ [One] *tuḫurai-* [bread], one BAR.DÙ of a sheep, [one *tal*]*aimi-* [jug] of beer to the Tutelary Deity of [Mt. Šu]nnara,

§17′ [One *tuḫ*]*urai-* [bread], one right thigh[175] of a sheep, [one] *talaimi-* [jug] of beer to the Tutelary Deity of [the river Kummar]a,

§18′ One *tuḫurai-* bread, one right "double bone" of a sheep, [one *t*]*alaimi-* jug of beer to the Tutelary Deity of the river Kella,

§19′ One *tuḫurai-* bread, one front thigh of a sheep, one *talaimi-* jug of beer to the Tutelary Deity of Ḫallašša,

173. A body part in the groin used as a flesh offering. This festival utilizes a number of different parts of animals as flesh offerings; Goetze in his review of *KBo* 11, *JCS* 17 (1963) 63, notes this and compiles a list of them. ^{UZU}BAR.SÌL, ^{UZU}BAR.DÙ, and ^{UZU}*ḫarpi-* have not been identified.

174. See Friedrich, *HW 3. Erg.* 31, Goetze, *JCS* 17: 63.

175. See Otten apud Friedrich, *HW 2. Erg.* 16, Poetto, *KZ* 99 (1986) 220–22.

A = *KBo* 11.40 Obverse i (*transliteration cont.*)

§20′ 23′ [(1 NINDAtu-u-ḫ)]u-ra-i 1 UZUku-du-úr UDU EGIR-iz-zi
24′ [1 DUGta-l]a-i-mi-iš KAŠ URUTi-da-an-⸢da⸣-aš DLAMMA-ri[176]

§21′ 25′ [(1 NINDAtu-u-ḫ)]u-ra-i 1 UZUŠÀ-ya
B ii 26′ [(1 D)UGta-]la-i-mi-iš KAŠ URUAn-za-aš ⸢D⸣L[(AMMA-i)][177]

§22′ 27′ [1 NINDAtu-u-ḫ]u-[ra-i 1 UZU]x UDU x[
28′ [1 DUGta-la-i-mi-iš KAŠ UR]U[x DLAMMA-ri]

(the tablet breaks off)

A = *KBo* 11.40 Obverse ii[178] (*transliteration*)

§23′ x+1 p[í?-

§24′ 2′ 1 NINDAt[u-u-ḫu-ra-i 1 UZUx]
3′ ḪUR.SAGI[š-ki-ša-aš DLAMMA]

§25′ 4′ 1 NINDAtu-u-ḫu-r[a-i 1 UZUx *ŠA* La-ba-ar-na]
5′ ḫu-u-it-na-aš [DLAMMA-aš]
6′ 1 NINDAtu-u-ḫu-r[a-i 1 UZUx *ŠA* La-ba-ar-na]
7′ in-na-ra-u-wa[-aḫ-ḫu-u-wa-aš DLAMMA-aš]

§26′ 8′ 1 NINDAtu-u-ḫu-ra[-i 1 UZUx *ŠA* La-ba-ar-na]
9′ pal-ta-na-aš[179] D[LAMMA-ri]

§27 10′ 1 NINDAtu-u-ḫu-ra-⸢i⸣ [1 UZUx *ŠA* La-ba-ar-na]
11′ wa-li-pa-at-ta-a[š-ši-iš DLAMMA-aš]
12′ 1 NINDAtu-u-ḫu-ra-i [1 UZUx *ŠA* La-ba-ar-na]
13′ pa-ra-a ḫa-⸢an-da⸣-a[n-da-an-na-aš DLAMMA]

§28′ 14′ 1 NINDAtu-u-ḫu-ra-i 1 [UZUx *ŠA* La-ba-ar-na]
15′ TI-an-na-aš DLAMMA-ri x[
16′ 1 NINDAtu-u-ḫu-ra-i 1 UZUḫ[ar-pí-iš *ŠA* La-ba-ar-na]
17′ tar-ḫu-i-la-an-na-aš DLAM[MA-ri]

§29′ 18′ 1 NINDAtu-u-ḫu-ra-i 1 UZUŠÀ [*ŠA* La-ba-ar-na]
19′ tu-uz-zi-ya-aš DLAMMA-r[i]
20′ 1 NINDAtu-u-ḫu-ra-i 1 UZU[x *ŠA* La-ba-ar-na]
21′ za-aḫ-ḫi-ya-aš DLAMMA-ri x[
22′ ⸢1 NINDAtu⸣[-u-ḫ]u-ra-i 1 UZUŠ[À *ŠA* La-ba-ar-na]
23′ [pí-ra-an ḫu-]⸢u-i-ya⸣[-u-wa-aš? DLAMMA-ri]

(the tablet breaks off)

176. Text B ii 7′: DLAMMA-*i*.
177. Bottom of tablet in text B.
178. After a gap of an undetermined number of paragraphs.
179. The parallel *KUB* 2.1 ii 18 has UZUZAG.UDU-*aš*.

A = *KBo* 11.40 Obverse i (*translation cont.*)

§20′ One *tuḫurai-* bread, one rear thigh of a sheep, [one *tal*]*aimi-* [jug] of beer to the Tutelary Deity of Tidanda,

§21′ One *tuḫurai-* bread, one heart, one [*ta*]*laimi-* jug of beer to the Tutelary Deity of Anza,

§22′ [One *tuḫ*]*u*[*rai-* bread, one (flesh] offering) of a sheep x, [one *talaimi-* jug of beer to the Tutelary Deity of ...

(the tablet breaks off)

A = *KBo* 11.40 Obverse ii[180] (*translation*)

§23′ Traces only.

§24′ One *t*[*uḫurai-*] bread, [one (flesh offering) (to) the Tutelary Deity of] Mt. I[škiša],

§25′ One *tuḫur*[*ai-*] bread, [one (flesh offering) (to) the Tutelary Deity] of the animals [of the Labarna],
One *tuḫur*[*ai-*] bread, [one (flesh offering) (to) the Tutelary Deity of] the strengthen[ing of the Labarna],

§26′ One *tuḫurai-* bread, [one (flesh offering) to the Tutelary Deity] of the shoulder [of the Labarna],

§27′ One *tuḫurai-* bread, [one (flesh offering) (to) the Tutelary Deity o]f encircling(?) [of the Labarna],
One *tuḫurai-* bread, [one (flesh offering) (to) the Tutelary Deity of] the divine pow[er of the Labarna],

§28′ One *tuḫurai-* bread, one [(flesh offering)] to the Tutelary Deity x of the life [of the Labarna],
One *tuḫurai-* bread, one *ḫ*[*arpi-* to] the Tutelary Dei[ty] of the heroism [of the Labarna],

§29′ One *tuḫurai-* bread, one heart t[o] the Tutelary Deity of the army [of the Labarna],
One *tuḫurai-* bread, one (flesh [offering)] to the Tutelary Deity x of battle [of the Labarna],
One *tuḫurai-* bread, one hea[rt to the Tutelary Deity of] runnin[g before of the Labarna],

(the tablet breaks off)

180. After a gap of an undetermined number of paragraphs.

E = *KBo* 12.60[181] (*transliteration*)

§30′ x+1 ^{D}LAMMA-⸢i⸣[1 ^{NINDA}tu-ḫ]u?[-ra-i 1 ^{UZU}TI? *ŠA* La-ba-ar-na]
2′ $^{HUR.SAG}$Ki-da-u-wa-an-da-aš [^{D}LAMMA-i]
3′ 1 ^{NINDA}tu-ḫu-ra-i 1 ma-ni-in-ku-w[a-an-da ^{UZU}TI[182] *ŠA* La-ba-ar-na]
4′ pí-ḫa-ad-da-aš-ši-iš ^{D}LAM[MA-i]
5′ 1 ^{NINDA}tu-ḫu-ra-i 1 ^{UZU}da-an-ḫ[a-aš-ti *ŠA* La-ba-ar-na]
6′ šar-la-da-aš-ši-iš ^{D}LA[MMA-i]
7′ [1] ⸢^{NINDA}⸣tu!-ḫu-ra-i 1 ^{UZU}ḫar-pí-i[š *ŠA* La-ba-ar-na ^{GIŠ}TUKUL-aš ^{D}LAMMA-i]
8′ [1 ^{NINDA}t]u-ḫu-ra-i 1 ^{UZU}ḫar-pí-i[š *ŠA* La-ba-ar-na mu-wa-ad-da-la-ḫi-da-aš]
9′ [^{D}LAMMA-i] 1 ^{NINDA}t[u-ḫu-ra-i 1 ^{UZU}x

(the tablet breaks off)

F = *KUB* 55.25

Obverse[183] (*transliteration*)

§31′ x+1 [ ] x [
2′ (completely abraded away)

---

§32′ 3′ (completely abraded away)
4′ [ ] x [ ] ^{D}A-a-la[-aš]

---

§33′ 5′ [1 ^{NINDA}tu-ḫu-r]a-i 1 ^{UZU}BAR.SÌL [
6′ [ ] ⸢x⸣ ^{D}A-la- [aš]

---

§34′ 7′ [1 ^{NINDA}tu-ḫu-r]a-⸢i⸣ 1 ^{UZU}ḫar-pí-iš x[
8′ [gi-im-ra-aš] ^{D}A-a-la- a[š]

---

§35′ 9′ [1 ^{NINDA}tu-ḫu-ra-i] ⸢1 ^{UZU}⸣ḫar-piš KI.MIN mi-nu-ma[-aš ^{D}A-a-la-aš]

---

§36′ 10′ [1 ^{NINDA}tu-ḫu-ra-i] ⸢1 ^{UZU}⸣ḫar-pé-eš KI.MIN aš-šu-la-aš ^{D}⸢A⸣[-a-la-aš]

---

§37′ 11′ [1 ^{NINDA}tu-ḫu-ra-i 1 ^{UZU}ḫar-piš? K]I.MIN ^{D}A-la-aš *Š*[*A* ^{URU}*ḪA-AT-TI*]

---

§38′ 12′ [1 ^{NINDA}tu-ḫu-ra-i 1 ^{UZU}ḫar-piš? KI.MIN ^{D}A-l]a KARA[Š]

(the tablet breaks off)

181. After a gap of an undetermined number of paragraphs. Restored from the parallel *KUB* 2.1 iii 8–15.

182. See *CHD* sub *man(n)i (n)kuwant-* 1.a.2′.

183. After a gap of an undetermined number of paragraphs. Restored from the parallel *KUB* 2.1 iii 29–35. The reverse is almost completely lost, although we may read ^{D}*A-*]*la*[(-) in line 4′, $^{U]ZU}$*ku-du-úr* in 5′, and ^{D}*A-*[*la-* in 8′. Such minimal data have not allowed placement of the reverse into the main text of either festival.

E = *KBo* 12.60[184] (*translation*)

§30′ To the Tutelary Deity of [x],[185] [one *tuḫ*]*u*[*rai*- bread, one rib(?) to the Tutelary Deity] of Mt. Kidawanda [of the Labarna],

3′ One *tuḫurai*- bread, one shor[t rib(?) to] the Tutelary De[ity] of the *piḫadda*- [of the Labarna],

5′ One *tuḫurai*- bread, one "double [bone" to] the Tutelary [Deity] of praise [of the Labarna],

7′ [One] *tuḫurai*- bread, one *ḫarpi*- [to the Tutelary Deity of the weapon of the Labarna],

8′ [One *t*]*uḫurai*- [bread], one *ḫarpi*- [to the Tutelary Deity of the awe-inspiring ability(?) of the Labarna],

9′ One *t*[*uḫurai*-] bread, [one (flesh offering) ...

(the tablet breaks off)

F = *KUB* 55.25[186]

Obverse (*translation*)

§31′ Traces only.

§32′ Ala [of ...

§33′ [One *tuḫur*]*ai*- [bread], one BAR.SÌL, (to) Ala of x,

§34′ [One *tuḫur*]*ai*- [bread], one *ḫarpi*-, x (to) Ala [of the countryside],

§35′ [One *tuḫurai*- bread], one *ḫarpi*-, the same (to) [Ala of] kindliness,

§36′ [One *tuḫurai*- bread], one *ḫarpi*-, the same (to) A[la] of favor,

§37′ [One *tuḫurai*- bread, one *ḫarpi*-(?), the s]ame (to) Ala o[f Ḫatti],

§38′ [One *tuḫurai*- bread, one *ḫarpi*-(?), the same] to [Al]a of the arm[y],

(the tablet breaks off)

184. After a gap of an undetermined number of paragraphs.

185. From preceding lines now lost.

186. After a gap of an undetermined number of paragraphs.

B = *KUB* 40.108 Reverse v[187] (*transliteration*)

§39′ 1 1 ^{NINDA}tu-ḫu-ra-i! 1 ^{UZU}ḫar-pí-iš 1 ^{DUG}ta[-la-i-mi-iš KAŠ]
2 ^{D}A-a-la-aš pa-ra-a ḫa-an-da-an-da-a[n-na-aš]
3 1 ^{NINDA}tu-ḫu-ra-i 1 ^{UZU}ḫar-pí-iš 1 $^{DU[G}$ta-la-i-mi-iš KAŠ]
4 ^{D}A-a-la-aš ša-ra-a ḫal-zi-ya-⸢u⸣-w[a-aš]
5 1 ^{NINDA}tu-ḫu-ra-i 1 ^{UZU}x [1 ^{DUG}ta-la-i-mi-iš KAŠ]
6 ^{D}A-a-la-aš x[
7 ⸢x x⸣[

C = *KUB* 40.101 Obverse[188] (*transliteration*)

§40′ x+1 [^{D}A-a-la-aš *ŠA* ^{m}Tu-ut?-]⸢ḫa?-li?⸣-ya ^{D}A-a-la-aš
2′ [*ŠA* É.LUGAL *ŠA* ? ^{m}T]u-ut-ḫa-li-ya 1 ^{GIŠ}BANŠUR[189]

- - - - - - - - - - - - ————————————————————

§41′ 3′ [*ŠA* ^{m}Tu-ut-ḫa-l]i-ya *A-NA* ḪUR.SAG.MEŠ! da-pí-aš
4′ [1 ^{NINDA}tu-ḫu-ra-]⸢i⸣ 1 ^{UZU}TI GUD
5′ [*A-NA* $^{ḪUR.SAG}$Ḫ]u-ul-la 1 ^{NINDA}tu-ḫu-ra-i
6′ [1 ^{UZU}]x *A-NA* $^{ḪUR.SAG}$Tu-ut-ḫa-li-ya

A = *KBo* 11.40 Reverse v (*transliteration*)

C 2′ 1 ^{NINDA}tu-ḫu-ra-i 1 ^{UZU}da-an[190]-ḫ[(a-aš-ti)]
3′ *A-NA* $^{ḪUR.SAG}$Kam-ma-li-ya[Ø]
4′ 1 ^{NINDA}tu-ḫu-ra-i 1 ^{UZU}ku-du-úr [(*A-NA* $^{ḪUR.SAG}$Da-a-ḫa)]
5′ 1 ^{NINDA}tu-ḫu-ra-i 1 ^{UZU}ku-du-úr [$^{ḪUR.SAG}$P(iš-ku-ru-nu-wa)]
6′ 1 ^{NINDA}tu-ḫu-ra-i 1 ^{UZU}ḫar-pí-i[(š $^{ḪUR.SAG}$Da-ag-gur-qa)]
7′ 1 ^{NINDA}tu-ḫu-ra-i 1 ^{UZU}ku-du-úr [($^{ḪUR.SAG}$Ḫa-aḫ-ḫar-wa)]
8′ 1 ^{NINDA}tu-ḫu-ra-i 1 ^{UZU}ḫar-pí-iš [($^{ḪUR.SAG}$Šar-pa-aš)]
9′ 1 ^{NINDA}tu-ḫu-ra-i 1 ^{UZU}ḫar-pí-iš [$^{ḪUR.SAG}$Za-(li-ya-nu-ú)]
10′ 1 ^{NINDA}tu-ḫu-ra-i 1 ^{UZU}ḫar-pí-iš [($^{ḪUR.SAG}$Ša-re-eš-ša)]
11′ 1 ^{NINDA}tu-ḫu-ra-i 1 ^{UZU}ḫar-p[í-iš ^{f}(^{D}Ma-ra-aš-ša-an-da-aš)]
12′ 1 ^{NINDA}tu-ḫu-ra-i 1 ^{UZU}ḫar-p[í-iš *ŠA*]
13′ Ḫa-te-en-zu-wa a[(l-da-an-ni)]
14′ 1 ^{NINDA}tu-ḫu-ra-i 1 [(^{UZU}*MÁŠ*!-*QA* GUD)][191]
15′ *A-NA* $^{ḪUR.SAG}$K[(aš-šu-ú)]
16′ 1 ^{NINDA}tu-ḫu-ra[-i 1 ^{UZU}*MÁŠ-QA* GUD]
17′ *A-NA* $^{ḪUR.S}$[(^{AG}Ar-nu-wa-an-da)]

187. After a gap of an undetermined number of paragraphs.
188. After a gap of an undetermined number of paragraphs.
189. Restored from similar passages in the parallel festival, *KUB* 2.1 iii 21–25 and v 1–5, which have a different order.
190. Collation confirms this reading.
191. In text C the next three offerings are prescribed as KI.MIN, "the same."

B = *KUB* 40.108

Reverse v[192] (*translation*)

§39′ One *tuḫurai-* bread, one *ḫarpi-*, one *ta*[*laimi-*] jug [of beer] (to) Ala [of] divine power,
One *tuḫurai-* bread, one *ḫarpi-*, one [*talaimi-* jug of beer] (to) Ala [of] calling up,
One *tuḫurai-* bread, one (flesh [offering), one *talaimi-* jug of beer] (to) Ala [of x],
(Traces)

C = *KUB* 40.101

Obverse[193] (*translation*)

§40′ [(For) Ala of Tud]ḫaliya, Ala [of the palace of T]udḫaliya, one offering table.

---

§41′ To all the mountains [of Tudḫal]iya:
[One *tuḫura*]*i-* [bread], one rib of an ox [to Mt. Ḫ]ulla, one *tuḫurai-* bread, [one (flesh offering)] to Mt. Tudḫaliya,

A = *KBo* 11.40

Reverse v (*translation*)

One *tuḫurai-* bread, one "double bone" to Mt. Kammaliya,
2′ One *tuḫurai-* bread, one thigh to Mt. Daḫa,
One *tuḫurai-* bread, one thigh to [Mt. P]iškurunuwa,
6′ One *tuḫurai-* bread, one *ḫarpi-* to Mt. Daggurqa,
One *tuḫurai-* bread, one thigh to Mt. Ḫaḫḫarwa,
8′ One *tuḫurai-* bread, one *ḫarpi-* to Mt. Šarpa,
One *tuḫurai-* bread, one *ḫarpi-* (to) [Mt. Za]liyanu,
10′ One *tuḫurai-* bread, one *ḫarpi-* to Mt. Šareššа,
One *tuḫurai-* bread, one *ḫar*[*pi-*] (to) the river Maraššanda,
12′ One *tuḫurai-* bread, one *ḫarp*[*i-*] to the spring [of] Ḫatenzuwa,
14′ One *tuḫurai-* bread, one ox hide to Mt. Kaššu,
16′ One *tuḫurai-* bread, [one ox hide] to Mt. Arnuwanda,

---

192. After a gap of an undetermined number of paragraphs.

193. After a gap of an undetermined number of paragraphs.

A = *KBo* 11.40

Reverse v (*transliteration cont.*)

§41′ 18′ 1 ^{NINDA}tu-ḫ[u-ra-i 1 ^{UZU}*MÁŠ-QA* GUD $^{\text{ḪUR.S}}$(^{AG}A-ma-na)]
(*cont.*) 19′ 1 ^{NINDA}tu-ḫ[u-ra-i 1 ^{UZU}*MÁŠ-QA* GUD $^{\text{ḪUR.S}}$(^{AG}Da-ḫal-mu-na-aš)]
20′ 1 ^{NINDA}tu-ḫ[u-r(a-i 1 ^{UZU}ku-du-úr) $^{\text{ḪUR.SA}}$($^{\text{G?}}$[194]Na-ḫu-ra-an-x-an-ta-aš)]
21′ 1 ^{NINDA}tu[-ḫu-ra-(i 1 ^{UZU}ŠÀ) *A-N*(*A*? x[195] I-šu-wa-an-da-aš)]
22′ 1 ^{NINDA}tu[-ḫu-ra-i 1 ^{UZU}x $^{\text{ḪUR.SA}}$($^{\text{G?}}$[196] x-ya-aš)]
C 23′ 1 ^{NINDA}t[u-ḫu-ra-i (1 ^{UZU}ku-du-úr)
24′ 1 ^{NINDA}[tu-ḫu-ra-i 1 ^{UZU}x

(the tablet breaks off)

D = *KUB* 40.107

Reverse iv[197] (*transliteration*)

§42′ x+1 1 ^{NINDA}tu-ḫu-ra-i ^{UZU}ḫar-pí-i[š *A-NA*
2′ 1 ^{NINDA}tu-ḫu-ra-i ^{UZU}ELLAG.GÙN.A [*A-NA*
3′ 1 ^{NINDA}tu-ḫu-ra-i ^{UZU}TI *A-N*[*A*
4′ 1 ^{NINDA}tu-ḫu-ra-i ^{UZU}TI *A-N*[*A*
5′ 1 ^{NINDA}tu-ḫu-ra-i ^{UZU}ḫar-pí-iš [*A-NA*
6′ 1 ^{NINDA}tu-ḫu-ra-i ^{UZU}ku-du-úr [*A-NA*
7′ 1 ^{NINDA}tu-ḫu-ra-i ^{UZU}ḫar-pí-iš *A*[*-NA*
8′ 1 ^{NINDA}tu-ḫu-ra-i ^{UZU}ḫar-pí-iš p[u?-[198]
9′ 1 ^{NINDA}tu-ḫu-ra-i ^{UZU}ḫar-pí-iš[
10′ 1 ^{NINDA}tu-ḫu-ra-i ^{UZU}ḫar-pí-i[š
11′ 1 ^{NINDA}tu-ḫu-ra-i ^{UZU}ḫar-p[í-iš
12′ 1 ^{NINDA}tu-ḫu-ra-i ^{UZU}[
13′ 1 ^{NINDA}tu-ḫu-ra-i ^{UZU}ḫ[ar-pí-iš
14′ *ŠA* KUR.KUR.ḪI.A ḫu-u-ma-an-da-a[š] $^{\text{⸢D⸣}}$UTU-*ŠI* [ku-i-e-eš
ši-ya-at-tal-li-iš-ki-iz-zi][199]
15′ 1 ^{NINDA}tu-ḫu-ra-i ^{UZU}ḫar-pí-iš ḪUR.SAG.ḪI.⸢A⸣ [ḫu-u-ma-an-da-aš
16′ ⸢x x⸣[ ]⸢x x⸣ *MA-ḪAR* ^{D}UTU-*ŠI* ku-i-⸢e⸣[-eš

---

194. Or ^{f}(^{D}?
195. The sign looks like *ar*, which I cannot interpret meaningfully.
196. Or ^{f}(^{D}?
197. After a gap of an undetermined number of paragraphs.
198. Or *še*?[- ...
199. This is the expected restoration here and in 16′, although it would assume a wider column than is indicated by the restorations in §43′.

A = *KBo* 11.40

Reverse v (*translation cont.*)

18′ One *tuḫ*[*urai-*] bread, [one ox hide] to [M]t. Amana,
One *tuḫ*[*urai-*] bread, [one ox hide] (to) [M]t. Daḫalmuna,
20′ One *tuḫurai-* bread, one thigh (to) [M]t.(?)[200] *Naḫuran-x-anta*?
One *tu*[*ḫura*]*i-* bread, one heart [t]o? «x?» *Išuwanda* ??
22′ One *tu*[*ḫurai-*] bread, [one (flesh offering)] (to) [M]t.(?)[201] *X-ya-aš*,
One *t*[*uḫurai-*] bread, one thigh [to DN],
24′ One [*tuḫurai-*] bread, [one (flesh offering) to DN],

(the tablet breaks off)

D = *KUB* 40.107

Reverse iv[202] (*translation*)

§42′ One *tuḫurai-* bread, (one) *ḫarpi-* [to
2′ One *tuḫurai-* bread, (one) kidney [to
One *tuḫurai-* bread, (one) rib t[o
4′ One *tuḫurai-* bread, (one) rib t[o
One *tuḫurai-* bread, (one) *ḫarpi-* [to
6′ One *tuḫurai-* bread, (one) thigh [to
One *tuḫurai-* bread, (one) *ḫarpi- p*[*u-* to
8′ One *tuḫurai-* bread, (one) *ḫarpi-* [to
One *tuḫurai-* bread, (one) *ḫarpi-* [to
10′ One *tuḫurai-* bread, (one) *ḫarp*[*i-* to
One *tuḫurai-* bread, (one) *ḫarp*[*i-*
12′ One *tuḫurai-* bread, (one) (flesh [offering) to
One *tuḫurai-* bread, (one) *ḫ*[*arpi-* to x]
14′ of all the land [which] His Majesty [regularly hunts]
One *tuḫurai-* bread, one *ḫarpi-* to all the mountains, ... which before His Majesty [...]

---

200. Or river.
201. Or river.
202. After a gap of an undetermined number of paragraphs.

A = *KBo* 11.40 Reverse vi (*transliteration*)

§43′ x+1 [ ]x[203]

D iv 17′ 2′ [1 ^{NINDA}tu-ḫu-r(a-)]⸢i⸣ 1[204] ^{UZU}ḫar-pí-iš ḪUR.⸢SAG.MEŠ⸣[205] ḫu-u-ma-an-te-eš

3′ [^{D}UTU-*Š*(*I* ku-)]i-e-eš ši-ya-at-tal-li-iš-ki-iz-zi[206]

4′ [1 ^{NINDA}t(u-ḫ)]u-ra-i 1 ^{UZU}ḫar-pí-iš ḪUR.SAG.MEŠ ḫu-u-ma-an-te-eš

5′ [*ŠA* KU(R ^{UR})]^{U}UGU-*TI*[207] ^{D}UTU-*ŠI* ku-i-e-eš

6′ [(ši-y)a-a]t-ta-al-li-iš-ki-iz-zi

7′ [1 ^{NINDA}t(u-ḫ)]u-ra-i 1 ^{UZU}ḫar-pí-iš *A-NA* ^{ÍD}Ma-a-la

8′ [1 ^{NINDA}t(u-ḫ)]u-ra-i 1 ^{UZU}TI *A-NA* ^{ÍD}Ma-am-ma-ra-an-da

9′ [1 ^{NINDA}t(u-ḫ)]u-ra-i 1 ^{UZU}TI *A-NA* ^{ÍD}Gur-ma-li-ya

10′ [1 ^{NINDA}t(u-ḫ)]u-ra-i 1 ^{UZU}ḫar-pí-iš ḪUR.SAG.MEŠ ḫu-u-ma-an-te-eš

11′ [ÍD.MEŠ[208]] ḫu-u-ma-an-te-eš *ŠA* KUR ^{URU}Ḫur-ri

12′ [^{D}UTU-*ŠI*]⸢ku-i-e⸣-eš ši-ga!-at-tal-li-<(iš)>-ki-iz-zi

13′ [(1 ^{NINDA}t)u-ḫ]u-ra-i 1 ^{UZU}pár-ku-i ḫa-aš-ta-i

14′ [ḪUR.SAG.MEŠ] ḫu-u-ma-an-te-eš ÍD.MEŠ ḫu-u-ma-an-te-eš

15′ [*ŠA* KUR ^{UR}]^{U}Ar-za-u-wa ^{D}UTU-*ŠI* ku-i-e-eš

16′ [ši-ya-ta]l-li-iš-ki-iz-zi

17′ [1 ^{NINDA}tu-ḫu-r]a-i 1 ^{UZU}⸢ÉLLAG⸣[209] ḪUR.SAG.MEŠ ÍD.MEŠ

D iv 30′ 18′ [*ŠA* KUR ^{UR}]^{U}Ma-a-ša ^{D}UTU-*ŠI* ku-i-e-eš

19′ [ši-ya-a]t-tal-li-iš-ki-iz-zi

20′ [1 ^{NINDA}tu-ḫ]u-ra-i ^{UZU}ZAG.UDU ḪUR.SAG.MEŠ ÍD.MEŠ

21′ [*ŠA* KUR ^{UR}]^{U}Lu-uq-qa-a ^{D}UTU-*ŠI* ku-i-e-eš

22′ [ši-ya-tal-l]e-eš-ki-iz-zi

23′ [1 ^{NINDA}tu-ḫu-r]a-i 1 ^{UZU}ḫar-pí-iš

24′ [ḪUR.SAG.MEŠ Í]D.MEŠ *ŠA* KUR ^{URU}Ga-aš-ga

25′ [^{D}UTU-*ŠI*] ku-i-e-eš ši-ya-tal-le-eš-ki-iz-zi

26′ [1 ^{NINDA}tu-ḫ]u-ra-i ^{UZU}ÉLLAG.GÙN.A ḪUR.SAG.MEŠ ÍD.MEŠ

27′ [*ŠA* KUR ^{URU}*Ḫ*]*A-AT-TI A-NA* ^{D}LAMMA ku-i-e-eš

28′ [KUR.KUR.MEŠ ḫu-u-ma-]an-te-eš 1 ^{GIŠ}BANŠUR

- - - - - - - ——————————————

- - - - - - - ——————————————

Colophon (*transliteration*)

29′ [DUB] 1 KAM *Ú-UL QA-TI*

30′ [*I-NA*] É ^{D}LAMMA gi-im-ma-an-d[a-aš

31′ [*A-NA*] ^{GIŠ}ḪUR-kán ḫa-an-d[a-an

203. This line is probably the same as D (*KUB* 40.107) iv 16′. There is no paragraph line in *KBo* 11.40.
204. Although text D prescribes the same flesh offerings as the main text, it does not specify a number.
205. From the Festival of Group Offerings, Bo 6113 iv 17′ and elsewhere: ḪUR.SAG.ḪI.A.
206. Text D iv 18′: *ši-ya-tal-li-iš-ki-iz*[*-zi*].
207. Text D iv 20′: [*ŠA* KU]R ^{URU}*I-LI-TI.*
208. Text D iv 25′: [ÍD.ḪI.]⸢A⸣.
209. Text D iv 29′: ^{UZU}ÉLLAG.GÙN.A.

A = *KBo* 11.40

Reverse vi (*translation*)

§43′ [One *tuḫur*]*ai*- [bread], one *ḫarpi*- (to) all the mountains which His [Majesty] regularly hunts:

4′ [One] *tuḫurai*- [bread], one *ḫarpi*- (to) all the mountains [of] the upper [la]nd which His Majesty regularly hunts,

7′ [One] *tuḫurai*- [bread], one *ḫarpi*- to the river Mala,

8′ [One] *tuḫurai*- [bread], one rib to the river Mammaranda,

[One] *tuḫurai*- [bread], one rib to the river Gurmaliya,

10′ [One] *tuḫurai*- [bread], one *ḫarpi*- (to) all the mountains (and) all [the rivers] of the Hurrian land which [His Majesty] regularly hunts,

13′ One *t*[*uḫ*]*urai*- bread, one bare bone(?) (to) all [the mountains] (and) all the rivers [of the land] of Arzawa which His Majesty regularly [hu]nts,

17′ [One *tuḫur*]*ai*- [bread], one kidney (to) the mountains (and) rivers [of the land of] Maša which His Majesty regularly [hu]nts,

20′ [One *tuḫ*]*urai*- [bread], one shoulder (to) the mountains (and) rivers [of] the Luqqa [land] which His Majesty regularly [hu]nts,

23′ [One *tuḫur*]*ai*- [bread], one *ḫarpi*- (to) [the mountains (and) r]ivers of the Kaškean land which [His Majesty] regularly hunts,

26′ [One *tuḫ*]*urai*- [bread], one kidney (to) the mountains (and) rivers [of the land of Ḫ]atti. For the Tutelary Deity of [al]l of which [lands], one offering table.

Colophon (*translation*)

One [tablet], not finished. [In] the winter temple of the Tutelary Deity. Tru[e to] the wooden tablet.

FESTIVAL TEXTS OF UNCERTAIN ATTRIBUTION

CTH 682.3: *KBo* 12.59

This tablet is included here because the festival described therein shows some resemblance to sections of the Festival for All the Tutelary Deities. The festival of *KBo* 12.59 does not, however, mention tutelary deities except Zitḫariya once in broken context. The similarity occurs in the portion of the festival in which the gods to be worshipped are geographical locations described as those in which the king regularly hunts or campaigns. The same formula is used for some of the deities in the Festival for All the Tutelary Deities.[210] The use of *tuḫurai-* bread for the bread offerings also parallels the Festival of Individual Offerings. These similarities do not necessitate taking this text as part of the Festival for All the Tutelary Deities, but it may have been a part of the ceremony now lost.

Transliteration

Obverse i

§1′ x+1 [LUGAL-uš ku-i-e-eš ši-ya-tal-li-i]š-ki-i[z-zi ḫu-ur-ni-iš-ki-iz-zi]

§2′ 2′ [MÁŠ.GAL-]aš 1-an Ša-lu-wa-an-ta ḪUR.SAG-i ^{m}T[u-ut-ḫa-li-ya-aš]
3′ [LUGAL-u]š ku-in ši-ya-tal-li-iš-ki-iz-zi ḫu-ur[-ni-is-ki-iz-zi]

§3′ 4′ [MÁŠ.GA]L-aš 1-an Ḫa-le-en-zu-wa ÍD-i ^{m}Tu-ut-ḫa-li[-ya-aš LUGAL-uš]
5′ [ku-i]n la-aḫ-ḫi-iš-ki-iz-zi Ku-um-ra ÍD-i Ke-e[l-la ÍD-i]
6′ [^{m}T]u-ut-ḫa-li-ya-aš LUGAL-uš ku-i-e-eš ši-ya-tal-li[-iš-k]i-iz-zi
7′ [ḫ]u-u-wa-ar-ni-iš-ki-iz-zi Šal-ma-ku[211] ÍD-i
8′ [^{D}G]AZ.BA.A.A-aš a-aš-ši-ya-an-ti Še-ḫi-ri-ya ÍD-i
9′ [^{m}T]u-ut-ḫa-li-ya-aš a-aš-ši-ya-an-ti

§4′ 10′ [ŠU.NIGIN] 14 MÁŠ.GAL

§5′ 11′ [o o o o] ^{UZU}NÍG.GIG-ši ^{NINDA}tu-ḫu-u-ra-i ^{D}Za-aḫ-pu-na-i
12′ [^{m}Tu-ut-ḫ]a-⸢li-ya⸣-aš LUGAL-wa-aš pí-ra-an ti-an-ti![212] (eras.)

§6′ 13′ [o o o o o o o o o]⸢x x⸣ ^{NINDA}tu-ḫu-ra-i ^{D}x[
14′ [o o o o o o o o o o]x-iz-zi LUGAL-u[š

(the tablet breaks off)

210. Utilized in both the Festival of Group Offerings, *KUB* 2.1 vi 1–9, and the Festival of Individual Offerings, *KBo* 11.40 vi 2′–26′.

211. Or *Šal-ma-ma*. Del Monte and Tischler, *RGTC* 6:546, read *Šal-ma-ku* for this hapax legomenon.

212. Scribal error for *ti-an-zi*.

Translation

Obverse i

§1′ [... which the king reg]ula[rly hunts (and) chases].

§2′ One [billy goat] to the mountain Šaluwanta which T[udḫaliya the kin]g regularly hunts (and) cha[ses].

§3′ One [billy goa]t to the river of Ḫalenzuwa in [whi]ch Tudḫali[ya the king] regularly campaigns.
To the river Kumra (and) [to the river] Kel[la] which Tudḫaliya the king reg[ula]rly hunts (and) chases.
To the river Šalmaku, the beloved of Ḫuwaššana, to the river Šeḫiriya, the beloved of Tudḫaliya.

§4′ [Total:] 14 billy goats.

§5′ [x], liver, *tuḫurai-* bread for Zaḫpuna they place before [Tudḫ]aliya the king.

§6′ [x], x, *tuḫurai-* bread to D[N ...] he/she x-s. The king[...

(the tablet breaks off)

CTH 682.3: *KBo* 12.59 (*transliteration cont.*)

Reverse iii[213]

Only a few signs are preserved from the beginnings of the lines of **§§7′–10′**.

Reverse iv[214]

§11′	x+1	[^{UZU} o o o o ZA]G-na-an ^{NINDA}tu-ḫu-⸢ra-i⸣-y[a da]-a-i $^{⸢D?⸣}$[o o o]
	2′	[o o o]x An-zi-ya TÚL-i ^{m}Tu-ut-ḫa-li-ya-aš LUG[AL-wa-aš]
	3′	[a-aš-ši-ya-a]n-ta-aš ú-e-te-na-aš [ ]
§12′	4′	[^{UZU} o o o ^{NI}]^{NDA}tu-ḫu-ra-i-ya Ḫa-ri-nu-um-ma ḪUR.SAG-i
	5′	[^{m}Tu-ut-ḫ]a-li-ya-aš LUGAL-uš ku-in ^{GIŠ}ER[IN w]a-ar-ḫu-«wa-»nu-ut
§13′	6′	[^{UZU} o o o]x-an ḫa-aš-ta-i ^{NINDA}tu-ḫu-ra-i-ya :ḫi-iš-da-a
	7′	[o o o o o -]li ^{m}Tu-ut-ḫa-li-ya-an LUGAL-un
	8′	[o o o o o]x URU-an [k]u-i-e-eš uš-kán-zi
§14′	9′	[o o o o o r]a?-an-ta i-ya-an-zi
§15′	10′	[^{UZU}o o o o]x ^{NINDA}tu-ḫu-u-ra-i-ya da-a-i nu kiš-an me-ma-i
	11′	[o o o o o o]x ^{D}Za-aḫ-pu-na-a ḫu-u-ma-an-ta-aš
	12′	[o o o o o LUGAL SA]L.LUGAL-aš
§16′	13′	[^{UZU}o o ^{NINDA}tu-ḫu-r]a-i-ya da-a-i nu kiš-an me-⸢ma-i⸣
	14′	[o o o o o ^{D}Zi-i]t-ḫa-ri-ya-aš in-x[o o o]

(the tablet breaks off)

213. After a large gap of an undetermined number of paragraphs.

214. After a large gap of an undetermined number of paragraphs.

Reverse iii[215]

§§ 7′–10′ continue the flesh offerings of the festival.

Reverse iv[216]

---

§11′ He places a [ri]ght [(flesh offering)] (and) *tuḫurai-* bread. [To] D[N ...] To the spring Anziya of the beloved water(?) of Tudḫaliya the ki[ng].

---

§12′ [(Flesh offering)], *tuḫurai-* [br]ead to the mountain Ḫarinumma which [Tudḫ]aliya the king has planted with ced[ar].

---

§13′ [x]-bone, *tuḫurai-* bread, *ḫišda*, the [x] who regularly see Tudḫaliya the king (and) the [x] city.

---

§14′ They make [... *-r*]*anta*.

---

§15′ [(Flesh offering)] and *tuḫurai-* bread he places. He recites as follows: [x?], Zaḫpuna, all[217] [the x, the king and qu]een.

---

§16′ [(Flesh offering)] and [*tuḫur*]*ai-* [bread] he places. He recites as follows: [x] of [Zi]tḫariya *in-x*[...].

(the tablet breaks off)

215. After a large gap of an undetermined number of paragraphs.

216. After a large gap of an undetermined number of paragraphs.

217. Although *ḫumantaš* in normal syntax would follow the word it modifies, sense and morphology indicate that it should modify not ᴰZaḫpuna, but rather whatever followed in the break.

CTH 682.4: *KUB* 51.36

This and the following text fragment have been published and identified as part of a festival dedicated to all the tutelary deities since Archi's article was published. They are too fragmentary to be identified as duplicates to preserved portions of the attributed festival texts. It is not even certain that either of them is part of the same festivals described by the main texts.

The obverse is not sufficiently well preserved to yield a coherent translation of the festival procedure. The mention of [all] the names of Ala in line 11 and Karzi and Ḫapa[ntaliya] in line 14 indicate that this text may be part of the festival for all the LAMMA and Ala deities, but with so little preserved text we cannot match it with any part of that festival as preserved.

Transliteration

Obverse

§1 1]x MÁŠ.GAL.ḪI.A an-da x[
2 *A-NA*? $^{\text{LÚ.M}}$]^{EŠ}MUḪALDIM 2 UGULA $^{\text{LÚ.MEŠ}}$NA[.GADA p]í-ra-an e[-ša-an-ta-ri]
3] 3 *ME* 50 MÁŠ.GAL [ḫ]u-u-kán-na-aš
4 EGIR?-p]a da-a-u-wa-x[ḫu-u-m]a?-an 3-*ŠÚ* ḫu-⸢u⸣[-kán-zi?]

§2 5]x-kán pa-⸢a⸣[-iz -z]i

§3 6 LUGAL?-]uš ti-ya-z[i o o o -a]n BAL-ti

§4 7 LUGAL-]uš ti-ya[-zi o o o o]
8]x ši-ip-pa-an-d[a-an-zi 1 U]DU 1 ⸢GUD.ŠE⸣ x[
9]2[218] GUD.AMAR.MAḪ x[o o o] [ ]x[
10]x-ar 1 UDU! ŠE 1 [o o]x x[ ]
11 ḪUR.SAG.ḪI.]A ^{URU}*ḪA-AT-TI ŠUM*$^{\text{ḪI.A}}$ ⸢^{D}⸣A-la-⸢a⸣[-aš ḫu-u-ma-an-da-aš]
12] ḪUR.SAG.ḪI.A ÍD.MEŠ [ ]

§5 13] x 2 SILA$_4$ É.ŠÀ KÙ.GA ši-i[p-pa-an-da-an-zi]

§6 14 -m]a?-aš-ma ^{D}Kar-zi ^{D}Ḫa-pa[-an-ta-li-ya]
15]x pé-en-ni-ya-an-z[i]
16]x ap-pa-an-z[i

(the tablet breaks off)

Reverse

§7′ x+1 (Only traces preserved.)
2′ (-)p]é?-eš-ša-na[(-)
3′–4′ (Only traces preserved.)

218. Or 3.

CTH 682.5: *KUB* 52.100

This text does not fit as a duplicate into the preserved portion of any of the other texts of the festival. It is a fragment of what looks like an extensive list of tutelary deities and therefore is likely to be part of the same festival. Like the Festival of Individual Offerings it contains descriptions of the offerings for individual deities.

Transliteration

x+1] x[

2′] ⌈^{D}⌉LAMMA ^{GIŠ}TIR ^{D}G[AL.ZU?

3′] ^{D}LAMMA.LÍL GUB-aš 1-*ŠU* ⌈e⌉[-ku-zi

4′]x ^{D}LAMMA É.DINGIR-*LIM* ^{D}LAMMA [

5′]x ^{D}LAMMA *AŠ-RI* ^{D}LAMMA LUGAL x[

6′]x ^{D}LAMMA ^{KUŠ}gur-ša-aš GUB-aš 1-*Š*[*U* e-ku-zi

7′] ^{D}Ḫa-pa-li$_{x}$-ya-an TUŠ-aš 1[-*ŠU* e-ku-zi

8′] ^{D}Du-uḫ-ka-ma-x[

9′] NINDA KAŠ x[

(the tablet breaks off)

COMMENTARY

Each of the two versions of this festival requires a long and involved ceremony. The evidence of *KUB* 44.16, which duplicates part of *KBo* 22.189 on its obverse and part of *KUB* 2.1 on its reverse, indicates the presence of at least one tablet before *KUB* 2.1 in the series required to complete the Festival of Group Offerings. The Festival of Individual Offerings probably also required at least a two tablet series to complete its description. The festivals are long because they strive for completeness in circumscribing the province of the tutelary deity, and they are the best evidence we have for the Hittite conception of what tutelary deities might be expected to protect. Their great interest stems from the theological exploration embodied in their ceremony. This is most clear in *KUB* 2.1, which as preserved is almost exclusively a list of very precisely described LAMMA and Ala deities.

In the festivals the tutelary deities are organized in groups to some extent; for instance in *KUB* 2.1 the first column is mostly LAMMA deities of various locations and the second column is devoted to LAMMA deities mostly of Labarna's attributes and possessions. Following this are the Ala deities of various attributes and areas of the kingdom intermingled. The last major element in the list is a series of offerings to the major regions of the king's domain.

The list of Ala deities begins only after that for LAMMA deities is completed, and it duplicates some of the characteristics and epithets of the LAMMA deities. DLAMMA and DAla are two distinct representations of the protective spirit; so much is clear from the overlap in this text, in which there are for example both a LAMMA and Ala tutelary deity of the army, of divine power (*para ḫandandatar*), and of many cities and mountains. However, the majority of epithets in this systematized list of gods as preserved occur with either the LAMMA or the Ala deities, which indicates the different spheres in which these two manifestations of the protective genius might operate. In *Chapter 1* it is argued that DLAMMA and DAla are a divine couple, both tutelary deities. Here we see them together in a few cases but in general controlling different areas. These texts are the only extensive evidence we have for how these two gods differed in Hittite perceptions. Many of the epithets of LAMMA and Ala deities are unique or very rare. This at times renders their understanding difficult but also serves as an indication of how far-ranging was this description of the nature of the tutelary deity in the Hittite universe. This is not a list of the standard divine epithets haphazardly applied to tutelary deities but rather a catalogue of very specific and distinctive deities to guard and protect narrowly defined aspects of the king's and the state's life.

In §33′ of the Festival of Group Offerings (*KUB* 2.1 iii 26), the point at which the Ala deities begin to be listed, there is a noticeable change in syntax in the titles. Whereas in the list of LAMMA epithets, the name LAMMA almost always came last in the phrase, with the names of the Ala deities they tend to come first in the phrase "to Ala of ... ," in Akkadian or Sumerian syntax. This use of Akkadian syntax with the Ala names conditioned my understanding of the names beginning in iv 5 which include the Labarna element.

Many of the LAMMA titles are complemented DLAMMA-*i* or DLAMMA-*ri*, some are DLAMMA-*aš*, and the others occur without complement. In *KBo* 11.40 i 24′ DLAMMA-*ri* has the variant in the duplicate *KUB* 40.108 ii 7′ DLAMMA-*i*. This kind of inconsistency demonstrates the care needed in deriving meaning from the morphology of these phonetic complements. Perhaps some of the differences in Hittite complementation on the Sumerogram LAMMA are important and reflect different underlying Hittite names for these gods. Because of the great consistency in using the Sumerian name for this god, we cannot draw on much outside evidence to indicate what those names may be. In several of the texts treated in this work there are examples of the name Inara alternating with DLAMMA. This name could be behind the writing DLAMMA-*ri*, but it is not necessarily so. Because the emphasis in this text is on the variety of epithets, I see no need to postulate different Hittite names behind the different complementations of the Sumerogram in the festival. Most of the LAMMA deities in the list have been understood as dative case; see Güterbock, *SBo* II: 8 with n. 28, on understanding these names as dative. Ala is portrayed in a unique way in this text. In other texts Ala is the name of one particular deity and does not occur with epithets. She is a goddess who needs no further identifying title. In this festival, however, the name Ala serves as a kind of title in parallel structure with DLAMMA. As mentioned in the translation, the case of D*A-a-la-aš*, the form consistently used throughout the text, is problematic. On the analogy of the preponderance of the dative-locative case for the LAMMA deities, one could take ^{D}*Alaš* as plural dative-locative. However, the use of the Luwian genitival adjective in the nominative case in *KUB* 2.1 iii 44-48 and elsewhere indicates that singular nominative should be understood for the form ^{D}*Alaš*. I have preserved in the translation distinctions of case in the Hittite, although in lists such as this the cases often get confused, so we should not ascribe too much meaning to this.

The list of deities presents some difficult points of translation, primarily because the syntax of the epithets varies considerably and because most of the epithets are expressed with nouns in a genitive construction. Some of them are expressed with Luwian genitival adjectives, which consistently appear in the nominative regardless of the case of the noun that they modify. Because of the way the genitive constructions are strung together in the titles, it becomes problematic in places to determine the relationship between the various elements. The primary problem is deciding whether certain attributes belong to the Labarna or to the tutelary deity. There has been some discussion of this in past scholarship, although there has been no comprehensive statement put forward by any scholar that all the ambiguous phrases are to be interpreted either as Labarna's attributes or the attributes of the tutelary deity. Güterbock[219] suggests that at least some of the lines are to be interpreted as listing tutelary deities of the various attributes of Labarna. Friedrich,[220] interpreting a few isolated lines of *KUB* 2.1, consistently takes the genitives as indicating attributes of ^{D}LAMMA, for example ii 23-24: [*ŠA Labarn*]*a tuziyaš* ^{D}LAMMA-*ri* [*ŠA Labar*]*na zaḫḫiyaš* ^{D}LAMMA-*ri* "[Seiner Majestä]t Schutzgotte des Heeres, (24) [Seiner Majes]tät Schutzgotte der Schlacht." Forrer[221] and Goetze[222] show evidence for interpreting selected lines as listing attributes of Labarna, not of the tutelary deity. We should not attempt to interpret all the phrases including both Labarna and ^{D}LAMMA in the genitive one way or the other; each line must be interpreted individually according to the best sense. The varied syntax, seen especially in §31′ of the Festival of Group Offerings (*KUB* 2.1 i 42-51), with both Hittite and Akkadian word order, indicates the variation in the text and the consequent need for flexibility in interpreting for sense.[223]

Given the unique nature of these festivals, we naturally wonder about the date of their composition. Are they an early manifestation of Hittite theological speculation, or do they demonstrate a late development and thus an increasing sophistication in Hittite religious perceptions? Archi[224] suggests that all the texts which he treats are to be dated to the reign of Tudḫaliya IV in the late 13th century. All of the copies are New Script; they may all

219. *SBo* II: 8.

220. *ZA* NF 1 (1924) 10–11.

221. *KlF* 1 (1930) 275–76.

222. *KlF* 1: 406–08.

223. Archi, pp. 90–91 mentions some of these difficulties, but he contents himself with pointing out that some of the epithets are ambiguous without giving his own opinion in every case. His translating of the epithets out of context does not always allow him to make his interpretation clear.

224. *SMEA* 16 (1975) 92.

even date from a period as late as Tudḫaliya IV.[225] However, indications in the language of some of the copies suggest an older, perhaps even Old Hittite, original of this text. *KUB* 44.16 of the Festival of Group Offerings has in ii 8′ an Old Hittite sentence particle in the sequence *ta-at*, and *KUB* 11.21 v 15′ has *ta-an-kán*. In *KUB* 40.107+ of the Festival of Individual Offerings, we have *ta-aš-kán* in i 12′ and [*t*]*a* in i 23′. *KBo* 22.189 ii 8 of the Festival of Group Offerings has ᴰ*Inaraš parna paizzi*, an example of the Old Hittite allative case. In *KBo* 12.59 i 12′ the postposition *piran* governs the genitive LUGAL-*waš*, an Old Hittite construction. Thus *KUB* 44.16, *KUB* 11.21, and *KBo* 22.189 of the Festival of Group Offerings, *KUB* 40.107 of the Festival of Individual Offerings, and *KBo* 12.59 of uncertain attribution may go back to Old Hittite prototypes.

The name of Tudḫaliya is quite prominent in most of the copies of the Festival for All the Tutelary Deities, a feature which is rather striking, as festivals usually transcended a given king's reign and therefore did not specify monarchs by name. His presence in the descriptions of this festival indicate his role in at least the commissioning of the copying of the tablets. However, in *KBo* 11.40 he does not appear. In column vi, which parallels the description in *KUB* 2.1 column vi of Tudḫaliya's hunting grounds, the king is denoted simply by ᴰUTU-*ŠI* "His Majesty." The consistency of his presence in the other exemplars emphasizes his absence in *KBo* 11.40; had this text been written or copied during his reign his name surely would have appeared in the catalogue of the kingdom's districts in column vi. This one copy of the festival therefore may represent a tablet antecedent to Tudḫaliya IV. Perhaps it is even the model that he used in the copies made during his reign. His use of older models is suggested also by *KBo* 12.59, in which the Old Hittite construction of genitive plus postposition is retained (i 12′), but which also mentions Tudḫaliya (i 12′, iv 2′, 5′, 7′) specifically. There must have been an Old Hittite archetype for the festival, possibly in both of its forms. Or the original festival may have been the Festival of Individual Offerings, based on the absence of Tudḫaliya in *KBo* 11.40. The Old Hittite forms in some texts of the Festival of Group Offerings could have been copied when that festival was being composed on the earlier model.

This exploration of tutelary deities is thus an early manifestation of the Hittite quest to perceive (and placate) all of their gods and not a special expression of Tudḫaliya's unique concentration on the religion of his kingdom.[226] That notwithstanding, the fact remains that he took a great interest in this festival. One of the last Hittite kings, he was extremely active in religious reorganization by making one of his major priorities a census of the religious resources of his kingdom.[227] He evinced a deep concern for maintaining the cult ceremony which ensured the prosperity of his realm by keeping the gods satisfied. The great number of copies of the Festival for All the Tutelary Deities from his reign attest to

225. The new texts *KUB* 51.36, *KUB* 52.100, and *KUB* 55.25 are not securely datable but could all be Empire period texts.

226. Kammenhuber, *ZA* 66 (1976) 74, suggests that Tudḫaliya IV was trying to simulate a god-pair with ᴰLAMMA and Ala but does not speculate on why he might have done so. The antiquity of the pairing of ᴰLAMMA and Ala in the Hittite cult is discussed in *Chapter 1*.

227. See Carter, Diss. 21–25, and Laroche in Dunand and Lévêque, eds., *Les Syncrétismes dans les Religions de l'Antiquité* (Leiden, 1975) 87–95.

the appeal which this systematic listing of tutelary deities held for this monarch in his role as priest and overseer of Hittite religious life.

The mention of both LAMMA and Ala deities of Alatarma as well as tutelary deities of the lands in which the king campaigns is interesting in light of the redating by Singer[228] to Tudḫaliya IV of *KBo* 4.14 ii 11, in which the king mentions Alatarma as part of the lands in which he has campaigned.[229] This strengthens Singer's argument for assigning *KBo* 4.14 to Tudḫaliya IV, as we know that the writer of that text had been in Alatarma, and in *KUB* 2.1 i 45 and iii 35 we have Tudḫaliya IV including gods from there in the offering list. Alatarma does not occur in the other copies of the festival. It could therefore be a later addition by Tudḫaliya after his campaigns there. Unfortunately the portion of *KBo* 11.40 which would parallel the *KUB* 2.1 column i occurrence of Alatarma is broken away, and *KUB* 55.25 obverse, which parallels *KUB* 2.1 obverse iii breaks one line before it might have mentioned Ala of Alatarma. The focus of the final section of the list (*KUB* 2.1 column vi and *KBo* 11.40 column vi) is to celebrate the gods of the lands which the king controls. Here the king's emphasis is on his prowess as a warrior and hunter.

Laroche in commenting on this festival suggests that we really have no longer to do with a deity at all, but rather with the development of a concept.[230] Certainly it is the concept of protection or guarding which the Hittites are developing and exploring in this festival. The festival has as its primary purpose the listing of and offering to protective deities associated with the king's well-being. Implicit in this is the Hittite conception of the king as the state.[231] The festival then is of special importance for the state's well-being. Although Tudḫaliya obviously promoted the celebration of this festival that provides for the worshipping of deities protective of the king, he himself recognized Šarruma as his own personal protective god as evidenced in the relief of the king and god at Yazılıkaya. The king's interest in the Festival for All the Tutelary Deities may simply have been part of his efforts to organize the religious administration of the realm, it may indicate a special interest in these tutelary deities, or it may be a reflection of some particular concern on his part which resulted in his desire to placate or supplicate the tutelary deities which he believed to be protecting his interests.

228. *ZA* 75 (1985) 100–23.

229. Hoffner, personal communication, pointed out the relevance of *KBo* 4.14 with its mention of the rare place name Alatarma.

230. *RLA* 6 (1980–83) 458.

231. The title "Labarna" used throughout refers to whoever the reigning king is. I am not certain why Labarna is used instead of "the king."

CHAPTER 4

THE FESTIVALS FOR RENEWING THE ^{KUŠ}*kurša*-s

INTRODUCTION

Another group of festival texts which describes a part of the cult dedicated to tutelary deities is one which provides for the renewing of the cult symbols of certain tutelary deities, which take the form of *kurša*-s, or hunting bags.[1] These festivals are extremely important as evidence of the Hittite use of implements associated with a particular god as the actual cult representation of that god. Sections of the ceremony make it clear that the *kurša*- is the god itself. The festivals thus describe for us how the Hittites renewed or replaced representations of the divine.

THE TEXTS

KUB 55.43[2]

Bo 2393+Bo 5138 = *KUB* 55.43 is a rather large tablet measuring 14.6 cm high and 20 cm across at its widest point. Portions of its reverse are blackened by fire. The surface of the tablet is abraded in many places and is in general not well preserved. The contour of the preserved portion of the tablet indicates that less than half of each column is preserved; on the obverse the tops of columns i and ii are preserved, but the tablet's thickness is still increasing at the point at which it breaks off.

The script of the tablet shows many older forms. There is not much of the crowding together of signs which is typical of Old Script, although one may note the irregular word spacing with occasional crowding together of separate words, for example *ḫantezzi palši* in obv. ii 1, and ^{URU}*Zapatiškuwa* GUB-*aš* in obv. ii 13. The *da* and *it* signs have very clearly broken middle horizontals, i.e., they do not show their very latest forms. They do not, however, show the indentation of the left edge typical of an Old Script form. Signs like

1. See *Appendix B* on the $^{(KUŠ)}$*kurša*- and its interpretation.
2. The festival is catalogued by Laroche as *CTH* 683, "Renouvellement de la 'toison' des dieux KAL." My treatment of it in this chapter includes texts not catalogued under *CTH* 683. See p. 7 in the *Introduction* for this festival's text scheme. Lines i 1–27 and l.e. 4–8, the colophon, are edited by Otten in *FsFriedrich* 351–59.

URU, *e*, KUŠ, *zu*, *ra*, and *LAM* show a first vertical wedge much shorter than the second vertical, an Old and Middle Script characteristic. In rev. iv 17′ there are two rather different URU signs, with the second one looking more like New Script. Rev. iv 26′ also contains a newer looking URU. The *al*, *li*, and *ak* signs do not occur in their later forms. The *šar* is written with the earliest of its forms. Consistent with these early forms is the writing of *ANA* in rev. iv 8′ as a ligature. See table 5 in *Appendix C* for drawings of some of the more distinctive signs.

Although the script shows older characteristics, I do not think this is an Old Script tablet. Against an Old Script dating is the lack of the characteristic crowding, and examples of *uk* and *az* signs with subscripts. The other older characteristics of the ductus suggest a Middle Script dating for this tablet. Such a dating has already been tentatively suggested by Melchert, who assigned a Middle Script(?) dating to the tablet without any comment on the evidence for it.[3]

Transliteration

KUB 55.43 Obverse i

§1 1 [ma-a-an *ŠA*] ^{D}Zi-it-ḫa-ri-ya *Ù* ^{D}LAMMA ^{URU}Ḫa-te-en-zu-wa
2 [2 ^{KU}]^{Š}kur-šu-uš EGIR-pa ne-e-u-wa-aḫ-ḫa-an-zi
3 ma-a-an *I-NA* MU 9 KAM ma-a-na-aš ku-wa-pí ku-wa-pí ne-wa-aḫ-ḫa-an-zi
4 me-ḫur *Ú-UL* du-uq-qa-a- ri[4]

---

§2 5 nu ma-aḫ-ḫa-an 2 ^{KUŠ}kur-šu-uš GIBIL-*TIM* *ŠA* ^{D}Zi-it-ḫa-ri-ya
6 *Ù ŠA* ^{D}LAMMA ^{URU}Ḫa-te-en-zu-wa ú-da-an-zi
7 na-aš-kán *I-NA* É ^{KUŠ}kur-ša-aš[5] an-da pé-e-da-an-zi
8 na-aš-ta 2 ^{KUŠ}kur-šu-uš *LA-BI-RU-TIM* kat-ta da-an-zi
9 nu pé-e-da-an du-uq-qa-a-ri *A-NA A-ŠAR*[6] DINGIR-*LIM*-pát
10 a-wa-an kat-ta ^{GIŠ}KAK.ḪI.A wa-al-ḫa-an-te-eš nu-uš a-pí-ya ga-an-kán-zi

---

§3 11 *A-ŠAR* DINGIR-*LIM*-ma 2 ^{KUŠ}kur-šu-uš GIBIL-*TIM* ga-an-kán-zi
12 na-aš-ta ma-a-an ^{URU}Ḫa-at-tu-ši EZEN.ḪI.A ḫu-u-da-a-ak
13 kar-pa-an-ta-ri na-aš-ta 2 ^{KUŠ}kur-šu-uš TIL-*TIM* pa-ra-a
14 ḫu-u-da-a-ak ne-ya-an-zi ma-a-an EZEN.ḪI.A-ma za-lu-ga-n[u-a]n-zi
15 nu ma-a-an ITU 1 KAM na-aš-ma ITU 2 KAM pa-iz-zi
16 2 ^{KUŠ}kur-šu-uš TIL.ḪI.A-ma-kán *I-NA* É kur-ša-aš-pát an-da
17 ga-an-kán-te- eš

---

§4 18 ma-aḫ-ḫa-an-ma-kán EZEN.ḪI.A kar-pa-an-ta-ri (erasure)
19 na-aš-ta 2 ^{KUŠ}kur-šu-uš TIL-⌈*TIM*⌉ pa-ra-a *QA-TAM-MA* ne-an-z[i]

---

3. Melchert, Diss. 98.
4. See *Appendix B* on *tukk-*.
5. See *Appendix B* on the É ^{KUŠ}*kuršaš*.
6. See *Appendix B* sub *AŠRU*.

Translation

KUB 55.43 Obverse i

§1 [When] they renew the [two] hunting bags [of] Zitḫariya and the Tutelary Deity of Ḫatenzuwa, whether in the ninth year, or whenever they renew them, the time is not prescribed.

---

§2 When they bring the two new hunting bags of Zitḫariya and the Tutelary Deity of Ḫatenzuwa, they take them into the temple of the hunting bag. They take down the two old hunting bags. The place is prescribed; the pegs are (already) driven in directly below the actual (*-pat*) place of the god. They hang them[7] there.

---

§3 In the place of the god, however, they hang the two new hunting bags. If in Ḫattuša the festivals will be completed promptly, they send[8] the two old hunting bags out immediately. If, however, they are postponing/prolonging the festivals, and one or two months pass, the two old hunting bags (remain) hanging in that same temple of the hunting bag.

---

§4 However, when the festivals (in Ḫattuša) are completed, they send out the two old hunting bags (to the provinces) in the same way.

---

7. The old hunting bags which have just been taken down from the "place of the god" so that the new ones can be hung there.
8. Compare *CHD* sub *nai-* for this meaning of *para nai-*, including citation of this passage: "they send off the old *kurša*-s right away."

KUB 55.43

Obverse i (*transliteration cont.*)

§5 20 ⸢nu⸣ *ŠA* ^{D}Zi-it-ḫa-[ri]-⸢ya ^{KUŠ}kur⸣-ša-an TIL *I-NA* ^{URU}Tu-u-ḫu-u[p-pí-ya]

21 ⸢pé⸣-e-da-an-zi na-⸢an-kán ma⸣-aḫ-ḫa-an ^{URU}Ḫa-at-tu-ša-az KÁ.GA[L o?[9]]

22 kat-[t]a ar-nu-an-zi na-an-za-kán KUR-ya an-da ^{D}LAMMA ^{KUŠ}kur-ša[-aš]

23 ḫal-⸢zi⸣-iš-ša-an-zi *ŠA* ^{D}LAMMA ^{URU}Ḫa-te-en-zu-wa-ma ^{KUŠ}kur-ša-a[n TIL]

24 *I-NA* ^{URU}Dur-mi-it-ta pé-e-da-an-zi na-an-kán ma-aḫ-ḫa-a[n [10]]

25 KÁ.GAL a-šu-ša-an?[11] kat-ta ar-nu-an-zi nu-uš-ši-kán *ŠUM-ŠU*

26 ar-ḫa da-an-zi na-an-za-an ^{D}LAMMA ^{URU}Za-pa-ti-iš-ku-wa

27 ḫal-z[i-iš-š]a-an- zi

§6 28 n[u-uš ma-a-an? .... -z]i ⸢MU-ti ne⸣-ya-an-zi nu-uš-ma-aš

29 [ar-ḫa-ya-an EZEN[12] a-pí?-]⸢ya⸣ *Ú-UL* ku-in-ki i-en[-zi]

30 [ma-a-an ^{KUŠ}kur-šu-uš-ma pa-ra-a? ḫu-u-da-]a-ak ne-ya-an-z[i]

31 [nu EZEN.ḪI.A ḫu-u-da-a-ak kar-pa-an-ta?-]ri ma-a-na-aš-kán

32 [o o o o o o o o o o o o o o o o y]a-⸢an⸣-zi

(the column breaks off)

Obverse ii[13] (*transliteration*)

§7′ 1 nu ⸢ḫa⸣-an-te-ez-zi pal-ši ^{D}UTU TUŠ-aš a-ku-w[a-an-zi]

2 [1 ^{N}]^{INDA}ta-kar-mu-un pár-ši-ya na-an-kán EG[IR-pa *A-NA* DINGIR-*LIM*]

3 iš-ka-ra-an-ta-aš še-er da-a-i EGIR-an-d[a-ma ^{D}IM? GUB-aš]

4 e-ku-zi 1 NINDA.KUR$_4$.RA pár-ši-ya na-an-ša-an EGIR-[pa]

5 *A-NA* DINGIR-*LIM* iš-⸢ka⸣-ra-an-ta-aš še-er da-a-i

§8′ 6 EGIR-an-da-ma ^{D}LAMMA ^{URU}*ḪA-AT-TI* GUB-aš e-ku-zi $^{\text{L}[\text{Ú.MEŠ}}$SÌR SÌR-*RU*]

7 LÚ.MEŠ UR.GI$_7$[14] wa-ap-pí-an-zi[15] 1 ^{NINDA}ta-kar-mu-un pár-š[i-ya]

8 na-an-kán EGIR-pa *A-NA* <DINGIR-*LIM*> iš-ga-ra-an-ta-aš še-er ti-an-z[i]

9 na-aš-ta ša-an-ḫa-an-zi nu ^{D}Zi-it-ḫa-ri-ya-an G[UB-aš]

10 a-ku-wa-an-zi $^{\text{LÚ.MEŠ}}$SÌR SÌR-*RU* LÚ.MEŠ UR.GI$_7$ wa-ap-pí-an-zi

11 1 ^{NINDA}ta-kar-mu-un pár-ši-ya na-an-kán EGIR-pa *A-NA* DINGIR-*LI*[*M*]

12 iš-ka-ra-an-ta-aš še-er ti-an-zi

9. Possibly something in the intercolumnium identifying the gate through which it was brought down, or a phonetic complement such as KÁ.GA[L-*az*].

10. There is no space for anything after *maḫḫa*[*n*], unless it was written up the intercolumnium. One might expect *Ḫattušaz* here on the analogy of line 21, or an Akkadian preposition to indicate the case of KÁ.GAL.

11. This is written over an erasure and is therefore somewhat unclear. Although not as good a reading, it could conceivably also be *a-šu-ša-aš*! Otten, *FsFriedrich* 353, reads *a-ṣu-ša-aṣ* without further comment.

12. Restored from the colophon, l.e. 7.

13. After a gap of an undetermined number of paragraphs.

14. See *Appendix B* on the LÚ.MEŠ UR.GI$_7$.

15. See *Appendix B* on *wappiya-*.

KUB 55.43

Obverse i (*translation cont.*)

§5 They take away the old hunting bag of Zitḫa[ri]ya to Tuḫu[ppiya]. When they bring it down from Ḫattuša, (through) the [x?] gate, in the land[16] they call it "the Tutelary Deity of the Hunting Bag." The [old] hunting bag of the Tutelary Deity of Ḫatenzuwa, however, they take away to Durmitta. When they bring it down [from Ḫattuša?] (through) the *ašuša*-gate,[17] they take its name away from it and c[al]l it the Tutelary Deity of Zapatiškuwa.

---

§6 [If] they send [them in the]x year, they do not celebrate any [festivals separately at that] time for them. [If, however,] they send [the hunting bags prom]ptly, [the festivals are complet]ed [promptly]. If they [...] them

(the column breaks off)

Obverse ii[18] (*translation*)

§7′ The first time t[hey] drink the Sungod, seated. He breaks [one] *takarmu*- bread and places it ba[ck for the god] upon the lined up ones. [But] afterwar[ds] he drinks [the Stormgod(?), standing]. He breaks one thick bread and places it back for the god upon the lined up ones.[19]

---

§8′ Afterwards he drinks the Tutelary Deity of Ḫatti, standing. The s[ingers sing]. The dog-men bark. [He b]reaks one *takarmu*- bread. They place it back for <the god> upon the lined up ones. They sweep (it) off.[20] They drink Zitḫariya, st[anding]. The singers sing. The dog-men bark. He breaks one *takarmu*- bread. They place it back for the god upon the lined up ones.

---

16. That is, outside the capital, in the provinces.
17. Or "down [through] the *ašuša*- gate ... "
18. After a gap of an undetermined number of paragraphs.
19. That is, the hunting bags?
20. See *Line Commentary* below, line ii 9, on translating *n⸗ašta šanḫanzi*.

KUB 55.43

Obverse ii (*transliteration cont.*)

§9′ 13 EGIR-an-da-ma ^{D}LAMMA ^{URU}Za-pa-ti-iš-ku-wa GUB-aš a-ku-wa-a[n-zi]
14 $^{[L]Ú.MEŠ}$SÌR SÌR-*RU* LÚ.MEŠ UR.GI$_7$ wa-ap-pí-an-zi 1 [^{NINDA}ta-kar-mu-un]
15 [pár-]ši-ya na-an-ša-an EGIR-pa *A-NA* DINGIR-*LIM* iš-ka-r[a-an-ta-aš]
16 [še-e]r ti-an-zi EGIR-an-da-ma ki-pí-ik-ki-iš-d[u]
17 [^{D}Ka]p-pa-ri-ya-mu-un ^{D}LAMMA ^{URU}Ta-ta-šu-na [Ø]
18 [^{D}LAMM]A ^{URU}⌈Ta⌉-aš-ḫa-pu-na GUB-aš a-ku-wa-an-zi 3 ^{NINDA}[ta-kar-mu-uš]
19 [pár-ši-y]a! na-aš-kán EGIR-pa *A-NA* DINGIR-*LIM* iš-ka-r[a-an-ta-aš]
20 [še-er ti-an-]⌈zi $^{LÚ⌉.MEŠ}$SÌR SÌR-*RU* LÚ.MEŠ UR.GI$_7$ wa-a[p-pí-an-zi]

- - - - - - - - - - - - - - - - -

§10′ 21 [EGIR-an-da-ma ^{D}LAMMA $^{UR]U⌈}$Ḫa-te⌉-en-zu-wa GUB-aš a-ku[-wa-an-zi]
22 [$^{LÚ.MEŠ}$SÌR SÌR-*RU* LÚ.M]EŠ UR.GI$_7$ wa-ap-pí-an-zi
23 [1 ^{NINDA}ta-kar-mu-un pár-ši-y]a! na-an-ša-an EGIR-pa [*A-NA* DINGIR-*LIM*]
24 [iš-ka-ra-an-ta-aš še-e]r da-a-i EGIR-an-da-ma [^{D}Ḫa-aš-ga-la-an[21]]
25 [GUB-aš a-ku-wa-an-zi $^{LÚ.MEŠ}$SÌ]R SÌR-*RU* LÚ.MEŠ UR.GI$_7$ w[a-ap-pí-an-zi]
26 [1 ^{NINDA}ta-kar-mu-un pár-]ši-ya na-an-kán EGIR-pa [*A-NA* DINGIR-*LIM*]
27 [iš-ka-ra-an-ta-aš] še-er ti-an-zi EGIR-an-da[-ma DINGIR.MEŠ URU-*LIM*?[22]]
28 [TUŠ-aš e-ku-zi 1 ^{NINDA}]ta-kar-mu-un pár-ši-ya n[a-an-kán]
29 [EGIR-pa *A-NA* DINGIR-*LIM* iš-k]a-ra-an-ta-aš še-er ti-a[n-zi]

- - - - - - - - - - - - - - - - -

§11′ 30 [EGIR-an-da-ma[23] ir-ḫa-]a!-an-te-eš ḫi-iš-ša-al-la-a-a[n!-te-eš[24] TUŠ-aš ku-u-uš][25]
31 [DINGIR.MEŠ e-ku-zi[26] ^{D}Ḫa-aš-g]a-la-a-an ^{D}LAMMA ^{GIŠ}ŠUKUR ^{GIŠ}D[AG-an?]
32 [(DN) (DN) (DN) ^{D}Gu]l-še-eš ^{D}Ḫi-la-aš-še-eš ^{D}Ḫa-š[a-am-mi-li-in]
33 [^{ÍD}Ma-ra-aš-ša-an-ta[27] ḪUR.]⌈SAG.⌉MEŠ ÍD.MEŠ[28] ḫa-re-eš [o?]
34 [o o[29] $^{LÚ.MEŠ}$SÌR SÌR-*RU* LÚ.MEŠ U]R.GI$_7$ wa-ap-pí-an-zi [1? ^{NINDA}ta-kar-mu-un]
35 [pár-ši-ya na-an-kán EGIR-pa *A-N*]*A* DINGIR-*LIM* iš-ga-r[a-an-ta-aš]
36 [še-er ti-an-zi o o o o $^{LÚ.MEŠ}$SÌR SÌR-*RU*? L]Ú?⌈MEŠ⌉ UR.G[I$_7$ wa-ap-pí-an-zi][30]

(the column breaks off)

21. Restored from the analogous passage in iv 23′.
22. Restored from iv 32′; see *Line Commentary* below on ii 27.
23. Restored from iv 33′.
24. See *Appendix B* sub *ḫiššalla-*.
25. Restored from iv 34′.
26. Restored from iv 34′.
27. Restored from l.e. 1.
28. See *Appendix B* on ḪUR.SAG and ÍD in cultic contexts.
29. The spacing indicates that a short word, presumably the last item in this list, began this line, before $^{LÚ.MEŠ}$SÌR. The fact that there is no *-a*, "and," on *ḫareš* could indicate that there was at least one more item after it in this list.
30. This line is restored on the basis of the posited restoration of l.e. 2–3. There is too much space, however, for just $^{LÚ.MEŠ}$SÌR SÌR-*RU* in the first break. What else might have been there is unclear.

KUB 55.43

Obverse ii (*translation cont.*)

§9′ Afterwards th[ey] drink the Tutelary Deity of Zapatiškuwa, standing. The singers sing. The dog-men bark. He [br]eaks one [*takarmu-* bread]. They place it back for the god [upo]n the line[d up ones]. Afterwards they drink the *kipikkišdus*:[31] [Ka]ppariyamu, the Tutelary Deity of Tatašuna, and [the Tutela]ry Deity of Tašḫapuna, standing. He [break]s three [*takarmu-*] breads. The[y place] them back for the god [upon] the line[d up ones]. The singers sing. The dog-men ba[rk].

§10′ [Afterwards they] drink [the Tutelary Deity] of Ḫatenzuwa, standing. [The singers sing. The d]og-men bark. He [breaks one *takarmu-* bread] and places it back [for the god] up[on the lined up ones]. Afterwards [they drink Ḫašgala, standing. The sing]ers sing. The dog-men b[ark]. He br[eaks one *takarmu-* bread]. They place it back [for the god] upon [the lined up ones]. Afterward[s he drinks the gods of the city(?), seated]. He breaks [one] *takarmu-* [bread]. [They] place [it back for the god] upon the [li]ned up ones.

§11′ [Afterwards, seated, he drinks these gods, the ones (whose offerings have been) comp]leted in sequence (and) the ones (whose offerings are) plann[ed: Ḫašg]ala, the Tutelary Deity of the Spear, Ḫal[maššuitta, DN, DN, DN, the Fate] Deities, Ḫilašši, Ḫa[šammili, the Maraššanta river,] (divine) [mou]ntains, rivers, valleys [and x(?). The singers sing. The d]og-men bark. [He breaks one *takarmu-* bread. They place it back f]or the god [upon] the lin[ed up ones]. [... The singers sing(?). The d]og-me[n bark].

(the column breaks off)

31. See *Appendix B* on *kipikkišdu*.

KUB 55.43

Reverse iii[32] (*transliteration*)

§12′x+1 [o o][33] x ⸢du-uq-qa⸣-a-r[i o o o o o o o o o o o]
2′ [o o o (-)]da-an-zi nu ^{URU}Du[r-mi-it-ta? o o o o o o]
3′ [$^{LÚ.MEŠ}$]SANGA $^{SAL.MEŠ}$SANGA ^{LÚ}GUDÚ [o o o o o o o o o o]
4′ [o o]*A-NA* DINGIR-*LIM* NINDA.KUR$_4$.RA.ḪI.A me-n[a-aḫ-ḫa-an-da pár-ši-ya-an-zi]
5′ [o o]x ^{LÚ}DUGUD ZAG-aš *ŠA* LÚ.MEŠ U[R.GI$_7$ o o o o o o o]
6′ [o o]⸢*PA-NI*?⸣ DINGIR-*LI*[*M*!][34] ka-a-aš ḫal-z[i-iš-ša-an-zi?]
7′ [p]u[35]-⸢ur⸣-pu-ru-uš-ša iš-ḫu-iš-kán[-zi o o o o o o]

-----

§13′ 8′ [n]a-aš-ta DINGIR-*LAM* *I-NA* ^{É}ka-r[i-im-mi an-da ar-nu-an-zi]
9′ ⸢*IŠ-TU*⸣ 12 MÁŠ.GAL-ya-kán 1 MÁŠ.GA[L ^{É}ka-ri-im-mi an-da]
10′ [u-u]n-ni-ya-an-zi an-dur!-za-ma M[ÁŠ?GAL ši-pa-an-ti]
11′ [^{NINDA}p]u-ur-pu-ru-uš-ša a-pé-e[l ^{É}ka-ri-im-mi iš-ḫu-iš-kán-zi]
12′ ma-aḫ-ḫa-an-ma-kán DINGIR-*LAM* *I-N*[*A* ^{É}ka-ri-im-mi an-da]
13′ ar-nu-an-zi nu ^{LÚ}DUGUD NINDA.KUR$_4$.R[A *A-NA* DINGIR-*LIM* pár-ši-ya]
14′ ^{NINDA}[p]ur-pu-ru-uš-ša *A-NA* DINGIR-*L*[*IM* iš-ḫu-iš-kán-zi]

-----

§14′ 15′ nu DINGIR-*LAM* *A-NA* *A-ŠAR* DINGIR-*LIM* ga-a[n-kán-zi o o o o o o o o]
16′ pa-⸢ra-a⸣ pa-iz-zi na-aš-ta ^{L}[$^{Ú!?}$ o o o o o o o o o]
17′ ši-p[a-a]n-ti nu-uš-ša-an ⸢iš⸣-k[a-ra-an-ta-aš še-er?]
18′ ti-a[n-z]i šu-up-pa-ma ḫ[u-i-šu? o o o o o o o o]
19′ a-pu-u[-u]n-na ḫu-u-ma-an-t[e-eš[36] o o o o o o o ma-a-an?]
20′ a-ku-w[a-a]n-na *IŠ-TU* x[o o o o o o o o o o o]
21′ a-aš-š[u nu?]LÚ.MEŠ URU-*LIM* iš[[37]- o o o o]x ⸢ir⸣-ḫi-iš-⸢ki⸣-i[t-ta]
22′ nu EGIR[KA]SKAL!-ši ku-⸢i⸣[-uš? ir-ḫ]a-a-an-zi ḫé-ma-aš-x[o o]
23′ a-pí-y[a-y]a x[o o o o o] [ ]

-----

32. After a gap of an undetermined number of paragraphs.

33. In the other occurrences of *duqqari* in this text, it was preceded by *UL* or by *pēdan*, but the trace before *duqqari* in this line does not really look like *-U*]*L* or *-a*]*n*. It is unclear what is to be restored for the beginning of this line.

34. Collation indicates this as a possible reading. Also possible is ^{D}U 1[-*ŠU*], but DINGIR-*LI*[*M*] makes better sense. The sign immediately before DINGIR could be LÚ. Even if this is the correct reading the beginning of the line is still unclear.

35. One might expect [^{NINDA}*p*]*u-ur-pu-ru-uš-ša*, which is possible, although spacing would be quite tight. The difference in spacing between line 7′ and 11′ makes restoring NINDA at the beginning of line 7′ doubtful. A NINDA determinative is not necessary to indicate that the balls are bread; compare *KBo* 19.128 (AN.TAḪ.ŠUM fragment), ed. Otten, *StBoT* 13 (1971) 2–3, where the *purpura-* are bread, despite the absence of NINDA as a determinative. See *Appendix B* on *purpura-*.

36. A reading *ḫu-u-ma-an-t*[*i* is also possible, although *-t*[*e-* fits the traces better.

37. The index to *KUB* 55 cites this as $^{(URU)}$*Ši*-x[.

KUB 55.43

Reverse iii[38] (*translation*)

§12′ [...]x is prescribed. [...]they take. The city Du[rmitta ... The] priests, the priestesses, the GUDÚ priest [and x break] thick breads be[fore] the god. [The] x, the dignitary of the right, [the x] of the do[g-men, and the x] cal[l out] "*kaš*"[39] before the god. And [th]ey heap up (bread)-balls.

§13′ [They bring] the god[40] into the *kari*[*mmi*-] building. Out of twelve male goats they [d]rive one [into the *karimmi*- building]. Inside, however, [they sacrifice] the g[oat]. And [they heap up bread]-balls [in] his [*karimmi*- building]. When, however, they bring the god int[o the *karimmi*- building,] the dignitary [breaks] thick bread [to the god] and [they heap up] bread-balls to the go[d].

§14′ [They h]ang up the god in the god's place. [x] goes forth. The x[-functionary] sacrif[ic]es [x]. They place them [upon] the li[ned up ones(?)]. The r[aw(?)] flesh, however, [they x]. They al[l x] that one. [If] drinking from the [x] is goo[d], [then (for)] the men of the city *iš*[- ...]x is offered in sequence. The ones [whom] they treat in sequence the last [ti]me,[41] [they x] the *ḫemaš* at that time.

38. After a gap of an undetermined number of paragraphs.
39. The first part of the Hattic exclamation *kaš miš*(*š*)*a*.
40. That is, the hunting bag representing him.
41. Or perhaps "on a later occasion."

KUB 55.43

Reverse iii (*transliteration cont.*)

§15′ 24′ lu-uk-ka[t-ta-ma *IŠ-TU* É ^{LÚ}[42]]u-ri-ya-an-ni ZAG-aš 4 BÁN [o o]
25′ 5 ^{DUG}i[š-nu-u-ru-uš[43] ú-d]a-an-zi na-aš-ta 3 *ŠA-A-T*[*I*! o o o]
26′ a-wa-an a[r-ḫa da-an-z]i na-at *PA-NI* DINGIR-*LIM* šu-⸢un?⸣-n[a-an-zi]
27′ nu ^{DUG}iš-n[u-u-ra-aš pí-r]a-an kat-ta ^{LÚ}GUDÚ pí-da-an[-zi nu 1-*ŠU* ?]
28′ ši-pa-an-ti[na-aš? ^{DUG}iš-nu-]u-ri *PA-NI* DINGIR-*LIM* še-eš-zi [ ]
29′ nu a-pé-e-⸢da-ni UD-ti⸣ EZEN NU.GÁL ku-iš-ki

§16′ 30′ lu-uk-kat-ta-ma ka-ru-ú-a-ri-wa-ar ḫu-u-da[-a-a]k? [iš-na-an]
31′ ša-ra-⸢a⸣ kar!-pa-an-zi na-an É.UDUN pé[-e-da-an-zi]
32′ nu 3 NINDA.KUR$_4$.RA *ŠA ŠA-A-TI* i-en-zi ma-aḫ-ḫa-an-ma[-at ze-ya-an-ta-ri]
33′ na-aš-kán ^{GIŠ}pa-a-pu-li ti-an-zi še-er-ma-aš-š[a-an GAD-it]
34′ ^{LÚ}⸢GUDÚ⸣ ka-ri-ya-az-zi na-aš *I-NA* ⸢É⸣[DINGIR-*LIM*[44] ú-da-an-zi?]
35′ nu pí-ra-an pal-ú-iš-kán-zi $^{\text{LÚ.MEŠ}}$SÌ[R]
36′ SÌR-*RU IŠ-TU* É ^{LÚ}u-ri-ya-an-ni-y[a ... [45]]
37′ d[a-a-a]n-zi nu a-pu-u-un-na pí-ra-an BA[L-an-zi?]

(bottom of tablet)

Reverse iv[46] (*transliteration*)

§17′x+1 [o o o o o o o o o o o o o o o o o o o (-)d]a?-an-zi [ ]
2′ [o o o o o o o o o o o o o o o o o o o *I*]*Š-TU* ⸢É⸣?-*ŠU* [ ]
3′ x-x [o o o o o o o o o o o o o o ^{DUG}iš-pa-a]n-du-uz-zi ú-da-a[-an-zi]

§18′ 4′ ma-aḫ[-ḫa-an-ma-aš-]ša-an a-ku-wa-an-na a-ri nu ^{D}UTU TUŠ-aš a-ku-wa-an-zi
5′ 1 ^{NINDA}t[a-kar-m]u-un pár-ši-ya na-an-kán EGIR-pa *A-NA* ^{KUŠ}kur-ši
6′ ^{D}LAMM[A ^{U}]^{RU}Za-pa-ti-iš-ku-wa ti-an-zi nu ^{D}IM GUB-aš a-ku-wa-an-z[i]
7′ nu 1 ^{NINDA}ta-kar-mu-un pár-ši-ya na-an-ša-an EGIR-pa
8′ *A-NA* ^{D}LAMMA ^{URU}Za-pa-ti-iš-ku-wa ti-an-zi nu ^{D}LAMMA ^{URU}Za-pa-ti-iš-ku-w[a]
9′ GUB-aš a-ku-wa-an-zi $^{\text{LÚ.MEŠ}}$SÌR SÌR-*RU* LÚ.MEŠ UR.GI$_7$ wa-ap-pí-an-zi
10′ 1 ^{NINDA}ta-kar-mu-un pár-ši-ya na-an-kán ^{KUŠ}kur-ši še-er da-a-i

42. Restored on the basis of line 36′ of this same column. Spacing on the tablet fits this restoration quite well. See *Appendix B* on the *uriyanni-*.

43. Or ^{DUG}*i* [*šnurit*. See *Line Commentary* below on this line.

44. Or possibly ⸢É⸣[^{KUŠ}*kur-ša-aš* ...

45. A sacrificial animal was probably named in the break here, based on what follows in line 37′.

46. After a gap of an undetermined number of paragraphs.

KUB 55.43

Reverse iii (*translation cont.*)

§15′ In the mor[ning] they [br]ing four BÁN-measures of [x] (and) five *i*[*šnura*-] vessels[47] [from the house of] the *uriyanni*- official of the right. From it they [tak]e ou[t] three *SŪTU* [of x]. [They] fill them[48] before the god. Th[ey] take the GUDÚ priest down [in fr]ont of the *išn*[*ura*-] vessel(s).[49] He libates [once]. He (the GUDÚ priest) spends the night by [the *išn*]*ura*- before the god.[50] There is no festival of any kind on that day.

§16′ The following day in the morning they immedi[atel]y take up [the dough. They ta]ke it (into) the bakery. They make three thick breads of one *SŪTU* (each). And when [they are baked], they place them on the bread tray(?).[51] The GUDÚ priest covers them over [with a cloth]. [They take] them into the te[mple].[52] They recite(?)[53] before (them). The sing[ers] sing. They also take [(a sacrificial animal)] from the house of the *uriyanni*- official, and that one they sa[crifice] before (the god).

(bottom of tablet)

Reverse iv[54] (*translation*)

§17′ [ ] they x. [f]rom his house(?) x[Th]ey bring the [lib]ation vessel(s).

§18′ Wh[en, however,] the drink arrives, they drink the Sungod, seated. He breaks one *t*[*akarm*]*u*- bread. They place it back upon the hunting bag of the Tutela[ry Deity] of Zapatiškuwa. They drink the Stormgod, standing. He breaks one *takarmu*- bread. They place it back upon the Tutelary Deity of Zapatiškuwa. They drink the Tutelary Deity of Zapatiškuwa, standing. The singers sing. The dog-men bark. He breaks one *takarmu*- bread and places it upon the hunting bag.

47. Or possibly … [in] five *i*[*šnura*-] vessels … "
48. That is, the DUG*išnura*-s.
49. LÚGUDÚ is singular, the verb is plural. If the verb's number is correct, we could translate "The GUDÚ priest(s) bring the *išn*[*ura*-] vessels down in front."
50. Or perhaps "It (the dough) spends the night in the [*išn*]*ura*- before the god."
51. See *Appendix B* sub GIŠ*papul*-.
52. Or perhaps "into the temple [of the Hunting Bag]."
53. Or "shout"; see *Appendix B* on *palwai*-.
54. After a gap of an undetermined number of paragraphs.

KUB 55.43

Reverse iv (*transliteration cont.*)

§19′ 11′ nu ^{D}LAMMA ^{URU}*ḪA-AT-TI* GUB-aš a-ku-wa-an-zi $^{LÚ.MEŠ}$SÌR SÌR-*RU*
12′ LÚ.MEŠ UR.⸢GI$_7$⸣ wa-ap-pí-an-zi 1 ^{NINDA}ta-kar-mu-un pár-ši-ya
13′ na-an-ká[n ^{K}]^{UŠ}kur-ši še-er da-a-i na-aš-ta ša-an-ḫa-an-zi
14′ nu ^{D}⸢Zi-it⸣-ḫa-ri-ya-an GUB-aš[55] a-ku-wa-an-zi $^{LÚ.MEŠ}$SÌR SÌR-*RU*
15′ LÚ.MEŠ UR.GI$_7$ wa-ap-pí-an-zi 1 ^{NINDA}ta-kar-mu-un pár-ši-ya
16′ na-an-kán EGIR-pa ^{D}Zi-it-ḫa-ri-ya da-a-i nu ^{D}Kap-pa-ri-ya-⸢mu⸣
17′ ^{D}LAMMA ^{URU}Ta-ta-šu-na ^{D}LAMMA ^{URU}Ta-aš-ḫa-pu-na GUB-aš a-ku-wa-an-zi
18′ 2 ^{NINDA}ta-kar-mu-uš pár-ši-ya na-aš-kán-«kán» EGIR-pa ^{KUŠ}kur-ši da-a-i
19′ $^{LÚ.MEŠ}$SÌR SÌR-*RU* LÚ.MEŠ UR.GI$_7$ wa-ap-pí-an-zi

---

§20′ 20′ na-aš-ta ša-an-ḫa-an-zi nu ^{D}LAMMA ^{URU}Ḫa-te-en-zu-wa GUB-aš a-ku-wa-an-zi
21′ $^{LÚ.MEŠ}$SÌR SÌR-*RU* LÚ.MEŠ UR.GI$_7$ wa-ap-pí-an-zi 1 ^{NINDA}ta-kar-mu-un pár-ši-ya
22′ na-an-kán ^{KUŠ}kur-ši še-er da-a-i na-aš-ta ša-an-ḫa-an-zi
23′ nu ^{D}Ḫa-aš-ga-la-a-an GUB-aš a-ku-wa-an-zi $^{LÚ.MEŠ}$SÌR SÌR-*RU*
24′ LÚ.MEŠ UR.GI$_7$ wa-ap-pí-an-zi 1 ^{NINDA}ta-kar-mu-un pár-ši-ya
25′ na-an-kán ^{KUŠ}kur-ši še-er da-a-i

---

§21′ 26′ nu nam-ma ^{D}LAMMA ^{URU}Za-pa-ti-iš-ku-wa GUB-aš a-ku-wa-an-zi $^{LÚ.MEŠ}$SÌR
27′ SÌR-*RU* LÚ.MEŠ UR.GI$_7$ wa-ap-pí-an-zi 1 ^{NINDA}ta-kar-mu-un pár-ši-ya
28′ na-an-kán ^{KUŠ}kur-ši še-er da-a-i na-aš-ta pé-e-da-aš $^{LÚ.MEŠ}$SÌR
29′ an-da ú-wa-an-zi na-aš-ta GUNNI 1-*ŠU* wa-ḫa-an-zi SÌR-ya
30′ nu-uš-ma-aš a-ku-wa-an-na pí-an-zi na-at-kán pa-ra-a pa-a-an-zi
31′ nu-za EGIR-pa EGIR ^{GIŠ}AB.ḪI.A *A-ŠAR-ŠU-NU* ap-pa-an-zi

---

§22′ 32′ [E]GIR-an-da-ma DINGIR.MEŠ URU-*LIM* TUŠ-aš e-ku-zi 1 $^{NINDA!}$ta-kar-mu-un
pár-ši-ya
33′ [na-]an-kán ^{KUŠ}kur-ši še-er da-a-i EGIR-an-da-ma ir-ḫa-a-an-te-eš
34′ [ḫi-i]š-ša-al-la-a-an-te-eš TUŠ-aš ku-u-uš DINGIR.MEŠ e!-ku-zi

---

(bottom of tablet)

55. Written in above the line.

KUB 55.43

Reverse iv (*translation cont.*)

§19′ They drink the Tutelary Deity of Ḫatti, standing. The singers sing. The dog-men bark. He breaks one *takarmu-* bread and places it upon the hunting bag. They sweep (it off). They drink Zitḫariya, standing. The singers sing. The dog-men bark. He breaks one *takarmu-* bread and places it back upon Zitḫariya. They drink Kappariyamu, the Tutelary Deity of Tatašuna, and the Tutelary Deity of Tašḫapuna, standing. He breaks two[56] *takarmu-* breads and places them upon the hunting bag. The singers sing. The dog-men bark.

§20′ They sweep (it off). They drink the Tutelary Deity of Ḫatenzuwa, standing. The singers sing. The dog-men bark. He breaks one *takarmu-* bread and places it upon the hunting bag. They sweep (it off). They drink Ḫašgala, standing. The singers sing. The dog-men bark. He breaks one *takarmu-* bread and places it upon the hunting bag.

§21′ They again drink the Tutelary Deity of Zapatiškuwa, standing. The singers sing. The dog-men bark. He breaks one *takarmu-* bread and places it upon the hunting bag. The singers of the place come in. They go once round the hearth and sing. They give them (something) to drink. They go out and again take their places behind the windows.

§22′ Afterwards he drinks the gods of the city, seated. He breaks one *takarmu-* bread and places it upon the hunting bag. Afterwards, seated, he drinks these gods, the ones (whose offerings have been) done in sequence (and) the ones (whose offerings are) [pl]anned:

(bottom of tablet)

56. One would expect three breads to be broken, since there are three gods being honored here. In the parallel occurrence of these three gods in §9′, three breads are broken.

KUB 55.43

Left edge (*transliteration*)

§23′ 1 [... ^{D}Ḫa-aš-ga-la-an ^{D}LAMMA ^{GIŠ}ŠUKUR ^{GIŠ}DAG-an? (DN) (DN) (DN)
^{D}Gu]l-še-eš[57] ^{D}Ḫi-la-a[š-š]i-in ^{D}Ḫa-ša-am-mi-li-in ^{fD}Ma-⌈ra⌉-aš-ša-an-ta [

2 [ḪUR.SAG.MEŠ ÍD.MEŠ ḫa-re-eš ... (?)[58] $^{\text{LÚ.MEŠ}}$SÌR SÌR-*RU* LÚ.MEŠ UR.GI$_7$
wa-ap-pí-an-zi 1 ^{NINDA}ta-kar-mu-u]n pár-ši-ya n[a-a]n-kán ^{KUŠ}kur-ši še-er da-a-i
$^{\text{LÚ.MEŠ}}$SÌR SÌR-*RU*

3 [LÚ.MEŠ UR.GI$_7$ wa-ap-pí-an-zi[59] ...]x

Colophon (*transliteration*)

4 [DUB 1 KAM *QATI*?[60] ^{URU}Ḫa-at-tu-ša-a]z[61] ma-aḫ-ḫa-an *ŠA* ^{D}LAMMA
^{URU}Ḫa-te-en-zu-wa ^{KUŠ}kur-ša-an TIL-*RA* [Ø]

5 [*I-NA* ^{URU}Dur-mi-it-ta pé-e-da-an-zi? n]a-an *ŠA* ^{D}LAMMA ^{URU}Za-pa-ti-iš-ku-wa
^{KUŠ}kur-ša-an i-ya-an-zi [Ø]

6 [ma-aḫ-ḫa-an-ma-an? pé-e-tum-ma-an-]zi[62] an-da uk-tu-u-ri-pát *A-NA* EZEN *I-NA*
^{URU}Dur-mi-it-ta [Ø]

7 [da-an-zi *A-NA* ^{D}Zi-it-ḫa-ri-ya-ma-aš?-t]a ar-ḫa-ya-an ⌈EZEN⌉ *Ú-UL* ku-in-ki

8 [[63] i?-]en-zi[64]

57. The names in the break are restored from obv. ii 31–32, the same list. Ḫašgala has been restored in this list because he probably occurs in ii 32; one should note, however, that he has already been honored individually in iv 23′–25′.

58. The evidence from ii 34 indicates that there is probably at least one more element in this list after *ḫareš*.

59. Restored thus because this phrase almost invariably accompanies the phrase $^{\text{LÚ.MEŠ}}$SÌR SÌR-*RU*. However, there is more space than this available in this line; if the dog-men were here, they were probably at the beginning of line 3, and the end of the line then had something else. On the other hand, since all that is left is the colophon, and the remaining text to be written is quite small, it is quite possible that the scribe just centered this last short line. The trace on the tablet does not really look like *-z*]*i*, but there is so little preserved that LÚ.MEŠ UR.GI$_7$ *wa-ap-pí-an-z*]*i* is not absolutely precluded.

60. Or *UL QATI*.

61. Restoration of *Ḫattuša*]*z* by Otten, *FsFriedrich* 353.

62. Otten, *FsFriedrich* 358, restores *pé-e-tum-ma-an-zi* on the basis of *KUB* 7.36 iv 4, edited below (cited by Laroche as *CTH* 685).

63. The location of the point of maximum thickness on the tablet indicates that the tablet was getting thinner here. Thus line 8 would have had less room to the left of the preserved portion than line 7 does. For this reason, it is possible that there was no room for anything besides [*i*]*enzi* in line 8, which would fit very well as a direct continuation of line 7.

64. Much less has been restored in the breaks in the colophon than in l.e. 1–3. The colophon was restored based on sense; the disparity between the length of its lines and those of l.e. 1–3 may cast doubt on the restoration of one or the other. The colophon only seems to mention one of the two hunting bags which were renamed and sent out to other cities. The restoration of the entire left edge must remain tentative.

KUB 55.43

Left edge (*translation*)

§23′ [Ḫašgala, the Tutelary Deity of the spear, Ḫalmaššuitta, DN, DN, DN, the Fate] Deities, Ḫila[šš]i, Ḫašamili, the Maraššanta river, [(divine) mountains, rivers, valleys, and x. The singers sing. The dog-men bark. One *takarmu-* bread] he breaks and places upon the hunting bag. The singers sing. [The dog-men bar]k.

Colophon (*translation*)

[First tablet, finished(?)[65] ...] How [they bring] the old hunting bag of the Tutelary Deity of Ḫatenzuwa fr[om Ḫattuša to Durmitta and] make it into the hunting bag of the Tutelary Deity of Zapatiškuwa. [When, however, they take it up in order to bri]ng it for the regular festival in Durmitta, they do not perform any festival separately [for Zitḫariya].

Comments on Individual Lines

Obverse i

i 9–10 (§2). The use of the participle *walḫanteš* instead of a finite form such as *walḫanzi* is significant; it indicates a completed action, i.e., that the pegs are driven in before the work on the *kurša*-s begins. A finite form would imply that the pegs were driven in as part of the ceremony. The pegs were driven in permanently and never moved because the place was already prescribed. In the phrase *ANA AŠAR* DINGIR-*LIM*-*pat*, the *-pat* is there to indicate the contrast between the actual place of the god and the area below it where the pegs are fixed and where the old hunting bags are hung to make room for the new ones in the place of the god. See Hoffner, *FsOtten* 105, for a discussion of how *-pat* attaches itself to the modifier in a word+modifier construction. Although it is attached here to DINGIR-*LIM*, it modifies the whole phrase, "place of the god." The phrase *AŠAR* DINGIR-*LIM* occurs nowhere else in the published Hittite corpus except in this text, i 9 and iii 15′. There is, however, at least one other text in which the places of the god are mentioned: *nu*-*za BELTI* É-*TI AŠRI*ᴴᴵ·ᴬ *ŠA* DINGIR-*LIM IŠTU* DINGIR-*LIM arḫa ariezzi* "The mistress of the house makes an oracular inquiry from the deity concerning the places of the deity" *KUB* 17.24 ii 9–10 (*witašš*(*iy*)*aš* Festival).[66]

i 13 and 18 (§§3 and 4): *karp-*. See Neu, *StBoT* 5 (1968) 80–82 for the medio-passive use of *karp-* and discussion of this passage.

i 20 (§5): ᵁᴿᵁTuḫuppiya. Otten, *FsFriedrich* 357–58, suggests that Tuḫuppiya and Durmitta, the two cities to which they take the old hunting bags after renaming them, must

65. Or "not finished."

66. *CHD* first draft on *peda-*.

be close to each other. See also Goetze, *RHA* XV/61 (1957) 93–99, on a "Reiseroute" that includes Tuḫuppiya. Tuḫuppiya is attested in Old Assyrian documents from Kültepe; see Bilgiç, *AfO* 15 (1945–51) 36.

i 23 and 27 (§5): *ḫalzai-*. The verb *ḫalzai-* occurs often in festivals, but usually with the meaning "to cry out" or "to call (by name)." Here it is used to indicate declaring a new identity for something. Such a meaning for *ḫalzai-* is attested in the Instructions for Temple Personnel:[67] *nu*-*za* A.ŠÀ DINGIR-*LIM šumēl ḫalziyatteni šumēl*-*ma*-*za* A.ŠÀ A.ŠÀ DINGIR-*LIM ḫalziyatteni* "(If) you call the god's field your own and your field the god's field." Its use with this meaning is unusual in a festival context, although there is at least one other similar example: *ANA* $^{LÚ.MEŠ}$SANGA-*TIM ḫumandaš* DUMU.MEŠ É.GAL LÚ.MEŠ *MEŠEDI* [ ] ^{UZU}NÍG.GIG *ḫuišu piyanz[i]* § *n*-*an*-*za* ^{UZU}NÍG.GIG *taḫalai[n] ḫalziššanzi* "The palace attendants and the royal bodyguards give the raw liver to all the priests. § They call it the *taḫalai-* liver."[68] In this text as in *KUB* 55.43 the construction involves the use of the sentence particle *-za*, a doubled object, and the iterative-durative form *ḫalziššanzi*.

i 25 (§5): KÁ.GAL *ašušan*. Although the basic semantic range of *ašuša-* as some kind of ornament is certain, a more precise meaning for it has not been agreed upon. See most recently Tischler, *HEG* Lief. 1 (1977) 90, as "ein Schmuckstück, Ohrgehänge"; Kammenhuber, *HW*² Lief. 6/7 (1982) 537–38, listing *ašuša-* in a genitive construction with KÁ.GAL as *ašuša-*¹ and a separate word *ašuša-*² for *ašuša-* as some kind of ornament, perhaps "Ohrgehänge"; and Puhvel, *HED* 1–2 (1984) 220–22, with the meaning "ring."

Otten in his commentary on this line in *FsFriedrich* 357 has already pointed out that *ašuša-* on the one hand is sometimes associated with a gate but on the other hand also appears in connection with cultic equipment, a point similar to the one made by Kammenhuber by dividing *ašuša-* into two distinct words. As noted in the transliteration, this word is sufficiently unclear on the tablet that both *a-šu-ša-an* and *a-šu-ša-aš* are possible readings. If it is to be read *a-šu-ša-an*, it cannot be an accusative, as we already have the object of the sentence expressed with the enclitic pronoun *-an-* at the beginning of the sentence. It must be taken rather as an Old Hittite genitive plural, "gate of the *ašuša*-s." If the reading *a-šu-ša-aš* is correct, it would also be a genitive (plural?). The existence of an *ašuša-* gate was noted by Alp, *Beamt.* (1940) 14 n. 1, and Otten *FsFriedrich* (1959) 355 and 357, and has been accepted by Kammenhuber, *HW*² 1: 537 and Puhvel, *HED* 1–2: 220. See Ünal, *FsBittel* (1983) 528–29, on the *ašuša-* gate as one of several gates at Ḫattuša whose names are known, and for a possible hieroglyphic reading for this gate name.

i 25 (§5): *ŠUMŠU*. There are no other definite examples in the published corpus of taking the name away from a god, or in fact from anything or anybody. "Calling" (*ḫalzai-*) and "speaking" (*te-*) the name are quite common, but this is the only text in which a name is taken away. This is so unusual and so concrete an expression that we may wonder if

67. *KUB* 13.4 rev. iv 16–17, ed. Sturtevant, *Chrest.* 162–63; Süel, *Direktif Metni* 76–77.

68. *KUB* 25.36 v 35–39 (Festival Celebrated by the Prince). For some reason the text shows both neuter (*ḫuišu*) and common (*-an-*, *taḫalain*) agreement for ^{UZU}NÍG.GIG.

there were names actually written on the *kurša*-s, perhaps on a medallion which was attached to the bag.

i 28 (§6). Restoring the broken section [... -*z*]*i* MU-*ti* has proved quite difficult. There are no examples of an ordinal number whose complement ends in -*zi*. The only adjective which might be appropriate to restore would be [*ḫantezz*]*i*. The problem with such a restoration is that [*ḫantezz*]*i* in i 28 would mean that sending out the hunting bags in the first year was being contrasted to sending them out promptly. This does not express the required contrast between the two different cases being described, so the restoration of i 28 remains uncertain.

Obverse ii

ii 2 (§7′): ^{NINDA}***takarmu-*.** See Jakob-Rost, in H. Klengel, ed., *Beiträge zur sozialen Struktur des alten Vorderasien* (Berlin, 1971) 114, and Hoffner, *AlHeth* (1974) 185. Jakob-Rost points out that, in texts in which the "singer from Kaneš" sings, the two breads almost invariably offered are NINDA.KUR$_4$.RA and ^{NINDA}*takarmu-*. This and Hoffner's idea in *AlHeth* that the word is probably Hattic might be an indication that ^{NINDA}*takarmu-* is an offering bread used from at least the earliest times of the Hittite cult and probably even earlier in Hattic festivals.

ii 3 and passim: *išgar-*. In column ii of *KUB* 55.43 this verb occurs a number of times, always in the same phrase and as a participle used substantively. The form *iškarantaš* could be either genitive or a dative-locative plural. There is little help to be gained from other texts; the *iškarantaš* occurs only two other times in the corpus, both in broken or unclear context. Translating it as a genitive, "for the god of the lined up one(s)," yields little sense. I have taken it as a plural dative-locative in a construction with *šer* as "upon the lined up ones," probably the lined up hunting bags.

The use of the participial form *išgarant-* as a substantive is attested elsewhere: *nu* ^{GIŠ}PA *kue išgaranta n*〃*at*〃*kan ḫuittianzi n*〃*at*〃*kan ANA* ^{NINDA}*paršulli šer ANA* ^{D}U *tianzi ŠA* ^{D}ZA.BA$_4$.BA$_4$ *išgaranta ḫuittiyanzi n*〃*at*〃*šan ANA* 6 ^{NINDA}*paršulli šer ANA* ^{D}ZA.BA$_4$.BA$_4$ *tianzi* "They pull the staff(s) which are lined up. They place them on the broken pieces of bread for the storm god. And the lined up ones (i.e., staffs) of ZA.BA$_4$.BA$_4$ they pull and place on 6 broken pieces of bread for ZA.BA$_4$.BA$_4$" *KBo* 11.45 iv 9′–15′ (Festival Celebrated by the Prince).

ii 3 (§7′). Either ^{D}IM or ^{D}LAMMA ^{URU}*Zapatiškuwa* could be restored at the end of the line, based on the similar list of gods in col. iv. Spacing would favor the restoration of the shorter name ^{D}IM. This is reinforced by the fact that the Tutelary Deity of Zapatiškuwa receives drink offerings further down in this list, in ii 13. The Tutelary Deity of Zapatiškuwa is less prominent and occurs further down in the order here than it does in col. iv; for possible reasons for this see the comments on the festivals below.

ii 9 (§8′). The phrase *n*〃*ašta šanḫanzi* is frequently used as an abbreviation for *n*〃*ašta daganzipan/uš šanḫanzi* "They sweep the floor(s)." Normally the ^{LÚ}ŠU.I would perform this task. Since the amount of crumbs generated during the ceremonies described in columns ii and iv would eventually necessitate the sweeping of the floor, it is quite possible that *n"ašta šanḫanzi* in this text is to be understood as "They sweep (the floor)." A passage from a ritual procedure provides another possible interpretation for *KUB* 55.43 ii 9 and rev. iv 13′, 20′, and 22′: ("They take away the broken thick breads from the tables") *n"ašta* ^{GIŠ}BANŠUR.ḪI.A *arḫa šanḫanzi* É-*ir"a"kan PANĪ* DINGIR-*LIM šanḫanzi* "They wipe/brush off the tables. They also sweep the house in front of the deity" *KBo* 24.57 i 6–8 with dupl. *KBo* 23.43 i 6–8 (Ritual of *šarraš*). Here *šanḫ-* is used for cleaning off bread crumbs after they have been broken and set out as part of the cultic activity. Because in column ii there may be only two and in column iv only one hunting bag on which the bread offerings are placed, perhaps this phrase here indicates that they wipe/brush off the hunting bags periodically before putting on more bread offerings. However, the *KUB* 55.43 passages do not express an object of *šanḫ-* as the *KBo* 24.57 passage does, so the correct interpretation may be that the floors are being swept.

ii 27 (§10′). The whole of column ii as preserved is a list of gods to whom are given drink and bread offerings; an almost identical list begins in the second preserved paragraph (§18′) of column iv and continues onto the left edge. Although this second list helps restore ii 27, the list of gods in column ii contains one less item than that of column iv. We must therefore choose between the last two elements of the column iv list, ^{D}LAMMA ^{URU}Zapatiškuwa and DINGIR.MEŠ URU-*LIM* to restore in ii 27. I restore DINGIR.MEŠ URU-*LIM* from iv 32′ rather than ^{D}LAMMA ^{URU}Zapatiškuwa of iv 26′ for two reasons: (1) There is very little space at the end of ii 27, making the shorter restoration more likely. (2) In all the places in which the Tutelary Deity of Zapatiškuwa receives offerings, they sing and bark as part of the ceremony. Because this does not happen with the offerings for the deity or deities broken away in ii 27, and because it is similarly omitted in iv 32′f. with the DINGIR.MEŠ URU-*LIM*, this seems the likelier possibility.

ii 30f. (§11′). The ceremonies of §11′ and §§21′–22′ involve the same sequence of activities and gods being honored. The sequence reconstructed from these two examples makes it clear that cultic singing by the $^{\text{LÚ.MEŠ}}$SÌR and barking by the LÚ.MEŠ UR.GI$_{7}$ accompany both drink offerings and bread offerings.

ii 33–34 (§11′). Although there may not be enough space for it, a possible restoration after *ḫareš* here would be [^{URU}*Ḫattušaš*] / [*LIM* DINGIR.MEŠ-*ya*], "and the thousand gods of Ḫatti," a logical way to end a list like this. Such a list is attested in *KUB* 9.28 i 7′–9′ (ritual for Heptad): [^{D}*IŠT*]*AR-iš* ^{D}*Ninattaš* ^{D}*Kulittaš* [^{D}*T*]*arauwaš* ^{D}*Gulšeš* ^{D}*Ḫilaššiš* [ḪU]R.SAG.MEŠ ÍD.MEŠ ^{URU}*Ḫattušaš LIM* DINGIR.MEŠ. Note here also that the Fate Deities and Ḫilašši again occur next to each other, making the restoration of [^{D}*Gul*]*šeš* in ii 32 even more likely.

Reverse iii

iii 8′ (§13′). The ^{É}*karimmi-* also occurs in the Ritual for the Tutelary Deity of the Hunting Bag in 523/t rev? 8′. The exact meaning of ^{É}*karimmi-* has not been agreed upon, but it is clear that it is a kind of sacred building.[69] The restoration ^{É}*kar*[*immi* makes good sense here, as we could expect the god to be taken to the ^{É}*karimmi*- or have something done for him there. There are, however, no other examples of a phrase like the one which we have in line 8′, *nu* DINGIR-*LAM INA* ^{É}*kar*[*immi* ... , so we cannot use the evidence of an analogous passage to restore the end of the line.

iii 22′ (§14′). The word beginning *ku*-⌈*x*⌉-[could be *ku*-⌈*e*⌉-[*da-ni, ku-i*[*š, ku*-⌈*e*⌉, *ku*-⌈*i*⌉-[*e-eš*, or *ku*-⌈*i*⌉-[*uš*. The translation reflects the last of these readings. The word *ḫé-ma-aš-x*[is a hapax legomenon; there are no occurrences even of a word beginning **ḫé-ma-*. The trace after -*aš* does not suggest any possible reading to me; it looks most like a *na* sign without the vertical wedge, even though the break is such that the vertical would be visible if the sign were *na*. There are at least four occurrences in the corpus of *ḫé* or *ḫé-e* followed by a break, some of which could conceivably be this same word. The broken nature of *KUB* 55.43 at this point makes it difficult to say even what function the word served in the sentence; it was probably the subject or object of the action performed. The reading *GAN-*ma-aš-x*[has not been considered because GAN never occurs by itself.

iii 25′ (§15′). Hoffner suggests restoring a form of ^{DUG}*išnura*- here on the basis of the trace in line 28′ in a context that seems to be referring to the same vessel and which could be read ^{DUG}*iš-nu-*]*u-ri*. In addition, the ^{DUG}*išnura*- is the vessel into which one puts *išna*-, "dough," which is the case here. This could also conceivably be ^{DUG}*i*[*šnurit*], with a translation "They [br]ing four BÁN [x] [in] five *i*[*šnura*-] vessels." There is not space in the break for an enclitic "and" on the end of *išnuruš* if we restore [*ud*]*anzi* instead of [*d*]*anzi*. The former verb has been restored here because *uda*- is frequently used in festival context with the expression *IŠTU* É ^{LÚ}*uriyanni*, while *da*- is not attested with this particular phrase.

iii 28′ (§15′). As indicated in the translation, it is unclear whether the subject of the sentence [*n*=*aš* ^{DUG}*išn*]*uri PĀNI* DINGIR-*LIM šešzi* is the GUDÚ priest or the dough whose preparation is described in this paragraph. Each interpretation can be supported by a passage which shows similarities to it. Although there are no other occurrences of *išna*- "dough" with *šeš*- "sleep, spend the night," similar foodstuffs/cultic materials do rarely occur with this verb, for example: § *nu šuppa PANI* DINGIR-*LIM šešzi lukkatta*=*ma*=*at šara daḫḫi n*=*e arḫa adanzi* "The flesh spends the night before the god. In the morning I take it up and they eat (it)" *KUB* 7.1+*KBo* 3.8 i 17–18 (Ritual of Ayataršа). "The king drinks the gods of the city, standing. (They play) the large INANNA instrument. He breaks sour thick bread. The cupbearer brings it forth." § ^{GIŠ}BANŠUR.ḪI.A *pēdi*=*pat kurkanzi* GAD-*it kariyanzi pedi*=*pat šešzi* "They keep the tables in the same place and cover (them) with a linen cloth. It (the sour thick bread) passes the night in the same place" *KBo* 19.128 vi 25′–29′ (fragment of AN.TAḪ.ŠUM Festival), ed. Otten, *StBoT* 13 (1971) 16–17. Otten translates the critical sentences "sie bedecken (sie) mit einem Linnen (und alles) bleibt an

69. Discussions of the ^{É}*karimmi*- include Alp, *Tempel* (1983) 102; Melchert, *Die Sprache* 29 (1983) 11–12; Pieri, *Atti e Memorie dell'Accademia Toscana di scienze e lettere "La Colombaria"* 47 (1982) 8–9; Haas and Wilhelm, *AOATS* 3 (1974) 44; and Güterbock, *CRRAI* 20 (1972) 125. Melchert's work is the latest to reaffirm Güterbock's point that the ^{É}*karimmi*- is not strictly the temple but rather has a more general meaning, perhaps best translated "sacred building."

seinem Ort," by which he seems to mean that the sour thick bread as well as the tables remain for the night. In any case this is an example of NINDA.KUR$_4$.RA as the subject of *šeš-*. In these examples the subjects of *šeš-*, both *šuppa-* "flesh" and NINDA.KUR$_4$.RA *EMṢA* "sour thick bread," support the interpretation of *išna-* as the subject of the sentence in iii 28′ in that they also are foodstuffs that are used in the cult.

In contrast to the interpretation of *išna-* as the subject of this sentence, it is also possible that it is the ^{LÚ}GUDÚ involved in the preparation of the dough in §15′ who watches over it through the night. There are a number of examples of the client for whom a ritual is being performed (*BĒL* SISKUR) spending the night in a ritually significant locus, for example: *maḫḫan nekuzzi nu-za BĒL* SISKUR.SISKUR ^{GIŠ}[BA]NŠUR-*pat piran šešzi* ^{GI}[^{Š}N]Á-*aš-ši* ^{GIŠ}BANŠUR-*pat piran katta tiyanzi* "When it becomes night the ritual's client sleeps before that same table. They place a bed for him down in front of that same table" *KUB* 7.5 ii 14′–16′ (Ritual of Paškuwatti), ed. Hoffner, *Aula Orientalis* 5 (1987) 271–87.[70] This and other examples like it differ from the proposed interpretation of the *KUB* 55.43 passage in that in the latter the GUDÚ priest is not a client for whom a ritual is being performed, and his spending the night before the god is therefore not done for his benefit. Rather the purpose would have been to watch over the carefully prepared dough until morning. The ritual client spending the night in a prescribed place does not guard anything, and the whole procedure is of course being performed in his interest and not as part of a state festival. In the absence of any more closely analogous passage to that of *KUB* 55.43 iii 28′ we must remain undecided as to exactly who or what spent the night before the god by/in the *išnura-*.

iii 29′ (§15′). The sentence in line 29′ is unique, although there are examples of somewhat similar expressions. The only other possible example which I have been able to find of EZEN NU.GÁL *kuiški* is: ^{URU}*Katapi* DINGIR.MEŠ-*aš ḫazziu* EZEN[-*ya* NU.GÁ]L? *kuiški* "[There is n]o kind of ceremony or festival of the gods in the city Katapa" *KUB* 30.39 obv. 9 (AN.TAḪ.ŠUM outline), ed. Güterbock, *JNES* 19 (1960) 80 and 87. Güterbock reads the broken section as EZEN[-*ya Ú-U*]*L ku-iš-ki*, which may very well be the correct reading, especially when we consider the example which he cites of a similar phrase in *IBoT* 3.40:5′ (AN.TAḪ.ŠUM Festival, first day), which reads [EZE]N-*ya Ú-UL ku-i*[*t-ki*].[71] Although Güterbock's reading may be correct, the trace in the copy is such that it could also be the end of a GÁL (*ik*) sign. Evidence for the reading [NU.GÁ]L *kuiski* in *KUB* 30.39 obv. 9 is the duplicate text *KBo* 10.20 i 12, which has at this point *ḫazziwi* NU.GÁL *kuitki*. I have found only one example of a sentence similar to that of iii 29′ with regard to time specification: *apēdani* UD-*ti ḫazziwe* NU.GÁL *kuitki* "There is no kind of ceremony on that day" *KUB* 27.66 ii 13′–14′ (frag. of *witašš*(*iy*)*aš* Festival).

iii 31′ (§16′). This passage is the only one in the published Hittite corpus in which the É.UDUN occurs. Its meaning, however, seems quite obvious from its component parts. See

70. See Hoffner, *Aula Orientalis* 5 (1987), especially p. 282, for a discussion of incubation, i.e., spending the night in a sacred location to facilitate access to a deity.

71. EZEN regularly takes common agreement, so the neuter *kui*[*tki*] here is unexpected. The trace on the tablet as copied, however, does not allow the possibility of reading *kui*[*ški*].

Hoffner, *AlHeth* 137f., for comments on the UDUN. He points out there that explicit references to the oven in Hittite are rare, so we should not be too surprised that the É.UDUN is otherwise unattested. He also notes, based on *KBo* 15.33 ii 17 and iii 29–30, that the UDUN was the type of oven used to bake NINDA.KUR$_4$.RA/*ḫarši-*, which accords well with our text, in which NINDA.KUR$_4$.RA is baked in the É.UDUN.

iii 36′ (§16′). The sentence beginning *IŠ-TU* É ... requires an object in the break to make sense. This object is something which in the following sentence the celebrants sacrifice (BAL). For this reason a sacrificial animal of some kind is suggested for the break. I take the *-ya* at the end of *uriyanni-* as the conjunction *-ya*, "and, also" and not as part of a form such as *^{LÚ}*uriyanniy*[*aš*] because such a form is unattested, while there are numerous examples of É ^{LÚ}*uriyanni.* See *Appendix B* for more on the morphology of *uriyanni-*. A stem form such as this is not uncommon in what we might call a quasi-Akkadographic writing. The conjunction *-ya-*, "also," marks the contrast between the ceremony with the bread in the first part of the paragraph and the animal sacrifice that follows it.

iii 37′ (§16′). The trace read BA[L could conceivably be *aš-š*[*i-*, but no Hittite word then suggests itself as a likely restoration. The verb *aššiya-* "to love" would make little sense here. With the exception of one occurrence, *aššiya-* is always written beginning *a-aš-ši-* ... One expects a verb denoting the action performed on the antecedent of *apūn*, thus BA[L as a logogram for *šipant-* seems to be the best reading. Given the similarity to the sentence in line 35′, it might have been possible to restore the verb *palwai-*, but the accusative form *apūn* in the sentence makes this impossible, as *palwai-* is always intransitive.

Reverse iv

iv 29′ (§21′). The verb *weḫ-* occurs in other festivals, especially in the festivals naming the NIN.DINGIR, *CTH* 649, but this passage is the only occurrence with GUNNI as an apparent object of *weḫ-* in the active voice, or with $^{LÚ.MEŠ}$SÌR, "singers" as the subject. This festival is thus unique in prescribing ritual "turning" for the singers, who normally just sing. There is one example of a similar ceremonial prescription: *n=ašta* GUNNI *ú-e-ḫa-an-ta-ri nu kiššan* SÌR-*RU* "'They' circle the hearth and sing as follows" *IBoT* 1.29 rev. 21′–22′ (*ḫaššumaš* Festival). Because line 21′ of the *IBoT* 1.29 passage begins a new paragraph, it is not clear who are circling the hearth and singing. Here as in the *kurša-* Festival the cultic singing is done while performing some kind of ceremonial dance or procession around the hearth.

Although this use of *weḫ-* with the hearth is extremely rare, there are a number of occurrences of running around the hearth (*ḫaššan ḫuwai-*). This is attested with uncomplemented GUNNI: GUNNI=*kan ḫūyanzi*, *KBo* 11.32 obv. 15 (Festival for the Earth Deities); with GUNNI-an: GUNNI-*an=kan ḫūiyanzi*, obv. 9 of the same text; and with *ḫaššan*: *n=ašta ḫaššan ḫuyanzi*, *KUB* 53.14 ii 7 (Festival for Telipinu). Although normally *ḫuwai-* is intransitive, here it takes an accusative and is translated "They run (around) the hearth." In the same way, in *KUB* 55.43 iv 29′, the normally intransitive verb *weḫ-* takes GUNNI as its direct object: "They circle the hearth."

In cultic ceremonies various functionaries run around the hearth, including the DUMU.MEŠ É.GAL, "palace attendants" *KUB* 55.39 i 9′–10′ (Festival for the Earth Deities), translit. (as Bo 2372) Neu, *StBoT* 26: 366; the LÚ.MEŠSANGA, "priests" *KUB* 10.39 obv. iii 7–8 (fest. fragment); and the LÚ.MEŠ*ḫapeš* (cult functionaries), *KBo* 25.46:10′ (Festival of Tetešḫapi). Often the subject of *ḫuwai-* is not expressed in this construction but is simply the impersonal "he/she" or "they" so common in festival procedure. Singing does not usually accompany the ceremony of running around the hearth. The one example of singers running around the hearth, interesting because it is singers who circle the hearth in *KUB* 55.43 iv 29′, is in *KUB* 55.28 iii 8′ (Building ritual),[72] in which the LÚ.MEŠNAR run around the hearth.

Left edge

l.e. 4 (colophon): TIL-*RA*. The complementation is for Akkadian *LABIRA*. This is a very unusual form, as TIL at Boğazköy is almost never provided with an Akkadian phonetic complement. The more frequent Sumerogram for "old" is LIBIR.RA.

l.e. 6 (colophon): *ukturi-*. Some festivals are described in their colophons as "regular" or "fixed," to be celebrated on a regular basis at the appropriate time of the year.[73] The ceremony for renewing the hunting bags was not regular; the introduction to the festival tells us that it was done as needed when replacing the hunting bags. There was, however, a regular festival related to the hunting bag which was performed in Durmitta, which is the city to which the old hunting bag of the Tutelary Deity of Ḫatenzuwa was taken. The word [*petumman*]*zi*, restored from line 4′ of the colophon of *KUB* 7.36 (*CTH* 683.3), is somewhat difficult to fit into the sentence, and the restorations and translation for l.e. 6 and 7 are therefore tentative.

A = *KBo* 13.179 B = *KBo* 22.168

Bo 55/u = *KBo* 13.179 is a fragment measuring 8.5 cm wide by 6.3 cm high. Although there is some abrasion of the surface, its state of preservation is in general quite good. The ductus of *KBo* 13.179, like that of *KUB* 55.43, looks like Middle Script. Even in such a small fragment we can see examples of older and newer forms of the same sign; the *da* sign for example shows forms both with and without a broken middle horizontal. The *e* sign occurs in an old form. The *nam* and *en* signs are not drawn in their very latest forms. The *ik* sign is written with the old form. The verticals have some of the typical Old Script slant to their tops, but there is no crowding together of signs. I suggest a Middle Script dating for this tablet as well.

Bo 412/u = *KBo* 22.168 is a small fragment approximately 6 cm wide by 3.2 cm high. Its surface is very well preserved, and the tablet is written in a neat, careful script. The

72. Edited by Ünal, *JCS* 40 (1988) 97–106.

73. See Singer, *StBoT* 27 (1983) 40 and 43, for comments on the concept of "regular" festivals.

tablet's small size makes it impossible to date the script precisely. The URU and *ik* signs occur in later forms, while *nam* does not have its very latest form. There is no slant to the tops of the vertical wedges. There is nothing definite to indicate anything but a New Script dating for this tablet.

Text Scheme

A. *KBo* 13.179.
B. *KBo* 22.168. Duplicates *KBo* 13.179 ii 2′–13′.

Transliteration

Obverse ii[74]

§1′ x+1 x x x x x[
B 2′ 2 KUŠ GUD SA$_5$ 2 KUŠ ⸢BABBAR? GUD? pa-an⸣[-zi?[75]]
3′ nu ku-e-da-ni URU-ri ^{KUŠ}kur-šu-uš [Ø]
4′ EGIR-pa ne-wa-aḫ-ḫa-an -zi [Ø]
5′ na-at a-pí-ya a-ša-an -zi [Ø]

§2′ 6′ na-aš-ta![76] 1 MÁŠ.GAL an-da u-un-ni-ya-an[(-zi)]
7′ nam-ma-an wa-ar-pa-an-zi na-an-kán
8′ *ŠA* É.GAL-*LIM* É.MEŠ ku-e-da-aš an-da
9′ pé-en-na-an-zi na-at-kán ša-an-ḫa-an-zi
10′ nam-ma-at ḫar-nu-wa-an -zi[77]

§3′ 11′ [na-a]š-ta MÁŠ.GAL LÚ.MEŠ UR.GI$_7$
12′ [(a-pí-ni-i)š-ša-an ku-wa-aš-kán-zi
B 13′ [o o o]x-kán *Ú-UL* ku-e-da-<(ni)>-ik-ki
14′ [o o o o o-z]i? nu KUŠ (eras.) *A-NA* $^{\text{LÚ.MEŠ}}$AŠGAB
15′ [pí-ya-an-zi? na-aš-t]a? ⸢^{KUŠ}kur-šu⸣-uš (eras.)
16′ [GIBIL-*TIM* $^{\text{LÚ.MEŠ}}$AŠGAB i-ya-an?-z]i

(the tablet breaks off)

Translation

Obverse ii

§1′ [...] two hides of red oxen (and) two white(?) oxen hides go(?). In whatever city they renew the hunting bags, they remain there.

74. Only traces of two or three signs preserved from column i.

75. Only the barest traces are preserved here; *pa-an-* is restored from text B 1′: *p*]*a-a*[*n*-. See *Line Commentary* below on this line on the possibility of objects such as cowhides going.

76. Text has -*ša*.

77. Or *ḫur-nu-wa-an-zi*. See *Appendix B* sub *ḫa/urn*(*uw*)*ai*-.

§2′ [Th]ey drive in one billy goat and then wash it. They sweep and then sprinkle the buildings of the palace into which they drive it.

---

§3′ The dog-men kill the goat in the same way. [...] to no one [they(?) x. They give] the hide to the leatherworkers. [Fro]m (it) [the leatherworkers mak]e the [new] hunting bags.

Comments on Individual Lines

2′ (§1′). The traces after the second KUŠ look good for ⸢BABBAR⸣, and one would expect a color here to parallel the SA_5. However, if GUD is read correctly here, why would the word order be different from the preceding phrase? One expects (number) KUŠ (animal type) (color). Whatever the traces may be, it is clear that they cannot be read as some form of ^{KUŠ}*kurša-*. Collation of *KBo* 13.179 indicates that the trace after ⸢BABBAR⸣ would also fit ⸢LÚ.MEŠ⸣, which suggests the restoration 2 KUŠ ⸢BABBAR LÚ.MEŠ x x⸣[*danzi*]. This is ruled out by the duplicate, which has 2 KU[Š o o o *p*]*a-a*[*n-* ... , possibly to be restored *ap-p*]*a-a*[*nzi*. The verb *ep*(*p*)-, "seize," would make sense here with the hides as direct object.

However, *appanzi* does not fit the preserved traces in the main text. We therefore restore *panzi*, which brings up the question of how cowhides may be said to go. In a possibly analogous situation the hunting bag goes, for example *KBo* 10.23 v 15′ (KI.LAM Festival), ed. Singer, *StBoT* 28 (1984) 14: *kunnanaš kuršaš p*[*aiz*]*zi*, "the beaded bag goes."[78] This passage allowed Singer to restore another part of the KI.LAM Festival: $^{\text{NA}_4}$*kunnanaš* [*kurš*]*eš panzi KBo* 10.25 vi 3′–4′, ed. Singer, *StBoT* 28: 52. In a similar vein are these passages: (24) *lukkatti⸗ma* ^{URU}*Arinnaz* ^{KUŠ}*kuršaš uizzi* "But in the morning the hunting bag comes from Arinna"; (26) [*lukkatti⸗ma* ^{KUŠ}*kurš*(*aš* ^{URU}*Taui*)]*niya paizzi* "But in the morning the hunting bag goes to Tawiniya"; (33) *nu* ^{KUŠ}*kur*[*šaš*] *INA* É ^{D}NISABA *uizzi* "The hunting bag comes into the temple of Nisaba" *KBo* 10.20 obv. i, restored from *KUB* 30.39 (outline of AN.TAḪ.ŠUM Festival), ed. (as 126/p+271/p+433/p+) Güterbock, *JNES* 19 (1960) 80–81. The verbs "go" and "come" describe the movements of the hunting bag as cult image while it is carried in procession. In *KBo* 13.179 obv. ii 2′ the cowhides (as prospective hunting bags?) were carried into the city in which the hunting bag was going to be renewed, and this was expressed in the same way as is the carrying of the hunting bag totem in the KI.LAM and AN.TAḪ.ŠUM Festivals.

The phrase KUŠ GUD SA_5 occurs in at least one other Hittite text: 9 ^{GIŠ}KAK ZABAR 9 ^{URUDU}*waršiniš* 2 KUŠ GUD SA_5 2 KUŠ GUD BABBAR 2 ^{DUG}*kantašualliš* ZABAR § "nine pegs of bronze, nine copper *waršini*-s, two red cowhides, two white cowhides, two *k.*-vessels of bronze," a list of equipment in *KUB* 7.29 obv. 10–11 (Ritual of ^{m}Yarri). In line 20 of the same text we have: [*A*]*NA PANĪ* ^{GIŠ}ŠÚ.A⸗*ma* 1 KUŠ GUD SA_5 *dai* "He places one red cowhide in front of the throne." There are no other occurrences of KUŠ GUD SA_5, so apparently red cowhides were only very rarely used as cultic equipment or as material

78. Güterbock, *FsKantor* 116 with n. 23, suggests that *kunnanaš kuršaš* means "beaded bag."

from which to make such equipment.[79] There are a number of examples of black cowhides, KUŠ GUD GE_6, and white cowhides, KUŠ GUD BABBAR. These examples demonstrate the Hittite preference for the hides of white or black cattle in ritual procedures. They also used the hides of other animals; there is attested for instance a goathide, KUŠ ÙZ in the ritual fragment *KBo* 17.78 ii 14. The fact that white cowhides were used in cultic procedures lends support to the idea of reading the broken sign after the second KUŠ as BABBAR; the problem with this is that I can find no examples of the word order *KUŠ BABBAR GUD. This reading must therefore remain tentative, although the *KUB* 7.29 passage quoted above is another clear example of red and white cowhides occurring together.

8′–9′ (§2′): É.GAL. There are no other occurrences in the published Hittite corpus of this phrase *ŠA* É.GAL-*LIM* É.MEŠ. There are many examples of É.GAL "palace" in the genitive, *ŠA* É.GAL(-*LIM*), but none in which the regens is "house" or "houses." This expression must refer to the individual buildings or rooms of the palace complex. There are also no other occurrences of É.GAL with the verb *penna*-; driving animals into the palace was not part of normal cult procedure.

12′ (§3′): *kuen*-. Although Friedrich, *HW* 113, gives the more common form of the iterative of *kuen*- as *kuennešk*-, in fact almost all of the rather few occurrences of this iterative are of the form *kuwaški*-. The form *kuwaškanzi* is ambiguous; there are occurrences of it which appear from context to be the verb *kuwaš*- "to kiss," which does not fit in *KBo* 13.179. The form *kuwaškanzi* could also be from the verb *kuš*-, *kuwaš*-, "to crush," but that also is less likely in this context than "kill." Because the dog-men are nowhere else attested killing, kissing, or crushing anything, we cannot derive any help from similar passages in other texts. Here the dog-men kill the goat to get its hide, from which the $^{LÚ.MEŠ}$AŠGAB will make the ^{KUŠ}*kurša*-.

14′ (§3′). The signs read KUŠ (eras.) could be KUŠ.MEŠ! If the MEŠ is there, it is not very well preserved; there are one too few verticals for KUŠ.MEŠ, and only two instead of three winkelhakens are visible for MEŠ. Another very good possibility is that the scribe started to write ^{KUŠ}*kuršuš* out of force of habit and then realized his error. The erased sign could easily have been *kur*. If we accept this last idea, we must also assume that the scribe, after erasing the beginning of *kuršuš*, forgot to write MEŠ; the mention of plural *kurša*-s in the next line implies that several hides were given to the leatherworkers to work on. See *Appendix B* sub *kurša*- for evidence that several hides might be used to make one *kurša*-.

14′ (§3′): ^{LÚ}AŠGAB. There are not a great number of occurrences of the ^{LÚ}AŠGAB, and only one other example in which he clearly receives a "hide" (KUŠ): KUŠ!GUD.ḪI.A UGULA $^{LÚ.MEŠ}$AŠGAB G[AL $^{LÚ.MEŠ}$x] / *dan*[*zi*] "The overseer of the leatherworkers and the chief of the [x] tak[e] the cowhides" *KBo* 20.23 rev. 5′–6′ (Cult of Nerik fragment). The general context of the tablet is sufficiently broken that we cannot tell just what the chief of the leatherworkers did with the hides. Nevertheless, on the basis of lines 3′–5′, it may be understood that in 15′–16′ the leatherworkers are making the new hunting bags.

79. Is this because they had to be dyed red and so were less convenient than naturally occurring colors?

KUB 7.36[80]

Bo 4912 = *KUB* 7.36 is a fragment approximately 9.8 cm wide by 9 cm high. Its surface is quite well preserved. The writing shows very strongly the crowding together of signs and words typical of Old Script. However, the *az* sign is written with a subscript *za* and the URU and SAG signs occur in later forms. These few observations do not constitute sufficient evidence to assign a dating to the script.

Transliteration

Reverse right

- - - - - - - - - - - - - - - - - - - -

§1′ x+1 [na-aš?-]ta ḫa-an-te-ez-zi [pal-ši *A-NA* (DN$_1$)]
2′ [ši-p]a-an-ti EGIR-an-da-ma-k[án[81] 1 MÁŠ.GAL *A-NA* (DN$_2$)]
3′ ši-pa-an-ti 1 MÁŠ.GAL-ma-kán [*A-NA* (DN$_3$) ši-pa-an-ti]
4′ 1 MÁŠ.GAL-ma-kán *A-NA* ^{D}Kap-[pa-ri-ya-mu ^{D}LAMMA ^{URU}Ta-ta-šu-na][82]
5′ ^{D}LAMMA ^{URU}Ta-aš-ḫa-pu-na [*Ù A-NA* (DN$_7$)]
6′ ši-pa-an-ti na-aš iš-ta-n[a-ni pí-ra-an da-a-i?]

- - - - - - - - - - - - - - - - - - - -

§2′ 7′ nu DINGIR-*LUM* EGIR-pa *A-NA A-AŠ-RI-Š*[*U*[83] pé-e-da-an-zi? na-aš-ša-an?]
8′ *A-NA* DINGIR-*LUM* SAG.DU-*ŠU* še-er d[a-an-zi[84]
9′ ke-e-ez ke-e-ez-zi-ya *A-N*[*A*
10′ na-at-kán še-er *A-NA* SAG.DU[-*ŠU* ti-an-zi?]
11′ *A-NA* NINDA.KUR$_4$.RA.ḪI.A-ma-kán še-er x[… ti-an-zi?]
12′ na-aš-ša-an še-er *A-NA* DINGIR-*LIM* SA[G.DU-*ŠU* se-er ti-an-zi?]

- - - - - - - - - - - - - - - - - - - -

§3′ 13′ *A-NA* DINGIR-*LIM*-ma pí-ra-an kat-ta da[-a-i]
14′ nu-uš-ša-an *ŠA* 3 MÁŠ.GAL ^{UZU}x[da-a-i? nu-uš-ša-an]
15′ *ŠA* ^{D}LAMMA ^{URU}Za-pa-ti-iš-ku-wa ^{K}[^{UŠ}kur-ši še-er da-a-i nu-uš-ša-an ^{UZU}x *A-NA*]
16′ ^{D}Kap-pa-ri-ya-mu ^{D}LAMMA ^{URU}T[a-ta-šu-na]
17′ ^{D}LAMMA ^{URU}Ta-aš-ḫa-pu-na ⸢*Ù*⸣[*A-NA* (DN)]
18′ ^{KUŠ}kur-ši še-er da-a-⸢i⸣[
19′ [ ]⸢ x x x ⸣[

(the tablet breaks off)

80. Catalogued by Laroche as *CTH* 685, "Fragments de fêtes pour les dieux KAL."
81. Collation reveals a trace of one or possibly two horizontals after *ma* which would fit *kán*.
82. Restored on the basis of *KUB* 55.43 ii 17–18.
83. This is the only occurrence of a plene spelling of *AŠRU* in the published Hittite corpus.
84. Or *da-a-i* "he places"?

KUB 7.36

Translation

Reverse right

§1′ The first [time] he [sac]rifices [to DN_1]. Then he sacrifices [one goat to DN_2] and one goat [to DN_3]. One goat he sacrifices to Kap[pariyamu, the Tutelary Deity of Tatašuna,] the Tutelary Deity of Tašḫapuna, [and to DN_7[85]]. [He places(?)] them [before(?)] the alt[ar].

---

§2′ [They carry] the god back to h[is] place. [They ta]ke(?) up its head away from the god.[86] On this side and that t[o ... They place(?)] it on [his] head. Upon the thick bread, however, [they place(?)] x[...]. [They place(?)] them up on the god's he[ad].

---

§3′ [He pu]ts (it) down before the god. [He sets out(?)] the x[...][87] of the three goats.[88] [He places them on] the hu[nting bag] of the Tutelary Deity of Zapatiškuwa. He places [x] on the hunting bag for Kappariyamu, the Tutelary Deity of T[atašuna], the Tutelary Deity of Tašḫapuna, an[d for DN[89]].

(the tablet breaks off)

85. The deity to whom the preceding three gods are *kipikkišdus*. See *Appendix B* sub *kipikkišdu* for the identification of Kappariyamu, the Tutelary Deity of Tatašuna, and the Tutelary Deity of Tašḫapuna as *kipikkišdus*.

86. Or "[He] pl[aces] its head up for the god."

87. A flesh part.

88. This refers to the three goats offered as sacrifices to deities in §1′.

89. The deity to whom these three are *kipikkišdus*.

KUB 7.36

Reverse left (colophon)[90]

x+1 [DUB 2? KAM *QATI*?[91] ^{URU}Ḫa-at-tu-ša?-]az
2′ [ma-aḫ-ḫa-an *ŠA* ^{D}LAMMA ^{URU}Ḫa-te-en-zu-wa ^{KUŠ}k]ur-ša-an TIL-*RA*
2a′ [*I-NA* ^{URU}Dur-mi-it-ta pé-e-da-an-zi][92]
3′ [na-an *ŠA* ^{D}LAMMA ^{URU}Za-pa-ti-iš-ku-wa ^{KUŠ}]kur-ša-an
4′ [i-ya-an-zi … p]é-e-tum-ma-an-zi
5′ [… d]a-an-zi
6′ [*A-NA* ^{D}Zi-it-ḫa-ri-ya-ma-aš-ta] ar-ḫa-an
7′ [EZEN *Ú-UL* ku-in-ki i-ya-an-zi …]x-pí[93]

(the tablet breaks off)

KUB 20.13[94]

Bo 2130 = *KUB* 20.13 is a fragment 9.1 cm wide by 7.8 cm high whose surface is not particularly well preserved. Its script shows a mixture of older and newer forms and is probably to be dated to early New Script or conceivably Middle Script.

Transliteration

Obverse i

§1′x+1 x [

---

§2′ 2′ na-aš-kán [o o o o o o o o o o o o]
3′ na-aš i-ya-a[n-na-i?[95] o o o o o o o]
4′ na-aš-ta ^{URU}L[a?- o o o o o o o o o o]
(one line blank)
5′ DINGIR-*LUM*-ma-kán ^{GIŠ}[GIGIR-az kat-ta ú-wa-da-an-zi?[96] o o]
6′ ap-pé-eš-kir na-aš-ta [o o o o o o o o]
7′ nu-uš-ša-an iš-ga-ra-an-t[a-aš? še-er ti-an-zi?]
8′ MÁŠ.GAL-ma ḫa-ap-pí-ni-i[t za-nu-an-zi]

---

90. After a gap of an undetermined number of paragraphs.
91. Or *UL QATI.*
92. There is room for this line on the tablet, and the sense of the colophon as reconstructed requires it.
93. This could conceivably be *-d*]*u-pí* or G]AL KAŠ, neither of which is meaningful in the context of a colophon.
94. Catalogued by Laroche as *CTH* 685, "Fragments de fêtes pour les dieux KAL."
95. Or perhaps *na-aš i-ya-a*[*n-zi.*
96. See *CTH* 685.2, *KUB* 9.17:24′–25′, edited in *Appendix A*.

KUB 7.36

Reverse left (colophon)[97]

[Second(?) tablet, finished(?).[98] How they take] the old [hu]nting bag [of the Tutelary Deity of Ḫatenzuwa] from [Ḫattuša to Durmitta and make it] the hunting bag [of the Tutelary Deity of Zapatiškuwa]. [... f]or carrying [...] they [t]ake. [For Zitḫariya, however, they do no] separate [festival]. [...]x-*pi*(?)

(the tablet breaks off)

KUB 20.13

Translation

Obverse i

§1′ (Only one trace preserved.)

§2′ He [...]. He goe[s(?)[99] ...]. There the city L[a- ...]. And they [bring(?)] the god [down on a chario]t. [...] they seized. And [...]. [On(?)] the lined up ones [they place(?)] them. But the billy goat [they cook with] flame.

97. After a gap of an undetermined number of paragraphs.
98. Or "unfinished."
99. Or "[They] make them."

KUB 20.13

Obverse i (*transliteration cont.*)

§3′ 9′ nu ḫa-an-te-ez-zi pal-ši ^{D}[UTU? TUŠ-aš/GUB-aš e-ku-zi]

10′ nu ^{D}U TUŠ-aš e-ku-zi $^{LÚ.MEŠ}$S[ÌR? SÌR-*RU* nu (DN)]

11′ ⸢GUB⸣-aš e-ku-zi $^{LÚ.MEŠ}$ALAN.Z[U$_{9}$ o o o o o]

12′ [nu ^{D}Zi-i]t-ḫa-ri-ya-an GU[B-aš e-ku-zi]

13′ [nu ^{D}LAMMA ^{URU}Ta-t]a-šu-na GUB-aš [e-ku-zi]

14′ [nu ^{D}Kap-pa-ri-ya-m]u-un GUB[-aš e-ku-zi]

15′ [nu ^{D}LAMMA ^{URU}Ḫa-te-e]n-zu-wa ^{D}[x GUB-aš]

16′ [e-ku-zi o o o o]x *IŠ-TU*[o o o o o]

17′ [o o o o o o o o NIND]A.KUR$_{4}$.R[A?[100] o o o o o]

(the tablet breaks off)

Reverse iv[101] (*transliteration*)

§4′x+1 ⸢ x x x ⸣[

2′ a-pé-e-da-aš-pát DINGIR.MEŠ-aš zi-ik-ká[n-zi

3′ ḫa-aš-ši-i iš-tar-na pé-e-di da-a-i ⸢*A-NA*?⸣[

4′ da-a-i ^{GIŠ}AB-ya 4 *AŠ-RA* ^{GIŠ}DAG-ti ^{D}Ḫi-la-a[š-ši

5′ še-ra-aš-ša-an ^{UZU}NÍG.GIG ^{UZU}ŠÀ ku-ra-a-an- z[i]

---

§5′ 6′ ^{UZU}Ì-ma TU$_{7}$.ḪI.A i-en-zi ma-aḫ-ḫa-an-ma-aš-ša[-an o o o]

7′ nu-kán wa-al-la-aš ḫa-aš-ta-i ^{DUG}UTÚL-az [da-an-zi]

8′ na-at-kán EGIR-pa *A-NA* DINGIR-*LIM* ti-an-zi [Ø]

9′ nu DINGIR.MEŠ a-ku-wa-an-na a-pu-u-uš-pát ir-ḫ[a-a-an-zi]

10′ ma-aḫ-ḫa-an-na ^{D}LAMMA[102] ^{URU}Ḫa-ti-en-zu-wa [

11′ nu ne-ku-ma-an-te-eš ú-wa-an-zi [

---

§6′ 12′ lu-uk-kat-ta-ma šu-up-pa-aš UD-a[z

13′ ⸢ x x x-zi⸣ nu *QA-TAM-MA* i-e[n-zi[103]

14′ [o o o o o]ni?[

(the tablet breaks off)

100. Collated.

101. After a large gap of an undetermined number of paragraphs.

102. The copy shows *ḫal*, but collation shows that the tablet actually has DINGIR as expected.

103. There is a very faint line across the tablet between 13′ and 14′. It looks like a paragraph line, but it is so faint that it is unclear whether it was actually intended to mark a new paragraph or not.

KUB 20.13

Obverse i (*translation cont.*)

§3′ The first time [he drinks the Sungod(?), seated/standing]. He drinks the Stormgod, seated. The sin[gers sing]. He drinks [DN], standing. The ALAN.Z[U$_9$]-men[104] [...]. [He drinks Zi]tḫariya, stand[ing]. [He drinks the Tutelary Deity of Tat]ašuna, standing. [He drinks Kappariyam]u, standi[ng]. [He drinks the Tutelary Deity of Ḫate]nzuwa (and) D[N, standing]. [...] from/with [... th]ic[k bread ...]

(the tablet breaks off)

Reverse iv (*translation*)

§4′ [...] [The]y place [x] for those same gods. [...] he places on the hearth in the middle. On [...] he places. To the window, the four places, the (deified) throne, (and) Ḫilaš[ši ...] On (it) they cut up the entrails (and) heart.

---

§5′ The fat, however, they make into stew. When, however, [...], [they take] the bone of the shank from the stew-pot. They place it back for the god. [They tr]eat in sequence the gods, i.e., those same ones, for drinking. And when the Tutelary Deity of Ḫatenzuwa [...] The naked ones come [and(?) ...]

---

§6′ The next morning, the day of the meat [...] he ⌈x's⌉. In the same way th[ey make]. (traces)

(the tablet breaks off)

104. On the ^{LÚ}ALAN.ZU$_9$ see most recently Güterbock, *JNES* 48 (1989) 307–09. The ALAN.ZU$_9$-man is a cult functionary who most often "recites" in festivals.

A = *KBo* 21.89+*KBo* 8.97[105] B = *IBoT* 2.69[106]

The fragment 402/d+230/m = *KBo* 21.89+*KBo* 8.97 measures approximately 12.5 cm wide by 13.2 cm high. The smaller *KBo* 8.97 piece adds greatly to the preserved portion of column i but does not supplement column iv at all. The tablet must have been rather long originally; tablet thickness indicates that the preserved portion is less than half the height of the original tablet. The tablet is a distinctive brick red color and has a very hard, smooth surface. The script shows very cramped signs, small word spaces, and a great deal of slant to the tops of the verticals. The *a*, *e*, *ra*, *zu*, KAL, and URU signs occur in a form in which all but the last vertical are very short. The *ak*, *ik*, *tar*, and *du* signs occur in their older forms. All of the evidence indicates that the tablet is Old Script. See table 6 in *Appendix C*.

Bo 504 = *IBoT* 2.69 is a small fragment, approximately 1.9 cm wide by 4.0 cm high, with a well-preserved surface. Although the fragment is small, the preserved "Randleiste" and the angled surface discernible on the reverse allow us to securely assign obverse and reverse and column numbers. There are too few signs to date this piece, although one can see older forms of *ḫa*, *li*, *da*, and URU. The few available signs are consistent with a pre-New Script dating.

Text Scheme

A. *KBo* 21.89+*KBo* 8.97.
B. *IBoT* 2.69. Obverse i duplicates *KBo* 21.89+*KBo* 8.97 i 10′–18′. Reverse too small to interpret.

Transliteration

Obverse i[107]

§1′ x+1 [ ]x x ḪI.A

- -

§2′ 2′ [ ] É NA₄KIŠIB
3′ [ ]x a-ap-pa
4′ [ ]x-ḫa(-)la?-am-mi-iš-na
5′ [ ]x wa-a-tar
6′ [ ]x

- -

§3′ 7′ [ ] ⸢ḪI.A?⸣[o o o o o o]wa-aḫ-nu-an-zi

105. *KBo* 8.97 preserves part of column i. An unpublished duplicate to *KBo* 8.97 is Bo 5572, noted by Otten in *RLA* 4 (1972–75) 134 sub Ḫaškala.

106. Catalogued by Laroche as *CTH* 685, "Fragments de fêtes pour les dieux KAL."

107. This column is labeled Rs? iv in the copy. The obverse of text B, *IBoT* 2.69, duplicates part of what is labeled reverse in *KBo* 21.89. Because *IBoT* 2.69 preserves the "Randleiste," its assigned obverse and reverse are secure, and the obverse and reverse of *KBo* 21.89+*KBo* 8.97 are to be switched. *KBo* 8.97 joins §§3′ and 4′ of this column. Otten, *FsFriedrich* 356 and 358 n. 1, has already briefly compared *IBoT* 2.69 with *KUB* 55.43 and has noted the similarities between the two texts.

KBo 21.89+*KBo* 8.97 (*cont.*)

Obverse i (*cont.*)

§3′ 8′ [ ]x ú-wa-⸢an⸣-[zi? o o o w]a-ar-pa-an-zi
(*cont.*) 9′ [*I-N*]*A* TÚL ar-ra-an-z[i n]a-aš-ta ^{LÚ}SANGA
obv. i 10′ [*A-NA* ^{D}Zi-it-ḫ]a[108]-ri-ya da-ma-in MÁŠ.G[A]L ši-pa-an-ti
11′ [ḫa-ap-pí-ni-it? a]n-da ^{UZU}NÍG.GIG-ya za-nu-an-zi
12′ [ ]x iš-ga-ra-an-ta *A-NA* ^{D}Zi-it-ḫa-ri-ya[109]
13′ [o-d(a EGIR-pa ti-an-z)]i nu 3-*ŠU* ši-pa-an-ti ḫa-aš-ši-ya 1-*ŠU*
14′ [ši-pa-an-ti[110] ^{UZU}NÍG.G]IG-ma ^{UZU}ŠÀ ku-er-zi na-at
15′ [EGIR-pa *A-NA*? DING(IR?M)]EŠ da-a-i

- -

§4′ 16′ [nu *A-NA* ^{D}UTU ^{D}IM? ^{D}LAMM]A ^{URU}*ḪA-AT-TI* ^{D}Kap-pa-⸢ri⸣-ya-mu-ú-i
17′ [^{D}LAMM(A ^{URU}Ta-aš-ḫa-pu-n)a[111]] ^{D}LAMMA ^{URU}Ta-a-ta-šu-⸢na⸣
obv. i 18′ [^{D}(LAMMA ^{URU}Ḫa-ti-en-zu)-wa] ⸢^{D}⸣Ḫa-aš-ga-la-a-i ^{D}L[AMMA ^{URU}]Za-pa-t[i-i]š-ku-wa
19′ -]ti-ya ḫa-aš-ši-i [^{D}Ḫi-l]a-aš-š[i]
20′]x ^{D}LAMMA ^{GIŠ}Š[UKUR[112] o o o o]x-li

(traces in the intercolumnium and then the tablet breaks off)

Obverse ii[113]

§5′x+1 x[
2′ nu[
3′ nu x[
4′ ^{D}LAM[MA
5′ ^{D}LAMMA [
6′ 3-*ŠU* ši[-pa-an-ti
7′ *A-NA* ZAG[.GAR.RA-ni?

- -

108. Collation indicates that the only trace visible here is a single winkelhaken which would fit *ḫa*.

109. Text B 3′: [*iš-ga-ra-an-t*]*a-ša-an A-NA* ^{D}*Z*[*i-it-ḫa-ri-ya*.

110. Text B 5′ has *n*]*u*? *ḫa-aš-ši-i* 1-*ŠU* BAL-*t*[*i*. I restore *šipanti* here because text A uses syllabically spelled *šipant-* rather than the logogram BAL.

111. Restored from text B 10′. Although text B has ^{D}LAMMA ^{URU}Ḫatenzuwa before ^{D}LAMMA ^{URU}Tašḫapuna, the transliteration reflects the suggestion that they were in reverse order from this in text A. This keeps the triad of Kappariyamu, ^{D}LAMMA ^{URU}Tatašuna, and ^{D}LAMMA ^{URU}Tašḫapuna together, as they are in *KUB* 55.43 ii 16–18 and iv 16′–17′. See *Appendix B* sub *kipikkišdu* for discussion of the reasons for these three deities occurring together as a group. The transliteration is also based on a proposed consistency in the order of the listing of the tutelary deities as seen in the two main lists in *KUB* 55.43 ii and iv. In *KUB* 55.43 iv 23′ Ḫašgala occurs between ^{D}LAMMA ^{URU}Ḫatenzuwa and ^{D}LAMMA ^{URU}Zapatiškuwa; this same order is preserved in the restoration of *KUB* 55.43 ii 24 and here in *KBo* 21.89+*KBo* 8.97.

112. Collation shows a definite GIŠ sign as read.

113. After a gap of an undetermined number of paragraphs.

KBo 21.89+*KBo* 8.97 (*cont.*)

Obverse ii (*cont.*)

§6′ 8′ nu ^{D}Ḫa-x[
9′ nu ^{D}LAMMA ^{UR}[^{U}
10′ nu ^{D}Ir-ḫa-a[-an-du-uš ^{D}Ḫi-iš-ša-al-la-an-du-uš-ša e-ku-zi]
11′ NINDA.KUR$_4$.RA NU.GÁL [
12′ nu-uš-kán É.ŠÀ [

---

§7′ 13′ nam-ma-aš-kán pa-ra[-a
14′ ḫal-zi-iš-ša-an-z[i
15′ ḫar-kán-zi na-aš-t[a
16′ na-aš-ta 2 MÁŠ.GAL KUR?[(-)
17′ an-da u-un-ni-ya-an[-zi

---

§8′ 18′ nu DUG.GAL ta-an-na-ra[(-)
19′ la-a-ḫu-i nam-ma-kán x[
20′ ^{NA_4}pa-aš-ši-la-an-na-ká[n
21′ nu ^{KUŠ}kur-šu-uš tuḫ-ḫ[u-
22′ a-ap-pa-ma-aš ú-e-eḫ-z[i
23′ nu *IŠ-TU* É ^{NA_4}KIŠI[B
24′ 1 *ŠA-A-DU ZI-KU-KI*[114] x[

---

§9′ 25′ nu-kán MÁŠ.GAL.ḪI.A [
26′ kur-ak-kán-zi [
27′ pa-ra-a ú-[
28′ ⸢x x⸣ DINGIR.MEŠ [

(the tablet breaks off)

Reverse iii[115]

§10′ x+1 x[

---

§11′ 2′ ma-a-an [
3′ nu-uš ḫu-u-d[a-a-ak?[116]
4′ ^{KUŠ}kur-šu-uš x[
5′ ^{KUŠ}kur-šu-uš x[
6′ ga-an-kán-[zi

---

114. A Hittite rendering of Akkadian *isqūqu*, a type of flour, for which see *CAD* I/J: 202–03.

115. After a gap of an undetermined number of paragraphs.

116. Collation shows a second horizontal trace on the broken edge which would fit *da* quite well.

KBo 21.89+*KBo* 8.97 (*cont.*)

Reverse iii (*cont.*)

§12′ 7′ nu 6 NINDA Kap-pa-r[i-ya-mu-ú-i?
8′ nu-uš-ša-an 3 x[
9′ EGIR-pa ti-an-z[i
10′ *A-NA* ^{D}LAMMA ^{URU}Ḫa-t[e-en-zu-wa

---

§13′ 11′ na-aš-ta MÁŠ.GAL.ḪI.A [
12′ nu-uš-ša-an iš-ga-r[a-an-ta-aš
13′ še-er ti-an-zi UZ[U
14′ ke-e-da-aš DINGIR.MEŠ x[
15′ ḫu-u-ma-an-da-aš t[i-
16′ x[117].MEŠ da-an-z[i

---

§14′ 17′ na-at *A-NA* [
18′ pí-di ti-an-z[i
19′ 3-*ŠU* ši-p[a-an-ti
20′ nu *A-N*[*A*
21′ nam-ma [
22′ *QA-TAM-M*[*A*

---

§15′ 23′ nu-kán [
24′ ^{NINDA}pu-u[r-pu-ru-uš?
25′ SAL.MEŠ x[
26′ MÁŠ.GA[L
27′ ⌈x ḪI.A⌉[

(the tablet breaks off)

Reverse iv preserves only the very ends of the lines. ^{D}]⌈LAMMA⌉ ^{URU}*Ḫa-te-en-zu-wa* may be read in line 15′.

A tiny portion of B rev. iv? is preserved, which presumably duplicates some lost portion of the reverse of text A and cannot be integrated into the main copy of the text:

B = *IBoT* 2.69 Reverse iv
1]x nam-ma-aš [
2 ^{KUŠ}ku]r?-ša-aš pé-e[-
3]x-i-li-y[a?
4]⌈x x x⌉[

(the tablet breaks off)

117. This sign has resisted all attempts at interpretation. It looks a little like *uk/az*, neither of which would make any sense. It could conceivably be GÌR! with one superfluous vertical, but it would be unusual in this type of text. There is not enough context to guess at what the scribe intended.

COMMENTARY

The existence of the festival for renewing the *kurša-* cult images preserved in *KUB* 55.43 has been known about since Otten published an edition of the first column and the colophon in 1959.[118] Laroche in *CTH* 683 titles this text "The renewing of the 'fleece' ('toison') of the gods KAL." Actually the text describes a festival not so much for the actual process of renewing or replacing the *kurša-* as for officially "installing" the new *kurša*-s, that is effecting the transfer from the old to the new hunting bags, including a description of what to do with the old hunting bags that have been replaced.

The main text is inscribed in four columns and an edge of one tablet; a partially broken colophon on the left edge would have made it clear whether the whole festival was described on this one tablet. Our understanding and interpretation of this festival are limited by not knowing whether it is complete on this tablet and by the fact that only half of the tablet is available to us. The four columns of the text divide up the different parts of the festival quite neatly. The first column describes the preparation for the festival and the disposition of the old hunting bags. When column ii picks up the description after a break in column i, a description of the actual festival activities has begun. The *ḫantezzi palši*, "the first time," of ii 1 may indicate that column ii initiates the description of offerings. This column is an offering list of gods who receive offerings of drink and *takarmu-* bread. These offerings are accompanied in most cases by singing and "barking" by cult functionaries. Seven of the ten gods receive individual offerings, while three are sacrificed to as a group. With the exception of the Sungod and Stormgod, the gods worshipped in this way are tutelary deities.

After this list of gods come the gods of the city, who receive their offerings as a group, followed by another list of deities, very broken, which are also offered to corporately. This last group is quite diverse, encompassing protective deities, specific deified localities, and mountains and rivers in general. The column breaks off here. There may have been more gods listed with drink and bread offerings, although this last group of deities at the end of the preserved portion of column ii were probably the last of the gods to be worshipped in that round of cultic offerings.

When the third column picks up after a large gap the festival has moved on to other cultic activities involving different equipment and materials: breaking other kinds of bread, taking the god (the *kurša-*) into the *karimmi-* building, sacrificing animals, and preparing a special dough which is then made into offering bread, accompanied by cultic activities like singing and reciting or shouting (*palwai-*). Two occurrences of the word *lukkatta*, "the following morning," indicate that it required at least three days to complete that portion of the festival described in the third column of the text.

The fourth column's beginning lines are also lost. The first readable lines indicate that libation vessels, the vessels containing the drink offerings for the gods, are being provided from someone's establishment. The festival then moves into a time "for drinking," a session of systematic drink offerings to various gods. The order of the ceremony in column

118. Otten, *FsFriedrich* 351–59.

iv is very similar to that of column ii; the two have been used in the transliteration to restore each other. There are some significant differences, however. In column iv, in the list of gods honored individually, the Tutelary Deity of Zapatiškuwa has been moved in front of the Tutelary Deity of Ḫatti to the first place in the list after the Sungod and Stormgod. The list in column iv contains eleven gods, not the ten of column ii, because this Tutelary Deity of Zapatiškuwa appears not only at the beginning, but at the end of the list as well, before the gods of the city, with the word *namma*, best translated here "again." He thus appears twice in the column iv ceremony, but only once in column ii. Furthermore, the list in column iv is followed by an extra ceremony in which the "singers of the place" come in, go once round the hearth while singing, are given something to drink, and then go and take their places again behind the windows. There is a distinction made here between the "singers," who occur throughout the text without further specification, and the "singers of the place," the local singers who occur only here. They are outside for most of the ceremony and therefore must come in before they sing.

Another significant difference between the cultic procedures described in these two columns of text is that in column ii the broken bread is placed "for the god on the lined up ones" (*išgarantaš*), while in column iv it is placed on the *kurša-* (singular). Although it is not explicitly stated what the "lined up ones" are, they may be the two new hunting bags, lined up to have the bread offerings of the various deities placed on them. In §14′, after the *kurša*-s have gone into the *karimmi*- cult building for some bread offerings, they are hung up in the place of the god in the temple of the hunting bags. Before this they could have been "lined up" to receive offerings. The proposed restoration of an offering [on] the l[ined up ones] in *KUB* 55.43 iii 17′–18′ soon after they hang up the god in iii 15′ raises difficulties for the interpretation of the two new *kurša*-s as the lined up ones. However, two partially broken lines intervene between the hanging up of the god and the offerings on the lined up ones, so it is possible the *kurša*-s were taken somewhere else and lined up again. Alternatively, since almost all of the gods in the ceremony are tutelary deities, they may all have had cult images in the form of hunting bags. The adjective *išgarantaš* could refer to all the images, lined up. Would only two hunting bags be considered a sufficient number to be "lined up?" In the column iv ceremony there probably were only two hunting bags involved, those of the Tutelary Deity of Zapatiškuwa and of Zitḫariya. The different terminology of the two descriptions strengthens the idea that column ii with its use of *išgarantaš* was referring to a larger number of hunting bags.[119]

However we interpret the *išgarantaš* of column ii, the differences between the column ii and column iv descriptions indicate that these two columns represent two distinct ceremonies. The first one (column ii) is for the new hunting bags and takes place in Ḫattuša. The similarity of the second ceremony (column iv) to that of column ii indicates that its general purpose was the same. The consistent use of a singular *kurša-* throughout the column iv ceremony, the explicit reference to the (*kurša-* of) the Tutelary Deity of

119. Another possibility is that sacrificial breads were *iškarant*-, "lined up" to receive the offerings, as is the case for example in another festival procedure, *KUB* 11.23 v 5–8 (AN.TAḪ.ŠUM Festival, 33rd/34th day).

Zapatiškuwa (the new name for the old *kurša-* of the Tutelary Deity of Ḫatenzuwa) in iv 5′–6′ and 8′, and the above-mentioned prominence given to the Tutelary Deity of Zapatiškuwa in the order of gods who receive offerings suggest that the ceremony described in column iv was performed in honor of the new hunting bag of the Tutelary Deity of Zapatiškuwa. This must be its installation ceremony in its new home. In the rites of column ii the Tutelary Deity of Ḫatti was the first god after the Sungod and Stormgod to receive offerings; perhaps this precedence was dictated by the fact that the festival was taking place in his home city. In column iv the Tutelary Deity of Zapatiškuwa is the first to receive offerings after the Sungod and Stormgod, perhaps again because the festival was in his home city. Because §5 tells us that this new home was Durmitta, I suggest that this ceremony took place there rather than in Ḫattuša.

The idea that the column iv ceremony took place somewhere other than Ḫattuša would help explain the rather curious phrase *pedaš* LÚ.MEŠSÌR "singers of the place," who must be the local singers of Durmitta. Their specific mention near the end of the Durmitta ceremony implies that the singers who sing throughout the ceremony previous to this are not local singers, but those from Ḫattuša. One wonders how much of the cultic personnel and equipment from the ceremony in the capital was brought to Durmitta for the local festival. The phrase DUG*išpa*]*nduzzi udanzi* in iv 3′ may refer to the bringing of libation vessels from Ḫattuša for offerings. The gods themselves would not necessarily have been brought from Ḫattuša, as they could have received drink offerings without actually being there, or they could have had images in Durmitta as well. The bread offerings all seem to have been put on the one hunting bag, that of the Tutelary Deity of Zapatiškuwa. The *kurša*-s of all the other gods given offerings in the column iv ceremony were not present; instead the offerings for these gods were in each case placed on the hunting bag of the Tutelary Deity of Zapatiškuwa.

Another possible interpretation of the column iv ceremony is that the offerings for each god were put on his own *kurša-* symbol. The text lists them one at a time, so in each case the *kurša-* would still be in the singular. But then how would column iv differ from the column ii ceremony, where the terminology is different? In column iv, if each deity gets offerings on his own hunting bag, are they not then "lined up" just like the ones in column ii? It seems rather that although many of these gods probably had a *kurša-* symbol in Ḫattuša, they were not all brought to Durmitta for the festival. This idea is strengthened by the fact that even when a group of gods receives offerings together in lines 16′–18′, the form is still the singular *kurši*, indicating that only one hunting bag was used. The one exception to this is in iv 6′, in which the bread offering to Zitḫariya is placed not "on the *kurša-*," but rather "on Zitḫariya." We know from §1 that Zitḫariya had his own hunting bag; is this a reference to his new hunting bag, brought from Ḫattuša for the ceremony? From §1 it is clear that the Tutelary Deity of Ḫatenzuwa also had his own *kurša-*, and yet this god, when he receives his bread offering, receives it simply "on the *kurša-*" with the same term used as with the other gods. Could this reference in iv 16′ conceivably be to the *old* hunting bag of Zitḫariya, which participated in the Durmitta ceremony before going on to its new home in Tuḫuppiya? If so, why is it not called by its new name, the Tutelary

Deity of the Hunting Bag, as is the old Tutelary Deity of Ḫatenzuwa, now the Tutelary Deity of Zapatiškuwa? In the individual offering lists in columns ii and iv, the other three deities associated with the old or the new hunting bags, Zitḫariya, the Tutelary Deity of Ḫatenzuwa, and the Tutelary Deity of Zapatiškuwa, each receive offerings, but the Tutelary Deity of the Hunting Bag does not and in fact never again appears in the text as preserved after §5.

In these ceremonies of providing offerings for the gods, there are few deviations from the standard procedure; almost every god is honored the same way. However, there are a few gods who get slightly different treatment. Almost all of the gods in the list are protective deities, both Hattic deities listed by name and tutelary deities denoted with the title ^{D}LAMMA. The exceptions to this are the Sungod, the Stormgod, the gods of the city, and some of the deities in the large group at the end of the list. The ceremony of presenting offerings to the gods includes in most cases ceremonial singing and "barking." This singing and barking does not, however, accompany the offerings for the Sungod and Stormgod, the first two gods in the list, or those for the gods of the city, the next to last item in the list. Perhaps this was because the singing (and/or barking?) was in Hattic and was considered appropriate only for the local, Hattic, tutelary deities and not for the more "universal" deities like the Sungod and Stormgod. Perhaps the tutelary deities' association with the hunt conditions the role of the $^{LÚ.MEŠ}$UR.GI$_7$, "dog-men," in their worship, while the Sungod and Stormgod have no such association.

One other minor point of difference is the use of NINDA.KUR$_4$.RA "thick bread" instead of *takarmu-* bread for the [Stormgod's] offerings in column ii. Again the significance of this is unclear; this is the only use of thick bread in the round of offerings detailed in columns ii and iv. The Stormgod does not always receive NINDA.KUR$_4$.RA for his bread offerings, as is shown by the fact that his bread offering in column iv is performed with *takarmu-*.

There is also a difference in the way the celebrants "drink" the various gods; they drink the tutelary deities standing, but they are seated for the drink offerings to the Sungod, gods of the city and the large group of gods at the end of the list. We might expect the same treatment for the Stormgod, the other non-tutelary deity of the group, but according to the text the celebrants give his drink offering standing. This may have been a slip by the scribe after writing GUB-*aš* so many times; column iv is broken at this point and cannot be checked against column ii. In addition to this difference between drinking standing and seated, there is some variation between singular and plural forms of the verb *eku-* "to drink." In the Ḫattuša ceremony the Stormgod and the Tutelary Deity of Ḫatti receive drink offerings from a single celebrant. The significance of this is elusive; the same gods are honored with drink offerings by several celebrants in the Durmitta ceremony. The last two groups of gods, the gods of the city and the large group, are drunk by a single celebrant in the Durmitta ceremony, where the prescription is preserved. The spacing in both line 28 and line 31 in column ii, the Ḫattuša ceremony, requires that the singular verb be restored there as well. For some reason then, these gods who were given a drink offering as a group received it from an individual rather than several celebrants.

What is not clear, regardless of whether the verb is singular or plural, is who is performing these drink offerings. Nowhere in *KUB* 55.43 as preserved is the subject of *eku-* specified. The only place where we know who is drinking is iv 30′, in which the local singers are given something to drink, but this is an isolated case, the only place where these local singers appear in the text. In Hittite festivals it is often the king who drinks the gods, or the king and queen when the verb is plural. This may have been assumed in our text and thus the subject was never expressed. This would imply that the king and queen also went to Durmitta for the ceremony there.

In both columns ii and iv the phrase *irḫanteš ḫiššallanteš* occurs modifying the long list of gods who receive offerings as a group. The verb *ḫiššalla-* and this particular phrase are discussed in *Appendix B*. The use of this phrase here indicates that the gods in the list that follows it are all included in the group and receive offerings, whether or not they have already received offerings individually. For example, Ḫašgala receives individual offerings in column ii (line 24, restored) and column iv (line 23′). The same god occurs (partially restored) in ii 31 as part of the final group of gods, along with a number of gods who definitely did not receive individual offerings in the first part of the ceremony. This final group thus includes gods who have and gods who have not previously received offerings in the ceremony.

In addition to the festival activities carried over from column iv onto the left edge of the tablet, the colophon is also inscribed on the left edge. Its preserved portion identifies the text as the festival performed when the old hunting bag of the Tutelary Deity of Ḫatenzuwa is [replaced] and made into the hunting bag of the Tutelary Deity of Zapatiškuwa. Although we know from the first paragraphs of the text that Zitḫariya, whose hunting bag becomes the Tutelary Deity of the Hunting Bag, is also involved, the colophon as preserved and restored does not mention Zitḫariya. Its reference to the old hunting bag of the Tutelary Deity of Ḫatenzuwa does confirm that item's importance in the festival and explains its important role in column iv.

The first paragraph of the text tells us that the hunting bags were periodically replaced; this was perhaps due to the fact that they were made from leather, a perishable material. The procedure for actually making the new hunting bags is not described at all. The text simply begins by describing how to proceed once the new *kurša*-s have been made. The time for replacing the hunting bags is not prescribed; the reference to nine years since the *kurša-* was installed may indicate a general expectation as to the duration of this cult symbol's use in Ḫattuša. The reason for changing the *kurša*-s is not given. It does not seem to be because the old ones were worn out; leather does not normally deteriorate extensively in nine years, and we know that the old hunting bags were sent out and used in the provinces with new names. After disposing of the matter of the *making* of the new hunting bags in the first two lines by using the verb "renew," the text concerns itself with describing how to proceed once they are ready and can take the place of the old ones. When the text says "the time is not prescribed," it seems to be referring to the time for making the new *kurša*-s, not necessarily to the time assigned to celebrating the festival for the official installation.

All of §2 and the first line of §3 give background information on how and where the hunting bags were kept and how to effect the physical changing of the *kurša*-s from old to new. This was done with a total lack of ceremony; the new ones were taken into the Temple of the Hunting Bags and the old ones taken down whenever "they" (presumably the workmen assigned to the task of making new *kurša*-s) brought them. Hanging up these new hunting bags is thus not part of the actual festival. In the Temple of the Hunting Bags there is a special location, called the "place of the god," where the new hunting bags are hung. There are pegs already in place below this "place of the god" for keeping the old ones until they are sent out to the provinces. The phrase *AŠAR* DINGIR-*LIM*, unique to the two occurrences (i 9 and iii 15′) in this text, indicates that in this festival the "place of the god" plays an essential role, because the god is strongly associated with a particular locus.

Paragraphs 3–4 clarify the status of the old hunting bags until the festivals for installing the new ones (the "festivals" of i 12) can be performed. The old hunting bags must be retained, hung below the place of the god in the Temple of the Hunting Bags until the installation festivals are ready to be celebrated. It does not seem to matter if the new hunting bags must wait for a while in the temple of the hunting bags before being made official, and it is only when the new hunting bags are to be officially installed and thus become effective as deities that it is possible to get rid of the old ones. The old and new hunting bags wait together in the temple of the hunting bags until the old ones are no longer needed. When they become superfluous in Ḫattuša they are sent out to the provinces, to serve as cult symbols, but with new names. They are called by their new names "in the land" (the provinces), in contrast to their role in the capital Ḫattuša.

Although a number of the deities sacrificed to in the course of the festival are known to be tutelary deities, only two, Zitḫariya and the Tutelary Deity of Ḫatenzuwa, are specifically said to have *kurša*-s in Ḫattuša. Otten points out that these two deities are very closely related, citing the evidence of Muršili's annals, in which Muršili identifies Ḫatenzuwa as the city of Zitḫariya.[120] The evidence of the two old hunting bags which go to two different places indicates, however, that each of these two gods had a hunting bag as cult symbol and that they were therefore two separate deities.[121] The only other *kurša*- specifically identified in the text is that of the Tutelary Deity of Zapatiškuwa in iv 5′–6′ and 8′, where it is being used in the ceremony at Durmitta. In the two sentences in which it occurs the first reads *ANA kurši* ^{D}LAMMA ^{URU}*Zapatiškuwa* while the second one omits *kurši*. This is very good evidence that the hunting bag was the image for these tutelary deities and thus perceived as the deity itself.

Further evidence from this text also demonstrates its equation of the god with the *kurša*-. In §13 they take "the god" into the *karimmi*- building and also heap up bread-balls to it. After doing this they take it back and in line iii 15′ hang it up in the "place of the god," which i 11 tells us is the place where they hang the new hunting bags. The text thus uses DINGIR-*LAM* "god" and *kurša*- "hunting bag" interchangeably. The hunting bag of the

120. Otten, *FsFriedrich* 355. See comments on Zitḫariya in *Chapter 1*.

121. In the late period under Tudḫaliya IV the image of the Tutelary Deity of Ḫatenzuwa was redone as an anthropomorphic statue. See discussion in *Chapter 1* sub ^{D}LAMMA ^{URU}Ḫatenzuwa.

Tutelary Deity of Zapatiškuwa of column iv is simply the old hunting bag of the Tutelary Deity of Ḫatenzuwa after it has been renamed. Concerning the renaming of the old *kurša*-s, we may note that although the old hunting bag of the Tutelary Deity of Ḫatenzuwa is named the Tutelary Deity of Zapatiškuwa, it is taken not to Zapatiškuwa, but to Durmitta. It is unclear why only these deities are explicitly said to have hunting bags as cult representations, nor is it certain how many other deities had these symbols; in column ii the dative-locative plural *išgarantaš* modifying (apparently) the hunting bags allows the possibility that many or all of the deities involved in this festival had their own hunting bag as a cult symbol.

In the festival at Durmitta from column iv, by contrast, the consistent use of the dative-locative singular form *kurši* may indicate that only one hunting bag, that of the Tutelary Deity of Zapatiškuwa, was involved. A second hunting bag, of Zitḫariya, very possibly was used in the offerings for that god only. Other Hittite religious texts attest to other deities who had their own *kurša*-s, for example: *ŠA* ^{D}*Kantipuitti* ^{KUŠ}*kuršan kuiš karpan ḫarzi* " ... the one who has carried the hunting bag of Kantipuitti" *KUB* 10.13 obv. iii 19′–21′ (fest. fragment); ^{LÚ}SANGA ^{D}LAMMA-*za* ^{KUŠ}*guršan ŠA* ^{D}LAMMA ^{URU}*Pitamma karapzi* "The priest of the Tutelary Deity lifts the hunting bag of the Tutelary Deity of Pitamma" *KUB* 20.80 iii? 14′ (Festival Celebrated by the Prince); *mān* ⌈ŠE$_{12}$⌉-*anti* ITU 12 KAM $^{\text{D.KUŠ}}$*kurša*[*š*] *ŠA* ^{D}U ^{URU}*Zipalanda ANA* KASKAL.IM.GÀL.LU *paizzi* "If in the [wi]nter, in the twelfth month, the hunting bag of the Stormgod of Zipalanda goes on the south road" *KUB* 10.75+*KUB* 20.25:2–5 (Journey of the *kurša*- in Winter), ed. Güterbock, *JNES* 20 (1961) 92. This last example is somewhat tentative, because, as Güterbock points out, this could alternatively be translated "'The Shield goes on the South Road of the Storm-god of Z.?'"

Music was an integral part of the festival, as indicated by the singing after each round of offerings in columns ii and iv. Another distinctive feature of this festival is the central role of the dog-men, who bark as part of the ceremony of giving offerings to the gods. Their importance in this text affirms the close ties of hunting to the tutelary deities and is understandable in a festival devoted to gods whose cult symbols are hunting bags.

The colophon indicates the integral nature of the renaming ceremony in the festival. Here, at least in the preserved portion, this festival is identified by this act of replacing the old hunting bag of the Tutelary Deity of Ḫatenzuwa and making it into the hunting bag of the Tutelary Deity of Zapatiškuwa. We may say therefore that the description of the festival proper begins with §5, which tells how the old hunting bags were renamed.

We thus have preserved approximately half of one tablet which originally described all or part of a festival designed to install new cult symbols in the form of hunting bags, both in Ḫattuša, where the new ones were probably made, and in the provinces, where the "new" hunting bags were used ones from the capital, new in the sense of having newly come to their respective provincial cities. The *kurša*- is an old, Hattic cult symbol as may be seen in the Hattic-based Old Hittite mythological text *KUB* 33.59[122] of the disappearing deity

122. OH/MS, translit. Laroche, *Myth.* 1: 149–50, under the title "Recherche d'une 'égide.'"

pattern, in which it is the *kurša-* that is being searched out. Hattic elements such as the use of the exclamation "*kaš*" in iii 6′, the occurrence of Hattic tutelary gods such as Ḫapantali(ya) and Zitḫariya, and the extensive offerings of *takarmu-* bread, which was possibly Hattic in origin,[123] also make it likely that the festival was based on an earlier Hattic prototype. The tablet itself dates from the Middle Hittite period and represents a later rescension of what is probably a very old festival antedating the formation of the Hittite state. The festival may have continued on further tablets; *KUB* 7.36 may even be a later tablet of the same festival as indicated below in the comments on that text. Because the colophon is broken, we cannot know just how long the festival was, but the installing of new hunting bags in the capital was a major event requiring a specific festival lasting several days. Although not an enormous proceeding like the spring AN.TAḪ.ŠUM Festival, it was nevertheless extensive enough to provide an indication of the importance placed on these deities and their cult symbols by the Hittites.

This festival presents unusual or unique features in its ceremony and purpose. Outside of the very late cult inventory texts discussion of replacing cult images is rare, and the reuse of the old images is unique to this ceremony. One other description of cultic procedure in the Hittite corpus presents some interesting points of comparison. *KUB* 25.31, a tablet which describes some of the preparations for the *purulli-* festival, reads in obverse 6–13:[124] ^{KUŠ}*kuršuš Ù* 2 ^{GIŠ}*ḫupp[ar]uš warnuanzi nu* EGIR-*pa* GIBIL-*an iyanzi* § (A paragraph about cultic equipment brought from the house of the scribe of wooden tablets.) § 6 MÁŠ.GAL GE_6 2 MÁŠ.GAL BABBAR *nu* ^{KUŠ}*kuršuš iyanzi* UGULA $^{LÚ.MEŠ}$SIPAD *pai* ŠÀ.BA 2 MÁŠ.GAL BABBAR ^{LÚ}SIPAD.GUD DINGIR-*LIM dai* 2 MÁŠ.GAL GE_6 ^{LÚ}SANGA ^{D}*Telipinu dai* 2 MÁŠ.GAL BABBAR ^{LÚ}SANGA ^{D}ZA.BA_4.BA_4 2 MÁŠ.GAL GE_6 ^{LÚ}SIPAD DINGIR-*LIM dai nu* ^{KUŠ}*kuršuš ienzi* "They burn the hunting bags and two basins. They make new (ones). § (Paragraph concerning other cult paraphernalia.) § Six black billy goats, two white billy goats. They make (them into) hunting bags. The overseer of the shepherds gives (them) out. From them the cowherd of the god takes two white ones, the priest of Telipinu takes two black ones, the priest of ZA.BA_4.BA_4 two white ones, (and) the shepherd of the god takes two black ones. They make hunting bags."

Although this prescription shares with the *kurša-* Festival the goal of replacing the hunting bag images, the contrasts to the *kurša-* Festival are more striking than the similarities. Here we learn about the making of the new hunting bags, something not described in the *kurša-* Festival. Cult personnel, including both priests and tenders of the gods' flocks, are responsible for making the new cult images. In contrast to the careful preservation, renaming, and reuse of the old hunting bags in the *kurša-* Festival, the *purulli-* preparations specify the thorough destruction of the old totems by burning. The *kurša-* Festival also prescribes a cultic procedure lasting several days for the installation of the new hunting bag images, and the old ones may not leave the temple until the new ones are

123. Hoffner, *AlHeth* 185.

124. Noted by Gaster, *Thespis* (New York 1950) 336; Popko, *AOF* 2 (1975) 69 with n. 29; and idem, *Kultobjekte* 109. Transliterated by Otten and Rüster, *ZA* 62 (1972) 234–35. Translated by Güterbock, *FsKantor* 116.

ceremonially installed. In *KUB* 25.31, the old hunting bags may be destroyed before new ones are even made, and there is no specific mention of a ceremony for installing the new ones. The hunting bags in *KUB* 25.31 are associated with Telipinu and his temple, and there is no mention of tutelary deities. Why the *kurša*-s of different deities should be treated so differently is unclear, and this emphasizes the special nature of the care taken with the *kurša*- images of Zitḫariya and the Tutelary Deity of Ḫatenzuwa in the festival of *KUB* 55.43.

The fragment *KBo* 13.179 with its duplicate *KBo* 22.168 is concerned with *kurša*-s and may or may not be directly related to the *kurša*- Festival. It does not duplicate any of the preserved portion of *KUB* 55.43. The oxhides of the first paragraph and the goats who are driven in, washed, and killed indicate that this is a text describing some of the procedure for the actual making of the new hunting bags. This process may very well have been ceremonially prescribed, but as noted above it would have been a separate cultic operation from the festival of dedication for the hunting bag cult symbols described in *KUB* 55.43.

The third paragraph is very unusual; the LÚ.MEŠ UR.GI$_7$, here described as killing the animals from whose hides the hunting bags will be made, are nowhere else attested killing anything. We have here an example of the "dog-men" doing something out of the ordinary for them, but we see from *KUB* 55.43 that they are quite involved in the festival for installing the new hunting bags, so it is likely that they would help in preparing them as well. There are no other examples in the known Hittite corpus of *apeniššan kuen*- "kill in the same way." This phrase refers to an earlier, now lost, description of killing other animals occurring above the preserved portion of our text; it was probably a description of how to kill the cattle who provided the cowhides of line 2′.

The beginning of the preserved fragment was probably the last paragraph of a section that described preparing the cowhides and bringing them to the place where the new hunting bags were made. In §§2′ and 3′ the text had moved on to describe the preparation of goathides for the same purpose. The goats were killed in the same way as the cattle, and the making of the hunting bags required hides of both cattle and goats. Perhaps certain gods had hunting bags made of goathide and others had their hunting bags made of cowhide.

The sweeping and sprinkling mentioned in §2′ seems to have been more than a cleansing for cultic purity only, because the goat would have fouled these "rooms of the palace" while in them, and the room in which he was washed would have become dirty during that process. In contrast to many instances of cultic purification when the thing being cleansed is not necessarily physically dirty, there was a very good practical reason to sweep and sprinkle these rooms into which the goat had been driven.

The fragment *KUB* 7.36 bears a certain resemblance to *KUB* 55.43, especially in the occurrence of the Tutelary Deity of Zapatiškuwa and two occurrences of the otherwise unattested triad Kappariyamu, the Tutelary Deity of Tatašuna, and the Tutelary Deity of Tašḫapuna. The fragment describes what may have been another part of the festival for renewing the *kurša*-s, now lost in *KUB* 55.43, in which the deities receive flesh offerings. In the broken portion of *KUB* 55.43 the deities probably received flesh offerings. In §3′ of

KUB 7.36 the offerings are placed upon the hunting bag, just as were the bread and drink offerings in *KUB* 55.43 column iv.

The most striking point of similarity between *KUB* 55.43 and *KUB* 7.36 is in the colophons. Although in each text the colophon is only partially preserved, enough remains to show that they are very similar; restorations from *KUB* 55.43 fit very well in *KUB* 7.36. This text may very well be a duplicate of *KUB* 55.43 and as such would provide evidence that the festival for renewing the *kurša-* included flesh offerings, now lost in the missing sections of *KUB* 55.43. Alternatively, the festival description may have required more than one tablet, and *KUB* 7.36 may be the second (or later) tablet describing the same festival.

The fragment *KUB* 20.13 shows strong resemblances to *KUB* 55.43 and may be part of this same festival of installation. The second paragraph, too poorly preserved to interpret meaningfully, is possibly a description of part of a cultic journey. It bears certain similarities to §§3′–4′ of the festival fragment *KUB* 9.17.[125] The *išgarant*[*aš*] of ii 7′ is reminiscent of column ii of *KUB* 55.43. It is quite likely that this participle here in *KUB* 20.13, as in *KUB* 55.43 column ii, refers to hunting bags lined up to receive offerings.

The third paragraph shows similarities to columns ii and iv of *KUB* 55.43. The preserved deities who receive drink offerings in this paragraph are all deities who occur in the lists of gods in *KUB* 55.43. The ALAN.ZU_9-men, seen here in *KUB* 20.13 i 11′, do not, however, participate in the preserved ceremonies of *KUB* 55.43.

In §§4′–5′, which are on the reverse and therefore follow §§1′–3′ by an undetermined amount of text, the cultic activities have moved from drink offerings to flesh offerings. The celebrants cut up entrails and make stew. There is an unusual reference to "the naked ones" in close proximity to the Tutelary Deity of Ḫatenzuwa. This god is one of the two deities for whom a new *kurša-* is dedicated in *KUB* 55.43, but it is unclear how he is related to the *nekumanteš* here in *KUB* 20.13. In §6′ the word *lukkatta* indicates another day in the celebrating of the festival, which day seems to be the "day of the meat." The flesh offerings continue, although the text breaks off here, making it impossible to follow the course of the festival any further.

Although *KBo* 21.89+*KBo* 8.97 is too broken to allow a coherent translation, it shows items of interest. There are three occurrences of the ^{KUŠ}*kurša-*, in ii 21′ and iii 4′ and 5′, each time in the accusative plural. The example in iii 5′ is followed in iii 6′ by *gankan*[*zi*] "th[ey] hang." This hanging up of the hunting bags is reminiscent of §§3 and 14′ of *KUB* 55.43. Also similar to the main text of the *kurša-* Festival are the two places (i 12′ and iii 12′) in *KBo* 21.89+ in which *išgarant-* occurs. In i 12′ the form is neuter plural nominative-accusative and is used either as a substantive ("the lined up ones") or as an adjective modifying the broken word preceding it ("the lined up [...]x's"). The second occurrence is mostly broken away, and we therefore do not know its case, but the *šer tianzi* which occurs after it in iii 13′ probably indicates that something was being placed upon "the lined up (x)."

125. *CTH* 685.2, edited in *Appendix A*.

In §12′ two gods who play a role in *KUB* 55.43 are mentioned. The Tutelary Deity of Ḫatenzuwa (iii 10′) is one of the two gods for whom new hunting bags were made in the main text. In iii 7′, because no bread name beginning *kappa-x* is known, I read the divine name Kappariyamu despite the absence of a DINGIR determinative. In *KUB* 55.43 Kappariyamu is one of a triad of deities who are *kipikkišdu*s of some other deity.[126] In ii 10′ ᴰ*Irḫa[nduš* has been restored because there is no other divine name in the published Hittite corpus that begins *Ir-ḫa-* ... Although the participle *irḫant-* is attested a number of times in festival context,[127] the restoration here is based on the only text in which *irḫanduš* appears with a DINGIR determinative: "They give to the queen to drink." *nu* ᴰAMAR.UTU ᴰ*Ir-ḫa-a-an-du-uš* ᴰ*Ḫi-iš-ša-al-la-an-du-uš-ša ekuzi* "She drinks Marduk, the divine ones offered to in sequence, and the divine ones (whose offerings are) planned" *KUB* 43.56 ii 19′–21′ (frag. of the Ritual for the Stormgod of Kuliwišna). The phrase *irḫanduš ḫiššallanduš* occurs twice in the main text and is therefore another point of similarity between that text and *KBo* 21.89+. In each festival, part of the ceremony includes offerings to groups of deities prescribed by this rare phrase.

In §§3′, 5′, and 14′ libating (*šipant-*) is part of the cultic procedure. Libation offerings are not preserved in *KUB* 55.43. However, other items in *KBo* 21.89+ which call to mind the main text are the list of gods in §4′, all of which occur in the main text in a list of gods to receive drink and bread offerings (columns ii and iv of *KUB* 55.43), the *ḫalziššanzi* in ii 14′, which is reminiscent of the renaming of the old hunting bags in §5 of *KUB* 55.43, and the *purpura-* bread (bread-balls) of iii 24′ (cf. *KUB* 55.43 iii 7′, 11′, and 14′).

There are also elements in *KBo* 21.89 which do not occur in the extant portions of the main text. The É.ŠÀ of ii 12′ is something not paralleled in *KUB* 55.43. So are the references to the ᴺᴬ⁴*paššilla-* in ii 20′; the seal-house, i 2′ and ii 23′; and "storing up," ii 26′. This does not of course mean that *KBo* 21.89+*KBo* 8.97 is not part of the *kurša-* Festival; the tablet pieces copied in *KUB* 55.43 and *KBo* 21.89+*KBo* 8.97 each represent only approximately half of their original texts and therefore preserve different portions either of the same tablet or of different tablets of the festival.

This chapter presents several different texts which describe festivals devoted to a greater or lesser extent to the *kurša-*, a hunting bag which functioned as cult symbol for certain tutelary deities both in the capital, center of the state cult, and in provincial cult centers. This particular cult symbol required "renewing" periodically, perhaps because of the nature of the material (leather) from which it was made, or for other reasons which the Hittites did not specify within the ceremony. This very unusual ritual of replacing cult symbols is coupled with the equally rare practice of recycling these old cultic symbols by a ceremonial renaming that allows them to continue to function as divine representations. The Hittites perceived their representations of the divine as the deity itself but could also envision a genius or spirit separate from the representation that could animate a new cult symbol through the proper ceremony of offerings and incantations.

126. See *Appendix B* sub *kipikkišdu.*

127. See *Appendix B* sub *ḫiššalla-*.

CHAPTER 5

THE FESTIVALS FOR THE TUTELARY DEITIES OF THE RIVER

INTRODUCTION

There are several festivals or fragments thereof which include offerings to a tutelary deity of the river.[1] These ceremonies do not show a great deal of uniformity, but they do afford some points of interest and have been collected for this chapter in order to explore this particular aspect of the concept of tutelary deities among the Hittites.

THE TEXTS

A = *KUB* 9.21 B = *ABoT* 3[2]

Bo 3576 = *KUB* 9.21 is a fragment measuring approximately 5.6 by 7 cm. The signs are large and inscribed very clearly. There is no crowding together of the signs, and the scribe has left very large word gaps. It is difficult to assign a firm dating to such a small tablet, especially since the preserved portion contains almost none of the diagnostic signs which are most helpful in dating the script. The URU in line 8′ is certainly a New Script form, and on the basis of this and the absence of evidence to the contrary I would posit a New Script date for the tablet.

An 6998 = *ABoT* 3 is a small fragment measuring approximately 4.5 by 4.2 cm. Its surface is unusually well preserved, and the signs are somewhat small and very neat. The signs are not crowded together, and the word spaces are large. The paucity of preserved signs makes dating the script impossible; the only sign which might be said to be distinctive is *ir* in line 3′, which has five small verticals inscribed in it.

1. These festivals are grouped together as *CTH* 684 by Laroche. See p. 7 in the *Introduction* for a complete text scheme of this festival.
2. Lines 3′–10′ of text A and 4′–5′ of text B (as 11′–12′) have been transliterated and translated by Goetze, *Language* 29 (1953) 273–74.

Text Scheme

A. *KUB* 9.21.
B. *ABoT* 3. Duplicates *KUB* 9.21:8′–10′ and adds two lines after it breaks off.

Transliteration

§1′x+1 [o o]⌈ x x x ⌉ [
2′ [SÌR]-*RU* [

- -

§2′ 3′ [EGIR-*ŠU*-]ma ÍD-an ÍD-aš ᴰLAMMA *ŠA* Í[D DINGIR.MEŠ]
4′ [DINGIR.MEŠ ḫ]a-an-ti-ya-aš-ša-aš TUŠ-aš 3-*ŠU* e[3][-ku-zi]
5′ [3 ᴺᴵᴺᴰᴬt]a-kar-mu-uš pár-ši-ya ᴸᵁN[AR ᵁᴿᵁKa-ni-eš SÌR-*RU*]

- -

§3′ 6′ [EGIR-*ŠU*-m]a wa-ap-pu-u-wa-aš ᴰGul-še[-eš DINGIR.MAḪ.MEŠ]
7′ [TUŠ-aš? 3-*Š*]*U* e-ku-zi 3 ᴺᴵᴺᴰᴬta-k[ar-mu-uš pár-ši-ya]
B 1′ 8′ [ᴸᵁNA]R ᵁᴿᵁKa-ni-eš SÌ[(R-*R*)*U*]

- -

§4′ 9′ [EGIR-*ŠU*-m]a ÍD ÍD-a[(š ᴰLAMMA <*ŠA*> ÍD DINGIR.ME)Š]
B 3′ 10′ [DINGIR.MEŠ ḫa-an-]⌈ti-ya⌉-a[(š-ša-aš ir-ḫa-an-d)u-uš]
B4′ [ḫi-iš-ša-al-la-an-d]u-uš 3-*ŠU* e[-ku-zi][4]
B5′ [3 ᴺᴵᴺᴰᴬta-kar-mu-uš pá]r-ši-ya ᴸᵁNA[R ᵁᴿᵁKa-ni-eš SÌR-*RU*]

(the tablet breaks off)

3. Collated.
4. See *Line Commentary* below on the restoration of this line.

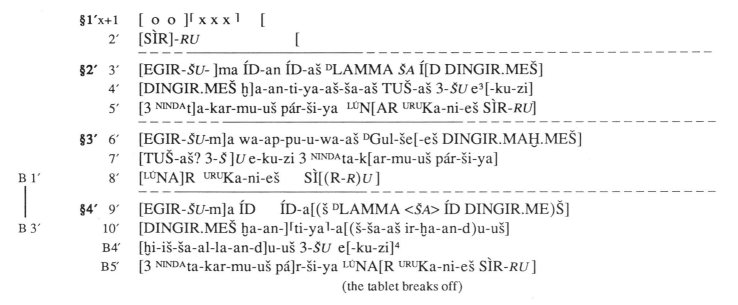

A = *KUB* 9.21 B = *ABoT* 3

Translation

§1′ [... They] sing [...]

§2′ [Nex]t [he drin]ks, seated, the river, the Tutelary Deity of the River, [the gods] of the ri[ver], (and) the gods of the *ḫantiyašša*-,[5] 3 times. [He] breaks [3 *t*]*akarmu*-breads. The sin[ger of Kaneš sings.]

§3′ [Nex]t he drinks the fat[e][6] deities of the riverbank [and the MAḪ deities, seated, 3 t]imes. [He breaks] 3 *tak*[*armu*-] breads. [The sin]ger of Kaneš sin[gs].

§4′ [Nex]t [he drin]ks the river, the Tutelary Deity of the River, the god[s] of the River, [the gods] of [the *ḫan*]*tiyašša*-, the (gods who have been) offered to in sequence (and) (the gods whose offerings are) [plann]ed,[7] three times. He brea[ks three *takarmu*- breads]. The sing[er of Kaneš sings].

(the tablet breaks off)

Line Commentary

10′. The restoration is from text B (*ABot* 3) 3′. Collation of text B indicates that the spacing at the end of line 3′ is somewhat different than copied. The spacing between *ḫa*, *an*, and *d*[*u* is more uniform than drawn, and in fact the *an* just barely touches the *du* sign. Thus the spacing of the signs requires reading this all as one word. Lines 4′ and 5′ of B follow immediately after the point at which text A breaks off. In line B4′, the -*d*]*u* of [*ḫi-iš-ša-al-la-an-d*]*u-uš* is more clear than the copy shows. See *Appendix B* on *ḫiššalla*-.

5. See *Appendix B* on *ḫantiyašša*-.

6. See *Appendix B* sub ᴰGulšeš.

7. Goetze, *Language* 29 (1953) 274, translates *irḫanduš ḫiššalanduš* as "those to be included and those to be excluded." See *Appendix B* sub *ḫiššala*- for commentary on this translation.

IBoT 1.2

Bo 63 = *IBoT* 1.2 measures approximately 9.7 by 10 cm. The shape of the preserved portion indicates that the original tablet had six columns. The script, while not distinctive, mixes older and newer forms to some extent. In signs such as *a*, *e*, and KAL the first vertical is sometimes significantly shorter than the second and sometimes equal in height. The *ḫa* sign has only a single winkelhaken, and *eš* sometimes has four winkelhakens, both later forms. The *da* and *en* signs show later forms. The URU sign occurs in its latest form. However, the *li* sign occurs only in the older form, and *nam* does not have its very latest form. On the basis of this somewhat sparse evidence I would assign this tablet an early New Script date. See table 7 in *Appendix C.*

Transliteration

Obverse ii

§1′ 1 [ ]-zi
2 [*PA-NI*? ^{N}]^{A_4}ZI.KIN
3 [*UŠ-GE-*] *EN*?
4 [-m]u ^{NA_4}ZI.KIN
5 [GU]D? UDU šu-up-pí-ya-aḫ-ḫi
6 [nam-ma šu-up-pí-y]a-aḫ-ḫu-u-wa-aš
7 [*A-WA-TE*^{MEŠ} m]e-ma-i

§2′ 8 [tuḫ-ḫ]u-eš-šar[8]
9 [ ]
10 [ ]
11 [ ]

§3′ 12 [ ]
13 [ ]

§4′ 14 [ ]

(the tablet breaks off)

Translation

Obverse ii

§1′ [...]he/they x. [... before(?) the s]tela [... he bow]s(?). [...] the stela [... (a number) catt]le and sheep he consecrates. [Furthermore,] he [sp]eaks [the words of cons]ecration.

§§2′–4′ (not enough preserved of these paragraphs to translate, although §2′ probably described a cleansing ceremony involving *tuḫḫueššar*)

8. See *Line Commentary* below on the restoration of lines 5–8 based on *KUB* 20.59 ii 6f.

Transliteration

IBoT 1.2 Obverse iii[9]

§5′ 1 LUGAL-uš *PA-NI* $^{\text{NA}_4}$ZI.KIN
2 2-*ŠU* ši-pa-an-ti
3 GUNNI 1-*ŠU*
4 ^{KUŠ}[k]ur-ši 1-*ŠU*
5 ^{GIŠ}DAG-ti 1-*ŠU*
6 ^{GIŠ}AB-ya 1-*ŠU*
7 ḫa-tal-wa-aš GIŠ-⸢i⸣ 1-*ŠU*
8 nam-⸢ma⸣ ḫa-aš-ši-i
9 ta-pu-uš-za 1-*ŠU*

---

§6′ 10 LUGAL-uš 3-e[10]
11 ir-ḫa-a-u-wa-an-zi
12 ^{ÍD}Ma-ra-aš-ša-an-da
13 ^{D}LAMMA ÍD ka-lu[11]-ti (eras.) <ti-ya-zi>

---

§7′ 14 [šu-u]p?[12]-pa ti-an-zi
15 [GAL.ḪI.A? u]k-⸢tu⸣-re-eš
16 [ir-ḫa-an- z]i?[13]

(the tablet breaks off)

Translation

IBoT 1.2 Obverse iii[14]

§5′ The king libates twice before the stela, (and) once to the hearth, once to the hunting bag, once to the throne, once to the window, once to the wood of the door bolt, (and) further once next to the hearth.

---

§6′ The king <proceeds> to treat three with offerings in sequence: the Maraššanda river, the Tutelary Deity of the River, and (their) circle.

---

§7′ [The me]at(?) they set out.[15] Th[ey take round in offering the r]egular [cups(?)].

(the tablet breaks off)

9. After a gap of an undetermined number of paragraphs.
10. See *Appendix B* sub "three" for the unusual complementation 3-e.
11. Collation indicates *lu* as a good possible reading of this sign, although it may have been written over an erasure. There is an erased winkelhaken after *kaluti* and an erased *ir* sign below it.
12. After collating this sign remains problematic. A horizontal trace below the winkelhaken suggests the restoration [*šu-u*]*p-pa*. Spacing to the edge of the column is very good for this, and it would also make sense with the verb *tianzi*.
13. Possible restoration of 15–16 based on 315/t i 6′; see Alp, *Tempel* 228–31.
14. After a gap of an undetermined number of paragraphs.
15. Bossert, *Heth.Kön.* 48 translates "Zu den [rei]nen Dingen treten sie (??)."

IBoT 1.2

Reverse iv[16] (*transliteration*)

§8′x+1 ⸢x ^{fD}Ma-ra-aš-ša⸣-an-da-an[17]
2′ wa-ar-šu- li
3′ 1-⸢*ŠU* [18]⸣ e-ku-zi
4′ 2 EN.MEŠ-ya-aš-ši
5′ wa-ar-šu- li
6′ IGI-an-da a-ku-wa-an-zi
7′ ⸢6⸣[19] NINDA.KUR$_4$.RA ⸢pár-ši-ya⸣
8′ $^{\mathrm{LÚ.MEŠ}}$NAR ^{URU}Ka-ni-eš
9′ SÌR- *RU*

---

§9′ 10′ LUGAL-uš GUB-aš
11′ ^{D}LAMMA ÍD 1-*ŠU* e-ku-zi
12′ 3 NINDA.KUR$_4$.RA pár-ši-ya
13′ $^{\mathrm{LÚ.MEŠ}}$NAR ^{URU}Ka-ni-eš SÌR-⸢*RU*⸣

(bottom edge of tablet)

Reverse v[20] (*transliteration*)

§10′x+1 [ ]x

- - - - - - - - - - - - - -

§11′ 2′ [ ]x
3′ [ ]x-an še-er i-ya-zi
4′ [^{fD}]Ma-ra-aš-ša-an-da
5′ [(-)]an-da i-ya-an-zi

- - - - - - - - -

§12′ 6′ [ ]
7′ [ ]
8′ [-]ni
9′ [ ] -zi

- - - - - - - - - - - -

(bottom edge of tablet)

16. After a gap of an undetermined number of paragraphs.
17. Bossert, *Heth.Kön.* 48, suggests [^{fD}*Ma-ra-aš-š*]*a-an-da-an*, but both spacing and preserved traces require a reading ⸢x ^{fD}*Ma-ra-aš-ša*⸣*-an-da-an*.
18. There are no traces preserved in this abraded area after 1-*ŠU*, nor would anything be expected between 1-*ŠU* and *ekuzi*; why then is there so much space here? It may be that the shortness of the lines in general affected the way the scribe spaced his words for lines in which he could only fit two or three words.
19. Collation indicates 6 as a better reading over Bossert's 5 (*Heth.Kön.* 48).
20. After a gap of an undetermined number of paragraphs.

IBoT 1.2

Reverse iv[21] (*translation*)

§8′ He drinks [x the Marašš]anda river by smelling, once, and two lords drink in the smell, facing him (i.e., the king).[22] He breaks six thick breads. The singers of Kaneš sing.

§9′ The king, standing, drinks the Tutelary Deity of the River, once. He breaks three thick breads. The singers of Kaneš sing.

(bottom edge of tablet)

Reverse v[23] (*translation*)

§10′ (not enough preserved to translate)

§11′ He worships [...]x up [in ...]. [... the river] Maraššanda [...] they worship.

§12′ (not enough preserved to translate)

(bottom edge of tablet)

Line Commentary

Obverse ii

ii 5–8. The restoration of these lines is based on Goetze's recognition of a similar passage in *KUB* 20.59.[24] Although the *IBoT* 1.2 and *KUB* 20.59 passages appear to be sufficiently alike that they may be used to restore each other, it is not quite as obvious as he indicates. *KUB* 20.59 i 13′–15′ reads: 2-*ŠU šuppiyaḫḫi* GUD-*ya* UDU[ ] / *šuppiyaḫḫi namma šuppi*[-] / *AWATE*^MEŠ^ *memai.* We do not have the word *šuppiyaḫḫuwaš* preserved whole in either text; we get its first half from *KUB* 20.59 and supply its ending from *IBoT* 1.2. Line 8 is restored on the basis of *KUB* 20.79 i 16; Goetze points out that in both texts the *tuḫḫueššar* ceremony follows the passage about speaking the words of purifying.

Obverse iii

iii 1. On the ^{NA_4}ZI.KIN = *ḫuwaši-* see Darga, *RHA* XXVII/84 (1969) 5–20, and idem, *Belleten* XXXIII/132 (1969) 493–504. Darga does not take up the question of occurrences

21. After a gap of an undetermined number of paragraphs.
22. Compare *CHD* sub *menaḫḫanda* 2c3′, citing a very similar passage from *IBoT* 1.1. On *waršula-* as "smell, aroma," see *HW 3. Erg.* 36, and Güterbock, *JKF* 10 (1986) 212, who suggests that *waršula-* in the context of drink offerings means to do an offering by sniffing the aroma of the wine being offered.
23. After a gap of an undetermined number of paragraphs.
24. Review of *IBoT* 1 in *JCS* 1 (1947) 87: "The passage II 6ff. can be restored from XX 59 I 13f. and in turn yields for that passage the reading *šu-up-pí-ia-aḫ-ḫu-u-wa-aš A-WA-TE*^MEŠ^ 'the certa verba that go with purifying.'"

of the *ḫuwaši-* stela inside a building, which is the situation in this passage. See Popko, *Kultobjekte* 124, on the *ḫuwaši-* stela in the temple. There are several other festivals in which, like this ceremony, a celebrant (usually the overseer of cooks) libates before the stela and then immediately libates to the holy places. In one example, *KBo* 30.56 obv. iii 31′–35′ (fest. fragment), the stela actually occurs in the list of holy places to which the overseer of cooks is libating. The fact that the celebrant libates to the holy places immediately after libating before the stela indicates that in these instances the stela must be in the temple. A silver ^{NA_4}ZI.KIN, attested in *KUB* 17.35 ii 6, *KUB* 38.17 iv 6, and *KBo* 2.1 ii 12, would probably be located not outside the city but rather in a building where it could be guarded. *KUB* 11.22 i 2–3 (AN.TAḪ.ŠUM Festival) offers further evidence for a stela indoors: *ŠA* ^{D}U ^{URU}*ḪATTI* ^{NA_4}*ḫuwaši INA* ^{É}*tarnui artari* "The stela of the Stormgod of Ḫatti stands in the *tarnu-* building."

iii 10–13. For the extreme rarity of the expression 3-*e* see the discussion of "three" in *Appendix B*. The infinitive *irḫawanzi* is also only rarely attested. Besides our text, there is only one other occurrence of *irḫawanzi* in a sentence without a finite verb: 1 ^{DUG}*PURZITUM* ^{TU_7}*ḫurutel* NINDA.KU$_7$ ½ *UPNI* 1 ^{NINDA}*punnikeš* ½ *UPNI* 9 AN.TAḪ.ŠUM.ḪI.A *AŠRI*$^{ḪI.A}$ *irḫauwanzi* EGIR-*ŠU* AN.TAḪ.ŠUM.ḪI.A-*it* ^{TU_7}*ḫurutel* NINDA.KU$_7$-*it* ^{NINDA}*punnikit AŠRI*$^{ḪI.A}$ *irḫanzi* "One *PURZITUM* container of stew, sweet bread of one half *UPNI*, one *punniki-* bread of one half *UPNI*, (and) nine AN.TAḪ.ŠUM plants (are) for treating the places with offerings in sequence. Then they treat the places with offerings in sequence, with AN.TAḪ.ŠUM, stew, sweet bread, (and) *punniki-* bread" *KUB* 2.8 obv. ii 21–24 (AN.TAḪ.ŠUM Festival, 32nd day). This text is different from *IBoT* 1.2 iii 10–13 in that the infinitive occurs in a nominal sentence whose sense does not require the addition of a verb such as *tiyazi*. In this text the persons doing the offerings are not specified; it is simply an impersonal "they" who perform this activity. In all of the other occurrences of *irḫawanzi* in unbroken context it occurs as LUGAL-*uš irḫawanzi tiyazi* "The king proceeds in order to treat with offerings." This is the only example in which the king is designated as the one performing the offerings without some finite verb such as *tiyazi*. Such a verb was certainly intended. Bossert, *Heth.Kön.* 48, translates this paragraph "Der König gibt, um die drei (Trias?) abzufertigen, dem Fluss Maraššanda (und) der Schutzgottheit des Flusses ein Opfer (unbekannter Art)." Goetze, *Language* 29 (1953) 274, translates "The king (proceeds) to treat three: the Marassandas River, Inar of the River, and (their) circle."

iii 15. Bossert, *Heth.Kön.* 48, restores [DINGIR.MEŠ *uk-*]*tu-ri-eš*. Collation of this text shows that a slightly oblique horizontal wedge preserved at the beginning of the line suggests the reading *u*]*k-*. Bossert translates this line "Die [e]wigen [Götter]."

A = *KUB* 51.79 B = *IBoT* 2.19 C = 412/s(+?)457/s

Bo 858 = *KUB* 51.79 is a fragment measuring 9 by 13.2 cm. The surface of the tablet is badly abraded, with the obverse! being in worse condition than the reverse! The signs are rather large and show a good deal of the slant on the tops of the vertical wedges which is one of the characteristics of older script. The *li* sign occurs in a very unusual and distinctive old form with only three horizontal wedges. The *e* sign shows an Old Script form. The *da* sign occurs both with and without a broken middle horizontal. The *al* sign does not have its latest form. However, the *az*, *tar*, and URU signs occur in later forms. The tablet is probably Middle Script or early New Script. See table 8 in *Appendix C* for specific sign shapes.

Bo 1108 = *IBoT* 2.19 is a fragment measuring approximately 6.9 by 6 cm. Its surface is somewhat unevenly preserved; the left side is in good condition, while the right side shows some abrasion. The signs are quite small, with large word spaces. The tops of the verticals have some slant to them. Although this is a small fragment, it contains some diagnostic signs for dating. The *a* and *e* signs occur in an older form. The *ḫa*, *ak*, and *li* signs show their older forms. The *al* sign does not occur in its latest form. The *du* sign shows what seems to be a later form, with a long oblique wedge instead of a winkelhaken. The URU sign occurs in what may be an intermediate form, with two verticals of equal height, but no indenting of its left edge. These considerations suggest a date for this tablet of early New Script or perhaps Middle Script.

KUB 44.2,[25] *IBoT* 2.19, and portions of *KUB* 51.79 (as Bo 858) are transliterated and translated by Lebrun, *Samuha* 176–78; in *Hethitica* 5 (1983) 51–57 Lebrun again worked on *KUB* 51.79 after it was published in hand copy. In this same article he also identifies the duplicate 412/s. Otten has very graciously supplied me with pre-publication copies done by Ms. Christel Rüster of 412/s, for which I would like to thank him. Included in this copy is a note that 412/s probably joins indirectly to 457/s, a copy of which Otten also provided. See the footnote to reverse! 12′ of the main text for more on 457/s. *IBoT* 2.19 is also transliterated and translated in Goetze, *Language* 29 (1953) 273. Otten already in a review of *IBoT* 2[26] had noted that Bo 858 (*KUB* 51.79) was parallel to *IBoT* 2.19. The preserved portion of text B is also preserved in text A. This is helpful in that it allowed the texts to be identified as duplicates but unfortunate in that they do not supplement one another to provide restorations. The obverse and reverse of the copy of *KUB* 51.79 are to be switched.

Text Scheme

A. *KUB* 51.79.
B. *IBoT* 2.19. Duplicates *KUB* 51.79 rev! 10′–15′.
C. 412/s(+?)457/s. Obverse duplicates *KUB* 51.79 obv! 4′–15′ and reverse 1′–7′ duplicate *KUB* 51.79 rev! 14′–18′.

25. Treated below.
26. *ZA* 49 (1950) 345.

A = *KUB* 51.79 B = *IBoT* 2.19 C = 412/s(+?)457/s

Transliteration

Obverse!

§1′ x+1 [o o o o o o o o o GIŠ ^{D}INAN]NA.GAL
2′ [ḫa-az-zi-kán-zi? $^{\text{LÚ.MEŠ}}$ḫal-li-ya-r]e-eš SÌR-*RU*
3′ [o o o o o o o]x ap-pa-an-zi
C obv. 1 4′ [(nam-ma-aš-kán pa)-r]a-a pé-e-da-an-zi
5′ [(NINDA.KUR$_4$.RA *EM-Ṣ*)]*A* ^{É}ḫi-i-li pár-ši-ya-an-zi

§2′ 6′ [(nam-m)]a-⸢kán?⸣ ^{LÚ}SAGI.A[27] *IŠ-TU* NINDA.KUR$_4$.RA
7′ [(2 ^{NINDA}pár-šu-u)]l-li pár-ši-ya nu-uš-kán
8′ [(^{NINDA}pí-y)]a-an-ta-al-li da-a-i
9′ [(nu-uš-ká)]n an-da-an pé-e-da-a-i[28]
10′ [1 (^{NINDA}pár)]-šu-ul-li LUGAL-i pa-a-i
11′ [LUGAL-uš-k]án wa-a-ki nam-ma-an-za-an
12′ [*A-NA* ^{GIŠ}B(ANŠ)]UR-*ŠU* da-a-i 1 ^{NINDA}pár-šu-ul-li-ma
13′ [(*A-NA* SAL.LUGAL[29])] pa-a-i SAL.LUGAL-kán wa-a-ki
14′ [(nam-ma-an-za-a)]n *A-NA* ^{GIŠ}BANŠUR-*ŠU* da-a-i

C obv. §3′ 15′ [1 UDU-ma-kán *A-NA*] ^{D}É.A ^{D}DAM.KI.NA ^{D}AG
16′ [^{D}NISABA ^{D}M]a-a-ti ^{D}Ḫa-az-zi-iz-zi
17′ [ši-pa-an-ti[30] o o tar-u-y]a-al-li
18′ [o o o o o o o o o o *PA-N*]*I* ? GUNNI
19′ [o o o o o o o o o o o ^{LÚ}]SANGA
20′ [o o o o o o o o tar-u-ya-a]l-li-in
21′ [o o o o o o o o o o o o o]tar-u-ya-al-li-in
22′ [o o o o o o o o o o o]x e-ku-zi
23′ [o o o o o o o o o o o o o S]ÌR-*RU*
24′ [o o o o o o o o o o o o o o]
25′ [o o o o o o o o o o o o o o o]
26′ [o o o o o o o o o o o o o o o o o]⸢x x x x⸣

(bottom of tablet broken away)

27. Text C has, instead of ^{LÚ}SAGI.A, ^{LÚ}SANGA ^{D}x[, probably ^{D}⸢É⸣.[A.

28. Text C 7: *pé-e-da-*⸢*i*⸣.

29. Text A may have had SAL.LUGAL-*ri* instead of *ANA* SAL.LUGAL, based on obv! 10′, in which "to the king" is written LUGAL-*i*, with Hittite phonetic complement for the d.-l. rather than an Akkadian preposition.

30. Lines 15′ through *šipanti* are restored from the same list in *KUB* 20.59 i 25–27 (AN.TAḪ.ŠUM Festival, 29th day, "for Ea and his group") and text C, 412/s rev. 10′–11′ (Lebrun, *Hethitica* 5 [1983] 56).

A = *KUB* 51.79 B = *IBoT* 2.19 C = 412/s(+?)457/s

Translation

Obverse!

§1′ [...] [They play] the large [INAN]NA instrument. [The *ḫalliyar*]*i-* men sing. They hold [ ]x. Then they carry them out. They break sour thick bread in the courtyard.

---

§2′ Then the cupbearer breaks 2 morsels from thick bread and places them on the *piyantalli-* bread. He brings them in. He gives [one] bread morsel to the king. [The king] bites (it). He then places it [on] his table. One bread morsel, however, he (the cupbearer) gives to the queen. The queen bites (it). She [then] places [it] on her table.

---

§3′ [One sheep, however, he sacrifices to] Ea, Damkina, Nabû, Nisaba, Māti, (and) Ḫazzizzi. [... *taruy*]*alli-* (d.-l.) [... befo]re(?) the hearth [... the p]riest. [... *taruya*]*lli-* (acc.) [...]*taruyalli-* (acc.) [...]x he drinks. [...] They sing. [...]
(Not enough preserved of the last three lines to yield anything.)

(bottom of tablet broken away)

A = *KUB* 51.79 B = *IBoT* 2.19 C = 412/s(+?)457/s Reverse! (*transliteration*)

§4′x+1 [[31]o o o o o o o o o o ^{D}É.A ^{D}D]AM.KI.NA
2′ [o o o o o o o ^{D}Ma-a-t]i?
3′ [o o o o o o ^{URU}Š]a-mu-u-ḫa-aš
4′ [^{D}*IŠTAR*? o o o o o -]li-i-li
5′ [o o o o o o o] $^{ḪUR.SAG}$Da-a-⸢x(-)[32] o o o-e⸣
6′ [o o o o o o]x-za $^{ḪUR.S}$[^{AG}[33] o o o o o o]
7′ [o o o o o ^{T}]^{ÚL}Pí-in-na-a-at [o o o]
8′ [^{D}Ka-a-re-pa] ^{TÚL}Ka-re-e-pa-a-at-ti[34] ⸢^{D}⸣[o o]
9′ [an-da tar-na-[35]]an-du-uš PA$_5$.ḪI.A-uš ⸢^{D}⸣[o o]
B 1′ 10′ [^{URU}Ša-mu-u]-ḫa-aš ^{D}Ḫu-u-wa-ri-ya-an-zi-pa-aš
11′ [KÁ.GAL.ḪI.]A!-aš[36] ^{D}Ša-li-wa-nu-uš[37]
12′ [^{ÍD}(N)]a-ak-ki-li-ya ÍD-aš ^{D}I-na-ra-an[38]
13′ [an-d]ur-za[39] a-ku-wa-an-zi

---

31. The tablet edge and therefore the length of the break is determined from the parallel text *KUB* 44.2, which in lines x+1–6′ almost exactly duplicates what is preserved in lines 8′–13′ of this text.
32. No attested mountain name suggests itself here. The mountain $^{ḪUR.SAG}$Taḫa (*RGTC* 6: 374–75) is precluded by the trace, which is not a *ḫa* sign. The one mountain name which could possibly fit is $^{ḪUR.SAG}$Tapala. However, this name is never written T/Da-a-pa-la.
33. The trace looks more like *k*[*a*-, but we expect another mountain name in such a list.
34. See *Appendix B* sub Karepa/Karepati for these names and a discussion of the *RGTC* 6 citations.
35. Restored from the parallel *KUB* 44.2:2′, which has *anda tarnandaš* PA$_5$.ḪI.A[-*aš*.
36. See *Line Commentary* below on rev! 11′ for this restoration.
37. Text B 2′: ^{D}*Ša-li-wa-ni-iš*.
38. Text B at this point has another three lines of deities and deified locations not included in the offering list of the main text. This section of text B is duplicated by the left column of 457/s (text C), which has [^{D}]*Zi-li-pu-ra-an* in place of the unreadable DN after GUNNI in text B 4′, the trace of which cannot be a *zi* sign. 457/s preserves traces of one line after *ḫiššalanduš*, which reads]x GAL x[. The right column of 457/s preserves only the first few signs of 5 lines, in which ^{D}Ḫilašši can be recognized. The extra lines of the offering list added by text B read:

    B 4′ [o o DING]IR?MEŠ *ŠA* ^{D}É.A GUNNI ^{D}x[o o]
    5′ [^{D}Ḫi-]⸢i⸣-li-aš-ši-in ir-ḫa-a-<an>-⸢du⸣-[uš]
    6′ [ḫi-iš-š]a-al-la-an-du-uš ^{D}[o o o o]

    "the [... go]ds(?), the hearth of Ea, the god x, [Ḫ]iliašši, (the gods who have been) treated with offerings in sequence (and) (the gods whose offerings are) [pla]nned, the god [x]." Collation notes for *IBoT* 2.19: At the beginning of line 4′ there are very clearly two verticals, not just one as copied. They are close together and suggest the restoration DING]IR.MEŠ. Goetze, *Language* 29 (1953) 273, reads [DINGIR.LÚ].MEŠ; the collation does not allow such a reading. The traces at the end of line 5′ very closely resemble the *du* sign in line 6′.

    The phrase *irḫanteš ḫiššallanteš* occurs in the *kurša*- Festival and is discussed in *Appendix B* sub *ḫiššalla*-. The phrase is also attested in other texts with the participles in the accusative plural, such as we have restored here. Lebrun, *Samuha* 177, reads *ir-ḫa-a*[-*an-zi*? in line 5′ and [ ]*ša-al-la-an-du-uš* in line 6′.
39. Text B 7′ as copied looks like -*ḫ*]*a a-ku-an-zi*. Collation reveals that what in the copy looks like a winkelhaken is probably an unintentional gouge in the clay. Text B thus may be read [*an-dur-z*]*a*.

A = *KUB* 51.79 B = *IBoT* 2.19 C = 412/s(+?)457/s[40]

Reverse! (*translation*)

§4′ [Ins]ide, they drink [... Ea, D]amkina, [... Māt]i, [...], [Ištar] of Šamuḫa, [... x-]*lili*, [...], Mt. *Dā-x*, [... -]*e*, [...]x-*za*, M[t.(?) x], [...] the spring Pinnat, [DN], [the spring Karepa], the spring Karepatti, ^{D}[x], the canals that join together,[41] ^{D}[x], Ḫuwariyanzipa[42] of Šamuḫa, the Šaliwani[43] gods of [the gate]s, the river Nakkiliya,[44] (and) Inara of the River.

---

40. After a gap of an undetermined number of paragraphs.
41. See *Line Commentary* below on *KUB* 51.79 rev! 8′–9′ for interpretations of this line.
42. See *Appendix B* sub ^{D}Ḫu(wa)riyanzipa.
43. See *Appendix B*.
44. See comments in *Appendix B*.

A = *KUB* 51.79 B = *IBoT* 2.19 C = 412/s(+?)457/s

Reverse! (*transliteration cont.*)

C rev. §5′ 14′ [$^{\text{LÚ.M}}$]^{EŠ}NAR ^{URU}Ka-ni-eš SÌR-*RU*[45]
B 9′ 15′ [LUGAL-u]š? NINDA.KUR$_4$.RA *EM-ṢA* pár-ši-ya
16′ [na-a]t?-ša-an [(EG)]IR-pa iš-ta-na-ni[46]
17′ [*A-N*]*A PA-NI* DINGIR-*LIM* ^{LÚ}AZU da-a-i

C rev. §6′ 18′ [LUGAL (SAL.LUGAL)] a-[k]u-an-na ú-e-kán-zi[47]
19′ [$^{\text{LÚ.MEŠ}}$SAGI.]⸢A⸣ a-aš-ka-az a-ku-wa-an-na
20′ [*BI-IB-RI*$^{\text{ḪI.A?}}$ ú-da-a]n-zi GIŠ ^{D}INANNA.GAL
21′ [ḫa-az-zi-kán-zi $^{\text{LÚ.MEŠ}}$ḫal-li-y]a-re-eš SÌR-*RU*
22′ [o o o o o o o o]⸢a??-ku?⸣-an-zi
23′ [o o o o o o o o o o o o -z]i

(bottom of tablet broken away)

45. Text B has its paragraph line one line further down, after this reference to the singer of Kaneš. Text C has no paragraph line here.

46. Text C rev. 4′: ^{GIŠ}ZAG.GAR.RA-*ni*.

47. Text C rev. 6′–7′: *a-ku-wa-an-na* [*ú-*]⸢e⸣*-ga-an-zi*. After this it diverges from text A, reading

8′ ⸢nu⸣ DINGIR.MEŠ ḫu-u-ma-an-te-eš [Ø]
9′ ir-ḫa-a-iz- zi
10′ ^{D}É.A ^{D}DAM.KI.N[A]
11′ ^{D}AG ^{D}NISA[BA ^{D}Ma-a-ti?]

(bottom of tablet)

The list of deities looks like the same group as that of text A obv! 15′–17′. It continued onto the next column, now lost.

A = *KUB* 51.79 B = *IBoT* 2.19 C = 412/s(+?)457/s

Reverse! (*translation cont.*)

§5′ The singers of Kaneš sing. The [kin]g(?) breaks sour thick bread. The seer puts [th]em back on the altar before the god.

---

§6′ [The king (and) queen] request (something) to drink.[48] [The cupbearer]s [bri]ng [rhyta(?)] from outside[49] for drinking. [They play] the large INANNA instrument. The [*ḫalliy*]*ari*- men sing. They drink(?) [...] (and) th[ey ...]

(bottom of tablet broken away)

Line Commentary

Obverse!

obv! 5′: ^{É}*ḫila-*. There are no other examples of breaking bread offerings in the courtyard. Most of the occurrences of this word involve a verb of motion "to the courtyard." In this text the distinction between the courtyard, which is "outside," and the "inside" locus (the temple) where most of the cultic activity is carried out, is emphasized by the action of "carrying them out" in obv! 4′, immediately preceding the breaking of the sour thick bread in the courtyard, and "bringing them in" in obv! 9′.

obv! 15′–17′. The gods worshipped together here are encountered as a group elsewhere, particularly in the twenty-ninth day of the AN.TAḪ.ŠUM Festival, which Laroche, *CTH* 616, describes as "pour Ea et son groupe." This same group occurs in several duplicates of this portion of the AN.TAḪ.ŠUM Festival; of these texts *KUB* 20.59 is utilized to restore the passage in *KUB* 51.79. See Laroche, *GLH* 100 and 163, for his observations that ^{D}Ḫazzizzi and ^{D}Māti almost always occur with Ea and that these are actually deified attributes of Ea. There are a number of examples of Māti used as a personal name.

^{D}AG, although a rarely attested god, is not a hapax legomenon in this text, as Lebrun, *Hethitica* 5 (1983) 56, claims. This god also occurs in *KBo* 13.128:2′ and *KUB* 20.59 i 25 (AN.TAḪ.ŠUM Festival, 29th day); and *KBo* 13.193:11′ (Ritual for the Ancient Gods). In the AN.TAḪ.ŠUM Festival passages ^{D}AG occurs in the same list as we have in *KUB* 51.79 obv! 15′–16′. Lebrun, *Hethitica* 5: 56, points out that this logogram stands for the god Nabû, a god associated with wisdom and scribes. For ^{D}Damkina, see Laroche, *Rech.* 126. A number of different spellings of her name are attested; to the examples of unusual spellings cited by Laroche add [(^{D}*Dam-k*)]*e-en-na*, 210/w:4′+*KUB* 47.37:9′ (Hurrian-Hittite ritual of *šarraš*), restored from *KBo* 24.57 iv 7′: ^{D}*Dam-ki-na*; and ^{D}*Dam-gi-na*, *KUB* 17.20+ iii 10′

48. For the construction *akuanna wek-* see Laroche, *RHA* XXVIII (1970) 41–42, and Kammenhuber, *Materialien*, Lief. 4, Nr. 5, p. 75.

49. Literally "from the gate."

(Ritual for the Ancient Gods). Damkina occurs quite a few times in festival texts of which perhaps seventy-five percent are in conjunction with Ea.

obv! 17′, 20′, 21′: *taruyalli*. This word is uncertain in both reading and meaning. It may be acephalic, or incorrectly restored in lines 17′ and 20′. If it is complete as we have it in line 21′, it is still difficult to identify it with a known Hittite word. There is a word *taruyalliš* which occurs only in two bird oracles, spelled *tar-u-ya-al-li-iš* in *KUB* 50.1 iii 12′ and 21′, *tar-u-ya-li-iš* in *KBo* 22.263:6′ and *KUB* 50.1 iii 17′ and 21′, and *tar-u-ya-le-e-eš* in *KBo* 22.263:4′. There may be a further example in *KBo* 4.2 ii 27 (Ritual of Ḫuwarlu, the ^{LÚ}MUŠEN.DÙ): *nu* ^{LÚ}MUŠEN.DÙ *ḫuwanzi mān tar-ú-i-ya-al-li-iš tiyazi mān=kan* EGIR-*an šara aššuaz uizzi n=at gimri araḫza panzi.* These examples may well be the full spelling of the term which occurs quite often in bird oracles and is spelled *tar-liš/tar-li*$_x$, *tar-u-ya*, and perhaps *tar-u.*[50] This word looks like a common gender *i*-stem noun, with both singular and plural nominative forms attested in the oracle texts, in which case *taruyallin* and *taruyalli* in *KUB* 51.79 could be accusative and dative-locative forms of the same word. It is unlikely, however, that we would have a bird oracle term in this festival text.

There is also a word $^{(GIŠ)}$*tar(u)wal(l)i-*, discussed by Hoffner, *EHGl* 68–69 with n. 141, with the meaning "pestle" and briefly by Starke, *KZ* 95 (1981) 156 with n. 62, who rejects "pestle" and proposes "mortar." The word does occur in festival texts and could conceivably be the same word as the *taruyalli-* of *KUB* 51.79. Against such an equation, however, there are at least two objections: First, $^{(GIŠ)}$*tar(u)wal(l)i-* seems to be neuter. In seven of its eight occurrences the form is $^{(GIŠ)}$*taruwal(l)i.* Although some of those could be d.-l., in *KBo* 25.32 iii 13′ and *KUB* 42.107 iv? 8′–9′ it is definitely neuter nom.-acc. If *taruyallin* is the same word, it would be the only unambiguously common gender example of it. Secondly, $^{(GIŠ)}$*tar(u)wal(l)i-* is never spelled with a *y* glide but rather always has the form *tarwal(l)i-* or *taruwal(l)i-*. Although *taruyalli-* in *KUB* 51.79 superficially resembles this word, the differences in morphology are too great to suggest that they are the same word. Lebrun, *Hethitica* 5 (1983) 56–57, although commenting on *taruyalli-* briefly, does not offer a translation.

Reverse!

rev! 7′. Although three occurrences of the spring name ^{TÚL}Pinnat are cited in *RGTC* 6: 542, two of them have only the beginnings of a name preserved and are quite conjectural. The *KUB* 51.79 passage is the only definite example of this spring in the published corpus. This list of deities contains several names which occur only in this text.

rev! 8′–9′: *anda tarna-*. Lebrun, *Samuha* (1976) 178, translates 9′ as "les canaux qui se rejoignent les uns les autres[" and the parallel text *KUB* 44.2, from which this text was restored, as "les canaux qui sont joints les uns aux autres[." In *Hethitica* 5 (1983) 53 he translates the *KUB* 51.79 passage as "les canaux [creu]sés"; in his commentary he elaborates on this translation as "les canaux creusés (dans le sol)." Lebrun does not

50. Güterbock, personal communication.

comment on the unusual syntax, in which this participle precedes the word it modifies, "canals."

Lebrun's two different translations of the *KUB* 51.79 passage reflect the uncertainty of the meaning of *anda tarnant-* in this context. There are no other occurrences of participles of *tarna-* used to modify names of deities or divine places such as we have here. None of the few examples of this preverb-verb combination *anda tarna-* resemble the context of *KUB* 51.79 rev! 8′–9′ or the parallel, but they can provide some clue to its meaning. The most helpful is the use of *anda tarna-* in certain rituals such as the Ritual of Uḫḫa-muwa against plague:[51] *nu* SÍG ZA.GÍN SÍG SA_5 SÍG SIG_7.SIG_7 SÍG GE_6 SÍG BABBAR-*ya anda tarnanzi* "They join together blue wool, red wool, yellow wool, black wool, and white wool. (They make it into a crown and crown the ram with it.)" Clearly here *anda tarna-* means "to join/twine together." Because canals too join together as they flow one into another, I favor Lebrun's earlier translation in *Samuha* 178 over his later idea.

rev! 9′: PA_5. This word is comparatively rare in the Hittite corpus and is only attested once in a cultic context outside of this festival for the Tutelary Deity of the River, in the Ritual for the Sungoddess of the Earth.[52] Since the occurrence in the Sungoddess ritual text is broken, the occurrences in this festival are the only definite examples of canals as deities receiving drink offerings.

rev! 11′. Restored from the parallel *KUB* 44.2:4′. The traces in the hand copy of *KUB* 51.79 read -]*za-aš*. Lebrun, *Samuha* 177, reads ^{GIŠ}K]Á-*aš* without comment, but in *Hethitica* 5: 55 (published after *KUB* 51 appeared), he reads [KÁ.GAL.ḪI.]A-*aš* and notes that Neu suggests A as a better reading than ZA after collating a photograph of the tablet.

A = *KUB* 44.2 B = *KUB* 44.3

Bo 539 = *KUB* 44.2 is a small fragment measuring approximately 6.1 by 6 cm. Even in such a small fragment there are some signs which provide evidence for dating. The script shows consistent late forms; *ḫa*, *li*, *tar*, and URU are the most distinctive and provide a definite New Script date for this tablet.

Bo 4489 = *KUB* 44.3 is also a small fragment, measuring 5.7 by 5.8 cm. The script is fairly large and not particularly cramped. Of the few signs that provide any clue to dating the tablet, the *ak*, *e*, *ḫa*, and *li* signs show older forms, while there are no specifically New Script forms on the preserved portion of the tablet. On the basis of the occurrence of older sign forms combined with a lack of the crowding of signs typical of Old Script, I would assign this fragment a Middle Script date.

This text has not been translated separately because its first paragraph differs so little from that of the parallel *KUB* 51.79, which has been translated above, while its second paragraph is too fragmentary to translate.

51. *HT* 1 ii 20–21, trans. Goetze, *ANET* 347.
52. *IBoT* 2.126:5′.

Text Scheme

A. *KUB* 44.2. Parallel to *KUB* 51.79 rev! 7′–13′.
B. *KUB* 44.3. Adds one line to the beginning of *KUB* 44.2 and duplicates 1′–7′ of that tablet.

Transliteration[53]

	§1′	B 1′	[o o o o $^{TÚ]L}$Pí-i[n-na-at[54] ^{D}o-o]
B 2′		A 1′	⌈*A-NA*? ^{D}Ka-a-re-pa ^{D}Ka⌉-r[(e-e-pa-ti)[55] ^{D}o-o]
		2′	an-da tar-na-an-da-aš[56] PA$_{5}$.ḪI.A[-aš ^{D}o-o]
		3′	^{URU}Ša-mu-u-ḫa-aš ^{D}Ḫu-u-wa-ri-an[-zi-pa-aš[57]]
		4′	KÁ.GAL.ḪI.A-aš ^{D}Ša-la-wa-na-a[š]
		5′	$^{⌈ÍD⌉}$Na-ak-ki-li-ya-aš ÍD-aš-š[a]
		6′	$^{⌈D⌉}$LAMMA-ri[58] ši-pa-an-ti
B 9′	§2′	7′	[ ]⌈x x-an⌉ DINGIR.MEŠ-ya x[[59]
		8′	[ ]⌈ar-ḫa⌉ da-a-⌈i⌉[
		9′	[ ]⌈x⌉-r[u?[60]

(bottom of tablet broken away)

COMMENTARY

There is not enough preserved of any of the texts here treated to allow a detailed look at the festivals described in them. The various texts have been gathered in this chapter because they are all festivals celebrated for gods associated with rivers, including the Tutelary Deity of the River. As preserved they have little else in common that is distinctive to them. In all of these festivals the giving of offerings is accompanied by cult music from the singer of Kaneš. Without more preserved text, however, we cannot say if the various tablets are describing different festivals or if some are actually different parts of the same festival.

53. Even though it contains the same list of deities and places to be offered to, *KUB* 44.2 with its duplicate seems to be only a parallel to *KUB* 51.79. *KUB* 44.2 has the verb *šipant-* where *KUB* 51.79 has *eku-*, and the paragraphs following these lists in the two texts are not the same.
54. Restored from *KUB* 51.79 rev! 7′.
55. Restored from text B 3′. See *Appendix B* sub ^{D}Karepa/Karepati.
56. Text B 4′: [*tar-na-a*]*n-ta-aš.*
57. Restoration from the parallel *KUB* 51.79 rev! 10′.
58. Text B 8′: [^{D}LAM]MA ÍD.
59. At this point text B breaks off, preserving from this line only *-š*]*a* $^{⌈D}$x⌉. It is unclear how this fits into line 7′ of text A.
60. Lebrun, *Samuha* 176, reads SÌ]R-*R*[*U*? The trace before *ru*, however, is not consistent with a reading SÌR.

The existence of these festivals focusing on deities associated with rivers, springs, and canals points up how essential a role bodies of water played in Hittite economy and society. These festivals demonstrate the state's concern with ensuring adequate water supply by propitiating the deities associated with various sources of water. They point up also the distinctively Hittite fascination with water sources seen in the number of monuments erected near water which still exist today.[61] The Mesopotamian kings chronicled their building and clearing of irrigation canals; the Hittites provided festivals for the deities who provided water.[62]

The singers of Kaneš occur in each of the festivals treated in this chapter. See Jakob-Rost in Klengel, ed. *Beiträge zur sozialen Struktur des alten Vorderasien* (Berlin, 1971) 111–15, for a discussion of these cult functionaries. As Jakob-Rost points out (ibid., p. 113), although we would expect the singer(s) of Kaneš to sing only for Hittite gods, they seem to sing not only for deities which have genuine Hittite names but also for a number of Hattic gods. Their occurrence in these festival texts cannot therefore be used as evidence for the ethnic background of the river deities being honored by the festivals.

KUB 9.21 is dedicated specifically to gods of the river. The use of *takarmu-* bread for the bread offerings is interesting in view of the very important role of that bread in the *kurša-* Festival.[63] The use of this bread, thought by Hoffner[64] to be Hattic in origin, may be evidence that this was a very old festival, perhaps antedating the Hittite state. There is nothing characteristically Old Hittite in the small amount of text preserved, and the copy probably dates to the Empire period. The festival provides evidence about conceptions of tutelary deities by distinguishing between the river, the tutelary deity of the river, and the gods of the river. The tutelary deity of a place or object is distinct from that object, whether it is divine or not. Among the deities receiving offerings are "the fate deities of the riverbank," who sound intriguing but difficult to conceptualize.

In *IBoT* 1.2, with more preserved text than in *KUB* 9.21, we may note more distinctive prescriptions in the festival procedure. The ceremony preserved in obverse ii, probably near the beginning of the festival, takes place at a cult stela and concerns the consecrating and purifying of cattle and sheep preparatory to sacrifice.

When obverse iii resumes the description after a gap, the celebrants, including the king, are still at the cult stela. The libations to the holy places of the temple immediately after those at the stela indicate that the stela is in the temple. How then do we understand the following paragraph in which the king treats with offerings the Marašš anda river[65] and the Tutelary Deity of the River? Possibly §6′ describes activities done at the river, although usually festival descriptions detail the processions required to move to different cult loci within a ceremony. These offerings of §6′ were therefore probably done in the temple as

61. For example Eflatun Pınar, Fraktin, and Sirkeli.
62. Lebrun, *Hethitica* 9 (1988) 151, suggests that a distinctive epithet of the Stormgod in Anatolian festivals from Emar is "the Stormgod, provider of life-giving water."
63. See *Chapter 4*.
64. *AlHeth* 185.
65. The classical Halys, modern Kızıl Irmak.

well. This is good evidence that deified geographical features such as the river Maraššanda had images in the temple and could thus receive regular offerings.

In §8′ the rare *waršula-* drink offering is prescribed. Not only is this unusual type of offering part of the ceremony, but the celebrants are unusual; only rarely are "lords" specifically included in Hittite cultic ceremony. The preserved section of column iv seems to be an elaboration of the rather cryptic provisions of §6′. In §§8′ and 9′ we see similar offerings for two of the three receivers of offerings indicated in §6′. The top of column v probably continued with analogous offerings for their *kaluti* or "circle."

In this festival as in *KUB* 9.21, all the deities, with the exception of the holy places, are associated with the river. The copy was written in the early Empire period; I find nothing in the text to provide evidence as to when the festival itself was developed.

The festival in *KUB* 51.79 presents some distinctive features, most notably the extensive list in §4′ of gods who are to receive drink offerings. The gods here worshipped are predominantly those having to do with sources of water: rivers, springs, and canals. Although the water motif dominates the selection of gods of this festival, there are also other deified geographical locations (mountains), and other gods both from the provinces and from the central cult. I do not see a unifying factor that holds all of these deities together, besides a concern for offering to all sources of ground water. Despite the predominance of deified locations, the ceremony takes place not at an outdoor cult site, but in a temple, as seen by the carrying of offerings from outside to inside and specific prescriptions for performing offerings inside. The king and queen are the primary celebrants of the festival.

Other points that distinguish *KUB* 51.79 and its parallel *KUB* 44.2 from the other texts in this chapter (as they are preserved) include the role of the seer in breaking and placing the bread offerings and the use of sour thick bread for those offerings. Although all the festivals of this chapter are done to the accompaniment of cult music of Kaneš, only in this text was other music used, the large INANNA instrument and the *ḫalliyari-* singers. There is also a rather unusual ceremony in which the "cupbearer" (^{LÚ}SAGI.A) breaks thick bread into crumbs (an action denoted by a phrase unique to this text), and then gives a morsel each to the king and queen, who bite it and place it on their tables.

There is more linguistic evidence for dating to be gained from this festival than from the others in this chapter. Most of the copies were written in Middle Script and New Script, and there is evidence from the main text, *KUB* 51.79, for an Old Hittite or Middle Hittite dating for the text itself. In obv! 7′ the use of the older form *-uš-* for the common accusative plural pronoun in *nu-uš-kan* suggests an Old Hittite or Middle Hittite date. In obv! 11′, *nam-ma-an-za-an*, the latter *-an* may be the rather rare Old Hittite sentence particle cited in Kammenhuber, *HW*² 69–70, and Puhvel, *HED* 1–2: 51.[66] Goetze, *ArOr* 5 (1933) 30–31,

66. To the literature cited in these two dictionary entries add Kammenhuber, *FsLaroche* 187, and Melchert, Diss. 110–11.

points out that the sequence *-za-an* actually stands for *-za-šan* in some cases, an idea followed by Friedrich, *HE* 1 (1960) §42b, and Carruba, *SMEA* 12 (1970) 71. Lebrun, *Hethitica* 5 (1983) 56, interprets this passage thus without discussing the reasons for it. Hoffner, *FsGüterbock*[2] 93–94, points out that *-an* in this position can also be a doubled enclitic pronoun. I would not take this *-an* as such because, as Hoffner notes, such a feature only occurs in late New Hittite texts, which this text, based on other evidence, does not seem to be. I see no reason not to read it as the sentence particle *-an*, which would then indicate an Old Hittite date for *KUB* 51.79, as the use of this particular particle died out very early. The same particle almost certainly occurs in obv! 14′. This festival thus seems to be an old one, although the inclusion of Mesopotamian gods such as Ea may argue against a pre-Hittite Hattic prototype.

While the festivals of this chapter touch only obliquely on tutelary deities of the river, they are important evidence for the existence of this particular manifestation of the tutelary deity. This deity is distinguished from the river itself, which can also be deified. As noted in *Chapter 1*, divine beings may themselves have a protective deity, and in the Hittite conception of their world the rivers which represented such an important resource were provided with special gods to ensure their well being.

CHAPTER 6

CONCLUSIONS

The Hittites accorded within the extensive cult that was so essential an element of the state's institutional framework a rather large position to a type of god that we conventionally label tutelary or patron. Such gods may be identified either by a common title, ᴰLAMMA, by explicitly protective functions, or simply by close association in the pantheon with other tutelary deities. Like much of Hittite culture, the worship of tutelary or patron deities can be perceived most readily in foreign religious traditions. The Hattians, the non-Indo-European Anatolians who antedate the Hittite entry into central Anatolia, had a very strong tradition of tutelary deities. All of the tutelary deities called by name in the texts seem to go back to Hattian prototypes. Many are attested from the earliest days of the Hittite kingdom. In the Old and Middle Hittite periods, when Hattian influence was strongest, the Tutelary Deity (ᴰLAMMA) and the Tutelary Deity of Ḫatti seem to have had their greatest prominence within the pantheon. In Mesopotamia, another culture that influenced the Hittites greatly, the tradition of patron deities was also quite strong. Patron deities mediated between humankind and the divine realm on cylinder seals, colossal deities guarded the gates of Assyrian palaces, and the very title used by the Hittites to name many of their tutelary deities was borrowed from the Sumerian tradition. The third major tradition contributory to Hittite culture, the Hurrian, seems not to have had the same pattern of deities specifically tutelary. If anything, as Hurrian influence increased in the Empire period while Hattian influences decreased, the prominence accorded to tutelary deities may have waned somewhat. I know of no examples of a tutelary deity with a clearly Hurrian name, either spelled out or implied in a phonetic complementation for ᴰLAMMA. An exception to this trend is the importance of the Festival for All the Tutelary Deities in the late period, under Tudḫaliya IV, attested in the many copies of this text datable to that king's reign. Even there, this active religious reorganizer may have been building on an older festival procedure.

The evidence for the Hittite interest in tutelary deities involves both festivals devoted primarily to them and numerous references to them in a variety of texts. Their importance at the state level is manifest from the rather prominent place given them in the catalogue of deities who witnessed treaty oaths. Religious festivals, as the vehicle for corporate worship, as the primary index of Hittite official piety, and as the institution that provided for systematic sacrificial offering, are a striking testimonial to the centrality in Hittite culture of maintaining the state's relationship with the divine. As such, the major state festivals were very elaborate ceremonial procedures which might last for weeks and require an enormous expenditure of the state's primary economic resource, agricultural produce, for offerings. In the great state festivals not specifically ordained for one particular deity the tutelary deities play a role similar to their role in the oath deity lists, never supplanting more universal gods like the Stormgod or the Sungod or Sungoddess but often receiving offerings in these festivals. The festivals celebrated primarily for tutelary deities, treated in this volume, are not of the magnitude of the great festivals like the KI.LAM or AN.TAḪ.ŠUM. However, the Festival for All the Tutelary Deities and the *kurša-* Festival are long ceremonies which almost certainly required the presence of the king and queen, the highest priests of the land, for their celebration. The *kurša-* Festival was sufficiently complex to require several days for its celebration.

Some of these festivals for tutelary deities are quite distinctive. The "Festivals of Karaḫna" text represents a characteristically Hittite concern that local festivals be recorded and performed. The Festival for All the Tutelary Deities is a monument of spiritual and intellectual investigation, a document manifesting the human desire for exploration of the divine realm and the need to know that world in order to relate better to it. The festival for renewing the hunting bag totems differs from the majority of Hittite festival descriptions, which usually prescribe processions, sacrificial offerings, and accompanying liturgy to be done on a regular basis. The *kurša-* Festival is performed only as needed and has the unusual (in Hittite culture) function of installing new divine images and providing for the recycling of the old ones. Some of these festivals go back to Old Hittite or perhaps earlier prototypes; the tradition of worship for tutelary deities is as old as the Hittite state. Some of the older compositions are extant in New Script copies, indicating how these cults were maintained throughout the history of the Hittite kingdom.

The great variety of tutelary deities is important evidence for the Hittite view of their world. In general the Hittites accepted any new deity they encountered as they confronted different cultures. Although in the later period especially, perhaps due to the influence of the well-developed and centralized Hurrian culture, the Hittite state had a clear conception of gods whose sway was universal; they maintained throughout their history a vital interest in localized deities and their individual cults. In all ancient civilizations local religious traditions flourished simultaneously with the state-sponsored religion, but few states consciously fostered and recorded in the state archives these local traditions as assiduously as the Hittites. The great number of tutelary deities deriving from the Hattian pantheon is probably a function of the political fragmentation of the Hattian cities, which produced a plethora of different gods, many of whom were taken over by the Hittites as they incorporated Hattian principalities into their united polity. For many of these deities the Hittites did nothing more than make them part of the pantheon, including them in the lists of gods who witnessed treaties and received offerings in the state cult. For some they apparently borrowed or adapted an entire cultic ceremony and performed it in the capital.

An excellent example of this is the *kurša*- Festival, which was performed in the capital for two gods who came originally from other cult centers. Maintaining these two gods in Ḫattuša required providing a place for them, the "house of the hunting bags," their temple. Thus the cults of certain provincial deities were transferred to the capital.

In other cases the variety of tutelary deities has its origins in the essential idea of protection inherent in the concept of a tutelary deity. In a festival involving the tutelary deity of the river,[1] the river, the gods of the river, and the tutelary gods of the river are all separately named. The distinction between the river, itself divine, and its tutelary deities is carefully maintained. Almost anything, human, divine, or inanimate, may have a deity assigned to its protection. Although many of these tutelary deities occupied only a minor place in the state pantheon, the Tutelary Deity, the Tutelary Deity of Ḫatti, and Zitḫariya were at times accorded a prominent place. The Tutelary Deity in the earlier period was even at times addressed or worshipped as part of a triad with the Stormgod and Sungod(dess). He was apparently a universal god recognized throughout the empire, as attested by his worship in local cults as well as at the capital.

The existence of this body of tutelary or protective gods can readily be traced in the Hittite documents. What is more problematic is to discern their nature, what it is that makes them "tutelary." As noted in *Chapter 1*, some deities are understood as tutelary deities because they occur with other better known gods of this general type in treaty witness lists or offering lists. Laroche[2] discusses the difficulty in recognizing a common trait among the gods grouped together in the treaty oath lists. The evidence of names is the most obvious clue; gods with ᴰLAMMA in their name or title are understood as tutelary deities. Iconography helps somewhat here, as some uniformity of representational conventions may be perceived among Hittite images of these gods. Two main iconographic traditions pertain to tutelary deities. Those tutelary deities who had anthropomorphic images about which we know something show fairly uniform elements. These include standing on a stag, carrying weapons, and holding animals in their hands. The second iconographic tradition for tutelary deities involves the use of a totem, a hunting bag. That hunting bag for the Hittites was the god, just as a statue of the deity was referred to as the deity. The use of an everyday object as a totem is distinctive and provides an iconographic clue for identifying tutelary gods.

Both types of representation of tutelary deities point up another characteristic which some tutelary deities seem to share: an association with the hunt. The anthropomorphic images portray a god whose close association with animals suggests the hunt. The use of the hunting bag as a totem strongly suggests that gods for whom it is a representation are gods who oversee hunting. The scene on the Schimmel rhyton portrays what is clearly a hunting scene, with the results of the chase represented. The scene contains as hunting equipment the bag, the spear, and the quiver. There is a tutelary deity of each attested in the Hittite corpus; probably all of these were therefore perceived as aiding the hunter. In the *kurša*- Festival, in which many tutelary deities are worshipped, the "dog-men" play a

1. *KUB* 9.21 and *ABoT* 3, *Chapter 5* above.
2. *RLA* 6 (1980–83) 456–57.

prominent role. These are probably handlers of hunting dogs, and their "barking" as a ritual litany to accompany offerings to these gods emphasizes the association of some tutelary deities with the hunt. This association demonstrates a protective side to the tutelary deity's nature; gods who assist in the hunt are helping provide the Hittites with one of their most basic needs.

The very term "tutelary" or "protective" deity implies the modern understanding of these as deities who watch over the interests of people or gods. Their protective nature can be seen in the Festival for All the Tutelary Deities, in which there is, for example, a tutelary deity of running in front of the king, presumably to protect him.[3] Their protective nature is also inferred from the fact that they are at times portrayed as personal gods. The Festival for All the Tutelary Deities lists tutelary deities for many personal attributes of the king. A Zitḫariya of the king and a Tutelary Deity of the king are attested outside this festival. A few references in instructions and festivals to "my tutelary deity" (ᴰLAMMA-*aš⸗miš*) or "your tutelary deity" (ᴰLAMMA-*KUNU*) also indicate the potentially personal nature of a god of this type. Perhaps the clearest example of a tutelary deity's protective nature is in the Instructions for Temple Personnel,[4] in which the personal tutelary deity of an accused temple servant is given credit if that person is acquitted. Even other gods may have a personal tutelary deity.

There is a great deal of variation in status within the body of tutelary deities. Some occur only in listings of gods. Local tutelary deities like ᴰLAMMA *šarlaimi-* play no role at all in the state cult and yet are one of the major gods for a local cult, in this case that of Ḫuwaššana of Ḫupišna. Many local cults clearly had their own tutelary deities; only a few are attested in the state archives. Sometimes a distinctive name, Hattic or Luwian, indicates the local cultural milieu from which they come. The Tutelary Deity (ᴰLAMMA) and to some extent the Tutelary Deity of Ḫatti seem most important if one judges by their place in the lists of treaty oath witnesses or offerings. The Tutelary Deity is at times part of a triad of the highest gods of the land with the Stormgod and Sungod(dess). Yet this impression is not borne out by other textual attestations; the Hittites may have officially accorded the Tutelary Deity a high place in the pantheon, but they rarely singled him out for special attention or individual supplication. While occurrences of the Stormgod and the Sungod(dess) throughout the Hittite corpus attest to their real importance in Hittite religious consciousness, ᴰLAMMA appears primarily in lists of gods. It is Zitḫariya who on the basis of his activities may be the most prominent tutelary deity. He is very often included in the cultic journeys as part of festivals. Even more significantly he is the god whom the king takes on campaign and for whom a festival is celebrated when the king returns successfully.

Important for our understanding of the Hittite response to the tutelary deities is their conspicuous absence in prayers. Deities who are personal and protective might be expected to be an important part of Hittite personal piety and petition, but such is not the case. The

3. *KUB* 2.1 ii 25, edited in *Chapter 3*.

4. *CTH* 264, *KUB* 13.4 iv 32, 54. See *Chapter 1* sub ᴰLAMMA.

prayers tend to be addressed to more universal gods of the pantheon. Thus, although the Hittite corpus provides a few examples of very personal tutelary deities, it is fewer than we might expect for gods who are supposed to be protectors for the individual. Perhaps the tutelary deities in general never attain the same status as the Stormgod and Sungod(dess) because they are gods of hunting while the latter two are gods who control the primary area of Hittite production, agriculture. The tradition of tutelary gods in the Hittite cult is to a great extent a borrowed tradition, which may also explain why they play such a small role in individual religious life as recorded in prayers and vows. The festivals treated in this work testify to the role played by the tutelary deities in the official cult, but at the individual level, where one might expect a special interest in protective deities, it is the major universal gods of the pantheon to whom the Hittites turn for special attention or protection.

APPENDIX A

FRAGMENTS OF FESTIVALS FOR TUTELARY DEITIES

INTRODUCTION

A number of tablet fragments of festivals appear to belong to festivals for tutelary deities.[1] They range from fairly substantial fragments that clearly feature tutelary deities as the object of the festival to small pieces of text which merely mention a ^{D}LAMMA. A transliteration of all the pertinent fragments identified by Laroche, as well as those discovered since *CTH* was published, are included here. Translations are provided for texts that are sufficiently substantial or interesting enough to warrant them. Each of the *CTH* 685 fragments was examined for the possibility that it belonged to one of the known festivals for tutelary deities. In a few cases a fragment was identified as a duplicate or parallel to one of those other festivals, and such texts are treated with their appropriate festival.

THE FRAGMENTS[2]

KUB 7.36

The text *KUB* 7.36, catalogued by Laroche under *CTH* 685, was determined to be part of the *kurša-* Festival, *CTH* 683, and is therefore treated in *Chapter 4*.

KUB 7.40

Bo 3334 = *KUB* 7.40 is a small fragment approximately 6.2 cm wide by 5.4 cm high. The scribe has left very large spaces between words. It is difficult to assign a firm dating to such a small fragment; the only really characteristic sign for dating purposes is an *az* with subscript *za* in 8′, indicating an Empire date for the copy.

1. Laroche catalogues fragments of festivals for tutelary deities as *CTH* 685. See p. 8 in the *Introduction* for a revised text scheme of *CTH* 685.
2. The fragments are presented in the order in which they are catalogued as *CTH* 685.

In this fragment a tutelary deity, possibly the goddess Inara with her name written logographically ᴰLAMMA-*ri*, receives offerings of bread, a libation, and meat. The festival represented is part of the state cult, as seen by the presence of the [king] and queen. The royal pair go down from somewhere during the ceremony and may be the ones who go up to the roof and come back down again. The occurrence of *ḫūkanzi* in 9′ probably indicates the slaughtering of the sacrificial sheep but could also refer to a cultic recitation, as there are two Hittite verbs which take this form in the third person plural.

KUB 7.40

Transliteration

§1′ x+1] x x [
2′]x-ya [

- -

§2′ 3′ -i]n?[3] ᴰLAMMA-ri 3 NINDA [… pár-ši-ya
4′] 2-*ŠÚ* BAL-an-ti UDU.NITÁ-y[a
5′ LUGAL-uš S]AL?LUGAL-aš-ša kat-ta pa-a-an-[zi
6′] pé-e-da-an-zi ku-it-t[a
7′ -ká]n?-zi na-at-kán šu-uḫ-ḫi [ša-ra-a pé-e-da-an-zi?
8′ EGIR-an-da?-]ma-at-kán šu-uḫ-ḫa-az k[at-ta ú-wa-an-zi?[4]
9′ UDU.NITÁ?] ḫu-u-kán-zi nu-za a-d[a-[5]
10′]⌈ x x x x x ⌉[

(the tablet breaks off)

Translation

§1′ (Not enough preserved to translate.)

---

§2′ […] three [x] breads for the Tutelary Deity [he breaks]. He libates [x] twice. An[d] the wether […] [The king] and [q]ueen go down. […] they carry. And that which they [ ]x, [they carry(?)] it [up] to the roof. [But afterwards they come dow]n from the roof. [… The wether(?)] they slaughter.[6] (traces)

KUB 9.17

This text describes a cultic journey that includes several stops at which tutelary deities are worshipped. The copy dates from the early Empire period. In §1′ the Tutelary Deity of Ḫatti and Zitḫariya receive offerings. This portion of the festival probably took place in

3. Collation indicates a winkelhaken trace not shown on the copy which would suggest *-i*]*n* or]*x-ni*.
4. See *KUB* 55.39 i 11 for a similar prescription, which provided this restoration.
5. Possibly *a-d*[*a-an-zi* or *a-d*[*a-an-na*. Another possibility is *a-p*[*í-ya*.
6. Or "[…] They do an incantation."

Ḫattuša; we know from the *kurša-* Festival that Zitḫariya had a cult image there, as of course does the Tutelary Deity of Ḫatti. The following paragraph describes a ceremony, still in the capital, at the temple of the Tutelary Deity. This ceremony involves three different types of attendants to the cult: the dog-men, barbers, and the ᴸᵁ́*palwatalla-*. For *palwai-*, the verb from which this last functionary's title is formed, see *Appendix B.*

In §3′ the cultic journey has begun, leaving the capital and stopping first at Tauriša, where local deities receive offerings. The sacred grove of Tauriša is one of the places where the cultic ceremonies take place. Groves occur throughout Hittite cultic literature as sacred places where local gods often have a stela or altar. The grove keeper (LÚ ᴳᴵŠTIR) is presumably responsible for maintenance of the grove and assists in the local cult centered there. In this role he provides the sacrificial loaves for the ceremony. Given the importance of groves in local cults, one would expect the LÚ ᴳᴵŠTIR to be attested frequently, but in fact he occurs very rarely. He does occur twice in a ritual fragment in broken context.[7] There is also a [L]Ú EN.NU.UN ᴳᴵŠTIR ᵁᴿᵁ*Ner*[*ik*] attested once in a list of personnel.[8] This must be a guard for the grove and is probably not the same thing as the LÚ ᴳᴵŠTIR, who in the *KUB* 9.17 passage is a kind of priest who takes a role in the cultic ceremonies.

The third and fourth paragraphs begin with the expression *n*=*aš iyannai,* "He sets out," but do not specify the subject. Line 24′ indicates that the god traveled on this cultic journey, so he could be the subject of *iyannai.* The Hittite gods often traveled to cult sites. This would necessitate a change of subject in line 13′, as it must have been the king or some cult functionary who drank Kalimma and the Tutelary Deity of Tauriša. It may be that the king is the understood subject of the prescription "he sets out." His role in cultic journeys is sufficiently universal that the scribe setting down this ceremony may have felt it superfluous to specify him as the subject.

Based on §2′, which takes place at the temple of the Tutelary Deity, and the fact that the text features several other tutelary deities, it is likely that "DINGIR-*LUM*" in 24′, the god who is taking the cult journey, refers to the image of the Tutelary Deity.

In 20′ we have a first person plural verb, which is unusual in a festival text. Apparently the cultic personnel involved in the festival put some type of garment on the god's image before it "stepped" into the chariot to continue the cultic journey. Unfortunately the broken nature of the tablet does not allow us to learn how long this cultic journey was or what other locations and deities were involved. What it does contribute is a clear example of the importance not only of maintaining local cults but also of bringing along gods from the state cult to participate. The Hittite concern for maintaining the proper relationship with the divine manifests itself not simply in providing encouragement and funding for gods and their cult centers outside the capital, but rather in the active participation of the king as chief priest and of god(s) who had temples at the capital. The image of the god rides in a wagon, but the king appears to have walked, indicating that this is probably a cult site close to the capital.

7. 173/q ii 5′, 7′.
8. *KBo* 12.65 v 6′.

KUB 9.17

Transliteration

§1′x+1 [p]í-an-z[i o o o o o]
2′ [e-k]u-zi $^{\text{LÚ.MEŠ}}$ALA[N.ZU$_9$ SÌR-*RU*]
3′ [o o o o o o ^{D}LAMMA? ^{U}]^{RU}*ḪA-AT-TI* e-ku-zi nu ^{D}Zi[-it-ḫa-ri-ya-an]
4′ [e-ku-zi nu $^{\text{LÚ.MEŠ}}$A]LAN.ZU$_9$-pát SÌR-*RU* [Ø]

- -

§2′ 5′ ⸢x x⸣.ḪI.A ku-it *IŠ-TU* É ^{D}LAMMA ta-pí-⸢ša!⸣-a-ni-it K[Ù.o[9] o o o]
6′ $^{\text{LÚ.MEŠ}}$ta-ḫi-i-ya-li-iš ú-da-an-zi nu *A-NA* LÚ.MEŠ UR.G[I$_7$ [10]]
7′ a-ku-wa-an-na 3-*ŠU* pí-an-zi *A-NA PA-NI* DINGIR-*LIM*-ma ku-it[o o o o o[11]]
8′ pé-e ḫar-kán-zi nu *A-NA* $^{\text{LÚ.MEŠ}}$ta-ḫi-ya-la-aš a-ku-wa-an[-na 3-*ŠU*?]
9′ a-pa-a-at pí-an-zi nu $^{\text{LÚ.MEŠ}}$ta-ḫi-i-ya-li-iš EGIR-p[a]
10′ ne-ya-an-ta-ri *A-NA* ^{LÚ}pal-wa-tal-li-ya *ŠA* É ^{D}[LAMMA]
11′ 1 NINDA.KUR$_4$.RA pí-an-zi nu-za-kán a-pa-a-aš-ša EGIR-pa ne-ya[-ri]

---

§3′ 12′ na-aš i-ya-an-na-i na-an-kán $^{\text{LÚ.MEŠ}}$ALAN.ZU$_9$ EGIR-an a[p-pa-an-zi?]
13′ na-aš ^{URU}Ta-ú-ri-ša ti-i-e-ez-zi nu ^{D}LAMMA ^{URU}Ta-ú-r[i-ša]
14′ ^{D}Ka-li-im-ma-an-na e-ku-zi na-aš i-ya-an-na-i [Ø]
15′ nu ^{GIŠ}TIR ^{URU}Ta-ú-ri-ša pí-ra-an wa-aḫ-nu-zi nu LÚ ^{GIŠ}T[IR]
16′ ^{NINDA}ú-i-iš-ta-aš NINDA-an ú-un-ga-na-an-ta-an ḫar-zi pal-ú-i[š-ki-iz-zi-ya?]
17′ na-an-ši-kán ^{LÚ}SANGA ar-ḫa da-a-i na-an pár-ši-ya
18′ nu ^{D}U ^{GIŠ}TIR e-ku-zi na-an LÚ.MEŠ UR.GI$_7$ EGIR KASKAL-pát a-da[-[12]an-zi?]

---

§4′ 19′ na-aš i-ya-an-na-i na-aš-ša-an a-ú-ri-ya še-er ti-i-e-ez-z[i]
20′ na-an wa-aš-šu-ú-e-ni na-aš-ša-an ^{GIŠ}GIGIR-ya ti-i-e-ez-zi [Ø]
21′ na-aš ma-aḫ-ḫa-an ^{URU}Ḫa-a-ḫi-ša a-ri nu me-na-aḫ-ḫa-an-da
22′ $^{\text{[SAL.]⸢MEŠ⸣}}$ḫa-az-ga-ra-a-i ú-iz-zi[13] NINDA.KUR$_4$.RA-ya ^{DUG}ḫu-u-up-pár KAŠ
23′ [me-na-]aḫ-ḫa-an-da ú-da-an-zi nu ^{NINDA}pur$^{\text{u-ur}}$-pu-ru-uš[14] kat-ta-a[n]
24′ [iš-ḫu-ú-]wa-an-zi na-aš-ta DINGIR-*LUM IŠ-TU* ^{GIŠ}GIGIR kat-ta
25′ [ú-wa-da-an?-z]i nu $^{\text{ḪUR.SAG}}$Ta-ḫa-an 1-*ŠU* e-ku-zi

- -

§5′ 26′ [na-aš *A-NA* ^{GIŠ}ZAG.GA]R?RA.MEŠ ša-ra-a ti-i-e-ez-zi
27′ [o o o o o o o n]a?-aš *QÍ-RU-UB* ^{URU}Ma-na-zi-ya-ra ti-i-e-ez[-zi]
28′ [o o o o o o o] x [o o]⸢ar-ḫa⸣ 6 DUG KAŠ 16 NINDA a-a-an
29′ [o o o o o o o o o o o o o]x ú-da-an-zi
30′ [o o o o o o o o o o o o o]x EGIR KASKAL-*NI* x[o o o]
31′ [o o o o o o o o o o o o o o] ši-⸢pa⸣[-an-ti?

(the tablet breaks off)

9. Either K[Ù.GI] or K[Ù.BABBAR].
10. Space for three or four signs, but nothing is required for sense.
11. There was a vessel or beverage name of neuter gender here.
12. The signs *a-da-* are written over an erasure.
13. The plural form $^{\text{[SAL.]⸢MEŠ⸣}}$*ḫazgarāi* often occurs with a singular verb.
14. See *AlHeth* 179 for Hoffner's comments on why the scribe used this redundant writing.

KUB 9.17

Translation

§1′ [... t]hey giv[e ...] He drin[ks DNs]. The ALA[N.ZU_9]-functionaries [sing. The x] drinks [the Tutelary Deity of] Ḫatti. [He drinks] Zi[tḫariya]. The same [A]LAN.ZU_9-functionaries sing.

---

§2′ They give the [x']s which[15] the barbers[16] bring from the temple of the Tutelary Deity in a g[old]/si[lver] *tapišana*- vessel to the dog-me[n] to drink three times. They give that [x] which they hold out before the god to the barbers to drin[k three(?) times]. The barbers turn around. They give one thick bread of the temple of [the Tutelary] Deity[17] to the reciter(?). He also turns around.

---

§3′ He (the king[?]) sets out. The ALAN.ZU_9-functionaries f[ollow(?)] him. He arrives at Tauriša and drinks the Tutelary Deity of Taur[iša] and the god Kalimma. He (again) sets out. The grove of Tauriša assumes the first position(??).[18] The grove keeper holds *wišta*- breads (and) **unganai*-ed[19] bread [and] recites(?). The priest takes it (the bread) away from him and breaks it. He drinks the Stormgod of the Grove. The dog-men ea[t(?)] it on the return trip(?).[20]

---

§4′ He sets out. He steps up on the lookout tower. We clothe him and he steps into the chariot. When he arrives at Ḫāḫiša the *ḫazgara*- women come to (meet) (him). They bring forward thick bread (and) a *ḫuppar* vessel of beer. They heap up bread balls down (at his feet). They [bri]ng the god down on a chariot. He drinks Mt. Taḫa once.

---

§5′ He proceeds up [to the alt]ars(?). [...] He procee[ds] into the center of the city Manaziyara. [...] six vessels of beer, 16 warm breads [...]x they bring. [...]x on the return trip x[...] [...] he lib[ates].

(the tablet breaks off)

15. One would expect a plural relative pronoun here because of the [ ].ḪI.A at the beginning of the sentence. The noun which is broken away is probably neuter plural, which usually takes singular agreement.

16. This functionary occurs with tutelary deities or in analogous situations elsewhere. He is loosely associated with the Tutelary Deity and Ḫapantali(ya) in *KBo* 25.176 obv. 17–18 (KI.LAM outline tablet), translit. Singer, *StBoT* 28 (1984) 93, and with the priest of the Tutelary Deity in *IBoT* 2.91 obv. iii 11′–12′ (fest. fragment). They "release" the command of Inara, passim in the NIN.DINGIR Festival (*CTH* 649). They also hold the hunting bag in the NIN.DINGIR Festival (*KBo* 20.32 ii 7): $^{\text{LÚ.MEŠ}}$*daḫiyaleš* TÚG-*aš kuršan ḫarkanzi* "The barbers hold the hunting bag of cloth."

17. That is, provided by the temple of the tutelary deity.

18. That is, "becomes the first place to visit(?)."

19. There is no verb **unganai*- attested elsewhere in the Hittite corpus, but *unganantan* looks like a singular common accusative participle of such a verb. It follows a noun in the same case, which lends support to the idea that it is a participle, the first occurrence of a previously unattested verb **unganai*-.

20. *CHD* first draft of *palši*- notes the use of EGIR.KASKAL as "return journey, return," and cites this passage as one which seems to require such a translation. Another possibility would be "after the trip."

KUB 10.29

There is not enough preserved of this tablet to produce a coherent translation. It is a festival which involves drink and bread offerings to a number of deities in succession; the three preserved gods are tutelary deities. As in the *kurša-* Festival Zitḫariya and the Tutelary Deity of Ḫatti receive drink and bread offerings. Another deity who receives offerings in the *kurša-* Festival is the Tutelary Deity of Ḫatenzuwa; ^{D}Ḫatenzawu of *KUB* 10.29:7′ is probably the same deity. Laroche, *Rech.* 24, in his entry for ^{D}Ḫatenzawu (attested only in this text and *KUB* 58.13 obv. 6′[21]) considered this possibility: "On songe au nom de ville Ḫatenzuwa dont ^{d}LAMA est précisément le patron ... "

Transliteration

§1′x+1]⸢x-x⸣[
2′ -t]a? pí-an-z[i
3′ ^{D}Zi-it-ḫ]a-ri-ya[22] GUB-aš ⸢e⸣[23][-ku-zi
4′ M]EŠ?-in pár-ši-y[a

- -

§2′ 5′]x ^{D}LAMMA ^{URU}*ḪAT-TI* ⸢e⸣[-ku-zi?
6′ -i]n pár-ši-ya [

- -

§3′ 7′] ^{D}Ḫa-ti-en-za-wu$_{\acute{u}}$(-)ú? [
8′ -i]n pár-ši-ya [

- -

§4′ 9′]⸢ x x x ⸣[

(the tablet breaks off)

21. ^{D}*Ḫa]-ti-en-za-*⸢*wu*$_{\acute{u}}$?⸣-[*u*]*n*. Read ^{D}Ḫatenzawu by Popko, *KUB* 58 p. V, Inhaltsübersicht and p. IX, index.
22. Collated.
23. Collation shows two possible horizontal traces which would fit *e* perfectly.

KUB 10.93[24]

Bo 2420 = *KUB* 10.93 is a fragment 16 cm wide by 9.9 cm tall. The back of column ii has been broken away, so that none of reverse iii is preserved. The tablet is inscribed in a large, very neat script which shows a mixture of older and newer forms. Although the signs *gi* and LAMMA occur in older forms, *az, da, ḫa, id, li,* and URU show their newer forms. The tablet is New Script, written in the early Empire period.

In addition to some standard drink and bread offerings, the first column involves a cultic meal, at which a variety of male and female cultic personnel eat. The conclusion of the meal is a series of drink and bread offerings. We cannot tell how extensive this series of offerings was, because column i ends after three rounds of offerings, and almost all of column ii is lost. The very end of column ii offers only tantalizing phrases of a somewhat unusual ceremony in which the throne is perhaps moved. In an unusual prescription the celebrant offers a drink offering to the name of the king.

In column iv we have two almost identical paragraphs which set out as part of the ceremony the performance by two different "old priests of the Tutelary Deity" of this festival for that god in Ḫattuša. It is important that it be done twice by two different priests; any tendency to save time and expense by cutting either ceremony short is specifically interdicted. The festival is to be celebrated in the autumn. However, the last paragraph in which anything readable is preserved mentions the festivals of spring. Perhaps the remainder of the fourth column described the special festivals for the Tutelary Deity and the duties of his priest in the spring festivals. The references to Ḫattuša and Ḫatti throughout the text suggest that the festivals described here took place in the capital and did not involve a cultic journey through the countryside.

24. Lines iv 1–2 are transliterated and translated by Sommer, *HAB* (1938) 175 with n. 3, and by Goetze, *JCS* 17 (1963) 100.

KUB 10.93

Transliteration

Obverse i

§1′x+1 [o o o o o o o o o]x-du-x[o o o o o o o o]
2′ [o o o o o o o o-m]a? GUNNI ta-⌈pu-uš⌉-[za]
3′ [o o o o o o o o] ši-pa-an- t[i]

§2′ 4′ [nu *A-NA* LÚSANGA DL]AMMA a-ku-wa-an-na pí-ya-an-zi
5′ [nu DLAMMA GUB-aš/TUŠ-aš]⌈e⌉-ku-zi DIM DWa$_a$-še-ez-za-le-e[n][25]
6′ [TUŠ/GUB-aš? e-ku-zi] SÌR-*RU*

§3′ 7′ [nu LÚ.MEŠMUḪALDIM? TU]$_7$?ḪI.A i-en-zi GIM-an-ma-aš-ša-an
8′ [zé-ya-an-ta-r]i nu *A-NA* LÚSANGA DLAMMA LÚ.MEŠta-ḫi-ya[-li-ya-aš]
9′ [*A-NA*? LÚ.MEŠša]r?-mi-ya-aš LÚ.MEŠKISAL.LUḪ-*TIM* EN.É.GAL
10′ [*Ù*?]*A-NA* SAL URU*ḪA-AT-TI* SALENSI kal-li-iš-šu-u[-an-zi?]
11′ [u-]⌈i⌉-e-an-zi na-at-za ú-wa-an-zi a-da-an-na
12′ ⌈e⌉-ša-an-ta-ri GIM-an-ma a-da-an-na zi-in-na-a[n-zi]

§4′ 13′ nu DU GUB-aš e-ku-zi GIŠ INANNA.GAL SÌR-*RU*
14′ 1 NINDA.KUR$_4$.RA pár-ši- ya

§5′ 15′ DUTU-aš TUŠ-aš e-ku-zi GIŠ INANNA.GAL SÌR-*RU* 1 NINDA.KUR$_4$.RA pár-⌈ši-ya⌉

§6′ 16′ nu nam-ma DU TUŠ-aš e-ku-zi GIŠ INANNA.GAL SÌR-*RU*
17′ 1 NINDA.KUR$_4$.RA pár-ši- ya

(bottom of tablet)

Obverse ii[26]

§7′x+1 [o o o o o o] x x [

§8′ 2′ [o o o o o]URUKÙ.BABBAR-⌈*TI*⌉[
3′ ⌈GIŠDAG-ti?⌉-in ZAG.GAR.RA-ni p[í-ra-an da-a-i?
4′ nu *ŠUM-MI* LUGAL-*RI* DZA.BA$_4$.[BA$_4$ e-ku-zi?
5′ nu tu-u-wa-az i-e-e[z-zi
6′ DKa-taḫ-ḫa-an ZAG.GAR.[RA-ni pí-ra-an?

25. Collated. Laroche, *Rech.* 37, notes this form of the Hattic god, Wašizzil, also in *KUB* 10.86 i 5.

26. After a gap of an undetermined number of paragraphs.

KUB 10.93

Translation

Obverse i

§1′ (The fragmentary paragraph describes libations to the holy places in the temple.)

§2′ They give [to the priest of the Tutel]ary Deity to drink. He drinks [the Tutelary Deity, standing/seated]. [He drinks] the Stormgod (and) Wašezzali, [standing/seated]. They sing.

§3′ [The cooks] prepare [ste]ws(?). When [they are cooke]d, they [se]nd in order [to] call the priest of the Tutelary Deity, the barb[ers], the [*ša*]*rmi*- men, the washers of the court, the lord of the palace, [and] the woman of Ḫatti, the prophetess. They come and sit down to eat. When they have finished eating, however,

§4′ he drinks the Stormgod, standing. (They play) the large Inanna instrument. They sing. He breaks one thick bread.

§5′ He drinks the Sungod, seated.[27] (They play) the large Inanna instrument. They sing. He breaks one thick bread.

§6′ Further, seated, he drinks the Stormgod. (They play) the large Inanna instrument. They sing. He breaks one thick bread.

(bottom of tablet)

Obverse ii[28]

§7′ (Nothing preserved to translate.)

§8′ [...] Ḫatti [...] [He places(?)] the throne b[efore] the altar. [He drinks(?)] the name of the king, ZA.BA$_4$.[BA$_4$, ...] He worsh[ips] from afar.[29] [...] Kataḫḫa [before(?)] the alta[r].

27. The ending for ^{D}UTU-*aš* is unexpected, but this formula is so typical that we must understand it as accusative. Perhaps the scribe was thinking ahead to the phonetic complement on TUŠ-*aš*.

28. After a gap of an undetermined number of paragraphs.

29. This is the only attested example of *tuwaz* with *iya*-; the translation is tentative.

KUB 10.93

Obverse ii (*transliteration cont.*)

§9′ 7′ GUNNI-*NI*[30] ta-pu-uš-za[

(bottom of tablet)

Reverse iii lost

Reverse iv[31] (*transliteration*)

§10′ 1 pa-ra-a-ma-aš-ša-an *Ú-UL* ku-it-ki na-a-i
2 EGIR-pa-ya-kán *Ú-UL* ku-it-ki pé-eš-še-ya- zi

§11′ 3 EGIR-an-da-ma ú-iz-zi ^{LÚ}SANGA ŠU.GI
4 *ŠA* ^{D}LAMMA ku-u-un[32] EZEN-an a-pé-el
5 *I-NA* É-*ŠU* ^{URU}Ḫa-at-tu-ši zé-e- ni
6 ⸢*A-NA*⸣ ^{D}LAMMA ki-iš-ša-an i-e-ez- zi
7 [pa-r]a-a-«ša»-ma-aš-ša-an *Ú-UL* ku-it-ki na-a-[i]
8 [EG]IR-pa-ya-kán *Ú-UL* ku-it-ki pé-eš-še-y[a-zi]

§12′ 9 [EGI]R-an-da-ma nam-ma ta-ma-a-iš ^{LÚ}SANG[A ŠU.GI]
10 [*Š*]*A* ^{D}LAMMA ku-u-un EZEN-an a-pé-el *I*-[*NA* É-*ŠU*]
11 [*A-N*]*A* ^{D}LAMMA ^{URU}Ḫa-at-tu-ši zé-e[-ni]
12 [ki-i]š-ša-an i-e-ez-zi pa-ra-a-m[a!?-aš-ša-an]
13 [*Ú-U*]*L* ku-it-ki na-a-i EGIR-pa-m[a? o o o o o]
14 [EGIR-p]a-ya-kán *Ú-UL* ku-it-k[i pé-eš-še-ya-zi]

§13′ 15 [nu ḫa-me-eš-ḫ]a-[33]⸢an⸣-ta-aš EZEN.ḪI.A[o o o o o o o]
16 [o o o o o ^{D}LAMM]A? ⸢^{URU}⸣*ḪA-A*[*T-TI* o o o o o o o]

§14′ 17 [o o o o o o o]⸢ x ⸣[o o o o o o o o o]

(the tablet breaks off)

30. This unusual complementation for GUNNI (Hittite *ḫašša-*) is probably for Akkadian *KINŪNI*. Friedrich notes this spelling in this passage in *HW* 276.
31. After a large gap of an undetermined number of paragraphs.
32. Written partly over an erasure.
33. Collated.

KUB 10.93

Obverse ii (*translation cont.*)

§9′ Next to the hearth [...]

(bottom of tablet)

Reverse iii lost

Reverse iv[34] (*translation*)

§10′ But he postpones(?) nothing, nor does he neglect(?) anything.[35]

§11′ Afterwards the old priest of the Tutelary Deity comes and celebrates this festival in this way in his (the Tutelary Deity's) temple[36] in Ḫattuša in the autumn for the Tutelary Deity. But he postpones nothing, nor does he neglec[t] anything.

§12′ Afterwards, again another [old p]riest of the Tutelary Deity celebrates this festival [in th]is way i[n his temple] in Ḫattuša in the autu[mn for] the Tutelary Deity. But he postpones [no]thing. He [...] back. [And he neglects] nothing.

§13′ The festivals of [spr]ing [...] [... the Tutelary De]ity of Ḫa[tti ...].

§14′ (Only one trace preserved.)

(the tablet breaks off)

KUB 12.52

Bo 2997 = *KUB* 12.52 is a small fragment approximately 7.8 cm wide by 7 cm high. There is not enough of it preserved to allow a meaningful translation, but it contains several items of interest. In i 2 we have the verb *lipšaizzi*; on *lipšai-*, whose meaning is still uncertain, see *CHD* for a possible meaning in this passage "break off" or "split open" in context with the fruit in i 1. See also Poetto, *AIΩN* 1 (1979 [1980]) 120–21 with n. 13 and 14 for an additional attestation of *lipšai-* in a fragment of Hurrian ritual unpublished when the *CHD* came out.[37] Poetto suggests "eat, consume" for this verb, but the evidence is still insufficient to make a definite judgement; Eichner[38] suggests "abnutzen" or "abstoßen" for this verb in the same contexts as those used by Poetto. The Tutelary Deity of Tauriša or his priest is mentioned twice in column i and perhaps in ii 2.

In column ii we may note little beyond the description of the priest of the Tutelary Deity [of Tauriša(?)] using a vessel stand (*zeriyalli-*) as part of the cultic procedure. The

34. After a large gap of an undetermined number of paragraphs.
35. Goetze, *JCS* 17 (1963) 100, translates "He does not add anything nor does he leave off anything." Sommer, *HAB* 175, translates "er verabsäumt nichts und vernachlässigt nichts."
36. Or " ... in his (the priest's) own house ... "
37. Poetto's Bo 2133 is now *KUB* 55.35.
38. *Die Sprache* 27 (1981) 65.

zeriyalli- is used in both the AN.TAḪ.ŠUM and KI.LAM Festivals. It is certainly possible that this text fragment is not from a festival for tutelary deities, but rather from one of these two major state festivals. The occurrences of the Tutelary Deity of Tauriša, or his priest, are almost the only distinctive feature of this fragment. That priest occurs elsewhere, most notably in the description of the sixteenth day of the AN.TAḪ.ŠUM Festival, for the Tutelary Deity of Tauriša. This is further evidence that this fragment could be a part of that festival.

Column iii does not add much information beyond the fact that once again some of the activities took place at a sacred grove, which is reminiscent of *KUB* 9.17 §3′ (*CTH* 685.2). The word *takkuwa*[*r*] in iii 6′ is difficult; it does not admit of ready recognition as a known Hittite word. It could conceivably be the verbal substantive of *takk-* "to be similar to," although how that would fit in this context is unclear.

Transliteration

Obverse i

§1 1 ḫa-me-]eš-ḫi *IN-BA*-⸢*AM*⸣
2]li-ip-ša-iz-zi
3 ^{LÚ}SANGA? ^{D}LAMM]A ^{URU}Ta-ú-ri-ša
4 ^{LÚ}SANGA? ^{D}LAMM]A ^{URU}Ta-ú-ri-ša
5 -a]z-zi

§2 6 *A-N*]*A* ? É-*ŠU* pa-a-i
7]x ⸢ x ⸣ kiš-an
8] (traces)

(the tablet breaks off)

Obverse ii[39]

§3′ 1 ka-ru-ú x[
2 ^{LÚ}SANGA ^{D}LAM[MA ^{URU}Ta-ú-ri-ša?
3 zé-ri-ya-al[-li(-)
4 kat-ta *I-NA* É[
5 pé-e-da-an [-zi?

§4′ 6 nu GIM-an ^{L}[^{Ú}
7 kat-ta *I-NA* ⸢É?⸣[
8 na-aš-kán x[
9 nu-uš-ši x[
10 na-aš-k[án

(the tablet breaks off)

39. After a gap of an undetermined number of paragraphs.

Reverse iii[40]

§5′x+1 nu[

§6′ 2′ GIM-a[n

3′ pí-ra-a[n

4′ nu *A-NA*[

5′ [GI]ŠTIR-aš [

6′ ták[41]-ku-wa-a[r

7′ ti-an-zi?[42] [

8′ nu *A-NA* LÚSANGA x[

9′ GAL-in *IŠ-T*[*U*

10′ LÚNAR-ma UR[U?

(bottom of tablet)

Reverse iv

(The preserved portion of column iv is uninscribed.)

KUB 20.13

This text is catalogued by Laroche as *CTH* 685. It is part of the *kurša*- Festival and is treated in *Chapter 4.*

IBoT 2.22[43]

Bo 4001 = *IBoT* 2.22 is a small piece 7.4 cm wide by 7.6 cm high. Part of its surface is completely broken away, leaving only a small area still inscribed. The portion of a festival which it describes is difficult to follow; without any part of either edge preserved, we can only conjecture how wide the column was originally and thus how the preserved sections relate to one another. The right edge indicated in the transliteration is very tentative, the left somewhat less so.

The only tutelary deity who definitely occurs in the text is the Tutelary Deity of the Hunting Bag (line 3′); the same god probably occurs in line 4′. Some of §2′ resembles §§2′ and 3′ of *KUB* 9.21, *CTH* 684.1, a festival for gods of the river treated in *Chapter 5.* That resemblance is not sufficiently close to identify this fragment with *KUB* 9.21. The LÚMUŠEN.DÙ, the augur, although very active in the taking of oracles which were pivotal in Hittite decision making and their relationship with the divine, does not usually participate in religious festivals. The references to animal skins in §2′ combined with the

40. After a gap of an undetermined number of paragraphs.

41. Collated.

42. The *zi* sign was written over an erasure.

43. Lines 4′–8′ are treated by Goetze in *Language* 29 (1953) 275–26. His transliteration indicates a paragraph line after line 8′ which is not on the tablet.

Tutelary Deity of the Hunting Bag could indicate that this text had to do with the making of new hunting bags (*kurša-*) as cult representations.

IBoT 2.22

Transliteration

§1′x+1 [o o] x x x [
2′ [o] x-zi a-pa-a-ša-a[z
3′ [^{LÚ}MUŠ]EN?DÙ[44] ^{D}LAMMA ^{KUŠ}kur-š[a-aš

- - -

§2′ 4′ [nu LU]GAL-uš GUB-aš GAL-it ^{D}L[AMMA ^{KUŠ}kur-ša-aš e-ku-zi]
5′ [ir-ḫ]a-u-wa-a-ar ir-ḫa-an-du-uš [ḫi-iš-ša-al-la-an-du-uš?[45]]
6′ [e-k]u-zi $^{\text{LÚ.MEŠ}}$NAR ^{URU}Ka-ni-i[š SÌR-*RU* ...]
7′ [1 ^{NINDA}t]a-kar-mu-un pár-ši-ya na-an x[
8′ [*A-NA PA-*]*NI* DINGIR-*LIM* da-a-i nu a-ap-pa l[a-
9′ [o o o -u]š ša-ra-a da-an-zi x[
10′ [*PA-NI*? DINGI]R?-*LIM* pé-e-da-an-zi ^{UZU}[
11′ [o o o ḫu?-]⌈i⌉-šu KUŠ.UDU KUŠ.MÁŠ.GAL [
12′ [o o o o] x la-aḫ-ḫur-nu-zi x[
13′ [o o o o o o] x KASKAL-az [

(the tablet breaks off)

Translation

§1′ [...] He x[...] That one (nom.) [... the aug]ur(?) [x's] the Tutelary Deity of the Hunting B[ag].

---

§2′ [The k]ing, seated, [drinks] with a cup the Tutel[ary Deity of the Hunting Bag. (As part of) tre]ating with offerings in sequence, he [dri]nks the (gods whose offerings have been) done in sequence [(and) the (gods whose offerings are) planned(?)].[46] The singers of Kaneš [sing ...] He breaks [one *t*]*akarmu-* bread and places it x[... bef]ore the god. Behind, *l*[*a-* ...] They take up the [x]'s. x[...] they bring [before(?) the g]od. The [(some flesh part) ...] [ra]w(?) [x], a sheepskin, a billy goat skin, [...]x, greenery, x[...] [...]x from the road [...]

44. The augur would be very unusual in a festival text, but see below, *CTH* 685.8: *KBo* 8.59:6′.

45. Goetze restores [DINGIR.MEŠ-*uš*] here, and his translation takes *irḫanduš* as modifying [DINGIR.MEŠ-*uš*].

46. Goetze, *Language* 29: 275, following his somewhat different transliteration, translates: "The king 'drinks' in a standing position with a cup Inar [of the shield] (and) [the gods] due for treatment." This translation seems to ignore [*irḫ*]*awar*.

IBoT 3.18

Bo 1528 = *IBoT* 3.18 is a very small fragment measuring 4.4 cm wide by 4 cm high. Although there are only a few signs preserved, the late forms of signs such as *al*, *li*, and URU indicate that the tablet is New Script.

The text is obviously part of a festival description and resembles *KUB* 10.29[47] in form, being a kind of formulaic listing of standard offerings to a series of gods given in succession. The [Tutelary Deity of K]araḫna (line 2′) and the Tutelary Deity of the City (line 4′) receive drink and bread offerings. The Tutelary Deity of Karaḫna may be mentioned again in line 7′. The fragmentary nature of *IBoT* 3.18 precludes any attempt at establishing a definite connection with the festivals of Karaḫna (*CTH* 681) treated in *Chapter 2.*

Transliteration

§1′x+1 [ ] x x [

§2′ 2′ [^{D}LAMMA ^{URU}K]a!-ra?-aḫ-na GU[B-aš e-ku-zi
3′ [pár]-ši-ya GIŠ ^{D}INANNA!GAL [SÌR-*RU*]

§3′ 4′ [nam-m]a ^{D}LAMMA URU-*LIM*-ya GUB-aš [e-ku-zi
5′ [pár-ši-y]a? GIŠ ^{D}INANNA.GAL SÌR-*R*[*U*]

§4′ 6′ [^{DUG}ḫar-]ši-ya-al-li-aš-ma UDU x[… *A-NA* ^{D}LAMMA?]
7′ [^{URU}K]a-ra-aḫ-na pé-eš-ká[n-zi
8′? [ ] (There is just space at the bottom of the tablet for another short line.)

(bottom of tablet)

Translation

§1′ (Only traces preserved.)

§2′ [He drinks the Tutelary Deity of K]araḫna, stan[ding]. [(A bread type) he b]reaks. (They play) the large wooden Inanna instrument. [They sing.]

§3′ [The]n [he drinks] the Tutelary Deity of the City as well, standing. [(A bread type) he break]s. (They play) the large wooden Inanna instrument. They sin[g].

§4′ In(?) the storage vessels, however, a sheep x[…] [… to the Tutelary Deity(?) of K]araḫna they gi[ve …]

(bottom of tablet)

47. *CTH* 685.3, treated above.

KBo 8.59

The fragment *KBo* 8.59 is too small and broken to yield a meaningful translation. The $^{\text{LÚ.MEŠ}}$MUŠEN.DÙ mentioned in 6′ do not usually play a role in the festivals.[48] There is in fact little in this text to indicate definitely that it is a festival. The one occurrence of the Tutelary Deity of the Hunting Bag without much preserved context is the only mention of a deity in the text. The imperative *ḫuyanza eš* "be running" in 8′ is certainly not expected in a festival. We may say that the text has something to do with the Tutelary Deity of the Hunting Bag, but we cannot on the basis of the preserved context definitely state that this is a festival for that or any other deity. It could be a ritual or a conjuration.

Transliteration

§1′	x+1	[o-]x-la[
	2′	ar-ḫa ⸢x⸣[o o o]⸢a-ra?⸣[-
§2′	3′	na-aš-ta[o o o] x tu-uk[(-)
	4′	LUGAL-i-ya-kán [SAL].LUGAL-ri x[
	5′	nu-uš-ma-aš-kán ZI-an-za an-d[a
	6′	*A-NA* $^{\text{LÚ.MEŠ}}$MUŠEN.DÙ-ya-kán z[i-
§3′	7′	[nu] LUGAL-i SAL.LUGAL-ri *A-NA* x[
	8′	[ḫ]u?-ya-an-za e-eš nu KUR.KUR.ḪI.A[
	9′	[LUG]AL-ša SAL.LUGAL-wa-ša tu-x[
	10′	[nu] ^{D}LAMMA ^{KUŠ}kur-ša-aš u-x[
§4′	11′	(traces only)

(the tablet breaks off)

KBo 21.89+*KBo* 8.97

This text, with duplicate *IBoT* 2.69, is catalogued by Laroche as *CTH* 685. It is part of the *kurša-* Festival and is treated in *Chapter 4.*

48. *IBoT* 2.22:3′ (*CTH* 685.6) may be another example of the augur participating in festival proceedings.

KUB 44.24

Bo 235 = *KUB* 44.24 is a fragment broken and abraded in such a way that no complete sentences are preserved. There is not enough material to posit even a tentative dating of the script of this piece. The tablet contains tantalizing references to the É.DU$_{10}$.ÚS.SA, "cultic washing house," and the ^{GIŠ}*kalmu-* "lituus"; the ceremony was a somewhat unusual one, making it all the more unfortunate that it is so poorly preserved. The best preserved portion of the tablet is the colophon. Even there the portion that would describe the ceremony's distinctive features is broken away. The priest of a tutelary deity is mentioned in i 9′ in very broken context; we cannot tell which tutelary deity this was. The colophon indicates that some or all of the cult proceedings took place in the temple of a tutelary deity. That this was a major cult ceremony is indicated by the fact that after one six-column tablet the description of the festival was not completed. Obverse i resembles portions of the AN.TAḪ.ŠUM Festival, and this text could belong to *CTH* 617, the AN.TAḪ.ŠUM Festival for the Tutelary Deity of Tauriša.

Transliteration

Obverse i

§1′x+1 [nu? LUGAL-uš *IŠ-TU*] É.DU$_{10}$.ÚS.SA ú[-iz-zi
2′ [o o o o DUMU]⸢É.GAL⸣ ^{GIŠ}kal-mu-uš [
3′ [2 DUMU.MEŠ É.GAL] 1 ^{LÚ}*ME-ŠE-DI*[
4′ [o o pí-ra-a]n ḫu-u-i-ya-an-z[i[49]

- -

§2′ 5′ [o o] x É? ⸢ x x ⸣[
6′ [1 UGULA $^{LÚ.ME]Š}$MUḪALDIM 1 ⸢UGULA $^{LÚ.⸣MEŠ}$[
7′ [ ]x *A-NA* LÚ.MEŠ[pí-ra-an]
8′ [ḫu-u]-i-ya-an- [zi

- -

§3′ 9′ [^{LÚ}SAN]GA ^{D}LAMMA [
10′ $^{[L]Ú.MEŠ}$⸢SANGA⸣[
11′ [ ]x $^{URU?}$x[
12′ ⸢x x x⸣
13′ [o o]⸢ḪI.A⸣[
14′ [o]⸢x x ⸣[

- -

(the tablet breaks off)

Reverse vi[50]

§4′ (No signs preserved.)

- -

49. This first paragraph is restored from the similar festival description *IBoT* 1.3:8–11 (AN.TAḪ.ŠUM Festival).
50. After a large gap of an undetermined number of paragraphs.

KUB 44.24

Reverse vi (*cont.*)

§5′x+1 [o o o o o] 7 *ŠUM*!$^{\text{ḪI.A}}$ [

§6′ 2′ [o o o]x LAL 2 UDU *A-N*[*A*[51]

3′ [o o o]x-la-aš ši-pa[-an-ti?

Colophon

4′ DUB 1 KAM *Ú-UL* [*QA-TI*]

5′ ma-a-an LUGAL-uš [

6′ *I-NA* É ^{D}LAMM[A

7′ iš-tar-ni-ya-aš [EGIR-an tar-nu-um-ma-aš]

8′ *A-NA* GIŠ.ḪUR-ká[n ḫa-an-da-a-an]

9′ KASKAL ^{m}Pí-ḫa-U[R.MAḪ DUB.SAR.GIŠ

10′ ^{m}Pal-lu-wa-[r]a(-)LÚ [DUB.SAR

11′ ^{m}Ḫu-ul-la LÚ[

(smaller script)

12′ ŠU ^{m}Ḫe-eš-ni[

13′ ^{m}Na-ni-y[a[52]

KUB 51.40

Bo 1229 = *KUB* 51.40 is a fragment approximately 14 cm wide by 8.1 cm high, with a great deal of surface abrasion which obscures many of the signs. Although the paucity of signs makes dating the script tentative, the absence of any slant on the tops of the verticals, the even height of the verticals in the *a*, *e*, and *ya* signs, and the subscript *za* in the *az* sign all point to a very likely New Script date.

A coherent translation is not possible because of the broken nature of the text. This is a festival text that includes drink and bread offerings, some of which are for deified mountains. The first word of obverse iii 6′ is read as a mountain name on the basis of the similar name $^{\text{ḪUR.SAG}}$*Ḫu-wa-aḫ-ḫar-ma* in *KUB* 1.15 obv. iii 5 (Festival of the Month) and $^{\text{ḪUR.SAG}}$*Ḫu-u-wa-ḫa*[*r-ma* in its duplicate *KUB* 40.104 obv. iii 6′.

The reverse of the tablet yields even less preserved context. Line 8′ indicates that part of the ceremonies took place at a *ḫuwaši-* stela. In line 10′ occur the *ḫazgara-* women, who

51. Or 2! x[.

52. This colophon is transliterated by Mascheroni, *Hethitica* 5 (1983) 97, with a discussion of it and similar colophons on pp. 98–104. Restorations are from Mascheroni's transliteration. See further comments on this relatively common type of colophon by del Monte, *OA* 22 (1983) 320–21 (review of *Hethitica* 5), and Singer, *StBoT* 27 (1983) 40–42. Güterbock, *JNES* 26 (1967) 79 n. 7, and private communication, suggests that the phrase EGIR-*an tarnummaš* most probably refers to an excerpt tablet.

also occur in much fuller context meeting the god's image or the king in Ḫaḫiša in *KUB* 9.17:21′–22′.[53]

KUB 51.40

Transliteration

Obverse iii

§1′	x+1	] x [
	2′	] (traces only) [
	3′	-]a? (traces)
§2′	4′	GUB/ TU]Š-aš 1-*ŠU* a-ku-wa-an-zi
	5′	]x
	6′	ḪUR.SAGḪ]u-uḫ-ḫar-ma-an GUB-aš
	7′	[a-ku-wa-an-zi ...]x 1 NINDA.KUR$_4$.RA pár-ši-ya
§3′	8′	]x-⸢zi⸣ nu ḪUR.SAGDa-a-ḫa-an
	9′	ḪUR.SA]GDa-a-ḫa GUB-aš
	10′	a-k]u-wa-an-zi
	11′	a-ku-wa?-a]n-zi
	12′	*P*] *A-NI* DINGIR-*LIM* ti-ya-zi
§4′	13′	]x DLAMMA-an TUŠ-aš
	14′	[a-ku-wa-an-zi ... NINDA.]KUR$_4$.RA pár-ši-ya
	15′	]TUŠ-aš 1-*ŠU* a-ku-wa-an-z[i]
	16′	E]GIR-*ŠU*-⸢ma x(-)⸣ ḫa-an-x[
	17′	] (traces) [
	18′	] (traces) [

(the tablet breaks off)

Reverse iv[54]

§5′	x+1	] x [
	2′	] x [
	3′	-z]i [
	4′	]x PA ZÍD.DA ⸢È⸣[.A]
	5′	DUGK]A.DÙ.A [Ø]
	6′	-]ši[55]
	7′	a-k]u?-wa-an-zi
§6′	8′	]x NA4?ḫu-u-wa-⸢ši!?⸣

53. *CTH* 685.2, treated above.

54. After a gap of an undetermined number of paragraphs.

55. There is an erased *-pát* after *ši*.

KUB 51.40

Reverse iv (*cont.*)

9′]
10′ SAL]ḫa-az-ga-ra-i-kán
11′ -i]z-zi
12′ -š]a-an-zi
13′]x GEŠPÚ-*ŠI*[56]
14′]x-ya-an-zi
15′] x x x x [

(the tablet breaks off)

KUB 53.11[57]

Bo 2309 = *KUB* 53.11 is a fairly large fragment measuring 13 cm wide by 13.7 cm high. Its script shows consistent use of older sign forms and is, I believe, an Old Script tablet.

The festival described in this fragment involves a variety of different types of offerings. In §§1′–7′ there is not enough preserved to know exactly what is happening beyond the fact that bread and drink offerings are being given. In §8′, after a break of several paragraphs, the ceremony has moved on to animal sacrifice and very specific flesh offerings. The following paragraphs, §§9′–10′, prescribe bread and meal offerings, §11′ again describes flesh offerings, and in §§12′–13′ drink offerings are performed with *tawal* and with beer. Thus in this one fragment of festival are detailed a rather diverse range of offerings, with every major type of offering represented.

To what deities were these various offerings given? Again in §§1′–7′ we can make little sense of the preserved portion, although in i 7′ the Tutelary Deity of Ḫatti may be receiving offerings, and in i 12′ the Maraššanda river has been restored as the recipient of a drink offering. In §8′ the flesh offerings are described without specifying for what deity they were being prepared. The next four paragraphs, §§9′–12′, however, all specify offerings to the holy places of the temple, offerings of bread, meal, flesh, and drink. In each case Kappariyamu[58] is included in the list of the holy places, and these four paragraphs of *KUB* 53.11 are the only example in the published corpus of this deity occurring in such a list. In ii 9′–10′, her first occurrence in the text, this goddess receives her offering "on the pegs." This is reminiscent of the pegs in *KUB* 55.43 i 10, the *kurša*-Festival,[59] where the pegs are driven in below the "place of the god" to hold the old *kurša*-s until they are sent out to the provinces. In that same text Kappariyamu appears in ii 17 and

56. Akkadian *umāšu*.

57. Lines ii 9′–15′ are transliterated and translated by Neu, *StBoT* 12 (1970) 71. Lines ii 29′–iii 5 are transliterated and briefly commented on (as Bo 2309) by Ehelolf, *ZA* 43 = NF 9 (1936) 183–84.

58. On this deity see *Chapter 1* and *Appendix B* sub *kipikkišdu*.

59. Treated in *Chapter 4*.

iv 16′, both times in a group with the Tutelary Deity of Tatašuna and the Tutelary Deity of Tašḫapuna, the three of whom are *kipikkišdu*s to some other deity and who receive offerings together as a group.[60] *KUB* 53.11 ii 9′–10′ does not specify what the pegs have to do with Kappariyamu. However, we know from the *kurša*- Festival[61] that pegs are associated with the place where the *kurša*-s are normally hung, that the *kurša*- very frequently appears in the list of holy places such as we have in *KUB* 53.11 §§9′–12′, and that Kappariyamu nowhere else occurs in the list of holy places which receive offerings. In view of the consistent writing of the name Kappariyamu where one would normally expect the *kurša*- in all the paragraphs describing offerings to the holy places, and the fact that Kappariyamu receives her offerings at least once "on the pegs," it seems that we have here an otherwise unattested use of Kappariyamu as a name for the *kurša*-, or perhaps more accurately an occurrence of the specific *kurša*- symbol of Kappariyamu included in the enumeration of the holy places. This particular use of a specific *kurša*- image may be seen in the fairly common use of Zitḫariya's *kurša*- in the offerings to the holy places.[62] Popko has briefly noted this unusual occurrence of Kappariyamu: "In ... Kol. II 29ff. ... steht der Name ^{D}*Kapparijamu* statt ^{KUŠ}*kurši* (Sg. Dat.) in der Aufzählung der 'heiligen Stätten.'"[63]

After these offerings to the holy places there follow in §13′ offerings to a group of gods, not necessarily tutelary deities, although the Tutelary Deity and Ḫapantali(ya) are included in the list. These offerings to deities are accompanied by music. Although the holy places received a series of offerings, including bread, meal, flesh, and drink, this group of gods in §13′ receives only a drink offering at this point in the ceremony. This is performed by the mayor of the city and accompanied by cult music.

After this offering, the celebrants seat themselves for a cultic meal that includes several kinds of bread, *marnuan*, and beer. The conclusion of this refreshment is a drink offering by the mayor and another celebrant (lost in the break) for a deity whose name is lost in the break and Telipinu, and a bread offering by the priest of the Tutelary Deity of Ḫatti(?). The offerings are again accompanied by music.

The last two readable paragraphs, §§15′–16′, are the only ones in the text that show the repetition typical of festival texts. The two paragraphs seem to be identical except for the gods who receive the offerings in each case. Paragraphs 14′–16′ are important for our understanding of the duties of the priest of the Tutelary Deity of Ḫatti. In each case, although this priest is the one who places the bread offering, it is not the Tutelary Deity of Ḫatti or indeed any tutelary deity who receives the offering. The one possible exception to this could be iii 18, in which the name of the deity is broken away, but there is no evidence to suggest that it was a tutelary deity who occurred in conjunction with Telipinu. Although the priest of the Tutelary Deity of Ḫatti plays a prominent role in the festival, the Tutelary Deity of Ḫatti, if he occurs at all, is only one of many deities worshipped in the festival.

60. See *Appendix B*, commentary on *kipikkišdu*.

61. *KUB* 55.43 §2.

62. See discussion of this in *Chapter 1* sub Zitḫariya.

63. Popko, *Acta Antiqua Academiae Scientiarum Hungaricae* 22 (1974) 310 n. 6. In 1978 (*Kultobjekte* 112 with n. 77) he again notes that Kappariyamu in this text is worshipped in the form of a *kurša*-.

KUB 53.11

Transliteration

Obverse i

§1′x+1] x x x x x x[

§2′ 2′ NIN]DA!? KU$_7$? *ŠA* 1 *UP-NI* BA.BA.ZA
3′ NINDA *L*]*A-AB-KU* 30-li
4′ a-ku-w]a-an-na-ma 1 DUG KAŠ
5′ -e]l *ME-EL-QÍ-TIM*-ma
6′] x $^{\text{[L]Ú}}$SANGA ^{D}LAMMA ^{URU}*ḪA-AT-TI*
7′ ^{D}LAM]MA ^{URU}*ḪA-AT-TI*
8′ ^{URU}*ḪA-A*]*T-TI-YA*
8a′ (space on tablet for one more line)

§3′ 9′] pí-an-zi
10′] e-ku-zi

§4′ 11′ T]UŠ-aš e-ku-zi

§5′ 12′ ^{fD}Ma-ra-aš-ša?-a]n-ta GUB-aš
13′ [e-ku-zi … NINDA.KUR$_4$.RA? N]U.GÁL

§6′ 14′]x-tu-ya-an-na
15′]x

§7′ 16′]x
17′]

(the tablet breaks off)

Obverse ii[64]

§8′x+1 [o o](-)ri[65]-⌈x⌉-še-šar x[o o o o] x x x[
2′ [o]-x-kán-zi nu-kán ḫ[u-i-šu? ^{UZ}]^{U}šu-up-pa ^{UZU}[
3′ ^{UZU}ZAG.UDU.ḪI.A SAG.DU.ḪI.A[o o]KUŠ.UDU.ḪI.A da-a[š-kán-zi?
4′ na-at iš-ta-na-a-ni pí-ra-an kat-ta da-x[[66]
5′ ^{UZU}NÍG.GIG.ḪI.A-ma ^{UZU}ŠÀ.ḪI.A ḫa-ap-pí-ni-it za-nu[-an-zi]
6′ ma-a-an ^{UZU}NÍG.GIG.ḪI.A zé-e-a-ri [Ø]

64. After a gap of an undetermined number of paragraphs.

65. The tablet shows a word space, but no Hittite words begin with *r*.

66. The trace does not fit *da-a*[*-i* or *da-a*[*š-kán-zi*.

Translation

KUB 53.11 Obverse i

§1′ (Only traces preserved).

§2′ [...] sweet [bre]ad(?) of one handful, groats [...] moist bread of 30,[67] [...] But one vessel of beer for [drin]king [... *e*]*l*. The offering materials, however [...] the priest of the Tutelary Deity of Ḫatti [... the Tutelary] Deity of Ḫatti [...]x-*ti-ya*.

§3′ [...] they give. [... DN] he drinks.

§4′ [...] drinks [DN], seated.

§5′ [The x drinks the Maraššа]nda river(?), standing. [...] There is no [thick bread(?)].

§§6′–7′ (Only traces.)

(the tablet breaks off)

Obverse ii[68]

§8′ (First line not capable of interpretation.) They [...] They t[ake(?)] r[aw(?)] flesh, [(a flesh part)], the shoulders, the heads, [x], (and) the sheepskins. [They] x[...][69] them down in front of the altar. The livers and hearts, however, [they] cook with flame. When the livers are cooked,

67. Presumably 30 units of some weight or volume which was not deemed necessary to be included here.

68. After a gap of an undetermined number of paragraphs.

69. One expects "he places" or "they place," but the traces do not allow such a reading.

KUB 53.11

Obverse ii (*transliteration cont.*)

§9′ 7′ nu ^{LÚ}SANGA ^{D}LAMMA ^{URU}*ḪA-AT-TI* 3 NINDA *LA-AB-KU* 30-l[i]
8′ pár-ši-ya na-aš-ša-an iš-ta-na-a-ni *PA-NI* DINGIR-*LIM* [da-a-i]
9′ 1 NINDA *LA-AB-KU*-ma pár-ši-ya na-an-ša-an ^{D}Kap-p[a-ri-ya-mu-i]
10′ ^{GIŠ}KAK.ḪI.A-aš da-a-i 1 NINDA *LA-AB-KU* pár-ši-ya nu-uš-š[a-an]
11′ ḫa-aš-ši-i iš-tar-na pé-e-di da-a-i ⸢ta⸣-ra-⸢a⸣[-u-ur[70]]
12′ pár-ši-ya nu 1 pár-šu-ul-li ^{GIŠ}ḫal-ma-as-⸢šu-it-ti⸣ [Ø]
13′ 1 pár-šu-ul-li-ma ^{GIŠ}lu-ut-ti-ya 1 NINDA *LA-AB*[-*KU*]
14′ pár-ši-ya nu ta-ra-u-ur ^{GIŠ}ḫa-at-ta-lu-wa-aš GIŠ-r[u-i]
15′ da-a-i ta-ra-u-ur-ma ḫa-aš-ši-i ta-pu-uš-za da-a-i

---

§10′ 16′ na-aš a-ap-pa ti-i-e-ez-zi nu-kán ^{GIŠ}e-er-ḫu-⸢ya-az?⸣
17′ me-ma-al ḫa-aš-šu-un-ga-a-iz-zi nu-uš-ša-an iš-ta-na-a-⸢ni⸣
18′ 3-*ŠU* šu-uḫ-ḫa-a-i ^{D}Kap-pa-ri-ya-mu-ú-i 1-*ŠU*
19′ ḫa-aš-ši-i iš-tar-na pé-e-di 1-*ŠU* ^{GIŠ}ḫal-ma-aš-šu-it-ti
20′ 1-*ŠU* ^{GI}[^{Š}l]u-ut-ti-ya 1-*ŠU* ^{GIŠ}ḫa-at-ta-lu-wa-aš GIŠ-ru-i
21′ 1-*ŠU* nam-ma ḫa-aš-ši-i ta-pu-uš-za 1-*ŠU* šu-uḫ-ḫa-a-i

---

§11′ 22′ nu-uš-ša-an *ŠA* GUD UDU.ḪI.A-ya ^{UZU}NÍG.GIG.ḪI.A ^{UZU}ŠÀ.ḪI.A
23′ iš-ta-na-a-ni *A-NA* NINDA.KUR$_4$.RA.ḪI.A še-er *PA*-⸢*NI* DINGIR!-*LIM*⸣ da-a-i
24′ 1 ^{UZU}NÍG.GIG-ma 1 ^{UZU}ŠÀ ar-ḫa kur!?-aš-ki-i[z-z]i
25′ nu-uš-ša-an ^{D}Kap-pa-ri-ya-mu-i da-a-i ḫ[a-aš-š]i-⸢i⸣
26′ iš-tar-na pé-e-di da-a-i ^{GIŠ}ḫal-ma-aš-šu-it-ti [Ø]
27′ ^{GIŠ}ḫa-at-ta-lu-wa-aš GIŠ-ru-i nam-ma ḫa-aš-ši-i [Ø]
28′ ta-pu-uš-za da-a- i [Ø]

---

§12′ 29′ nu-za ^{LÚ}SANGA ^{D}LAMMA ^{URU}*ḪA-AT-TI* 1 ^{DUG}*KU-KU-UB* ta-a-u-w[a-la-aš][71]
30′ da-a-i nu iš-ta-na-a-ni pí-ra-an 3-*ŠU* ši[-pa-an-ti]
31′ ^{D}Kap-pa-ri-ya-mu 1-*ŠU* ḫa-aš-ši-i iš-tar-na pé[-e-di][72]
32′ 1-*ŠU* ^{GIŠ}ḫal-ma-aš-šu-it-ti 1-*ŠU* ^{GIŠ}lu-ut-ti-ya 1[-*ŠU*]

(bottom of tablet)

70. Neu, *StBoT* 12 (1970) 71, reads *ta-ra-u̯-*[*ur*.

71. Ehelolf, *ZA* 43 = NF 9 (1936) 183, reads *ta-a-u-w*[*a-al*]. My restoration is based on line iii 2 of the text.

72. Ehelolf, *ZA* 43 = NF 9: 183, reads *p*[*í-di*].

KUB 53.11

Obverse ii (*translation cont.*)

§9′ the priest of the Tutelary Deity of Ḫatti breaks three moist breads of 30. [He places] them on the altar before the god. One moist bread, however, he breaks and places [for] Kapp[ariyamu] on the pegs.[73] He breaks one moist bread and places (it) in the middle place of the hearth. He breaks (one) meas[uring vessel[74] of x], one morsel for the throne and one morsel for the window. He breaks one moi[st] bread. He sets out a measuring vessel for the wood of the door bolt. And a measuring vessel he sets out next to the hearth.

§10′ He steps back. He cleans/sifts(?) the meal by means of a basket[75] and scatters (it) three times on the altar.[76] He scatters (it) once to Kappariyamu, once to the middle place of the hearth, once to the throne, once to the [w]indow, once to the wood of the door bolt, and, further, once next to the hearth.

§11′ He places the livers and hearts of the cattle and sheep on the altar, on top of the thick breads, before the god. One liver and one heart, however, he cu[ts] up. He sets out (the pieces) for Kappariyamu, (and) he sets (them) out for the middle place of the hearth, (and) he sets (them) out for the throne, the wood of the door bolt, and, further, next to the hearth.

§12′ The priest of the Tutelary Deity of Ḫatti takes one jug of *taw*[*al*]. He lib[ates] three times before the altar, and once (to) Kappariyamu, once to the middle pl[ace] of the hearth, once to the throne, o[nce] to the window,

(bottom of tablet)

73. Neu, *StBoT* 12: 71, translates "(der) Gottheit K.[15] [ ] zu den Pflöcken," with footnote 15 reading "Vielleicht ^{D}Kapparii̯amu."

74. See Riemschneider, *FsGüterbock* 276 with n. 61, and Neu, *StBoT* 12 (1970) 70–73, on *taraur* as "measuring vessel."

75. That is, uses a basket as a sieve?

76. See *CHD* sub *memal* a4′b′ for treatment of this passage.

KUB 53.11 Reverse iii (*transliteration*)

§12′ (*cont.*)
^{GIŠ}ḫa-at-tal-wa-aš GIŠ-i 1-*ŠU* nam-ma ḫa-aš-š[i-i ta-pu-uš-za][77]
1-*ŠU* ši-pa-an-ti nu ^{DUG}*KU-KU-UB* ta-a-u-wa-la-aš k[at-ta da-a-i]
nu-za ^{DUG}*KU-KU-UB* KAŠ da-a-i nu ta-a-u-wa-li-i[t GIM-an]
ir-ḫa-a-it si-i-e-es-ni-it-ta *QA-TAM-MA* ir!-ḫ[a-a-iz-zi]
nu ^{DUG}*KU-KU-UB* KAŠ kat-ta da-a- i [Ø]

§13′[78]
[n]u *A-NA* ^{LÚ}*ḪA-ZA-AN-NI* a-ku-an-na pí-an-zi n[u ^{LÚ}*ḪA-ZA-AN-NU*]
[k]u-u-uš DINGIR.MEŠ ir-ḫa-a-iz-zi ^{D}Ḫal-ki-in ⸢^{D}⸣[Te-li-pí-nu-un]
⸢^{D}⸣UTU ^{D}UTU ^{URU}A-ri-in-na ^{D}IM ^{D}IM ^{UR}[^{U}Zi-ip-la-an-da][79]
⸢^{D}⸣LAMMA ^{D}Ḫa-ba-an-ta-li-ya-an ^{D}Ḫal-ma-aš-š[u-it-ta-an][80]
⸢^{D}⸣ZA.BA$_{4}$.BA$_{4}$ ^{D}GAL.ZU ^{D}IM É-*TIM* ^{D}K[án-di-wu$_{u}$-it-ti-en][81]
⸢^{D}⸣Ka-at-tar-ma-na-a-an ^{D}IM KI.LAM ^{D}Wa$_{a}$-a[-še-ez-za-al-li-in e-ku-zi][82]
[GI]Š ^{D}INANNA.GAL SÌR-*RU* [Ø]

§14′
[n]a-at-za wa-ga-a-an-na e-ša-an-ta-r[i o o o o]
[x[83] NIN]DA a-a-an *ŠA* ½ *ŠA-A-TI* 3 NINDA.KU$_{7}$ x[o o o o]
5 NINDA *LA-AB-KU* 30-li 5 NINDA ZÍD.DA.ŠE [1? ^{DUG}ḫu-u-up-p]ár KAŠ
⸢x⸣[84] ^{DUG}ḫu-u-up-pár mar-nu-an *IŠ-TU* É x[o ú-da-an-zi?]
nu-za a-da-an-zi nu *A-NA* ^{LÚ}*ḪA-ZA-AN-N*[*I* o o o o o]
a-ku-an-na ták-ša-an pí-an-zi nu ⸢^{D}⸣[o o o o o]
^{D}Te-li-pí-nu-un-na TUŠ-aš a-ku-an-z[i o o o o o]
[p]ár-ši-ya na-an-ša-an ^{LÚ}⸢SANGA ^{D}LAMMA⸣ [^{URU}*ḪA-AT-TI*?]
[*PA-N*]*I* DINGIR-*LIM* da-a-i GIŠ ^{D}INANNA.GA[L SÌR-*RU*]

§15′
[EGI]R-an-da-ma ^{D}UTU ^{D}UTU ^{URU}A-r[i-in-na a-ku-an-zi]
[GIŠ ^{D}IN]ANNA.GAL SÌR-*RU* 1 ^{NINDA}ta-kar-m[u-un pár-ši-ya]
[na-an-š]a-an ^{LÚ}SANGA ^{D}LAMMA ^{URU}*ḪA-AT-T*[*I* Ø?]
[*PA-NI* DINGIR-*LIM*] da-a- i [Ø]

77. Ehelolf, *ZA* 43 = NF 9: 183, reads *ḫa-aš-š*[*i-i iš-tar-na pí-di*]. This is unlikely to be the correct restoration because this phrase has already occurred in this listing of the holy places, in ii 31′. Because the beginning of column iii is an immediate continuation of the list at the end of column ii, we must restore the element of this standardized list which has not yet occurred and which is normally (in this text) the last item in the list.

78. Paragraph 13′ is restored from the very similar list in a festival fragment, *KUB* 41.50 iii 6′–12′, noted by Otten, *RLA* 5 (1976–80) 390. In *KUB* 41.50 the celebrant who performs the drink offerings is called the EN ^{URU}*ḪA-AT-TI*, "the lord of Ḫattuša."

79. *KUB* 41.50 iii 8′: ... ^{D}UTU ^{D}UTU ^{URU}TÚL-*na* ^{D}U ^{D}U ^{URU}*Zi-*⸢*ip-la*⸣*-a*[*n-da*].

80. *KUB* 41.50 iii 9′: ^{D}LAMMA ^{D}*Ḫa-pa-an-da-li* ^{D}DAG-*in* ...

81. *KUB* 41.50 iii 10′: ^{D}GAL.ZU ^{D}U É-*TIM* ^{D}*Kán-di-wu$_{u}$-it-ti-en.*

82. *KUB* 41.50 iii 11′–12′: ^{D}*Ka-at-*⸢*tar*?*-x*⸣*-na-an* ^{D}U KI.LAM ^{D}*Wa$_{a}$-a-še-ez-za-al-li-in e-ku-zi* GIŠ ^{D}INANNA.GAL SÌR-*RU.*

83. A number.

84. A number.

KUB 53.11

Reverse iii (*translation*)

§12′ (*cont.*) once to the wood of the door bolt, (and), further, once [next to the h]earth he libates. [He puts dow]n the jug of *tawal*. He takes a jug of beer. [As] he offered in sequence with the *tawal*, so he also offe[rs in sequence] with beer in the same way. He puts down the jug of beer.

---

§13′ They give to the mayor to drink. [The mayor] treats these gods with offerings in sequence: [He drinks] Ḫalki, [Telipinu], the Sungod, the Sungoddess of Arinna, the Stormgod, the Stormgod of [Ziplanda], the Tutelary Deity, Ḫapantaliya, the deified thr[one], ZA.BA$_4$.BA$_4$, GAL.ZU, the Stormgod of the House, K[antipuitti], Kattarmana, the Stormgod of the Gatehouse, (and) Wa[šezzil]. (They play) the large INANNA instrument. They sing.

---

§14′ They sit down for some refreshment.[85] [...] [(a number)] warmed breads of ½ *SŪTU* each, three sweet breads, x[...], five moist breads of 30, five breads of barley flour, [one(?) bo]wl of beer, ⌈x⌉ bowls of *marnuan* from the house of x[[86] they bring(?)]. They eat. They give to the mayor [and the x] to drink together. They drink the god [x] and Telipinu, seated. [...] he breaks. The priest of the Tutelary Deity of [Ḫatti(?)] places it [befo]re the god. (They play) the lar[ge] INANNA instrument. [They sing.]

---

§15′ [Aft]erwards, however, [they drink] the Sungod (and) the Sungoddess of Ar[inna]. (They play) the large [IN]ANNA instrument. They sing. [He breaks] one *takarm*[*u*-] bread. The priest of the Tutelary Deity of Ḫatti places [it before the god].

---

85. Literally "They sit down to bite." On the use of the infinitive of *wak-* as "for refreshment, for a snack," see Friedrich, *ArOr* 6 (1934) 375.

86. In this break is either the title of an official whose estate provided materials for the festival, or the name of a god, whose temple (house) provided the offering materials.

KUB 53.11

Reverse iii (*transliteration cont.*)

§16′ 26 [EGIR-an-da] ^{D}IM ^{D}IM ^{URU}Zi-ip-p[a-la-an-da a-ku-an-zi]
27 [GIŠ ^{D}INANNA.GAL SÌR-*R*]*U* 1 ^{NINDA}ta-kar-mu-u[n pár-ši-ya]
28 [na-an-ša-an ^{LÚ}SANGA] $^{⌈D⌉}$LAMMA ^{URU}*ḪA-AT-TI* [*PA-NI* DINGIR-*LIM*]
29 [da-a-] [i]

- -

§17′ 30 [o o o o ^{URU}*ḪA-A*]*T-TI* $^{⌈D⌉}$[o o o o o o o o o]
31 [o o GIŠ ^{D}INANNA.GAL S]ÌR-*RU* [o o o o o o o o o]
32 [o o o o o o o] ^{D}LAMM[A o o o o o o o o o]

(the tablet breaks off)

KUB 53.11

Reverse iii (*translation cont.*)

§16′ [Afterwards they drink] the Stormgod (and) the Stormgod of Zipp[alanda. (They play) the large INANNA instrument. They sin]g. [He breaks] one *takarmu-* bread. [The priest] of the Tutelary Deity of Ḫatti [places it before the god].

---

§17′ (Another round of offerings and cult music too broken to translate.)

(the tablet breaks off)

Reverse iv not preserved

APPENDIX B

PHILOLOGICAL COMMENTARY

HITTITE

ḫantiyašša-

KUB 2.1 ii 47 (*Chapter 3*); *KUB* 9.21:4′, 10′; *ABoT* 3:3′ (*Chapter 5*). Friedrich, *HW 1. Erg.* 4, gives the definition "männlich(?)" for this word, citing *KUB* 2.1 ii 47 and *KUB* 9.21:4′. He understands the form *ḫantiyaššaš* in *KUB* 9.21:4′ as plural accusative(?) common gender. He derives the meaning for this word from what he tentatively calls a parallel to *KUB* 9.21:4′, *KUB* 20.48 vi 13 (spring festival on Mt. Tapala), where the form is DINGIR.LÚ.MEŠ. His final comment on the situation is "alles sehr unklar!" The meaning of this word is indeed unclear, and in my opinion the *KUB* 20.48 passage is not sufficiently close to *KUB* 9.21 to provide a meaning for the word. The meaning "masculine" was difficult even when the only two texts in which *ḫantiyašša-* occurred were *KUB* 9.21 (with duplicate) and *KUB* 2.1 ii 47, where its meaning is also obscure. In the *KUB* 9.21 passage, although the text elsewhere consistently uses forms in *-uš* for accusative plural, the form of the word is *ḫantiyaššaš*. It therefore does not look like an adjective in the accusative plural as Friedrich parsed it but rather a noun in the genitive in the phrase [DINGIR.MEŠ *ḫ*]*antiyaššaš* "gods of the *ḫantiyašša-*." In the *KUB* 2.1 passage the form *ḫanteyaššaššiš* is the Luwian genitival adjective modifying ^{D}LAMMA. In neither text does the context provide conclusive evidence for a meaning for *ḫantiyašša-*.[1]

Since Friedrich's dictionary was published, two more examples of *ḫantiyašša-* have come to light, both in *KBo* 20.107+*KBo* 23.50 (Ritual for the Tutelary Deity of the Hunting Bag). Obverse ii 9–13 read: *kāša* ^{D}LAMMA ^{KUŠ}*kuršan araḫzenaš* KUR.KUR.MEŠ-*az ḫūmandaz* [Ḫ]UR.SAG.MEŠ-*az ḫāriyaz* ÍD.MEŠ-*az ḫa*[*nti*]*yaššaz* TÚL.MEŠ-*az welluwaz* [*talli*]*škiwen mukiškiwen* "We have implored (and) petitioned the Tutelary Deity of the

1. Archi, *SMEA* 16 (1975) 96, translates *ḫantiyaššaššiš* as "del particolare" without citing his reasons.

Hunting Bag from all the neighboring lands, from the mountains, the valleys, the rivers, the *ḫantiyašša*-s, the springs (and) the meadows." The same list is repeated in iii 26′–28′. The *ḫantiyašša-* is part of a list of locations from which the Hittites are petitioning the god to return. In these passages it could be a noun, or an adjective modifying either ÍD.MEŠ or TÚL.MEŠ. If it is an adjective, the meaning "masculine" does not seem likely to modify rivers or springs. Neu notes this in his review of Tischler's glossary.[2] He also indicates there that the use of *ḫantiyašša-* in *KUB* 9.21 may denote a "landschaftliche Region." In the *KBo* 20.107+*KBo* 23.50 passages *ḫantiyašša-* almost certainly is a noun denoting another topographical term, another place from which the Hittites called and petitioned the Tutelary Deity of the Hunting Bag. The one topographical term which occurs to me as missing from this list is "lake" or "pond," for which there is no known Hittite word.[3] The idea that *ḫantiyašša-* is not an adjective but a topographical term, perhaps "lake, pond," fits well in the *KUB* 9.21 passages and provides a parallel structure with the "gods of the river" in both passages there. In *KUB* 2.1 ii 47 the context does not provide conclusive evidence for or against this idea.

ḫa/urn(uw)ai-

KBo 13.179:10′, dupl. *KBo* 22.168:6′ (*Chapter 4*). This verb is attested as *ḫa/urn(uw)ai-*, *ḫa/urniya-*, and *ḫarnāi-*. See Friedrich, *HW* 76 and *2. Erg.* 13, on the latter two stems and Neu, *StBoT* 26 (1983) 55 n. 261, for evidence that one should read the last of the stems listed as *ḫarnai-* and not *ḫurnai-* as *HW* 76 cites it. There are no examples as yet of either of the first two stems spelled with anything but an initial *ḫar/ḫur* sign. Their vocalization thus remains uncertain, but all three stems seem to convey the same meaning. They are treated here as one verb.

The verb *ḫa/urnuwai-* occurs quite rarely and almost exclusively in ritual or festival contexts. Although it occurs once as a participle in a passive construction with ^{GIŠ}*taršeš* as the subject[4] and possibly once with *nakkušši-* as its object,[5] it usually takes as its object some kind of building. The one passage outside of rituals or festivals in which *ḫa/urnuwai-* occurs is: *INA* É ^{LÚ}NINDA.DÙ.DÙ *″ma″aš″kan kuedaš andan eššanzi n″at″kan šanḫan ḫarnuwan ešdu* "Let the bakery in which they make them (breads) be swept and sprinkled."[6] In the rituals and festivals there are several examples of É.DINGIR-*LIM* as the object of *ḫa/urnuwai-*, one of É-*TIM* as object, and our passage, *ŠA* É.GAL-*LIM* É.MEŠ as the object. It occurs with *šanḫ-* "sweep" in some of the other examples; it was the practice as a prelude to performing certain cultic procedures to sweep and sprinkle the room. In our passage the sweeping and sprinkling cleanses the room after the goat is washed and before

2. Review of Tischler, *HEG* in *IF* 82 (1977) 274.
3. Hoffner, *EHGl*, does not list any Hittite, Akkadian, or Sumerian words for "lake" or "pond."
4. *KUB* 30.19++ i 15–16 (Totenritual), ed. Otten, *HTR* 32–33.
5. [*na*]-*a*[*k-k*]*u-uš-ši-in-na* x[/ [*na*]*m-ma-an ḫa/ur-nu-u-wa-an-z*[*i*, *KBo* 9.111:6′–7′ (rit. frag.).
6. *KUB* 13.4 i 18–20 (Instructions for Temple Personnel), ed. Sturtevant, *Chrest.* 148–49, and Süel, *Direktif Metni* 22–23. The phrase *šanḫan ḫarnuwan ešdu* also occurs in iii 60 of the same text.

it is (ritually?) killed. It makes sense that the Hittites would want to clean the room before cutting up meat. Sweeping and sprinkling the room in this case was done probably both for reasons of cultic purity and also for the very practical reason of cleansing a room in which an animal had been washed before killing and perhaps butchering it. The cleansing of a room could be a kind of final cleanup as the last cultic activity of the day, for example in *KBo* 24.45 obv. 22′, in which after the prescription for sprinkling the temple the paragraph ends with UD 1 KAM *QATI* "First day, finished."

ḫiššala-

KUB 55.43 ii 30, iv 34′; *KBo* 21.89 ii [10′] (*Chapter 4*); *KUB* 9.21:[11′] and *IBoT* 2.19:6′ (*Chapter 5*). Goetze, *Language* 29 (1953) 273 with n. 78, cites *KBo* 4.14 iii 13–16 (Tudḫ. IV treaty)[7] and *KUB* 31.136 rev. 3 (frag. of a prayer to the god of Nerik) as evidence for a meaning "to block" for *ḫiššalla-*, while in *IBoT* 2.19:6′ and *KUB* 9.21:10′–11′ he translates *irḫanduš ḫeššallanduš* as "included and excluded." Friedrich, *AfO* 17 (1954–56) 99, rejects Goetze's translation and offers a different interpretation of *KUB* 31.136 rev. 3, demonstrating that this is not an example of *ḫišalla-*. Goetze reads *tu-uk ḫé-e-ša-la*??*-t*[*i*?*-iš*], taking the broken word as a participle of *ḫiššalla-*, while Friedrich reads *tu-uk ḫé-e-ša-te-e*[*š*], understanding it as a participle (for *ḫešanteš*) of *ḫaš-* "to open." The copy supports Friedrich's reading. As additional evidence that the word in *KUB* 31.136 rev. 3 is not the verb *ḫiššalla-* Friedrich notes that *ḫiššalla-* is always written with initial *ḫi* and doubled *š*.[8] Laroche, *DLL* (1959) 45, simply cites the occurrence in *KBo* 4.14 iii 15 without positing a meaning. Otten, in a review of *KUB* 46 in *ZA* 66 (1976) 299, notes the other occurrences *KUB* 2.8 v 29′, *KUB* 43.56 ii 21′, Bo 2646 (now *KUB* 56.57) ii 21′, and Bo 4086 (now *IBoT* 4.337:5′). He reads ^{D}*Ḫ*]*iššalanduš* in *KUB* 46.18 obv. 17′, but there is no compelling reason to restore a DINGIR determinative; it may be *ḫ*]*i-iš-ša-la-an-du-uš*. As Otten notes, Jakob-Rost's restoration [*P*]*iššalandu-* in the *KUB* 46 Inhaltsübersicht and index of divine names is less likely than reading *ḫiššala-* here.

In all of its occurrences except *KBo* 4.14 iii 15,[9] *ḫiššalla-* occurs as a participle in a ritual or festival context, and with the same one exception, it always (where preserved) follows a participle of *irḫai-*.[10] The *KBo* 4.14 passage is thus unique in several ways in that only here does *ḫiššalla-* occur a) in a non-cultic context, b) in a non-participial form, c)

7. See Singer, *ZA* 75 (1985) 100–23, on redating this text to Tudḫaliya IV from Šuppiluliuma II as Laroche has it in *CTH*.
8. The first of these two points must now be amended; in *IBoT* 4.337:5′ it is written [*ḫ*]*é-eš-ša-al-la-an-te-eš*.
9. Lines iii 13–15 of this treaty read: [*ma-a-an-n*]*a* LUGAL-*i kuitki nakkiešzi naššu* LUGAL GIG-*zi* [*našma*] ″*kan* KUR.KUR *niyari našma* ″*kan* ^{LÚ}KÚR ŠÀ KUR.KUR *uizzi* [*nu QA*]*TAMMA* :*ḫi-iš-ša-al-la QATAMMA*″*ta* :*naḫḫuwayadu* "If something becomes troublesome for the king: either the king falls ill, or lands defect, or the enemy invades the lands, in the same way plan(?), in the same way let there be concern to you!" Translation of the passage is adapted from the *CHD* discussion of *:nahhuwa-*, which treats this passage but not the sentence containing *:ḫiššalla*.
10. In *KUB* 56.57 ii? 4′ *irḫanteš* is to be restored in the break at the end of the line.

without *irḫai-*, and d) with a glossenkeil. Friedrich, in treating *KBo* 4.14 iii 15 briefly,[11] declines to offer even a tentative translation of *ḫiššalla-*. In *AfO* 17 (1954–56) 99 he tentatively translates it as "ins Auge fassen," positing a meaning for the use of the paired participles of *irḫai-* and *ḫiššalla-* in cultic contexts as "die (schon) abgefertigten (und) die (noch zur Beopferung) vorgesehenen(??), ins Auge gefassten(??) Götter." He retains this idea in *HW 1. Erg.* 6, where he cites the word as *ḫeššalla-*, translates it as "ins Auge fassen(??), planen(??)," and adds a note rejecting Goetze's idea in *Language* 29. Stefanini edits *KBo* 4.14 iii 15 in *AANL* 20 (1965) 44–45 but does not translate *:ḫiššalla-*, merely noting in his translation that the form is a second person singular imperative. Friedrich's idea seems to me to fit the evidence best, with the participle *irḫant-* denoting the gods whose offerings have been performed, and *ḫiššallant-* denoting those for whom offerings have been prescribed but not yet completed.

kariya-

KUB 25.32+*KUB* 27.70 ii 39 (*Chapter 2*); *KUB* 55.43 iii 34′ (*Chapter 4*). The occurrence of *kariya-* in *KUB* 55.43 is somewhat unusual; this verb is not often attested in the third person singular present and very rarely attested with this particular spelling. This is to date the only occurrence in the published Boğazköy corpus of the ^{LÚ}GUDÚ "covering." This covering action occurs frequently in other festivals and very often includes the phrase *IŠ-TU* GAD or GAD-*it* "with a linen (cloth)." The verb *kariya-* does not require the adverb *šer* to have the meaning "to cover up" but *šer* is often used in combination with *kariya-*, for example: *nu⸗kan* ^{D}*Āpin šer kariyazi* "He covers up the ritual pit";[12] *n⸗at⸗kan šer kariya*[(-) "They/He cover(s) it up."[13] As in the *kurša-* Festival, so also in the Festival of Karaḫna the bread is covered while being transported: *nu IŠTU* É ^{LÚ}NINDA.DÙ.DÙ NINDA.KUR$_4$.RA *udanzi nu⸗kan* NINDA.KUR$_4$.RA *IŠTU* GAD *ka-ri-ya-an-za* $^{\text{LÚ.MEŠ}}$NAR *pian ḫūyanzi* 3 NINDA.KUR$_4$.RA *paršiya* "They bring the thick bread from the house of the baker. The thick bread (is) covered with a linen (cloth). The singers run in front (of it). He breaks three thick breads."[14] Here not only is the NINDA.KUR$_4$.RA covered with a linen cloth, but musicians go in front of it, bringing to mind the prescription *piran palwiškanzi*, "they recite(?)" in the *kurša-* Festival.

kipikkišdu

KUB 55.43 ii 16 (*Chapter 4*). This word occurs only a few times in the entire Hittite corpus, in the two basic forms *kipik*(*k*)*išdu* and *kipik*(*k*)*ašdu*.[15] It occurs both with and without a DINGIR determinative. The presently known examples are: [LUGAL

11. *JCS* 1 (1947) 304.
12. *KUB* 41.8 iii 16–17 (Ritual for the Underworld Deities).
13. *KUB* 4.47 i 15 (Ritual against Insomnia).
14. *KUB* 25.32+*KUB* 27.70 ii 38–40 (Festival for the Tutelary Deity of Karaḫna), edited in *Chapter 2*.
15. Hoffner points out to me that *kipik*(*k*)*išdu* and *kipik*(*k*)*ašdu* must be variant forms of the same word and also suggests the idea put forward here that this word denotes a relationship between deities.

SA]L.[L]UGAL TUŠ-*aš* 2 ᴰ*ki-pí-ik-aš-du ŠA* ᴰU [*a-k*]*u-wa-an-zi* "[The king (and) qu]een, seated, drink the two *kipikašdu*s of the Stormgod" *KUB* 20.19 iv 12′–13′ (fest. frag.); SAL.LUGAL TUŠ-*aš* [(ᴰ*k*)]*i-pí-ig-ga-aš-du* ᴰUTU ᴰ*Mezzulla Ù* ᴰUTU *ekuzi* "The queen, seated, drinks the [*k*]*ipiggašdu* of the Sungod, (namely) Mezzulla, and the Sungod" *KUB* 27.69 i 6′–9′ (Festival of the Month), restored from the duplicate *KUB* 10.89 ii 27; 3 *ki-pí-ki-iš-tu* ᴰ[UTU *ekuzi*?] [*nam*]*ma* ᴰUTU GIŠ ᴰINANNA GAL *walḫa*[*nzi*] "[He drinks] the three *kipikištu*s of the [Sun]god (and) [fur]ther the Sungod (himself). [They] play the large Inanna instrument" *KBo* 20.81 v 17′–18′ (fest. frag.); [*nu*? ᴰ]*ki-pí-ki-iš-tu* ᴰIM ᴰIM *ma-x*[... *ekuzi*] "[He drinks] the *kipikištu* of the Stormgod (and) the Stormgod *ma-x*[...]" *KBo* 30.46:5′ (fest. frag.); DUMU-*aš* ᴰ*Tuḫašai*[*l* TUŠ-*aš ekuzi* DUMU-*aš* DN TUŠ-*aš ekuzi*] DUMU-*aš* ᴰ*Zuliya* TU[Š-*aš ekuzi*] § ⸢1?⸣ DUMU-*aš* 3 *ki-pí-ki-iš-du Š*[*A* ᴰUTU TUŠ-*aš ekuzi*] *namma* ᴰUTU TUŠ-*aš ek*[*uzi*] "The DUMU-*aš* [drinks] Tuḫašai[l, seated. The DUMU-*aš* drinks DN, seated.] The DUMU-*aš* [drinks] Zuliya, sea[ted]. § One(?) DUMU-*aš* [drinks] the three *kipikišdu*s o[f the Sungod, seated]. Then he drin[ks] the Sungod, seated" *KBo* 21.83 rev. 1′–4′ (Festival Celebrated by a DUMU-*aš*);[16] [SAL.LUGAL TUŠ-*aš ki-pí-i*]*k-ki-iš-du* [*ŠA*? ᴰUTU ᴰ*Me-ez*]-⸢*zu-ul-la*⸣[*Ù*] [ᴰUTU *e-ku-zi*] "[The queen, seated, drinks the *kipi*]*kkišdu* [of the Sungod, (namely) Mez]zulla, [and the Sungod]" *KUB* 60.21:11′–13′ (fest. frag.). This word also occurs as ᴰ*Ki-pí-ki-iš-du* in *KBo* 25.67 iii 18′ (Festival Celebrated by a DUMU-*aš*) in context too broken to aid our understanding of it.

From the evidence of the examples cited above and the passage in the *kurša*- Festival, we may make some general observations about *kipikkišdu*. Despite the many variations in its spelling, the word always has the same ending, and shows no signs of Hittite noun inflection. Although it always functions as an accusative within its sentence, it never shows the expected accusative form, nor does it change its inflection for the plural in the *KUB* 20.19 and *KBo* 21.83 examples. These points could be explained by positing a neuter gender for *kipikkišdu*, but such a *u*-stem neuter would be very unusual and inappropriate to designate divine beings. It is more likely that *kipikkišdu* is a foreign word which the Hittites did not decline according to their inflectional system. The *KUB* 27.69 example, in which the *kipikkišdu* is Mezzulla, the *KBo* 21.83 passage, in which Zuliya is one of the *kipikkišdu*s, and the *KUB* 55.43 passage, in which the *kipikkišdu*s are Kappariyamu, the Tutelary Deity of Tatašuna, and the Tutelary Deity of Tašḫapuna, suggest that the word is Hattic, as all of these deities have Hattic antecedents.

It is clear that *kipikkišdu* is a designation of divine beings, as half of its occurrences have the DINGIR determinative. It usually occurs in the genitive construction "*kipikkišdu*(s) of DN," and this suggests that *kipikkišdu* denotes some kind of relationship between deities, i.e., that certain deities are the *kipikkišdu*s of other deities. The evidence is not sufficient for us to determine what that relationship was. Most of the deities thus described are not understood well enough for us to define their relationship to the deities for whom they are *kipikkišdu*s. Of the few gods attested as *kipikkišdu*s, we know that

16. The first paragraph of this passage has been restored based on the idea that the "three *kipikišdu*s" of the second paragraph are named in the first.

Mezzulla is female[17] and that Kappariyamu[18] probably is as well. In the case of Mezzulla we also know that she is the daughter of the Sungoddess of Arinna. The ᴰUTU in *KUB* 27.69 i 8′ and 9′ may be the Sungoddess of Arinna, with *kipikkišdu* in that passage expressing Mezzulla's relationship as her daughter. This is however not the only possible interpretation, especially since we would expect the Sungoddess of Arinna to be more explicitly identified. The surrounding context of this passage gives no further clue as to what particular sun deity is being referred to, so it is quite possible that ᴰUTU in the *KUB* 27.69 passage is referring to some other sun deity, such as Ištanu, and that *kipikkišdu* denotes some other relationship to that deity, perhaps "consort."

In the *kurša-* Festival (*KUB* 55.43 ii 16–18), Kappariyamu, the Tutelary Deity of Tatašuna, and the Tutelary Deity of Tašḫapuna receive offerings as a group and are referred to as *kipikkišdu*s. The text does not indicate whose they are, but one possibility is that they are *kipikkišdu*s to the deity occurring immediately before them in the list, the Tutelary Deity of Zapatiškuwa. We learn in §5 of *KUB* 55.43 that this is the new name for the old hunting bag of the Tutelary Deity of Ḫatenzuwa. In iv 16′–19′ of the same text, the three *kipikkišdu* gods again receive offerings as a group, but without the label *kipikkišdu*. Despite this absence of the actual word, here also these gods are grouped together to receive their offerings because they share the characteristic of being *kipikkišdu*s to some other deity. The Tutelary Deity of Zapatiškuwa no longer immediately precedes the *kipikkišdu* group, having been moved to a more prominent place in the offering list for the column iv ceremony. His *kipikkišdu*s (if they are indeed his), however, remain in the same position in the offering list that they occupied in the column ii list.[19] The same group of three deities occurs again in §1′ and §3′ of *KUB* 7.36, another text of the *kurša-* Festival. This tablet is too broken to offer any more evidence beyond that of *KUB* 55.43 concerning the deity for whom they are *kipikkišdu*s, but these occurrences do provide confirmation of the consistent grouping of these three gods together.

kurša-

KUB 2.1 ii 32, iv 22 (*Chapter 3*); *KUB* 55.43 passim; *KBo* 13.179:3′, 15′; *KBo* 22.168:2′ *Chapter 4*). Early translations for this word were "shield" or "fleece." The *kurša-* has been written about extensively. Important recent discussions include: Popko, *AOF* 2 (1975) 65–70, and idem, *Kultobjekte* (1978) 108–20; Bittel, *Beitrag zur Kenntnis der hethitischen Bildkunst*, SHAW 1976/4: 16; Alp, *Tempel* (1983) 98–99; Dinçol, *JKF* 9 (1983) 221 with n. 3; Beal, "The Organization of the Hittite Military," Ph.D. diss. Chicago, 1986, 621–25; Güterbock, *FsKantor* 113–19; and idem, *FsAkurgal* Part 2 1–5.[20] Popko

17. Laroche, *Rech.* 30.
18. Laroche, *Rech.* 27.
19. The fact that they do not move with the Tutelary Deity of Zapatiškuwa in the rearrangement of the order of the gods for the provincial festival described in column iv weakens the argument that they are his *kipikkišdu*s. No other obvious possibility presents itself.
20. My thanks to Güterbock for allowing me to utilize his ideas in the *FsKantor* and *FsAkurgal* articles before they appeared in print.

rejects the meaning shield and accepts the *kurša-* as a "fleece." His very complete entry on this word in *Kultobjekte* collects most of the texts in which the *kurša-* occurs and thereby makes it convenient for other scholars to examine the evidence. He discusses the unusual nature of the *kurša-* as a cult symbol and points out the important text *KUB* 25.31 obv. 6–7 and 11–13, in which the *kurša-*s are burned and new ones made. Although he notes that it probably took the form of a "Schlauch" and even suggests that it may have been a container, he does not develop this idea but continues to refer to the *kurša-* as a fleece. Alp's contribution (*Tempel* [1983] 98–99) is especially important because he is the first to suggest that the object on the Schimmel rhyton which Bittel describes as a hunting bag is the *kurša-*, although he continues to call it a fleece.[21] Dinçol, using evidence from seals, concludes that the *kurša-* is a bag with a handle, represented in the cult scene on the Schimmel stag rhyton and on a number of seals in very similar cult scenes. Güterbock supports Dinçol's conclusion (*FsAkurgal*) and further specifies this as a hunting bag (*FsKantor*).

I concur with Dinçol and Güterbock that the *kurša-* is a bag. The *kurša-* may be made of several different materials; determinatives for leather, wood, and reed are attested. The ^{KUŠ}*kurša-*, the leather bag, occurs frequently in cultic texts and is the subject of the festival in *KUB* 55.43. The discussion here applies specifically to the ^{KUŠ}*kurša-*. One interesting piece of evidence for the ^{KUŠ}*kurša-* is in the Old Hittite vanishing deity myths and rituals, in which the hunting bag is hung on an *eya-* tree, after which good things designed to please the god are placed in it. Popko, who rejects the old translation "shield" but retains the meaning "fleece," himself points out that the *kurša-* functions as a kind of cornucopia filled with a variety of goods.[22] A bag certainly could hold the things mentioned in these rituals. However, the *kurša-* in these texts is described as being that of a sheep: ^{GIŠ}*eyaz⸗kan* UDU-*aš* ^{KUŠ}*kuršaš kankanza* "A *kurša-* of a sheep is hung from an *eya-* tree" *KUB* 17.10 iv 28 (Tel. myth). In this case the bag is not just leather but is actually made of a sheepskin. It would not be difficult to stitch up a sheepskin to make a bag out of it, and it therefore seems that in the rituals connected with the vanishing deity myths a particular kind of *kurša-*, a sheepskin bag, was used. The integral nature of the *kurša-*'s role in Old Hittite mythology and ritual, including a ceremony done in the temple of the Hunting Bag in an Old Script text containing Hattic,[23] indicates that it was a cult symbol deriving originally from the Hattic tradition.

The *kurša-* made of leather is the most common; all the passages that mention the making of a *kurša-* discuss the preparation of oxhides or goathides. In *KBo* 13.179[24] red and white(?) oxhides are mentioned in conjunction with renaming of the *kurša-*s, probably the raw materials for their manufacture. The same text also describes the killing of a goat and the use of the hide by the leatherworkers to make *kurša-*s. The other texts of the *kurša-*

21. For the Schimmel rhyton see Muscarella, ed., *Ancient Art: The Norbert Schimmel Collection* (1974) no. 123; Alp, *Tempel* figs. 6a–h; Bittel, *Hethiter* 160, fig. 169; and Güterbock, *FsAkurgal* Part 2 1–5.

22. Popko, *Acta Antiqua Academiae Scientiarum Hungaricae* 22 (1974) 309.

23. *KBo* 20.69+*KBo* 25.142:6′–7′.

24. *CTH* 683.2 with duplicate *KBo* 22.168, *Chapter 4*.

Festival treated in *Chapter 4* have to do with the ceremony for installation of the new hunting bags and not with their manufacture. Although in the Telipinu myth the *kurša-* was probably made from one sheepskin, elsewhere it appears to require several hides for its manufacture. An inventory text[25] provides evidence on the composition of the *kurša-*: 6 KUŠ MÁŠ.GAL *warḫui* SIG$_5$-*anda* GAL $^{\text{LÚ.MEŠ}}$SIPAD *AN*[(*A* UGULA $^{\text{LÚ.MEŠ}}$AŠ)GAB *pai*] [*nu* ?] *ŠA* DINGIR-*LIM* ^{KUŠ}*kuršan iyazzi* "Six billy goat hides, rough (and) well worked, the chief of the shepherds gives to the head of the lea[therworkers]. He makes a hunting bag of the god." Popko[26] interprets this as distributive, i.e., one bag from each hide. This may well be the correct understanding, but we could interpret this brief inventory entry as a description of the making of one *kurša-* out of six goathides. Haas and Wäfler understand the prescription as six goathides for one *kurša-*,[27] as does Güterbock.[28] Here the color is apparently not important, but another characteristic is specified, that the skins be rough,[29] that is with the hair left on. A description of preparations for the *purulli-* Festival[30] provides information on how many hides might be used to make a *kurša-*: 6 MÁŠ.GAL GE$_6$ 2 MÁŠ.GAL BABBAR *nu* ^{KUŠ}*kuršuš iyanzi* UGULA $^{\text{LÚ.MEŠ}}$SIPAD *pai* ŠÀ.BA 2 MÁŠ.GAL BABBAR ^{LÚ}SIPAD.GUD DINGIR-*LIM dai* 2 MÁŠ.GAL GE$_6$ ^{LÚ}SANGA ^{D}*Telipinu dai* 2 MÁŠ.GAL BABBAR ^{LÚ}SANGA ^{D}ZA.BA$_4$.BA$_4$ 2 MÁŠ.GAL GE$_6$ ^{LÚ}SIPAD DINGIR-*LIM dai nu* ^{KUŠ}*kuršuš ienzi* "Six black billy goats, two white billy goats. They make (them into) hunting bags. The overseer of the shepherds gives (them) out. From them the cowherd of the god takes two white ones, the priest of Telipinu takes two black ones, the priest of ZA.BA$_4$.BA$_4$ two white ones, (and) the shepherd of the god takes two black ones. They make hunting bags." Presumably each functionary makes one hunting bag from the two hides allotted to him.

In *KUB* 55.43 and other festival texts, the ^{KUŠ}*kurša-* functions as the symbol of a deity and is therefore treated as a god. Güterbock points out that the protective deity Zitḫariya's representation is a *kurša-*.[31] Popko, *Kultobjekte* 110, discusses the evidence of the *kurša-* Festival in showing that the *kurša-* of the tutelary deity is to be identified with that tutelary deity itself. This is most clear in *KUB* 55.43 iv 5′–6′ and 8′, where the phrase "the hunting bag of the Tutelary Deity of Zapatiškuwa" alternates with "the Tutelary Deity of Zapatiškuwa." He also interprets the personal name ^{m}Kurša-^{D}LAMMA as evidence that

25. *KUB* 30.32 i 9–10, with duplicate *KBo* 18.190:4′–5′, *CTH* 241, edited somewhat differently by Haas and Wäfler, *UF* 8 (1976) 97–99; see also Košak *THeth* 10 (1982) 63–64. Noted by Popko, *AOF* 2: 66, and idem, *Kultobjekte* 109.
26. *AOF* 2: 66 and *Kultobjekte* 109: "'Sechs? Ziegenbockfelle, (jedes) zottig (und) gut behandelt, der Oberste der Hirten fü[r ... (von jedem Fell)] macht er ein göttliches Vlies.'"
27. *UF* 8: 97 "Sechs(?) struppige Ziegenbockfelle von guter Qualität macht der Oberste der Hirten für den Vorsteher der Hir[ten(?)] als Schild der Gottheit."
28. *FsKantor* 116 with n. 18 " ... and he makes the god's *kurša*."
29. See Košak, *THeth* 10: 64.
30. *KUB* 25.31 obv. 11–13, noted by Popko, *AOF* 2 (1975) 69 with n. 29, and idem, *Kultobjekte* 109, and Güterbock, *FsKantor* 116.
31. *NHF* 68, translated by him there as "Schild."

the *kurša-* itself is divine with his translation "'Vlies (ist) Schutzgottheit.'" Laroche, *NH* p. 283, interprets this name differently, arguing that it is of a familiar type in which a toponym or genitive precedes a divine name, and interprets this name as "'dieu tutelaire de/à l'égide.'" Laroche's comparisons to similar names are convincing, but Popko's interpretation is not impossible and in fact seems likely.

The hunting bag was frequently included in the list of "holy places" within the temple, together with the throne, the hearth, the window, etc., to which the Hittites libated. There are a number of occurrences of the expression $^{\text{D(KUŠ)}}$*kurša-*, both in and out of the context of the offerings to the holy places. This is not necessarily conclusive evidence that the hunting bag was identified with the deity, because other items in the list of holy places also sometimes occur with a DINGIR determinative, but it is in accord with the idea of the *kurša-* being thought of as the god itself. The *kurša-* image of a particular god might be used as one of the holy places in ceremonial offerings. Almost always this was Zitḫariya's *kurša-*, although that of Kappariyamu was used at least once.[32]

One unusual text seems to describe a festival being provided(?) before the *kurša-*: [... *-y*]*a-*⌜x⌝*-ša-an INA* É *ABI ABI* ^{D}UT[U-*ŠI*] [... -]*i n*⸗*ašta apiya maḫḫan* [... *A*]*NA PANI* ^{KUŠ}*kurši* EZEN *aššanuzz*[*i*] § "He [...] the [...] in the house of His Majesty's grandfather. How he complete[s]/prepare[s](?) a festival there [...] before the hunting bags §" 2011/u rev. 1–3 (catalogue, X *ṬUP-PU*), ed. Alp, *Tempel* 224–25. Alp identifies the text not as a catalogue but as part of a festival, perhaps the great festival of Arinna. The second sentence in this passage is quite an unusual construction. There are a few examples of similar but not identical expressions. There is an example of cups being prepared (*aššanu-*) *PANI* ^{D}U *piḫaššašši* *Ù PANI* ^{D}UTU ^{URU}TÚL-*na* "before the Stormgod *piḫaššašši* and before the Sungoddess of Arinna,"[33] which resembles the 2011/u passage in that the action of *aššanu-* is performed before (a representation of) a deity. In the Ritual Against Epidemic in the Army[34] a ritual (SISKUR) is *aššanu*-ed. One of the few clear examples of EZEN as the object of *aššanu-* is: *nu*⸗*kan maḫḫan INA* É *ḫešti* GAL-*in* EZEN-*an aššanunun* "When I completed(?) the great festival in the *ḫešti-* house" *KBo* 2.5+ iii 46–47 (Detailed Annals of Muršili), ed. Goetze, *AM* 190–91, translating *aššanu-* as "ausrichten." Despite the lack of other occurrences of a construction *ANA PANI* DN EZEN *aššanu-*, it seems clear that the hunting bag in 2011/u was being honored with a festival.

The hunting bag was involved in other festivals besides this festival performed before it and the one celebrated for its installation, described in the texts of *Chapter 4.* Although its normal resting place was the "house of the hunting bags,"[35] we know that a hunting bag was carried around to various temples and cult centers during the celebration of both the KI.LAM and AN.TAḪ.ŠUM festivals; see *Chapter 4*, commentary on *KBo* 13.179:2′ for examples from each of these festivals. In at least one instance it was taken to the *ḫalentu-*

32. See *Appendix A*, *KUB* 53.11 §§9′–12′.

33. *KBo* 10.20 iii 10–11, AN.TAḪ.ŠUM Festival outline, ed. (as 126/p+) Güterbock, *JNES* 19 (1960) 83 and 86.

34. *KUB* 7.54 iii 3.

35. See the entry on É ^{KUŠ}*kuršaš* in this appendix.

building: [É]*ḫalentuwaš*⸗*ma*⸗*kan anda* [Ø?] *ŠA* SAL.LUGAL [D]*Zitḫariyaš* [Ø] [*k*]*arū gankanza* [Ø?] "In the *ḫalentu-*, however, Zitḫariya of the queen (is) already hung."[36] The use of the verb *gank-* here makes it clear that it was the hunting bag of Zitḫariya as his cult symbol which was hung in the *ḫalentu-* during the festival procedures. In the Festival for the Infernal Deities,[37] besides receiving offerings as part of the regular list of holy places, the hunting bag was honored with individual drink offerings: UGULA [LÚ.MEŠ]MUḪALDIM *kuršaš piran* [GI][Š]BA]NŠUR *katta* [3-*ŠU*] *šipanti* "The chief cook libates [3 times] before the hunting bag (and) under the [ta]ble."

In *KUB* 55.43 column iv the offerings are placed directly on the hunting bag. So also in part of the AN.TAḪ.ŠUM Festival[38] the offering for Zitḫariya is placed on the *kurša-*. Another example of an offering provided specifically for the hunting bag is *KBo* 21.85 i 51′ (Festival of Moon and Thunder), in which an offering of a bread morsel is placed on it. The hunting bag also received offerings regularly in the various festivals in which it occurs as one of the holy places, for example: *nu*⸗*kan* UGULA [LÚ]MUḪALDIM *kattapalan dai ḫaššī* 1-*ŠU* [KUŠ]*kurši* 1-*ŠU* [GIŠ]DAG-*ti* 1-*ŠU* [GIŠ]*ḫattalwa*<*š*> GIŠ-*rui* 1-*ŠU ḫašši tapušza* 1-*ŠU dāi* "The chief cook sets out the *kattapala-*. On the hearth once, on the hunting bag once, on the throne once, on the wood of the door bolt once, (and) next to the hearth once, he places (it)" *KUB* 10.21 v 19–22 (fest. frag.), ed. Jestin, *RA* 34 (1937) 49 and 54.

newaḫḫ-

KUB 55.43 i 2, 3; *KBo* 13.179:4′ (*Chapter 4*). Examples of simple *newaḫḫ-* are quite rare, as this verb is usually combined with the preverb *appa*. There seems in general to be no difference in meaning between *newaḫḫ-* and *appa newaḫḫ-*; they both normally mean "to renew."[39] Friedrich, *HW* 151, proposes, "wieder erneuern" for *appa newaḫḫ-* and simply "erneuern" for *newaḫḫ-* without preverb, but he also translates *appa newaḫḫ-* "wiederherstellen," showing that this preverb-verb phrase could mean simply "renew, restore." The occurrences of *newaḫḫ-* in *KUB* 55.43 are instructive as to the use and meaning of this verb. First of all, we may note that in its two occurrences in §1, referring to the same action, one occurs as EGIR-*pa newaḫḫ-* and the other simply as *newaḫḫ-*, without *appa*. Thus within this one text we have parallel examples, requiring the same meaning, of *newaḫḫ-* with and without the adverb *appa*. We may also note that although *newaḫḫ-* is normally translated "renew," in our text at least "renew" means "replace." This is clear from the discussion in the following paragraphs of the text about the old hunting bags and what is done with them.

36. 315/t i 12′–14′ (fragment of a festival celebrated by the queen), ed. Alp, *Tempel* 230–31.
37. *CTH* 645, *KUB* 43.30 obv. ii 9′–10′.
38. *KBo* 19.128 ii 35–37, ed. Otten, *StBoT* 13 (1971) 6–7.
39. The *CHD* does not specifically comment on *appa newaḫḫ-* but does comment without giving examples that the use with EGIR-*pa* emphasizes "'making new again.'"

The objects which can be "renewed" are quite diverse. In *KUB* 13.7 iv 3–6 (law text of a king Tudḫaliya), a scribe *appa newaḫḫ*-s a broken tablet. In a fragment of a prayer[40] translated by the *CHD* sub *mayantaḫḫ-*, it is the king's frame (*ešri*〃*ššet*). In the *BĒL MADGALTI* instructions[41] they renew the É.MEŠ LUGAL, the É.MEŠ GUD, the É $^{\text{NA}_4}$KIŠIB, and the ^{É}*tarnui-* by replastering. Two examples apply more directly to our text: in the Prayer of Arnuwanda and Ašmunikal[42] they renew both the statues (ALAM.ḪI.A) and implements (*UNŪTE*) of the gods, so this verb is utilized elsewhere for renewing cultic equipment.

In the tablet catalogue *KUB* 30.56 rev. iii 6–7[43] we have: $^{\text{[UR]U}}$KÙ.BABBAR-*az* GIM-*an* ^{D}LAMMA ^{URU}*Ḫalinzuwa* ^{URU}*Tu*[*ḫuppiya*] [GI]BIL-*anzi paizzi* "How the Tutelary Deity of Ḫalinzuwa goes from Ḫattuša to Tuḫuppiya for renewing." This is so similar to what is happening in *KUB* 55.43 that it could be a reference to this tablet. It does not quite fit, however, because in the catalogue the Tutelary Deity of Ḫalinzuwa (Ḫatenzuwa in *KUB* 55.43) goes to Tuḫuppiya for renewing, while §5 of *KUB* 55.43 indicates that it is the hunting bag of Zitḫariya that goes to Tuḫuppiya, with that of the Tutelary Deity of Ḫatenzuwa going to Durmitta. Perhaps this catalogue is not after all referring to the tablet *KUB* 55.43, but to a similar festival text. The situation is made somewhat more complicated by evidence in the Annals of Muršili,[44] in which Muršili refers to Ḫatenzuwa as the city of the deity Zitḫariya. One might suggest, based on this passage, that there was actually only one god, and that Zitḫariya is the syllabic name of the Tutelary Deity of Ḫatenzuwa. However, the evidence of *KUB* 55.43, especially §5, in which different destinations are assigned to the two old hunting bags being sent out to the provinces, makes it clear that the hunting bags of Zitḫariya and of the Tutelary Deity of Ḫatenzuwa are distinct. See a discussion of this in the comments on Zitḫariya in *Chapter 1*.

palwai-

KUB 55.43 iii 35′ (*Chapter 4*). Although this verb occurs very frequently in festival texts as well as occasionally in other genres, its meaning is still unsure and has been the subject of some discussion. Güterbock[45] prefaces his own comments on *palwai-* by noting Alp's[46] view, that *palwai-* usually seemed to be "eine Art kultisches Vortragen." He points out, however, that the translation "to recite" does not fit the passage in the Song of Ullikummi[47] concerning Tašmišu's actions, which were a spontaneous response and not a memorized recitation. He also cites *KBo* 4.9 obv. i 45–50, a portion of the AN.TAḪ.ŠUM

40. *KUB* 43.63 obv. 13–14.
41. *KUB* 13.2 ii 13–15, ed. von Schuler, *Dienstanw.* 44–45.
42. *KUB* 17.21++ obv. i 18′–22′.
43. Ed. Laroche, *CTH* pp. 181–82.
44. *KUB* 19.39 ii 7, ed. Goetze, *AM* 164–65.
45. *Kum.* (1946) 79–80.
46. Alp, *Beamt.* 77f.
47. *KUB* 33.106 rev. iv 15–18, now recopied with new joins as *KBo* 26.65 rev. iv.

Festival, which involves the ^{LÚ}ALAN.ZU$_9$ standing next to the king, holding his hands up, turning in place, and performing the action of *palwai-*. He notes that "recitation" is hardly likely when a turning movement is prescribed. He enumerates the following characteristics for *palwai-*: 1) It is an expression of joy, 2) it is audible, and 3) it can be done two or three times (as in the Kumarbi passage about Tašmišu, where he *palwaizzi* three times and then two times). Hence he understands it as a short repeatable sound and suggests either to "emit a cry" or to "clap," with the latter more likely in view of the *KBo* 4.9 passage. He translates the relevant part of the Song of Ullikummi, *KUB* 33.106 rev. iv 15–18, as "er klatschte(?) dreimal."[48]

Güterbock later translates the same passage as "three times he *shouted*," with the italics indicating uncertainty of translation.[49] He explains this change in his understanding of *palwai-* in *JCS* 6: 42 by citing the text 274/c (now *KBo* 24.76), in which the verb is followed by ^{D}*Le-el-lu-u-ri-iš-wa-kán*. The *-wa-* direct speech particle in this phrase caused him to note that "... the following speech with *-wa-* clearly shows that *palwai-* is a verbum dicendi";[50] he therefore gives up the idea of "clap" and opts for a verb of speech. Along these same lines, in his article on "The Hittite Temple According to Written Sources,"[51] he defines the ^{LÚ}*palwatallaš*, a cult functionary who most often performs this verb's action and whose title is obviously related to it, as "a kind of reciter." When I was preparing the present work as a dissertation, I noted the suggestion in an early draft of the *CHD* article on *palwai-* that the *KBo* 24.76 passage was not compelling evidence for *palwai-* being a *verbum dicendi*, since in Hittite the *verbum dicendi* is frequently omitted. The occurrence of the sentence particle *-wa-* does not invariably mean that the preceding sentence contained a *verbum dicendi*. Güterbock at that time (1987) accepted the idea that *palwai-* was not necessarily a *verbum dicendi*. Singer, in his glossary to his edition of the KI.LAM Festival, remains neutral by giving the definition "to recite(?), clap(?)."[52] I therefore used the translation "clap(?)" primarily on the basis of the *KBo* 4.9 passage. In the interval between completion of the dissertation and its submission for publication Badalì has published a thorough study of this verb.[53] Based on his many examples of *palwai-* in different text genres, he concludes that it must be a *verbum dicendi* and further that it means "to recite" ("recitare"). In my opinion this very specific translation is still problematic for the Song of Ullikummi (Badalì translates *palwai-* in those passages as "shout" [gridare]), and a number of his examples do not conclusively require a meaning "recite" versus "clap." However, as he notes on pages 141–42, *KBo* 15.48 ii 5′–9′,[54] in which the ^{LÚ}*palwattallaš palwai-*s but is also described as holding a cup of water and an eagle's wing, is very strong evidence that

48. *Kum.* 28.
49. Ullik. (*JCS* 6 [1952]) 31.
50. Ullik. (*JCS* 6 [1952]) 42.
51. *CRRAI* 20 (1972) 125–32; see p. 131 for this comment on the ^{LÚ}*palwatallaš*.
52. *StBoT* 28 (1984) 158.
53. "Il significato del verbo ittito *palwae-*," *Or* 59 (1990) 130–42.
54. His example III.11, a passage from the (*ḫ*)*išuwaš* Festival.

palwai- does not mean "clap." His examples III.4 and III.10 also argue, somewhat less conclusively, against a meaning "clap." I therefore accept his conclusion that *palwai-* must be a *verbum dicendi.*

GIŠ*papul-*

KUB 55.43 iii 33′ (*Chapter 4*). This word is a hapax legomenon. Although the signs on the tablet are somewhat difficult to read because of abrasion of the surface, GIŠ*pa-a-pu-li* seems to be the best reading. Although such a word is not attested elsewhere, no other word which would fit these signs suggests itself.[55] This word looks like a nomen instrumenti in *-ul* (*HE* §47) declined here as a dative-locative.

There is one occurrence of a word GIŠ*papu-* that may be related to GIŠ*papul-*.[56] From this single context all one can say about the meaning of GIŠ*papu-* is that it is used in a bakery.[57] This strengthens the possible connection between GIŠ*papu-* and GIŠ*papul-*, because the latter occurs in *KUB* 55.43 iii 33′ as an implement on which bread is placed when it comes out of the oven. The fact that the bread is then covered and taken to a temple indicates that the GIŠ*papul-* is not just a cooling tray, but something that is used to deliver bread from the bakery to its final destination.

purpura-

KUB 55.43 iii 7′, 11′, 14′ (*Chapter 4*); *KUB* 9.17:23′ (*Appendix A*). See Otten, *StBoT* 13 (1971) 35; Hoffner, *AlHeth* (1974) 151, 178–79, and 207; G. Jucquois and R. Lebrun, *Heth. u. Idg.* (1979) 106 n. 8; and Košak, *FsGüterbock*² (1986) 126. This word, whose semantic content primarily denotes a shape, a ball or lump, almost always occurs with some indication of the material from which it is made, either with a determinative or with a genitive of material. That material may be one of many different things. Košak discusses *purpura-* made of iron and points out that elsewhere in the corpus this word refers "to lumps of dough, bread, cheese, clay, or soap … ." Hoffner discusses *purpura-* made of bread and dough, points out other materials from which *purpura-* are made, and makes note of the common cultic practice of scattering *purpura-* of dough or bread at the feet of the king and queen in a procession. I would note the further distinction which the Hittites made between a bread-ball, NINDA*purpura-*, and ball(s) of dough, written *purpurēš išnaš* in *KBo* 4.2 i 63 (Ritual of Ḫuwarlu), *išnaš purpuran* in i 56 of the same text, and *išnaš purpurēš* in *KUB* 27.67 ii 9 and iii 16 (Ritual of DTarpattašši). The Ritual of Ḫuwarlu contains the best evidence for the distinction between NINDA*purpura-* and *išnaš purpura-*, as it makes use both of bread-balls (*KBo* 4.2 i 19) and of balls of dough (passages cited above). Clearly

55. Hoffner suggests reading the *KUB* 55.43 passage as GIŠ*papuli* and points out to me the existence of GIŠ*papu-* and its possible relation to this word in the *kurša-* Festival.

56. *KUB* 16.34 i 14 (oracle question).

57. *CHD* first draft. Sommer, *KlF* 1 (1930) 344, on the basis of the similar passage *KUB* 5.7 obv. 24–25, suggests the possibility of GIŠ*papu-* as the Hittite word underlying GIŠBANŠUR "table." As pointed out in the *CHD* first draft on GIŠ*papu-*, this identification, although not impossible, is not compelling, and GIŠ*papu-* could be any wooden object likely to be found in a bakery.

purpura- išnaš/išnaš purpura- is to be distinguished from ^{NINDA}*purpura-* and understood as (unbaked) balls of dough.[58] The "bread-balls," ^{NINDA}*purpura-*, occur only in festival or ritual texts, and are most often used in the KI.LAM Festival. They are usually poured/heaped up, taking the verbs *išḫuwa(i)-* or *šuḫḫa-*. Since we have the verb *išḫuwa(i)-* preserved in *KUB* 55.43 iii 7′, we may restore the same verb in the broken lines 11′ and 14′ as well. Despite the lack of a determinative on *purpura-* in line 7′, it is clear, because of the mention of ^{NINDA}*purpura-* in lines 11′ and 14′, that "bread-balls" were also intended here. There is at least one other similar example of *purpura-* in festival context without any determinative or indication of material, that is, Bo 68/215+ v 5′–6′, *[pu-u]r-pu-ru-uš* LUGAL-*i kattan išḫuwanzi* "They pour out (bread?) balls for the king."

$^{LÚ.MEŠ}$*šarmiya-*

KUB 10.93 i 9′ (*Appendix A*): There is no entry in *HW* or any of the Ergänzungshefte for the word *šarmi-*. Pecchioli Daddi, *Mestieri* 146–47 does not give a definition but cites this title in her section "Personale Palatino e Templare" and gives examples of the ^{LÚ}*šarmi-* in both palace and temple context. The *šarmi-* man or men occur once as a witness in a deposition,[59] once in the inventory of Maninni,[60] once in a fragment of a cult inventory,[61] and approximately eight times in cultic texts, including the example in *KUB* 10.93 i 9′. Beyond the fact that he usually occurs in a list of cult functionaries and therefore must also be some kind of cult functionary, the contexts in which he occurs do not provide a clue as to his function. Jakob-Rost, Werner, and Neu[62] all decline to attempt a translation of $^{LÚ.MEŠ}$*šarmi-* in their treatments of passages in which they occur.

tukk-

KUB 55.43 obv. i 4, 9, iii 1′ (*Chapter 4*). Friedrich in *HW* 227 gives for this verb the meanings "to be visible, to be seen, to be of importance," with more bibliography in *HW 3. Erg.* 21 for the meaning "to be seen." Neu, *StBoT* 5 (1968) 178–80, does not add any new meanings, giving the two basic translations "to be seen/be visible" and "to be considered/be of importance." Other occurrences of the verb indicate that in addition to these meanings it can also mean "to be prescribed, specified." A passage which seems to require this meaning occurs in a birth ritual:[63] ^{GIŠ}BANŠUR*-ma-kan ANA* ^{LÚ}*MUTIŠU-ya [tu-ug-g]a-a-ri [AN]A* DAM-*ŠU-ya-at-kan tu-ug-ga-a-ri* ^{DUG}LIŠ.GAL*-ya-šmaš-kan tu-ug-ga-a-ri* "A table for her husband also [is pre]scribed and [fo]r the wife one is also prescribed. And a bowl for (each of) them is prescribed." Beckman translates *tuggari* as "is required." See *CHD* sub *meḫur* f, for a translation of *KUB* 55.43 obv. i 4 as "the time is not

58. *CHD* first draft, used with the permission of the editors.
59. *KUB* 13.34++ iv 21, ed. Werner, *StBoT* 4 (1967) 40–42.
60. *ABoT* 108 iv 8′.
61. *KUB* 38.129 obv. 2, ed. Jakob-Rost, *MIO* 9 (1963) 188–89.
62. Jakob-Rost, *MIO* 9 (1963) 188, Werner, *StBoT* 4 (1967) 42, Neu, *StBoT* 18 (1974) 115.
63. *KBo* 17.65 obv. 21–22, ed. Beckman *StBoT* 29 (1983) 134–35.

important." The passage is also translated by Haas and Jakob-Rost, *AOF* 11 (1984) 16: "der Zeitpunkt ist ohne Belang." The occurrence of *meḫur* with *duqqari* is quite rare; it occurs in only one other passage, *KUB* 32.123 rev. iii 12 (Ištanuvian festival): -]*wanzi*=*ma meḫur* UL *kuitki tuqqari* "No particular time, however, is prescribed for [x]-ing."

LÚ*uriyanni-*

KUB 55.43 iii 24′, 36′ (*Chapter 4*). This title denotes a fairly important official of the Hittite court. Weidner already in 1923, commenting on the occurrence of LÚ*uriyanni-* in the Talmi-Šarruma Treaty,[64] in a list of officials in Ḫatti before whom this treaty was written, noted that it occurs often in the texts and that it probably denoted a "bestimmte Priesterklasse."[65] Laroche[66] favored identifying the LÚ*uriyanni-* with the LÚ*KARTAPPU*, a groom or charioteer, while Goetze[67] considered an identification with *TARTĒNU*, a word which von Soden[68] translates tentatively as "Mann an zweite Stelle?" Friedrich[69] proposed simply "(Art höherer Priester oder Tempelfunktionär?)," without providing any morphology information for this word. Liverani proposes *uriyanni-* as the Hittite reading of LÚḪAL, the diviner.[70] However, his evidence for this, the existence of an *uriyanni-* oracle bird and a possible connection with the seal Tarsus 43,[71] is tenuous. Liverani rejects Laroche's and Goetze's ideas on the LÚ*uriyanni-* because they do not take into account all the various functions of this official, but his identification of the *uriyanni-* as the LÚḪAL also does not really allow for the diverse duties attested for this official.

Pecchioli Daddi in 1975 commented briefly on the *uriyanni-* official, pointing out that he was an official of some importance, based on his appearance as a witness in land donations and international treaties and as an owner of land himself.[72] In addition, she suggested that this official probably belonged to the sacred sphere of the Hittite court, based on his participation in the festivals and the mention of an *uriyanni-* official together with a GAL SANGA. Although she referred to some of Liverani's observations on the duties of the *uriyanni-* official, she did not comment on his or other previous proposals for identifying the LÚ*uriyanni-* with any Sumerographic or Akkadographic title. Two years later, in her article on the LÚ*KARTAPPU*,[73] she specifically rejected Laroche's and Goetze's suggestions. Still later, in *Mestieri* (1982) 266–68, Pecchioli Daddi provided a very useful

64. *KBo* 1.6 rev. 19.
65. *BoSt* 8 (1923) 88.
66. *RA* 43 (1949) 70–71.
67. *RHA* XII/54 (1952) 9.
68. *AHw* 3 (1981) 1332.
69. *HW* (1952) 235.
70. *Storia di Ugarit* (Rome, 1975) 73–74.
71. For this seal see Gelb in Goldman, *Excavations at Gözlü Kule, Tarsus II* (Princeton, 1956) 251. For the reading of the seal see Laroche, *Syria* 35 (1958) 259.
72. *OA* 14 (1975) 119–20 n. 93.
73. *SCO* 27 (1977) 187–88 n. 83.

summary of the available evidence for the *uriyanni-* official, including citation of occurrences, inflection, proper names attested for the *uriyanni-* official, and other details about this official.[74] The entry in *Mestieri* provides a listing of occurrences divided according to the *uriyanni-* official's various functions; its location in the section of the book devoted to specific terms for religious personnel reaffirms Pecchioli Daddi's opinion as to his role as a religious official. To her section c (pp. 267–68) on his role in festivals may now be added Bo 3238 iii 11′, transliterated in *KBo* 30 p. IV sub number 73. Here the ^{LÚ}*uriyanni-* occurs with a number of other cult functionaries such as the ^{LÚ}*palwatalla-*.

Pecchioli Daddi's entry in *Mestieri* effectively demonstrates that the *uriyanni-* official's two main duties were participation in the official cult and acting as a witness in treaties and land donations. In addition to the texts cited in *Mestieri*, the *uriyanni-* official also occurs as a witness in the İnandık tablet,[75] along with the GAL LÚ.MEŠ GEŠTIN "chief of the wine stewards," DUMU.LUGAL "prince," and UGULA 1 *LI* ^{LÚ}IŠ.M[EŠ] "overseer of 1,000 grooms." Balkan does not comment on this word. The word occurs also in one Akkadian text from Ugarit.[76] The *uriyanni-* official's duties at Ugarit included carrying out orders for the king and placing boundary stones on the border between Ugarit and Siyannu. At Ugarit at least his duties seem to be those not of a religious official but rather of a high level administrator. Nougayrol does not attempt a translation of the word, simply inserting it in his translation as "l'*uriyannu*." Von Soden, *AHw* 3 (1981), maintains a very noncommittal position, defining the ^{LÚ}*uriyanni-* as "ein Funktionär." Based on the occurrences of the word at Ugarit and in the İnandık tablet, he suggests that it may be a Hittite loan word into Akkadian. It can hardly even be termed a loan word, as it is presently attested only twice in Akkadian texts.

This word does occasionally occur declined as a Hittite *i*-stem noun, for example ^{LÚ}*u-ri-an-ni-iš* in *KBo* 3.34 i 5 (Palace Chronicle), and ^{LÚ}*u-ri-ya-an-ni-in* in *KUB* 23.87 i 3 (letter). In the expression "the house of the *uriyanni-*," in which it occurs most frequently, it seems to be frozen in an Akkadographic writing É ^{LÚ}*uriyanni*, without a Hittite genitive case ending. In the Ugarit example it is written as ^{LÚ}*uriyannu*, with the correct vowel for the Akkadian nominative required in the sentence. In the İnandık tablet it is written ^{LÚ}*urianni*, genitive following the *ANA PANI* which governs it.

Past scholars have attempted to place the *uriyanni-* official in either the religious or secular sphere. Although it is true that some officials at the Hittite court had duties which were almost exclusively one or the other, the Hittites did not observe the same sharp distinction between sacred and secular duty that some societies draw. Many Hittite officials occur in all types of Hittite texts and clearly have both "religious" and "secular" duties. Rather than trying to categorize the ^{LÚ}*uriyanni-* as either a sacred or secular official, we may simply note his various duties and realize that they included responsibility in what we would term the sacred as well as the secular sphere.

74. Her list of occurrences does not include *SBo* I.2 rev. 11, RS 17.368 rev. 5′, or İnandık rev. 25.

75. Balkan, *İnandık* 43.

76. RS 17.368 rev. 5′. See J. Nougayrol, *PRU* 4 (1956) 77, and Liverani, *Storia di Ugarit* (Rome, 1962) 73–74.

The phrase which concerns us in *KUB* 55.43 is É [LÚ]*uriyanni* "the house of the *uriyanni*-official." Aside from a very brief mention in *Mestieri* 268, this phrase has hardly been discussed in the previous literature on this official. It occurs a number of times in festival texts, in a context where something is being brought or driven out "from the house/estate of the *uriyanni*- official," (*IŠTU* É [LÚ]*uriyanni*). See for example *KUB* 53.49 obv. 9′–10′ (fragment of the Nerik cult): *IŠTU* É [LÚ]*u-ri-ya-an-ni* x[...] *unniyanzi* "They drive x[...] from the house of the *uriyanni*- official"; Bo 3418:10′–11′ (fest. frag.):[77] [*ta* 1 UD]U.ŠE *IŠTU* É [LÚ]*u-r*[*i-ya-an-ni*] [*un*]*ianzi* "They [dr]ive [one] fattened [she]ep from the house of the *ur*[*iyanni-*] official." In the latter text the following paragraph, although quite broken, seems to indicate that the king sacrificed this fattened sheep provided from the house of the *uriyanni*- official. In the Festival for Telipinu[78] animals again must be supplied from the house of the *uriyanni*- official, although not for sacrifice: *INA* UD 4 KAM *mān lukkatta nu* DINGIR-*LAM-aš* [GIŠ]*ḫulugannin* GUD.ḪI.A [LÚ]*BĒL* É [URU]*Ḫanḫana turizzi* 2 GUD.APIN.LAL-*ma* [*I*]*ŠTU* É [LÚ]*u-ri-ya-an-ni* [LÚ]*BĒL* É [URU]*Ḫanḫana pai* "On the fourth day, at dawn, the lord of the house of Ḫanḫana harnesses the chariot of the god (with) oxen. And the two draft oxen the lord of the house of Ḫanḫana gives from the house of the *uriyanni*- official." Clearly É here does not mean literally "house" but rather "household" or "estate," the resources or property of a domestic establishment. Another text of the Festival for Telipinu[79] demonstrates not only the involvement of the "house of the *uriyanni*- official" in the cult but also indicates that this can mean a physical "house:" *para-ma* KÁ É [LÚ]*u-ri-ya-an-ni* 1 UDU *appanzi n-an* [É]*ḫilamnaš* [D]UTU-*i* [*ḫuk*]*anzi* "Further, they seize one sheep (at) the door of the house of the *uriyanni*- official and [sacri]fice it to the Sungod of the gatehouse."

In addition to animals, there are several passages in which sacrificial bread is supplied by the house of the *uriyanni*- official, for example: *IŠTU* É [LÚ]*u-ri-ya-an-ni* GÙB-*laš-ma* 3 [NINDA]*paršulli karu udanteš n-at-šan* GUNNI *ištarna pidi kianta* "Three bread morsels have already been brought from the house of the *uriyanni*- official of the left. They are placed on the hearth, in the middle" *KUB* 53.13 iv 16′–19′ (Festivals Celebrated by a DUMU-*aš*); [*I*]*ŠTU* É [LÚ]*u-ri-ya-an-ni* x[... ?] 3 NINDA.KUR_4.RA-*ya udanz*[*i* ...] "They bring x[... (?)] and three thick breads from the house of the *uriyanni*- official" *KUB* 53.49 rev. 2–3 (cult of Nerik).

What light do these various examples of the É [LÚ]*uriyanni* shed on the occurrences in *KUB* 55.43? First of all, we may note that the house of the *uriyanni*- official often incurs the responsibility of supplying animals and bread for offerings in the cult. Bo 3418:10′–11′, cited above, in which sacrificial animals are brought from the house of the *uriyanni*-official, is good evidence that in *KUB* 55.43 iii 36′ some sacrificial animal is also to be restored in the break at the end of the line as the item which they take from the house of the *uriyanni*- official. In addition, the occurrence of the "*uriyanni*- official of the left" in

77. Edited by Alp, *Tempel* 20–21, transliterated in *KBo* 30 p. IV sub number 74.

78. *KUB* 53.3 obv. i 18′–22′.

79. *KUB* 53.12 rev. iv 1–2, ed. Haas and Jakob-Rost, *AOF* 11 (1984) 49–52.

KUB 53.3 rev. 16′ (cited above) implies that there was an "*uriyanni*- official of the right," which we now have attested in line 24′ of our text. The text *SBo* 1.2 is quite interesting in this regard, as it includes in rev. 11, in a list of witnesses, two *uriyanni*- officials: ᵐ*Zū*[*z*]*zu* *Ù* ᵐ*Maraššā* ᴸᵁ́·ᴹᴱŠ*urianni*. We very probably have here the names of the *uriyanni*- official of the right and the *uriyanni*- official of the left.

wappiya-

KUB 55.43 passim in columns ii and iv (*Chapter 4*). See also the discussion of the LÚ.MEŠ UR.GI$_7$ below. Although this verb is rarely attested, the contexts in which it occurs make its meaning clear. Goetze notes that this verb, cited by him as *wapp*-, is undoubtedly "bellen."[80] Friedrich notes the phrase LÚ.MEŠ UR.GI$_7$ *wappianzi* in the AN.TAḪ.ŠUM Festival[81] and translates "sie bellen."[82] The thirteen occurrences of *wappiya*- in the preserved portion of *KUB* 55.43 constitute approximately half of all known occurrences of this verb. Of the examples outside of this text that occur in clear context, three have as subject UR.GI$_7$, two the LÚ.MEŠ UR.GI$_7$, and two are uncertain. The three examples with UR.GI$_7$ are most useful in determining the meaning of *wappiya*-: KA x[ ] = *A-MU-U* = UR.GI$_7$ *ku-it wa-ap-pé̌š-k*[*i-iz-zi*] Hittite: "what the dog barks";[83] [UR.GI]$_7$ *wappiyazi* ŠAḪ-*aš ḫuntarnuzzi* [*nu* DINGIR]-*LAM le kuelqa ištamašti* "[The do]g barks, the pig grunts. Do not, [O g]od, hear (the sounds) of these";[84] UR.GI$_7$-*aš wappiyazi apiya*″*ma*″*aš ari n*″*aš karuššiyazi* "The dog barks, but (when) he comes there (the stonehouse), he is silent."[85] Both of the examples of the LÚ.MEŠ UR.GI$_7$ with *wappiya*- outside of our text are in festivals.[86] With the publication of *KUB* 55.43 we now have the dog-men well attested with *wappiya*-. Beyond establishing quite clearly that the dog-men do indeed *wappiya*- as part of certain cult ceremonies, these examples do not provide any further context that might be used to complement the occurrences of *wappiya*- with UR.GI$_7$ in determining the meaning of this word. The very designation dog-men indicates that these men in cultic contexts imitate the actions of dogs. Whatever the meaning of *wappiya*-, we may expect the dog-men to do it because dogs are attested doing it. Thus it is reasonable to assume that the dog-men barked as part of their cultic role.

The other two occurrences of *wappiya*- in relatively unbroken context are both in column iv of *KUB* 20.90 (frag. of fest. naming the NIN.DINGIR): iv 4′–7′: [*ta*? ᴰ*Z*]*itḫariyan* TUŠ-*aš ekuzi* [*ašešš*]*ar arta wappiyanzi* [o-o-]x-*uzzaš uizzi* ᴸᵁ́·ᴹᴱŠ*ḫapiyaš*

80. *Madd.* (1928) 145.
81. *KBo* 4.13 vi 7.
82. *ZA* 15 (1950) 253 n. 3.
83. *KBo* 1.44+*KBo* 13.1+*KBo* 26.20 ii 30 (Erimḫuš Boğ.), edited in *MSL* 17: 108.
84. *KBo* 12.96 i 12′–13′ (Ritual of the Tutelary Deity of the Hunting Bag), ed. Rosenkranz, *Or* 33 (1964) 239 and 241; and Neu, *StBoT* 5 (1968) 105; also compare *CHD* sub *lē* a2′b′.
85. *KUB* 13.8:7 (Instructions of Ašmunikal to the Guardians of the Stonehouses).
86. *KBo* 4.13+ vi 7 (AN.TAḪ.ŠUM) and 158/o:2′ (fest. frag.), translit. Otten and Rüster, *ZA* 68 (1978) 277–78.

[^{TÚG}š]*iknuš peššiyanzi* "He drinks [Z]itḫariya, seated. [The asse]mbly stands. 'They' bark. He comes to(?)[87] the [...]x-*uzza*-s. The *ḫapiya*- men throw (off) the(ir) cloaks(?)." Because the assembly here is a collective noun and occurs with a singular verb, it should not also be the subject of *wappiyanzi*.[88] That subject is not expressed, although it is clearly a group of cultic personnel and therefore (because of the singular form *ekuzi*) different from the celebrant who drinks Zitḫariya. The passage does not provide any further clues as to who was barking as part of the ceremony. A paragraph concerning the NIN.DINGIR and further activities involving the assembly follows the above-cited passage, and then comes the last paragraph of the tablet, iv 14′–16′: ^{D}*Zaiun* TUŠ-*aš IŠTU BIBRI* KÙ.G[I GEŠ]TIN *pianzi ašeššar arta* ^{TÚG}*šiknuš peššiyanzi wappianzi* ŠU-*i* "They give the deity Zaiu (to drink) from a gol[d] rhyton of [wi]ne. The assembly stands. 'They' throw (off) the(ir) cloaks and bark. To the hand ... " (continued on the next column, which is now broken away). The assembly is consistently construed as a collective noun with a singular verb. The subject of these two plural verbs is not expressed, although we know from the earlier paragraph of this same text cited above that it is the *ḫapiya*- men who throw off their cloaks after the barking takes place. They may well be the understood subject, again throwing off their cloaks as they did two paragraphs earlier. They must then also be the ones who bark, as the verb *wappianzi* immediately follows the sentence concerning the throwing off of the cloaks. It is uncertain what significance the throwing off of the cloaks has for the barking, especially as the sequence is different in the two examples. In the first case, the barking occurs before the throwing off of the cloaks, with a sentence concerning the [...]x-*uzza*-s in between these two actions. In the second example the barking follows the throwing off of the cloaks with no intervening activity. Although these examples from a festival involving the NIN.DINGIR do not provide evidence either to confirm or to call into question our understanding of the meaning of *wappiya*-, they are important evidence for showing that the use of this verb is not restricted to dogs and dog-men and for confirming that "barking," not by a dog but by a cult functionary, can be a part of cult procedure, as it is throughout *KUB* 55.43.

SUMERIAN

^{GIŠ}AB

KUB 55.43 iv 31′ (*Chapter 4*). Only rarely in the Hittite cult are functionaries placed behind the windows as in this portion of the *kurša*- Festival. A fragment describing part of the AN.TAḪ.ŠUM Festival contains a similar prescription:[89] [GIŠ] ^{D}INANNA.GAL $^{LÚ.MEŠ}$*ḫalliyareš* [SÌ]R-*RU* ^{LÚ}SAGI.A-*aš* 1 NINDA.KUR$_4$.RA KU$_7$ [*ašg*]*az pai* LÚ.MEŠ UR.GI$_7$ E[G]IR ^{GIŠ}AB.ḪI.A "(There is) the large Inanna instrument. The cult singers sing.

87. Or "It (the assembly) comes ... ."

88. Goetze, *Madd.* 145, notes briefly that *wappiya*- occurs with three possible subjects, dogs, dog-men, and, in his interpretation of these passages, the assembly. Friedrich, *ZA* 15 (1950) 253 n. 3, also interprets the *KUB* 20.90 passages as referring to the assembly.

89. *KBo* 19.128 iv 50′–53′, ed. Otten, *StBoT* 13 (1971) 12–13.

The cupbearer gives out one sweet thick bread from outside. The dog-men behind the windows ... " Otten translates the relevant passage "Die Hunde-Leute hinter den Fenstern," taking the verb of this sentence to be lost in the break at the beginning of column v. This is almost certainly correct, even though there is space in iv 53′ after ^{GIŠ}AB.ḪI.A for one more word of 4–5 signs. Perhaps this sentence resembled iv 31′ of *KUB* 55.43, with the dog-men rather than the local singers taking their places behind the windows. On the analogy of the passage cited below, they may also have sung behind the window, but if the end of the sentence was simply SÌR-*RU*, why did the scribe not write it in the empty space available at the end of iv 53′? This is one of the very few occurrences of uncomplemented ^{GIŠ}AB.ḪI.A outside of the Old Hittite mythological texts. A similar passage, also from a possible fragment of the AN.TAḪ.ŠUM Festival is: [LUGAL SAL].LUGAL TUŠ-*aš* ^{D}LAMMA *ašgaza akuwanzi* [LÚ.MEŠ U]R.GI$_7$ EGIR ^{GIŠ}AB-*ya* SÌR-*RU* 1 NINDA.KUR$_4$.RA *paršiya* "[The king (and) qu]een drink the Tutelary Deity, seated, outside. [The d]og-[men] sing behind the window. He breaks 1 thick bread."[90]

There is a clear example of a festival celebrant moving *to* the window in the Festival of the Month: SAL.LUGAL*=kan anda paizzi n=aš ištanani* DINGIR.MEŠ-*naš UŠGEN n=aš šarazzi* ^{GIŠ}AB-*ya tapušza tiyazzi* § *n=ašta* DUMU É.GAL.ḪI.A $^{\text{LÚ.MEŠ}}$*MEŠEDI anda uwanzi nu=za=kan ANA* SAL.LUGAL *menaḫḫanda* ZAG-*az AŠARŠUNU appanzi* $^{\text{LÚ.MEŠ}}$ALAN.ZU$_9$-*az* EGIR GUNNI *AŠARŠUNU appanzi* "The queen goes in. She does reverence at the altar of the gods. She steps to the side of the upper window. § The palace attendants (and) the royal bodyguards come in. They take their places before the queen on the right. The ALAN.ZU$_9$-men take their places behind the hearth."[91]

The window is one of the "sacred places" in the temple that receives offerings regularly as part of most festival celebrations. As a kind of ceremonially fixed locus it can also serve as a reference point by which those celebrating festivals navigate and find their proper places for a ceremony. In the Festival of the Month example the queen, having come into the cella first, establishes her position at the window. The other cult functionaries can then find their assigned places for the ceremony relative to her or to another of the fixed sacred places, the hearth. In the other examples cited the windows seem to be a kind of partial border between sacred and secular loci. In the *kurša-* Festival the local singers take part in the ceremony but only for a short period. They are involved throughout, but for most of the ceremony only by watching from the windows while cult personnel from the capital perform a state ceremony in the local temple.

É ^{KUŠ}*kuršaš*

KUB 55.43 i 7, 16 (*Chapter 4*). The phrase "temple/house of the hunting bags" is written É ^{KUŠ}*kuršaš* in our text, É ^{D}*kuršaš*,[92] É *kur*[*šaš*],[93] *kuršaš* É-*irza*,[94] and ^{KUŠ}*kuršaš*

90. *KBo* 4.13+ v 39–40.
91. *KUB* 27.69 rev. v 1–14.
92. *KBo* 14.76 i 13′ (*nuntarriyašḫaš* Festival).
93. *KBo* 25.142+*KBo* 20.69 obv? 6′ (chant in Hattic), ed. Neu, *StBoT* 25: 229.
94. *ABoT* 5+ ii 18′ (KI.LAM Festival), ed. Singer, *StBoT* 28: 34.

parna.[95] The house of the hunting bags occurs only in cultic context, either in festivals or festival descriptions in oracles. The two questions that have most occupied scholars concerning the house of the hunting bags are: 1) is it a separate building or part of a cult building complex? and 2) is it a temple where cult activity takes place or merely a house/room where the hunting bags are kept until they are needed elsewhere for some cultic ceremony? Otten in 1959 suggested that the É ^{KUŠ}*kuršaš* was probably not a building, but just a room within the sanctuary.[96] Güterbock has pointed out the role of the house of the hunting bags in furnishing all the offering materials at the various stations of a cultic journey of the hunting bag, as well as the fact that a festival takes place in the house of the hunting bags upon Zitḫariya's return from his cultic journey on the third day of the *nuntarriyašḫaš* Festival.[97] He refuted Otten's idea and suggests not only that the house of the hunting bags was a building of its own but further, based primarily on the fact of its providing offering materials, that it was a temple. Güterbock reiterates this position, using ^{KUŠ}*kuršaš parna* as an example of *parna-* meaning "temple,"[98] and translates É ^{KUŠ}*kuršaš* in the festival fragment *KBo* 10.27 iii 18 as "temple ... of the Divine Shield."[99] Popko favors Otten's idea, suggesting that the house of the hunting bags was a permanent resting place for the hunting bag and that it was probably a room within the temple, although he does not cite any specific evidence for this position.[100] Most recently Singer cites the Old Hittite example *ABoT* 5+ ii 18′ (with many duplicates): *kuršaš* É-*irza* DINGIR.MEŠ *uenzi* and translates "the gods come from the 'house of the fleece,'" without commenting on what that might be.[101]

As noted most emphatically by Güterbock, there are several examples of offering materials being supplied from the house of the hunting bags, in for example *KUB* 22.27 iv 35 and *KUB* 50.82:9′, 13′ (both oracles about festivals). There are also a number of examples of cultic activity being performed in the house of the hunting bags. Examples include: *kuedani″ma* UD-*ti* ^{D}UTU-*ŠI IN*[*A* o o o]x *paizzi INA* É ^{D}*kuršaš″ma* EZEN *nu* x[o o o]x.ḪI.A LÚ.MEŠ UR.GI$_7$ *unniyanzi* KUR-*eaš ḫuma*[*ndaš a*]*rkammaš IŠTU* É ^{D}*kuršašš″a* 1 GUD ŠE 3 G[UD? *unni*]*yanzi ḫalkueššar ŠA* É ^{D}*kuršaš″pat* "On the day that the king goes to [x], (there is) a festival in the house of the hunting bags. The dog-men drive (in) [...]x's. (It is) the [t]ribute of al[l] the lands. And from the house of the hunting bags they [driv]e one fattened ox (and) three o[xen(?)]. (They are) the offering materials of that same house of the hunting bags";[102] NIN.DINGIR *″ma šara INA* É ^{KUŠ}*kuršaš paizzi piran* ^{D}*Kantipuittiyaš* ^{KUŠ}*kuršaš iyatta* $^{\text{LÚ.MEŠ}}$*ḫapeš ú-nu-wa*!?-*an-t*[*e-eš*?] *iyanta* LÚ.MEŠ

95. *KUB* 57.59 ii 9′, cited as Bo 805:10 in *KBo* 20 p. VII n. 10.
96. *FsFriedrich* (1959) 356.
97. *NHF* (1964) 68 with n. 63.
98. *CRRAI* 20 (1972) 125 with n. 4.
99. *CRRAI* 20: 126 with n. 8.
100. *Acta Antiqua Academiae Scientiarum Hungaricae* 22 (1974) 309.
101. *StBoT* 27 (1983) 91.
102. *KUB* 22.27 iv 16–20 (oracle about festivals).

^{URU}*Anunuw[a* SÌR]-⸢*RU*⸣ $^{\text{SAL.MEŠ}}$*zintuḫiyaš* EGIR-*a[n* SÌR]-⸢*RU*⸣ $^{\text{SAL.MEŠ}}$*arkammiyaleš* ^{GIŠ}*arkammi galgalturi* GUL-*aḫḫannieškanzi* § *mān* NIN.DINGIR *INA* É ^{KUŠ}*kuršaš ari n⸗ašta* ^{É}*ḫilamni andan* ⸢x x x⸣ SÌR-*R[U]* NIN.DINGIR⸗*kan andan paizzi* "The NIN.DINGIR goes up to the house of the hunting bags. The hunting bag of Kantipuitti[103] goes before. The *ḫapiya-* functionaries, adorned(?), proceed. The men of Anunuw[a si]ng. The female singers [si]ng afterwa[rds]. The female *arkammi-* players play the *arkammi-* and *galgalturi-* instruments. § When the NIN.DINGIR arrives at the house of the hunting bags, the ⸢x x x⸣ sing in the gate house. (Then) the NIN.DINGIR goes in." (A cult ceremony follows.)[104] Otten, commenting on this last passage, interprets it as evidence that the house of the hunting bags was near the gatehouse.[105] Güterbock refutes this idea, citing other evidence that the house of the hunting bags was a "selbständiges Gebäude" and interpreting ^{É}*ḫilamni* in this passage as the gate house of the house of the hunting bags, where some cult functionaries stop and sing before the NIN.DINGIR actually enters the building.[106] In several passages in the KI.LAM Festival and other festivals cult ceremonies are described, after which comes the prescription "The gods come from the house of the hunting bags."[107] Important also is an Old Script chant in Hattic[108] "When the priest [co]mes from the house of the huntin[g bags]." Thus both priests and gods went into the house of the hunting bags, presumably (based on the other evidence of cult ceremonies there) for celebrating festivals or parts of festivals.

All of this is evidence that this structure was some kind of temple. The writings É $^{\text{D/KUŠ}}$*kuršaš* and ^{KUŠ}*kuršaš parna* exactly parallel the normal forms used for writing the names of other temples.[109] Several examples demonstrate the role of the house of the hunting bags in providing offering materials. These may also indicate that the house of the hunting bags was not simply a room in a larger temple complex but a free-standing building. Certainly the passage about the gate house of the house of the *kurša*-s cited above, if interpreted correctly by Güterbock, is good evidence for this. In addition, the examples of cultic ceremonies being held in the house of the hunting bags lead to the conclusion that this structure is a temple.[110]

103. That is, the image of Kantipuitti as a hunting bag. Popko, *Kultobjekte* 112, points out the importance of this passage as an example of the *kurša-* as a divine image.
104. *KBo* 10.27 iii 10′–20′ (Festival naming the NIN.DINGIR).
105. *FsFriedrich* 356.
106. *NHF* 68 n. 63.
107. For examples in the KI.LAM, see *ABoT* 5+ ii 18′ (Singer, *StBoT* 27: 91, "from the house of the fleece"), *KBo* 20.33+ obv. 13–16, translit. Singer, *StBot* 28: 89. The same prescription occurs in another festival fragment: *KBo* 20.5 rev? 6′ with duplicate *KBo* 22.224 obv. 4′. Popko, *Kultobjekte* 110, understands these references to the gods coming from the house of the *kurša*-s as the *kurša*-s themselves, as gods, coming out, which seems quite likely.
108. *KBo* 25.142+*KBo* 20.69 obv? 6′–7′, *CTH* 742, edited by Neu, *StBoT* 25: 229.
109. Pointed out by Güterbock, *CRRAI* 20: 125–26.
110. Houwink ten Cate, *FsOtten*² 190, mentions the festival for Zitḫariya in what he calls the "Temple of the (Divine) 'Fleeces.'"

The additional evidence from the text treated in *Chapter 4*, *KUB* 55.43, allows for three main conclusions. First, the house of the hunting bags is the place where the hunting bags were normally hung, with a regular place, the *AŠAR* DINGIR-*LIM*, "place of the god," prepared for them. This evidence of a special locus for the hunting bags to reside is supplemented by one reference to the "place of the *kurša*-s" (*kuršaš⸗pat pedi*) in a festival fragment.[111] The context of this fragment does not really provide information about what the place of the *kurša*-s might be, but in light of the opening passages of the *kurša*- Festival it is clear that the place of the *kurša*-s is the same as the *AŠAR* DINGIR-*LIM* "place of the god" of the *kurša*- Festival. There were of course occasions when the hunting bags like any other divine image were taken out of their own temple to other cult sites for a particular festival celebration, for example: É*ḫalentuwaš⸗ma⸗kan anda* [Ø] *ŠA* SAL.LUGAL D*Zitḫariyaš* [Ø] [*k*]*arū gankanza* [Ø] "In the *ḫalentu*- building, however, Zitḫariya of the queen (is) already hung."[112] The use of the verb *gank*- here indicates that it was the hunting bag of Zitḫariya as his cult symbol which was hung in the *ḫalentu*- during the festival procedures. In the Thunder Festival[113] the *kurša*- is moved out of a cult site: [L]Ú*ḫuldalaša* É*ḫa*[(*lentiuaz kurš*)]*an dai* "The *ḫuldala*- functionary takes the hunting bag from the *ḫalentu*- building." Second, more than one hunting bag was hung there, and therefore we must take *kuršaš* in the construction É KUŠ*kuršaš* (and other writings of the phrase) as a genitive plural and translate accordingly as "temple of the *kurša*-s." Third, the *kurša*-s function as the cult symbols for certain tutelary deities and therefore would be kept in a temple.

It is possible that the "house of the *kurša*-s" may be the same structure as the temple of Zitḫariya discussed in *Chapter 1* under that god. Popko[114] implies this understanding of the house of Zitḫariya. Since Zitḫariya is represented as a hunting bag and resides according to the *kurša*- Festival in the Temple of the Hunting Bags, the occurrences of Zitḫariya's house may be another way of referring to this temple.

ḪUR.SAG

KUB 55.43 ii 33, [l.e. 2] (*Chapter 4*). (Deified) mountains occur in lists of gods in several different kinds of texts, including treaties (list of oath deities), prayers, and festivals. Since in such a context ḪUR.SAG.MEŠ almost always occurs with ÍD.MEŠ, it is discussed together with ÍD.

ÍD

KUB 55.43 ii 33, [l.e. 2] (*Chapter 4*); *KUB* 9.21:3′, 9′, *IBoT* 1.2 iii 13, iv 11′, *KUB* 51.79 rev! 12′, *KUB* 44.2:5′ (*Chapter 5*). Besides occurring in the list of oath deities in treaties, in evocatios, and in prayers, ÍD.MEŠ, "rivers," as deities appear also in the

111. *KUB* 34.130 ii? 11, noted by Popko, *Kultobjekte* 109–10.

112. 315/t i 12′–14′ (fragment of a festival celebrated by the queen), ed. Alp, *Tempel* 230–31.

113. *KBo* 17.74 i 33, *CTH* 631, edited by Neu, *StBoT* 12 (1970) 14–15.

114. *Kultobjekte* 112.

festival texts. Rivers are sacrificed to in several different ways. Offerings in general: DINGIR.MEŠ-*naš ḫumandaš ANA* ḪUR.SAG.ḪI.A ÍD.MEŠ *ḫumandaš šippanti* "He makes offerings (or "libates") to all the gods and all the mountains (and) rivers."[115] These offerings to the mountains and river were considered important enough to be included in the *BĒL MADGALTI* instructions: *ANA* ḪUR.SAG.ḪI.A ÍD.ḪI.A *kuedaš* SISKUR.SISKUR *ešzi n〃aš šipanzakandu* "The mountains and rivers for which there is a ritual, let them regularly (iterative) make offerings to them."[116]

Some texts are more specific in describing the offerings for the mountains and rivers: 1 UDU *A*[*NA*] ḪUR.SAG[.MEŠ 1 UD]U *ANA* ÍD[.MEŠ 1 UDU] ... "One sheep t[o] the mountain[s, one she]ep to the river[s 1 sheep ...]."[117] In addition to animals being sacrificed, bread was broken to the mountains and rivers on a few occasions: [*n*]*〃ašta kī kue* ḪUR.SAG.MEŠ ÍD.MEŠ [*n*]*epiš tekan ŠUM-it ḫalzišai* [NIN]DA.Ì NINDA.KU$_7$-*ya paršiyannai* "These mountains (and) rivers, sky (and) earth which he calls by name, he regularly breaks fat bread and sweet bread (to them)."[118] Later in the same festival drink offerings for the mountains and rivers are again called for: EGIR-*ŠU〃ma nepiš tekan* GUB-*aš* 1-*ŠU ekuzi* EGIR-*ŠU-ma* ḪUR.SAG.MEŠ ÍD.MEŠ [GU]B?-*aš* 1-*ŠU ekuzi* "Afterwards he drinks the sky (and) earth once, standing. Afterwards he drinks the mountains (and) rivers once, standing."[119]

One might expect ÍD.MEŠ to occur frequently with *ḫareš* "valleys," but in fact there is only one other occurrence of ÍD with *ḫare-* besides *KUB* 55.43 ii 33 and [l.e. 2]. Although also in a text devoted to a tutelary deity, the Ritual for the Tutelary Deity of the Hunting Bag, the context is different:[120] ᴰLAMMA ᴷᵁŠ*kursa*[*n*] *araḫzenaš* KUR.KUR.MEŠ-*az ḫumandaz* [Ḫ]UR.SAG.MEŠ-*az ḫariyaz* ÍD.MEŠ-*az ḫan*[*t*]*iyaššaz* TÚL.MEŠ-*az uelluwaz* [*talli*]*škiwen mukiškiwen* "We called and implored the Tutelary Deity of the Hunting Bag from all the surrounding lands, from the mountains, the valleys, the rivers, the lakes(?),[121] the springs, (and) the meadows."[122]

LÚ.MEŠ UR.GI$_7$

KUB 55.43 ii passim, iii 5′, iv passim; *KBo* 13.179:11′ (*Chapter 4*). See Friedrich, *ZA* 15 (1950) 253 with n. 3; Jakob-Rost, *Or* 35 (1966) 417–22; Kammenhuber, *HbOr* I Abt., II Bd., 1. und 2. Abschnitt, Lief. 2 (1969) 435; and Pecchioli Daddi, *Mestieri* (1982) 376–78. Friedrich notes that in the Kešši myth LÚ UR.GI$_7$ must mean "hunter." Jakob-Rost summarizes, with text citations, the available evidence for the "dog-men," pointing out that

115. *KBo* 4.1 i 6–7 (Ritual by the Enemy Border).
116. *KUB* 13.2 iii 8 (*BĒL MADGALTI* Instructions), ed. von Schuler, *Dienstanw.* 47.
117. *KUB* 2.2+ iv 18 (Hattic bilingual for the consecration of a temple), ed. Schuster, *HHB* 76.
118. *KUB* 10.72 ii 19′–21′ (fest. frag.).
119. *KUB* 10.72 v 20–22 (fest. frag.).
120. The broken passage in *KUB* 55.43 is the only one in which "valleys" receive offerings.
121. See above discussion of *ḫantiyašša-* in this appendix.
122. *KBo* 20.107+*KBo* 23.50+ ii 10–13.

they almost always occur in cultic context, the exceptions being the laws (§88) and the myth of Kešši (*KUB* 33.121 ii 3′), and that their primary role in the cult is to bark or to sing. Pecchioli Daddi in *Mestieri* suggests that LÚ UR.GI$_7$ can mean two different things, "hunter" and "dog-man."

These studies summarize the available information about the LÚ(.MEŠ) UR.GI$_7$ very well. What the new evidence from *KUB* 55.43 adds to our knowledge of this title is the close association of the LÚ.MEŠ UR.GI$_7$ with the hunting bag as seen in their important role in the *kurša*- Festival. Another passage in which the dog-men are involved with the hunting bag is in an oracle about festivals: *INA* É ^{D}*kuršaš*-*ma* EZEN x[o o UD]U.ḪI.A LÚ.MEŠ UR.GI$_7$ *unniyanzi* "The dog-men drive [the she]ep into the temple of the hunting bags for the festival of [x]."[123] This passage not only associates the dog-men once again with the hunting bag but also demonstrates that one of their duties was driving sheep into the temple of the hunting bags during the performing of a festival. It is even possible that the festival being inquired about in *KUB* 22.27 iv 17 was in fact the festival of the renewing of the *kurša*-s, since the dog-men are nowhere else attested in festival context driving animals, and the temple of the hunting bags and the dog-men both play important roles in the *kurša*- Festival. This brings to mind *KBo* 13.179:11′–12′, treated in *Chapter 4*, in which the dog-men kill a goat after it has been driven into certain "buildings of the palace." The evidence from the *KUB* 22.27 passage leads us to ask if the impersonal "they" who drive in the goat in *KBo* 13.179 §2 were the dog-men. The most important point to be derived from the *KUB* 22.27 passage is not the fact that the LÚ.MEŠ UR.GI$_7$ are attested in this one text driving animals, but that, as in *KUB* 55.43, they are closely associated with the hunting bag.

Perhaps the most important evidence for understanding the role of the dog-men in the cult is the fact that, as noted in the comments on *wappiya*-, the dog-men are one of only three possible subjects attested for *wappiya*-, which, from its occurrences with UR.GI$_7$ is secure in its meaning "to bark." With the new examples from *KUB* 55.43 of the dog-men barking, they are by far the most common subject of *wappiya*-. In addition, these occurrences in the *kurša*- Festival are the most examples of dog-men barking in one festival. Their barking throughout the festival (and in other festivals) might indicate that they are representing dogs, but it may also show nothing more than that they bark as part of their duties. This could be expected of hunters who use hunting dogs or of professional dog-handlers.[124] If they are hunters, Pecchioli Daddi's distinction between hunters and dog-men becomes unnecessary. The prominent role of the dog-men in the *kurša*- Festival points out their close connection with the tutelary deities and the hunting bag and reinforces the idea that they may very well be hunters or handlers of hunting dogs.

123. *KUB* 22.27 iv 17.

124. Güterbock, *FsKantor* 118, suggests that they were perhaps the men in charge of the hunting dogs.

Numbers

3-*e*

IBoT 1.2 obv. iii 10 (*Chapter 5*). The form 2-*e* also occurs and is more frequent than 3-*e*. The complementation 3-*e* is most unusual; it only occurs in four other places. The best preserved of these is *KUB* 11.30+*IBoT* 4.197 rev. iii 22′–23′ (Festival of Zippalanda): LUGAL-*uš irḫawanzi tiyazi* 3-*e*! *irḫaizzi* "The king proceeds in order to treat with offerings. He makes offerings in sequence to 3 (gods)." Reverse iv 6′–7′ of the same text reads: LUGAL-*uš irḫaw*[*anzi tiyazi*] 3-*e*! NINDA *irḫaizz*[*i*] "The king [proceeds] in order [to] treat with offerings. He makes offerings in sequence to 3 (gods) (with) bread." I would restore the third example, 355/t rev. 7′–8′ as follows: *ta* LUGAL-*u*[*š irḫawanzi tiyazi*] 3-*e* *irḫa*[*izzi*] on the basis of the *KUB* 11.30+ passage. In the only other occurrence of 3-*e* outside of our text, *KBo* 25.66 obv. ii 2′, the word after 3-*e* is broken away, leaving only a trace of the first sign, which is consistent with the *ir* sign. This third attestation thus probably also occurs with a form of the verb *irḫai-*. In the *IBoT* 1.2 passage 3-*e* also occurs with *irḫai-*. This consistent use of 3-*e* only with the verb *irḫai-* provides a clue as to what this particular complementation of "three" denotes, although the examples are too few to posit a definite meaning for this complementation of the numeral "3." Friedrich, *HW* 302, lists 3-*e* as an alternate form of the accusative. This may be correct, as it could be interpreted in its known attestations as an object of *irḫai-*, considering an understood (gods) as the actual object and 3-*e* the adjective modifying this understood object. It is also possible that it is a locative, "in three places," which also would make sense in the examples which we have of 3-*e*.

Akkadian

AŠRU (*AŠAR* DINGIR-*LIM*)

KUB 55.43 i 9, 11, iii 15′ (*Chapter 4*). This phrase, "the place of the god," is attested only in this one text. The place of the god, which in this text is a location assigned as the place where the hunting bag was normally hung, was not something that needed to be specified in other cultic texts. Lines i 9 and 11 when taken together are instructive as to its nature, as they describe how the old hunting bags are hung below the *AŠAR* DINGIR-*LIM*, and the new ones on it. The only examples known to me of *AŠAR* in a phrase similar to this occur in *KUB* 53.12 obv. iii 22′ and 24′ (Festival for Telipinu), which describe holding a sheep in the *AŠAR* ᴰ*Kattaḫḫa* "place of Kattaḫḫa." This is the only text which specifies the place of a particular deity. Otten comments on *AŠAR* DINGIR-*LIM*=*pat* in i 9, with the tentative translation "Götterbild, Götterstatue, göttlicher Ort" and the alternative suggestion that the phrase indicated a "Kultplatz" where the hunting bag was hung.[125] Presumably the place of the god is normally the niche where his cult statue was placed. Because of the unusual (if not unique) nature of the hunting bag as a cult representation, it

125. *FsFriedrich* 356.

required a special sacred locus or "place of the god." Hence this text, which describes the festivals for the gods thus represented, uses a term unnecessary for most cultic prescriptions. This locus is also prescribed in the festival fragment *KUB* 34.130 ii? 11:[126] [KU]Š*kuršan* KUŠ*kuršaš⸗pat pedi ka*[*nkanzi*] "[They ha]ng the hunting bag in the very place of the hunting bags."

Divine Names

DḪu(wa)riyanzipa

KUB 51.79 rev! 10′ and all duplicates; *KUB* 44.2:3′ with duplicate *KUB* 44.3:5′ (*Chapter 5*). See Laroche, *RHA* VII/45 (1945–46) 7; idem, *Rech.* (1947) 67; Kammenhuber, *KZ* 77 (1961) 187–88 with n. 2; Otten and von Soden, *StBoT* 7 (1968) 28 n. 3; Frantz-Szabó, *RLA* 4 (1972–75) 503–04. This god is very poorly attested; Laroche comments, *RHA* VII/45 (1945–46) 7, that "Ḫurijanzipaš est très obscur." He later catalogues this name with those divine names that are formed with a suffix *-šipa*, a substantive with the sense of "genie or demon," and proposes a tentative meaning "genie du *ḫurija* ?"[127] This god's name is attested in two different stems. As Ḫuriyanzipa- he occurs once in a Ḫurri bird oracle question (*KUB* 5.7 obv. 17) and three times in festival texts (*KBo* 22.192 rev. 9, *KUB* 20.4 i 13′ and 16′). As Ḫuwariyanzipa- he occurs in one of the fragments naming the SAL.MEŠ*zintuḫeš* (*KBo* 30.164+*KUB* 44.13 obv. iii 24′), in two different festival fragments (*KBo* 20.101:14′ and *IBoT* 2.30:7′), and in our text, a festival for the Tutelary Deity of the River. The specifically localized deity "Ḫuwariyanzipa of Šamuḫa" which we have in the tutelary deity festival does not occur in any of the other examples.

DGulšeš

KUB 9.21:6′ (*Chapter 5*). On DGulšeš in general see Otten, *RLA* 3 (1957–71) 698, with previous literature cited there. More recently the Gulšeš are discussed by Otten and Siegelová, *AfO* 23 (1970) 32–38, and Beckman, *StBoT* 29 (1983) 80 n. 196 and 241–45. The expression that concerns us in *KUB* 9.21:6′, *wappuwaš* D*Gulšeš*, is extremely rare, occurring in two other places. One is in a ritual fragment: *n⸗aš* EGIR-*pa tuk AN*[(*A* ÍD *wap*)]*wašša* D*Gulašša* DINGIR.MAḪ.MEŠ *paiz*[(*zi*)] "He goes to you, the river, and to the fate deities of the riverbank, (and) the MAḪ deities."[128] The second passage is in a ritual against sorcery: *ezzatten wappuwaš* D*Gulšuš*, *KUB* 17.27 ii 20′, translated by Goetze, *ANET* 347 as "Eat, ye demons of the clay pit!" Goetze translates the *KUB* 9.21:6′ passage

126. Noted by Popko, *AOF* 2 (1975) 68, and idem, *Kultobjekte* 109–10.

127. Laroche, *Rech.* 67.

128. A = Bo 3617 obv. i 15′–16′, B = Bo 3078 obv. ii?, C = *KBo* 13.104+Bo 6464 obv. ii, ed. Otten and Siegelová, *AfO* 23 (1970) 33, with the translation "so kommt er zu dir, dem Fluš, und zu den Gulš-Gottheiten des Ufers und den MAḪ-Gottheiten."

as "[Afterwards] he 'drinks' the Gulšeš of the clay pit."[129] The occurrence of *wappuwaš* ^{D}*Gulšeš* in *KUB* 9.21 in a festival for the Tutelary Deity of the River and in a context where gods of the river are receiving drink offerings argues for a translation "fate deities of the riverbank" instead of the "clay pit."

^{D}LAMMA.

See *Chapter 1* for a discussion of the various names and titles of the tutelary deities.

^{D}Šalawani-

KUB 51.79 rev! 11′; *IBoT* 2.19:2′; *KUB* 44.2:4′; *KUB* 44.3:6′ (*Chapter 5*). On this group of gods see Laroche, *NH* 259 n. 25; Otten, *StBoT* 7 (1968) 28; Jakob-Rost, *THeth* 2 (1972) 83; and Kammenhuber, *HW*², Lief. 6/7 (1982) 411b, 412b sub *aška-*. This name always occurs in the plural denoting a group of gods, they occur only in festival and ritual texts, and they are always (where the text is sufficiently well preserved) described as "of the gate(s)." In almost every case the gate is unspecified, but in *KBo* 10.27 iv 28–29 (fest. frag. naming the NIN.DINGIR) we have KÁ.GAL *ašušaš* ^{D}*Šalawanaš*, "the Šalawani-deities of the gate of the *ašuša*-s," in a list of gods who are to receive offerings.

GEOGRAPHICAL NAMES

^{D}Karepa/Karepati

KUB 51.79 rev! 8′; *KUB* 44.2:1′ with duplicate *KUB* 44.3:2′–3′ (*Chapter 5*). As with other geographical locations, these names can occur as deified loci with a divine determinative. Concerning these names two questions suggest themselves: First, are these two separate entities or simply variants of one name? Second, what kind of name(s) are they? They are attested only in *CTH* 684.3, in the main text, the parallel, and a duplicate to the parallel text. The only other passage cited in *RGTC* 6: 533, *KBo* 11.21 (right column) 3′, should be read ^{TÚL}*Ka-ri-t*[*a*(-). Tischler treats Karepa and Karepati as one name under the rubric Karipa and categorizes it as a "Quellname," but the evidence suggests that the situation with these names is more complex than he indicates in *RGTC* 6.

KUB 44.3:2′–3′ is the most important passage for answering our first question. There we have secure evidence that there are two separate names,]^{x}*Ka-re-e-*[*pa* in line 2′ and $^{?}$*Ka-*]*re-e-pa-ti* in line 3′. Although he cites both of these passages in *RGTC* 6: 533, Tischler does not take *KUB* 44.3 as evidence that Karepa and Karepati may actually be two different names. As *KUB* 44.3 is a fragment of a list of deities who are to receive offerings, it is unlikely that there would be variant spellings of the same name in one list. *RGTC* 6 reads line 2′ as]*x ka-ri-e*[-, but there is no word space before the *ka* sign, so the broken sign preceding it is probably a determinative. The preserved trace of this determinative is ambiguous but would allow either ^{DING}]^{IR} or ^{TÚ}]^{L} to be read. In *KUB* 44.3:3′ the beginning of the name, including the determinative, is completely lost. *KUB* 44.3 thus

129. *Language* 29 (1953) 274.

serves to demonstrate the existence of the two distinct names Kare[pa] and [Ka]repati but provides no evidence for our second question as to what type of name these are, whether they be divine name, spring name, or something else.

For this second question we have the evidence of *KUB* 51.79 rev! 8′ and *KUB* 44.2:1′. The *KUB* 51.79 passage is the only place in which either word occurs with a preserved TÚL determinative. The *RGTC* 6 citation of Bo 858 is now *KUB* 51.79 rev! 8′ and should be corrected to ^{TÚL}*Ka-re-e-pa-a-at-ti*. This one clear example is sufficient to indicate that there was indeed a spring named Karepat(t)i. In *KUB* 44.2:1′, although most of the signs in the first line are partially broken away, the line is sufficiently readable for us to be sure that the determinative for Karepa is DINGIR, and that Kar[epati], if correctly restored from the duplicate *KUB* 44.3, also has a DINGIR determinative. *RGTC* 6 reads *KUB* 44.2′: as]*x ka-a-ri-pa-an*, but there is a word space after *ka-a-ri-pa*, and the following *an* sign may therefore be read as a DINGIR determinative. Tischler's reading as an accusative form would be suspect in this text anyway, as all the other names in the list are d.-l. forms, indirect objects of *šipant-*. In *KUB* 44.2:1′, in a list of deities such as this, one would expect another divine name. Lebrun, *Samuha* 176, reads the sign as a DINGIR determinative but restores ^{D}*Ka-aš*[*-ta-ma*. The duplicate *KUB* 44.3:3′ and the parallel *KUB* 51.79 rev! 8′ indicate, however, that the correct restoration must be ^{D}Kar[(epati)].

This occurrence of ^{D}Kar[(epati)] in *KUB* 44.2:1′ in conjunction with ^{TÚL}Karepatti in *KUB* 51.79 rev! 8′ indicates that Karepat(t)i was the name of a spring, like many others a holy place whose name could be written either with a TÚL or a DINGIR determinative. Although the name Karepa may also have been a spring name in *KUB* 44.3:2′, where the trace of the determinative is inconclusive, and in *KUB* 51.79 rev! 8′, where the name has been completely restored, the only attested determinative for Karepa is DINGIR, in *KUB* 44.2:1′. It is quite possible then that Karepa is the name of a deity only, in which case the (divine) spring name Karepat(t)i may be derived from that deity's name. Using the evidence discussed above, I restore [^{D}Karepa] in *KUB* 51.79 rev! 8′.

^{ÍD}Nakkiliya

KUB 51.79 rev! 12′; *IBoT* 2.19:3′; *KUB* 44.2:5′; *KUB* 44.3:7′ (*Chapter 5*). All but one of the occurrences of this river cited in *RGTC* 6: 540–41 are from the various duplicates of this text. The exception is Bo 983, now *KUB* 57.32, which is a small fragment that does not seem to be related to our text. The *KUB* 57 passage is the only one in which a clear ÍD determinative is preserved to indicate that this is definitely a river name. The list of deities receiving drink offerings in *KUB* 51.79 §4′ is an unusual list because it contains several deified locations which are either unique in this text or at least extremely rare, and this river is one of those. Tischler points out in *RGTC* 6: 541 that ^{ÍD}Nakkiliya is very probably the same river as ^{ÍD}Nakkiliyata. This latter form of the name is also very rare; all the occurrences which he cites are in *KUB* 36.89 (Ritual to bring back the Stormgod of Nerik). *KUB* 57.32, which contains the only occurrence of the river Nakkiliya outside of *CTH* 684.3, is a duplicate of this ritual. To the *RGTC* 6 references for ^{ÍD}Nakkiliyata add *KUB* 36.88 obv. 12 (Prayer to the god of Nerik) and *KUB* 36.49 obv. i 11 (mythological fragment). There is a personal name *Nakili*(*a*)*t* (*NH* #850) on which Laroche, *NH* 309, comments briefly in relation to this river name.

URUZapatiškuwa

KUB 55.43, passim; *KUB* 7.36 rev. rt. 15′, rev. left [3′]; *KBo* 8.97+*KBo* 21.89 iv 18′ (*Chapter 4*). All occurrences of this city name are in the phrase DLAMMA URUZapatiškuwa, "the Tutelary Deity of Zapatiškuwa," and the passages cited above are the only occurrences of this phrase. Thus the city of Zapatiškuwa is never mentioned outside of cultic texts for tutelary deities, and its only importance seems to have been in connection with its own Tutelary Deity. The fact that the old hunting bag of the Tutelary Deity of Ḫatenzuwa is renamed the Tutelary Deity of Zapatiškuwa but is taken to Durmitta may indicate that Zapatiškuwa was a Hattian city which had at some point given its name to this particular tutelary deity but had since diminished in its importance in the cult to the point that even the tutelary deity named for the city no longer resided there but was now taken to Durmitta.

APPENDIX C

TABLES OF SIGN SHAPES FOR SELECTED TABLETS

As noted in the *Introduction*, paleography of script is an essential aid in the dating of individual Hittite tablets and, in turn, an essential part of reconstructing Hittite history. The paleography of many of the festival texts is discussed in the commentaries of *Chapters 2–5*. The following tables of selected sign shapes for eight of the larger texts are intended to supplement those discussions. Signs that are generally agreed upon as "diagnostic," whose changes over the course of Hittite scribal history have been traced by modern scholars, are included. Numbers refer to the system developed by Rüster and Neu, *Hethitisches Zeichenlexikon*.

Table 1. Bo 3298+*KUB* 25.32+*KUB* 27.70+1628/u

Sign	*Examples*	*Sign*	*Examples*
7 tar	none	187 e*	ii 10, iii 14′, iii 42′ 
30 gi	none	192 SAG	i 39, iii 14′ 
39 nam	none	197 un	iii 32′, iv 4 
40 en	none	209 zu	none
43 ru	none	214 da*	i 54, ii 2, ii 24, iii 24′ 
44 ip*	i 52, iii 6′, iii 39′, iii 44′ 	215 it	none
67 ik	i 35, ii 14 	229 URU*	i 25, i 40 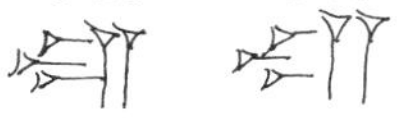
69 KÙ	none	265 *Ù*	none
72 ni*	i 33, iii 31′ 	313 ki	i 32, iii 15′, iii 17′ 
81 ak	none	343 li*	i 33, ii 22 
92 az	i 27 	353 šar	none
93 uk	ii 19 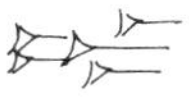	357 me*	i 42, ii 30, iv 3 
115 LUGAL*	ii 46, iii 15′ 	360 MEŠ*	i 32, ii 16, iii 12′ 
128 du	ii 47, iii 30′ 	364 *ANA**	i 29, ii 36 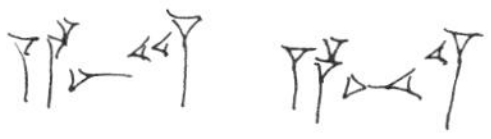
183 al*	i 43, ii 30, iii 19′ 	367 ḫa*	i 27, ii 4 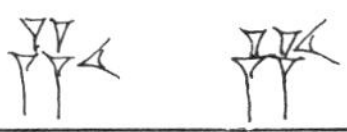

*More than four examples

Table 2. *KUB* 2.1

Sign	*Examples*	*Sign*	*Examples*
7 tar*	i 45, ii 22, iii 2 	187 e*	ii 40, iii 28, iii 29 
30 gi	iii 26, iii 31, iii 42 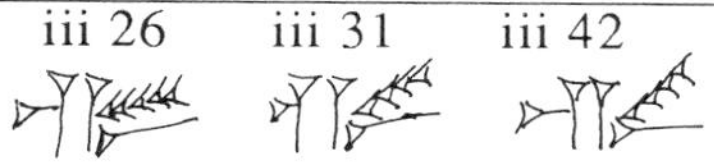	192 SAG*	i 45, ii 38, iv 37, vi 7 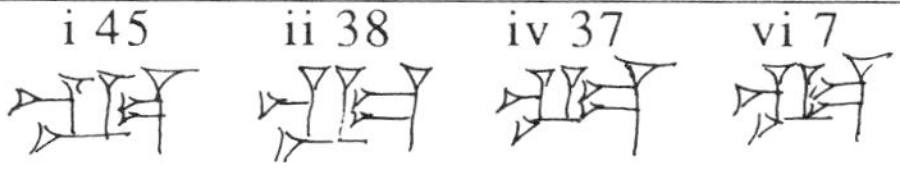
39 nam	none	197 un	i 50, ii 49 
40 en	none	209 zu	none
43 ru	ii 35 	214 da*	i 42, i 45, ii 20, iv 6 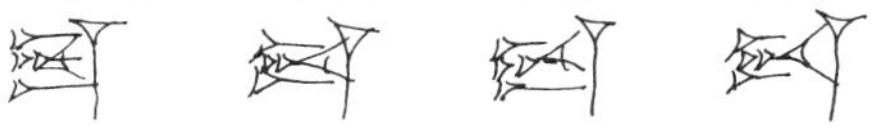
44 ip	none	215 it	ii 16 
67 ik	none	229 URU*	i 43, i 48, i 51 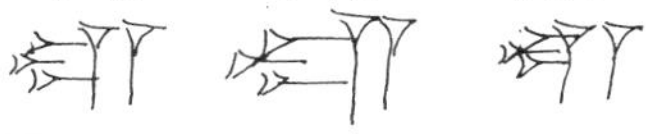
69 KÙ	none	265 *Ù*	none
72 ni	ii 50 	313 ki*	ii 29, ii 37, vi 3, vi 8 
81 ak	iii 5 	343 li*	i 44, ii 38 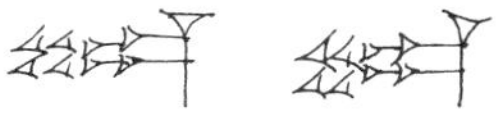
92 az	none	353 šar	iii 12, iv 2 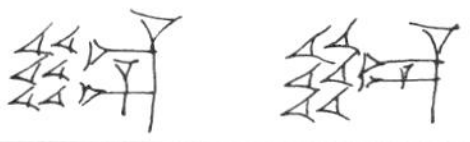
93 uk	none	357 me	iii 25, iii 29 
115 LUGAL	vi 5 	360 MEŠ	ii 13 
128 du	iv 33, iv 33 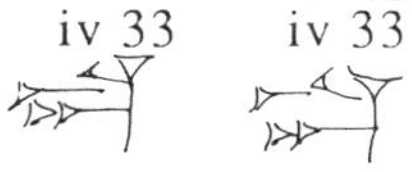	364 *ANA*	i 42 
183 al	iv 1 	367 ḫa*	i 43, ii 20 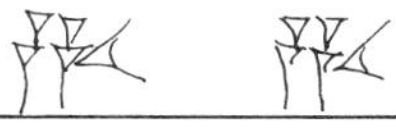

*More than four examples

Table 3. *KBo* 22.189

Sign	Examples	Sign	Examples
7 tar	v 2′ 	187 e*	ii 13, ii 13 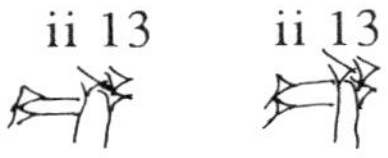
30 gi	none	192 SAG	none
39 nam	none	197 un	none
40 en	iv 5′ 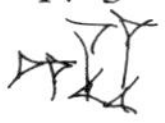	209 zu	none
43 ru	none	214 da*	ii 11, ii 13, iii 10, v 4′ 
44 ip	none	215 it	none
67 ik	ii 11 	229 URU	none
69 KÙ	iii 6 	265 *Ù*	none
72 ni	ii 9, ii 10, vi 2′ 	313 ki	ii 1, iii 5 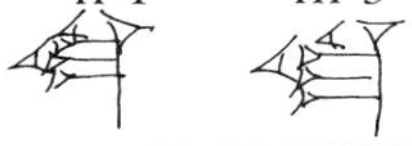
81 ak	none	343 li	ii 12 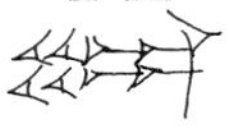
92 az	v 6′ 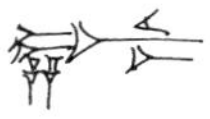	353 šar	none
93 uk	none	357 me*	ii 4, ii 13, iv 9′ 
115 LUGAL*	ii 2, iv 4′, iv 7′ 	360 MEŠ*	ii 10, v 7′, v 11′, v 12′ 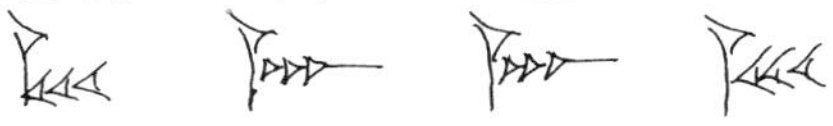
128 du	none	364 *ANA*	none
183 al	none	367 ḫa*	ii 10, iv 5′, iv 7′, v 9′ 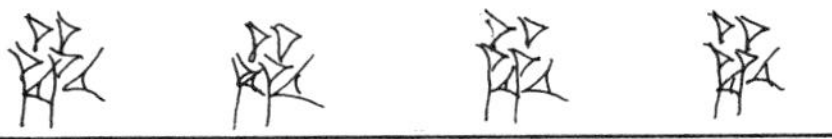

*More than four examples

Table 4. *KBo* 11.40

Sign	*Examples*	*Sign*	*Examples*
7 tar	ii 17′ 	187 e*	vi 3′ vi 21′ vi 27′ 
30 gi	vi 30′ 	192 SAG*	ii 3′ v 15′ vi 10′ vi 26′ 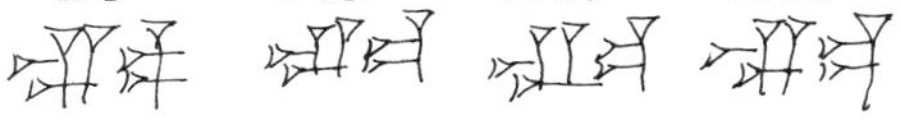
39 nam	none	197 un	none
40 en	v 13′ 	209 zu	v 13′ 
43 ru	none	214 da*	i 5′ i 24′ 
44 ip	none	215 it	ii 5′ 
67 ik	none	229 URU*	i 26′ vi 11′ 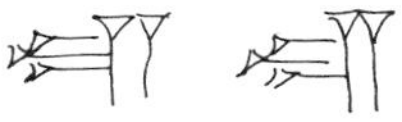
69 KÙ	none	265 *Ù*	none
72 ni	none	313 ki*	vi 3′ vi 12′ vi 16′ vi 22′ 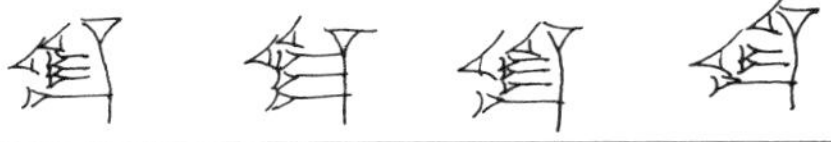
81 ak	none	343 li*	ii 11′ v 3′ vi 6′ vi 12′ 
92 az	none	353 šar	none
93 uk	none	357 me	none
115 LUGAL	none	360 MEŠ*	vi 14′ 
128 du*	i 21′ v 5′ 	364 *ANA**	v 17′ vi 7′ 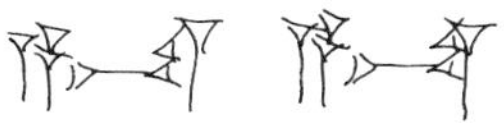
183 al	i 10′ 	367 ḫa*	v 13′ vi 13′ 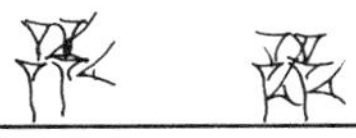

*More than four examples

Table 5. *KUB* 55.43

Sign	*Examples*	*Sign*	*Examples*
7 tar	none	187 e	i 7, i 21, ii 4, iii 29′ 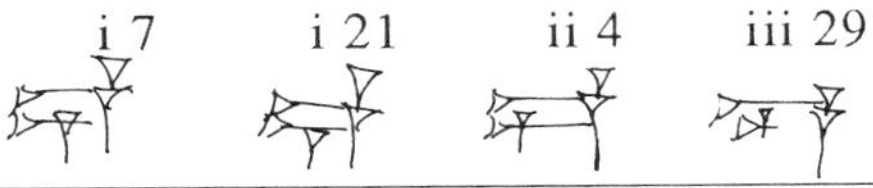
30 gi	none	192 SAG	none clear
39 nam	none	197 un	ii 17, iv 5′, iv 27′ 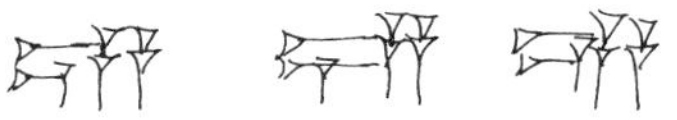
40 en	i 1, i 6, iii 32′, iv 20′ 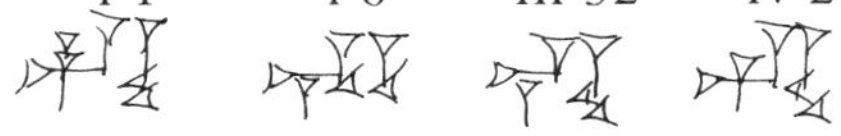	209 zu	i 1, i 23, ii 21, iv 20′ 
43 ru	i 8, iii 14′, iii 30′ 	214 da	i 8 
44 ip	iii 33′ 	215 it	i 1, i 5 
67 ik	ii 16, iii 29′ 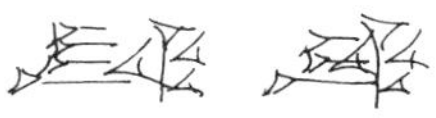	229 URU	i 6, i 12, i 20, i 24 
69 KÙ	none	265 *Ù*	i 1, i 6 
72 ni	iii 24′, iii 36′ 	313 ki	i 29, ii 16, ii 16 
81 ak	i 12 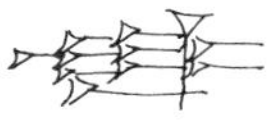	343 li	iii 33′ 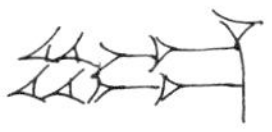
92 az	i 21, iii 34′ 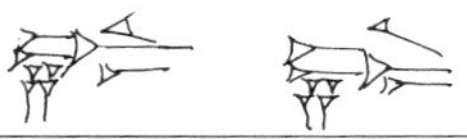	353 šar	i 11, iv 31′ 
93 uk	i 4, iii 30′ 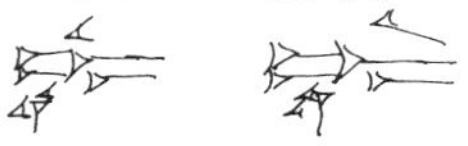	357 me	iii 4′ 
115 LUGAL	none	360 MEŠ*	ii 7, ii 20, ii 33(1st), iv 27′ 
128 du	i 9, iv 26′ 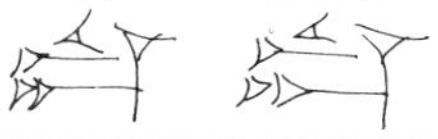	364 *ANA**	i 9, iv 8′ 
183 al	i 10, iv 34′ 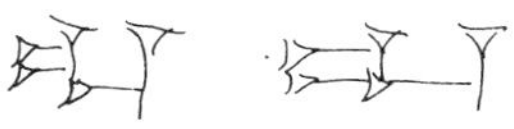	367 ḫa	i 2, iii 12′ 

*More than four examples

Table 6. *KBo* 21.89+*KBo* 8.97

Sign	*Examples*	*Sign*	*Examples*
7 tar	i 5′ 	187 e	ii 22′  iii 14′ 
30 gi	none	192 SAG	none
39 nam	ii 13′  iii 21′ 	197 un	ii 17′ 
40 en	iv 15′ 	209 zu	iv 15′  iv 22″ 
43 ru	none	214 da*	i 10′  ii 17′ 
44 ip	none	215 it	i 12′ 
67 ik	ii 11′ 	229 URU	i 16′  i 17′ 
69 KÙ	none	265 *Ù*	none
72 ni	ii 17′ 	313 ki	ii 24′ 
81 ak	ii 26′ 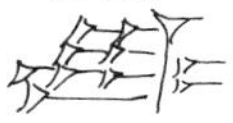	343 li	i 20′ 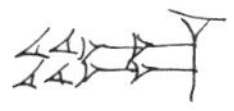
92 az	none	353 šar	none
93 uk	none	357 me	none
115 LUGAL	none	360 MEŠ	iii 14′ 
128 du	ii 24′ 	364 *ANA**	i 12′  ii 7′ 
183 al	none	367 ḫa*	i 12′ 

*More than four examples

Table 7. *IBoT* 1.2

Sign	*Examples*	*Sign*	*Examples*
7 tar	none	187 e	iii 10  iv 11′ 
30 gi	none	192 SAG	none
39 nam	iii 8′ 	197 un	none
40 en	ii 3 	209 zu	none
43 ru	iv 9′ 	214 da*	iii 12  iv 6′ 
44 ip	none	215 it	none
67 ik	none	229 URU	iv 8′  iv 13′ 
69 KÙ	none	265 *Ù*	none
72 ni	iv 13′ 	313 ki	none
81 ak	none	343 li	iv 2′ 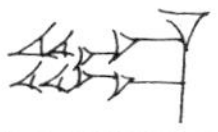
92 az	none	353 šar	ii 8 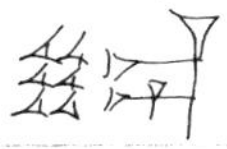
93 uk	none	357 me	none
115 LUGAL	iii 10 	360 MEŠ	iv 8′  iv 13′ 
128 du	none	364 *ANA*	none
183 al	none	367 ḫa	iii 7 

*More than four examples

Table 8. *KUB* 51.79

Sign	*Examples*	*Sign*	*Examples*
7 tar	obv! 21′ 	187 e*	obv! 4′ rev! 8′ 
30 gi	none	192 SAG	rev! 5′ 
39 nam	obv! 11′ 	197 un	none
40 en	none	209 zu	none
43 ru	obv! 2′ obv! 23′ rev! 21′ 	214 da*	obv! 9′ obv! 9′ rev! 17′ 
44 ip	none	215 it	none
67 ik	none	229 URU	rev! 14′ 
69 KÙ	none	265 *Ù*	none
72 ni	rev! 16′ rev! 17′ 	313 ki*	obv! 11′ rev! 1′ rev! 12′ 
81 ak	rev! 12′ 	343 li*	obv! 5′ obv! 10′ rev! 11′ 
92 az	obv! 16′ 	353 šar	none
93 uk	none	357 me	none
115 LUGAL	obv! 10′ 	360 MEŠ	none
128 du	rev! 9′ 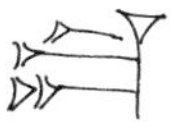	364 *ANA*	obv! 14′ 
183 al	obv! 8′ obv! 21′ 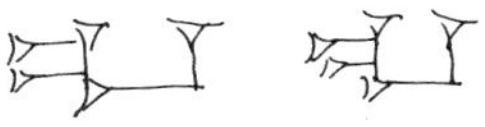	367 ḫa	obv! 16′ rev! 10′ 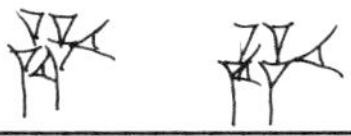

*More than four examples

BIBLIOGRAPHY

Alp, Sedat. *Untersuchungen zu den Beamtennamen im hethitischen Festzeremoniell. Sammlung Orientalischer Arbeiten* 5. Leipzig: Otto Harrassowitz, 1940.

———. *Beiträge zur Erforschung des hethitischen Tempels.* Ankara: Türk Tarih Kurumu Basımevi, 1983.

———. "GIŠ*kalmuş* 'Lituus' and ḪUB.BI 'Earring' in the Hittite Texts." *Belleten* XII/46 (1948) 320–24.

———. "Die Lage der heth. Kultstadt Karaḫna im Lichte der Maşat-Texte." *FsBittel*, pp. 43–46.

———. "Hititlerin dinsel törenlerinde kullanılan temizlik maddesi *tuḫḫueššar* üzerinde bir inceleme." *Belleten* XLVI/182 (1982) 247–59.

———. "Zu den Körperteilnamen im Hethitischen." *Anadolu* 2 (1957) 1–48.

Archi, A. "Das Kultmahl bei den Hethitern." *Kongreye Sunulan Bildiriler, 1. Cilt*, pp. 197–213. Published by Sekizinci Türk Tarih Kongresi, 11–15 Ekim 1976. Ankara: Türk Tarih Kurumu Basımevi, 1979.

———. "Divinità Tutelari e *Sondergötter* Ittiti." *SMEA* 16 (1975) 89–117.

———. "Fêtes de printemps et d'automne et reintégration rituelle d'images de culte dans l'Anatolie hittite." *UF* 5 (1973) 7–27.

———. "Note sulle feste ittite–I." *RSO* 52 (1978) 19–26.

Archi, A. and Klengel, H. "Ein hethitischer Text über die Reorganisation des Kultes." *AOF* 7 (1980) 143–57.

Ardzinba, V. G. "On the Structure and the Functions of Hittite Festivals." *Gesellschaft und Kultur im alten Vorderasien*, pp. 11–16. H. Klengel, ed. Berlin: Akademie Verlag, 1982.

Badalì, Enrico. "LÚALAM.ZU$_x$: Adoratore di Statue o Clown?" *Bibbia e Oriente* 139/(1984)/ XXVI Anno 45–53.

———. "Il significato del verbo ittito *palwae-*." *Or* 59 (1990) 130–42.

Balkan, Kemal. *İnandık'ta 1966 Yılında Bulunan Eski Hitit Çagına ait bir Bağış Belgesi.* Ankara: Türk Tarih Kurumu Basımevi, 1973.

Bayburtluoğlu, Ceydet. *Akurgal'a Armağan (Festschrift Akurgal).* Part 1: *Anadolu (Anatolia)* 21 (1978/1980). Ankara: Dil ve Tarih-Çoğrafya Fakültesi Basımevi, 1987.

———. *Akurgal'a Armağan (Festschrift Akurgal).* Part 2: *Anadolu* 22 (1981/1983). Ankara: Dil ve Tarih-Çoğrafya Fakültesi Basımevi, 1989.

Beckman, G. "A Contribution to Hittite Onomastic Studies." *JAOS* 103 (1983) 623–27.

———. *Hittite Birth Rituals.* 2nd rev. ed. *StBoT* 29. Wiesbaden: Otto Harrassowitz, 1983.

Beckman, G. and Hoffner, Harry A. *Hittite Fragments in American Collections. JCS* 37 (1985) 1–60.

Beal, Richard. *The Organization of the Hittite Military.* Ph.D. diss., University of Chicago, 1986.

Bilgiç, E. "Die Ortsnamen der 'kappadokischen' Urkunden im Rahmen der alten Sprachen Anatoliens." *AfO* 15 (1945–51) 1–37.

Biran, A., ed. *Temples and High Places in Biblical Times. Proceedings of the Colloquium in Honor of the Centennial of Hebrew Union College.* Jerusalem: Hebrew Union College, 1981.

Bittel, K. *Beitrag zur Kenntnis hethitischer Bildkunst. SHAW* 1976/4. Heidelberg: Carl Winter Universitätsverlag, 1976.

———. *Die Hethiter.* Munich: Verlag C. H. Beck, 1976.

———. "Hittite Temples and High Places in Anatolia and North Syria." *Temples and High Places in Bibilical Times. Proceedings of the Colloquium in Honor of the Centennial of Hebrew Union College*, pp. 63–73. A. Biran, ed. Jerusalem: Hebrew Union College, 1981.

Bittel, K. and Güterbock, H. G. *Boğazköy 1. Neue Untersuchungen in der Hethitischen Hauptstadt.* Berlin: Verlag der Akademie der Wissenschaften, 1935.

Bittel, K., Houwink ten Cate, Ph. H. J., and Reiner, E., eds. *Anatolian Studies Presented to Hans Gustav Güterbock on the Occasion of his 65th Birthday.* Istanbul: Nederlands Historisch-Archaeologisch Instituut in het Nabije Oosten, 1973.

Bittel, K., Boessneck, J., Damm, B., Güterbock, H. G., Hauptman, H., Naumann, R., and Schirmer, W. *Das hethitische Felsheiligtum Yazılıkaya. Boğazköy-Ḫattuša* 9. Berlin: Gebr. Mann Verlag, 1975.

Boehmer, R. M. and Gauptmann, H., eds. *Beiträge zur Altertumskunde Kleinasiens. Festschrift für Kurt Bittel.* Mainz: Verlag Philipp von Zabern, 1983.

Borger, R. *Assyrisch-babylonische Zeichenliste.* 2nd ed. *AOAT* 33/33A. Neukirchen-Vluyn: Verlag Butzon und Bercker Kevelaer, 1981.

Bossert, H. T. *Ein hethitisches Königssiegel. Istanbuler Forschungen* 18. Berlin: 1944.

Brandenstein, C.-G. von. *Hethitische Götter nach Bildbeschreibungen in Keilschrifttexten. MVAeG* 46.2. Leipzig: J. C. Hinrichs Verlag, 1943.

Brock, Nadia van. "Dérivés Nominaux en *L* du Hittite et du Louvite." *RHA* XXII/71 (1962) 69–168.

Carruba, O. "Anatolica *Runda*." *SMEA* 4 (1968) 31–41.

———. "Di nuove e vecchie particelle anatoliche." *SMEA* 12 (1970) 68–87.

Carter, C. *Hittite Cult Inventories.* Ph.D. diss., University of Chicago, 1962.

Coşkun, Y. *Boğazköy metinlerinde geçen bazı seçme kap isimleri. AnYayın* 285. Ankara: Ankara Üniversitesi Basımevi, 1979.

Crepon, P. "Le thème du cerf dans l'iconographie anatolienne des origines à l'epoque hittite." *Hethitica* 4 (1981) 117–55.

Daddi Pecchioli, F. See Pecchioli Daddi, Franca.

Danmanville, J. "Le rituel d'Ištar de Tamininga." *RHA* XX/70 (1962) 51–61.

Darga, M. "Hitit Metinlerinde Geçen ^{NA_4}ZI.KIN=^{NA_4}*ḫuwaši* Kelimesinin Anlamı Hakkında bir Araştırma." *Belleten* XXXIII/132 (1969) 493–504.

———. "Hititlerin Kült Törenlerinde Kadınların Yeri ve Görevleri." *Tarih Enstitüsü Dergisi* 4–5 (1974) 231–45.

———. "*LÚ.MEŠ ḪILAMMATTI* Kelimesinin Anlamı." *Tarih Enstitüsü Dergisi* 1 (1970) 121–30.

———. "Über das Wesen des *ḫuwaši*- Steines nach hethitischen Kultinventaren." *RHA* XXVII/84–85 (1969) 5–20.

Deighton, Hilary J. *The 'Weather-God' in Hittite Anatolia.* British Archaeological Reports International Series, 143. Oxford: British Archaeological Reports, 1982.

Deimel, Antonius. *Pantheon Babylonicum.* Rome: Sumptibus Pontificii Instituti Biblici, 1914.

Dinçol, Ali. "Ašḫella Rituali (CTH 394) ve Hititlerde Salgın Hastalıklara karşı Yapılan Majik Işlemlere Toplu bir Bakış." *Belleten* XLIX/193 (1985) 1–40.

———. "Hethitische Hieroglyphensiegel in den Museen zu Adana, Hatay und Istanbul." *JKF* 9 (1983) 213–49.

Dinçol, A. and Darga, M. "Die Feste von Karaḫna." *Anatolica* 3 (1969–70) 99–118.

Dressler, Wolfgang. *Studien zur verbalen Pluralität.* Vienna: Hermann Böhlaus Nachf., 1968.

Dunand, F. and Lévêque, P., eds. *Les Syncrétismes dans les Religions de l'Antiquité.* Leiden: E. J. Brill, 1975.

Edel, Elmar. *Ägyptische Ärzte und ägyptische Medizin am hethitischen Königshof.* Göttingen: Westdeutscher Verlag, 1976.

Ehelolf, H. "Hethitisch-akkadische Wortgleichungen." *ZA* NF 9 (1936) 170–95.

Eichner, H. "Brief Comments on *lipšai-*." *Die Sprache* 27 (1981) 65 §142.

Emre, Kutlu. *Anatolian Lead Figurines and Their Stone Moulds.* Ankara: Türk Tarih Kurumu Basımevi, 1971.

Engelhard, David. *Hittite Magical Practices: An Analysis.* Ph.D. diss., Brandeis University, 1970.

Ertem, H. *Boğazköy metinlerine göre Hititler devri Anadolu'sunun Faunası.* Ankara: Ankara Üniversitesi Basımevi, 1965.

———. *Boğazköy metinlerine göre Hititler devri Anadolu'sunun Florası.* Ankara: Türk Tarih Kurumu Basımevi, 1974.

Fauth, Wolfgang. "Ištar als Löwengottin und die Löwenköpfige Lamaštu." *WO* 12 (1981) 21–36.

Ferm, Vergilius. *Forgotten Religions.* New York: Philosophical Library, n.d. (ca. 1950).

Florilegium Anatolicum: Mélanges offerts à Emmanuel Laroche. Paris: Éditions E. de Boccard, 1979.

Forrer, E. "Das Abendmahl im Hatti-Reiche." *Actes du XXe Congrès International des Orientalistes. Bruxelles 5–10 Septembre 1938,* pp. 124–28. Louvain: Bureaux du Muséon, 1940.

———. *Die Boghazköi-Texte in Umschrift. WVDOG* 41/42. Leipzig: J. C. Hinrichs'sche Buchhandlung, 1922, 1926.

———. *Forschungen.* Berlin: Privately published, 1926–29.

———. "šakija(ḫ) = 'verfinstern!'" *KlF* 1 (1930) 273–85.

Foxvog, D., Heimpel, W., Kilmer, A. D. "Lamma/Lamassu. A.I. Mesopotamien. Philologisch." *RLA* 6 (1980–83) 447–53.

Frantz-Szabó, G. "ᴰḪu(wa)riyanzipa." *RLA* 4 (1972–78) 503–04.

———. "Kapparijamu." *RLA* 5 (1976–80) 400.

Friedrich, J. "Alte und neue hethitische Wörter." *ArOr* 6 (1934) 358–76.

———. "Churritische Märchen und Sagen in hethitischer Sprache." *ZA* 49=NF 15 (1950) 213–55.

———. "Grammatische und lexikalische Bemerkungen zum Hethitischen." *ZA* 35=NF 1 (1923) 9–21.

———. *Hethitisches Elementarbuch.* 2nd ed. Heidelberg: Carl Winter Universitätsverlag, 1974.

———. *Hethitisches Keilschrift-Lesebuch.* Teil II. Heidelberg: Carl Winter Universitätsverlag, 1960.

———. *Hethitisches Wörterbuch.* Heidelberg: Carl Winter Universitätsverlag, 1952.

———. "Reinheitsvorschriften für den hethitischen König." *MAOG* 4 (1925) 46–58.

———. *Staatsverträge des Hatti-Reiches in hethitischer Sprache.* Parts I and II. *MVAeG* 31.1, 34.1. Leipzig: J. C. Hinrichs'sche Buchhandlung, 1926, 1930.

———. "Zu den hethitisch *ḫeššalla-* (*ḫiššalla-*)." *AfO* 17 (1954–56) 99.

———. "Zum hethitische Lexikon." *JCS* 1 (1947) 275–306.

Friedrich, J. and Kammenhuber, Annelies, eds. *Hethitisches Wörterbuch,* 2nd ed. Heidelberg: Carl Winter Universitätsverlag, 1975–

Furlani, Giuseppe. "The Basic Aspect of Hittite Religion." *Harvard Theological Review* 31 (1938) 251–62.

Gaster, T. *Thespis: Ritual, Myth and Drama in the Ancient Near East.* New York: Henry Schuman, 1950.

Goetze, A. *Die Annalen des Muršiliš. MVAeG* 38. Leipzig: J. C. Hinrichs'sche Buchhandlung, 1933.

———. *Ḫattušiliš. Der Bericht über seine Thronbesteigung nebst den Paralleltexten. MVAeG* 29.3. Leipzig: J. C. Hinrichs'sche Buchhandlung, 1925.

———. "Hittite Couriers." *RHA* XII/54 (1952) 1–14.

———. "Hittite *šipant-*." *JCS* 23 (1970) 76–94.

———. *Kultur-Geschichte Kleinasiens*. Munich: C. H. Beck, 1957.

———. "The Linguistic Continuity of Anatolia as Shown by Its Proper Names." *JCS* 8 (1954) 74–81.

———. *Madduwattaš. MVAeG* 32.1. Darmstadt: Wissenschaftliche Buchgesellschaft, 1968.

———. "Nochmals *šakiiaḫ(ḫ)-*." *KlF* 1 (1930) 401–13.

———. "Postposition and Preverb in Hittite." *JCS* 17 (1963) 98–101.

———. Review of *İstanbul Arkeoloji Müzelerinde Bulunan Boğazköy Tabletlerinden Seçme Metinler* 1, by H. Bozkurt, M. Çığ, and H. G. Güterbock. *JCS* 1 (1947) 87–92.

———. Review of *Keilschrifttexte aus Boghazköi* 11, by H. G. Güterbock and H. Otten. *JCS* 17 (1963) 60–64.

———. "The Roads of Northern Cappadocia in Hittite Times." *RHA* XV/61 (1957) 91–103.

———. "The Theophorus Elements of the Anatolian Proper Names from Cappadocia." *Language* 29 (1953) 263–77.

———. "Über die Partikeln *-za*, *-kan* und *-šan* der hethitischen Satzverbindung." *ArOr* 5 (1933) 1–38.

Goldman, H. *Excavations at Gözlü Kule. Tarsus II*. Princeton: Princeton University Press, 1956.

Gonnet, Hatice. "La 'Grande Fête d'Arinna.'" *Mém.Atatürk*, pp. 43–71.

———. "Remarques sur un geste du roi Hittite lors des fêtes agraires." *Hethitica* 4 (1981) 79–94.

Gordon, E. I. "The Meaning of the Ideogram ^{d}KASKAL.KUR='Underground Watercourse.'" *JCS* 21 (1967) 70–88.

Güterbock, H. G. "The Composition of Hittite Prayers to the Sun." *JAOS* 78 (1958) 237–45.

———. "Das dritte Monument am Karabel." *IM* 17 (1967) 63–71.

———. "The God Šuwaliyat Reconsidered." *RHA* XIX/68 (1961) 1–18.

———. "Hethitische Götterbilder und Kultobjekte." *FsBittel*, pp. 203–17.

———. "Hethitische Götterdarstellungen und Götternamen." *Belleten* VII/1 (1943) 295–317.

———. "The Hittite Conquest of Cyprus Reconsidered." *JNES* 26 (1967) 73–81.

———. "Hittite *kursa* 'Hunting Bag.'" *FsKantor*, pp. 113–19, pls. 16–19.

———. "Hittite Mythology." *MAW*, pp. 141–79.

———. "The Hittite Palace." *CRRAI* 19 (1971) 305–14.

———. "Hittite Religion." *Forgotten Religions*, pp. 81–109. Vergilius Ferm, ed. New York: Philosophical Library, n.d.

———. "The Hittite Temple according to Written Sources." *CRRAI* 20 (1972) 125–32.

———. *Kumarbi. Mythen von churritischen Kronos. Istanbuler Schriften* 16. Zurich, New York: Europaverlag, 1946.

———. "Marginal Notes on Recent Hittitological Publications." *JNES* 48 (1989) 307–11.

———. "North-central Area of Hittite Anatolia." *JNES* 20 (1961) 85–97.

———. "A Note on the Frieze of the Stag Rhyton in the Schimmel Collection." *FsAkurgal* Part 2, pp. 1–5.

———. "Notes on Luwian Studies (A propos B. Rosenkranz' Book *Beiträge zur Erforschung des Luvischen*)." *Or* 25 (1956) 113–40.

———. "An Outline of the Hittite AN.TAḪ.ŠUM Festival." *JNES* 19 (1960) 80–89.

———. "Religion und Kultus der Hethiter." *NHF*, pp. 54–73.

———. "A Religious Text from Maşat." *Anadolu Araştırmaları (JKF)* 10 (1986) 205–14.

———. Review of *Hethitische Götter nach Bildbeschreibungen in Keilschrifttexten*, by C.-G. von Brandenstein. *Or* 15 (1946) 482–96.

———. *Siegel aus Boğazköy I. AfO* Beiheft 5. Berlin: 1940; reprint ed., Osnabrück: Biblio-Verlag, 1967.

———. *Siegel aus Boğazköy II. AfO* Beiheft 7. Berlin: 1942; reprint ed., Osnabrück: Biblio-Verlag, 1967.

———. "Some Aspects of Hittite Festivals." *CRRAI* 17 (1969) 175–80.

———. "The Song of Ullikummi." *JCS* 5 (1951) 135–61; *JCS* 6 (1952) 8–42.

———. "To Drink a God." Paper given at the Rencontre Assyriologique Internationale, Istanbul, 1987.

———. "Yazılıkaya: Apropos à New Interpretation." *JNES* 34 (1975) 273–77.

Güterbock, H. G. and Alexander, Robert L. "The Second Inscription on Mount Sipylus." *AnSt* 33 (1983) 29–32.

Güterbock, H. G. and Hoffner, Harry A., eds. *The Hittite Dictionary of the Oriental Institute of the University of Chicago.* Chicago: The Oriental Institute of the University of Chicago, 1980–

Gurney, O. R. "The Hittite Title *tuḫkanti*." *AnSt* 33 (1983) 97–101.

———. *Some Aspects of Hittite Religion.* Oxford: Oxford University Press for the British Academy, 1977.

Haas, V. *Der Kult von Nerik.* Rome: Päpstliches Bibelinstitut, 1970.

———. "Leopard und Biene im Kulte 'hethitischer' Göttinnen. Betrachtungen zur Kontinuität und Verbreitung altkleinasiatischer und nordsyrischer religiöser Vorstellungen." *UF* 13 (1981) 101–16.

———. "Substratgottheiten des westhurrischen Pantheons." *RHA* 36 (1978) 59–69.

Haas, V. and Jakob-Rost, L. "Das Festritual des Gottes Telipinu in Ḫanḫana und in Kašḫa. Ein Beitrag zum hethitischen Festkalender." *AOF* 11 (1984) 204–36.

Haas, V. and Thiel, H. *Die Beschwörungsrituale der Allaituraḫ(ḫ)i und verwandte texte. AOAT* 31. Neukirchen-Vluyn: Neukirchener Verlag, 1978.

Haas, V. and Wäfler, M. "Bemerkungen zu [É]*heštī/ā-*." (1.Teil). *UF* 8 (1976) 65–99. (2. Teil). *UF* 9 (1977) 87–122.

———. "Yazılıkaya und der Grosse Tempel." *OA* 13 (1974) 211–26.

Haas, V. and Wilhelm, G. *Hurritische und luwische Riten aus Kizzuwatna. AOATS* 3. Neukirchen-Vluyn: Neukirchener Verlag, 1974.

Hallo, W. W., Moyer, J. C., and Perdue, L. G., eds. *Scripture in Context II.* Winona Lake, Indiana: Eisenbrauns, 1983.

Hammond, N. G. L. and Scullard, H. H., eds. *The Oxford Classical Dictionary.* Oxford: Oxford University Press, 1970.

Hanfmann, George. "A 'Hittite' Priest from Ephesus." *AJA* 66 (1962) 1–4, pls. 1–4.

Haussig, H. W., ed. *Wörterbuch der Mythologie.* Stuttgart: Ernst Klett Verlag, 1965.

Hawkins, J. D. and Davies, Anne Morpurgo. "Studies in Hieroglyphic Luwian." *FsGüterbock*², pp. 69–81.

Hellenkemper, Hansgerd and Warner, Jörg. "The God on the Stag." *AnSt* 27 (1977) 167–73, pls. XXXI–XXXIV.

Hoffmann, Inge. "Zur Wortbedeutung des EZEN *ḫaššumaš*." *Or* 52 (1983) 98–101.

Hoffner, Harry A., Jr. *Alimenta Hethaeorum. Food Production in Hittite Asia Minor.* New Haven: American Oriental Society, 1973.

———. "An Anatolian Cult Term in Ugaritic." *JNES* 23 (1964) 66–68.

———. "The *Arzana* House." *FsGüterbock*, pp. 113–21.

———. *An English-Hittite Glossary. RHA* XXV/80. Paris: Librairie C. Klincksieck, 1967.

———. "Histories and Historians of the Ancient Near East: The Hittites." *Or* 49 (1980) 283–332.

———. "The Hittite Particle *-pat*." *FsOtten*, pp. 99–117.

———. "Hittite *tarpiš* and Hebrew *terāphîm*." *JNES* 27 (1968) 61–68.

Hoffner, Harry A., Jr. (*cont.*)

———. "The Hittites and Hurrians." *Peoples of Old Testament Times*, pp. 197–228. D. J. Wiseman, ed. Oxford: Oxford University Press, 1973.

———. "The Hurrian Story of the Sungod, the Cow and the Fisherman." *FsLacheman*, pp. 189–94.

———. "Paskuwatti's Ritual against Sexual Impotence (CTH 406)." *Aula Orientalis* 5 (1987) 271–87.

———. Review of *Hethitisches Wörterbuch*, 2nd ed., Lief. 2–3, by J. Friedrich and A. Kammenhuber. *BiOr* 37 (1980) 198–202.

———. Review of *The Records of the Early Hittite Empire (c. 1450–1380 B.C.)*, by Ph. H. J. Houwink ten Cate. *JNES* 31 (1972) 29–35.

———. "Second Millennium Antecedents to the Hebrew *'ÔḆ*." *JBL* 86 (1967) 385–401.

———. "Studies in Hittite Grammar." *FsGüterbock²*, pp. 83–94.

Hoffner, Harry A., Jr. and Beckman, Gary M., eds. *Kaniššuwar—A Tribute to Hans G. Güterbock on His Seventy-Fifth Birthday, May 27, 1983. AS* 23. Chicago: The Oriental Institute of the University of Chicago, 1986.

Hout, Th. P. J. van den. "Kurunta und die Datierung einiger hethitischer Texte." *RA* 78 (1984) 89–92.

Houwink ten Cate, Philo H. J. "Brief Comments on the Hittite Cult Calendar: The Main Reçension of the Outline of the *nuntarriyašḫaš* Festival, especially Days 8–12 and 15′–22′." *FsOtten²*, pp. 167–94.

———. *The Luwian Population Groups of Lycia and Cilicia Aspera during the Hellenistic Period.* Leiden: E. J. Brill, 1961.

———. *The Records of the Early Hittite Empire (c. 1450–1380 B.C.).* Istanbul: Nederlands Historisch-archaeologisch Instituut in het Nabije Osten, 1970.

Jakob-Rost, Liane. "Bemerkungen zum 'Sänger von Kaneš.'" *Beiträge zur sozialen Struktur des alten Vorderasien*, pp. 161–65. H. Klengel, ed. Berlin: Akademie Verlag, 1971.

———. *Das Ritual der Malli aus Arzawa gegen Behexung (KUB XXIV 9+). THeth* 2. Heidelberg: Carl Winter Universitätsverlag, 1972.

———. "Zu den hethitischen Bildbeschreibungen." I. Teil *MIO* 8 (1963) 161–217. II. Teil *MIO* 9 (1963) 175–239.

———. "Zu einigen hethitischen Kultfunktionären." *Or* 35 (1966) 417–22.

Jestin, Raymond. "Texte Religieux Hittite (KUB n° 21)." *RA* 34 (1937) 45–58.

Jucquois, Guy and Lebrun, René. "Louvite *ḫuwarti-* 'decoction' et *ḫuwartalli-* 'mélange.'" *Heth.u.Idg.*, pp. 105–14.

Kammenhuber, A. "Das Hattische." *HbOr*, I Abt., II Bd., 1. and 2. Abschnitt, Lief. 2 (1969) 428–546.

———. "Hattische Studien I." *RHA* XX/79 (1962) 1–29.

———. "Die hethitische Göttin Inar." *ZA* 66 (1976) 68–88.

———. "Inar." *RLA* 5 (1976–80) 89–90.

———. *Materialien zu einem hethitischen Thesaurus.* Heidelberg: Carl Winter Universitätsverlag, 1973–

———. "Nominalkomposition in den altanatolischen Sprachen des 2. Jahrtausends." *KZ* 77 (1961) 161–218.

———. "Zwischenbilanz zu den hethitischen Enklitika-Ketten." *FsLaroche*, pp. 185–96.

Kantor, H. "A 'Syro-Hittite' Treasure in the Oriental Institute Museum." *JNES* 16 (1957) 145–62, pls. XX–XXVI.

Kapelrud, Arvid S. "The Interrelationship Between Religion and Magic in Hittite Religion." *Numen* 6 (1959) 32–50.

Kellerman, G. "Towards the Further Interpretation of the *purulli*-festival." *Slavica Hierosolymitana* 5–6 (1981) 35–46.

Kienle, R. von, Moortgat, A., Otten, H., von Schuler, E., and Zaumseil, W. eds. *Festschrift J. Friedrich zum 65. Geburtstag gewidmet.* Heidelberg: Carl Winter Universitätsverlag, 1959.

Klengel, H. *Beiträge zur sozialen Struktur des alten Vorderasien.* Berlin: Akademie-Verlag, 1971.

———. "Zur ökonomischen Funktion der hethitischen Tempel." *SMEA* 16 (1973) 181–200.

———. *Gesellschaft und Kultur im alten Vorderasien.* Berlin: Akademie Verlag, 1982.

Korošec, Victor. "Einiges zur inneren Struktur hethitischer Tempel nach der Instruktion für Tempelleute (KUB XIII, 4)." *FsGüterbock*, pp. 165–74.

Košak, Silvin. "The Gospel of Iron." *FsGüterbock²*, pp. 123–35.

———. *Hittite Inventory Texts (CTH 241–250). THeth* 10. Heidelberg: Carl Winter Universitätsverlag, 1982.

———. "The Hittites and the Greeks." *Linguistica* 20 (1980) 35–47.

Kramer, S. N., ed. *Mythologies of the Ancient World.* Garden City, New York: Anchor Books, 1961.

Kühne, C. "Hethitisch *auli-* und einige Aspekte altanatolischer Opferpraxis." *ZA* 76 (1986) 85–117.

Kümmel, Hans M. *Ersatzrituale für den hethitischen König. StBoT* 3. Wiesbaden: Otto Harrassowitz, 1967.

———. "Gesang und Gesanglosigkeit in der hethitischen Kultmusik." *FsOtten*, pp. 171–78.

Landsberger, B., et al. *Materialien zum sumerischen Lexikon.* Rome: Pontificium Institutum Biblicum, 1937–.

Laroche, E. *Catalogue des Textes Hittites.* 2nd ed. Paris: Éditions Klincksieck, 1971.

———. "Les Dénominations des Dieux 'Antiques' dans les Textes Hittites." *FsGüterbock*, pp. 175–85.

———. *Dictionnaire de la langue louvite.* Paris: Librairie Adrien-Maisonneuve, 1959.

———. "Les dieux de la Lycie classique d'après les textes lyciens." *Actes du colloque sur la Lycie antique*, pp. 1–6. H. Metzger, ed. Paris: Maisonneuve, for the Bibliothèque de l'Institut Français d'Études Anatoliennes d'Istanbul, 1980.

———. "Documents en langue Hourrite provenant de Ras Shamra." *Ugar.* 5 (1968) 448–544.

———. "Documents hiéroglyphiques hittites provenant du palais d'Ugarit." *Ugar.* 3 (1956) 97–160.

———. "Études de linguistique anatolienne III." *RHA* XXVII (1970) 22–71.

———. "Études de vocabulaire." *RHA* IX/49 (1948–49) 10–25.

———. "Études de vocabulaire VI." *RHA* XV/60 (1957) 9–29.

———. "Études sur les hiéroglyphes hittites." *Syria* 31 (1954) 99–117; ##4–7: *Syria* 35 (1958) 252–83.

———. *Glossaire de la langue hourrite. RHA* 34–35. Paris: Éditions Klincksieck, 1976–77.

———. "Ḫattic Deities and Their Epithets." *JCS* 1 (1947) 187–216.

———. *Les hiéroglyphes hittites.* Paris: Éditions du Centre National de la Recherche Scientifique, 1960.

———. "Hittite *-nš-/-nz-*." *RHA* VII/45 (1945–46) 3–11.

———. "Lamma/Lamassu. C. Anatolien." *RLA* 6 (1980–83) 455–59.

———. "Langues et civilisation de l'Asie Mineure." *Annuaire du College de France* 82 (1981–82) 521–27.

———. *Les Noms des Hittites.* Paris: Librairie C. Klincksieck, 1966.

———. "Le panthéon de Yazılıkaya." *JCS* 6 (1952) 115–23.

———. *Recherche sur les noms des dieux hittites. RHA* VII/46. Paris: Éditions Klincksieck, 1947.

———. *Recueil d'Onomastique Hittite.* Paris: Librairie C. Klincksieck, 1951.

———. "La Réforme Religieuse du Roi Tudhaliya IV et sa Signification Politique." *Les Syncrétismes dans les Religions de l'Antiquité*, pp. 87–95. F. Dunand and P. Lévêque, eds. Leiden: E. J. Brill, 1975.

———. Review of *Keilschrifttexte aus Boghazköi* 11, by H. G. Güterbock and H. Otten. *OLZ* 58 (1963) 245–48.

———. Review of *Keilschrifturkunden aus Boghazköi* 44, by H. Kengel. *OLZ* 72 (1977) 32–34.

———. "Teššub, Ḫebat et leur cour." *JCS* 2 (1948) 113–36.

———. *Textes mythologiques hittites en transcription. RHA* XXIII/77, XXVI/82. Paris: Librairie C. Klincksieck, 1965, 1968.

———. "Le Voeu de Puduḫepa." *RA* 43 (1949) 55–78.

Lebrun, R. "Deux textes hittites représentant la version impériale tardive de fêtes anatoliennes." *Hethitica* 2 (1977) 7–23.

———. "Divinités louvites et hourrites des rituels anatoliens en langue akkadienne provenant de Meskene." *Hethitica* 9 (1988) 147–55.

———. *Hymnes et Prières Hittites.* Louvain-la-Neuve: Centre d'Histoire des Religions, 1980.

———. *Samuha, Foyer religieux de l'empire hittite.* Louvain-la-Neuve: Institut Orientaliste, 1976.

———. "Studia ad civitates Lawazantiya et Samuha pertinentia II." *Hethitica* 5 (1983) 51–62.

Leinwand, N. W. "Archaeological Evidence for Hittite Cult Statuary." *AJA* 89 (1985) 338–39.

Leonard, A., Jr. and Williams, Bruce B., eds. *Essays in Ancient Civilization Presented to Helene J. Kantor.* Chicago: The Oriental Institute of the University of Chicago, 1989.

Liverani, M. *Storia di Ugarit.* Rome: Centro di Studi Semitici, 1962.

Loon, Maurits van. *Anatolia in the Second Millennium B.C.* Iconography of Religions XV, 12. Leiden: E. J. Brill, 1985.

de Martino, S. "La funzione del *tarša(n)zipa* nelle cerimonie cultuali ittite." *Hethitica* 5 (1983) 75–94.

———. "La posizione del coppiere presso la corte ittita." *SCO* 32 (1982) 305–18.

———. "Il LÚALAN.ZÚ come 'mimo' e come 'attore' nei testi ittiti." *SMEA* 24 (1984) 131–48.

Mascheroni, Lorenza M. "À propos d'un groupe de colophons problématiques." *Hethitica* 5 (1983) 95–109.

Melchert, H. C. *Ablative and Instrumental in Hittite.* Ph.D. diss., Harvard University, 1977.

———. "'God-Drinking': A Syntactic Transformation in Hittite." *JIES* 9 (1981) 245–54.

———. "A 'New' PIE **men* Suffix." *Die Sprache* 29 (1983) 1–26.

Mémorial Atatürk. Études d'Archéologie et de Philologie Anatoliennes. Éditions Recherche sur les civilisations, Synthèse nº 10. Paris: Institut Français d'Études Anatoliennes, 1982.

Meriggi, P. *Hieroglyphisch-hethitisches Glossar.* 2nd ed. Wiesbaden: Otto Harrassowitz, 1962.

Metzger, H., ed. *Actes du colloque sur la Lycie antique.* Paris: Maisonneuve, 1980. (Bibliotheque de l'Institut Français d'Études Anatoliennes d'Istanbul).

Milgrom, Jacob. "The Shared Custody of the Tabernacle and a Hittite Analogy." *JAOS* 90 (1970) 204–09.

Monte, G. F. del. Review of *Hethitica* 5, by E. Laroche, E. Neu, Y. Duhoux, G. Jucquois, and R. Lebrun, eds. *OA* 22 (1983) 319–21.

Monte, G. F. del and Tischler, J. *Répertoire géographique des Textes Cunéiformes*, vol. 6. Wiesbaden: Dr. Ludwig Reichert Verlag, 1978.

Moore, George C. Review of *Hethitica* 2, by G. Jucquois and R. Lebrun, eds. *JAOS* 102 (1982) 180–81.

Morrison, M. A. and Owen, D. I., eds. *Studies on the Civilization and Culture of Nuzi and the Hurrians in Honor of Ernest R. Lacheman.* Winona Lake, Indiana: Eisenbrauns, 1981.

Moyer, J. C. "Hittite and Israelite Cultic Practices: A Selected Comparison." *Scripture in Context II*, pp. 19–38. W. W. Hallo. ed. Winona Lake, Indiana: Eisenbrauns, 1983.

Muscarella, Oscar White, ed. *Ancient Art: The Norbert Schimmel Collection.* Mainz: Verlag Philipp von Zabern, 1974.

Neu, Erich. *Ein althethitisches Gewitterritual. StBoT* 12. Wiesbaden: Otto Harrassowitz, 1970.

———. *Der Anitta-Text. StBoT* 18. Wiesbaden: Otto Harrassowitz, 1974.

———. *Glossar zu den althethitischen Ritualtexten. StBoT* 26. Wiesbaden: Otto Harrassowitz, 1983.

———. *Interpretation der hethitischen mediopassiven Verbalformen. StBoT* 5. Wiesbaden: Otto Harrassowitz, 1968.

———. Review of *Hethitisches etymologisches Glossar*, by J. Tischler . *IF* 82 (1977) 269–75.

Neu, Erich, ed. *Investigationes Philologicae et Comparativae. Gedenkschrift für Heinz Kronasser.* Wiesbaden: Otto Harrassowitz, 1982.

Neu, Erich and Meids, Wolfgang. *Hethitisch und Indogermanisch. IBS* 25. Innsbruck: Institut für Sprachwissenschaft der Universität Innsbruck, 1979.

Neu, Erich and Rüster, Christel, eds. *Documentum Asiae Minoris Antiquae. Festschrift für Heinrich Otten zum 75. Geburtstag.* Wiesbaden: Otto Harrassowitz, 1988.

———. *Festschrift Heinrich Otten.* Wiesbaden: Otto Harrassowitz, 1973.

Neve, Peter. "Die Kulträume in den Hethitischen Tempeln Hattusas." *FsOtten*, pp. 253–72.

Nougayrol, Jean. *Textes Accadiens des Archives Sud. PRU* 4. Paris: Librairie C. Klincksieck, 1956.

Nowicki, H. "Zur Etymologie von heth. *paluae-*." *Or* 59 (1990) 239–42.

Oettinger, Norbert. *Die Stammbildung des hethitischen Verbums.* Nürnberg: Verlag Hans Carl, 1979.

Orthmann, W. *Untersuchungen zur Späthethitischen Kunst.* Bonn: Rudolf Habelt Verlag, 1971.

Osten, Hans Henning von der. *Ancient Oriental Seals in the Collection of Mr. Edward T. Newell. OIP* 22. Chicago: The University of Chicago Press, 1934.

Otten, H. "Der Anfang der *ḪAZANNU*-Instruktion." *Or* 52 (1983) 133–42.

———. "Eine Beschwörung der Unterirdischen aus Boğazköy." *ZA* 54 (1961) 114–57.

———. *Ein hethitisches Festritual (KBo 19.128). StBoT* 13. Wiesbaden: Otto Harrassowitz, 1971.

———. "dKAL=dInar(a)." *AfO* 17 (1956) 369.

———. "Die Götter Nupatik, Pirinkir, Ḫešue und Ḫatni-Pišaišapḫi in den heth. Felsreliefs von Yazılıkaya." *Anatolia* 4 (1959) 27–37.

———. "DGulšeš." *RLA* 3 (1957–71) 698.

———. "Ḫapantali(ia)." *RLA* 4 (1972–75) 111–12.

———. "Ḫaškala." *RLA* 4 (1972–75) 134.

———. *Hethitische Totenrituale. VIO* 37. Berlin: Akademie-Verlag, 1958.

———. "Kantipuitti." *RLA* 5 (1976–80) 390.

———. "Karzi." *RLA* 5 (1976–80) 459.

———. "Kurunta." *RLA* 6 (1980–83) 372–73.

———. "Neue Quellen zum Ausklang des Hethitischen Reiches." *MDOG* 94 (1963) 1–23.

———. Review of *İstanbul Arkeoloji Müzelerinde Bulunan Boğazköy Tabletleri* 2, by H. Bozkurt, M. Çığ, and H. G. Güterbock. *ZA* 49 (1950) 344–47.

———. Review of *Keilschrifturkunden aus Boghazköi* 46, by L. Jakob-Rost. *ZA* 66 (1976) 298–301.

———. "Ritual bei Erneuerung von Kultsymbolen hethitischer Schutzgottheiten." *FsFriedrich*, pp. 351–59.

———. *Die Überlieferungen des Telepinu-Mythus. MVAeG* 46.1. Leipzig: J. C. Hinrichs Verlag, 1942.

———. "Zu einem hethitischen Bauterminus: (GIŠ)*šarḫuli-*." *IM* 19/20 (1969/1970) 85–91.

Otten, H. and Röllig, W. "Karaḫna." *RLA* 5 (1976–80) 403.

Otten, H. and Rüster, C. "Textanschlüsse und Duplikate von Boğazköy-Tafeln (11–20)." *ZA* 62 (1972) 230–35; ##31–40: *ZA* 64 (1975) 241–49; ##61–70: *ZA* 68 (1978) 270–79.

Otten, H. and Siegelová, J. "Die hethitischen Gulš-Gottheiten und die Erschaffung der Menschen." *AfO* 23 (1970) 32–38.

Otten, H. and von Soden, W. *Das akkadisch-hethitische Vokabular. KBo I 44+KBo XIII 1. StBoT* 7. Wiesbaden: Otto Harrassowitz, 1968.

Özgüç N. *The Anatolian Group of Cylinder Seal Impressions from Kültepe.* Ankara: Türk Tarih Kurumu Basımevi, 1965.

Pecchioli Daddi, Franca. "Il *ḫazan(n)u* nei testi di Hattusa." *OA* 14 (1975) 93–136.

———. "Il LÚ*KARTAPPU* nel Regno Ittita." *SCO* 27 (1977) 169–91.

———. *Mestieri, Professioni e Dignita' Nell'Anatolia Ittita.* Rome: Edizioni dell'Ateneo, 1982.

Pieri, F. C. "L'edificio 'Sinapsi' nei rituali ittiti." *Atti e Memorie dell'Accademia Toscana di Scienze e Lettere "La Colombaria"* 47 (1982) 1–37.

Poetto, Massimo. "Eteo *sappu-*." *AIΩN* 1 (1979 [1980]) 117–21.

———. "Eteo $^{(UZU)}$*kudur*." *KZ* 99 (1986) 220–22.

Popko, Maciej. "Anatolische Schutzgottheiten in Gestalt von Vliesen." *Acta Antiqua Academiae Scientiarum Hungaricae* 22 (1974) 309–11.

———. "Die hethitische Gottheit ^{D}KAL ^{URU}*Tauriša*." *AOF* 8 (1981) 329–31.

———. *Kultobjekte in der hethitischen Religion.* Warsaw: Wydawnictwa Universytetu Warszawskiego, 1978.

———. "Zum hethitischen $^{(KUŠ)}$*kurša-*." *AOF* 2 (1975) 65–70.

Pritchard, James B., ed. *Ancient Near Eastern Texts Relating to the Old Testament.* 3rd ed. Princeton: Princeton University Press, 1969.

Przeworski, Stefan. "Notes d'Archéologie Syrienne et Hittite." *Syria* 21 (1940) 62–76.

Puhvel, Jaan. *Hittite Etymological Dictionary.* Berlin: Mouton Publishers, 1984–

———. Review of *Hethitisches Wörterbuch*, 2nd ed., Lief. 1, by J. Friedrich and A. Kammenhuber. *JAOS* 97 (1977) 596–99.

Riemschneider, Kaspar K. "Die Glasherstellung in Anatolien nach hethitischen Quellen." *FsGüterbock*, pp. 263–78.

Riemschneider, Margarete. *Der Wettergott.* Leipzig: Koehler and Amelang, 1956.

Rochberg-Halton, Francesca, ed. *Language, Literature and History: Philological and Historical Studies Presented to Erica Reiner. AOS* 67. New Haven: American Oriental Society, 1987.

Rosenkranz, Bernhard. "Kultisches Trinken und Essen bei den Hethitern." *FsOtten*, pp. 283–89.

———. "Ein neues hethitisches Ritual für ^{D}LAMA ^{KUŠ}*kuršaš*." *Or* 33 (1964) 238–56.

Rost, Liane. See Jakob-Rost.

Rüster, Christel and Neu, Erich. *Hethitisches Zeichenlexikon. StBoT* Beiheft 2. Wiesbaden: Otto Harrassowitz, 1989.

Schuler, Einar von. *Hethitische Dienstanweisungen für Höhere Hof- und Staatsbeamte. AfO* Beiheft 10. Graz: 1957; reprint ed., Osnabrück: Biblio-Verlag, 1967.

———. "Inar(a)." *Wörterbuch der Mythologie*, pp. 178–79. H. W. Haussig, ed. Stuttgart: Ernst Klett Verlag, 1965.

———. *Die Kaškäer.* Berlin: Walter de Gruyter, 1965.

———. "Die Würdenträgereide des Arnuwanda." *Or* 25 (1956) 209–40.

Schuster, Hans-Siegfried. *Die hattisch-hethitischen Bilinguen I/1. DMOA* 17. Leiden: E. J. Brill, 1974.

Sekizinci Türk Tarih Kongresi, 11–15 Ekim 1976. *Kongreye Sunulan Bildiriler, 1. Cilt.* Ankara: Türk Tarih Kurumu Basımevi, 1979.

Sergent, B. "Panthéons hittites trifonctionnels." *Revue de l'histoire des religions* 200 (1983) 131–53.

Singer, Itamar. "The Battle of Niḫriya and the End of the Hittite Empire." *ZA* 75 (1985) 100–23.

———. *The Hittite KI.LAM Festival. StBoT* 27 and 28. Wiesbaden: Otto Harrassowitz, (Part One) 1983, (Part Two) 1984.

———. "Western Anatolia in the Thirteenth Century B.C. According to the Hittite Sources." *AnSt* 33 (1983) 205–17.

Soden, Wolfram von. *Akkadisches Handwörterbuch.* Wiesbaden: Otto Harrassowitz, 1958–81.

———. "Die Schutzgenien Lamassu und Schedu in der babylonisch-assyrischen Literatur." *BagM* 3 (1964) 148–56.

Sommer, F. *Die Aḫḫijavā-Urkunden*. Munich: Bayerische Akademie der Wissenschaften, 1932.

———. Review of *Keilschrifturkunden aus Boghazköi* 14–17, by A. Götze, J. Schiele, A. Walther, and H. Ehelolf. *KlF* 1 (1930) 335–49.

Sommer, F. and Falkenstein, Adam. *Die hethitisch-akkadische Bilingue des Ḫattušili I. (Labarna II)*. Munich: Verlag der Bayerischen Akademie der Wissenschaften, 1938; reprint ed. Hildesheim: Verlag Dr. H. A. Gerstenberg, 1974.

Souček, V. "Soziale Klassen und Schichten in der hethitischen Tempelwirtschaft." *ArOr* 47 (1979) 78–82.

Spycket, A. "Lamma/Lamassu. B. Archäologisch." *RLA* 6 (1980–83) 453–55.

Starke, Frank. "Die keilschrift-luwischen Wörter für 'Insel' und 'Lampe.'" *KZ* 95 (1981) 141–57.

Stefanini, R. "KBo IV 14=VAT 13049." *AANL* 20 (1965) 39–79.

Steiner, G. "'Gott' nach hethitischen Texten." *RLA* 3 (1957–71) 547–75.

Stephens, F. *Personal Names from Cuneiform Inscriptions of Cappadocia*. Yale Oriental Series, Researches, 13, 1. New Haven: Yale University Press, 1928.

Sturtevant, E. H. and Bechtel, G. *A Hittite Chrestomathy*. Philadelphia: Linguistic Society of America, 1935.

Süel, A. *Hitit kaynaklarında tapınak görevlileri ile ilgili bir direktif metni*. Ankara: Ankara Üniversitesi Dil ve Tarih-Çoğrafya Fakültesi Basımevi, 1985.

Sürenhagen, Dietrich. *Paritätische Staatsverträge aus hethitischer Sicht*. *StMed* 5. Pavia: Gianni Iuculano Editore, 1985.

Şahin, Sencer, Schwertheim, Elmar, and Wagner, Jörg, eds. *Studien zur Religion und Kultur Kleinasiens*. Leiden: E. J. Brill, 1978.

Tischler, Johann. *Hethitisches etymologisches Glossar*. *IBS* 20. Innsbruck: Institut für Sprachwissenschaft der Universität Innsbruck, 1977–

Tischler, Johann, ed. *Serta Indogermanica: Festschrift für Günter Neumann zum 60. Geburtstag*. *IBS* 60. Innsbruck: Institut für Sprachwissenschaft der Universität Innsbruck, 1982.

Ünal, Ahmet. *Ein Orakeltext über die Intrigen am hethitischen Hof*. *THeth* 6. Heidelberg: Carl Winter Universitätsverlag, 1978.

———. "'You Should Build for Eternity:' New Light on the Hittite Architects and Their Work." *JCS* 40 (1988) 97–106.

———. "Zu neu entdeckten kuriosen Graffiti in der näheren Umgebung von Boğazköy-Ḫattuša." *FsBittel*, pp. 523–35.

Ünal, A. and Kammenhuber, A. "Das althethitische Losorakel KBo XVIII 151." *KZ* 88 (1974) 157–80.

Vavroušek, P. "Letzte Beiträge zu heth. [É]*ḫalentu(wa)-*, *ḫilammar, und* [É]*arkiu-*." *ArOr* 52 (1984) 190–93.

Vieyra, Maurice. "Fragments de Boghaz-Köy." *RA* 59 (1965) 131–32.

Walser, G., ed. *Neuere Hethiterforschung*. Wiesbaden: Franz Steiner Verlag GMBH, 1964.

Weidner, E. *Politische Dokumente aus Kleinasien*. *BoSt* 8–9. Leipzig: J. C. Hinrichs'sche Buchhandlung, 1923.

Werner, Rudolf. *Hethitische Gerichtsprotokolle*. *StBoT* 4. Wiesbaden: Otto Harrassowitz, 1967.

Willemaers, Noëlle. "Contribution iconographique à l'histoire du rituel hittite. II. Confrontation avec les textes." *Hethitica* 2 (1977) 53–78.

Wiseman, D. J. *Peoples of Old Testament Times*. Oxford: Oxford University Press, 1973.

LEXICAL INDEX

This index includes words for which I have suggested new meanings, provided information about attestations in the corpus, or given a summary of other scholarly work. Foreign or loan words from languages other than Sumerian or Akkadian have been included in the Hittite section.

HITTITE

alilanza- 112 n. 146
-an 208–09
annari- 9–10, 107 n. 112
É*arkiu-* 87 n. 14
aššatta- 109 n. 123
aštaš 101 n. 79
ašuša- 146 n. 11, 158
ḫal(l)ašša- 101 n. 76
ḫalzai- 158
ḫantiyašša- 245–46
ḫa/urn(uw)ai- 246–47
DUG*ḫaršiyal* 56 n. 10
SAL*ḫazgarai* 220 n. 13
É*ḫila-* 88 n. 26, 203
É*ḫilammar* 266
ḫiššala- 182, 247–48
ḫuwaši- 195–96
É*ḫuwapraš* 107 n. 116
irḫai- 196
irḫatti 65 n. 50
išḫašarwannaš 105 n. 104
išgar- 159, 179 with n. 119
kariya- 248
É*karimmi-* 160–61
kaš 151 n. 39
kattapuzna- 87 n. 15
kipikkišdu 248–50
kuen- 167
kurraštarra- 107 n. 114
kurša- 20–22, 182–84, 250–54
GIŠ*kurtal* 65 n. 53
lipšai- 227
militaš 72 n. 68
newaḫḫ- 254–55
palwai- 255–57
GIŠ*papu-* 257
GIŠ*papul-* 257
:paraštarra- 107 n. 114
:parzaḫannaš 74 n. 71
:piḫaladdaššiš 106 n. 110
piḫaddaššiš 106 n. 110
purpura- 150 n. 35, 257–58
šakiyaḫḫ- 101 n. 78
šanḫ- 159–60
šarlaimi- 50 with n. 329
LÚ.MEŠ*šarmiya-* 258
šiyatalleški- 115 n. 159
šuwant- 103 n. 89
NINDA*takarmu-* 159
takšatar 105 n. 109
takkuwar 228
takkuwi- 107 n. 113
tarna- 204–05, 234 n. 52

SUMERIAN

NUMBERS

AKKADIAN

DIVINE NAMES

GEOGRAPHICAL NAMES

PERSONAL NAMES

INDEX OF TEXTS TREATED

Full Editions

Unpublished Texts

Cited Texts

KBo 1.35+ iii 3′–4′	9
KBo 1.44+ iv 35–36	9
KBo 3.8+ i 17–18	161
KBo 4.2 ii 27	204
KBo 4.13+ v 39–40	264 with n. 90
KBo 4.14 iii 13–15	247 n. 9
KBo 10.27 iii 10′–17′	17
iii 10′–20′	265–66 with n. 104
KBo 11.45 iv 9′–15′	159
KBo 13.1+ iv 35–36	9
KBo 14.70+ i 21′–22′	40
KBo 18.190:4′–5′	252 with n. 25
KBo 20.81 v 17′–18′	249
KBo 20.107+ ii 9–13	245–46
ii 10–13	268 with n. 122
iii 26′–28′	246
KBo 21.83 rev. 1′–4′	249
KBo 23.43 i 6–8	160
KBo 23.50+ ii 9–13	245–46
ii 10–13	268 with n. 122
iii 26′–28′	246
KBo 24.57 i 6–8	160
KBo 26.25+ iii 3′–4′	9
KBo 29.211 i? 7′–8′	13 with n. 30
KBo 30.46:5′	249
KUB 2.8 ii 21–24	196
KUB 7.1+ i 17–18	161
KUB 7.29 obv. 10–11	166
KUB 9.28 i 7′–9′	160
KUB 10.13 iii 16′–21′	17
iii 19′–21′	184
KUB 10.21 v 19–22	254
KUB 10.72 ii 19′–21′, v 20–22	268 with nn. 118–19
KUB 11.30+ iii 22′–23′	270
KUB 20.2 iv 24′–30′	29 with n. 168
KUB 20.19 iv 12′–13′	248–49

KUB 20.59 i 13′–15′	195
KUB 20.90 iv 4′–7′	262–63
iv 14′–16′	263
KUB 20.99 ii 6–10	13
KUB 22.27 iv 16–20	265 with n. 102
KUB 25.31 obv. 6–13	185
obv. 11–13	252 with n. 30
KUB 25.36 v 35–39	158 with n. 68
KUB 27.69 i 6′–9′	249
v 1–14	264 with n. 91
KUB 30.32 i 9–10	252 with n. 25
KUB 30.39 obv. 9	162
KUB 30.60+ i 21′–22′	40
KUB 31.121+ i! 11′–15′	33 with n. 200
KUB 32.123 iii 12	259
KUB 38.1 l.e. 1–2	12
KUB 38.2 ii 24′–26′	24 with n. 129
KUB 43.23 rev. 38–42	12, 25
KUB 43.30 ii 9′–10′	254 with n. 37
KUB 46.18 obv. 17′	247
KUB 53.3 i 18′–22′	261 with n. 78
KUB 53.12 iv 1–2	261 with n. 79
KUB 53.13 iv 16′–19′	261
KUB 53.49 rev. 2–3	261
KUB 60.21:11′–13′	249
IBoT 4.197+ iii 22′–23′	270

Unpublished Texts

Bo 3418:10′–11′	261 with n. 77
Bo 5728+ i! 11′–15′	33 with n. 200
315/t i 12′–14′	254 with n. 36, 267 with n. 112
355/t rev. 7′–8′	270
2011/u rev. 1–3	253
Bo 68/215+ v 5′–6′	258